Uncle Jo[illegible]
LEGENDARY LOST BATHROOM READERS®

The Bathroom Readers' Institute

Bathroom Readers' Press
Ashland, Oregon

UNCLE JOHN'S
LEGENDARY LOST
BATHROOM READER®

For information, write The Bathroom Readers' Institute,
P.O. Box 1117, Ashland, OR 97520
www.bathroomreader.com

Cover design by Michael Brunsfeld
Brunsfeld Designs, *brunsfeldo@home.com*

Uncle John's Legendary Lost Bathroom Reader®
by The Bathroom Readers' Institute

☆ ☆ ☆

Library of Congress Catalog Card Number: 99-095363

ISBN: 1-879682-74-5 UPC: 7-30258-50274-1

Printed in the United States of America
Seventh Printing 2001

17 16 15 14 13 12 11 10 9 8

Uncle John's Fifth Bathroom Reader

Uncle John's Sixth Bathroom Reader

"Reader's Article of the Year" excerpted from *THE POWER OF POSITIVE NONSENSE*, by Leo Rosten; published by McGraw Hill. Copyright © 1977. Reprinted by permission of the author.

"The King of Farts" reprinted from *IT'S A GAS: A STUDY OF FLATULENCE*, by Eric S. Rabkin, Ph.D., and Eugene M. Silverman, M.D., Manticore Books: 3644 Creekside Dr., Ann Arbor, MI 48105.

"Twisted Titles" originally appeared in the June 1993 and in 1994 issues of *CALIFORNIA MONTHLY*, published by the California Alumni Association. Reprinted by permission of the California Alumni Association.

* * * *

Uncle John's Seventh Bathroom Reader

The article, "There's No Such Thing as Smelly Feet," by Teo Furtado is reprinted by permission of *HEALTH* magazine. Copyright © 1993.

Excerpts reprinted with permission from "Diamond Voodoo," by Jack Connelly. Copyright © 1994 by Jack Connelly. Reprinted with permission.

"True Lies: Sweetened with Fruit Juice" originally appeared as "Stripped Juice Tease: Ingredients in Fruit Juice Are Not What's on the Label," by Stephen Schmidt in the *NUTRITION ACTION HEALTHLETTER*. Reprinted by permission.

Excerpts reprinted from *AMERICA AT RANDOM: A Multiple Choice Self-Quiz on Everything You Always Wanted to Know*

THANK YOU

The Bathroom Readers' Institute sincerely thanks the people whose advice and assistance made this book possible.

John Javna
Gordon Javna
Michael Brunsfeld
John Dollison
Jennifer & Sage
Jeff Altemus
Jay Newman
Sharilyn Hovind
Jack Mingo
Erin Barrett
Paul Stanley
Lonnie Kirk
Julie Roeming
Bennie Slomski
Nenelle Bunnin
Hi, Emily and Molly Bennett
Julie Bennett
Claudia Bauer
Larry Kelp
Peter Wing
Kelly Rogers
Ross Owens
Leo Rosten
Russel Schoch
Penelope Houston
Andrea Sohn
Lenna Lebovich
Mustard Press
Eric Lefcowitz
Jesse & Sophie, *B.R.I.T.*
...and all the
bathroom readers

A WORD FROM UNCLE JOHN

This book is a special edition, created for the thousands of fans who've called or written over the years trying to get copies of our *Fifth*, *Sixth*, or *Seventh Bathroom Readers*. Usually they tell us that they've looked in a number of stores, and even tried to order them. Sometimes they ask if the books really exist—or if we've just been playing games with them. For those folks, this really is the *Legendary Lost Bathroom Reader*.

The books do exist...But for years they've been next to impossible to find in bookstores. Here's why:

As you probably know, we've put out one new *Bathroom Reader* each year since 1988. The first four 220-page books were published by St. Martin's Press. Then, in 1992, we decided to take over the publishing ourselves. We found a great printer (Banta), a distributor who could get our books into stores (Publishers Group West, or PGW)...and the Bathroom Readers' Press was born.

Thanks to enthusiastic readers, we were successful right away. Nearly every copy of *Uncle John's Fifth Bathroom Reader* sold out in 1992. We were on a roll...but we still had a lot to learn. When PGW asked us to reprint the book, so they could fill the thousands of new orders they were getting, we just ignored them; we were busy writing our new edition, and thought that was more important. PGW didn't push the issue—they figured we were a little eccentric anyway.

So there were no new copies to ship.

The same thing happened in 1993 with *Uncle John's Sixth Bathroom Reader* and in 1994 with *Uncle John's Seventh Bathroom Reader*.

In the end, the three books were never reprinted.

A NEW ATTITUDE

In 1995, the BRI moved to Ashland, Oregon. We decided to take the publishing business more seriously, and made a series of changes. For example, we stopped numbering the book titles, so people wouldn't feel compelled to read them in order...and we made the *Bathroom Readers* longer, so they'd last a whole year. We started doing reprints of our latest books, too. (There have now been 10 editions of our 1995 volume, *The Best of Uncle John's Bathroom Reader.*)

We're happy to say that our books are getting more popular all the time. One of the offshoots of our growing readership is an interest in the older volumes.

Until recently, we could usually help the most insistent fans by scrounging a copy of one the *Fifth*, *Sixth*, or *Seventh BR* from somewhere. But now we're completely out. Not a single one can be found anywhere...so we've decided to finally give in, and reprint them. This single volume contains the text of all three books.

We've made a few changes—spelling and punctuation have been corrected whenever possible, and some of the running feet that were ridiculously outdated have been replaced. There are also a few replacement articles. But we've resisted the impulse to rewrite everything. These are reprints after all, and the important thing is simply to make them available—warts and all.

Looking at them now, 6 to 8 years after they were written, we can see that the books have a somewhat uneven quality. Some of our favorite pieces are included here...but so are a few things we'd rather forget about.

Overall, however, we're proud of the material. We think this volume—our biggest ever—is a lot of fun and great bathroom reading. And that's what counts, after all. Enjoy it...

and

Go With the Flow!

CONTENTS

NOTE

Because the BRI understands your reading needs, we've divided the contents by length as well as subject:

Short—A quick read

Medium—1 to 3 pages

Long—For those extended visits, when something a little more involved is required

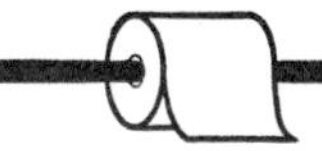

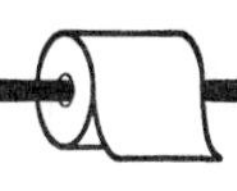

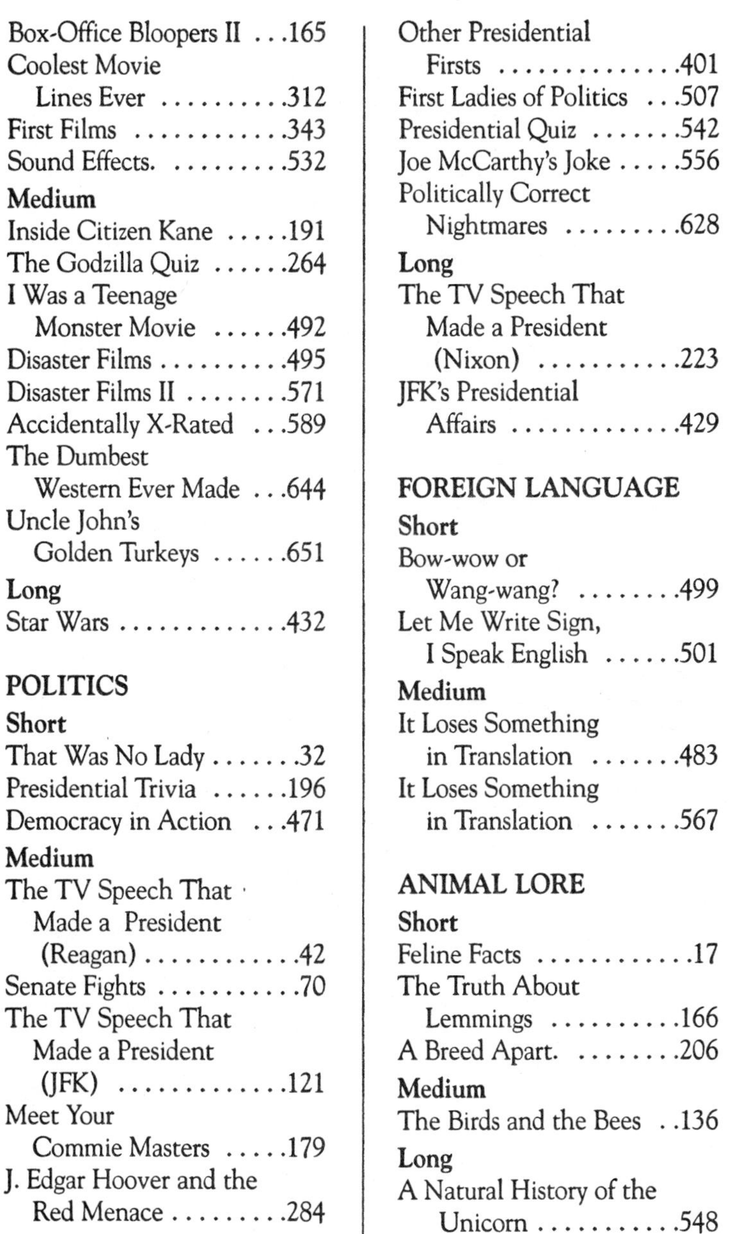

* * *

RANDOM THOUGHTS ON THE MILLENNIUM...

Patriotic Effort

"America must do more than the minimum on the millennium...I believe it should be celebrated with all the grandiosity, excess and overkill that we can muster. Our national pride is at stake. There is much planning to do. Why, just the logistics of recruiting and training enough Elvis impersonators boggles the mind."

—Lewis Grossberger,
***New York Times*, Aug. 14, 1989**

In 2000...

"Authors of self-help books will be required to provide proof that they have actually helped themselves."

—Jane Wagner,
***Ms.* magazine, 1990**

Big Whoop

"A lot of Chinese feel rather patronizing toward the millennium. The idea of a calendar with only 2000 years is rather charming."

—Charlie Chin,
New York Chinatown History Project

Uncle John's

FIFTH BATHROOM READER

First published October 1992

UNCLE JOHN'S NOTES:

This was the first book we ever published.

Reading it over now, I like the ideas and information but think the writing is still a little rough. This book clearly needed more editing—but frankly, we didn't know how to do it back then.

Still, you can see the BRI style developing. Compare the section called "Order in the Court," for example, with the "Court Transquips" in our current work. It's clearly on it's way to becoming a viable format.

We were also just starting to figure out that the length of the articles in a *BR* should vary. There are a few longer-than-average pieces (e.g., "The TV Speech that Made a President") here—but not enough. A number of articles would have been much better longer. For example: compare the section on *Citizen Kane* in this book (2 pages) with the one in *Uncle John's Absolutely Absorbing Bathroom Reader* (6 pages). It's night and day. But, then, we had to start somewhere.

Some of our favorites in this volume:

- Carnival Tricks
- The Myth-Adventures of Christopher Columbus
- Meet Dr. Seuss

FELINE FACTS

Cats are America's most popular pet. Here are six things you may not know about them.

THE INSIDE POOP

Nearly all domestic cats bury their feces—but in the wild, only timid cats do. Aggressive cats in the wild actually leave their droppings on tiny "advertising hills" that they create. This leads researchers to believe that domestic cats see themselves as submissive members of their human families and environments.

FAMILY FLAVOR

Does your cat lick its fur clean after it rubs against you? That's its way of "tasting" you—becoming familiar with the taste and scent of the people in its life.

CAT & MOUSE

Why do cats play "cat and mouse" with their victims? Experts believe it's because they're not hungry. Wild cats, who eat nothing but the food they catch, rarely, if ever, play cat and mouse.

PURR-FECT

Do cats purr because they are happy? Probably not, researchers say; even dying cats and cats in pain purr. The researchers think a cat's purr is a sign it is receptive to "social interaction."

THE BETTER TO SEE YOU WITH

Unlike human eyes, a cat's eyes have pupils that are shaped like vertical slits. These vertical slits work together with the horizontal slits of the cat's eyelid to give it greater control over how much light it allows into its eyes.

WHISKED AWAY

Because a cat's whiskers are sensitive to the slight air currents that form around solid objects (such as furniture and trees), they help it to "see" in the dark. This is especially helpful when the cat hunts at night.

Elvis Presley's favorite amusement park ride was the bumper cars.

WHERE-ING CLOTHES

Ever wonder how fabric designs and clothing styles get their names? Some are named after the places they were created or worn. For example…

CALICO. In the early 1700s, a fabric from India became so popular with the British public that they stopped buying English cloth and English weavers began losing their jobs. The weavers rioted. (In fact, they started attacking people wearing the cloth.) The result: Parliament banned imports of the fabric, and English weavers began making it themselves. They named it after the place it was originally made, the Indian town of Calicut. Eventually, *Calicut* cloth evolved into *calico* cloth.

PAISLEY. These amoebalike patterns were originally found on shawls imported into England from India in the 1800s. Scottish weavers in the town of Paisley began producing their own versions of the design.

BIKINI. Daring two-piece swimsuits were introduced at end-of-the-world parties inspired by America's 1946 A-bomb tests on the Bikini Atoll in the Pacific.

BERMUDA SHORTS. Bermuda, an island in the Atlantic, was a popular warm-weather tourist resort in the 1940s. But female vacationers had to use caution when they relaxed—a law on the island prohibited them from walking around with bare legs. The fashion solution: knee-length shorts, worn with kneesocks.

CAPRI PANTS. Fashion designer Emilio Pucci met a beautiful woman while vacationing on the Isle of Capri in the 1950s. The encounter inspired a line of beach fashions that featured these skin-tight pants.

JODHPURS. These riding pants were created by English horsemen living in Jodhpur, India.

FAMOUS FOR 15 MINUTES

We've included this feature—based on Andy Warhol's comment that "In the future, everyone will be famous for 15 minutes"—in almost every Bathroom Reader. *Here it is again, with new stars.*

THE STAR: Oliver Sipple, an ex-marine living in San Francisco

THE HEADLINE: "Man Saves President Ford's Life by Deflecting Assassin's Gun"

WHAT HAPPENED: President Gerald R. Ford was visiting San Francisco on September 22, 1975. As he crossed the street, a woman in the crowd, Sara Jane Moore, pulled out a gun and tried to shoot him. Fortunately, a bystander spotted Moore and managed to tackle her just as the gun went off. The bullet missed the president by only a few feet.

Oliver Sipple, the bystander, was an instant hero—which was about the last thing he wanted. Reporters investigating his private life discovered that he was gay—a fact he'd hidden from his family in Detroit. Sipple pleaded with journalists not to write about his sexual orientation, but they ignored him. The next day, the *Los Angeles Times* ran a front-page story headlined "Hero in Ford Shooting Active Among S.F. Gays."

THE AFTERMATH: The incident ruined Sipple's life. When his mother learned that he was gay, she stopped speaking to him. And when she died in 1979, Sipple's father would not let him attend the funeral. Sipple became an alcoholic. In 1979, he was found dead of "natural causes" in his apartment. He was 37.

THE STAR: Hiroo Onoda, a Japanese army lieutenant during World War II

THE HEADLINE: "Japanese Soldier Finally Surrenders...29 Years After the War"

WHAT HAPPENED: In February 1945, Allied forces overran Lubang Island in the Philippines. Most of the occupying Japanese

Q: What cable TV channel is available to the most American viewers? A: C-SPAN.

soldiers were captured, but a few escaped into the hills. There they waited to be "liberated," unaware that Japan had surrendered. They survived by living off the forest and raiding native villages for food. Villagers called them "the mountain devils."

The U.S. and Japanese governments knew there were holdouts on the island, and for more than 25 years they tried to reach them by dropping leaflets, organizing search parties, and bringing relatives to coax them out of hiding. But nothing worked.

By 1974, there was only one soldier left: 53-year-old Hiroo Onoda. One day, he spotted a young Japanese man drinking from a stream in the hills. The stranger turned out to be Norio Suzuki, a university dropout who'd come to the island specifically to find Onoda. Suzuki explained that the war had been over for 27 years and asked Onoda to return with him to Japan. But Onoda refused—unless his commanding officer came to the island and delivered the order personally. Suzuki returned to Japan, found the commanding officer, and brought him back to Lubang Island, where Onoda finally agreed.

THE AFTERMATH: Onoda was regarded as a curiosity in the world press, but in Japan he was a national hero. More than 4,000 people greeted him at the airport when he returned to Japan. He sold his memoirs for enough money to buy a 2,870-acre farm in Brazil, stocked with 1,700 head of cattle.

THE STAR: Roy Riegels, captain of the football team at the University at California, Berkeley during the 1929 season

THE HEADLINE: "Blooper of the Century: Cal Captain Runs Wrong Way, Gives Away Rose Bowl Game"

WHAT HAPPENED: It was the 1929 Rose Bowl game: U.C. Berkeley was playing Georgia Tech, and the score was 0-0 in the second quarter. Cal had the ball deep in Georgia Tech territory, but in four attempts, they failed to score. Now Tech took over the ball...but on first down, the Georgia quarterback fumbled. In the confusion, Roy Riegels recovered the ball and started running for a touchdown. The only problem was, he was running *the wrong way*.

Benny Lom, Cal's center, realized what was happening and chased Riegels, shouting and screaming. But Riegels outran him, carrying the ball 69½ yards down the field. Lom finally tackled him—six *inches* from the California goal line.

THE AFTERMATH: On the next play, Tech nailed Cal for a safety, making the score Georgia 2, California 0. They added a touchdown in the third quarter, but failed to make the extra point. Now the score was Georgia 8, California 0. In the fourth quarter, California scored a touchdown and made the extra point—but that was it. Final score: Georgia Tech 8, California 7. Riegels's blunder had cost Cal the game. The next day, Riegels was the most celebrated sports figure in the country. In fact, he's still known as "Wrong Way" Riegels.

THE STAR: William Figueroa, a 12-year-old student

THE HEADLINE: "New Jersey Student Makes Vice President Look Like a Foole"

WHAT HAPPENED: In June 1992, Vice President Dan Quayle visited a Trenton, New Jersey, elementary school where a spelling bee was being held. Quayle took over. Reading from a cue card, Quayle asked Figueroa, a sixth-grader, to spell the word "potato." The boy spelled the word correctly, but Quayle insisted that he change it, because "potato" was spelled with an 'e' at the end. "I knew he was wrong," Figueroa later told reporters, "but since he's the vice president, I went and put the 'e' on and he said, 'That's right, now go and sit down.' Afterward, I went to a dictionary and there was potato like I spelled it. I showed the reporters the book and they were all laughing about what a fool he was."

THE AFTERMATH: Figueroa became an instant celebrity. "Late Night with David Letterman" had him on as a guest, and he was asked to lead the pledge of allegiance at the 1992 Democratic National Convention. Afterwards, an AM radio station paid him $50 a day to provide political commentary on the Republican National Convention. He was also hired as spokesperson for a company that makes a computer spelling program.

TV QUIZ: THE ADDAMS FAMILY

1. What language drove Gomez crazy?

2. What did Gomez called Morticia?

3. How did Uncle Fester produce electric light?

4. What kind of creature was Wednesday's pet, Homer?

5. How was Itt, the four-foot ball of hair, related to Gomez?

Answers: 1. French; 2. Tish; 3. He put a bulb in his mouth; 4. Black widow spider; 5. Cousin.

FAMOUS PHRASES

Here's another of our regular Bathroom Reader *features—the origins of familiar phrases.*

NOT UP TO SCRATCH

Meaning: Inadequate, subpar

Background: In the early days of boxing, there was no bell to signal the beginning of a round. Instead, the referee would scratch a line on the ground between the fighters, and the round began when both men stepped over it. When a boxer couldn't (or wouldn't) cross the line to keep a match going, people said he was "not up to the scratch."

CAUGHT RED-HANDED

Meaning: Caught in the act

Background: For hundreds of years, stealing and butchering another person's livestock was a common crime. But it was hard to prove unless the thief was caught with the dead animal...and blood on his hands.

CAN'T HOLD A CANDLE TO (YOU)

Meaning: Not as good as (you)

Background: Comes from England. Before there were streetlights, when wealthy British nobles went walking at night they brought along servants to carry candles. This simple task was one of the least-demanding responsibilities a servant could have; people who weren't able to handle it were considered worthless. Eventually, the term "can't hold a candle" came to mean inferiority.

GIVE SOMEONE THE BIRD

Meaning: Make a nasty gesture at someone (usually with the middle finger uplifted)

Background: Originally referred to the hissing sound audiences made when they didn't like a performance. Hissing is the sound that a goose makes when it's threatened or angry.

Albert Einstein slept 10 hours a night.

INSIDE CHEERS

What was the best sitcom of the 1980s? Most TV critics say "Cheers." Did you know...

How it Started. Producers Glen and Les Charles and producer/director James Burrows were part of the team that created the successful 1970s sitcom, "Taxi." When they left that show, they decided to work together on a comedy set in a hotel... so they'd be able to bring in new characters whenever they wanted. However, when they sketched out plots, they found that most of the action would take place in the hotel bar. So they dumped the hotel and kept the bar.

The show debuted on September 30, 1982. But despite critical acclaim, it was a flop. The first episode was rated 60th out of 63 programs, and it didn't do much better for the rest of the season. To everyone's surprise, NBC decided to renew the sitcom anyway (because it had faith in its creators). Result: By the following season it was in the top 20, and a year later it was in the top 10.

INSIDE FACTS

• Ted Danson got his start on TV in the 1970s soap opera "Somerset." The turning point in his career was a guest appearance he did on "Taxi," playing an obnoxious beautician who gave Elaine Nardo a dreadful new-wave hairdo. He was so impressive that the producers took him aside and convinced him to audition for the lead role in a new series they were developing—"Cheers."

• The "Cheers" creators intentionally picked the name Norm for George Wendt's character because he's supposed to be the guy who represents the "norm."

• The exterior of the "Cheers" bar belonged to a real Boston bar called the Bull and Finch. Inside, however, the dimly lit, crowded interior was nothing like Sam Malone's place.

• Shelley Long was pregnant during most of the third season. It was covered up by strategically placed trays and by having her stand behind the bar a lot. "I'm sure," Long recalls, "there were times when the audience said, 'My God, she's pregnant.' "

In 1992, about 1 in 4 Americans who ate breakfast away from home ate it at McDonald's.

MADE IN AMERICA?

How can you be sure the "American" product you're buying is really made in the U.S.? According to a little volume called Buy American—Buy This Book, *by Eric Lefcowitz, it's not as easy as it might seem.*

THE TOWN CALLED USA

Some people say this is an urban legend, but according to Lefcowitz: "Before World War II, products stamped MADE IN USA were not necessarily made in the United States or its territories. Many items were made in the town of Usa, Japan (current pop: 27,994). Usa is known to tourists as the home of a beautiful Shinto shrine....However, prior to World War II it was notorious for manufacturing articles stamped MADE IN USA, which, according to the *Encyclopedia Americana*, was used "as a means of circumventing American boycotts of Japanese goods."

AMERICAN QUILTS

In 1992 the Smithsonian Institution contracted with a firm to manufacture reproductions of four antique quilts in its quilt collection. The company hired was in China—and the move infuriated the American quilt industry, which accused the Smithsonian of undercutting their business. The quilts were mass-produced at a price much lower than it would have cost to make them in the U.S. (thanks to cheap labor), and sold in the Smithsonian gift shop, as well as in Land's End and Speigel catalogs for $200-400. The only thing identifying them as Chinese: a removable tag. (One of the four quilts selected for reproduction was "America's Great Seal.")

AMERICAN FLAGS

An estimated 15% of all American flags are manufactured in other countries. "This phenomenon is not new," Lefcowitz writes. Before World War II, the American Legion chapter in Cambria County, Pennsylvania complained that was "unable to find any small American flags that were not made in either Germany or Japan." Today most foreign-made American flags come from Taiwan. It can be hard to tell whether a flag is foreign made or not, because the tag identifying them as such is usually removable. Experts advise examining the quality of the flag—stitched flags are more likely to be American made than printed flags, and the colors of imported flags "rarely" match the official Old Glory red, Old Glory white, and Old Glory blue.

FLORIDA ORANGE JUICE

Is your container of orange juice stamped with the Florida Seal of Approval? That doesn't necessarily mean that the juice inside comes from oranges grown in the United States. In 1991, for example, more than 300 million gallons' worth of frozen citrus concentrate was imported into the United States from Brazil, reconstituted and sold to U.S. consumers. *Any orange juice*, no matter where it comes from, can be given the Florida Seal of Approval if it meets Florida state standards. Only orange juice with the "100% Florida" label is certified to come from oranges grown in the United States.

* * * *

ASK THE EXPERTS

STAR-GAZING

Q: *What are those silvery, star-like spots I sometimes see in my eyes?*

A: "Those spots may look like tiny flickers of light or swarms of fireflies. Usually they last a second or two. You may see them after receiving a blow to the head, or after doing a somersault or making some other sharp head movement.

What happens is that the sudden movement increases the pressure in the blood vessels in your eyes for a few moments. That triggers the nerves of your eyes, fooling your brains into thinking you're seeing spots of light." (*Know It All!* by Ed Zotti)

POSSESSED

Q: *Why do cats' eyes shine in the dark?*

A: "[It's] due to the reflection of light by the *tapetum lucidum*—a part of a membrane layer between the retina and the outer covering of the pupils that enables [cats] to see even when there is very little light. In the domestic cat the tapetum lucidum is brilliant green or blue in color and has a metallic luster." (*Why Do Some Shoes Squeak? and 568 Other Popular Questions Answered*, by George W. Stimpson)

HOORAY FOR HOLLYWOOD

Hollywood is so closely identified with the "decadent" film industry, that it's hard to imagine that it started out as a prim Victorian town...but it did.

HISTORY. In 1886, Kansas prohibitionists Harvey and Daeida Wilcox "bought a 120-acre citrus farm in sleepy Cahuenga Valley, a suburb of Los Angeles, for $150/acre." They built an elaborate Victorian house in the middle of a fig orchard, then began subdividing the property. Liquor wasn't allowed, and only "well-educated, worldly, decent" people were offered the property.

In 1903 the subdivision was big enough to become the city of Hollywood. But that didn't last long. In 1910, the citizens voted to make Hollywood an official district of L.A. The reason: They wanted access to L.A.'s water system. Since then, one historian laments, "Hollywood has been reduced to a mere 'northwest sector of the city of Los Angeles.' "

NAME. While her California house was being built in 1886, Daeida Wilcox went East to visit her family. On the train, she met a woman who described a lovely Illinois summer estate, called Hollywood, that was sprinkled with holly trees.

Wilcox was taken with the idea. She repeatedly tried to grow holly on her citrus farm before deciding that the climate wasn't suitable. Perhaps to console herself, she named their ranch "Hollywood" anyway. In 1887 she registered the name with the Los Angeles recorder.

MAIN INDUSTRY. In the early 1900s, the film industry was centered in both New York City and Fort Lee, New Jersey. But soon movie companies were headed west.

The First West Coast Studio. In 1907, Col. William Selig was producing crude silent movies in Chicago, "whenever the sun was shining—which was not frequently enough to make [his business] a profound success." He happened to read a promotional pamphlet

The game of badminton used to be called "poona."

sent East by the Los Angeles Chamber of Commerce that mentioned the city was "bathed in sunshine some 350 days of the year." This impressed Selig, and he sent two men—Francis Boggs and Thomas Parsons—to see if it was true.

To give the area a test, Boggs and Parsons set up a temporary studio in L.A. and began making pictures, recruiting actors off the streets of the city. When they'd completed several pictures, they left to test another location—Colorado—where they compared the climate and photographic possibilities to those on the coast. The West Coast won. Not only was there almost unlimited sunshine, but the varied scenery—mountains, rivers, deserts, and ocean—was unbeatable. Boggs and Parsons shared their discovery with other filmmakers in the east, and in early 1909, Selig went to Los Angeles to build the first L.A. film studio.

The First Hollywood Studio. Ironically, it was the Wilcoxes' puritanism that brought moviemakers to Hollywood. When the couple subdivided their estate, one plot of land wound up in the hands of a tavern owner, who opened a bar there. The outraged Victorians passed a law prohibiting booze, bankrupting the bar. So when the Nestor Moving Picture Company arrived from New Jersey in 1911, it was able to buy the abandoned tavern cheap and convert it into the first Hollywood studio. Within a week, the company had produced Hollywood's first film, *Her Indian Hero*, a Western featuring real Native Americans. Within three months, it was sharing Hollywood with 14 other film companies—despite the "Actors Not Welcome" signs posted all over town.

HOLLYWOOD FACTS

- Early filmmakers who moved West weren't just looking for a place in the sun; they were looking for a place to hide. So many were violating Thomas Edison's motion picture patents that a legal battle known as the Patents War erupted. Southern California was the perfect refuge—as far from the federal government as possible and close enough to the Mexican border for a quick getaway.
- The famous "HOLLYWOOD" sign in the hills above the film capital originally said "HOLLYWOODLAND." It was built in 1923 to promote a real estate development. The last four letters fell down during WW II.

White is the most common color for houses in the United States.

THE LAST LAUGH: EPITAPHS

In the Second Bathroom Reader, *we included some unusual epitaphs sent to us by BRI members. Here's a bunch we've gotten since then.*

Seen in Medway, MA:
In Memory of Peter Daniels, 1688-1746
Beneath this stone, a lump of clay,
Lies Uncle Peter Daniels,
Who too early in the month of May
Took off his winter flannels.

Seen in Ribbesford, England:
Anna Wallace
The children of Israel wanted bread,
And the Lord he sent them manna.
Old clerk Wallace wanted a wife,
And the Devil sent him Anna.

Seen in Westminster Abbey:
John Gay
Life is a joke, and all things show it;
I thought so once and now I know it.

Seen in Death Valley, CA:
May Preston
Here lies the body of fat May Preston
Who's now moved to heaven
To relieve the congestion.

Seen in Falkirk, Scotland:
Jimmy Wyatt
At rest beneath this slab of stone
Lies Stingy Jimmy Wyatt;
He died one morning just at ten
And saved a dinner by it.

Seen in Thanet, England:
Against his will, here lies George Hill
Who from a cliff, fell down quite stiff.
When it happened is not known,
Therefore not mentioned on this stone.

Seen in Shutesbury, MA:
To the Four Husbands of Miss Ivy Saunders
Here lies my husbands, One, Two, Three,
Dumb as men could ever be.
As for my fourth, well, praise be God,
He bides for a little above the sod.
Alex, Ben and Sandy were the first three's names,
And to make things tidy I'll add his—James.

HAPPY BIRTHDAY!

It may come as a surprise to learn that celebrating birthdays is a relatively new tradition for anyone but kings and queens.

BIRTHDAY CELEBRATIONS. The first people known to celebrate birthdays were the ancient Egyptians—starting around 3000 B.C. But only the queen and male members of the royal family were honored. No one even bothered *recording* anyone else's birthdates.

• The ancient Greeks expanded the concept a little: they celebrated the birthdays of all adult males...and kept on celebrating, even after a man had died. Women's and children's birthdays were considered too unimportant to observe.

• The Greeks also introduced the birthday cake (which they got from the Persians) and birthday candles (which may have been used to honor Artemis, goddess of the moon, because they symbolized moonlight).

• It wasn't until the Middle Ages that German peasants became the first to celebrate the birthdays of everyone in the family. Children's birthday celebrations were especially important. Called *Kinderfestes*, they were the forerunner to our toddler birthday parties.

THE BIRTHDAY SONG. Mildred and Patty Smith Hill, two sisters from Louisville, Kentucky, published a song called "Good Morning to All" in a kindergarten songbook in 1893. They wrote it as a "welcoming" song, to be sung to young students at the beginning of each school day.

In 1924, a songbook editor changed the lyrics to "Happy Birthday to You" and published it without the Hill sisters' permission. The new lyrics made it a popular tune, but the Hill family took no action...until the song appeared in a Broadway play in 1933. Then Jessica Hill (a third sister) sued for copyright infringement. She won, but most singers stopped using the song rather than pay the royalty fee. In one play called *Happy Birthday*, for example, actress Helen Hayes *spoke* the words to avoid paying it.

Today, whenever "Happy Birthday" is sung commercially, a royalty still must be paid to the Hills.

What's the most popular candy bar in the U.S.? Snickers.

REAL-LIFE SONGS

Some pop songs are pure fiction, but some are inspired by real events in a songwriters life. Here are four examples of "pop autobiography" from Behind the Hits, *by Bob Shannon and John Javna.*

THE DOCK OF THE BAY—OTIS REDDING. One warm morning in late 1967, Redding relaxed on a houseboat he'd rented in Sausalito, across the bay from San Francisco. He was "just wastin' time"—and he could afford to. A few days earlier, he'd electrified the audience with his midnight show-closing performance at the Monterey Pop Festival. Then, he had headed north to the legendary Fillmore Auditorium in San Francisco and knocked out the audience there. He was definitely on his way to rock stardom. Satisfied, Redding kicked back in the sunshine, played a few chords on his guitar, and dreamed up a little tune: "Sittin' in the mornin' sun..."

When Redding got back to Memphis, he went into the studio and recorded his song. At the end he wasn't sure what to sing or say—so he just whistled, capturing the casual mood he'd been in on that houseboat in Sausalito.

For the Record: Three days later, Redding died in a plane crash near Madison, Wisconsin. "The Dock of the Bay" became the first posthumous #1 record in history—and Redding's only #1 pop hit.

ROXANNE—THE POLICE. On October 20, 1977, the Police—a starving "art rock" band—were scheduled to be the opening act for a punk band in a Paris club. So they loaded up their car with equipment and drove to France. But when they arrived at the club, they found that there was no gig. They weren't opening for anybody, and no one had come to watch them. They played to an empty house anyway, and left disconsolate, because they could scarcely afford to have made the trip for nothing.

Things got worse: As they drove around the city right after the gig, their car broke down; it had to be towed back to London.

Sting, their bass player and singer, decided that as long as he had to walk, he might as well take a stroll through Paris's famous red-light district. "It was the first time I'd seen prostitutes on the

Someone paid $14,000 for the bra Marilyn Monroe wore in *Some Like It Hot*.

streets," Sting recalls. "I imagined being in love with one of those girls. I mean, they do have fellas. How would I feel?" He translated the experience into a song called "Roxanne." Two years later it became the first big New Wave hit and established the Police.

For the Record: Where did he get the name? "It's a beautiful name, with such a rich history....Roxanne was Alexander the Great's wife, and Cyrano de Bergerac's girlfriend."

UP, UP AND AWAY—THE FIFTH DIMENSION. Here's songwriter Jimmy Webb's version of writing the song: "A friend of mine named William F. Williams, who was at radio station KMEN in San Bernardino, was using this hot air balloon for promotions in the...area. He and I were just kind of hanging out, and he took me up a couple of times. The first time, he and I started thinking about doing a film about hot air balloons...just because they were so colorful and so big and so different....He said, 'I've got a great idea for a title—*Up, Up and Away*.' And I said, 'Oh, that's good, I like that.' I was still going to San Bernardino Valley College, so that afternoon I sneaked into a practice room and I wrote 'Up, Up and Away.' The next time I saw him, I said, 'Well, I've got the music for the film.' As it turned out, there never was a film made. But the Fifth Dimension recorded it a few years later, and it worked out nicely for everybody."

SOMEONE SAVED MY LIFE TONIGHT—ELTON JOHN. "She was six feet tall and going out with a midget in Sheffield," Elton John told *Rolling Stone* about a woman he'd met in 1968. "He used to beat her up! I felt so sorry for her...I fell desperately in love." When they moved in together, "It was just like six months in hell....I tried to commit suicide. It was a very Woody Allen-type suicide. I turned on the gas and left all the windows open." Still, Elton planned to marry her. The night before the ceremony, his friend and manager, John Baldry, came over and convinced him to call it off. Some time later, Elton and Bernie Taupin wrote "Someone Saved My Life Tonight" about Baldry's eleventh-hour wedding intervention.

For the Record: Elton didn't like the record. "I thought it was the worst vocal of all time." But it hit #4 on the charts and was nominated for a Grammy.

Sammy Davis, Jr., was originally known professionally as "Silent Sam, the Dancing Midget."

THAT WAS NO LADY...

When Dolly Madison passed away, a critic noted that "the first lady of the nation" had died. Since then, we've referred to all presidents' wives as "First Ladies." Here are 10 facts about them.

1. Following doctor's orders, Eleanor Roosevelt ate three chocolate-covered garlic balls every day of her adult life. Her physician assured her it would improve her memory.

2. Lady Bird Johnson was such a fan of TV's "Gunsmoke" that she sometimes left official functions early to watch the show.

3. William McKinley's wife, Ida, suffered from seizures. (She was believed to be an epileptic.) She and her husband took the problem in stride: whenever she suffered a seizure during a state dinner, President McKinley would drape a handkerchief over her face. When the fit had passed, Ida would remove the handkerchief herself and continue as if nothing had happened.

4. Louisa Adams (John Quincy Adams's wife) had a unique hobby: she spun silk from silkworms living in the mulberry trees on the White House lawn.

5. Martha Washington was such a poor speller (she spelled the word "cat" with two t's) that George often wrote her letters for her.

6. Dolly Madison was addicted to snuff.

7. Edith Wilson (Woodrow Wilson's wife) was a direct descendant of Pocahontas.

8. Elizabeth Monroe, wife of James Monroe, liked to have the White House staff address her as "Your Majesty."

9. Zachary Taylor's wife hated public life so much that she rarely attended White House functions. Many people never even realized the president had a wife until he died in office in 1850...and she attended the funeral.

10. Harry Truman met his future wife, Bess, when both were only five years old. One thing he liked about her: she was the only girl in Independence, Missouri, who could whistle through her teeth.

Bad year: Nobody won the Nobel Peace Prize in 1972.

A TOY IS BORN

You've bought them. You've played with them. Now the BRI will satisfy your curiousity about where they came from and who created them.

WIFFLE BALLS

In 1953, David Mullaney noticed that his son and a friend were playing stickball in the small backyard of their Fairfield, Connecticut, home...but they were using one of Mullaney's plastic golf balls instead of a rubber ball. It seemed like a good idea; that way the ball couldn't be hit or thrown too far.

Intrigued, Mullaney began experimenting with the golf balls. He cut holes in some with a razor blade and discovered that, with the right configuration, players using a lightweight plastic ball could even throw curves and sliders. In 1955, he began manufacturing his new creation, marketing it as a Wiffle Ball—a name he adapted from the baseball term "to whiff," or strike out.

SUPERBALLS

In the early 1960s, a chemist named Norman Stingley was experimenting with high-resiliency synthetics when he discovered a compound he dubbed "Zectron." He was intrigued: When the material was fashioned into a ball, he found it retained almost 100% of its bounce—which meant it had six times the bounce of regular rubber balls. And a Zectron ball kept bouncing about 10 times longer than a tennis ball.

Stingley presented the discovery to his employer, the Bettis Rubber Company, but the firm had no use for it. So, in 1965, Stingley took his Zectron ball to Wham-O, the toy company that had created Hula Hoops and Frisbees. It was a profitable trip. Wham-O snapped up Stingley's invention, named it "Superball," and sold 7 million of them in the next six months.

Scientific Curiosity. Stingley wasn't the only "scientist" interested in Superballs. During the Superball craze, aficionados in Australia made a giant Superball and dropped it from a skyscraper to see if it would bounce all the way back up.

Unfortunately, the experiment went awry: when the ball hit the ground, it split in half and one part went crashing down the street, bouncing off cars and buildings until it crashed through the front window of a store.

PIGGY BANKS

"For almost 300 years," writes Charles Panati in *Extraordinary Origins of Everyday Things*, "the predominant child's bank has been a pig with a slot in its back." Yet, he points out, pigs have no symbolic connection to saving money. So why did people pick a pig?

According to Panati, "The answer is: by coincidence. During the Middle Ages, mined metal was scarce, expensive, and thus rarely used in the manufacture of household utensils. More abundant and economical throughout Western Europe was a type of dense, orange clay known as pygg. It was used in making dishes, cups, pots, and jars, and the earthenware items were referred to as pygg.

"Frugal people then as now saved cash in the kitchen pots and jars. A 'pygg jar' was not yet shaped like a pig. But the name persisted as the clay was forgotten. By the 18th century in England, pygg jar had become pig jar, or pig bank. Potters, not usually etymologists, simply cast the bank in the shape of its common, everyday name."

TROLL DOLLS

In the early 1950s, a Danish woodcarver named Thomas Dam made a wooden doll as a birthday gift for his teenage daughter.

The doll, Dam's interpretation of "the mythical Scandinavian elves visible only to children and childlike grown-ups," was so popular with local kids that a Danish toy store owner insisted he make more of them. Eventually, to keep up with European demand, Dam began mass-producing them out of plastic.

In the early 1960s, they were exported to the United States as Dammit Dolls...and quickly became a teenage fad, adapted to everything from key chains to sentimental "message" dolls. But since Dam had no legal protection for the design, dozens of manufacturers jumped on the troll-wagon with knockoffs called Wish Niks, Dam Things, Norfins, etc.

The original Dammit Dolls are now collectors' items.

OL' BLOOD 'N' GUTS

General George Patton was famous for his one-liners as he was for his military victories in World War II.

"In war, just as in loving, you've got to keep on shoving."

"To be a successful soldier you must know history.... What you must know is how man reacts. Weapons change but man who uses them changes not at all. To win battles you do not beat weapons—you beat the soul of the enemy man."

"Wars may be fought with weapons, but they are won by men. It is the spirit of the men who follow and of the man who leads that gains the victory."

"The most vital quality a soldier can possess is self-confidence, utter, complete, and bumptious."

"Never tell people *how* to do things. Tell them *what* to do and they will surprise you with their ingenuity."

"A pint of sweat will save a gallon of blood."

"Untutored courage is useless in the face of educated bullets."

"Take calculated risks. That is quite different from being rash."

"A piece of spaghetti or a military unit can only be led from the front end."

"Use steamroller strategy; that is, make up your mind on the course and direction of action, and stick to it. But in tactics, do not steamroller. Attack weakness. Hold them by the nose and kick them in the pants."

"There's one thing you men can say when it's all over and you're home once more. You can thank God that twenty years from now when you're sitting by the fireside with your grandson on your knee, and he asks you what you did in the war, you won't have to shift him to the other knee, cough and say, 'I shoveled crap in Louisiana.' "

Q: How long is the world's longest human foot? A: 27 inches.

THE MYTH-ADVENTURES OF CHRISTOPHER COLUMBUS

Who was Christopher Columbus and what did he really do? Much of what we were taught in school is untrue, according to The Myth-Adventures of Christopher Columbus, *by Jack Mingo. Here are some examples.*

THE MYTH: Columbus was born in Genoa, Italy.

BACKGROUND: The only documentary proof is a will written in 1498, purportedly by Columbus, that begins with "I, being born in Genoa..."

THE TRUTH: According to his son Fernando, Columbus never revealed where he was born; he preferred to call himself "a man of the sea." And historians doubt whether the 1498 will is genuine. Meanwhile, dozens of places claim to be Columbus's birthplace, including:

- **Corsica.** The town of Calvi claims both his birth and his remains; Columbus has a tombstone there.
- **France.** In 1687, French lawyer Jean Colomb claimed Chris was his ancestor.
- **England.** A book published in 1682 in London states that Columbus was "born in England, but lived in Genoa."
- **Spain, Armenia, Poland, and even Norway.** Norwegians say his real name was Christopher Bonde.

THE MYTH: Christopher Columbus was named...Christopher Columbus.

BACKGROUND: This name first appeared in 1553, long after his death, in a book by Petrus Martyr.

THE TRUTH: He was never called Columbus in his lifetime. In fact, when Columbus was alive he was known by at least five other names:

- **Cristoforo Colombo.** Most historians believe he was born Cristoforo Colombo (although one Genoese source referred to him as Christofferus de Columbo).
- **Christovam Colom.** When he settled in Portugal and became

a successful merchant-seaman, he was known as Christobal (or Christovam) Colom (or Colombo).

• **Cristobal Colon.** He adopted this name after he moved to Spain (also, occasionally, Christoual or Colamo). This was his name during his voyages and what he's still called in Spanish countries.

• **Christophorus Colonus.** This is the name preferred by his son Fernando, who wrote a biography of his dad. Other Latin forms of the name: Christoforus Colom, Cristoferi Colom.

• **Xpoual de Colon.** This is what he was called in his agreement with the King and Queen of Spain before his first voyage across the Atlantic. After 1493, he signed his name Xpo FERENS, using only his first name, in the fashion of royalty. Later he began to sign his name like this:

.S.
.S. A .S.
X M Y
: Xpo FERENS/

Nobody in the past 500 years has been able to explain what this signature means.

THE MYTH: Columbus's boats were officially named the *Nina*, the *Pinta*, and the *Santa Maria*.

BACKGROUND: Blame historians for spreading the story. For example, in *Three Ships at Dawn*, Augustus Heavy wrote: "*Pinta*, meaning 'Lovely Lady,' was called that because she floated so gracefully; *Nina*, meaning 'Baby,' was named that because it was so small; and the devoutly religious sailors called the last ship the *Santa Maria* in honor of Saint Mary."

THE TRUTH: In Columbus's time, if a ship had any kind of name at all, it was unofficial—usually something that the crew came up with. This was true of Columbus's ships as well:

• The *Pinta* might have been called that in honor of the Pinto family in Palos, where the ships were readied for the voyage. But a more likely explanation: "Pinta" also meant "Painted Lady"—a prostitute.

• The *Nina*, smallest of the three ships, had previously been known as the Santa Clara. "Nina" means "Little Girl"—sailor slang for a woman who's easy with sexual favors.

• And the *Santa Maria*? Many of the crew knew it under its longtime name of *La Gallega* ("Lady from Galicia"), so-called because it was built in that region of Spain. But it had picked up a newer nickname, *Marigalante*—"Dirty Mary." The devout Columbus objected to the name. He demanded that the crew call the boat *Santa Maria* in honor of Jesus' mother.

THE MYTH: Queen Isabella of Spain believed so firmly in Columbus's project that she pawned her jewels to finance it.

BACKGROUND: Two of Columbus's biographers—his son Fernando and Bartolome dé Las Casas—told this tale decades after his death.

THE TRUTH: Isabella didn't pawn a single pearl. The queen had a special fondness for Columbus: they were both in their mid-30s, fervently religious, enthusiastic about reforming the world, and may both have had fair complexions and red hair. Queen Isabella would listen to Columbus for hours as he laid out his maps of the world and described his plans for carrying Christianity across the ocean. Despite that, he couldn't get her to finance his plans, because the crown's funds were tied up in a holy war against the Islamic Moors in southern Spain.

Though Isabella had a great many virtues, religious tolerance wasn't one of them. She went to war with the Muslims and ordered all Jews expelled from Spain. Christians found to be "insincere" were burned alive at the stake while choir boys sang to protect the queen's ears from their screams.

With the fall of Granada, the last Islam stronghold, in January 1492, the queen was full of goodwill and generosity. Columbus saw his chance to plead his case again and received a more benevolent hearing this time. Isabella was now soundly behind his vision of taking Christianity across the waters to save thousands more souls.

But she didn't need to pawn her jewels. As monarch of Castile, she had plenty of her own resources. She used funds from her government coffers, fattened by confiscating property from Jews, Muslims, and "infidels." She even figured out a way to cut expenses. Shippers in the harbor town of Palos, Spain, had been caught smuggling African goods without paying royal duties. As punishment, the town was ordered to supply ships and provisions for Columbus's journey.

The screwdriver was first used to help knights put on their armor.

THE DEATH OF JIM MORRISON

Did Jim Morrison really leave the land of the living in 1971...or did he just slip out of the limelight? Some facts to consider from It's a Conspiracy! *by the National Insecurity Council.*

The Deceased: Jim Morrison, lead singer of the Doors, one of the most popular rock bands of the 1960s.

How He Died: In the summer of 1971, Morrison and his girlfriend, Pamela Courson, went to Paris on vacation. On July 5, Courson allegedly found him dead in the bathtub. Two days later, he was buried in a quiet service attended by five close friends. The official cause of death was listed as a heart attack. He was 27.

SUSPICIOUS FACTS

• Nobody but Courson ever saw Morrison's dead body; neither Morrison's friends nor his family were given the opportunity to view it. After Morrison died, Courson asked Bill Siddons, the Doors' road manager, to come to Paris. He said that when he arrived on July 6, he "was met at the flat by Pamela, a sealed coffin, and a signed death certificate." He never saw Morrison's body.

• When asked the name of the doctor who signed the death certificate, Siddons said he didn't know, and Courson said she didn't remember. Moreover, according to *No One Here Gets Out Alive*, a 1980 biography of Morrison, "There was no police report, no doctor present. No autopsy had been conducted."

• When Courson filed the death certificate at the U.S. Embassy on July 7, the day of the funeral, she claimed there were no living relatives—which meant that since there was no one to be notified, Morrison could be buried quickly. In fact, Jim's family lived in Arlington, Virginia.

• Morrison's friends kept the story of his death a secret for almost a week. Siddons told his story to the media six days after Morrison died, two days after the funeral. Beyond noting that Morrison had died of "natural causes," Siddons had no more to add.

It's auto-matic: according to recent polls 40% of American couples first discuss marriage in a car.

POSSIBLE CONCLUSIONS

• **Morrison is really dead.** His friends say they hushed up his death to protect his privacy. A statement prepared for the public said, "The initial news of his death and funeral was kept quiet...to avoid all the notoriety and circus-like atmosphere that surrounded the deaths of such other rock personalities as Janis Joplin and Jimmy Hendrix."

• **Morrison is hiding out.** At the time of his death, Morrison's life was a mess. He had been convicted on two counts of profanity and indecent exposure in Miami and faced a jail sentence if his appeal failed; he faced a possible 10-year sentence after being busted by the FBI for being drunk and disorderly on an airplane; and more than 20 paternity suits were pending against him. Facts:

✓ Morrison was sick of his life as a rock star and had been saying so for years. He said he wanted to start over anonymously, so he could just write. With Courson's help, he could easily have faked his own death to give himself a fresh start.

✓ For years, Courson had urged Morrison to quit the band and develop himself as a poet.

✓ She, or someone else, started a rumor that Morrison may have visited a Paris hangout earlier in the evening and obtained some heroin. That, mixed with alcohol, is what supposedly killed him. Yet for all the drugs he ingested, no friends ever mentioned heroin, and Morrison was afraid of needles.

✓ The absence of an autopsy and police report is very suspicious, and the lie about his parents and the quick "burial" forestalled any further inquiries. A doctor could have been bribed to fake a death certificate.

✓ Finally, Morrison had repeatedly talked about Paris. According to one close friend of the singer, "he thought it was a place where he could be himself and not have people hounding him and making a circus out of his life, making him something he wasn't."

RECOMMENDED READING

All of the quotes in this chapter are from *No One Here Gets Out Alive*, by Jerry Hopkins and Danny Sugerman (Warner Books, 1980).

According to mathematicians, the billionth digit of pi is 9.

PARKING METER TRIVIA

Fortunately for us, no one's figured out how to put parking meters in bathrooms...but it seems like they're everywhere else. Here's a little parking meter history, from The Little Book of Boston Parking Horrors, *by Michael Silverstein and Linda Elwood (Silverwood Publications, 1986).*

THE ORIGIN OF PARKING METERS

• In the early 1930s, Carl Magee, an Oklahoma City journalist, decided he was sick of looking for a parking space every time he drove to town.

• He was sure there was a way to build a machine that kept track of how long a car was parked in a space, but didn't know how to do it. So in 1933 he sponsored a contest at the Engineering Department of Oklahoma State University, offering to pay a cash prize to the student who designed the best working model. A number of students entered the contest, but none came up with a workable design.

• Finally, two engineering professors at the university submitted a design. Magee liked it so much that he formed a company to sell their "parking meters."

TAKING IT TO THE STREET

• The first parking meter, the "Park-O-Meter," was installed at the intersection of First and Robinson in July 1935. Cost: 5¢ an hour.

• When the first batch of 150 meters was installed, curious motorists came from miles around to witness the unveiling and try one out.

• One local farmer tied his horse to the meter (he told reporters it was cheaper than keeping the horse in a stable); another family pumped a day's worth of nickels into the meter, set up a card table, and spent the day playing bridge with their neighbors.

• The first person to get a ticket was Reverend H. C. North, a local clergyman. He was also the first person to talk his way out of a fine: He told the judge he'd gone to get change when the meter expired.

• R. H. Avant, another local, was the first person to actually *pay* a fine for a meter violation. He handed over $11, an enormous amount of money in 1935. (Not all early fines were that steep; one woman only had to pay $3—and her fine was suspended until she sold enough chickens to come up with the money.)

THE TV SPEECH THAT MADE A PRESIDENT

No one would have believed Ronald Reagan could be elected president—or even governor of California—until he gave a pro-Goldwater TV speech in 1964 called "A Time for Choosing." Then he was on his way.

BACKGROUND. In 1954, Ronald Reagan was having such a hard time getting acting jobs that he had to work as a Las Vegas emcee. Then came General Electric.

G.E. was looking for someone to host its new half-hour television show—"a man," says one historian, "who could act, sell General Electric products, help build the company's corporate image, and visit General Electric plants to improve company morale." Reagan's agent at MCA got wind of it; he thought the assignment was tailor-made for Ronnie...and G.E. agreed.

Reagan started at $125,000 a year...then got a quick boost to $150,000—because G.E. loved him. "He was a superb TV salesman," one biographer says. "There was a joke in Hollywood about someone who'd watched Reagan deliver an institutional advertisement for G.E.'s nuclear submarine, then remarked, 'I really didn't need a submarine, but I've got one now.'"

G.E. Spokesman

Between TV appearances on "G.E. Theater" from 1954 to 1962, Reagan traveled the country representing the company. He visited 125 G.E. plants, spoke to thousands of Rotary Clubs and other service organizations, and met with 250,000 workers. At each stop, he gave a standard address that became known as "The Speech." It was a conservative diatribe extolling free enterprise and warning against the evils of big government.

Republican

In 1962, G.E. canceled "G.E. Theater," and Reagan became host of "Death Valley Days." He also became more active in Republican politics, speaking on behalf of Richard Nixon (who ran for California governor in 1962) and right-wing causes like Dr. Fred Schwartz's Christian anti-Communist campaign. He even produced

Millie the White House dog earned more than four times as much as Pres. Bush in 1991.

Ronald Reagan Record Kits "to warn listeners of...the spreading virus of socialized medicine."

Goldwater Supporter

When Barry Goldwater was nominated for president in 1964, Reagan became co-chair of Californians for Goldwater.

"In late October," writes Larry Learner in his book *Make-Believe*, "Goldwater was unable to speak at the big $1000-a-plate dinner at the Ambassador Hotel in Los Angeles." Reagan was asked to pinch-hit.

"Asking Ronnie to talk about the 'cause,'" says Learner, "was like getting Billy Graham to discuss sin. He had been preparing his speech for more than a decade as he toured the country for General Electric. He had tried out each bit and piece scores of times. He had tested the response to each of his anecdotes, each of his stories of outrage, each of his shocking facts a score of times."

Naturally, the speech went over well. In fact, it raised so much money around the state that California Republicans decided to televise it nationally. They called it "A Time for Choosing."

THE SPEECH

"On October 27, 1964," writes Lou Cannon in *Ronald Reagan*, "a washed-up 53-year-old movie actor...made a speech on national television on behalf of a Republican presidential candidate who had no chance to be elected....Most of his address was standard, anti-government boilerplate larded with denunciations of communism and a celebration of individual freedom. His statistics were sweeping and in some cases dubious. His best lines were cribbed from Franklin Roosevelt." He only mentioned Goldwater five times in the entire half-hour speech. Yet it was a magic moment in TV political history. Here are a few excerpts:

• "You and I are told increasingly that we have to choose between a left or a right, but I would like to suggest that there is no such thing as a left or a right....There is only an up or a down: up to man's age-old dream—the ultimate in individual freedom consistent with law and order—or down to the ant heap of totalitarianism."

• "We have so many people who can't see a fat man standing beside a thin one without coming to the conclusion that the fat man got that way by taking advantage of the thin one! So they are going to

A scallop has 35 eyes—all of them blue.

solve all the problems of human misery through government and government planning."

• "We cannot buy our security, our freedom from the threat of the bomb, by committing an immorality so great as saying to a billion human beings now in slavery behind the Iron Curtain, 'Give up your dreams of freedom because to save our own skin, we are willing to make a deal with your slave-masters.'"

• "You and I have a rendezvous with destiny. We will preserve for our children this, the last best hope of man on Earth, or we will sentence them to take the last step into a thousand years of darkness. We will keep in mind and remember that Barry Goldwater has faith in us. He has faith that you and I have the ability and the dignity and the right to make our own decisions and determine our own destiny. Thank you."

THE REACTION

Before the speech, powerful California conservatives considered Reagan "little more than an after-dinner entertainer and cheerleader." Afterward, he was regarded as the new star of the Right.

"Everyone thought I'd done well," recalls Reagan, "but still you don't know always about these things. Then the phone rang about midnight. It was a call from Washington, D.C., where it was 3 a.m. One of Goldwater's staff called to tell me that the switchboard was still lit up from the calls pledging money to his campaign. I then slept peacefully. The speech raised $8 million [at that time, more than any speech in history] and soon changed my life."

Washington columnist David Broder called it "the most successful political debut since William Jennings Bryan electrified the 1896 Democratic convention." A group in Michigan immediately formed a Reagan for President committee. And legend has it that after watching the speech, President Johnson himself turned to aide Bill Moyers and drawled, "Y' know, the Republicans have the wrong damn boy runnin' for president." The direct result of the speech: California Republicans insisted that Reagan run for governor of California. He did, and won two times. His next elected office was the presidency.

"Fluency in English is something that I'm often not accused of."

—*George Bush*

DEFINITIONS

In previous Bathroom Readers *we've included some uncommon words, and their meanings, to help build weak vocabularies. Here's another batch.*

Ambivert: A person who's half introvert and half extrovert.
Backclipping: Shortening a longer word into a smaller one, like *chrysanthemum* to *mum.*
Boomer: A male kangaroo.
Callipygian: Having shapely buttocks.
Chad: The little circles of paper your hole-punch makes.
Furfurrate: What dandruff does when it falls from your scalp.
Genuglyphics: Painting or decorating a person's knees to make them more erotic.
Hypocorism: Baby talk.
Infix: A word placed inside another word to change its meaning, as in *fan-f------tastic.*
Izzard: The name of the letter "z."
Kith: Your friends.
Lecanoscopy: The act of hypnotizing yourself by staring into a sink filled with water.
Liveware: People who work with computer software and hardware.
Nidus: A place where bacteria multiplies.
Otoplasty: A surgical procedure to fix ears that stick out.
Otorhinolaryngologist: An ear, nose, and throat doctor.
Pandiculate: To yawn.
Paradog: A military dog that's been trained to parachute out of airplanes.
Paranymph: The bridesmaid or best man at a wedding.
Pica: A desire to eat nonfoods (like dirt).
Pilomotor reaction: What your hair does when it stands on end.
Pip: What an unhatched chick does to break through its eggshell.
Pullet: A female chicken one year old or younger.
Puwo: An animal that's half poodle and half wolf.
Taresthesia: The tingling sensation you get when your foot falls asleep.
Tautonym: A word consisting of two identical parts, like *tutu.*
Ucalegon: A neighbor whose house is burning down.
Zoonoses: Diseases humans can get from animals.

INSIDE "JEOPARDY!"

"If I had a TV in my bathroom," writes BRI member D. Ottati, "I'd be a regular 'Jeopardy!' watcher. How about a few pages on the program, so I can still think about 'Jeopardy!' in the john?" We aim to please, so here's some info from The Jeopardy! Book, *by Alex Trebek.*

ORIGIN. In 1963 Merv Griffin and his wife, Juliann, were on a flight to New York when they began discussing game shows. Griffin describes the conversation:

"After the quiz show scandals of the late fifties, the networks were leery of shows where contestants answered questions for money....I mentioned how much I liked the old quiz shows, but reminded her that the scandals had created credibility problems for producers.

"'So,' Juliann joked, 'Why not just give them the answers to start with?' She was kidding, but the thought struck me between the eyes. She said to me, '79 Wistful Vista.' And I replied, 'What's Fibber McGee and Molly's address?'" The "Jeopardy!" format was born.

THE SHOW GOES ON

As soon as the plane landed in New York, Griffin began working on the show. "I decided to create separate categories of answers, such as History, Literature, Motion Pictures. Put the categories in columns and assign dollar values to each square. That was it. One big board with ten categories and ten answers in each category. We called the game 'What's the Question?' and had a game board built to show to NBC."

The Name. "During the development process, I showed our efforts to network executive Ed Vane, who commented, 'I like what I see, but the game needs more Jeopardies,' " or portions of the game where the players risk losing it all. "I didn't hear another word he said after that. All I could think of was the name: goodbye 'What's the Question?,' hello 'Jeopardy!' "

Showtime. At first, NBC executives disliked the show. During the final sales presentation to the network, NBC head Mort Werner played the game, with Merv Griffin acting as host. Halfway through it, Werner threw up his hands and shouted, "I didn't get one ques-

Poll results: 62% of Americans say Monday is the worst day of the week.

tion right; it's too hard." But before he could reject the show, an assistant leaned over and whispered, "Buy it." Werner bought it. (The assistant, a man named Grant Tinker, eventually became head of NBC himself.)

THE HOSTS

Art Fleming. The first "Jeopardy!" host was an announcer Merv Griffin had seen on a TWA commercial. Fleming hosted the program for more than 12 years, ultimately appearing on 2,858 shows between 1964 and 1979.

Alex Trebek. Trebek took over when the show was revived in 1984. Earlier that year, Chuck Woolery, host of "Wheel of Fortune" (another Merv Griffin game show) became ill. The producer needed a replacement host, and he called Alex Trebek, who was emceeing a game show called "Battlestars." Trebek agreed to fill in, and did so well that he was hired to host the new "Jeopardy!"

ANSWERS & QUESTIONS

How do they come up with their questions?

- A research staff of 12 writers drafts the questions and provides at least two sources verifying the information.
- Then the show's editorial associate producer edits the questions and assigns dollar amounts.
- The questions are then sent back to a different researcher, who verifies them again.
- From there the questions are given to the show's producer, who can ask for even further verification.
- On game day Alex Trebek reviews the questions himself.

More than 300,000 questions have been through this review process.

CONTESTANTS

Where do they get the contestants?

- Every year, 250,000 people apply for an audition, either through the station that broadcasts the show in their area, or by contacting the show itself.
- Only 15,000 are chosen for the initial screening exam, and only 1,500 qualify to become contestants. Then, only 500 actually make it on the air.

IN THE BLINK OF AN EYE

In the time it takes to read this four-page article, you'll blink at least 30 times. Or at least that's what Jay Ingram says in his fascinating book, The Science of Everyday Life. *Here are some of the more fascinating tidbits on blinking and the eye from Ingram's book and others.*

IT CLEANS & MOISTENS!

"The typical eyeball is about 2.5 centimeters in diameter and seven grams in weight," reports Thinkquest. That translates to just about one inch wide, and about 1/4 of an ounce.

• The front, non-white part of the eye—the *cornea*—is covered by a transparent membrane called the *conjunctiva*, which functions along with the lachrymal (or tear) gland, to keep the eyeball moist.

• When we blink, the tear gland releases tears and the eyelid washes the eyeball clean while moistening it at the same time.

• From there the liquid collects in tear ducts at the sides of our eyes, and it eventually drains back into our bodies by way of the back of the nasal passages.

• Beyond keeping the eyeball moist, the blink serves other important functions. It protects the eyeball from nearby objects, like an oncoming finger. But primarily it acts as a cleaning device, washing out dust and dirt particles and killing germs and bacteria.

• A blink is an involuntary reaction, much like breathing and if you choose to not blink, your body will usually take over and do it for you when your eyes get dry enough.

FAST, FAST, FAST RELIEF!

• How often one blinks varies from person to person, but most scientists agree that we blink an average of 17,000 times in a day.

• That translates to roughly one blink every five seconds and rounds up to six-and-a-quarter million times in one year.

• Each blink lasts about three-tenths of a second.

• Author Jay Ingram: "Slow motion replays show that the eyelid

Astronaut Buzz Aldrin claims to have been the first man to "piss in his pants on the moon."

begins to drop, builds up speed to a maximum, then begins to slow again before your eye is actually closed."

• The eye-closing part of a blink lasts, on average, one-tenth of a second.

• Ingram, again: "The eyelid stays closed for about one-twentieth of a second, then it starts accelerating back upward again, leaving a film of tears behind. The odd thing is that even though your eye is partly or completely closed for three-tenths of a second or more, you aren't aware of missing anything."

BLINKIN' PSYCHOLOGY

• We tend to blink faster when we're excited or nervous. For instance, someone who's on television tends to average between 31 and 50 blinks per minute—twice the normal rate.

• But why? A chemical called dopamine is responsible. It's released in the brain when we're under stress...which triggers body arousal —faster heart rate, quicker breathing, and more rapid eyelid movement, or blinking.

• Knowing this, psychotherapists have long thought that excessive blinking in a patient can reflect, among other things, a deep-seated desire to hide. As a result, blink rates are used to gauge subjects taking polygraph tests as well. The normal blink rate is about twenty times per minute. A faster rate signifies anxiety, emotional distress, or that the "fight or flight" response is kicking in—all indicators that someone may be lying.

INSIDE INFO

• FBI Special Agent, Joe Navarro, has gone so far as to identify a specific type of blink that he directly associates with someone about to lie.

• In an online interview, Navarro explains: "On NBC's "Today Show," Matt Lauer talked about how Madonna had lied to him about her announced pregnancy just the other day. He showed the video and her response but he missed something to ponder about. She did what I call the eyelash flutter when asked, "Are you pregnant?"

• It's different under high speed camera from the eye-blink, we can see that it does not close completely and the speed is amazing. I first observed this eyelid behavior in 1985, and find that people who are troubled by a question or an event do this, especially if they have to answer and are about to lie.

• "I tell attorneys to look for the eyelash flutter when they have people on the stand; it means they really do not like the question at all. I even had a case where the individual picked out the route of escape for me when I went through several routes with him; I just waited for the flutter to pick out the way."

DEMOCRACY GOES ON THE BLINK

• With the advent of video closeups, political analysts have looked for signs in the blinking of politicians. Somebody with a video recorder and a stopwatch discovered that Richard Nixon blinked twice as much as normal when answering hostile questions about Watergate and that Bill Clinton's blinking rate went up from 51 blinks per minute to 71 when discussing Monica Lewinsky.

• During the television debates between Michael Dukakis and George Bush, somebody else discovered that both candidates blinked faster when questions were directed to them.

• Most recently, Boston College neuropsychologist Joe Tecce noted that George W. Bush blinked an average of 82 blinks a minute, indicating severe stress. Al Gore, on the other hand, blinked at a rate of 48 blinks a minute. Based on the previous six elections, where the slower blinker won, Tecce believed it was a sign that Gore was more likely to keep his head and win the election. However, as the election showed, the eyes didn't have it.

• The extremes of blinking in presidential debates? Bob Dole is "the fastest blinker among all world leaders I've studied," says Tecce. He clocked a record 147 blinks per minute in his 1996 debate with Clinton. The slowest? Ross Perot, who managed a meditative 9 bpm in the three-way 1992 debate.

DOCTOR, MY EYES

• Excessive blinking in children is one of the symptoms that pediatricians watch for. It can mean a number of things, including allergies, chronic exposure to cigarette smoke, extreme anxiety or eye problems.

• Rapid and habitual blinking is often the first symptom that appears in children who are developing Tourette's Syndrome. On the other hand, sometimes it's just a habit that a kid does because it gets him adult attention.

WITH A NOD AND A WINK

• Blinking eyes have many times been used as a signal. American prisoners of war appearing before movie cameras communicated secret messages in Morse code during the Vietnam War.

• While frozen within a block of ice, magician David Blaine answered questions by blinking once for yes and twice for no.

• However, the most extraordinary use of blinking for communication has to be writer Jean-Dominque Bauby. Profoundly paralyzed by a stroke, he lost all movement in his body except his left eyelid. Using 200,000 blinks and a very patient friend, Bauby wrote his memoirs. The book became an instant bestseller in France, but Bauby all-but-missed the excitement—he died two days after it was published.

HISTORY PASSES IN A BLINK OR TWO

• The Roman emperor Gaius screened gladiators based on whether they could go unblinking into the face of extreme danger. It wasn't a foolproof test—only two of 20,000 passed it.

• It was a blinking surgeon during the French Revolution who first demonstrated that a head lived for a short time after decapitation. Unfortunately, the head in question was his own. Antoine Lavoisier (1743–1794), a French chemist who discovered oxygen, was beheaded during the Reign of Terror. Ever the scientist, before being beheaded he told a friend that he would continue blinking for as long as possible after the guillotine struck to see how long he would remain conscious. His friend reported that Lavoiser's disembodied head blinked for about 15 seconds.

* * *

And Speaking Of Eyes.... According to a story in the *Washington Times*, "glass eyes" are no longer made from glass, but a hard, virtually unbreakable plastic. That's a good thing, since 17,000 to 18,000 people lose an eyeball every year. A good replacement eye is indistinguishable from a real one, but it doesn't come cheap—$1700 to $2500 for a custom-matched eye, made by an expert ocularist.

Galileo went blind studying the sun through telescopes.

10 CANDY BARS YOU'LL NEVER EAT

These tidbits about extinct candy bars come from Dr. Ray Broekel, "candy bar historian" and publisher of a newsletter called the Candy Bar Gazebo.

THE AIR MAIL BAR. Introduced in 1930 to honor the first airmail flight in the U.S.—in 1918, from Washington, D.C. to New York City. Ironically, the first flight never made it to New York. After takeoff, the pilot noticed someone had forgotten to fill the fuel tank. Then he got lost over Maryland and had to land in a cow pasture. The Air Mail candy bar had a similar fate.

FAT EMMA. In the early1920s, the Pendergast Candy Company in Minneapolis introduced a candy bar with a nougat center. They planned to call it the Emma bar. But when it wound up twice as thick as expected (they accidentally put too much egg white in the mixture), they changed the name to Fat Emma. Later, Frank Mars copied the idea to create the Milky Way bar.

THE SAL-LE-DANDE BAR. The first candy bar named after a stripper—Sally Rand, whose "fan dance" at the 1933-34 Chicago World's Fair in shocked and titillated the nation. In the 1960s, another stripper bar was available briefly: the Gypsy bar, named after Gypsy Rose Lee.

THE RED GRANGE BAR. Endorsed by Red Grange, the most popular football player of his day. After starring at the University of Illinois, he joined the Chicago Bears in 1925 and helped keep the National Football League in business. Unfortunately, he couldn't do the same for his candy bar.

THE VEGETABLE SANDWICH BAR. One of the weirdest "health" bars ever made, this 1920s vegetable concoction contained cabbage, celery, peppers, and tomatoes. Its makers claimed it aided digestion and "will not constipate."

The average American throws out 1,905 pounds. of garbage every year.

THE ZEP CANDY BAR. "Sky-High Quality." One of several candy bars that capitalized on the popularity of "lighter-than-air" dirigibles in the 1930s. This one featured a sketch of a Graf Zeppelin on the wrapper. It was taken off the market after the Hindenburg exploded in 1937.

THE CHICKEN DINNER BAR. One of the bestselling bars you've never heard of. It was introduced in the 1920s and remained on the market for about 50 years. The original wrapper featured a picture of a roasted chicken on a dinner plate—a bizarre way of suggesting it was a nourishing meal and encouraging consumers to associate it with prosperity ("a chicken in every pot"). The manufacturer, Sperry Candy Co., even dispatched a fleet of Model A trucks disguised as giant sheet-metal chickens to deliver the candy to stores. Several years after the bar's debut, Sperry dropped the chicken from the wrapper. But it kept the name.

THE BIG-HEARTED "AL" BAR. George Williamson, owner of the Williamson Candy Company, was a good Democrat and a good friend of New York governor Al Smith, Democratic nominee for president in 1928. Smith lost in a landslide to Herbert Hoover, and his candy bar soon followed.

THE SEVEN UP CANDY BAR. Got its name from having seven connected pieces, each with a different center. The bar came out in the 1930s, before the 7-Up Bottling Company began producing its soft drink—so the Trudeau Candy Company owned the trademark rights to the name. Eventually the 7-Up Bottling Company bought the bar and retired it, so they had exclusive use of the name no matter how it was spelled—*Seven Up* or *7-Up*.

THE "IT" BAR. The #1 female sex symbol of the silent movie era was Clara Bow—known as the "It Girl." (She had that special quality her movie studio called "It.") In 1927 the McDonald Candy Company of Salt Lake City tried cashing in on her popularity with a candy bar featuring her face on the wrapper. It did well for a few years, then disappeared along with Bow. (She wasn't able to make the switch to talkies, because although she was lovely to look at, her Brooklyn accent made her impossible to listen to.)

Also Gone: The Betsy Ross bar, the Lindy (for Charles Lindbergh), Amos 'n' Andy, Poor Prune, Vita Sert, and Doctor's Orders.

THAT'S A LOAD OF GARBAGE

You think it's a pain to take out the garbage at home? Just be glad you haven't got these problems.

Garbage: 400,000 pounds of "pizza sludge" (flour, tomato paste, cheese, pepperoni, etc.)

Location: Wellston, Ohio

Source: A Jeno's, Inc., frozen pizza plant

Problem: Jeno's produced so much waste in their pizza factory that the local sewage system couldn't accommodate it. They couldn't bury it either, because environmental experts said it would "move in the ground" once they put it there. They had to truck it out.

Garbage: 27 years' worth of radioactive dog poop

Location: Unknown

Source: Department of Energy experiments. For almost three decades, the DOE studied the effects of radiation by feeding 3,700 beagles radiation-laden food. Each ate the food for a year and a half, and was then left to live out its life.

Problem: No one anticipated that while the experiment was going on, the dog-doo would be dangerous and would have to be treated as hazardous waste. They saved it for decades...and finally took it to a hazardous waste facility.

Garbage: 1,000 pounds of raspberry gelatin and 16 gallons of whipped cream

Location: Inside a car in Provo, Utah

Source: Evan Hansen, a student at Brigham Young University. He won a radio contest for "most outrageous stunt" by cutting the roof off a station wagon and filling the car with the dessert.

Problem: Hansen couldn't find any way to get rid of the Jell-O. He finally drove to a shopping center parking lot, opened his car doors, and dumped it down a storm drain. He was fined $500 for violating Utah's Water Pollution Control Act.

WHAT, ME WORRY?

Mad magazine has a place in American pop culture as one of the most successful humor magazines ever published. It's also great bathroom reading. Here's a brief history.

BACKGROUND

In 1947 Max Gaines, owner of Educational Comics (which published biblical, scientific, and historical comic books), was killed in a boating accident. He left the business to his 25-year-old son, William, a university student.

The younger Gaines renamed the company Entertaining Comics (EC) and got rid of the stodgy educational stuff. Instead, he started publishing more profitable crime, suspense, and horror comics like *Tales from the Crypt*, *Vault of Horrors*, and *House of Fear*.

THE BIRTH OF *MAD*

Gaines paid his writers and artists by the page. Most of his employees preferred this—but not Harvey Kurtzman. Kurtzman was a freelancer who worked on *Frontline Combat*, a true-to-life battle comic that portrayed the negative aspects of war. He enjoyed writing it, but it took so long to research and write that he couldn't make a living doing it. So he went to Gaines and asked for a raise. Gaines refused, but suggested an alternative—in addition to his current work, Kurtzman could produce a satirical comic, which would be easier and more profitable to write. Kurtzman liked the idea and immediately started creating it.

The first issue of *Tales Calculated to Drive You Mad: Humor in a Jugular Vein* debuted in August 1952. It was a flop...and so were the next two issues. But Gaines didn't know it; back then, it took so long to get sales reports that the fourth issue—which featured a *Superman* spoof called *Superduperman*—was already in the works before Gaines realized he was losing money. By then, *Mad* had started to sell.

RED SCARE

Gaines didn't expect *Mad* to be as successful as his other comics, but it turned out to be the only one to survive the wave of anti-comic hysteria that swept the country during the McCarthy era.

In 1953, Frederic Wertham, a noted psychiatrist and self-proclaimed "mental hygienist," published a book called *The Seduction of the Innocents*, a scathing attack on the comic book industry. Few comics were left untouched—Wertham denounced Batman and Robin as homosexuals, branded Wonder Woman a lesbian, and claimed that words such as "arghh," "blam," "thunk," and "kap-ow" were producing a generation of illiterates. The charges were outlandish, but the public believed it; churches across the country even held comic book burnings.

To defend themselves, big comic book publishers established the Comics Code Authority (CCA) to set standards of "decency" for the comic industry and issue a seal of approval to comics that passed scrutiny. (Among the so-called reforms: only "classic" monsters such as vampires and werewolves could be shown; authority figures such as policemen, judges, and government officials could not be shown in a way that encouraged "disrespect for authority," and the words "crime," "horror," and "weird" were banned from comic book titles.) Magazine distributors would no longer sell comics that didn't adhere to CCA guidelines.

Gaines refused to submit his work to the CCA, but he couldn't withstand public pressure. By 1954, only four EC titles were left. Amazingly, *Mad* was one of them.

MAD LIVES

Gaines knew *Mad* wouldn't survive long unless he did something drastic to save it. So rather than *fight* the CCA, he avoided it: He dropped *Mad's* comic book format and turned it into a full-fledged, "slick" magazine. Thus, it was no longer subject to CCA censorship.

The first *Mad* magazine was published in the summer of 1955. "We really didn't know how *Mad*, the slick edition, was going to come out," one early *Mad* staffer later recalled, "but the people who printed it were laughing and getting a big kick out of it, so we said 'This has got to be good.' "

The first issue sold so many copies that it had to be sent back for a second printing. By 1960, sales hit 1 million copies, and *Mad* was being read by an estimated 58% of American college students and 43% of high school students.

In 1967, Warner Communications, which owned DC Comics,

The average bird's eyes take up 50% of the space in its skull.

bought *Mad*, but it couldn't affect sales or editorial content: as part of the deal, Warner had to leave Gaines alone. In 1973 sales hit an all-time high of 2.4 million copies; since then they've leveled off at 1 million annually in the United States. There are also 12 foreign editions. Gaines died in 1992, but *Mad* continues to thrive.

WHAT, ME WORRY?

Alfred E. Neuman has been *Mad* magazine's mascot for years. But his face and even his "What me worry?" slogan predate the magazine by 50 years. They were adapted from advertising postcards issued by a turn-of-the-century dentist from Topeka, Kansas, who called himself "Painless Romaine."

Mad artists were able to rationalize their plagiarism, according to Harvey Kurtzman, after they discovered that Romaine himself had lifted the drawing from an illustration in a medical textbook showing a boy who had gotten too much iodine in his system.

Kurtzman first dubbed the boy "Melvin Koznowski." But he was eventually renamed Alfred E. Neuman, after a nerdy fictional character on the "Henry Morgan Radio Show." Strangely enough, *that* character had been named after a real-life Alfred Newman, who was the composer and arranger for more than 250 movies, including *The Hunchback of Notre Dame* and *The Grapes of Wrath*.

MAD FACTS

• In 1965, *Mad* magazine was turned into an off-Broadway play called *The Mad Show*. Notices were sent out to New York theater critics in the form of ransom notes tied to bricks. The show gave performances at 3:00 p.m. and midnight, and sold painted rocks, Ex-Lax, Liquid Drano, and hair cream in the lobby. The play got great reviews from the press and ran for two years, with bookings in Los Angeles, Chicago, Boston, and other major cities. It was reportedly a major influence on the creators of "Laugh In."

• *The Mad Movie*, Gaines's first attempt to adapt *Mad* for the silver screen, was dumped before production began, and *Up the Academy*, Mad's second effort, was so bad that Gaines paid $50,000 to have all references to the magazine edited out of the film. An animated TV series in the early 1970s was pulled before it aired. In the mid-1990s, "Mad TV" debuted on the Fox network.

Bird droppings are the chief export of Nauru, an island nation in the western Pacific.

PRETTY FLAMINGOS

They're America's beloved symbol of bad taste—as designs for lawn ornaments, lamps, cups, and so on. BRI member Jack Mingo tells us how these strange-looking birds became as American as apple pie.

THE FLAMINGO BOOM

During the 1920s, Florida was the hottest vacation spot in the United States. Tens of thousands of real estate speculators and tourists swarmed to the semitropical state...and many brought home souvenirs bearing pictures of a bizarre pink bird that lived there—the flamingo.

In the North, these items—proof that their owners were rich enough to travel to exotic places—became status symbols. Everyone wanted them. So manufacturers started incorporating flamingos into a variety of new product designs.

They were so popular that by the 1950s, the image of a flamingo was as much a part of middle-class America as Wonder Bread or poodles.

THE LAWN FLAMINGO

In 1952, the Union Plastics Company of Massachusetts introduced the first flamingo lawn ornament. It was "flat and unappealing."

• To boost sales, the company decided to offer a more lifelike, three-dimensional flamingo. But the second generation of lawn flamingos "was made of construction foam and fell apart rather quickly," recalls a company executive. "Dogs loved to chew it up."

• Finally, in 1956, Union Plastics hired a 21-year-old art student named Don Featherstone to sculpt a new lawn flamingo. "I got a bunch of nature books and started studying them," says Featherstone. "Finally, I sculpted one, and I must say it was a beautiful looking thing."

• The first atomic-pink molded plastic lawn flamingo went on sale in 1957. It was an immediate success; in the next decade, Americans bought millions of them. But by the 1970s, lawn flamingos were, "gathering dust on the hardware store shelves along with other out-of-date lawn ornaments such as the scorned sleeping

Mexican peasant and the black jockey." In 1983, The *New York Times* ran an article titled "Where Did All Those (Plastic) Flamingos Go?"

• Then suddenly, lawn flamingos were flying again. 1985 was a record year, with 450,000 sold in the United States. Why the resurgence? Critics suggested a combination of nostalgia and the popularity of the television show "Miami Vice." "They are a must for the newest hot social events—'Miami Vice' parties," reported a California newspaper in 1986.

• Featherstone never got any royalties for his creation. But he did become a vice president of Union Plastics...and in 1987, he was honored when the company started embossing its flamingos with his signature. "I'm getting my name pressed into the rump of every flamingo that goes out the door," he announced proudly.

FLAMINGO: THE BIRD

History. Flamingos, looking pretty much as they do today, were roaming the earth 47 million years before humans came along.

• They were well known in Egypt during the pyramid-and-sphinx period. A flamingo played a prominent role in Aristophanes' 414 B.C. play *The Birds*.

• The American flamingo is extinct in the wild—captive flocks (most with wings clipped so they don't fly away) at zoos and bird sanctuaries are the only ones left.

Body. Flamingos' knees don't really bend backward. But their legs are so long that the joint you see where it seems the knee ought to be is really the flamingo's ankle, and it bends the same way yours does. The knee is hidden, high up inside the body.

• The flamingo is the only bird that eats with its head upside down—even while it is standing up.

Color. While flamingos are known to sometimes eat small fish, shrimp, and snails, they are primarily vegetarians. They consume vast quantities of algae, and this is what makes them pink. Without the "food coloring," flamingos are actually white.

• Flamingos in captivity are, as a result of algae deprivation, quite a bit paler than their wild cousins. Zoos attempt to keep their flamingo flocks in the pink by feeding them carotene to compensate for the algae they'd get in their natural habitats.

There are more plastic flamingos in America than real ones.

GIVE 'EM HELL, HARRY

Here are a few words from President Harry Truman.

"I never did give anybody hell. I just told the truth, and they thought it was hell."

"The C students run the world."

"The only things worth learning are the things you learn after you know it all."

"You know what makes leadership? It is the ability to get men to do what they don't want to do, and like it."

"You want a friend in this life, get a dog."

"The best way to give advice to your children is to find out what they want and advise them to do it."

"Men don't change. The only thing new in the world is the history you don't know."

"It's a recession when your neighbor loses his job; it's a depression when you lose yours."

"If you can't convince them, confuse them."

"A politician is a man who understands government—and it takes a politician to run a government. A statesman is a politician who's been dead ten or fifteen years."

"Whenever you have an efficient government, you have a dictatorship."

"Whenever a fellow tells me he's bipartisan, I know he's going to vote against me."

"Polls are like sleeping pills designed to lull voters into sleeping on election day. You might call them 'sleeping polls.' "

"I think there is an immense shortage of Christian charity among so-called Christians."

"I look with commiseration over the great body of my fellow citizens who, reading newspapers, live and die in the belief they have known something of what has been passing in the world around them."

"Secrecy and a free, democratic government don't mix."

SECRETS OF DISNEYLAND

Well, they're not really secrets—more like gossip. But most people don't know much about the history and operations of the original mega-theme park. And it's pretty interesting stuff.

INSPIRATION

In the 1940s, a couple of Walt Disney's top animators were real train buffs. They got Uncle Walt interested in the hobby and he set up a miniature steam railroad that circled his house and gardens (note: see *Bathroom Reader #2*, p. 62), big enough to ride. After several train-theme parties, Walt got the idea that if his friends got such a kick from this one ride, maybe a whole amusement park would lure vacationers who were visiting Hollywood to star-gaze.

HOW WALT GOT THE MONEY

Walt proposed the idea to his brother Roy, the Disney stockholders, and their bankers...but they rejected it. In fact, they thought he was nuts. (In those days, amusement parks were sleazy places full of carnival side-shows, rip-off games, and cheap mechanical rides.)

So Disney was on his own. He went on a relentless search for financing. He sold his Palm Springs home and cashed in his $100,000 life insurance policy to finance his research. He lined up corporate sponsors, who were willing to pay for exhibits and restaurants in exchange for name recognition.

But the turning point came when he made a deal with ABC-TV. At the time ABC, a relatively new network, was a distant third in the ratings. It was desperate for the high-quality, high-name-recognition programming Disney could provide. But Disney had already turned down offers from other networks. Why should he join forces with a loser like ABC? The answer: financing for his amusement park. In exchange for doing the show, Disney received a substantial sum of money and ABC agreed to call the show "Disneyland," virtually making the weekly show a one-hour commercial for the park. But perhaps more important, later, in an "unrelated" deal, ABC purchased a 34% interest in Disneyland, Inc., the company set up to build the park. (Ironically, Disney now owns ABC.)

When Roy saw the package Walt had put together, he changed his mind and hopped on the Disneyland bandwagon. In 1954, ground was broken in an Anaheim orange grove.

OPENING DAY

In the wake of its enormous success, people have forgotten that Disneyland's opening day was a disaster. Nearly 33,000 people—twice as many as the number invited—packed the park with the help of forged tickets and surreptitiously placed ladders. Not all the rides were operational, and the restaurants ran out of food after a few hours. In some parts of the park, concrete and asphalt hadn't hardened properly, and women walked out of their high-heel shoes.

Also, there had been a plumber's strike during construction, and there weren't enough drinking fountains. The press thought it was a ploy to get visitors to purchase soft drinks. What they didn't know was that, in order to be ready for opening day, Walt had to choose between installing toilets or drinking fountains.

Thanks to nationwide TV coverage emceed by Ronald Reagan, the entire country learned of the mess. The next day's headlines read, "Walt's Dream A Nightmare," and Disney seemed to agree: For the rest of his life he referred to opening day as "Black Sunday."

LAND OF ILLUSIONS

When Uncle Walt bought the property for Disneyland in Anaheim in the early 1950s, he couldn't afford to buy all the land he wanted. So, in order to fit everything in, he used movie makers' tricks to make everything look bigger.

One trick was to use things that are familiar, but make them smaller than normal. Unless you look carefully and measure with your eyes, you'll assume, for instance, that the Disneyland train is normal size. It isn't. It is built to 5/8 scale. Many of the Disney buildings use the same trick, but that's just the beginning.

If you look carefully at some of the Disney buildings, especially those on Main Street, you'll notice there's something a little odd about them. They are not only smaller than normal, but their second and third stories are smaller still. This is known in art and in

The praying mantis is the only insect that can turn its head.

movie making as "forced perspective." By tapering the upper stories, the designers fool your eye into believing that they are bigger and taller than they really are.

This is done especially skillfully on Sleeping Beauty's Castle, even to the point that the bricks get smaller and smaller with each level.

In making Disney World this was less of a problem, because by that time the company could afford to buy an area bigger than most cities. It used many of the same tricks, but on an even bigger scale.

DISNEYLAND DEATHS

According to an article in *Egg* magazine, at least 53 people have died at Disneyland. According to *Egg*:

• The first Disney death was apparently a suicide: In 1964, after an argument with his girlfriend, a passenger on the Matterhorn stood up on the ride and was catapulted onto the tracks when his car came to a sudden stop. He never regained consciousness, and died four days later.

• The Matterhorn killed again in 1984, when a 48-year-old woman fell out of the ride and was struck by the following car. (For the rest of the day the Matterhorn was closed due to "technical difficulties.")

• Two people have been killed in accidents in Tomorrowland's PeopleMover ride, two others drowned in the river surrounding Tom Sawyer's Island. Another person was run down by the Monorail when he tried to sneak into the park without paying; and a park employee was crushed by a moving wall in the "America Sings" attraction.

• The park's first homicide occurred in 1981, when a man was stabbed after touching another man's girlfriend. (Disneyland was found negligent in the death and fined $600,000 after a park nurse neglected to call paramedics—and instead had the victim driven to the hospital in a park van.)

• Not all of Disneyland's deaths happen inside the park: In 1968, 44 people were killed in two separate helicopter accidents traveling between Disneyland and Los Angeles International Airport; and in 1987 a teenage male was killed during a gunfight in the parking lot.

English word with the most different meanings in the dictionary: *Set*, with 464. (2nd place, *run*.)

WHAT'S IN A NAME?

You know these corporate and product names, but probably not where they come from. Well, the BRI will fix that. Here's a little trivia you can use to entertain store clerks next time you're shopping.

Kodak. No meaning. George Eastman, founder of the company, wanted a name that began and ended in the letter K. "The letter K has been a favorite with me," he explained. "It seems a strong, incisive sort of letter."

Chanel No. 5 Perfume. Coco Chanel considered 5 her lucky number. She introduced the perfume on the fifth day of the fifth month of 1921.

Lucky Strikes. Dr. R. A. Patterson, a Virginia doctor, used the name to sell tobacco to miners during the California Gold Rush in 1856.

Ex-Lax. Short for *Excellent Laxative.*

Reebok. An African gazelle, "whose spirit, speed, and grace the [company] wanted to capture in their shoes."

Avon Products. Named for Stratford-on-Avon, William Shakespeare's birthplace.

Random House. America's biggest publisher started out in the 1920s, offering cheap editions of classic books. But founder Bennett Cerf decided to expand the line by publishing luxury editions of books selected "at random."

Kent Cigarettes. Herbert A. Kent, a Lorillard Tobacco Company executive, was so popular at the office that the company named a cigarette after him in 1952.

Toyota. Sakichi Toyoda made the first Japanese power loom. His son Kiichiro expanded into the automobile business.

Xerox. The Haloid Company originally called its copiers "electrophotography" machines. In the 1940s, they hired a Greek scholar at Ohio State University to think up a new name. He came up with "Xerography" for the process (after the Greek words for dry and writing) and called the copier itself a *Xerox* machine.

There are nine members in the Official Rin Tin Tin Fan Club.

TANG TWUSTERS

Ready for a workout? Here are 20 difficult tongue twisters. Try to say each of them five times fast...and don't pay any attention to the people banging on the bathroom door, asking what's going on in there.

If you must cross a coarse cross cow across a crowded cow crossing, cross the coarse cross cow across the crowded cow crossing carefully.

Does this shop stock short socks with spots?

The sixth sheik's sixth sheep's sick.

"The bun is better buttered," Betty muttered.

Seven sleek sleepless sleepers seek sleep.

Sixty-six sickly chicks.

The sun shines on shop signs.

The shady shoe shop shows sharp sharkskin shoes.

A noise annoys an oyster, but a noisy noise annoys an oyster more.

Rush the washing, Russel!

The seething sea ceaseth seething.

Awful old Ollie oils oily autos.

Mummies munch much mush.

This is a zither.

Ike ships ice chips in ice chip ships.

She says she shall sew a sheet.

Feed the flies fly food, Floyd!

Miss Smith dismisseth us.

Ted threw Fred thirty-three free throws.

Rex wrecks wet rocks.

In Germany, a yuppie is known as a *Schicki Micki.*

THE STORY OF WALL STREET

Why is Wall Street the financial center of the United States? Why is it even called Wall Street? Here's the answer.

HISTORY. In the early 1600s, the southern tip of Manhattan Island was a Dutch settlement known as New Amsterdam. In 1653, the governor of the colony decided the best way to protect his thriving trading post from Indians and the British was to build a wall from the Hudson River to the East River.

However, the wall did little to deter the British. They attacked by ship in 1664, easily overwhelmed the Dutch, and renamed the city New York. Thirty years later, they tore down the wall and used it for firewood.

NAME. The dirt road that ran alongside the wall was—naturally enough—known as Wall Street. When the wall was destroyed, the road became a main thoroughfare in New York.

MAIN INDUSTRY. Wall Street has been a commercial center ever since the British took over.

• They immediately set up a number of "exchanges"—open, shed-like buildings used for trading commodities like fur, molasses, and tobacco—on Wall Street.

• About 100 years later, the first stocks and bonds were sold on the street. At the end of the Revolutionary war, the Colonies were so deeply in debt that the first Congress issued $80 million in bonds (government IOUs). Stocks were added two years later, when Alexander Hamilton (then Secretary of the Treasury) established the nation's first bank, the Bank of the United States, and offered shares to the public.

New York Exchange. Stocks and bonds soon became a booming business, and in 1792 a group of 24 brokers decided to create an informal exchange to specialize in these "paper transactions." They signed a document known as the "Buttonwood Agreement" (named after the tree on Wall Street where the group met), in which they agreed to trade only among themselves and to charge customers a minimum 25% commission. These men are considered the original members of the New York Stock Exchange.

• When conditions on the street got too crowded, the exchange moved into a coffeehouse, then rented a room at 40 Wall Street. New members were required to pay an initiation fee of not less than $25; the amount varied, depending on the location of their seat in the room. This is how traders came to buy "a seat on the exchange."

• By 1848, the prestigious New York Stock Exchange and Board had absorbed all other exchanges on Wall Street and was conducting business in an orderly and unexciting manner: the chairman called the name of each stock twice a day and any trading was completed before moving on.

American Exchange. Meanwhile, those who couldn't afford to become members continued to trade on the street after-hours, and became known as "curb brokers." For this army of opportunists, the action was in stocks considered too speculative by members of "The Big Board"—especially railroads and mining companies created after the discovery of gold in California.

• By the late 1890s, some of the brokers on "The Curb Exchange" could afford to rent offices in nearby buildings. Telephone clerks took orders and shouted them out the window to the brokers below, who wore loud checkered jackets and hats, from bright green derbies to pith helmets, so their clerks could spot them in the crowded street. When the shouting got out of hand, a system of hand signals (some of which are still used today) was developed to pass on price and volume information.

• This entire scene moved indoors in 1921. And in 1953, the New York Curb Exchange, its name since 1928, became the American Stock Exchange, the second largest exchange on Wall Street.

MISCELLANY. The term "broker" comes from the french *brochier*, meaning someone who broaches, or breaks, a wine keg. It was originally used to refer to entrepreneurs who bought wine by the barrel, "broke it open," and sold it by the cup.

MALCOLM X SPEAKS

Malcolm X was one of the most controversial—and significant—figures in recent American history.

"You're not supposed to be so blind with patriotism that you can't face reality. Wrong is wrong, no matter who does it or who says it."

"It's easy to become a satellite today without even being aware of it. This country can seduce God. Yes, it has that seductive power—the power of dollarism."

"I for one believe that if you give people a thorough understanding of what confronts them and the basic causes that produce it, they'll create their own program, and when the people create a program, you get action."

"I believe in the brotherhood of man, all men, but I don't believe in brotherhood with anybody who doesn't want brotherhood with me. I believe in treating people right, but I'm not going to waste my time trying to treat somebody right who doesn't know how to return that treatment."

"Power never takes a back step—only in the face of more power."

"Nobody can give you freedom. Nobody can give you equality or justice or anything. If you are a man, you take it."

"After you get your freedom, your enemy will respect you."

"You cannot seperate peace from freedom, because no one can be at peace until he has his freedom."

"Truth is on the side of the oppressed."

"Learn to see...listen...and think for yourself."

"The colleges and universities in the American education system are skillfully used to miseducate."

"There shouldn't be bars. Behind bars, a man never reforms. He will never forget. He will never get completely over the memory of the bars."

BOX-OFFICE BLOOPERS

We all love bloopers. Here are a bunch of movie mistakes to look for in popular films. You can find more in a book called Film Flubs, *by Bill Givens.*

Movie: *The Wizard of Oz* (1939)
Scene: Dorothy, the Tin Woodsman, and the Scarecrow dance down the Yellow Brick Road singing, "We're Off to See the Wizard."
Blooper: A crew member can be seen in the background among the trees. (For years, rumors circulated in Hollywood that the crew member had committed suicide and hung himself from one of the trees on the set. The rumors were false.) *Note:* Also pay close attention to the length of Dorothy's hair. Because the scenes were filmed out of sequence, her hair changes from mid-length to long to short as the movie progresses.

Movie: *Spartacus* (1960)
Scene: Peter Ustinov gets off of his horse.
Blooper: His jockey shorts are visible under his tunic as he climbs down.

Movie: *The Alamo* (1960)
Scenes: The battle sequences.
Bloopers: Though the movie is a Western, you can see several mobile trailers in the distance. (And in another scene, you can see a stuntman falling into a mattress.)

Movie: *Children of a Lesser God* (1986)
Scenes: Several occasions in which Marlee Matlin (who is deaf and portrays a deaf character) and co-star William Hurt sign to each other during conversations in which Hurt is speaking.
Blooper: The sign language has nothing to do with the movie—it's about Matlin's and Hurt's private life. (At the time the movie was made, Matlin and Hurt were having an affair.)

Movie: *Rambo III* (1988)
Scene: Rambo steals a "Russian" helicopter.
Blooper: A small American flag is clearly visible on the helicopter's rotor housing.

The average American senior citizen takes 14 prescription drugs.

SENATE FIGHTS

You've heard of floor fights in Congress...but you probably never imagined the kind where people get bloody noses and pull guns on each other. Here are a few instances when that's exactly what happened.

FOOTE VS. BENTON

Background: Senator Henry Foote of Mississippi had a reputation as a hothead and a fighter; he'd been injured in no less than three duels. His temper reached legendary proportions on April 17, 1850, when he drew a pistol on Thomas Hart Benton of Missouri in the Senate chamber.

What Happened: Benton had just finished delivering a stinging attack on Foote's recently deceased mentor, former Vice President John C. Calhoun of South Carolina. Suddenly Foote leaped to his feet and denounced Benton as a coward. When Benton advanced toward the offending senator, Foote retreated and pulled a pistol from his coat. Benton replied: "I have no pistols. Let him fire. Stand out of the way. Let the assassin fire."

Result: Chaos ensued. Finally, Senator Daniel Dickinson of New York took Foote's pistol away. Foote was later reprimanded for his behavior but no other charges were pressed.

BROOKS VS. SUMNER

Background: Civil War tensions boiled over in Congress on May 22, 1856, when South Carolina Representative Preston Brooks brutally attacked and injured Massachusetts Senator Charles Sumner with a cane. The incident followed a heated address by the anti-slavery Sumner, who had specifically attacked Brooks's relative, Senator Andrew Butler of South Carolina.

What Happened: When the Senate adjourned, Brooks approached Sumner—who was sitting at his desk—and began striking him on the head with a cane. Sumner was trapped. To avoid the blows, he tried to rise from his bolted-down desk. His effort was so great that he literally ripped the screws from the floor.

Result: Sumner was so badly injured that he spent the next three years recovering. Efforts to punish Brooks—who became a hero in the South—were unsuccessful. He died shortly after the attack.

TILLMAN VS. McLAURIN

Background: On February 28, 1902, the Senate was debating a bill relating to government aid for the Philippines.

What Happened: Senator Benjamin Tillman of South Carolina charged that "improper influences" had influenced his colleague, John McLaurin—also from South Carolina—to change his vote on the legislation. When McLaurin heard Tillman's charges, he ran back to the Senate chambers "pale with anger" and accused Tillman of lying. Tillman lunged at McLaurin and punched him in the eye. McLaurin came back with a blow to Tillman's nose.

Result: A doorkeeper and several senators intervened and the gallery was immediately cleared. Later that day, both were suspended for six days for "disorderly conduct." The fight eventually led to Senate Rule 19, which says "no Senator in debate shall, directly or indirectly, by any form of words impute to another Senator or to other Senators any conduct or motive unworthy or unbecoming a Senator."

ENGLE VS. THE FILIBUSTER

Background: On June 10, 1964, one of the most dramatic votes in Senate history took place. Democratic Senator Clair Engle of California, terminally ill with a brain tumor, cast a vote from his wheelchair that led to the passage of the Civil Rights Act of 1964. A Southern filibuster had stalled the bill on the floor of the Senate. Ending the filibuster required a two-thirds majority, and it looked like the Democrats were one vote short.

What Happened: "Then came the moment few had expected," *The New York Times* reported. "Seconds before his name was called, Senator Clair Engle of California was pushed into the chamber in a wheelchair. He was smiling slightly. 'Mr. Engle,' the clerk called. There was a long silence. Senator Engle, recuperating from two brain operations, tried to speak. He could not. Finally he raised his left arm, as though trying to point toward his eyes. He nodded his head, signaling that he was voting 'aye.' He was wheeled out of the chamber minutes later and taken by ambulance back to his home."

Result: The resolution passed by one vote. Nine days later, on June 19, 1964, the Senate passed the final version of the Civil Rights Act, again with Engle's vote. A month later, "Congressman Fireball"—as Engle had once been called—died at the age of 52.

WISE GUY

Have you ever heard of H. L. Mencken? In the 1920s, he was one of America's most famous newspaper columnists. His claim to fame was his acid-tongued social commentary... as these examples demonstrate.

"Imagine the Creator as a low comedian, and at once the world becomes explicable."

"Jury: a group of twelve men who, having lied to the judge about their hearing, health, and business engagements, have failed to fool him."

"Lawyer: one who protects us against robbery by taking away the temptation."

"The best years are the forties; after fifty a man begins to deteriorate, but in the forties he is at the maximum of his villainy."

"If I had my way, any man guilty of golf would be ineligible for any office of trust in the United States."

"Conscience is a mother-in-law whose visit never ends."

"Criticism is prejudice made plausible."

"A cynic is a man who, when he smells flowers, looks around for a coffin."

"Democracy is the art of running the circus from the monkey cage."

"On one issue, at least, men and women agree: they both distrust women."

"Every man is thoroughly happy twice in his life: just after he has met his first love, and just after he has left his last one."

"Wife: a former sweetheart."

"To die for an idea; it is unquestionably noble. But how much nobler it would be if men died for ideas that were true!"

"An idealist is one who, on noticing that a rose smells better than a cabbage, concludes that it will also make better soup."

Mike Wallace, investigative reporter on "60 Minutes," was once a game show host.

FAMILIAR NAMES

Some people achieve immortality because their names become commonly associated with an item or activity. You already know the names—now here are the people.

Alfredo di Lellio. A Roman restaurateur. His fettucine with butter, cream, and Parmesan cheese became famous in the 1920s after Hollywood stars Mary Pickford and Douglas Fairbanks ate in his restaurant every day during their honeymoon.

John Langon-Down. An English doctor of the late 19th century. He was the first doctor to describe, in medical literature, the genetic defect now known as Down's Syndrome. Down called it "mongolism," because physical characteristics related to the condition reminded him of the features of people of Mongolia.

Queen Mary I of England and Ireland. A fanatical Catholic, she brutally repressed Protestants in her realm. Her reputation earned her the nickname "Bloody Mary," and inspired a cocktail made with vodka and tomato juice.

Vyacheslav Mikhailovich Molotov. Soviet foreign minister, 1939-1949 and 1953-1956, and rabid Stalinist. Finnish resistance fighters battling Russian tanks in the 1940s named their primitive gasoline-filled bottle bombs "Molotov cocktails" in his "honor."

Sir George Everest. The surveyor-general of India from 1830 to 1843, he named the world's tallest mountain after himself.

Dr. A. M. Latan. A quack dentist and peddler of health tonics in Paris during the 1840s. He traveled the city in an opulent coach—usually with a man marching in front, blowing a horn to attract attention—selling his wares as he went. Parisians shouted "Voila, le char (car) de Latan"—later shortened to "charlatan."

Mickey Finn. A 19th-century San Francisco saloon keeper who ran a bar popular with sailors. When customers got too rowdy, he slipped drugs into their drinks to knock them out. Today, giving someone a knockout drink is called "Slipping them a Mickey."

Sam Ellis. A tavern keeper on what was later called Ellis Island.

Edward Stanley, 12th Earl of Derby. A British nobleman of the late 1700s and early 1800s. An avid horse lover, he hosted a 1.5-mile horse race in 1780 that he called the "Derby Stakes." Today the term "derby" is used to represent any horse race or other sporting event that has a strong local following.

Gabriel Daniel Fahrenheit. German scientist of the late 17th and early 18th centuries. Invented a new thermometer that used mercury instead of alcohol. Its new scale—which marks water's freezing point at 32° and its boiling point at 212°—was named Fahrenheit after him and became popular in English-speaking countries.

Anders Dahl. In 1789 Alexander von Humboldt, a German explorer, discovered a new species of flower while on an expedition to Mexico. He sent some of the plant's seeds to the Botanic Garden in Madrid, where the curator promptly named the plants *Dahlias*—after his close friend Anders Dahl, a famous Swedish botanist who had died earlier that year.

George Nicholas Papanicolaou. Pioneered the use of cervical tissue smear samples in detecting uterine cancer. Today that test is known as a "Pap smear."

Josiah Wedgwood. An English potter of the late 1700s. He developed a line of china famous for its white designs on a blue background, which later became known as "Wedgwood" china.

David Douglas. A 19th-century Scottish botanist and explorer of the western United States. He discovered a new species of tall evergreen trees that bear his name: Douglas firs.

Draco. A magistrate and lawmaker who wrote the first code of laws of ancient Athens in the seventh century B.C. The code was one of the strictest set of laws ever written; it gave the death sentence for nearly every crime—even petty theft. Today any punishment that seems too severe for the crime can be labeled "draconian."

Caspar Wistar. A professor of "anatomy and midwifery" who held regular Sunday tea parties for a wide variety of scientists. One of his frequent guests was Thomas Nuttall, curator of the Harvard University Botanical Garden. In appreciation, Nuttall named a species of climbing plant "wistarias" in Wistar's honor. But because of a spelling mistake, the plants became known as "wisterias."

THE TRUTH ABOUT THE PANAMA CANAL

The Panama Canal was a triumph of engineering—but it was also a triumph of political conspiracy. As one political wit said in the 1970s: "The Panama Canal belongs to us. We stole it fair and square."

THE MYTH: The Panama Canal was an American idea.

THE TRUTH: The idea of a building a canal through the Panama Strait was more than three centuries old before anybody actually did anything about it.

The possibility was first discussed just decades after Columbus landed in the New World, when the Spaniards realized how far around South America they had to go to get to the Pacific Ocean. Panama seemed to be an ideal spot for a canal, since it measured only 50 miles from coast to coast.

But the issue was put to rest in 1552 by King Philip, whose religious advisors reminded him that the scriptures warned: "What God has joined together let no man put asunder." Philip agreed. "If God had wanted a Panama Canal," he announced, "He would have put one here."

America's First Effort. In the 1850s, the U.S. sent a survey team to Panama to see if it was possible to build a canal. But the idea was dropped when the team reported that there wasn't "the slightest hope that a ship canal will ever be found practicable across any part of it."

The French Effort. That didn't stop the chief promoter of the Suez Canal from trying. In 1880 Ferdinand de Lesseps, backed by a group of French investors, began building a canal across the Isthmus of Panama. American President Rutherford Hayes was outraged that this was happening in "our" territory and decreed that France should cede control of the canal to the United States.

Before the issue became an international incident, however, the French project collapsed under the weight of corruption, poor planning, and the harsh Central American jungle environment: floods,

The 100 Years War lasted 116 years.

earthquakes, yellow fever, and malaria. The French abandoned their partly dug canal and left most of their heavy machinery to rust in the jungle.

THE MYTH: The U.S. signed a treaty with the legitimate government of Panama to build and lease the Canal Zone.

THE TRUTH: Panama wasn't even a country when the U.S. decided to build a canal there—it was a territory of Colombia.

Background. In 1898 the battleship *Oregon*, stationed off the California coast, was ordered to Cuba to prepare for battle in the Spanish American War. The voyage around South America took two months. Clearly, a faster route was needed.

When the war was over, President Theodore Roosevelt began pushing for a canal. He was partial to a canal through Nicaragua: Even though that route was longer, it appeared to be an easier dig, since it would run through Lake Nicaragua.

But Panama had its partisans in the fierce Senate debate about the canal. When the French—who wanted to unload the canal they'd begun—dropped the price for their unfinished assets from $109 million to $40 million, America decided on Panama.

The Colombia Problem. There was just one problem: Roosevelt found that the people he called "Dagos" in Colombia were asking too much for using their territory.

He decided the solution was simple—if the existing country was a problem, create a new country that would be more willing to compromise. The U.S. Army teamed up with a former director of the French canal company, who stirred up a "revolt" against Colombia. Meanwhile, the American battleship *Nashville* positioned itself off the Colombian coastline with guns ready, in case Colombia objected.

Friendly Nation. As soon as a new revolutionary government was announced, the U.S. recognized it and pushed through a deal: for $10 million, an annual fee of $250,000, and a guarantee of "independence," the United States received rights to the 10-mile-wide canal zone "in perpetuity." Since the new country of Panama was not much wider than that 10-mile-zone, the U.S. effectively controlled the country. Colombia did protest, but there wasn't much it could do. The canal was finished in 1914.

Couch potatoes: 25% of American adults say they never exercise.

FREE ADVICE

Here are a handful of helpful hints from high-profile heavyweights, found in Friendly Advice, *by Jon Winokur.*

"Never go out to meet trouble. If you will just sit still, nine cases out of ten someone will intercept it for you."

—Calvin Coolidge

"Don't put no restrictions on the people. Leave 'em the hell alone."

—Jimmy Durante

"The best way to keep money in perspective is to have some."

—Louis Rukeyser ("Wall Street Week in Review")

"The only way to keep your health is to eat what you don't want, drink what you don't like, and do what you'd rather not."

—Mark Twain

"If four or five guys tell you that you're drunk, even though you know you haven't had a thing to drink, the least you can do is lie down a while."

—Joseph Schenck

"A man is a fool if he drinks before he reaches fifty, and a fool if he doesn't drink afterward."

—Frank Lloyd Wright

"Never go to a doctor whose office plants have died."

—Erma Bombeck

"A woman's dress should be like a barbed-wire fence: serving its purpose without obstructing the view."

—Sophia Loren

"Never underestimate a man who overestimates himself."

—Franklin D. Roosevelt

"My father gave me these hints in speechmaking: Be sincere... be brief...be seated."

—James Roosevelt (FDR's son)

"The secret of dealing successfully with a child is not to be its parent."

—Mell Lazarus

"Saving is a very fine thing. Especially when your parents have done it for you."

—Winston Churchill

"Never put off until tomorrow what you can do the day after tomorrow."

—Mark Twain

Lee Harvey Oswald's cadaver tag sold at auction for $6,600 in 1992.

THE PLUMBER'S HELPER

While you're sitting on the john, take a moment to examine it. Do you notice a problem? If so, you're in luck: BRI plumber's helper is here. We can't guarantee or even recommend this advice, of course (we're writers, not plumbers), but it sounds good.

The Problem: Running water.

What It Could Mean: The chain connecting the handle to the flush valve—the hole at the bottom of the tank where the water enters the bowl—is too long. Remove a few links of the chain so that it hangs with only a little slack.

Other Possible Causes:

• The "float mechanism" that shuts off the water isn't working; it's letting water leak into the overflow pipe. If your mechanism is a "float ball" attached to a horizontal rod, bend the rod so that the ball hangs lower in the tank. If it's a plastic cylinder called a "float cup," adjust it so that it hangs lower in the tank.

• Your "flush valve" is leaking. This is most likely the problem if you have to jiggle the toilet handle a lot, or if the toilet hisses regularly. Your best bet is to replace the rubber bulb mechanism. Replace the flush valve with one that's the same size.

The Problem: A wet floor around the base of your toilet.

How To Fix It: Add several tablespoons of food coloring to the water in the bowl and in the tank. Wipe the floor around the toilet dry, and then wait for the moisture to reappear.

Mop up the area again, this time using white paper towels. If the moisture is colored, your toilet is leaking. If it isn't, you probably have a condensation problem, or a leak from another fixure.

• To fix a leaky toilet tank, drain it and use a wrench or screwdriver to tighten the nuts at the base of the tank. (If the washers around the bolts look worn, replace them.) Don't overtighten; if you do you'll risk cracking the tank.

• If the toilet still leaks, the flush valve may be loose. The only way to fix it: remove the tank from the bowl and tighten the valve.

A FAMILY AFFAIR

Did TV's "Brady Bunch" seem like a close family to you? According to actor Barry Williams (Greg Brady) in his book, Growing Up Brady (HarperCollins, 1992), *they were a lot closer than you think.*

"At some point throughout the five years of filming, every Brady (kid) paired up romantically with the opposite sex counterpart," Williams confesses, although as far as he knows, none of the encounters "went all the way." Still, here's the juicy details of some of the closer encounters of the Brady clan:

The Couple: Greg and Mrs. Brady (Barry Williams and Florence Henderson)

The Place: The Coconut Grove Club in Los Angeles

Kiss and Tell: After sharing a dirty joke about lollipops with her on the set, "I got a case of the hots for my mom," Williams confesses, "I just couldn't control myself anymore and wound up asking her out. Amazingly, she accepted." Williams describes their first kiss: "No tongue, but nice."

Why It Ended: They just never hit it off. Henderson later told Williams: "You were really cute, and I was tempted a few times. I think we're lucky Carol never slept with Greg, but...uh...it coulda been."

The Couple: Greg and Marcia (Maureen McCormick and Barry Williams)

The Place: Waikiki Beach, when the cast was in Hawaii filming the show's first Hawaiian special

Kiss and Tell: "I kissed her, and the floodgates opened; warm and hard and packed with the kind of osculatory excitement only teenagers can transmit....Years later, I'd find out that this had been Mo's first kiss."

Why It Ended: While on a cruise on the *Queen Elizabeth II*, Williams snuck into McCormick's bedroom, climbed into bed with her, and started caressing her. McCormick woke up and kicked him out of her room. According to Williams: "My desperate groping killed something between us that night."

The Couple: Jan and Peter (Eve Plumb and Christopher Knight)

The Place: Aboard the *Queen Elizabeth II*, and later in Knight's truck

Kiss and Tell: Unlike Williams, Knight didn't have to sneak into his female counterpart's stateroom in search of action—Plumb came to him. And Knight had better luck than Williams did: "Finally, as she nibbled on my ear, something clicked...I thought to myself, 'Oh, my God—now I understand what all the fuss is about!' I was 14."

A year after the show was canceled, Knight and Plumb had another encounter, an attempted "quickie" in Knight's truck. Says Knight: "*This* time, we quickly moved beyond the sensory pleasures of just making out."

Why It Ended: Before they could get very far, a police officer walked up to the truck and shined his flashlight in the window. The interruption killed the romance.

The Couple: Cindy and Bobby (Susan Olsen and Michael Lookinland)

The Place: Tiger's doghouse and Lookinland's dressing room

Kiss and Tell: "During our first season, Michael got the notion that he had a major crush on me. And he'd put his arm around me, and he'd kiss me, and...uh...I kinda liked it."

Why It Ended: "A couple years later...he seemed to have a kinda 'boob thing'....This is at like age 10 or 11....I of course had none, so he decided it was time to get rid of me and chase after Eve for a while. So we got a divorce."

* * * *

WHAT ABOUT MR. BRADY?

According to *USA Today*, Robert Reed was "too busy firing off angry memos to the show's creators about how asinine the scripts were" to indulge in the pleasures of Brady flesh: "To blow off steam over crummy storylines, he sometimes went to a nearby bar and came back to work loaded." Alice the maid (Ann B. Davis), now a born-again Christian, also remained Brady-celibate. No word on Tiger the dog (who was run down by a florist's truck one day after he wandered off the set "looking for a place to relieve himself").

LAST WISHES

Think it's tough planning ahead now? Try imagining what your dying wish will be. Here are some odd last requests from nine well-known people.

Eleanor Roosevelt: Fearful of being buried alive, the former first lady requested that her major veins be severed to eliminate the possibility of regaining consciousness after burial.

Harry Houdini: The famous escape artist asked to be buried in the "trick" coffin he used in his magic act—with letters from his mother tucked beneath his head.

William Shakespeare: Wanted his oldest daughter, Susanna, to inherit his favorite bed. He left his wife "my second best bed."

President Andrew Johnson: The president who came closest to impeachment asked to be wrapped in an American flag, with a copy of the U.S. Constitution placed beneath his head.

J. Paul Getty: Requested a burial on the property of the Getty Museum in Malibu. However, his lawyers never applied for burial permits, so his remains had to be refrigerated and stored in a nearby mausoleum for *three years* until the necessary paperwork was completed. (Getty left his son J. Paul, Jr. "the sum of $500, and nothing else.")

W. C. Fields: Wanted a portion of his estate to be used for a "W. C. Fields College for orphan *white* boys and girls." (The request was never honored.)

P. T. Barnum: Wanted to keep the Barnum name from dying with him...so he left his grandson, Clinton Seeley, $25,000—on the condition that he change his middle name to Barnum. Seeley did.

Janis Joplin: Asked friends to have a farewell party for her at her favorite pub, the Lion's Share, in California—and left $2,500 in her will to finance it.

Albert Einstein: No one knows what his last wishes were. On his deathbed, he said something in German to his nurse—but she didn't speak German.

Leonardo da Vinci painted only 17 paintings—and some of them were unfinished.

THE "WILD THING" STORY

"Wild Thing" is one of those ridiculously catchy tunes you can't forget. It's been a hit in three different decades and performed by some of the greatest—as well as some of the most forgettable—artists. This tale of how it was written comes from Behind the Hits, *by Bob Shannon.*

AN OPPORTUNITY

In 1966 Chip Taylor—actor Jon Voight's brother—was a songwriter working for a music publisher in New York City. One day he got a phone call from a friend who was producing a record by a group called Jordan Christopher and the Wild Ones. The friend explained that the songs he was supposed to use on the album weren't good enough. He wondered if Taylor had "something different, something unique."

Taylor said he'd work on it and send something over.

"It was around one o'clock when I spoke to my friend," Taylor recalls. "I was planning to go into the studio at five o'clock, so between that time and five, I had to figure out what I was gonna do. I didn't come up with anything until around four o'clock...and then I started to get this little riff on the guitar."

IMPROVISING AT THE STUDIO

It was almost 5:00, so Taylor headed for the recording studio. He says: "Between my office and the studio, which was about four blocks, I was humming this crazy little thing, 'Wild Thing, you make my heart sing,' and just had this groove going.

"I got to the studio and I asked the engineer just to let the tape roll, and I told him not to stop me, I was gonna do this nonsense thing and see what came out. I basically had the chorus already, so I just sang it over and over again, and every once in a while I stopped and said some things. What came out was exactly what you've heard on records.

"The next morning, I listened to this [terrible song]. I said, 'All right, send it over to my friend'—because I promised I'd send something over to him—[but] don't let anybody else hear this demo. I was really embarrassed."

THE FIRST VERSION

Eventually, Jordan Christopher and the Wild Ones did make the first recording of "Wild Thing."

"But they did it very differently, with horns," Taylor explains, "and they changed the rhythm and stuff like that. I didn't think it [was very] good, and I was kind of glad that it wasn't a hit. I was glad they recorded it, but I was a little embarrassed anyway."

IT'S A HIT

The music publisher Taylor worked for had a deal with a music company in England—they had to send everything they published to the British company. Taylor was horrified. "I asked them not to send it over," he says, "but somehow it was included with the other material they sent."

To his surprise, a few months later "Wild Thing," by a little-known group called the Troggs (from the word "troglodytes"), hit #2 in England and #1 in the United States. Even more surprising to Taylor, it later became a rock classic, recorded by everyone from Jimi Hendrix to X. Taylor himself got in on the fun in 1967 when he produced a "Wild Thing" satire performed by "Senator Bobby," a Robert Kennedy soundalike. Even *that* version was a Top 20 hit.

FOR THE RECORD

How did the Troggs pick "Wild Thing"?

• Taylor says: "The story I hear is that when they were presented the package to choose what songs to do, they were given a stack of about fifty tapes. They just kept listening to them until they got to 'Wild Thing,' and decided they wanted to do it."

• The leader of the Troggs, Reg Presley, tells a different tale. He recalls that their manager picked the song—and that he couldn't stand it. "I looked at the lyrics—'Wild thing, you make my heart sing...You make everything groovy'...and they seemed so corny and I thought, 'Oh God, what are they doing to us?'"

The ocarina solo on the Troggs' record was copied from Taylor's demo tape. But it was originally played on someone's hands, not an instrument. Taylor explains: "While the engineer, Ron Johnson, was playing the tape back in the studio, I heard him playing this little thing on his hands. I said to him, 'Go on out and do that in the middle part.' If you play my demo against the Troggs' record, you'll see it's almost exactly the same."

The index finger is the most sensitive finger on your hand.

LUCKY STRIKES

Some of the most important historical discoveries have been complete accidents. Here are four examples.

The Discoverer: A peasant farmer digging a well

What He Found: Lost cities of Pompeii and Herculaneum

Lucky Strike: In 1709 a peasant who was digging in the area that had been destroyed when Mount Vesuvius erupted in 79 A.D. brought up several pieces of sculpted marble from statues and other objects. When word of his discovery spread, an Italian prince bought the land and began the first large-scale excavation of the site. Today more than three-quarters of ancient Pompeii has been uncovered; the rest remains buried underneath the modern city of Pompeii.

The Discoverers: Some quarrymen digging in a cave

What They Found: Neanderthal man

Lucky Strike: In 1856 workers excavating a cave in Germany's Neander Valley unearthed a human skeleton more than 100,000 years old. The remains provided some of the earliest evidence supporting the theory that modern humans evolved from apes.

The Discoverers: A group of French army engineers in Egypt

What They Found: The Rosetta stone

Lucky Strike: In July 1799, French army engineers working near the Egyptian town of Rosetta noted that a section of the wall they were about to demolish had both Greek script and hieroglyphics carved into it. On a hunch, they saved it. The stone turned out to be the first Egyptian hieroglyphic document ever found that was accompanied by a translation into a modern language. With the aid of this "Rosetta stone," scientists finally cracked the code of the hieroglyphics—which had been indecipherable for more than 1,300 years.

The Discoverer: A Bedouin boy looking for a lost goat

What He Found: The Dead Sea Scrolls

Lucky Strike: In 1947 a Bedouin boy searching for his goat on cliffs near the Dead Sea idly tossed a rock into a cave. He heard some pottery shatter. Investigating, he found a number of large clay jars containing hundreds of scrolls, many of which were early versions of the Bible at least 1,000 years older than any other known copy.

Sweet tooth: 48% of Americans feel guilty after eating candy.

THE ADVENTURES OF SUPERMAN

"Look! Up in the sky...it's a bird...it's a plane...no, it's Superman!" "The Adventures of Superman," a syndicated TV show filmed from 1951 to 1957, has been on the air sporadically for almost 40 years. By modern standards, the special effects (and even the hero himself) are laughable. But if you've never seen the show, or don't remember it, you're missing a great slice of 1950s Americana. Check it out.

A TV SHOW IS BORN

"The Adventures of Superman" was actually just part of the Man of Steel's leap into every existing entertainment medium. In the early 1940s, Superman was the star of a popular radio show and a movie cartoon series. In 1948 and 1950, he became the star of movie serials. ("Now the one and only Superman at his mightiest as a real live hero on the serial screen!")

In 1951, DC comics agreed to a deal for a feature film and a TV series. The star of the serials, Kirk Alyn, was offered the lead role, but he declined. So the producers conducted an extensive—and unsuccessful—search for a new hero. They interviewed more than 200 actors; they became so desperate that they even checked out the 1951 Mr. America contest. They weren't impressed. They wanted brains, not just beef.

It wasn't until George Reeves strolled into their office one day that Our Hero was ready to fly again. Reeves, who'd played Brett Tarleton in *Gone with the Wind*, had been stuck in "B" films like *Sir Galahad* during the 1940s. Now he was hired to star in the first full-length Superman movie, *Superman and the Mole Men* ("America's favorite hero! His latest . . . his greatest!"), not because of his acting ability, but because of his profile and—most important—his chin, which looked like Superman's from the comics. Reeves wasn't particularly excited about the part, either. "I've played about every type of part you can think of," he said at the time. "Why not Superman?"

The low-budget film became the pilot episode of the TV series, which went on the air in 1953, sponsored by Kellogg's.

CHEAP SHOTS

"Superman" was filmed like an assembly-line product. Each episode cost only $15,000 to make, and four episodes were shot every 10 days. The cast always wore the same clothes, because several episodes were filmed at the same time; this way they didn't have to keep track of when they were supposed to change costumes.

SUPER SUITS

Reeves had naturally sloping shoulders, and Superman had big, broad ones—so the Superman costume had rubber and sponge padding built into it (which made it unbearably hot).

MAN AND SUPERMAN

• The show almost cost Reeves his life. In 1953, while Reeves was making an appearance as Superman in Detroit, a youngster aimed his father's loaded pistol at Reeves. (He wanted to watch bullets bounce off Superman.) George calmly talked the kid into giving up the gun, but stopped wearing the Superman suit in public.

• Reeves tried to give up smoking, believing he'd be setting a bad example if kids spotted him with cigarettes. He also tried to avoid being seen in public with women, a tall order for a bachelor TV star. In 1953 he toured the country speaking to kids about the dangers of jaywalking, bicycling...and trying to fly.

UP IN THE SKY

Special effects have come a long way since Superman flew in 1951:

• For takeoffs, Reeves jumped off a springboard so he'd look like he was propelled into the air.

• If he was jumping out a window, he just leaped onto a mattress.

• If he was flying, he was pulled into the air by wires and pulleys, and in later episodes by a hydraulic system.

• For Superman's dramatic landings, Reeves simply jumped from an off-screen stepladder.

TYPECASTING

Sadly, his success as Superman ruined Reeves's chances for other acting parts. He had a role in the Oscar-winning film *From Here to Eternity* (1953), for example...but his scenes were cut because audiences shouted "Superman!" every time he appeared in the film. In 1959, after trying singing and directing, he put a gun to his head and pulled the trigger. The headlines blared: "Superman Kills Self."

Until 1850, most golf balls were stuffed with feathers.

THE DEATH OF WARREN G. HARDING

Did Warren Harding die of a heart attack or was he poisoned? This piece on his suspicious death is from It's a Conspiracy!, *by the National Insecurity Council.*

The Deceased: Warren G. Harding, 29th president of the United States (1921-1923)

How He Died: In the summer of 1923, President Harding was visiting Vancouver when he became gravely ill. He was rushed to San Francisco and seemed to recover. But then, on August 2, 1923, he suddenly died of a heart attack. *The New York Times* reported: "Mrs. Harding was reading to the President, when utterly without warning, a slight shudder passed through his frame; he collapsed....A stroke of apoplexy was the cause of his death."

Although initial newspaper accounts didn't mention it, the White House physician, General Sawyer, was probably in the room as well when the president died.

SUSPICIOUS FACTS

Warren and the Duchess

• Harding owed his political success to his ambitious wife, Florence (nicknamed "the Duchess"). But his marriage wasn't a happy one; he strayed often. During the 1920 campaign, for example, the Republican National Committee paid a former lover of Harding's $20,000 for incriminating letters, paid her $2,000 a month for her silence, and sent her to Europe to keep her away from reporters.

• Harding had a child by Nan Britten, the daughter of a friend. In fact, they had regular trysts in a large White House closet.

• According to former Treasury agent Gaston Means, who worked for Mrs. Harding, the president's wife despised her husband for his affairs and his ingratitude. In his bestselling book about Harding's death, Means reported that when the president's wife found out Harding had fathered Britten's baby, she got hysterical and vowed revenge. "I made him, I made him president!" she raved. When she confronted her husband, there was a nasty scene. He roared that he had never loved her, was sick of the whole presidential charade, and wanted to live with Britten and his child.

After Harding's Death

• To everyone's surprise, Mrs. Harding refused to allow either an autopsy or a death mask.

• The *New York World* reported: "There will be no death mask made of President Harding....Although it is the usual custom, when a Chief Executive dies, to have a mask made that his features may be preserved for posterity, Mrs. Harding demurred."

• About a year later, while the president's widow was visiting General Sawyer, the former White House physician unexpectedly died in his sleep.

• According to the account in The *New York Times*: "General Sawyer's death was almost identical with the manner of death of the late Warren G. Harding when General Sawyer was with the President in San Francisco. Mrs. Harding was at White Oaks Farm (Sawyer's home) when General Sawyer was found dead. Members of his family had no intimation of the seriousness of the general's condition up to the moment he expired."

POSSIBLE CONCLUSIONS

Harding really did have a heart attack. His administration was riddled with scandals, and people called for his impeachment. The president, who'd previously had five nervous breakdowns, was said to be despondent. He may have succumbed to the stress.

Harding was poisoned by his wife. If Harding was really ready to give up his political career and marriage, then the Duchess may have poisoned him either to avoid disgrace or to exact revenge. She may have tried first in Vancouver; when Harding didn't die, the attempt was dismissed as food poisoning. Five days later, in San Francisco, she may have succeeded.

• Refusing a death mask and an autopsy is consistent with this scenario. (Poison victims sometimes die with horrible grimaces.)

• Sawyer's death is either a remarkable coincidence or proof of Mrs. Harding's guilt. Even if he wasn't involved in killing the president, as a physician Sawyer may have guessed what had happened and helped to cover it up. Mrs. Harding could have poisoned him to keep her secret safe.

The Empire State Building is only 265 feet taller than the Eiffel Tower.

STATE YOUR NAME

You know the names of all 50 states...but do you know where any of them come from? Here's the best information we could find on the origin of each.

ALABAMA. Possibly from the Creek Indian word *alibamo*, meaning "we stay here."

ALASKA. From the Aleutian word *alakshak*, which means "great lands," or "land that is not an island."

ARIZONA. Taken either from the Pima Indian words *ali shonak*, meaning "little spring," or from the Aztec word *arizuma*, meaning "silver-bearing."

ARKANSAS. The French somehow coined it from the name of the Siouan *Quapaw* tribe.

CALIFORNIA. According to one theory, Spanish settlers named it after a utopian society described in a popular 16th-century novel called *Serged de Esplandian*.

COLORADO. Means "red" in Spanish. The name was originally applied to the Colorado River, whose waters are reddish with canyon clay.

CONNECTICUT. Taken from the Mohican word *kuenihtekot*, which means "long river place."

DELAWARE. Named after Lord De La Warr, a governor of Virginia. Originally used only to name the Delaware River.

FLORIDA. Explorer Ponce de Leon named the state *Pascua Florida*—"flowery Easter"—on Easter Sunday in 1513.

GEORGIA. Named after King George II of England, who chartered the colony in 1732.

HAWAII. An English adaptation of the native word *owhyhee*, which means "homeland."

IDAHO. Possibly taken from the Kiowa Apache word for the Comanche Indians.

ILLINOIS. The French bastardization of the Algonquin word *illini*, which means "men."

INDIANA. Named by English-speaking settlers because the territory was full of Indians.

IOWA. The Sioux word for "beautiful land," or "one who puts to sleep."

KANSAS. Taken from the Sioux word for "south wind people," their name for anyone who lived south of Sioux territory.

KENTUCKY. Possibly derived from the Indian word *kan-tuk-kee*, meaning "dark and bloody ground," or *kan-tuc-kec*, "land of green reeds," or *ken-take*, meaning "meadowland."

LOUISIANA. Named after French King Louis XIV.

MAINE. The Old French word for "province."

MARYLAND. Named after Queen Henrietta Maria, wife of English King George I.

MASSACHUSETTS. Named after the Massachusetts Indian tribe. Means "large hill place."

MICHIGAN. Most likely from the Chippewa word for "great water," *micigama*.

MINNESOTA. From the Sioux word for "sky tinted" or "muddy water."

MISSISSIPPI. Most likely taken from the Chippewa words *mici* ("great") and *zibi* ("river").

MISSOURI. From the Algonquin word for "muddy water."

MONTANA. Taken from the Latin word for "mountainous."

NEBRASKA. From the Otos Indian word for "broad water."

NEVADA. Means "snow-clad" in Spanish.

NEW HAMPSHIRE. Capt. John Mason, one of the original colonists, named it after his English home county of Hampshire.

NEW JERSEY. Named after the English Isle of Jersey.

NEW MEXICO. The Spanish name for the territory north of the Rio Grande.

NEW YORK. Named after the Duke of York and Albany.

NORTH AND SOUTH CAROLINA. From the Latin name *Carolus*; named in honor of King Charles I of England.

NORTH AND SOUTH DAKOTA. Taken from the Sioux word for "friend," or "ally."

OHIO. Means "great," "fine," or "good river" in Iriquois.

OKLAHOMA. The Choctaw word for "red man."

OREGON. Possibly derived from *Ouaricon-sint,* the French name for the Wisconsin River.

PENNSYLVANIA. Named after William Penn, Sr., the father of the colony's founder, William Penn. Means "Penn's woods."

RHODE ISLAND. Named "Roode Eylandt" (Red Island) because of its red clay.

TENNESSEE. Named after the Cherokee *tanasi* villages along the banks of the Little Tennessee River.

TEXAS. Derived from the Caddo Indian word for "friend," or "ally."

UTAH. Means "upper," or "higher," and was originally the name that Navajos called the Shoshone tribe.

VERMONT. A combination of the French words *vert* ("green") and *mont* ("mountain").

VIRGINIA AND WEST VIRGINIA. Named after Queen Elizabeth I of England, the "virgin" queen, by Sir Walter Raleigh in 1584.

WASHINGTON. Named in tribute to George Washington.

WISCONSIN. Taken from the Chippewa word for "grassy place."

WYOMING. Derived from the Algonquin word for "large prairie place."

The story of Cinderella has been made into a movie 58 times.

WHO WERE HARLEY & DAVIDSON?

Here's the story behind two of the best-known names in America.

The first motorcycle was developed by Gottlieb Daimler, one of the founders of Daimler-Benz (maker of the Mercedes Benz) in Germany in 1885. Ten years later, two German brothers, Hildebrand and Alois Wolfmuller, began manufacturing motorcycles to sell to the public.

In 1901 news of the Wolfmullers' motorcycles reached Milwaukee, Wisconsin. Four young friends—21-year-old William Harley and the Davidson brothers, William, Walter, and Arthur—decided to build a small engine in the Davidsons' backyard and attach it to one of their bicycles. Legend has it that the engine was made from household castoffs, including a carburetor made of a tomato can.

After working out the bugs on their prototype, they built three more motorized bicycles in 1903 and began riding them around town. Their bikes were simple but reliable—one of them ultimately racked up 100,000 miles. People began asking if they were for sale.

The Harley-Davidson Motorcycle Company legally incorporated in 1909. More than 150 U.S. manufacturers eventually followed suit, but Harley-Davidson has outlasted them all. It's now the only American motorcycle company and sells more than 50,000 motorcycles a year.

THE HARLEY IMAGE

In the mid-1980s, Harley's "rough rider" image began hurting sales. So the company took steps to change it. They encouraged Harley execs to wear white or red shirts to biker rallies to dispel the notion that Harley riders wear only black. They formed the Harley Owner's Group (H.O.G.) and the Ladies of Harley club to offset outlaw biker clubs. And they licensed the Harley name and logo to $100 million worth of products as diverse as wine coolers, cologne, and removable tattoos. Still, the company prefers customers with permanent Harley tattoos: "If you can persuade the customer to tattoo your name on their chest," one executive admits, "they probably will not switch brands."

The smallest bones in your body are in your ear.

THE HONEYMOONERS

When TV critics are asked to pick the best sitcom in history, many select Jackie Gleason's 1955 one-season wonder, "The Honeymooners." Here are some facts about that classic program from Cult TV, *by John Javna.*

HOW IT STARTED

In the early days of TV, the three networks were CBS, NBC...and Dumont. This third network was founded in 1946 by the Allen Dumont Laboratories and limped along for nine years before finally disappearing in 1955. Its main contribution to television history was making Jackie Gleason a star.

In 1950 Gleason wasn't welcome on the major networks—he'd done poorly as star of NBC's sitcom "The Life of Riley" the previous season, and network executives were wary of his excessive lifestyle. But on Dumont, he flourished. As host of its 1950 variety show "Cavalcade of Stars"—performing his own comedy sketches as well as emceeing—he was a smash. His first two shows attracted a large audience and got rave reviews.

Inventing a Classic. For the third one, Gleason wanted to come up with something special. So he invented a husband/wife comedy sketch based on his childhood environment. "I knew a thousand couples like these in Brooklyn," Gleason said. "It was like the loudmouth husband... with the wife who's a hell of a lot smarter than [him]. My neighborhood was filled with them."

His writers wanted to call the skit "The Beast," but Gleason didn't like it. The husband might be a windbag, Gleason said, but he wasn't an animal—he and his wife really loved each other. So the writers suggested "The Lovers"—which was close, but not right. Finally, Gleason came up with "The Honeymooners."

The sketch, which featured Jackie as bus driver Ralph Kramden and Pert Kelton as his wife, Alice, was only on for a few minutes. But it elicited an enormous response from viewers. In fact, it was so popular that it became a regular feature on Gleason's show. Gleason added two neighbor characters: sewer worker Ed Norton and his wife, Trixie.

When Gleason moved to CBS in 1952, he brought "The Honeymooners" with him, and in 1955 it became a series. Thirty-nine episodes aired. Although it was a popular program, Gleason didn't want to continue it. He preferred variety shows, where "The Honeymooners" periodically surfaced. The last "Honeymooners" special aired in 1978. Gleason unveiled 75 "lost episodes" in the 1980s.

INSIDE FACTS

Belly Laughs. Gleason never rehearsed, and generally didn't need to because he had a photographic memory—one look at the script and he had it down. Nonetheless, he occasionally forgot his lines, which was a potential disaster in the days of live TV. When he did forget, Gleason would pat his stomach—a sign for someone else to think of something...quick. Once Alice snapped, "If you get any bigger, gas bag, you'll just float away." That wasn't in the script.

Another time, Gleason forgot to make an entrance. Art Carney (Ed Norton), who was onstage at the time, calmly went to the icebox, pulled out an orange, and began peeling it until Gleason realized his mistake.

One evening, Art Carney showed up for a performance completely plastered. Gleason, who'd memorized Carney's part as well as his own, did the whole show by asking a sitting (and incoherent) Carney yes or no questions.

Heeere's Alice. Pert Kelton, the first actress to play Alice Kramden, fell ill with a heart condition and could not continue in the role when Gleason moved to CBS. When another actress, Audrey Meadows, was asked if she knew anyone who could play the part of Alice, she said, "Me." Gleason turned her down because she was too pretty. That made her want the part more. She sent Gleason photos of herself as a "frumpy" housewife, and Gleason triumphantly announced he'd found the right actress—not realizing she was the same woman he'd already rejected.

You Can Do Better. Joyce Randolph played Ed Norton's wife, Trixie. But Randolph's mother didn't like her daughter playing the part—she thought Joyce "could do better than marrying a sewer worker."

At his heaviest, President James Madison weighed 98 pounds.

ONE-HIT WONDERS

You're listening to the radio, and you hear this great (or terrible) song by a new group. It rockets all the way to #1 and sells 5 million copies...but then you never hear anything by the artists again. They're one-hit wonders—part of a pop music phenomenon no one can explain. Here are a few case studies for BRI members to ponder.

The Artist: The Monotones

The Song: "The Book of Love" (1958, #5)

The Story: In 1955 six kids from Newark, New Jersey, formed a doo-wop band called The Monotones. One day a member of the group was looking at the sheet music for a song called "Book of Love," when he heard a Pepsodent toothpaste commercial on the radio: "You'll wonder where the yellow went, when you brush your teeth with Pepsodent." It inspired him to write: "Oh I wonder, wonder who...who wrote the book of love."

He and the group turned it into a song. "It was a joke to us," he explains. But when a rival group wanted to record it, The Monotones quickly made a demo and sold it to a record company. It became a Top 10 hit. Unfortunately, The Monotones didn't bother putting out a follow-up record until three months after "Book of Love" peaked. By then, their fans had moved on.

The Artist: David Soul

The Song: "Don't Give Up on Us, Baby" (1977, #1)

The Story: David Solberg dropped out of college in the 1960s to become a folk singer. He decided he needed a gimmick to get attention, so he wrote a song called "The Covered Man"—which he sang while wearing a ski mask. The stunt got him on "The Merv Griffin Show" more than 20 times, but he still couldn't sell any records. Solberg (now renamed Soul) did, however, get enough exposure to land a starring role on the TV show "Starsky & Hutch." The program's popularity encouraged him to try music again. He released "Don't Give Up on Us Baby" in 1977. It hit #1...but none of his follow-ups made it into the Top 40. He gave up recording about the same time "Starsky & Hutch" went off the air.

The average U.S. student attends school 180 days; in China, it's 251 days.

The Artist: Steam

The Song: "Na-Na, Hey, Hey, Tell Him Goodbye" (1969, #1)

The Story: In 1969 a singer named Gary DeCarlo recorded his first single for Mercury Records. Then he went back to the studio to record a throwaway "flip side"—something so bad no disc jockey would accidentally play it instead of the "A" side.

A few friends were at the studio that night; they suggested a tune they'd performed in a band in 1961. It was called "Kiss Him Goodbye," and it was perfect for the "B" side of the record...except that it had no chorus. No problem—they made one up on the spot, with "na-nas" instead of lyrics. They described it as "an embarrassing record...an insult."

But to everyone's horror, Mercury thought it was great and decided to release it as a single. No one wanted to be identified with the record, so it was credited to "Steam."

"Na-Na" sold more than a million copies, but DeCarlo wouldn't make another Steam record. Mercury got a different group to do the follow-ups, but the best they could come up with was "I've Gotta Make You Love Me," which reached #46 on the charts in 1970.

The Artist: Zager and Evans

The Song: "In the Year 2525 (Exordium & Terminus)" (1969, #1)

The Story: In 1968 Denny Zager and Rick Evans were playing folk music in a motel lounge in Lincoln, Nebraska. One of their most popular songs was "In the Year 2525," an up-tempo apocalyptic vision Evans had written four years earlier. They decided to record it. For $500, they got recording studio time and 1,000 copies of their single—which they sold to local record stores and passed out to Nebraska radio stations.

Zager and Evans were delighted when the song began getting airplay in Lincoln...and flabbergasted when it drew the attention of a hotshot management firm in Los Angeles. An executive with the firm flew to Lincoln and signed Zager and Evans to a personal contract; then he signed them to a recording contract with RCA.

A few weeks later, "In the Year 2525" was released nationally ...and a few weeks after that, it was #1 in America. However, Denny Zager had never really liked the song and wasn't interested in doing any more tunes in the same style. None of the pair's subsequent records even made it into the Top 100.

English is the official language of more countries than any other language. French is second.

MORE FREE ADVICE

Here are more helpful hints from high-profile heavyweights. From Friendly Advice, *by Jon Winokur.*

"Never kick a fresh turd on a hot day."
—Harry S Truman

"Never say anything on the phone that you wouldn't want your mother to hear at the trial."
—Sydney Biddle Barrows, *the "Mayflower Madam"*

"You can get much further with a kind word and a gun than you can with a kind word alone."
—Al Capone

"Never trust a man unless you've got his pecker in your pocket."
—Lyndon Baines Johnson

"To succeed with the opposite sex, tell her you're impotent. She can't wait to disprove it."
—Cary Grant

"Sleeping alone, except under doctor's orders, does much harm. Children will tell you how lonely it is sleeping alone. If possible you should always sleep with someone you love. You recharge your mutual batteries free of charge."
—Marlene Dietrich

"Anything worth doing is worth doing slowly."
—Gypsy Rose Lee

"Don't try to take on a new personality; it doesn't work."
—Richard Nixon

"There's nothing to winning, really. That is, if you happen to be blessed with a keen eye, an agile mind, and no scruples whatsoever."
—Alfred Hitchcock

"Rise early. Work late. Strike oil."
—J. Paul Getty

"Don't let your mouth write a check that your tail can't cash."
—Bo Diddley

"Never eat at a place called Mom's. Never play cards with a man named Doc. And never lie down with a woman who's got more troubles than you."
—Nelson Algren

"What is worth doing is worth the trouble of asking someone to do it."
—Ambrose Bierce

According to experts, "Elvis" is the most popular name for pet King snakes.

NIXON'S THE ONE?

Did Richard Nixon undermine LBJ's peace talks and keep the Vietnam War going in 1968, just to get elected? Here are some facts to consider from It's a Conspiracy!, *by the National Insecurity Council.*

Although President Lyndon Johnson wasn't running for reelection in 1968, he was still obsessed with ending the war in Vietnam. His decision was partly political, since any resolution would help the Democrats hold on to the White House. But more important, by finding an "honorable" settlement to the conflict, Johnson could avoid becoming the first American president to lose a foreign war.

In June Johnson came up with a plan: he proposed a halt to the U.S. bombing of North Vietnam, to be followed by negotiations with all parties. At first the proposal was rejected by the Communists. Then, after several months of secret meetings, the North Vietnamese suddenly agreed to his terms. The U.S. allies, the South Vietnamese, also accepted the plan—in fact, they insisted that talks begin immediately after the cease-fire went into effect.

Peace talks were scheduled to begin on November 2, three days before the presidential election. Democrats were sure the talks would help defeat Richard Nixon.

WHAT HAPPENED

• Suddenly, on October 29, South Vietnam—whose defense had already cost 29,000 American lives—backed out of the peace talks. According to former Defense Secretary Clark Clifford, South Vietnamese president Nguyen Van Thieu "reneged on everything he had previously agreed to," saying the peace talks were "too soon."

• Thieu said he would need "materially more time" to prepare for talks in Paris and that he "needed to consult the South Vietnamese National Security Council again."

• Johnson and his aides were livid. But they could do nothing to bring Thieu back to the negotiating table. When the peace talks were aborted, so was Democratic nominee Hubert Humphrey's bid for the presidency. On November 2, Richard Nixon won by 510,645 votes, or less than 1% of the total votes cast.

37% of Canadians think Canada will become part of the U.S. in the next 50 years.

SUSPICIOUS FACTS

• On July 12, 1968, Nixon, Bui Diem (the South Vietnamese ambassador to the U.S.), and Anna Chennault (a prominent right-wing Republican) met secretly in New York City.

• Chennault was an important figure in both Asian and American politics and had access to highly placed officials on the two continents. She was one of the mainstays of the China Lobby, a Taiwan-based group that fought to keep Red China out of the United Nations, and was chair of Republican Women for Nixon.

• At Nixon's request—perhaps made at the July 12 meeting—Ambassador Diem began regular and secret communications with Nixon's campaign manager, John Mitchell, and other senior members of the Nixon team.

• The White House knew what was going on. "Gradually," Defense Secretary Clark Clifford wrote later, "we realized that President Thieu's growing resistance to the agreement in Paris was being encouraged—indeed, stimulated—by the Republicans, and especially by Anna Chennault." (The *New Yorker*)

• According to former Assistant Secretary of State William Bundy: "Johnson and his inner circle...learned through intercepted South Vietnam Embassy cables, particularly one of October 27, that Anna Chennault was conveying via Bui Diem apparently authoritative 'Republican' messages urging Mr. Thieu to abort or cripple the deal by refusing to participate. That 'smoking gun' cable included promises of later favor from Mr. Nixon, including a possible visit to Saigon before the inauguration if he were elected." (The *New York Times*)

• Bundy also said that "on November 3, two days before the election, Mr. Johnson [confronted] Mr. Nixon with Mrs. Chennault's activities, and Mr. Nixon categorically denied any connection or knowledge—almost certainly a lie in light of later disclosures." (ibid.)

• Clifford reported that, on the day after the election, South Vietnamese Vice President Nguyen Ky "almost contemptuously" told U.S. Ambassador Ellsworth Bunker "that it might take two months—just about the length of time left to the Johnson administration—to resolve his government's problems with the negotiating

A shark can have as many as 24,000 teeth in its lifetime.

format." President Thieu finally agreed to resume peace negotiations on January 25, 1969—just days after Richard Nixon's inauguration.

WAS IT A CONSPIRACY?

Clark Clifford thought so. He said the secret Republican effort was "a plot—there is no other word for it—to help Nixon win the election by a flagrant interference in the negotiations."

• Clifford adds: "No proof...has ever turned up linking Nixon [himself] directly to the messages to Thieu....On the other hand, this chain of events undeniably began with Bui Diem's meeting with Richard Nixon in New York, and Nixon's closest adviser, John Mitchell, ran the Chennault channel personally, with full understanding of its sensitivity." (The *New Yorker*)

• "The activities of the Nixon campaign team," Clifford wrote, "went far beyond the bounds of justifiable political combat. They constituted direct interference in the activities of the executive branch and the responsibilities of the Chief Executive—the only people with authority to negotiate on behalf of the nation. [They] constituted a gross—and potentially illegal—interference in the national-security affairs by private individuals." (ibid.)

FOOTNOTE

Why didn't LBJ or Hubert Humphrey turn Nixon's alleged interference with the peace talks into a campaign issue? Bundy says that "in the circumstances, Mr. Johnson and Mr. Humphrey decided, separately, not to raise what would surely have been a highly divisive issue so late in the campaign."

RECOMMENDED READING

"Annals of Government: The Vietnam Years," by Clark Clifford and Richard Holbroke (*The New Yorker* magazine; May 6, May 13, and May 20, 1991). *A three-part article.*

Note: It's a Conspiracy! *is a 256-page book full of amazing and entertaining stories. Highly recommended as bathroom reading.*

THE MYTH-ADVENTURES OF THOMAS EDISON

Most Americans believe that Thomas Edison invented the lightbulb. He didn't. In fact, although he was a great inventor, there are a number of myths we commonly believe about Edison. Let's correct a few.

THE MYTH: Edison was the father of electric light.

THE TRUTH: Electric lighting had been made practical decades before Edison began his famous research. Although incandescent light (the kind that's made by charging a wire filament until it glows white hot with energy) had not yet been perfected, by the 1870s *arc* lighting (light that's created when a spark "arcs" across two highly charged electric rods) was already in use in lighthouses and in the street lamps of some major cities.

The only problem was, they used too much energy and generated too much light (300 times as much as the household gas lights of the day) to be practical in homes. A less-powerful source of light was needed.

THE MYTH: Edison invented the incandescent lightbulb.

THE TRUTH: Incandescent lightbulbs had been around as a laboratory curiosity since 1823, and the first incandescent bulb was patented by Joseph Swan, an English inventor, in 1845.

By the time Edison began experimenting with lightbulbs in 1878, scientists around the world had already spent 55 years trying to perfect them. Edison wasn't trying to invent the lightbulb; he was trying to find a long-lasting *filament* that would make the lightbulb practical for the first time.

Incandescent lightbulbs operate on the principle of electrically heating a tiny filament until it glows white hot with energy, creating light in the process. The main problem at the time: most substances either melted or burned up when heated to such a high temperature, causing the bulb to burn out after only a few seconds.

Vacuum bulbs, which had some of their air removed, solved part of the problem; by reducing the amount of oxygen in the bulb, they lengthened the time it took for the filament to burn up. Even so, in 1878 even the best bulbs only only lasted a short time...and *that's* where Edison came in.

THE MYTH: He perfected the incandescent bulb by himself.

THE TRUTH: He failed on his own, and had to bring in experts. Edison thought the secret to building a better light bulb was to design a switch inside the bulb that would function like a heater thermostat, turning off the electricity when the filament got too hot, and turning it on again as soon as the filament cooled off—a process that would take only a fraction of a second.

Edison thought (and announced) that he could develop the switch in a few weeks—but he guessed wrong. It didn't work at all.

More a scientific tinkerer than a scientist, his strategy had always been to blindly build prototype after prototype. He ignored work that other researchers had done and, as a result, often unwittingly repeated their failed experiments. That's what happened with the lightbulb. After a month of trying on his own, he threw in the towel and hired Francis Upton, a Princeton physicist, to help him.

As soon as Upton signed on, he had the lab's researchers study old patents, electrical journals, and the work of competing inventors to see what progress they had made. He also shifted the focus of the work from testing prototypes to methodically experimenting with raw materials (in order to understand their scientific properties and see which ones made the best filaments). Without this important shift in strategy, Edison's lab might never have developed a practical bulb at all...and certainly would have fallen behind competing labs.

THE MYTH: Edison made his critical breakthrough on October 21, 1879—known for many years as "Electric Light Day"—when he had kept a lightbulb lit for more than 40 hours.

THE TRUTH: The story is a fake. According to lab notes, nothing important happened on October 21—and it took another full year to produce a 40-hour bulb. The October 21 date was made up in late December 1879 by a newspaper reporter who needed a good story for the Christmas season.

Couch potato fact: 80% of people who own VCRs don't know how to program them.

INNOVATIONS IN YOUR HOME

You probably have some of these products around the house. Here's how they were created.

COPPERTONE SUNTAN LOTION

Background: In the early part of the 20th century, suntans were the mark of the lower classes—only laborers who worked in the sun, like field hands, had them. But as beaches became more popular and bathing suits began revealing more skin, styles changed. Suntans became a status symbol that subtly demonstrated that a person was part of the leisure class.

Innovation: The first suntan lotion was invented in the 1940s by Dr. Benjamin Green, a physician who'd helped develop a petroleum-based sunblock for the military to protect soldiers from the sun. After the war, Green became convinced civilians would buy a milder version of his product—one that protected them from the sun while letting them tan. He called his lotion Coppertone, because it produced a copper-colored tan on the people who used it.

RUNNING SHOES WITH "WAFFLE" SOLES

Background: In the late 1950s, Phil Knight was a track star at the University of Oregon. His coach, Bill Bowerman, was obsessed with designing lightweight shoes for his runners. "He figured carrying one extra ounce for a mile," Knight recalls, "was equivalent to carrying an extra thousand pounds in the last 50 yards."

When Knight began his graduate work at the Stanford Business School, he wrote a research paper arguing that lightweight running shoes could be manufactured cheaply in Japan and sold at a low price in the United States. Then he actually went to Japan and signed a distribution deal with a Japanese shoe company called Tiger. He and Bowerman each invested $500 to buy merchandise, and the Blue Ribbon Sports Company (later Nike) was founded.

Innovation: Bowerman developed Nike shoes to meet runners' needs. *Swoosh: The Story of Nike* describes the origin of the celebrated "waffle" shoe: "It occurred to Bowerman to make spikes out of rubber....One morning while his wife was at church, Bowerman sat at the kitchen table staring at an open waffle iron he had seen hundreds of times. But now, for some reason, what he saw in the familiar pattern was square spikes. Square spikes could give traction to cross-country runners sliding down wet, muddy hills.

"Excited, Bowerman took out a mixture of liquid urethane... poured it into about every other hole of the waffle iron in...just the right pattern, and closed the lid to let it cook. Legend had it that he opened the waffle iron and there was the waffle sole that became Nike's first signature shoe. But what really happened that morning is that when he went to open the smelly mess, the waffle iron was bonded shut....[He] switched to a plaster mold after that."

THERMOS JUGS

Background: In the 1890s, British physicist Sir James Dewar invented a glass, vacuum-walled flask that kept liquids hot longer than any other container in existence. Dewar never patented his invention, however; he considered it his gift to the scientific world.

Innovation: Reinhold Burger, a German glassblower whose company manufactured the flasks, saw their potential as a consumer product. Dewar's creations were too fragile for home use, so Burger built a sturdier version, with a shock-resistent metal exterior. He patented his design in 1903 and held a contest to find a name for the product. The contest was more of a publicity stunt than anything else, but Burger liked one entry so much that he used it: "Thermos," after the Greek word for heat.

S.O.S. SOAP PADS

Background: In 1917 Edwin W. Cox was peddling aluminum cookware door to door in San Francisco. He wasn't making many sales, though; aluminum cookware was a new invention, and few housewives would even look at it.

Innovation: In desperation, Cox began offering a free gift to any housewife who'd listen to his presentation—a steel-wool soap pad he made in his own kitchen by repeatedly soaking plain steel-wool pads in soapy water. (His wife used them in their own kitchen and loved them; she called them "S.O.S." pads, meaning Save Our Saucepans.) The gimmick worked—sort of. Housewives still weren't interested in the cookware, but they loved the soap pads. Eventually he dropped pots and pans and began selling soap pads full-time.

American chickens are direct descendants of the ones brought over by Columbus.

THE S&L SCANDAL: TRUE OR FALSE?

"I think we've hit the jackpot."
—Ronald Reagan to assembled S&L executives, as he signed the Garn–St. Germaine Act deregulating the savings and loan industry.

You, your children and your grandchildren are going to be paying for the savings & loan scandal for years, but how much do you know about it? See if you can tell which of the following statements are true:

1. The S&L scandal is the second-largest theft in the history of the world.

2. Deregulation eased restrictions so much that S&L owners could lend money to themselves.

3. The Garn Institute of Finance, named after Senator Jake Garn—who co-authored the S&L deregulation bill—received $2.2 million from S&L industry executives.

4. For his part in running an S&L into the ground, Neil Bush, George's son, served time in jail and was banned from future S&L involvement.

5. Rep. Fernand St. Germain, House banking chairman and co-author of the S&L deregulation bill, was voted out of office after some questionable financial dealings were reported. The S&L industry immediately sent him back to Washington...as its lobbyist.

6. When asked whether his massive lobbying of government officials had influenced their conduct, Lincoln Savings president Charles Keating said, "Of course not. These are honorable men."

7. The S&L rip-off began in 1980, when Congress raised federal insurance on S&L deposits from $40,000 to $100,000, even though the average depositor's savings account was only $20,000.

8. Assets seized from failed S&Ls included a buffalo sperm bank, a racehorse with syphilis, and a kitty-litter mine.

Benito Mussolini was a schoolteacher before he went into politics.

9. Working with the government in a bailout deal, James Fail invested $1 million of his own money to purchase 15 failing S&Ls. In return, the government gave him $1.8 billion in federal subsidies.

10. Federal regulators sometimes stalled as long as seven years before closing hopelessly insolvent thrifts.

11. When S&L owners who stole millions went to jail, their jail sentences averaged about five times the average sentence for bank robbers.

12. The government S&L bailout will ultimately cost taxpayers as much as $500 billion.

13. If the White House had admitted the problem and bailed out failing thrifts in 1986, instead of waiting until after the 1988 election, the bailout might have cost only $20 billion.

14. With the money lost in the S&L rip-off, the federal government could provide prenatal care for every American child born in the next 2,300 years.

15. With the money lost in the S&L rip-off, the federal government could have bought 5 million average houses.

16. The authors of *Inside Job*, a bestselling exposé of the S&L scandal, found evidence of criminal activity in 50% of the thrifts they investigated.

ANSWERS

(1) F; it's the *largest*. (2) T (3) T (4) F (5) T (6) F; actually he said: "I certainly hope so." (7) F; all true, except the average savings account was only $6,000. (8) T (9) F; it was only $1,000 of his own money. (10) T; partly because of politics, partly because Reagan's people had fired 2/3 of the bank examiners needed to investigate S&L management. (11) F; they served only a fifth of the time. (12) F; it may hit $1.4 *trillion*. (13) T (14) T (15) T (16) F; they found criminal activity in *all* of the S&Ls they researched.

SCORING

13-16 right: Sadder, but wiser.

6-12 right: Just sadder.

0-5 right: Charlie Keating would like to talk to you about buying some bonds.

This quiz is from *It's a Conspiracy!* by the National Insecurity Council. Thanks to *The Nation* and *Inside Job* for the facts cited.

DIRTY TRICKS

Why should politicians have all the fun? You can pull off some dirty tricks, too. This "dirty dozen" should inspire you to new lows.

POUND FOOLISH

Pay a visit to the local dog pound or SPCA, wearing a chef's hat and an apron. Ask to see one of the kittens or puppies that are available for adoption. Pick it up and act as if you're weighing it, then set it down and ask to see one that's "a little more plump."

SOCK IT TO 'EM

Tired of looking for that one sock you lost in the laundry? Pass on your anxieties: Stick the leftover sock in with someone else's washload. Let them look for the missing sock for awhile.

SOMETHING FISHY

If you have a (clean) aquarium, toss some thin carrot slices into the tank. Later when you have guests over, grab the slices out of the tank and eat them quickly. If you do it quick enough, your victims will assume you're eating a goldfish. (If you accidentally grab a *real* goldfish, toss it back in, grab the carrot slice, and complain to your victims that the first fish was "too small.")

LOST YOUR MARBLES?

Pry the hubcap off a friend's car, drop two or three steel ball bearings inside, and replace the hubcap. Then watch them drive off. The ball bearings will make an enormous racket for a few seconds, until they become held in place by centrifugal force. They'll stay silent until the victim applies the brakes, and then they'll shake loose again.

TV GUIDE

Got a friend who's a couch potato? Carefully remove the cover of their *TV Guide* (or weekly newspaper TV schedule), then glue it to an older schedule, so the TV listings are wrong. It'll drive a true TV fanatic crazy.

RETURN TO SENDER

Embarrass a coworker by buying a magazine they would *never* read (*High Times*, *Guns & Ammo*, and *Easy Rider* work well), and glue the mailing label from one of their regular magazines to the cover. Then stick it in the cafeteria or restroom where other coworkers can see it.

PRACTICE DRILLS

The next time you visit the dentist, scream really loud the minute you get seated in the dentist's chair. You'll send the patients in the waiting room running for cover.

MAD HATTER

If your friend wears a favorite hat, find out the manufacturer and buy two or more others of varying sizes. Then periodically switch them with your friend's hat. He'll be convinced his head is changing sizes. (Another hat trick: Fill your victim's hat with baby powder.)

AT A WEDDING

If you're a close friend of the groom, paint a message on the sole of his shoes (the raised part near the heel that doesn't touch the ground) without telling him. When he kneels at the altar, the message will be visible for everyone to see.

PARK PLACE

The next time you're walking through a crowded parking lot, pull out your car keys and act as if you're looking for your car. Walk in between cars across the rows; motorists looking for a parking space will race to keep up with you.

PARTY IDEA

Using superglue, glue someone's drink to the bar or to a table.

WAKE UP CALL

Gather as many alarm clocks as you can find and hide them in different places in your victim's room. Set one alarm so it goes off very early in the morning, and set the others so they go off every five minutes afterward. Guaranteed to make your victim an early riser.

There are approximately 720 peanuts in every pound of peanut butter.

THE ROCK 'N' ROLL RIOTS OF 1956

Were there really rowdy rockers in 1956 at Bill Haley and the Comets concerts? Did DJs really accuse him of being "a menace to life, limb, decency, and morals"? Believe it or not, they did. By the mid-1950s, parents were already sure rock 'n' roll had ruined their kids.

TEENS RIOT IN MASSACHUSETTS

Boston, Mass., March 26, 1956 (Wire service report)

"Record hops by disc jockeys featuring 'rock and roll' tunes were banned in Boston today after a riot at Massachusetts Institute of Technology's annual charity carnival.

"The disturbance involved nearly 3,000 students. It began when hundreds of teenagers who paid the 99¢ admission fee to see WCOP disc jockey Bill Marlowe discovered the carnival wasn't a record hop, and they couldn't dance.

"More than 20 officers were summoned to the scene, but they were unable to cope with the surging mob of teenagers who overturned booths, smashed records, and battled M.I.T. students who tried to keep order.

" 'Some of that music is crazy,' commented Mary Driscoll of the Boston licensing board. 'Teenagers have no business listening to disc jockeys at 12:00 at night. The way they're going, they'll have high blood pressure before they're 20.' "

WASHINGTON MELEE

Newsweek, *June 18, 1956*

"Even before the joint began to jump, there was trouble at the National Guard Armory in Washington, D.C. As 5,000 people, mostly teenagers, poured in for some rock'n'roll, knives flashed and one young man was cut in the arm. Inside the auditorium, 25 officers waited tensely for Bill Haley and his Comets to swing into the 'big beat.'

"Haley gave the downbeat, the brasses blared, and kids leaped into the aisles to dance, only to be chased back to their seats by the cops. At 10:50, the Comets socked into their latest hit, 'Hot Dog, Buddy, Buddy!' and the crowd flipped.

"Some of the kids danced, some scuffled, fights broke out, a chair flew. William Warfield, 17, a high school junior, was hit. Suffering from a concussion and a severe cut over one eye, he was rushed to the hospital. 'Before I knew it, everybody was pounding everybody,' he said later.

"The fight overflowed into the street. A 19-year-old was struck over the head, and a 16-year-old was cut in the ear. Two cars were stoned and one exuberant teenager turned in a false alarm.

" 'It's the jungle strain that gets 'em all worked up,' said Armory manager Arthur (Dutch) Bergman, surveying the damage."

THEATER ATTACKED

Hartford, Conn., March 28, 1956

"Hartford police have instituted action to revoke the license of the State Theater, as a result of a series of riots during rock'n'roll shows. The latest took place this weekend during performances of an Alan Freed show.

"The 4,000-seat theater has had five police riot calls since last November. Over this past weekend alone, a total of 11 people were arrested. Practically all arrests have been teenagers."

ROCK, ROLL, AND RIOT

Time, *June 18, 1956*

"In Hartford city officials held special meetings to discuss it....In Minneapolis a theater manager withdrew a film featuring the music after a gang of youngsters left the theater, snake-danced around town and smashed windows....At a wild concert in Atlanta's baseball park one night, fists and beer bottles were thrown, and four youngsters were arrested.

"The object of all this attention is a musical style known as 'rock'n'roll,' which has captivated U.S. adolescents.

"Characterisics: an unrelenting syncopation that sounds like a bullwhip; a choleric saxophone honking mating-call sounds; an electric guitar turned up so loud that its sound shatters and splits; a vocal group that shudders and exercises violently to the beat while roughly chanting either a near-nonsense phrase or a moronic lyric in hillbilly rhythm....

"Psychologists feel that rock'n'roll's appeal is to teenagers' need to belong; [in concert], the results bear passing resemblance to Hitler mass meetings."

QUEEN SCREENS

Scholastic Magazine, *Oct. 4, 1956*

"In England, over 100 youths were arrested in 'rock and roll' riots that broke out during showing of a 'rock and roll' film. Queen Elizabeth II, disturbed by the growing number of such arrests, has scheduled a private screening of the film at her palace for official study."

WILDE ABOUT OSCAR

Wit and wisdom from Oscar Wilde, one of the 19th century's most popular—and controversial—writers.

"The only way to get rid of temptation is to yield to it."

"It is better to have a permanent income than to be fascinating."

"The soul is born old but grows young. That is the comedy of life. And the body is born young and grows old. That is life's tragedy."

"Seriousness is the only refuge of the shallow."

"Children begin by loving their parents. After a time they judge them. Rarely, if ever, do they forgive them."

"There's no sin...except stupidity."

"Experience is the name everyone gives to their mistakes."

"Formerly we used to canonize our heroes. The modern method is to vulgarize them. Cheap editions of great books may be delightful, but cheap editions of great men are absolutely detestable."

"All women become like their mothers. That is their tragedy. No man does. That's his."

"Society often forgives the criminal; it never forgives the dreamer."

"It is better to be beautiful than to be good, but it is better to be good than to be ugly."

"The only portraits in which one believes are portraits where there is very little of the sitter and a very great deal of the artist."

"The youth of America is their oldest tradition. It has been going on now for three hundred years."

"One should always play fairly—when one has the winning cards."

"Discontent is the first step in the progress of a man or a nation."

"The well-bred contradict other people. The wise contradict themselves."

The three best-known western names in China: Jesus Christ, Richard Nixon, Elvis Presley.

A HANDY GUIDE TO THE END OF THE WORLD (Part I)

Most cultures have a tradition that predicts the end of the world... and many of their prophecies could apply to our era. The good news is that they're not all fire and brimstone. Here are three examples from Eastern cultures, reprinted from Uncle John's Indispensable Guide to the Year 2000.

BUDDHISM

Background: Founded in the sixth century B.C. in India. One of its primary teachings is observance of the 10 moral precepts (standards of conduct).

Signs the End Is Near: According to the Buddha in the *Sutta-pitaka* (Buddhist scriptures and sermons):

- The 10 moral courses of conduct will disappear...and people will follow the 10 *immoral* courses instead—"theft, violence, murder, lying, evil-speaking, adultery, abusive and idle talk, covetousness and ill will, wanton greed, and perverted lust." Poverty "will grow great."
- "The Dharma [universal law, or truth] will have disappeared from the world...as a counterfeit Dharma arises."

When the World Ends: Good news! A new Buddha "by the name Maitreya" will arise. This new Buddha will "replace the counterfeit Dharma of materialism and selfishness...and give new teachings to solve the social problems of the world."

ZOROASTRIANISM

Background: A Persian religion based on the belief that the universe is filled with good and evil spirits. There will be an ultimate battle between these forces, and evil will be eliminated.

Signs the End Is Near: The *Zand-i Vohuman Yasht* predicts:

- "(At the) end of thy tenth hundredth winter...the sun is more unseen and more spotted; the year, month, and day are shorter; and the earth is more barren; and the crop will not yield the seed; and men...become more deceitful and more given to vile practices; they have no gratitude."

• "Honorable wealth will all proceed to those of perverted faith...and a dark cloud makes the whole sky night...and [it will rain] more noxious creatures than water."

When the World Ends: Saoshyant, the Man of Peace, comes to battle the forces of evil. "The resurrection of the dead will take place—the dead will rise...the world will be purged by molten metal, in which the righteous will wade as if through warm milk, and the evil will be scalded."

At the end of the battle, the Final Judgment of all souls begins. Sinners will be punished (apparently for 3 days), then forgiven, and humanity will be made immortal and free from hunger, thirst, poverty, old age, disease, and death. The world "will be made perfect once again."

HINDUISM

Background: "Hindu" is a Western term for the religious beliefs of numerous sects in India dating back to 1500 B.C. Their goal: "liberation from the cycle of rebirth and suffering."

Signs the End Is Near: The world falls into chaos and degradation; there's an increase in perversity, greed, conflict. According to Cornelia Dimmit's translation of the *Sanskrit PurAnas:*

• "When deceit, falsehood, lethargy, sleepiness, violence, despondency, grief, delusion, fear, and poverty prevail...when men, filled with conceit, consider themselves equal with Brahmins...that is the *Kali Yuga* [present era]."

When the World Ends: A savior (avatar) will appear. "The Lord will again manifest Himself as the Kalki Avatar...He will establish righteousness upon the earth and the minds of the people will become pure as crystal....As a result the Sat or Krta Yuga [golden age] will be established."

* * *

"I am confident that [in 2000] the Republican Party will pick a nominee that will beat Bill Clinton."

—***Dan Quayle*, 1998**

"The Munsters" was created by the same people who created "Leave It to Beaver."

TV THEME SONG TRIVIA

For your bathroom reading pleasure: 10 facts you don't know about classic TV themes, from John Javna's TV Theme Song Sing-Along Songbook.

JUST THE FACTS

The first TV theme ever to become a Top 40 hit was the theme from "Dragnet." It was recorded by band leader Ray Anthony as "The Dragnet March" in 1953 and reached #3 on the national charts. At the time, "Dragnet" was the second-most popular TV program in America, behind "I Love Lucy."

HEY LOOOSY!

The theme song from "I Love Lucy" was also released as a single in 1953. But despite the fact that "Lucy" was the #1 program on TV at the time, the record flopped—perhaps because America knew it as an instrumental, and this version had *lyrics*. Desi Arnaz had commissioned Oscar-winner Harold Adamson to write words to the song ("I love Lucy, and she loves me / We're as happy as two can be"), and then sang it on the air. Arnaz and Columbia Records thought they had a sure smash, but America wasn't buying. It wasn't until 24 years later—20 years after "Lucy" had gone off the air—that it finally made the charts...as a *disco song*. (Performed by the Wilton Place Band, it reached #24 in 1977.)

THAT'S TER-R-RIBLE, WILBUR-R-R

The "Mr. Ed" theme song ("A horse is a horse, of course, of course") is one of the all-time classics. But for the strangest of reasons, it was almost dumped before the show aired.

To save money, the music for the "Mr. Ed" pilot episode was done in Italy...and the Italians who scored the show picked an opera singer to perform the theme song. His version was so bad that the show's producers planned to replace the whole song. "They thought it was the song, not the singer," explains the theme's composer, Jay Livingston. To prove the song was usable, he recorded his own version. The producers liked it so much they had Livingston sing the final version. That's him you hear on reruns.

NO, NO, NOT AGAIN!

"Bonanza" was one of the most popular TV shows of the 1960s. Its theme song—an instrumental by guitarist Al Caiola—hit #19 on the *Billboard* charts in 1961.

Most fans never knew that the theme song had lyrics, and that the Cartwright family had actually sung it once on the show: at the end of the "Bonanza" pilot episode, Ben, Adam, Little Joe, and Hoss rode into the sunset singing its ludicrous lyrics, "We got a right to pick a little fight, Bonanza..."

The rendition was so awful that it's been shown on TV blooper shows...but it was never sung on the show again.

HAPPY DAYS ARE HERE AGAIN

When the 1950s nostalgia show "Happy Days" made its debut in 1974, it didn't have a theme song. Instead, the producers used "Rock Around the Clock," by Bill Haley and the Comets—which had been #1 in 1955 but hadn't been on the charts since then. Such is the power of TV that "Rock Around the Clock" became a Top 40 hit again in 1974 and Haley—a "has-been"—was briefly resurrected as a star.

In 1976 a new theme was introduced. "Happy Days," sung by a duo named Pratt and McClain, immediately went to #5 on the national charts.

HERE ON GILLIGAN'S ISLE

"Gilligan's Island" creator Sherwood Schwartz had a hell of a time selling his show to CBS. Network executives insisted that while the basic idea was okay, it had one major flaw: viewers who turned in for the first time wouldn't understand what seven people were doing on an island together. They wanted Schwartz to turn "Gilligan" into a sitcom about a charter boat instead.

Schwartz desperately wanted to keep the original premise...and came up with a solution: he wrote a theme song that described who the characters were and how they wound up on the island. Then, in the middle of a formal meeting with CBS execs, he abruptly got up and performed the tune. They bought the show.

WE'RE #1

The first TV theme to hit #1 on the charts was "Davy Crockett," in 1955. The second was "Welcome Back Kotter," in 1976.

Americans bought almost a billion pounds of unpopped popcorn in 1990.

IT'S A MIRACLE!

The tabloids are full of stories of people who see images of Jesus in everything from a lima bean to a smudge on a car window. Could they be real? Here are the details of five sightings. Judge for yourself.

The Sighting: Jesus in a forkful of spaghetti, Stone Mountain, Georgia

Revelation: Joyce Simpson, an Atlanta fashion designer, was pulling out of a gas station in Stone Mountain when she saw the face of Jesus in a forkful of spaghetti on a billboard advertising Pizza Hut's pasta menu. Simpson says at the time she was trying to decide whether to stay in the church choir or quit and sing professionally. (She decided to stick with the choir.)

Impact: Since the sighting, dozens of other people called Pizza Hut to say that they, too, had seen someone in the spaghetti. But not all the callers agreed that the man in the spaghetti was Jesus; some saw Doors singer Jim Morrison; others saw country star Willie Nelson.

The Sighting: Jesus in a tortilla, Lake Arthur, New Mexico

Revelation: On October 5, 1977, Maria Rubio was making burritos for her husband when she noticed a 3-by-3-inch face of Jesus burned into the tortilla she was cooking. Local priests argued that the image was only a coincidence, but the Rubio family's faith was unshaken. They saved the tortilla, framed it, and built a shrine for it in their living room.

Impact: To date more than 11,000 people have visited it.

The Sighting: Jesus on a soybean oil tank, Fostoria, Ohio

Revelation: Rita Rachen was driving home from work along Ohio Route 12 one night in 1986 when she saw the image of Jesus with a small child on the side of an Archer Daniels Midland Company oil tank containing soybean oil. She screamed, "Oh, my Lord, my God," and nearly drove off the side of the road, but recovered enough to continue driving.

Impact: She spread the word to other faithful, and the soybean tank became a popular pilgrimage site. (Since then, however, the oil tank has been repainted. Jesus is no longer visible.)

The Sighting: Jesus on the side of a refrigerator, Estill Springs, Tennessee

Revelation: When Arlene Gardner bought a new refrigerator, she had the old one dragged out onto her front porch. A few nights later, she noticed several of her neighbors were standing around staring at the old fridge. They told her that the reflection from a neighbor's porch light had created an image of Jesus on the side of the fridge. Gardner took a look and agreed.

Impact: Soon thousands of faithful were making pilgrimages to the site—so many, in fact, that Gardner's neighbors had their porch light disconnected, so Jesus could be seen no more. (*Note:* Not everyone agreed that Jesus had really made an appearance; as one local skeptic explained to a reporter, "When the good Lord comes, he won't come on a major appliance.")

The Sighting: A 900-foot Jesus at the City of Faith, Tulsa, Oklahoma

Revelation: This vision—one of the most publicized Jesus sightings ever—came to famed televangelist Oral Roberts on May 25, 1980 ...but he inexplicably kept it secret for over five months. Then one day he shared his vision and explained what he'd seen to reporters: "He reached down, put His hand under the City of Faith (a city Roberts had built), lifted it, and said to me, 'See how easy it is for me to lift it?' "

On January 4, 1987, Roberts told his followers God had appeared again, this time demanding $8 million. Roberts warned that if the money wasn't sent in by March 31, "God would call me home."

Impact: Roberts's followers coughed up $9.1 million.

* * * *

Royal Gossip

Queen Elizabeth likes to do crossword puzzles. She also likes to read mysteries by Dick Francis and play parlor games like charades.

WHAT REALLY HAPPENED IN 1000 A.D.? (Part I)

As the clock ticks down to 2000, will people begin to lose control? Will panicky crowds stampede grocery stores? Isn't that what happened in the last millennium? Maybe not.

THE STORY

According to popular lore, Europeans in the year 999 A.D. were even more panicked about the apocalypse than people are today. As the year ticked away, they gave away or sold their possessions, set their animals loose, left their homes, and huddled in churches to pray for salvation.

A DETAILED HISTORY

In his book *Doomsday: 1999 A.D.*, Charles Berlitz describes "the year of doom" in detail.

> "As the year 999 neared its end a sort of mass hysteria took hold of Europe. All forms of activity became affected by the specter of impending doom...Men forgave each other their debts, husbands and wives confessed suspected and unsuspected infidelities to each other...poachers proclaimed their unlawful poachings to the lords of manors...
>
> As the year rolled on toward its end, commerce dwellings were neglected and let fall into ruin...There was a wave of suicides as people sought to punish themselves in advance of Doomsday or simply could not stand the pressure of waiting for Judgement Day....
>
> As the night of December 31 approached, the general frenzy reached new heights. In Rome, the immense Basilica of St. Peter's was crowded for the midnight mass which in the belief of many might be the last mass they would ever attend on earth.

MEANWHILE, IN ROME...

Frederick H. Martens writes in *The Story of Human Life* that there was a dramatic New Year's Eve climax at St. Peter's:

> "Pope Sylvester II stood before the high altar. The church was overcrowded, all in it lay on their knees. The silence was so great that the rustling of the Pope's white sleeves as he moved about the altar could be heard. And there was still another sound...that seemed to measure out the last minutes of the earth's thousand years of existence between towns and cities was largely interrupted; since the coming of Christ—the door of the church sacristy stood open, and the aùdience heard the regular, uninterrupted tick, tick, tock of the great clock which hung within....
>
> The midnight mass had been said, and a deathly silence fell. The audience waited....Pope Sylvester said not a word....The clock kept on ticking....Like children afraid of the dark, all those in the church lay with their faces to the ground, and did not venture to look up. The sweat of terror ran from many an icy brow, and knees and feet which had fallen asleep lost all feeling. Then, suddenly—the clock stopped ticking! Among the congregation the beginning of a scream of terror began to form in many a throat. Stricken dead by fear, several bodies dropped on the stone floor.

WHEW!

Berlitz picks up the narrative again: "Then the clock began to strike. It struck one, two, three, four. It struck twelve. The twelfth stroke echoed out, and a deathly silence still reigned! Then it was that Pope Sylvester turned around, and with the proud smile of a victor stretched out his hands in blessing over the heads of those who filled the church....Men and women fell in each other's arms, laughing and crying and exchanging the kiss of peace. Thus ended the thousandth year after the birth of Christ."

It's a pretty exciting story...but is any of it true?
Turn to page 293 for Part II.

"MADAM, I'M ADAM"

A palindrome is a word or phrase that spells the same thing backward and forward. Here are the best that BRI members have sent us. Try your own. If you come up with a good one, send it to us and we'll publish it in the next edition.

TWO-WORD PHRASES

No, Son.

Sue us!

Pots nonstop.

Dump mud.

Go, dog!

Stack cats.

Worm row.

Party trap.

LONGER PHRASES

Wonder if Sununu's fired now.

Never odd or even.

Ed is on no side.

Step on no pets.

Rise to vote, sir!

Naomi, did I moan?

"Desserts," I stressed.

Spit Q-Tips.

Roy, am I mayor?

A car, a man, a maraca.

Are we not drawn onward, we few, drawn onward to new era?

A man, a plan, a canal… Panama!

Live not on evil.

If I had a Hi-Fi…

A slut nixes sex in Tulsa.

Put Eliot's toilet up.

Pull up, Bob, pull up!

Pa's a sap.

Ma is as selfless as I am.

NONSENSE PHRASES

Did mom poop? Mom did.

We panic in a pew.

Yawn a more Roman way.

Mr. Owl ate my metal worm.

THE TV SPEECH THAT MADE A PRESIDENT

John Kennedy owed his 1960 nomination for the presidency to a carefully planned campaign...starting with the 1956 TV speech that made him a national political figure.

BACKGROUND. In 1956 John F. Kennedy—an ambitious freshman senator from Massachusetts—wanted the Democratic nomination for vice president. But his chances were slim; the favorite was Senator Estes Kefauver of Tennessee.

On the first night of the Democratic convention, Kennedy narrated a film on the history of the Democratic party, called *The Pursuit of Happiness*. It was well received, and when JFK went to take a bow, the applause "was surprisingly loud and long."

Adlai Stevenson, the Democrats' presidential candidate, was impressed. He asked JFK to give his nomination speech—a peace offering that meant JFK wasn't going to be his running mate. But Kennedy didn't give up. He saw the speech as an opportunity. "One last possibility remained," writes Herbert Parmet in *The Struggles of John F. Kennedy*, "—going before the convention with a performance...so effective that even Stevenson and the other skeptics would have no choice but to recognize Kennedy's attractions as a running mate."

Although Stevenson gave Kennedy a prepared speech, JFK discarded it and spent the next 10 hours working on a new one.

THE SPEECH. On August 16, 1956, JFK made his first nationally televised speech, placing Stevenson's name in nomination. A few excerpts:

- "We here today are selecting a man who must be more than a good candidate, more than a good politician....We are selecting the head of the most powerful nation on Earth—the man who will hold in his hands the power of survival or destruction, of freedom or slavery."
- "We must, therefore, think beyond the balloting of tonight and tomorrow to seek, beyond even the election of this November, and think instead of the four years ahead and of the crises that will come

in them....Let us be frank about the campaign in the days ahead. Our party will be up against two of the toughest, most skilled campaigners in American political history—one who takes the high road (Eisenhower) and one who takes the low road (Nixon)."

• "These are critical times—times that demand the best we have, times that demand the best America has. We have, therefore, an obligation to pick the man best qualified not only to lead our party but to lead our country....Ladies and gentlemen, it is now my privilege to present to the convention as a candidate for the president of the United States...the man from Libertyville...Adlai Stevenson."

THE REACTION. The speech, described as "Kennedy's second success of the convention," put Stevenson in a quandary: Should he pick Kennedy, Kefauver, Sen. Albert Gore, or Sen. Hubert Humphrey?

In the end, Stevenson decided not to pick anyone. He announced to the convention that *they* could select the vice presidential candidate with a roll-call vote. "The choice will be yours," he told them. "the profit will be the nation's."

Kennedy came within about 30 votes of the nomination on the second ballot. But in a wild scene on the convention floor, he eventually lost to Kefauver. On learning the news, he rushed to the convention center and pushed his way onto the stage. The chairman saw him and brought him up to the microphone.

THE CONCESSION. "TV coverage of conventions was still something fresh and new in 1956, and a hundred million Americans were watching," writes historian Ralph G. Martin. "They saw this freshman senator on the podium before a packed national political convention, listening to the roar, picking at some invisible dust on his boyish, handsome face, nervously dry-washing his hands, waving to yelling friends nearby, his smile tentative, but warmly appealing, his eyes slightly wet and glistening. He spoke without notes, and his words were short, gallant, and touching. For the TV audience, it was a moment of magic they would not forget."

AFTERMATH. The Stevenson/Kefauver ticket went down in a landslide, but JFK emerged as the Democrats' rising star. His performance on TV made him the most sought-after political speaker in America and opened the door for a 1960 presidential run.

Most engaged couples who split up do so between 9 p.m. and midnight.

WHO WROTE SHAKESPEARE'S PLAYS?

We include this to inspire you to add the Bard's writing to your bathroom reading. BRI members have a lofty image to uphold, after all.

William Shakespeare authored 36 plays, 154 sonnets, and 2 narrative poems between 1588 and 1616. Though his works are among the most influential literature of Western civilization, little is known about the man himself—and no manuscripts written in his own hand have ever been found.

• This fact has inspired speculation by pseudoscholars, cranks, and English society snobs that Shakespeare—the commoner son of a glovemaker—couldn't have been intelligent or educated enough to write "his own" works.

• Why would the real author have given the credit to Shakespeare? One theory: Many of the plays dealt with members of the English royal family and were politically controversial. It may have been too dangerous for the real author to take credit for the radical ideas they contained.

• The *real* William Shakespeare, according to this theory, was a third-rate actor, playwright, and theater gadfly who was more than happy to take credit for work he was not capable of producing.

• Whatever the case, more than 5,000 other authors (including Queen Elizabeth I and a Catholic pope) have been proposed as the *real* Shakespeare. Here are five of the more popular candidates:

1. SIR FRANCIS BACON. An English nobleman, trusted advisor to Queen Elizabeth I, and renowned writer, scholar, and philosopher.

Background: The Sir Francis Bacon-as-Shakespeare theory was popularized in 1852 by Delia Bacon (no relation), a 41-year-old Connecticut spinster who detested William Shakespeare, referring to him as "a vulgar, illiterate...deer poacher" and "stableboy."

• Bacon believed that Shakespeare had been buried with documents that would prove her theory. She spent much of her life struggling to get permission to open the crypt. She never succeeded and died insane in 1859.

Evidence: According to some theorists, a number of Shakespeare's plays demonstrate "profound legal expertise." But Shakespeare was not a lawyer—and according to one theorist, "A person of Shakespeare's known background could not have gained such knowledge." Sir Francis Bacon, on the other hand, was so gifted as a lawyer that he eventually became Lord Chancellor of England.

• Shakespeare's plays also show a strong familiarity with continental Europe, though there's no evidence the Bard himself ever left England. Bacon, an aristocrat, was well traveled.

• Bacon had a reason for hiding his authorship: In the 17th century, poetry and playwriting was considered frivolous and beneath the dignity of a nobleman. Bacon may have kept his identity a secret to protect his reputation (as well as his standing in the royal court, since a number of the plays dealt with English monarchs). So he paid William Shakespeare, a nobody, to take the credit.

2. CHRISTOPHER MARLOWE. An accomplished playwright of the 1500s. Author of such works as *Edward the Second* and *The Tragical History of Doctor Faustus*, Marlowe was considered as talented as Shakespeare by audiences of the day.

Background: Unlike most candidates for the Shakespearean crown, Marlowe was already dead by the time most of Shakespeare's plays were written; according to the official story, he was stabbed to death during a drunken brawl in a pub in 1593. Marlowe theorists disagree—they believe he *faked* his death:

• Marlowe had a reputation for rowdiness, was an alleged homosexual and atheist, and may have even been an English spy.

• His wild life and radical beliefs eventually got him into trouble, and in 1593 a warrant was put out for his arrest. Marlowe theorists believe that his alleged lover, Sir Thomas Walsingham, staged the pub fight, had someone else murdered, and then bribed the coroner to report that Marlowe was the man who'd been killed. Marlowe escaped to France to continue his writing career, and Sir Thomas hired Shakespeare to publish—under his own name—the manuscripts Marlowe sent back from France.

Evidence: Though the theory was first suggested by W. G. Zeigler, a California lawyer, in 1895, it wasn't until the early 1900s that an

Long-distance travelers: Hummingbirds can fly 500 miles without stopping.

Ohio professor, Thomas C. Mendenhall, checked to see if the claims were credible. He spent months analyzing more than 400,000 individual words from Shakespeare's plays and comparing them with words from Marlowe's known works.

• His stunning conclusion: The two men had similar writing styles, and for both Marlowe and the Bard, "the word of greatest frequency was the four-letter word." (One problem with the research: Mendenhall studied *contemporary* editions of Shakespeare's plays, which spelled many words differently than they had appeared in the original plays.)

• Other researchers dug up Sir Thomas's grave to see if it held any clues to whether Marlowe really was a homosexual. The search turned up nothing—not even Sir Thomas.

3. EDWARD DE VERE, 17th Earl of Oxford. Though none of his plays survive, de Vere was an accomplished author in his own right. He's also been described as a "hot-tempered youth, a spendthrift, and a philanderer specializing in the queen's maids-of-honor."

Background: J. Thomas Looney, father of the de Vere-as-Shakespeare theory, was an English schoolmaster and Bard buff in the early 1900s. Over time he came to believe that Shakespeare's descriptions of Italy in *The Merchant of Venice* could only have been made by someone who'd actually been there, and Shakespeare had not. Looney began researching the lives of other writers of Shakespeare's day to see if he could find the real author. He eventually settled on de Vere.

Evidence: De Vere had traveled abroad. After emitting "an unfortunate flatulence in the presence of the Queen," he was compelled to leave England and spent several years traveling in Europe. During his travels he spent a great deal of time in Italy and gained the knowledge Looney alleges he needed to write *The Merchant of Venice* and other plays.

• According to Looney, many of de Vere's relatives had names that were similar to the names of characters in Shakespeare's plays—too many relatives to be a coincidence.

4. SIR WALTER RALEIGH. Raleigh, an "author, adventurer, and explorer," was the founding father of the state of Virginia and,

When snakes are born with two heads, they fight each other for food.

like Bacon, was popular in Queen Elizabeth's court. But he fell out of favor when James I took the throne, and was beheaded in 1618.

Background: George S. Caldwell, an Australian, first advanced the theory that Raleigh wrote Shakespeare's plays in 1877. The theory later became popular with U.S. Senator Albert J. Beveridge, who made speeches supporting it in the 1890s. In 1914 Henry Pemberton, Jr., a Philadelphia writer, gave the theory new life in his book *Shakespeare and Sir Walter Raleigh*.

Evidence: Raleigh was familiar with the traditions of the royal court and the military, which were central themes in a number of Shakespeare's plays.

• Unlike Shakespeare, who was not known for being emotional, Raleigh was a passionate man, much like the characters in Shakespeare's plays.

5. MICHEL ANGELO FLORIO. Florio, an Italian, was a defrocked Franciscan monk who converted to Protestantism. A Calvinist, he lived in exile in England for much of his life. His son John Florio most likely knew William Shakespeare; many historians speculate that the two men were close friends.

Background: In 1925 Santi Paladino, a writer, visited a fortuneteller and was told that he would someday shock the world with an amazing discovery. Within four years he had published his book *Un Italiano Autore Delle Opere Shakespeariane*, which claimed that Michel Angelo Florio was the true author of Shakespeare's works.

Evidence: Again, the main body of circumstantial evidence is that Florio had an intimate knowledge of Italy that Shakespeare could not have possessed. Florio-as-Shakespearists believe that the elder Florio, whose experience as an exile made him leery of publishing in his own name, wrote Shakespeare's plays in *Italian*, had his son translate them into English, and paid Shakespeare to publish them under his own name.

• Shakespeare's supporters disagree, arguing that the Bard wrote the plays himself, but got a lot of his information on Italy from the Florios, who were writers themselves and owned a large library of Italian books. Shakespeare may have even borrowed from some of the Florios' writings, they say, but there's no hard evidence anyone other than Shakespeare wrote his plays.

MOOO: Most cows give more milk when they listen to music.

CARNIVAL TRICKS

Do the booths at carnivals and traveling circuses seem rigged to you? According to Matthew Gryczan in his book Carnival Secrets, *many of them are. Here are some booths to look out for—and some tips on how to beat them.*

The Booth: "Ring a Bottle"

The Object: Throw a small ring over the neck of a soft-drink bottle from a distance of about five feet.

How It's Rigged: The game isn't rigged, but it doesn't have to be—it's almost impossible to win.

• In 1978 researchers stood six feet away from a grouping of 100 bottles and tossed 7,000 rings at it. They recorded 12 wins—an average of one shot in every 583 throws. What's more, the researchers found that all of the 12 winning tosses were ricochets; not a single *aimed* shot had gone over the bottles. In fact, the light, plastic rings wouldn't stay on the bottles even if dropped from a height of three inches directly over the neck of the bottle.

How to Win: It appears that the only way to win is to throw two rings over a bottle neck at the same time. However, carnival operators usually won't let you throw more than one ring at a time.

The Booth: "The Bushel Basket"

The Object: Toss softballs into a bushel basket from a distance of about six feet.

How It's Rigged: The bottom of the basket is connected to the baseboard in such a way that it has a lot of spring to it, so the ball will usually bounce out.

• In addition, carnies sometimes use balls that weigh as little as 4 ounces, rather than the 6-1/4-ounce minimum weight of an official softball. The lighter ball makes the game harder to win.

• Some carnies use a heavier ball when demonstrating the game or to give to players for a practice shot. Then, when play begins, they switch to a lighter ball that's harder to keep in the basket.

How to Win: Ask to use the same ball the carny used.

A recent U.S. Army study estimates that 25% of U.S. troops cannot be taught to use a map.

• The best throw is to aim high, so that the ball enters the basket from a vertical rather than a horizontal angle. The worst place to put the ball is directly on the bottom of the basket.

• Aim for the lip or the sides of the basket. If the rules prohibit these shots, the game will be tough to win.

The Booth: "Shoot Out the Dots"

The Object: Using soft graphite bullets, shoot out all the red in three to five dots printed on a paper target.

How It's Rigged: The bullet, called an "arcade load," is discharged from the rifle barrel in little chunks. Propelled by a low-powder charge that ranges from a .22 cap to a .22-short, the chunks barely penetrate the target.

• Even if the bullet remained intact, it would not be able to take out all of the red of the .22 caliber–sized dots, because its diameter ranges from .15 caliber to .177 caliber. Besides, the chunks of graphite *tear* the paper target instead of punching out a clean hole. So there's always some red left on the target, even with a direct hit.

How to Win: In many cases, winning is impossible. During a trial, one carny testified that she'd never had one winner in 365,000 plays over five and a half years—despite the fact the game was frequented by U.S. naval personnel with experience in shooting guns.

The Booth: "The Milk Can"

The Object: Toss a softball into a 10-gallon milk can.

How It's Rigged: Most carnival cans aren't ordinary dairy cans. For the midway game, a concave piece of steel is welded to the rim of the can's opening, reducing the size of the hole the ball must travel through to anything from 6-1/2 inches down to 4-3/8 inches in diameter.

• At one game played at a state fair in 1987, there were 15 wins out of a total of 1,279 tries—one win for every 86 balls thrown.

How to Win: Carnies say the best way to win is to give the ball a backspin and try to hit the back edge of the can.

• Another way: Toss the ball as high as you can, so that it drops straight into the hole. This isn't always easy; operators often hang prizes from the rafters of the booth to make high tosses difficult.

There are an estimated 508,000 metric tons of tea in China.

THEY WENT THAT-A-WAY

Malcolm Forbes wrote a fascinating book about the deaths of famous people. Here are some of the weirdest stories he found.

FRANCIS BACON

Claim to Fame: One of the great minds of the late 16th century. A statesman, philosopher, writer, and scientist. Some people believe he's the real author of Shakespeare's plays (see page 123).

How He Died: Stuffing snow into a chicken.

Postmortem: One afternoon in 1625, Bacon was watching a snowstorm. He began wondering if snow might be as good a meat preservative as salt...and decided to find out. With a friend, he rode through the storm to a nearby peasant's cottage, bought a chicken, and had it butchered. Then, standing outside in the cold, he stuffed the chicken with snow to freeze it. The chicken never froze, but Bacon did. He caught a serious chill and never recovered. He died from bronchitis a few weeks later.

WILLIAM HENRY HARRISON

Claim to Fame: Ninth president of the United States; elected in 1841 at the age of 67.

How He Died: Pneumonia.

Postmortem: Harrison's advanced age had been an issue in his race against incumbent president Martin van Buren. Perhaps because of this—to demonstrate his strength—he rode on horseback in his inaugural parade without a hat, gloves, or overcoat. Then he stood outside in the snow for more than one and a half hours, delivering his inaugural address.

The experience weakened him, and a few weeks later he caught pneumonia. Within a week he was delirious, and on April 4—just one month after his inauguration—he died. He served in office long enough to keep only one campaign promise: not to run for a second term.

Queen Elizabeth and Prince Philip of Great Britain are 2nd, 3rd, 4th, and 5th cousins.

AESCHYLUS

Claim to Fame: Greek playwright in 500 B.C. Many historians consider him the father of Greek tragedies.

How He Died: An eagle dropped a tortoise on his head.

Postmortem: According to legend, an eagle was trying to crack open a tortoise by dropping it on a hard rock. It mistook Aeschylus's head (he was bald) for a rock and dropped it on him instead.

TYCHO BRAHE

Claim to Fame: An important Danish astronomer of the 16th century. His groundbreaking research enabled Sir Isaac Newton to come up with the theory of gravity.

How He Died: Didn't get to the bathroom on time.

Postmortem: In the 16th century, it was considered an insult to leave a banquet table before the meal was over. Brahe, known to drink excessively, had a bladder condition—but failed to relieve himself before the feast started. He made matters worse by drinking too much at the dinner, but was too polite to ask to be excused. His bladder finally burst, killing him slowly and painfully over the next 11 days.

JEROME IRVING RODALE

Claim to Fame: Founding father of the organic food movement, creator of *Organic Farming and Gardening* magazine. Founded Rodale Press, a major publishing company.

How He Died: On the "Dick Cavett Show," while discussing the health benefits of organic food.

Postmortem: Rodale, who bragged, "I'm going to live to 100 unless I'm run down by a sugar-crazed taxi-driver," was only 72 when he appeared on the "Dick Cavett Show" in January 1971. Partway through the interview, he dropped dead in his chair. Cause of death: a heart attack. The show was never aired.

ATTILA THE HUN

Claim to Fame: One of the most notorious villains in history. By 450 A.D., his 500,000-man army conquered all of Asia—from Mongolia to the edge of the Russian empire—by destroying villages and pillaging the countryside.

Uh-oh: 23% of Americans believe the president can suspend the Bill of Rights during wartime.

How He Died: He got a nosebleed on his wedding night.

Postmortem: In 453 Attila married a young girl named Ildico. Despite his reputation for ferocity on the battlefield, he tended to eat and drink lightly during large banquets. But on his wedding night he really cut loose, gorging himself on food and drink. Sometime during the night he suffered a nosebleed, but was too drunk to notice. He drowned in his own blood and was found dead the next morning.

JIM FIXX

Claim to Fame: Author of the bestselling *Complete Book of Running,* which started the jogging craze of the 1970s.

How He Died: A heart attack...while jogging.

Postmortem: Fixx was visiting Greensboro, Vermont. He walked out of his house and began jogging. He'd only gone a short distance when he had a massive coronary. His autopsy revealed that one of his coronary arteries was 99% clogged, another was 80% obstructed, and a third was 70% blocked—and that Fixx had had three other heart attacks in the weeks prior to his death (when he'd competed in 12-mile and 5-mile races).

HORACE WELLS

Claim to Fame: Pioneered the use of anaesthesia in the 1840s.

How He Died: Used anaesthetics to commit suicide.

Postmortem: While experimenting with various gases during his anaesthesia research, Wells became addicted to chloroform. In 1848 he was arrested for splashing sulfuric acid on two women outside his home. In a letter he wrote from jail, he blamed chloroform for his problems, claiming he'd gotten high before the attack. Four days later he was found dead in his cell. He'd anaesthetized himself with chloroform, then slashed open his thigh with a razor.

* * * *

And Now for Something Completely Different

• Elvis Presley was a big Monty Python fan; he saw *Monty Python and the Holy Grail* at least five times.

• The King's favorite board games were Monopoly and Scrabble. Neutrogena was his favorite soap.

THE ELVIS SIDESHOW

Hurry, hurry, step right up! See the amazing Elvis freaks!

Richard Tweddell III. Inventor of the Elvis Vegiform, a plastic garden mold that fits over young vegetables and gets them to grow into the shape of the King. He says, "[Elvis-shaped] vegetables are more weighty, and the flavor is enhanced."

Nicholas "S&L-vis" D'Ambra. An Elvis impersonator with a social conscience. "S&L-vis" takes on the savings and loan scandal with songs like "Tax-break Hotel." Sample lyrics: "The deal the bank board gave them; was too good to be true; for every dollar they put in there; there's 15 from you."

"Major" Bill Smith. Believes the King is still alive and claims to have regular phone conversations with him. Smith, a 68-year-old Texan, is a religious man; he sees Elvis as a sort of mini-messiah: "Elvis is coming back in the spirit of Elijah....Praise God, he's coming back....This thing's about to bust right open." He has devoted his life to paving the way for the Second Coming of Elvis, which he considers the Lord's work. "Like Elvis told me, 'I'm walkin' the line God has drawn for me.' It's what the Holy Spirit told me to do."

Peter Singh. A Sikh living in Wales, England, he croons Elvis hits, Indian-style, to customers at his pub. Favorites include "Who's Sari Now," "My Popadum Told Me," and "Singh, Singh, Singh."

Uri Yoali. An Israeli Arab, owner of a roadside diner called The Elvis Inn, located in the Holy Land just 7,000 miles from Memphis. "It's not just for tourists," Yoali says, "Elvis is my life." The diner is decorated with 728 pictures and posters of the King. It boasts a 12-foot, 500-pound, epoxy-and-plaster likeness of Presley outside its entrance. "I've always dreamed of seeing Elvis big," Yoali says, "In my mind he is so large, bigger even than this."

Danny Uwnawich. Owner of Melodyland, a small, three-bedroom version of Graceland in California's San Fernando Valley. Highlight: A white wrought-iron gate. Like the gate at Graceland, it's shaped like an open music book. According to Uwnawich, "The only people who have those gates is me and Him."

COWBOY TALK

Well, Hoss, maybe you can't be a cowboy, but you can still talk like one. Here are a few phrases to practice. Save 'em until you can find a way to use 'em in conversation. And smile when you say them, son.

"He's crooked enough to sleep on a corkscrew": He's dishonest.

"Raised on prunes and proverbs": A religious person.

"Coffin varnish": Whiskey.

"Fat as a well-fed needle": Poor.

"Deceitful beans": Beans that give you gas. (They talk behind your back.)

"Got a pill in his stomach that he can't digest": Shot dead.

"She's like a turkey gobbler in a hen pen": She's proud.

"He's like a breedin' jackass in a tin barn": He's noisy.

"Fryin' size but plumb salty": A senior citizen.

"Quicker 'n you can spit 'n holler 'Howdy!' ": Very fast.

"Studying to be a half-wit": Stupid or crazy.

"Built like a snake on stilts": Tall.

"Shy on melody, but strong on noise": A bad singer.

"Weasel smart": Very crafty.

"Scarce as bird dung in a cuckoo clock": Hard to find.

"Dry as the dust in a mummy's pocket": Very dry.

"In the lead when tongues was handed out": Talks too much.

"If he closed one eye he'd look like a needle": Very skinny.

"He lives in a house so small he can't cuss his cat without getting fur in his mouth": He's a tightwad.

"He died of throat trouble": He was hung.

Captain Kangaroo won five Emmy awards.

DUBIOUS ACHIEVERS

Here are some of the stranger people listed in the Guiness Book of World Records.

Randy Ober, Bentonville, Arkansas
Achievement: Spit a wad of tobacco 47 feet, 7 inches in 1982.

Joe Ponder, Love Valley, North Carolina
Achievement: Lifted a 606-pound pumpkin 18 inches off the ground with his teeth in 1985.

Neil Sullivan, Birmingham, England
Achievement: Carried a large bag of "household coal" 34 miles on May 24, 1986. It took him 12 hours and 45 minutes.

Travis Johnson, Elsberry, Missouri
Achievement: Held nine baseballs in his hand "without any adhesives" in 1989.

David Beattie and Adrian Simons, London, England
Achievement: Rode up and down escalators at the Top Shop in London for 101 hours in 1989. Estimated distance of travel: 133.19 miles.

Pieter van Loggerenberg, Hoedspruit, South Africa
Achievement: Played the accordion for 85 hours during a wildlife festival in 1987.

Michel Lotito, Grenoble, France
Achievement: Has been eating metal and glass since 1959; currently he eats more than two pounds of metal every day. Since 1966 he has eaten 10 bicycles, a supermarket food cart, 7 televisions, 6 chandeliers, a coffin, and a Cessna airplane.

"Country" Bill White, Killeen, Texas
Achievement: Buried alive in a coffin, more than six feet underground, for 341 days in July 1981. Only connection to the outside world: a four-inch tube used for feeding and breathing.

Name mentioned most frequently in the Bible: David. (Jesus is second.)

King Taufa'ahau, Tonga
Achievement: World's fattest king; weighed 462 pounds in 1976.

Alfred West
Achievement: Split a human hair into 17 different pieces "on eight different occasions."

Remy Bricka, Paris, France
Achievement: In 1988, using 13-foot-long floating "skis," he "walked" across the Atlantic Ocean from Tenerife, Spain, to Trinidad (a distance of 3,502 miles). The trip took 60 days.

Steve Urner, Tehachapi, California
Acheivement: Threw a dried, "100% organic" cow chip more than 266 feet on August 4, 1981.

N. Ravi, Tamil Nadu, India
Acheivement: Stood on one foot for 34 hours in 1982.

"Hercules" John Massis, Oostakker, Belgium
Achievement: Used teeth to stop a helicopter from taking off, 1979.

Zolilio Diaz, Spain
Achievement: Rolled a hoop from Mieres to Madrid, Spain, and back—a distance of more than 600 miles. It took him 18 days.

Nine employees of the Bruntsfield Bedding Centre, Scotland.
Achievement: Pushed a wheeled hospital bed 3,233 miles between June 21 and July 26, 1979.

Fred Jipp, New York City, New York
Achievement: Most illegal marriages. Between 1949 and 1981, using over 50 aliases, married 104 women in 27 states and 14 foreign countries. Sentenced to 34 years in prison and fined $336,000.

Octavio Guillen and Adriana Martinez, Mexico City, Mexico
Acheivement: Longest engagement: 67 years. They finally tied the knot in 1969. Both were age 82.

Sisters Jill Bradbury and Chris Humpish, London, England
Achievement: Made a bed (2 sheets, 1 undersheet, 1 blanket, 1 pillow, and a bedspread) in 19 seconds flat on October 8, 1985.

An estimated 70% of the hats sold in the United States are baseball caps.

THE BIRDS AND THE BEES

When people talk about "the birds and the bees," this probably isn't what they had in mind. Here are some of the weirder ways animals reproduce.

SQUID

The male squid's sperm are contained in 1/2-inch-long pencil-shaped "packages" called spermatophores, which are located in a pouch near his gills. When the male is ready to reproduce, he grabs some of the spermatophores with one of his tentacles and deposits them deep inside the gill chamber of a female squid. The spermatophores remain inside the female until she ovulates, when they explode into a cloud of sperm and fertilize the egg. (In some species the male's arm breaks off inside the female and remains there until it is absorbed by her body.)

SLOTHS

Sloths are the only land animals besides humans that regularly mate face to face. One important difference: they do it while hanging from tree branches by their arms.

SEA URCHINS

Sea urchins expel their semen directly into the surrounding seawater, doing nothing to ensure that it ever reaches an unfertilized egg. If the current is right, the semen will eventually be carried to an egg, and reproduction will take place.

"NOSE," OR "VAQUERO," FROGS

When the female is ready to reproduce, she lays 20 to 30 *un*fertilized eggs. Nearby male frogs surround the eggs, fertilize them, and then guard them for as long as two weeks. As soon as they can see tadpoles forming within the eggs, each frog immediately tries to "swallow" as many eggs as possible, depositing them in a large throat sac that extends from their chins to their thighs. The eggs remain there until the tadpoles metamorphosize completely into frogs, when they enter the world by crawling out of the father's mouth.

The gorilla's scientific name is "Gorilla gorilla gorilla."

MUD TURTLES

The female mud turtle has a pair of bladders connected to her intestines that she uses to build a nesting pit for her eggs. When she is ready to lay her fertilized eggs, she fills the bladders with water, and then partially empties them over the patch of dirt she wants to use for her nest. Then she starts digging, emptying the rest of the water in her bladders as she digs. When the bladders are empty, she returns to the water to refill them, then returns to the nest and continues digging. When she finishes, she kicks her eggs into the hole with her feet or tail, and covers the nest with fresh mud.

EUROPEAN CUCKOOS

Like all species of cuckoos, the European cuckoo does not build its own nest. Instead, it lays its eggs in the nests of other species of birds. Some types of cuckoos remove the original eggs from the nest, other types leave them in the nest, and the host mother raises all the young as if they were her own. But the offspring of the European cuckoo are more aggressive than most: a few hours after one is born it begins kicking uncontrollably, an involuntary response that lasts about four days. By that time, the fledgling has usually kicked everything out of the nest—including any other baby birds.

SNAILS

Snails practice a form of foreplay in which they shoot chalky "love darts" at each other to determine if they are members of the same species. Because snails are hermaphrodites—they have male and female sex organs—each snail will impregnate the other.

DUCKS

According to one study, young male ducks are often disinterested in sex—even to the point of resisting the advances of females who are "in the mood." Sometimes the ducks appear to make elaborate excuses for why they cannot have sex, such as chasing away an imaginary enemy, taking an unneeded bath, etc. But the male ducks make up for it in later life: after they select a mate.

AFRICAN ELEPHANTS

According to at least one study, female elephants act as midwives for one another when the hour of birth draws near. One researcher

Australia has more sheep than any other country on Earth.

reported observing three female elephants leaving their herd and approaching a thicket. One of the females went into the thicket, while the other two stood guard outside, driving away any elephant or other animal that tried to approach. After a while the sentries returned to the herd, followed shortly afterwards by the third elephant and her newborn.

SPIDERS

Because the male spider has no sex organ, he has to squeeze sperm from his belly onto his web, which he then picks up with his antennae before going off in search of a female spider. Male spiders also have to be careful once they find a female; if they aren't careful, the female will bite their head off during sex.

PRAYING MANTISES

As soon as the male praying mantis mounts the female, the female bites his head off. Undeterred, the male continues mating while the female eats his shoulders and upper abdomen. Unlike most other creatures, the male mantis's brain *prevents* him from releasing sperm, so the female *has* to bite his head off.

BEES

Only one male bee in a hive has the right to mate with the Queen, a process that takes about two seconds. When the male bee pulls away, his penis breaks off and remains inside the Queen, while he falls to the bottom of the hive and bleeds to death.

SNAKES

Female snakes mate with several male snakes during each mating cycle and can store sperm in their bodies for months. According to one theory, snakes do this in order to have a "sperm contest" inside their bodies, somehow allowing only the healthiest sperm to fertilize their eggs. This increases the number of live births per season, increasing the chance that the species will survive.

GREAT GREY SLUGS

Grey slugs are also hermaphrodites and engage in foreplay consisting of circling one another for hours, generating lots of slime in the process. Then they mate while hanging from ropes of slime.

Secret stash: FBI director J. Edgar Hoover kept a collection of pornography locked in his desk.

THE DUSTBIN OF HISTORY

Harold Stassen almost won the GOP nomination for president in 1948. Did something "snap" when he lost? No one knows for sure, but he kept on running...and running...and running...

BACKGROUND. Harold Stassen was the Republican "Boy Wonder" of Minnesota politics in the 1930s. He was elected governor of the state in 1937 at the age of 31, and re-elected in 1940 and 1942. He was widely regarded—by friends *and* foes—as presidential timber.

The Sure Thing. Nineteen forty-eight was the presidential election Republicans had been waiting for: FDR was dead, and Harry Truman's approval rating had slipped below 30%. The Republican nominee—whoever he was—was a shoo-in to claim the Oval Office. And Harold Stassen was a front-runner for the nomination.

Stassen steamrolled through the Nebraska, Wisconsin, and Pennsylvania primaries. And he lost New Jersey by only 600 votes, despite the fact that Governor Thomas E. Dewey of New York was the favorite son of a neighboring state. Next, he stormed West Virginia, winning 117,000 of the state's 139,000 votes. He looked unstoppable—until he got to Oregon.

The Loser. Stassen had agreed to debate Dewey on May 17, 1948—only days before the Oregon primary—on the single issue of whether or not the Communist Party should be banned in the U.S. Stassen debated in favor of the ban; Dewey opposed it.

Stassen was the first candidate to speak, and he ripped into the Reds. "These Communist organizations are not really political parties. They actually are fifth columns....Governor Dewey's position in effect means a soft policy towards Communism...we must not coddle Communism with legality." One broadcaster later described Stassen's delivery as being the "assured and authoritative delivery of a man comfortable with command."

Next came Dewey's turn to reply. He didn't defend Communism, but he urged restraint in dealing with it: "The people of this country are being asked to outlaw Communism. That means this: Shall we in America, in order to defeat a totalitarian regime which we detest, voluntarily adopt the methods of that system?...I am unalterably, wholeheartedly, unswervingly against any scheme to write laws outlawing people because of their religious, political, social, or economic ideas."

Dewey was an experienced district attorney, and his defense of his position was eloquent and masterful. In fact, he took such command of the debate that Stassen began to panic. Tom Swaford, a broadcaster who was there, described Stassen's reaction:

> The Minnesotan was a different man. As he responded, he was wearing the kind of half smile a boxer puts on after taking a damaging blow when he wants the judges to think it didn't hurt. The radio audience couldn't see that, of course, but it could hear the uncertain, diffident delivery that had replaced the earlier booming confidence. The smooth flow was gone. I thought at the moment that we were watching a man who had not done his homework and was now aware of it.

Stassen's rebuttal was so weak that Dewey shot back: "I gather from Mr. Stassen's remarks that he has completely surrendered." In a way, Stassen had. And in doing so, he lost more than just the debate: he lost the Oregon primary...and he lost his momentum. In the end, Dewey edged Stassen out for the Republican nomination.

World-Class Loser. Some politicians would have retired gracefully after such a humiliating defeat, but not Stassen. He showed the form that makes him a truly world-class loser, continuing to run in races he had no chance to win for the next *45 years!* He ran for president in 1952, 1964, 1968, 1976, 1980, 1984, 1988, and 1992. He lost races for mayor of Philadelphia (1962), senator of Minnesota (1978), another term as governor of Minnesota (1982), and a bid for Congress (1986).

Stassen became a national joke, usually referred to as "the perennial candidate." In the 1992 Republican National Convention, delegates made fun of him with "Stop Stassen" buttons. "The ridicule bothers me," said the 85-year-old candidate, "but it doesn't stop me....Every one of the ten times [I've run], there has been some solid result." Besides, he adds, "Winning is not the primary concern. My primary concern is to move America."

Pop singer Michael Jackson collects mannequins.

ONE NUCLEAR BOMB CAN RUIN YOUR WHOLE DAY

We don't want to make you paranoid, but all of these incidents really happened.

1. In July 1956, a B-47 aircraft plowed into a storage igloo 20 miles outside of Cambridge, England. The plane's jet fuel burst into flames almost immediately, but for some reason didn't ignite the contents of the igloo. A lucky thing, too—it contained three Mark 6 nuclear bombs.

2. In 1958 a B-47E accidentally dropped a nuclear bomb into a Mars Bluff, South Carolina, family's vegetable garden. The bomb didn't explode, but it did damage five houses and a church. Air Force officials apologized.

3. In 1961 a B-52 dropped two 24-megaton bombs on a North Carolina farm. According to one physicist: "Only a single switch prevented the bombs from detonating."

4. In 1966 another B-52 carrying four 20-megaton bombs crashed in Palomares, Spain—with one of the bombs splashing into the Mediterranean Sea. It took the U.S. 6th fleet—using 33 ships and 3,000 men—several weeks to find the missing bomb.

5. In 1980 a repairman working on a Titan II missile in Arkansas dropped a wrench—which bounced off the floor, punctured the missile, and set off an explosion that blew the top off the silo and threw the warhead 600 feet into the air.

6. Did June 3, 1980, seem tense to you? It did to the Strategic Air Command in Omaha, Nebraska. Their computers detected a Soviet submarine missile attack in progress. Within minutes, more than 100 B-52s were in the air, but the SAC soon called off the counterattack—the computers had made a mistake. The culprit: a 46¢ computer chip. Three days later the same mistake happened again.

According to the FBI, most burglaries occur in winter.

FAMILY HOLIDAYS

Every year, Americans set aside special days to honor our fathers, our mothers, our grandparents, and even our mothers-in-law. Where did these holidays come from? Here's a little background.

MOTHER'S DAY (Second Sunday in May)

ORIGIN: The result of a one-woman crusade launched in 1908 by Anna Jarvis, a West Virginia schoolteacher whose mother had died three years earlier. On May 10, 1908, she persuaded pastors in nearby Grafton, West Virginia, and Philadelphia, Pennsylvania, to hold Mother's Day services in their churches. (They handed out carnations, Anna's mother's favorite flower.) From there she launched a letter-writing campaign to U.S. governors, congressmen, clergy, media, etc. She wasn't immediately successful, but by 1914 Congress endorsed the idea. On May 9, 1914, President Wilson issued a proclamation establishing the holiday.

THE INSIDE SCOOP: Jarvis—who had no children—came to hate the holiday she had created. She railed against its commercialism, and especially loathed flowers and greeting cards. "Any mother would rather have a line of the worst scribble from her son or daughter," she complained, "than any fancy greeting card." She became a recluse who never left her house, posting "Warning—Stay Away" signs on her front lawn. She refused to give interviews, but a reporter posing as a deliveryman managed to speak with her. "She told me with terrible bitterness that she was sorry she had ever started Mother's Day," he revealed.

FATHER'S DAY (Third Sunday in June)

ORIGIN: Anna Jarvis's "success" inspired a number of other Americans to begin work for a Father's Day. First among them was Sonora Smart Dodd, a Spokane, Washington, housewife whose father had raised six children alone after her mother died in childbirth. She proposed making Father's Day the *first* Sunday in June (the month of her father's birthday), but local religious leaders vetoed the date; they needed more time to prepare sermons on fatherhood. So they settled on the third Sunday. The holiday was first celebrated in Spokane on June 19, 1910.

It took the all-male U.S. Congress longer to acknowledge Father's Day than it took them to recognize Mother's Day. The reason: They feared voters would think it was too self-serving. Although President Wilson personally observed the holiday, he refused to issue a proclamation making it official. In 1924 Calvin Coolidge encouraged state governments to enact their own Father's Days, but he too declined to make it a federal holiday. Finally in 1972, Father's Day was proclaimed a federal holiday by President Nixon.

THE INSIDE SCOOP: Although she turned down many offers to endorse products, Dodd had nothing against giving gifts on Father's Day. "After all," she said, "why should the greatest giver of gifts not be on the receiving end at least once a year?" When the day's commercialism was decried in the 1950s, Dodd defended it again: "I'm convinced that giving gifts is a sacred part of the holiday, as the giver is spiritually enriched in the tribute paid his father." Dodd died in 1978, but she'd probably be happy to know that 15% of the 7 million electric shavers sold in the U.S. every year are bought for Father's Day, and Americans annually spend some $20 million on Father's Day ties.

GRANDPARENT'S DAY (First Sunday after Labor Day)

ORIGIN: Michael Goldgar, a grandparent himself, came up with the idea after visiting his aunt in an Atlanta, Georgia, nursing home. Using $11,000 of his savings, he made 17 trips to Washington, D.C. over the next seven years to lobby for a national holiday. President Carter signed the holiday into law in 1978. Today Americans send more than 4 million Grandparent's Day cards a year.

MOTHER-IN-LAW'S DAY (Fourth Sunday in October)

ORIGIN: In 1981 the U.S. House of Representatives passed a resolution establishing Mother-in-Law's Day. But the Senate never passed a similar resolution, and the bill hasn't been signed into law. Some 800,000 Americans mail Mother-in-Law's Day cards annually.

"One word sums up probably the responsibility of any vice president. And that one word is 'to be prepared.'"

—*Dan Quayle*

THE DUKE

Some people call John Wayne an American hero, others call him a Neanderthal right-winger. Neither side really knows much about him. Here are some facts about the Duke.

As a boy, Wayne learned to handle a gun by shooting rattlesnakes while his father plowed the land. But, according to one biographer, the experience gave Wayne nightmares of "slithering, disembodied snake heads coming at him. [He] often awoke in a cold sweat in the middle of the night—but he kept these fears to himself."

After finishing high school, Wayne tried to get into the U.S. Naval Academy...but was turned down. In later years, referring to the Academy's rejection, Wayne claimed "I'd probably be a retired admiral by now." (However, during World War II, he received an exemption for being the father of four children.)

Wayne created his tough-guy image only because he didn't think he could act. Later in his career he explained to The *New York Times*: "When I started, I knew I was no actor and I went to work on this Wayne thing. It was as deliberate a projection as you'll ever see. I figured I needed a gimmick, so I dreamed up the drawl, the squint, and a way of moving meant to suggest that I wasn't looking for trouble but would just as soon throw a bottle at your head as not. I practiced in front of a mirror."

After attending Governor Ronald Reagan's inauguration in 1971, the Duke spotted a group of Vietnam War protesters waving Vietcong flags. Enraged, he charged into the crowd screaming, "You dirty no-good bastards," and punching wildly. Police intervened, and the scuffle quickly ended; however, the next day, one of the protesters filed a complaint with the local police, claiming Wayne had disturbed the peace. Police refused to prosecute.

Wayne died in 1979. His funeral was held at 5 a.m., and his body was buried in an unmarked grave to prevent fans from mobbing the burial site. Four fresh "decoy" graves were also dug to prevent anyone from positively identifying the real one.

Calling Mr. Sartre: 27% of U.S. male college students believe life is "a meaningless existential hell."

A SLICE OF LIFE

A slice of the history of the most popular "ethnic" food in America.

ORIGIN. The ancient Greeks invented pizza. The most accomplished bakers of the ancient world, they made a variety of breads topped with spices, herbs, and vegetables. Their first pizza was designed as a kind of "edible plate," with the thick crust around the edge serving as a handle.

How did pizza become Italian? The Greeks occupied part of Italy for 6 centuries; one of their legacies is the popularity of pizza there.

TOMATOES

• Early pizzas featured cheese, herbs, vegetables, and fish or meat—but no tomatoes. Tomatoes, a New World food, didn't reach Italy until the mid-1500s—and weren't popular until the late 19th century because people believed they were poisonous.

• In 1889 pizza maker Raffaele Esposito added tomatoes to pizza for the first time. The reason: He wanted to make a pizza for Italian Queen Margherita in the colors of the Italian flag—red, white, and green—and needed something red to go with white mozzarella cheese and green basil.

PIZZA IN THE UNITED STATES

• The first American pizzeria was opened in New York in 1905. By the early 1920s, family-run pizzerias were popping up all over the American Northeast...but it was still considered an exotic food.

• American G.I.s returning from Italy after World War II made pizza popular throughout the United States. But it wasn't until the 1960s that it became a fad...and a movie may have been responsible. In the controversial 1961 film *Splendor in the Grass*, Warren Beatty asks a waitress, "Hey, what is pizza?" The waitress takes him "out back," introducing him to pizza and a bit more.

• Today Americans eat more than 30 million slices of pizza per day—or 350 slices a second—and spend as much as $25 billion a year on pizza.

• Pepperoni is the most popular pizza topping nationwide; anchovies are the least favorite.

You're more likely to get stung by a bee on a windy day than in any other weather.

MEET THE BEATLES

The Beatles were personalities, as entertaining in interviews as they were on record. To prove it, here are excerpts from Beatle press conferences held in the mid-1960s, when the group had become popular. At the time, rock bands were still considered vacuous non-artists. It's interesting to see how the Beatles helped change that.

Reporter: Ringo, why do you think you get more fan mail than anyone else in the group?
Ringo: I don't know. I suppose it's because more people write me.

Reporter: Do you date much?
Ringo: What are you doing tonight?

Reporter: How do you like this welcome [in the U.S.]?
Ringo: So this is America. They all seem out of their minds.

Reporter: What do you do when you're cooped up in a hotel room between shows?
George: We ice skate.

Reporter: How did you find America?
Ringo: We went to Greenland and made a left turn.

Reporter: Why do teenagers stand up and scream piercingly and painfully when you appear?
Paul: None of us know. But we've heard that teenagers go to our shows just to scream. A lot of them don't even want to listen because they have our records. We kind of like the screaming teenagers. If they want to pay their money and sit out there and shout, that's their business. We aren't going to be like little dictators and say, "You've got to shut up." The commotion doesn't bother us anymore. It's come to be like working in a bell factory. You don't hear the bells after a while.

Reporter: Would you like to walk down the street without being recognized?
John: We used to do that with no money in our pockets. There's no point in it.

Not tonight, Dear: An estimated 1 in 5 American adults—some 38 million—don't like sex.

Reporter: Are you scared when crowds scream at you?
John: More so in Dallas than in other places perhaps.

Reporter: Is it true you can't sing?
John (pointing to George): Not me. Him.

Reporter: Why don't you smile George?
George: I'll hurt my lips.

Reporter: What's your reaction to a Seattle psychiatrist's opinion that you are a menace?
George: Psychiatrists are a menace.

Reporter: Do you plan to record any anti-war songs?
John: All our songs are anti-war.

Reporter: Does all the adulation from teenage girls affect you?
John: When I feel my head start to swell, I look at Ringo and know perfectly well we're not supermen.

Reporter: Do you resent fans ripping up your sheets for souvenirs?
Ringo: No I don't mind. So long as I'm not in them while the ripping is going on.

Reporter: Do you follow politics?
John: I get spasms of being intellectual. I read a bit about politics but I don't think I'd vote for anyone. No message from any of those phony politicians is coming through to me.

Reporter: What's the most unusual request you've had?
John: I wouldn't like to say.

Reporter: What do you plan to do next?
John: We're not going to fizzle out in half a day. But afterwards I'm not going to change into a tap dancing musical. I'll just develop what I'm doing at the moment, although whatever I say now I'll change my mind next week. I mean, we all know that bit about: "It won't be the same when you're twenty-five." I couldn't care less. This isn't show business. It's something else. This is different from anything that anybody imagines. You don't go on from this. You do this and then you finish.

Reporter: Do you like topless bathing suits?
Ringo: We've been wearing them for years.

Ronald Reagan is the only U.S. president to have performed in Las Vegas.

Reporter: Girls rushed toward my car because it had press identification and they thought I met you. How do you explain this phenomenon?
John: You're lovely to look at.

Reporter: How do you add up success?
John, Paul, George, Ringo: Money.

Reporter: What will you do when Beatlemania subsides?
John: Count the money.

Reporter: What do you think of the Bomb?
Paul: It's disturbing that people should go around blowing us up, but if an atom bomb should explode I'd say, "Oh well, no point in saying anything else, is there." People are so crackers. I know the bomb is ethically wrong but I won't go around crying. I suppose I could do something like wearing those "ban the bomb" things, but it's something like religion that I don't think about. It doesn't fit in with my life.

Reporter: What do you think of space shots?
John: You see one, you've seen them all.

Reporter: What do you think about the pamphlet calling you four Communists?
Paul: Us, Communists? Why, we can't be Communists. We're the world's number one capitalists. Imagine us. Communists!

Reporter: What's your biggest fear?
John: The thing I'm afraid of is growing old. I hate that. You get old and you've missed it somehow. The old always resent the young and vice-versa.

Reporter: What about the recent criticism of your lyrics?
Paul: If you start reading things into them you might as well start singing hymns.

Reporter: You were at the Playboy Club last night. What did you think of it?
Paul: The Playboy and I are just good friends.

Reporter: George, is the place you were brought up a bit like Greenwich Village?
George: No. More like The Bowery.

In 1980, a Las Vegas hospital suspended workers for betting on when patients would die.

Reporter: Ringo, how do you manage to find all those parties?
Ringo: I don't know. I just end up at them.
Paul: On tour we don't go out much. Ringo's always out, though.
John: Ringo freelances.

Reporter: There's a "Stamp Out the Beatles" movement underway in Detroit. What are you going to do about it?
Paul: We're going to start a campaign to stamp out Detroit.

Reporter: Who thought up the name, Beatles?
Paul: I thought of it.
Reporter: Why?
Paul: Why not?

Reporter: Beethoven figures in one of your songs. What do you think of Beethoven?
Ringo: He's great. Especially his poetry.

Reporter: Ringo, why do you wear two rings on each hand?
Ringo: Because I can't fit them through my nose.

Reporter: When you do a new song, how do you decide who sings the lead?
John: We just get together and whoever knows most of the words sings the lead.

Reporter: Do you think it's wrong to set such a bad example to teenagers, smoking the way you do?
Ringo: It's better than being alcoholics.

Reporter: What do you think of the criticism that you are not very good?
George: We're not.

Reporter: What do you believe is the reason you are the most popular singing group today?
John: We've no idea. If we did, we'd get four long-haired boys, put them together and become their managers.

Reporter: You've admitted to being agnostics. Are you also irreverent?
Paul: We are agnostics...so there's no point in being irreverent.

Some 4% of Americans are more likely to vote *for* a candidate who has an extramarital affair.

WORDPLAY

We use these words all the time, but most of us have no idea where they came from. Fortunately, we're on the job, ready to supply their history and make your brief (?) stay in the john an educational one.

POTLUCK. In the Middle Ages, cooks threw all their left-overs into a pot of water that was kept boiling most of the time. This makeshift stew was eaten by the family or fed to strangers when no other food was available. Since food was thrown in at random, its quality and taste depended entirely on luck.

JUKEBOX. The term "juke" was originally a New Orleans slang expression meaning "to have sex." Jukeboxes got their name because they were popular in houses of prostitution known as juke joints.

SLUSH FUND. "Slush" was originally the name for kitchen grease from the galleys of naval sailing ships. Most of this sludge was used to lubricate masts of the ship; the rest was sold with other garbage whenever the ship entered port. Money made from the sale was kept in a "slush fund," used to buy items for enlisted men.

HAYWIRE. Bales of hay are held together with tightly strung wire. If the wire snaps, it whips around wildly and can injure people standing nearby.

BROKE. Many banks in post-Renaissance Europe issued small, porcelain "borrower's tiles" to their creditworthy customers. Like credit cards, these tiles were imprinted with the owner's name, his credit limit, and the name of the bank. Each time the customer wanted to borrow money, he had to present the tile to the bank teller, who would compare the imprinted credit limit with how much the customer had already borrowed. If the borrower was past the limit, the teller "broke" the tile on the spot.

BOMB. The term "bomb," long in use as a name for explosive devices, was first used to describe a bad theater play by Grevile Corks, theater critic for the *New York Standard* in the 1920s. When one

Sherlock Holmes kept his tobacco in the toe of a Persian slipper.

particularly bad play closed after only two performances, Corks wryly observed: "Since the producers were so eager to clear the theater, they might have tried a smoke bomb instead. It would have been quicker for the audience, and less painful." The column was so popular that Corks started the "Bomb of the Year" award for the worst play on Broadway.

OUTSKIRTS. As medieval English towns grew too big to fit inside town walls, houses and other buildings were built outside them. These buildings surrounded the wall the same way a woman's skirt surrounds her waist—and became known as the town's "skirts." People living on the outer fringes of even *these* buildings were considered to be living in the *outskirts* of the town.

BANGS. In the early 19th century, it was common for English noblemen to maintain elaborate stables for their horses. But hard times in following years made stables an expensive luxury. Many nobles were forced to reduce their staffs—which meant that the remaining grooms had less time to spend on each horse. One innovation that resulted: instead of spending hours trimming each horse's tail, grooms cut all tail hair the same length, a process they called "banging off." Eventually the "banged" look became popular as a woman's hairstyle, too.

HUSBAND. Comes from the German words *Hus* and *Bunda,* which mean "house" and "owner." The word originally had nothing to do with marital status, except for the fact that home ownership made husbands extremely desirable marriage partners.

WIFE. Comes from the Anglo-Saxon words *wifan* and *mann,* which mean "weaver" and "human." In ancient times there were no words that specifically described males or females; one way Anglo-Saxons denoted the difference was to use the word *wifmann* or "weaver-human," since weaving was a task traditionally performed by women.

PENKNIFE. One problem with quill pens was that their tips dulled quickly and needed constant sharpening. Knife makers of the 15th century produced special knives for that purpose; their sharp blades and compact size made them popular items.

The heaviest bird in North America is the wild turkey.

ON A CAROUSEL

Just "sitting there watchin' the wheels go 'round and 'round?" While you're there, you might as well learn a little bit about the origin of the carousel and other rides, as told by BRI member Jack Mingo.

THE CAROUSEL

The name *carousel* originated with a popular 12th-century Arabian horseman's game called *carosellos*, or "little wars." The rules were simple: teams rode in circles throwing perfume-filled clay balls from one rider to another. If a ball of perfume broke, the team lost. Their penalty: they carried the smell of defeat with them for days after.

The game was brought to Europe by knights returning from the Crusades, and it evolved into elaborate, colorful tourneys called *carousels*.

Making the Rounds. In the 17th century, the French developed a device to help young nobles train for carousels. It featured legless wooden horses attached to a center pole. As the center pole turned (powered by real horses, mules, or people), the nobles on their wooden steeds would try to spear hanging rings with their lances. (This later evolved into the "catching the brass ring" tradition.) The carousel device gradually evolved into a popular form of entertainment. The peasants rode on barrel-like horses; the nobles rode in elaborate chariots and boats.

The Machine Age. Until the 1860s, carousels, which had become popular all over Europe, were still dependent on horses and mules for power. But that changed when Frederick Savage, an English engineer, designed a portable steam engine, which could turn as many as four rows of horses on a 48-foot-diameter wheel. Later, Savage also patented designs for the overhead camshafts and gears that moved the wooden horses up and down. This new type of carousel—called a "round-about" (later, merry-go-round)—was a huge success throughout Europe. Ads for carousels first appeared in America as early as 1800. Typically, offering fun was not enough—carousel owners also felt obliged to claim that doctors recommended the rides to improve blood circulation.

THE FERRIS WHEEL

A 33-year-old American engineer named George Washington Ferris designed a giant "observation wheel" for Chicago's World's Columbian Exhibition in 1893, as an American counterpart to the Eiffel Tower (which had been unveiled four years earlier). At 250 feet in diameter, this first Ferris wheel could carry more than 2,000 passengers high above the city...and bring them smoothly back down. It was the hit of the fair; some 1.5 million people rode in it.

It was such a success, writes Tad Tuleja in *Namesakes*, that "it fostered many imitators at the turn of the century, the most notable being a 300-foot wheel constructed for the 1897 London Fair and a 197-foot one built for Vienna's Prater Park in 1896....These giants proved impractical, of course, for the many carnival midways where Ferris's invention now prospers; the average traveling wheel today is about 50 feet in diameter."

In 1904 Ferris's original wheel, which cost $385,000 to build, was dismantled and sold for scrap. It brought in less than $2,000.

ROLLER COASTERS

The roller coaster was invented by an enterprising showman in Russia who built elaborate ice slides in St. Petersburg during the 15th century. Catherine the Great enjoyed the ice slides so much that she ordered tiny wheels added to the sleds so she could ride in the summer.

• The first "modern" roller coaster was built in Coney Island in 1884, more than 400 years later.

• Believe it or not, statistically, roller coasters are much safer than merry-go-rounds. One reason: People rarely decide to jump off a roller coaster while the ride is still moving. Also, the safety restraints work better. Despite that, 27 people died on roller coasters between 1973 and 1988.

• Designers purposely create the illusion that your head is in danger of being chopped by a low overhang at the bottom of a hill. Actually there's almost always a nine-foot clearance.

• Americans take more than an estimated 214 million roller coaster rides each year.

"We won't make a sequel, but we may well make a second episode."

—Jon Peters, *film producer*

OXYMORONS

Here's a list of oxymorons sent to us by BRI member Peter McCracken. In case you don't know, an oxymoron is a common phrase made of two words that appear to be contradictory.

Military Intelligence
Light Heavyweight
Jumbo Shrimp
Painless Dentistry
Drag Race
Friendly Fire
Criminal Justice
Permanent Temporary
Amtrack Schedule
Genuine Imitation
Mandatory Option
Protective Custody
Limited Nuclear War
Dear Occupant
Standard Deviation
Freezer Burn
Pretty Ugly
Industrial Park
Loyal Opposition
Eternal Life
Natural Additives
Student Teacher
Educational Television
Nonworking Mother
Active Reserves
Full-Price Discount
Limited Immunity

Death Benefits
Upside Down
Original Copy
Random Order
Irrational Logic
Business Ethics
Slightly Pregnant
Holy Wars
Half Dead
Supreme Court
Even Odds
Baby Grand
Inside Out
Fresh Frozen
Moral Majority
Truth in Advertising
Friendly Takeover
Good Grief
United Nations
Baked Alaska
Plastic Glasses
Peacekeeping Missiles
Somewhat Addictive
Science Fiction
Open Secret
Unofficial Record
Tax Return

According to zoologists, deer like to play tag. They tag each other using their hooves.

IT'S IN THE CARDS

Do you like to play poker?...gin rummy?...bridge...or (in the bathroom) solitaire? Then maybe we can interest you in a couple of pages on the origin of playing cards.

HISTORY

Origin. The first playing cards are believed to have come from the Mamelukes, people of mixed Turkish and Mongolian blood who ruled Egypt from 1250 to 1517. Like today's standard playing cards, the Mamelukes' deck had 52 cards and four suits (swords, polo sticks, cups, and coins), with three face cards and 10 numbered cards per suit. Mameluke decks did not include queens or jacks; they used "Deputy Kings" and "Second," or "Under-Deputy Kings," instead.

European Popularity. In the mid-1300s, the cards were introduced to Europe, where they spawned a gaming craze similar to the Monopoly or Trivial Pursuit fads of the 20th century. Historians measure their popularity not by how many times people wrote about them (cards received little or no mention) or by the number of decks that survive (few did), but by the number of cities that *banned* them. Paris was one of the first: it outlawed card-playing among "working men" in 1377. Other cities soon followed, and by the mid-1400s, anti-card sentiments reached a fervor. During one public demonstration in Nuremburg, led by the Catholic priest and future saint John Capistran (better known by his Spanish name, Juan Capistrano), more than 40,000 decks of cards, tens of thousands of dice, and 3,000 backgammon boards were burned in a public bonfire. None of the attempts to eliminate card-playing were successful; in fact, cards are one of only a few items of the 12th century that survive almost unchanged to this day.

THAT SUITS ME FINE

- The four modern suits—hearts, clubs, spades, and diamonds—originated in France around 1480, at a time when card makers were beginning to mass-produce decks for the first time.
- The simple single-color designs were easier to paint using stencils

and cheaper to produce than the more elaborate designs that had been popular in the past.

• Not all today's cards use diamonds, hearts, spades, and clubs as suit symbols. Traditional German cards use hearts, leaves, acorns, and bells; Swiss cards use roses, shields, acorns, and bells; and Italian cards use swords, batons, cups, and coins.

CARD FACTS

• For more than 500 years, playing cards were much larger than today's versions and didn't have the *indices* (the numbers, letters, and suit marks on the top left corners) that let you read the cards in a tightly held hand. Card players either had to hold their cards in both hands to read them (which made them easy for other players to see), or else had to memorize them and then play with none of the cards showing. In the mid-19th century, card makers began adding the indices in decks called "squeezers" (which let you hold the cards closely together).

• It was in "squeezer" decks that the jacks became a part of the deck. Earlier they had been called knaves, which, like kings, started with the letter "K". To avoid the confusion of having two types of cards with the letter "K", card makers changed *knaves* to *jacks* (a slang term for the knaves already) and used the letter "J" instead.

• The first face cards were elaborately painted, full-length portraits. While beautiful, they posed a serious disadvantage: when they were dealt upside down, novice players tended to turn them right-side-up—telling experienced players how many face cards were in their hand. Card makers corrected this in the 19th century, when they began making decks with "double-ended" face cards.

• The joker is the youngest—and the only American—card in the deck. It was added in the mid-19th century, when it was the highest-value card in an American game called Euchre. From there it gained popularity as a "wild" card in poker and other games.

• In November 1742, an Englishman named Edmond Hoyle published a rule book on the popular game of Whist. The book was so successful that dozens of writers plagiarized it, even using the name "Hoyle's" in the pirate editions. Today's "Hoyle's" rule books are descendants of the *plagiarized* versions, not the original.

• The word "ace" is derived from the Latin word *as*, which means the "smallest unit of coinage."

Ruling class: Winston Churchill and Franklin Roosevelt were seventh cousins once removed.

THE SINGING CHIPMUNKS

Alvin, Simon, and Theodore are the most famous chipmunks in the world. This mini-biography was taken from Behind the Hits, *by Bob Shannon and John Javna.*

THE WITCH DOCTOR

In 1957, a 38-year-old songwriter named Ross Bagdasarian (stage name: David Seville) was sitting in his study when an idea for a new song came to him.

"I looked up from my desk and saw a book called *Duel with the Witch Doctor*," he recalled. "All the teenage records seemed to have one thing in common back then—you couldn't understand any of the lyrics. So I decided to create a 'Witch Doctor' who would give advice to the lovelorn in his own language—a kind of qualified gibberish."

Bagdasarian quickly wrote and recorded the song...but was stumped about what kind of voice to use for the witch doctor (Whose advice consisted of: "Oo-ee, Oo-ah-ah, Ting-tang, Walla-walla Bing-bang.")

FINDING A VOICE

One day Bagdasarian was fooling around with a tape recorder, playing with the speeds. He sang into the machine while it was running at half-speed...and then played it back at full-speed. The result: It sounded like he'd swallowed helium...or played a 45-rpm record at 78 rpm. It was exactly the voice he'd been looking for. (*Note:* Remember this was 1957; today's sophisticated recording equipment hadn't been invented yet.)

Bagdasarian brought his finished tape to Liberty Records. "They flipped," he said. Before 24 hours had elapsed, "The Witch Doctor" was on its way to record stores. Within weeks it was the #1 song in the nation. In all, it sold about 1.5 million copies.

THE SINGING CHIPMUNKS

A year later, Liberty Records found itself in financial trouble. So they asked Bagdasarian to come up with another song like "The Witch Doctor." He agreed to try.

According to astronaut Neil Armstrong, the moon's surface is "fine and powdery."

He decided to turn the Witch Doctor's voice into several different characters. As his son recalls: "He didn't know whether to make them into hippos or elephants or beetles or what. He came up with the idea of chipmunks when he was driving in Yosemite National Park and this chipmunk almost dared him and his huge car to drive past. My dad was so taken with their audacious behavior that he decided to make these three singing characters chipmunks. He named them after three executives at Liberty Records. (Alvin: Al Bennett, the label president; Simon: Si Waronker, vice-chair; Theodore: Ted Keep, chief recording engineer.)

"Then he took the song he'd written, 'The Chipmunk Song,' to Liberty and the president, Alvin's namesake, said, 'We need hits, not chipmunks.' My dad said, 'You have nothing to lose, why don't you put it out?' In the next seven weeks they sold 4.5 million records."

Ultimately, the first Chipmunk record sold more than 7 million copies; at the time, it was the fastest-selling record in history.

LIFE AFTER DEATH

The Chipmunks outlived Bagdasarian. He died in 1972 of a heart attack; 11 years later, in 1983, the Chipmunks emerged as stars of their own Saturday morning TV cartoon show. Today they rank as three of the most lucrative characters ever created in a pop song.

* * * *

THE "PURPLE PEOPLE EATER"

In 1958 a friend of actor/singer Sheb Wooley told him a riddle he'd heard from his kid: "What flies, has one horn, has one eye, and eats people?" The answer: "A one-eyed, one-horned people eater." Wooley thought it was funny, and wrote a song based on it.

A short time later, he met with the president of MGM Records to decide on his next record. Wooley played every song he'd written, but there was nothing the guy liked. "You got anything else?" the president asked. "Well, yeah," Wooley said, "one more thing—but it's nothing you'd want to hear." The president insisted, so Wooley reluctantly played him "Purple People Eater." Three weeks later it was the #1 song in the country.

There isn't any sand in sandpaper.

THE SECRETS OF A HARLEQUIN ROMANCE

Romance novels account for a hefty chunk of the paperback book market. If you're looking for a few extra bucks, writing one may be a way to pick them up. So, for you aspiring "writers," here are some facts and guidelines about Harlequin Romances.

VITAL STATS

History: Harlequin Books was founded in Winnipeg, Manitoba, in 1949 to reprint romance novels put out by the British publisher Mills & Boon. In 1958 Richard and Mary Bonnycastle bought the company, rechristened it Harlequin Enterprises, and set up headquarters in Toronto. Now, with more than 10 billion romances sold, Harlequin is the McDonalds of paperback publishing. They print books in some 17 languages and ships to more than 100 different countries.

Sales: In 1970 Harlequin sold 3 million books. Now it sells more than 200 million a year. The company estimates that every six seconds, another Harlequin romance is sold.

Market: Romance is the biggest-selling area of the paperback book market—25% to 40% of all mass-market paperback sales...and Harlequin has an estimated 80% of that market. Surveys show that romance addicts will spend up to $60 a month on romances (and read them in less than two hours apiece).

Audience: More than 100 million people worldwide read romances regularly—mostly in the U.S., Germany, France, and the U.K. But Harlequin reports that sales are growing steadily in Asia. Company surveys indicate that 50% of its North American readers are college-educated, and a third make more than $30,000 a year.

YOU CAN WRITE A ROMANCE

Tired of reading other people's fantasies? Think you've got what it takes to pen prose powerful enough to promote palpitations? Want to try your hand at writing a romance novel? Here are excerpts from the editorial

To avoid being trapped in a burning building, Hans Christian Anderson always carried a rope.

guidelines for a basic Harlequin romance. This is the information Harlequin supplies to all prospective writers, and we provide it here as a service to you.

Guidelines: "What we are looking for are romances with...strong believable characters, not stereotypes; stories that center on the development of the romance between the heroine and hero, with the emphasis on feelings and emotions."

Style: "Keep 'strong' language (swear words) and highly provocative, sensual language to a minimum.

"Descriptions of sex or sexual feeling should be kept to a minimum in Romances. Love scenes are fine, but the descriptions of such, which should not go on for pages, should deal with how the heroine feels (perhaps the hero, too)—her emotional responses, not just purely physical sensations. Leave a lot to the imagination. A kiss and an embrace, if well told, can be just as stimulating to the reader as pages of graphically described sensual scenes."

Heroine: "Generally, younger than the hero, relatively inexperienced sexually, though this fact need not be stressed. She should hold traditional (not to be equated with old-fashioned) moral standards....The heroine need not be a career woman, nor even a woman with a fascinating, different job....She may hold just an average job, earning average income; she may be unemployed. If she works in a traditional woman's job—secretarial, nursing, teaching, etc.—that's okay, too.

Hero: "Try to avoid excessive age difference; for instance, the 17-year-old heroine and the 37-year-old hero. He should be very attractive, worldly and successful in his field and, unlike the heroine, quite sexually experienced, and this fact may be implied."

SEND NOW!

Want more info? Send for complete guidelines. Enclose a self-addressed, stamped envelope to Harlequin Enterprises, Ltd., 225 Duncan Mill Road, Don Mills, Ontario, Canada M3B 3K9. (Don't quit your day job: Publishers receive up to 1,000 unsolicited manuscripts every month. For the few books they do buy, they pay advances between $1,000 and $15,000, with royalties of 7% to 8%.)

Ride on: 10% of Californians own convertibles.

UNSUNG SUPERHEROES

Imagine inventing America's most popular comic character...and getting only $130 for it. That's what happened to these guys.

THE HEROES: Jerry Siegel and Joseph Shuster

WHAT THEY DID: Created Superman, the most popular comic book character in American history.

One night in 1934, 17-year-old Jerry Siegel, an aspiring comic book writer fresh out of high school, came up with the idea for Superman. He was so excited that at dawn he ran 12 blocks to his tell his friend and partner, Joseph Shuster.

The pair began drawing up cartoon panels showing their hero in action. They sent samples to newspaper comic strip editors all over the country, but no one was interested. Finally, in 1938, DC Comics agreed to print a Superman comic and paid Siegel and Shuster $130 ($10 a page for 13 pages of work) for it. In addition, the two were hired as staff artists to draw future Superman comics.

Superman made his first appearance in June 1938. He was an instant smash. Over the years he inspired a radio show, animated cartoons, a TV series, movies, and licensed products. In the 1970s alone, Superman products grossed about $1 billion.

THE SAD FACTS: When Siegel and Shuster sold the first comic to DC for $130 and signed on as staff artists, they effectively signed away all rights to Superman. From then on, all the money went to DC Comics.

They continued drawing the strip for DC until 1948, when the company fired them for asking for a share of the profits. Both men filed suits against DC...which they ultimately lost. By the 1970s, both were broke, living on money made by selling old comic books and other memorabilia they still owned. Shuster was unemployed, nearly blind, and living in a tiny apartment in Queens, New York.

Finally, in 1975, Warner Communications (owner of DC) voluntarily gave them pensions of $20,000 a year. In 1981 these were increased to $30,000—plus a $15,000 bonus after the first *Superman* film grossed $275 million. That was all the compensation the two men ever received for their creation.

Emergency rooms treat twice as many left-handed people for accidents as right-handed people.

PATRON SAINTS

The Roman Catholic Church has more than 5,000 saints, many of whom are "patron saints"—protectors of certain professions, sick people, even hobbies. Here are a few of the more interesting ones.

Saint Matthew: Patron Saint of Accountants. (He was a tax collector before becoming an apostle.)

Saint Joseph of Cupertino: Patron Saint of Air Travelers. (Nicknamed "The Flying Friar," he could levitate.)

Saint Fiacre: Patron Saint of Taxi Drivers, Hemorrhoid Sufferers, and Venereal Disease.

Saint Matrona: Patron Saint of Dysentery Sufferers.

Saint Louis IX of France: Patron Saint of Button Makers.

Saint Adrian of Nicomedia: Patron Saint of Arms Dealers.

Saint Anne: Patron Saint of Women in Labor. (Not to be confused with Saint John Thwing, Patron Saint of Women in *Difficult* Labor.)

Saint Nicholas of Myra (also known as Santa Claus): Patron Saint of Children and Pawnbrokers.

Saint Bernardino of Siena: Patron Saint of Advertisers and Hoarseness.

Saint Blaise: Patron Saint of Throats (he saved a child from choking) and Diseased Cattle (he also healed animals).

Saint Joseph: Patron Saint of Opposition to Atheistic Communism.

Saint Sebastian: Patron Saint of Neighborhood Watch Groups.

Saint Joseph of Arimathea: Patron Saint of Funeral Directors.

Saint Eligius: Patron Saint of Gas Station Workers. (He miraculously cured horses, the precursors to automobiles.)

Saint Martin de Porres: Patron Saint of Race Relations, Social Justice, and Italian Hairdressers.

Saint Martha: Patron Saint of Dietitians.

In 1992 former Panamanian pres. Noriega's wife was arrested in Miami for shoplifting buttons.

ACCIDENTAL DISCOVERIES

Not all scientific progress is the product of systematic experimentation. A number of important modern discoveries have been a matter of chance—which means you should keep your eyes and ears open, even while you're just sitting there on the john. You never know what might happen.

The Discovery: Insulin

How It Happened: In 1889 Joseph von Mering and Oscar Minkowski, two German scientists, were trying to understand more about the digestive system. As part of their experiments, they removed the pancreas from a living dog to see what role the organ plays in digestion.

The next day a laboratory assistant noticed an extraordinary number of flies buzzing around the dog's urine. Von Mering and Minkowski examined the urine to see why…and were surprised to discover that it contained a high concentration of sugar. This indicated that the pancreas plays a role in removing sugar from the bloodstream.

Legacy: Von Mering and Minkowski were never able to isolate the chemical that produced this effect, but their discovery enabled John J. R. MacLeod and Frederick Banting, two Canadian researchers, to develop insulin extracts from horse and pig pancreases and to pioneer their use as a treatment for diabetes in 1921.

The Discovery: Photography

How It Happened: The *camera obscura,* designed by Leonardo da Vinci in the early 1500s and perfected in 1573 by E. Danti, was a workable camera. It was widely used in the early 1800s—but not for taking photographs. The reason: The technology for photos didn't exist. People used the camera for tracing images instead, placing transparent paper over its glass plate.

In the 1830s, French artist L. J. M. Daguerre began experimenting with ways of recording a camera's images on light-sensitive photographic plates. By 1838 he'd made some progress; using silver-coated sheets of copper, he found a way to capture an image.

Aztec emperor Montezuma had a nephew, Cuitlahac, whose name meant "plenty of excrement."

However, the image was so faint that it was barely visible. He tried dozens of substances to see if they'd darken it...but nothing worked. Frustrated, Daguerre put the photographic plate away in a cabinet filled with chemicals and moved on to other projects.

A few days later, Daguerre took the plate out. To his astonishment, the plate had mysteriously darkened; now the image was perfectly visible. One of the chemicals in the cabinet was almost certainly responsible...but which one?

He devised a method to find out. Each day he removed one chemical from the cabinet and put a fresh photographic plate in. If the plate still darkened overnight, the chemical would be disqualified. If it didn't, he'd know he'd found the chemical he was looking for. It seemed like a good idea, but even after *all* the chemicals had been removed, the plate continued to darken. Daguerre wondered why. Then, examining the cabinet closely, he noticed a few drops of mercury that had spilled from a broken thermometer onto one of the shelves.

Legacy: Later experiments with mercury vapor proved that this substance was responsible. The daguerrotype's worldwide popularity paved the way for the development of photography.

The Discovery: Safety glass

How It Happened: In 1903 Edouard Benedictus, a French chemist, was experimenting in his lab when he dropped an empty glass flask on the floor. It shattered, but remained in the shape of a flask. Benedictus was bewildered. When he examined the flask more closely, he discovered that the inside was coated with a film residue of cellulose nitrate, a chemical he'd been working with earlier. The film had held the glass together.

Not long afterward, Benedictus read a newspaper article about a girl who had been badly injured by flying glass in a car accident. He thought back to the glass flask in his lab and realized that coating automobile windshields, as the inside of the flask had been coated, would make them less dangerous.

Legacy: Variations of the safety glass he produced—a layer of plastic sandwiched by two layers of glass—are still used in automobiles today.

BOX-OFFICE BLOOPERS II

Here are a few more movie mistakes to look for in popular films.

Movie: *Rear Window* (1954)
Scene: Jimmy Stewart, in a cast and sitting in a wheelchair, argues with Grace Kelly.
Blooper: His cast switches from his left leg to his right.

Movie: *Raiders of the Lost Ark* (1982)
Scene: German soldiers and Gestapo agents lift the ark.
Blooper: Paintings of C3P0 and R2D2, the androids from *Star Wars* (another George Lucas film), are included among the hieroglyphics on the wall.

Movie: *Close Encounters of the Third Kind* (1977)
Scene: Richard Dreyfus and Teri Garr smash through several road blocks as they near Devil's Tower.
Blooper: The license plate on their station wagon keeps changing.

Movie: *Abbot and Costello Go to Mars* (1953)
Blooper: In the movie they actually go to Venus.

Movie: *Camelot* (1967)
Scene: King Arthur (Richard Harris) praises his medieval kingdom while speaking to some of his subjects.
Blooper: Harris is wearing a Band-Aid on his neck.

Movie: *The Fortune Cookie* (1966)
Scene: Walter Matthau leaves one room and enters another—and appears to lose weight in the process.
Blooper: Matthau suffered a heart attack while this scene was being filmed; only half was completed before he entered the hospital. He returned five months later to finish the job—40 pounds lighter than he was in the first part of the scene.

Movie: *Diamonds Are Forever* (1971)
Scene: James Bond tips his Ford Mustang up onto two wheels and drives through a narrow alley to escape from the bad guys.
Blooper: The Mustang enters the alley on its two right wheels—and leaves the alley on its two *left* wheels.

At one North Carolina golf club, you can rent a llama to be your caddy for $100.

THE TRUTH ABOUT LEMMINGS

You've probably heard that lemmings commit mass suicide when they experience overpopulation. It turns out that isn't true...and you can blame the myth on the Walt Disney Company.

THE MYTH

In 1958 Walt Disney produced *White Wilderness*, a documentary about life in the Arctic. This film gave us the first close look at the strange habits of arctic rodents called lemmings.

• "They quite literally eat themselves out of house and home," says the narrator. "With things as crowded as this, someone has to make room for somebody somehow. And so, Nature herself takes a hand....A kind of compulsion seizes each tiny rodent and, carried along by an unreasoning hysteria, each falls into step for a march that will take them to a strange destiny."

• The film shows a pack of lemmings marching to the sea, where they "dutifully toss themselves over a cliff into certain death in icy Arctic waters." "The last shot," says critic William Poundstone, "shows the sea awash with dying lemmings."

• The narrator says: "Gradually strength wanes...determination ebbs away...and the Arctic Sea is dotted with tiny bobbing bodies."

THE TRUTH

• According to a 1983 investigation by Canadian Broadcasting Corporation producer Brian Vallee, *White Wilderness*'s lemming scene was sheer fabrication.

• Vallee says the lemmings were brought to Alberta—a landlocked province that isn't their natural habitat—where Disney folks put them on a giant turntable piled with snow to film the "migration segment."

• Then, Vallee reports, they recaptured the lemmings and took them to a cliff over a river. "When the well-adjusted lemmings wouldn't jump," writes Poundstone, "the Disney people gave Nature a hand [and tossed them off]....Lemmings don't commit mass suicide. As far as zoologists can tell, it's a myth."

TRANSLATED HITS

Here are six popular songs that originated in a foreign language and were translated into English—sometimes by people with no idea of what the original lyrics were. From Behind the Hits, *by Bob Shannon.*

IT'S NOW OR NEVER—ELVIS PRESLEY

Background: In 1901 Italian composer Eduardo di Capua wrote "*O Sole Mio.*" This operatic theme was eventually popularized in America by Mario Lanza (who sang it in Italian) and again by Tony Martin in 1949. Martin's version, an English "translation," was called "There's No Tomorrow." It hit #2 on the pop charts in 1949.

The Elvis Version: While Elvis was in the Army from 1958 to 1959, he decided to clean up his image by recording a new version of "*O Sole Mio*" that even teenagers' *parents* could love. (Although his fans didn't know it, Presley had always admired operatic voices like Mario Lanza's.) But Elvis didn't like the Tony Martin version—it "wasn't his style"—so he commissioned a new set of lyrics.

It took two New York writers 20 minutes to write the song. Elvis loved it (it became his favorite of all his records) and recorded it about two weeks after he got out of the Army. It hit #1 all over the globe, selling more than 20 million copies worldwide. For a few years, it was listed in the *Guinness Book of World Records* as the largest-selling single in the history of pop music.

MY WAY—FRANK SINATRA

Background: The lyrics of this song were written specifically with Sinatra in mind, but the melody belonged to a French tune called "*Comme d'habitude,*" or "As Usual."

The Sinatra Version: Paul Anka, who felt a growing affinity with Frank Sinatra, decided that if he ever had the chance, he'd write something special for ol' Blue Eyes. And at about three o'clock on a rainy Las Vegas morning, it happened. As he thought of the melody of "*Comme d'habitude*" (which he'd heard in France), the words of "My Way" spontaneously came to him. "[It was] one of the magic moments in my writing career," he says. "I finished it in an hour and a half." Sinatra loved the song and spent two weeks perfecting it. Within a year it had been recorded by over a hundred different artists. Elvis Presley did a live version in 1977 that sold over a million copies.

VOLARE—DEAN MARTIN, BOBBY RYDELL, & OTHERS

Background: The original Italian version, by Domenico Modugno, was a million-seller in the U.S. and the #1 record of 1958. The original title, however, was not "*Volare*," but "*Nel Blu, Dipinto di Blu*" (literal translation: "the blue, painted in blue"). The lyrics told the story of a man dreaming he was flying through the air with his hands painted blue.

The English Version: When Modugno's record started selling in the U.S., American artists clamored for an English-language version they could record. So Mitchel Parish wrote new lyrics, retitling the song "*Volare*." About a dozen versions were released right away, and combined sales of the song in 1958 alone were estimated at eight million. The bestselling U.S. renditions: Dean Martin's (#12 in 1958), Bobby Rydell's (#4 in 1960), and Al Martino's (#15 in 1975). Chrysler Corp. even named a car after the song.

SEASONS IN THE SUN—TERRY JACKS

Background: The song was originally written as "*Le Moribund*" (literal translation: "the dying man") by Jacques Brel in 1961.

The English Version: Rod McKuen adapted the song to English in 1964, and Terry Jacks heard it on a Kingston Trio record. In 1972 he took it to a Beach Boys' session he was producing, and the Beach Boys recorded it...but didn't release it. So Jacks, who was distraught over a friend's death, did his own version.

Jacks was playing his year-old recording of it one day at his house when the boy who delivered his newspapers overheard it; the boy liked it so much that he brought some friends over to Jacks's house to listen to it, and their enthusiastic response inspired him to release it on his own Goldfish record label. The result: It skyrocketed to #1 all over the world and sold 11.5 million copies.

THOSE WERE THE DAYS—MARY HOPKIN

Background: It was originally a Russian tune called "*Darogoi Dlimmoyo*," which means "Dear to Me." The original artist was Alexander Wertinsky, who recorded it in the 1920s.

Chickens can live as long as 14 years.

The English Version: In the 1950s, a Finnish singer translated it to her native language and recorded it. An American named Gene Raskin heard the record and wrote English lyrics (which were popularized in the U.S. by a folk trio called the Limeliters). In 1965 he and his wife performed the song in a London club called The Blue Angel. Paul McCartney was in the audience.

Three years later, McCartney heard about a 17-year-old Welsh singer named Mary Hopkin, who had appeared on the TV show "Opportunity Knocks" (a London version of "Star Search") and won three times. The Beatles had just formed Apple Records and were looking for people to record—so McCartney asked her if she wanted to audition. She did, and when she sang for Paul, her high soprano made him think of "Those Were the Days." He bought the rights to the song, and Hopkin recorded it. Her record was included in a specially boxed introductory set of the first four Apple releases. It became the second million-seller on Apple. ("Hey Jude" was the first.) Worldwide, it sold five million copies.

THE LION SLEEPS TONIGHT—THE TOKENS, ROBERT JOHN, & OTHERS

Background: The original title of this song was "*Mbube*" (which means "lion"); the subject was a sleeping lion. Sample lyrics: "Hush! Hush! If we will all be quiet, there will be lion meat for dinner." It was sung with a haunting Zulu refrain that sounded, to English-speaking people, like "wimoweh."

"*Mbube*" was popular on the boats of what is now Swaziland. In the 1930s, a South African singer named Solomon Linda recorded it; then the tune passed into the broad field of folk music. As the 1950s arrived, Miriam Makeba recorded the song in its original Zulu…and an American folk group called the Weavers adapted her version into a Top 15 hit called "Wimoweh."

The English Version: In 1961 a Brooklyn doo-wop group called the Tokens were offered a try-out with RCA. Caught up in the folk music boom of the time, they auditioned with "Wimoweh." The RCA executives liked the song but decided it needed new lyrics, so they wrote "The Lion Sleeps Tonight" for the Tokens—not knowing that the original version had also been about a lion. The Tokens' record hit #1 in 1961, and Robert John's was #3 in 1972.

If you're average, you'll keep your old magazines for 29 weeks before you toss them out.

MEN OF LETTERS

In his book Dear Wit, *H. Jack Lang collected celebrities' humorous correspondence. Here are a few examples.*

GIVE HIM A BRAKE

In 1872, George Westinghouse asked Cornelius Vanderbilt, multimillionaire president of the New York Central Railroad, to listen to his ideas about developing an "air brake." Vanderbuilt wrote back:

I have no time to waste on fools. —*Vanderbilt*

After the brake was successfully tested on another railroad, Vanderbilt wrote Westinghouse asking to see it. Westinghouse wrote back:

I have no time to waste on fools. —*Westinghouse*

FIERY WRITING

The celebrated author Somerset Maugham once received a manuscript from a young writer, accompanied by a letter that said:

Do you think I should put more fire into my stories?

Maugham replied: No. Vice versa.

GIVE HIM A SIGN

In the early 1960s, columnist Leonard Lyons complained to President John F. Kennedy that JFK's signature was only worth $65 to collectors—compared to $175 for George Washington and $75 for Franklin Roosevelt. Kennedy responded:

Dear Leonard: In order not to depress the market any further, I will not sign this letter.

NO JOKE

A publisher who wanted an endorsement for a humor book sent Groucho *Marx a copy and asked for Groucho's comments. Marx wrote back:*

I've been laughing ever since I picked up your book. Some day I'm going to read it. —*Groucho*

Joe Louis was the world heavyweight boxing champ for 11 years and 252 days.

MAKING THE BREAST OF IT

At dinner, Winston Churchill asked his American hostess, "May I have a breast?" She replied: "In this country, it is customary to ask for white or dark meat." The next day, as an apology, Churchill sent her an orchid, with a card that said:

Madam: I would be most obliged if you would pin this on your white meat. —*Winston Churchill*

ARE YOU SURE?

Playwright Eugene O'Neill received a cable from Hollywood bombshell Jean Harlow asking him to write a play for her. "Reply collect in 20 words," the cable requested. O'Neill cabled back:

NO NO NO NO NO NO NO NO NO NO
NO NO NO NO NO NO NO NO NO NO

FANCY FOOTWORK

Jack London's publisher sent him the following letter when the famous novelist missed a publishing deadline:

My dear Jack London: If I do not receive those stories from you by noon tomorrow, I'm going to put on my heaviest soled shoes, come down to your room, and kick you downstairs. I always keep my promises. —*Editor*

London wrote back:

Dear Sir: I, too, would always keep my promises if I could fulfill them with my feet. —*Jack London*

WHAT'S THE STORY?

After a news item reported that Rudyard Kipling was paid $5 a word for his magazine articles, an autograph collector sent him a check for $5 and a letter asking for a single word. Kipling wrote back:

Thanks. —*Rudyard Kipling*

Afterward the autograph-seeker wrote back:

Dear Mr. Kipling: I sold the story of your one-word reply to a magazine for two hundred dollars. The enclosed check is your half.

OH, KATE!

Here are a few of Katherine Hepburn's unscripted comments.

"When I started out, I didn't have any desire to be an actress or to learn how to act. I just wanted to be famous."

"Sometimes I wonder if men and women really suit each other. Perhaps they should live next door and just visit now and then."

"If you give audiences half a chance they'll do half your acting for you."

"Being a housewife and a mother is the biggest job in the world, but if it doesn't interest you, don't do it.... I would have made a terrible parent. The first time my child didn't do what I wanted, I'd kill him."

"I find men today less manly ...but a woman of my age is not in a position to know exactly how manly they are."

"Great performing in any field is total simplicity, the capacity to get to the essence, to eliminate all the frills and foibles."

"If you survive long enough, you're revered—rather like an old building."

"I don't care what is written about me as long as it isn't true."

"A sharp knife cuts the quickest and hurts the least."

"Life is to be lived. If you have to support yourself, you had bloody well better find some way that is going to be interesting. And you don't do that by sitting around wondering about yourself."

"What the hell—you might be right, you might be wrong... but don't just *avoid*."

"The male sex, as a sex, does not universally appeal to me."

"You can't change the music of your soul."

"Life's what's important. Walking, houses, family. Birth and pain and joy. Acting's just waiting for a custard pie."

OPENING LINES

Remember those great science fiction programs you watched on TV when you were a kid? They had some great opening lines, didn't they? Here a few of our favorites.

THE ADVENTURES OF SUPERMAN (1953–57)
"Look! In the sky!" "It's a bird!" "It's a plane!" "It's Superman!" "Yes, it's Superman, strange visitor from another planet who came to Earth with powers and abilities far beyond those of mortal men. Superman, who can change the course of mighty rivers, bend steel in his bare hands; and who, disguised as Clark Kent, mild-mannered reporter for a great Metropolitan newspaper, fights a never-ending battle for truth...justice...and the America way!"

CAPTAIN VIDEO (1949–56)
"Captain Video! Master of space! Hero of science! Captain of the Video Rangers! Operating from his secret mountain headquarters on the planet Earth, Captain Video rallies men of good will everywhere. As he rockets from planet to planet, let us follow the champion of justice, truth, and freedom throughout the universe."

ROD BROWN OF THE ROCKET RANGERS (1955–56)
"CBS television presents...'Rod Brown of the Rocket Rangers'! Surging with the power of the atom, gleaming like great silver bullets, the mighty Rocket Rangers' spaceships stand by for blast off!...Up, up, rockets blazing with white hot fury, the man-made meteors ride through the atmosphere, breaking the gravity barrier, pushing up and out, faster and faster and then...outer space and high adventure for...the Rocket Rangers!"

THE TIME TUNNEL (1966–67)
"Two American scientists are lost in the swirling maze of past and future ages during the first experiments on America's greatest and most secret project—the Time Tunnel. Tony Newman and Doug Phillips now tumble helplessly toward a new, fantastic adventure somewhere along the infinite corridors of time!"

10% of Americans read the *Bible* every day.

STAR TREK (1966–69)

"Space, the final frontier. These are the voyages of the starship Enterprise. Its five-year mission: to explore strange new worlds; to seek out life and new civilizations; to boldly go where no man has gone before."

TOM CORBETT, SPACE CADET (1950–56)

"Space Academy, USA, in the world beyond tomorrow. Here the Space Cadets train for duty on distant planets. In roaring rockets, they blast through the millions of miles from Earth to far-flung stars and brave the dangers of cosmic frontiers protecting the liberties of the planets, safeguarding the cause of universal peace in the age of the conquest of space!"

THE TWILIGHT ZONE (1959–63)

"There is a fifth dimension beyond that which is known to man. It is a dimension as vast as space and timeless as infinity. It is the middle ground between light and shadow, between science and superstition, and it lies between the pit of man's fears and the summit of his knowledge. This is the dimension of imagination. It is an area which we call the Twilight Zone."

SPACE PATROL (1950–56)

"High adventure in the wild, vast regions of space! Missions of daring in the name of interplanetary justice! Travel into the future with Buzz Corey, commander in chief of...the Space Patrol!"

THE OUTER LIMITS (1963–65)

"There is nothing wrong with your television set. Do not attempt to adjust the picture. We are controlling transmission. If we wish to make it louder, we will bring up the volume. If we wish to make it softer, we will tune it to a whisper. We will control the horizontal. We will control the vertical. We can roll the image; make it flutter. We can change the focus to a soft blur, or sharpen it to crystal clarity. For the next hour, sit quietly and we will control all you see and hear. We repeat: There is nothing wrong with your television set. You are about to participate in a great adventure. You are about to experience the awe and mystery which reaches from the inner mind to...the Outer Limits."

The U.S. minted 12,837,140 pennies and 2,240,355,488 dimes in 1989.

MORE CARNIVAL TRICKS

Here's more information about carnival booths to look out for—and some tips on how to beat them—from Matthew Gryczan's book Carnival Secrets.

The Booth: "Plate Pitch"

The Object: Players toss dimes onto plates sitting on the heads of large stuffed animals. If a dime remains on the plate, the player wins the animal.

How It's Rigged: Some carnival suppliers put their glass plates in a furnace for 48 hours. The heat makes the sides of the plates droop, so the surface of the plate is significantly flatter than that of the same style of plate found in stores. This makes it easier for the dimes to slip off the plates.

• Some operators polish the dishes with furniture wax to make them slippery, or set them on an angle so the coins slide off.

How to Win: It helps to practice at home for this one.

• The best pitches are thrown softly, in a low arc. According to one manufacturer, if the coin lands flat against the back edge of the plate in Plate Pitch, it will rebound back into the center.

• Toss the coin so it travels in a line to other plates if it skips off the first plate.

The Booth: "Spill the Milk"

The Object: Throw a ball and knock down a pyramid of three aluminum bottles shaped like old-fashioned glass milk bottles. Knocking all three pins completely off their stand wins you a prize.

How It's Rigged: The bottles look identical, but they don't always weigh the same amount. Some carnies set a heavier bottle on the bottom row. That way, the ball will hit the lighter two bottles first, and won't have enough energy to knock the heavy bottle off.

• Some unscrupulous operators fill the bottles with molten lead, so they're too heavy to be knocked over with a softball. Other operators cast lead in the *side* of the bottle so it can be knocked down, but not off the stand.

• If the player is allowed two shots, there may be a different setup. One bottle may be unweighted, while the remaining two are

In 1955 a book was returned to the Cambridge University library that was 288 years overdue.

different weights. The carny sets the unweighted bottle on top and gives the player a heavier softball. If the player strikes the center of the pyramid, the top bottle flies off, the lighter lower bottle is knocked over, and the heavier bottle remains standing. Then the player is given an ultralight ball that can't be thrown hard enough to knock over the heaviest bottle.

How to Win: Make sure the game isn't rigged. Ask about the weights of the bottles and the ball and don't play until you get a satisfactory answer. Ask to examine the bottles. Check whether they're all the same weight or if the weight is distributed in each bottle unevenly.

• Carnies say the best way to win at Spill the Milk is a direct hit in the triangular area where the three bottles meet.

The Booth: "High Striker"

The Object: Using an oversized rubber mallet, hit a cast-iron striker to the top of a 21-foot-high tower to ring the bell.

How It's Rigged: Most High Strikers in use today are honest, but, according to one manufacturer, some early models used several "guy wires" that held up the tower. Unknown to players, one of the guy wires led from a stake directly down the front of the tower. The striker traveled along this wire.

• The unscrupulous agent would lean up against the phony guy wire and keep it taut enough so a player could ring the bell on the first and second tries. But on the player's third swing (the one that could win the prize), the agent would stop leaning on the wire. With the wire slack, the striker brushed against the tower as it traveled skyward, and friction prevented it from reaching the gong. The player had no chance to win the grand prize for three rings.

How to Win: "The trade secret is to hit the pad squarely, just as if you were splitting wood," according to the manufacturer.

The Booth: "Basketball"

The Object: Toss the basketball into a hoop while standing behind a designated foul line.

How It's Rigged: Some operators overinflate the balls, so they have more bounce and are tougher to get through the hoop. Others don't attach the hoops securely to the backboard, so the rims vibrate when struck by the ball. This keeps rim shots from going in.

THE STORY OF LAS VEGAS

Have you ever wondered how Las Vegas became the gambling capital of the world? Here's the story.

NAME

"Las Vegas" means "the meadows" or "the fertile plains" in Spanish. The city acquired this name in the early 1800s, when it was a peaceful rest stop on the Old Spanish Trail.

HISTORY. Ironically, the Mormans were the first to settle Las Vegas, in 1855. They built the first church, first fort, and first school in Nevada, only to abandon them three years later. Pioneers were still using the site as a watering hole and, as one missionary noted, few could be induced to attend the church. "Only one man attended," he wrote. "The rest of them were gambling and swearing at their camps."

Las Vegas didn't become a real town until almost 50 years later. Because of its central location and ample water supply, the railroad decided it would make an ideal stop on the transcontinental train line. They bought the land and, one scorching hot day in 1905, auctioned it off to 1,200 eager settlers. A few days later, the town appeared: a haphazard assortment of canvas tent saloons, gambling clubs, and drinking parlors that quickly established the city's character and reputation.

Despite prohibitionist protests, Las Vegas maintained its early emphasis on night life and continued to flourish throughout the 1920s. "Such places as the Red Rooster, the Blue Goose, the Owl, and Pair-o-Dice were temporarily inconvenienced from time to time by raids from federal agents," writes one local historian. "But they were, of course, as safe as a church from local interference."

In 1931 the Nevada state legislature enacted two well-publicized "reforms": They liberalized divorce laws, changing residency requirements from six months to six weeks, and officially legalized gambling. Now Las Vegas had two unique attractions. While the

Every year, 5% of Americans go on cruises.

rest of the country was suffering through the Great Depression, Las Vegas casinos made a killing catering to the workers constructing nearby Boulder Dam, as well as the 230,000 tourists who came to see it. (Las Vegas also became a significant divorce center after movie star Clark Gable's wife, Rhea, chose it as the place to divorce him.)

The first full-fledged resort, the plush El Rancho Vegas, was built in 1940. Another (the New Frontier) followed, and the notorious Vegas "strip" was established. A military base and a magnesium plant were installed nearby in the early 1940s, and both brought more people to the area and kept the town prosperous through World War II. By 1970 more than half of Nevada's entire population lived in Las Vegas.

MAIN INDUSTRY. Las Vegas as we know it today might never have been born if it weren't for gangster Ben "Bugsy" Siegel. Wanted for murder in New York, Siegal was sent out West to set up a booking service for the mob and became obsessed with the idea of creating a "glittering gambling mecca in the desert." He borrowed $6 million in mob money and constructed the Flamingo Hotel, a lavish olive-green castle surrounded by a 40-acre garden that was planted literally overnight in imported soil brought in by truck.

Unfortunately for Bugsy, the Flamingo was initially a bust. To top it off, the mob found out he'd been skimming profits. They had him killed in 1947. But business at the Flamingo picked up, and over the next few years Mafia-owned resort casinos sprang up all along Highway 91, the Las Vegas strip.

According to *The Encyclopedia of American Crime*, for example:

✓ Meyer Lansky put up much of the money for the Thunderbird.

✓ The Desert Inn was owned by the head of the Cleveland mob.

✓ The Dunes "was a goldmine" for the New England mob.

✓ The Sahara "was launched by the Chicago mob."

"Despite the huge profits," the *Encyclopedia* adds, "by the mid-'50s the mob had started selling off its properties to individuals and corporations. In the 1960s billionaire Howard Hughes started buying one casino after another. In the early 1970s the mob's interest in Vegas was reportedly at a low point, but by the close of the decade, many observers concluded, mobsters were returning to the scene."

Fifty-eight percent of Americans believe they have above-average IQ's.

MEET YOUR COMMIE MASTERS

In 1984, when we were still fighting of the Cold War, Robert Conquest and Jon Manchip White wrote a book called What to Do When the Russians Come. *We may laugh now, but at one time, the threat of a communist takeover seemed very real to oddballs like these guys. These excerpts give you an idea of what they thought life in the U.S. would look like...after the invasion.*

You will be anxious to know how someone of your particular professional and ethnic and political and temperamental background is likely to fare [under Soviet rule]. In the pages that follow, we look into the special conditions facing a wide variety of these, of a reasonable representative nature, From Academic to Farmer, from Realtor to Industrial Worker, from Homosexual to Feminist...

ACADEMIC. When universities reopen after the crisis, student numbers will have gone down. Some will be dead, some in prison, some in the partisan movement. Private, religious and racially or ethnically oriented institutions will have been taken over by the state. All departments...will be purged of "incorrect" teachers with great thoroughness. Colleges will be run by Communist-appointed functionaries, including representatives of the secret police, and there will be no "academic freedom." If you are at the moment an academic with Communist or Marxist leanings, you can expect to become at least a dean or the head of your department....Sneaking and denunciation will be the order of the day, and since the arrest rate will be one of the highest in any field, you will be hard put to trust your colleagues, for you will not be able to tell which of them have become police informers, either of their own volition or through blackmail....Be generous with your grades, otherwise disgruntled students will denounce you.

BARBER/BEAUTICIAN. Any but the most orthodox haircuts will be heavily discouraged. You...will become standardized and paid as a public servant, under a new Department of Internal

Trade. Most beauty salons will close for lack of patrons with enough money to be able to afford such luxuries. A few will remain open to serve the new Communist elite and the wives of Soviet generals.

DENTIST. The level of dental care in the population will fall. Dental stocks will dwindle and dental equipment will deteriorate for lack of spare parts. Dental techniques will become basic, with extraction taking precedent over filling. Dentures will be poorly made and ill-fitting when available. Extractions will be performed without anesthesia because of the absence of supply. Many dentists will give up in despair.

ENVIRONMENTALIST. No public organization, demonstration, or other activity will, of course, be permitted. As for nuclear power stations, they will be developed to the limit. No sort of objection to them will be permitted under any circumstances. However, there will be one area in which improvement will have been made: The shortage of private cars will mean less pollution from gasoline.

FUNERAL DIRECTOR. Services will be speedy, drab, and uniform. Atheist forms of committal will be encouraged, religious forms banned or perfunctorily performed. Only in rare cases will services be carried out in churches or other religious buildings, the majority of which will be closed. However, Communist burials, while lacking frills, will at least be inexpensive.

GARAGE EMPLOYEE. There will be very few cars on the roads and consequently no need for a large number of gas stations.... Although there are fewer cars, production and servicing standards will be such that motor mechanics' skills will be saleable on the black market. And you may also try your hand at, and profit by, the repairing and refurbishing of bicycles.

JOHN BIRCH SOCIETY MEMBER. Your life will, of course, be automatically forfeit.

LAWYER. Lawyers, will, in general, be regarded as a hostile class element. This will be more so in their case because so many of them are...concerned with rights, balances, constitutionality, and common law—all totally opposed to the Communist principle. Casualties, therefore, will be high.

LIBRARIAN. Your old reference books, such as encyclopedias, will be withdrawn and pulped. You should keep handy a pair of sharp scissors and a supply of paste, as you will have to cut out or replace those entries that become politically inconvenient—a normal Soviet practice. As the years go by, even the more harmless books on your shelves will be gradually replaced as works commissioned and printed by the State begin to appear in adequate numbers. If you can safely save and secrete some of the books that are being discarded, well and good; although your superiors will be on the lookout for this, and it may be hazardous for you or your friends to be caught reading them.

PET SHOP OWNER. It is unlikely that families will be able to spare any scraps of food for feeding pets, let alone extra money for grooming them or purchasing accessories. Most cats and dogs will have to be put to sleep or allowed to run free and take their chances. After the fighting stops, there will be a serious infestation of ownerless dogs running in wild packs with which authorities will have to deal. Owners of pet shops should lose no time in making plans for alternative employment.

PSYCHOPATH. If you are able and prepared to control yourself in all matters where you might offend authorities, a wide field of activity of a type you will find rewarding will remain open to you. Those not afflicted with consciences will be in demand not only to occupations offering opportunities of violence, but also in all other institutions, where it will always be possible to denounce anyone who stands in the way of your desires or to blackmail them into submitting. Indeed, the Soviet system...has been described as a psychopathocracy. If your condition is of the right type, you may rise very high indeed in the new hierarchy.

SADIST. Although the secret police will have some use for torturers, such positions are unlikely to be open except to men with political acumen and training, but low-grade thugs, known as "boxers," are often employed for routine beatings....If you apply for the

First million-selling album in U.S. history: the soundtrack to *Oklahoma*, 1958.

post of an executioner, you might be enrolled in one of the municipal firing squads. Your opportunity to carry out individual executions, if that is your taste, will probably be somewhat limited. The traditional Soviet method of executing single offenders is by means of a bullet in the back of the neck and is invariably conducted neatly and expeditiously by a specialist of officer rank. Mass executions are bound, of course, to occur, and you may well be given a chance to participate in some of them.

YOUTH. You will find yourself under very heavy pressures of a type which your present life has not accustomed you.... The special Communist effort to indoctrinate you will mean that you will be under considerably higher pressures than your elders.... You will lose several hours a week at compulsory sessions in Marxist-Leninism, in addition to endless harangues about loyalty and the glorious future, which you will be expected to applaud. Still...you have one great point in your favor: unlike your parents, you may find that the overthrow of Soviet power will come when you are still in the full vigor of, perhaps, your forties, when you will provide the leaders to build a new America and a new world.

Just as the airlines hope that their passengers will never have to follow the instructions they give you on what to do in case of a disaster, so we, for our part, hope you may never have to follow the advice we have given you in the preceding pages. But time is running short. We would be deceiving you if we pretended that the nightmare we have described is not a real and deadly possibility. If it does come about, we have one last piece of advice:

BURN THIS BOOK.

* * *

"I didn't intend for this to take on a political tone. I'm just here for the drugs."

—Nancy Reagan, *referring to a "Just Say No" rally*

"The press says that the public has a right to know everything. That's a load of garbage."

—George Lauder, CIA *spokesman*

On any given day, 60 million U.S. females and 41 million U.S. males are dieting.

MORE EPITAPHS

More unusual epitaphs and tombstone rhymes from our wandering BRI tombstoneologists.

Seen in Oxfordshire, England:
**Here lies the body of
John Eldred,**
At least he will be here when
he is dead.
But now at this time, he is
alive,
The 14th of August, 1765.

Seen in Plymouth, Mass.:
Richard Lawton
Here lie the bones of Richard
Lawton,
Whose death, alas! was
strangely brought on.
Trying his corns one day to
mow off,
His razor slipped and cut
his toe off.
His toe, or rather, what it
grew to,
An inflammation quickly
flew to.
Which took, Alas! to mortify-
ing,
And was the cause of Richard's
dying.

Seen in Luton, England:
Thomas Proctor
Here lies the body of Thomas
Proctor,
Who lived and died without a
doctor.

Seen in Shrewsbury, England:
**Here lies the body of
Martha Dias,**
Who was always uneasy, and
not over-pious;
She lived to the age of three
score and ten,
And gave to the worms what
she refused to the men.

Seen in Marshfield, Vt.:
**Here lies the body of
William Jay,**
Who died maintaining his
right of way;
He was right, dead right, as he
sped along,
But he's just as dead as if he'd
been wrong.

Seen in Lee, Mass.:
**In Memory of Mrs. Alpha
White, Weight 309 lbs.**
Open wide ye heavenly gates
That lead to the heavenly
shore;
Our father suffered in passing
through
And Mother weighs much
more.

Seen in Putman, Conn.:
Phineas G. Wright
Going, But Know Not Where

It took 14 years to build the Brooklyn Bridge.

FAMILIAR MELODIES

Some tunes are so familiar that it seems like they've just always been around. Of course, every song has it's beginning. Here are the stories of how some old favorites were written.

DIXIE

Written in 1859 by Daniel Decatur Emmett for a blackface minstrel show. Ironically, though his song became the anthem of the South, Emmett was a northerner who detested the Confederacy. When he found out the song was going to be sung at Confederate President Jefferson Davis's inauguration, he told friends, "If I had known to what use they were going to put my song, I'll be damned if I'd have written it."

HERE COMES THE BRIDE

Composer Richard Wagner wrote the "Bridal Chorus" in 1848 for his opera *Lohengrin*. He used it to score a scene in which the hero and his new bride undress on their wedding night and prepare to consummate their marriage. It was first used as a bridal march in 1858, when Princess Victoria (daughter of England's Queen Victoria) married Prince Frederick William of Prussia. Interestingly, because of the sexual nature of the original opera scene, some religions object to using the song in wedding ceremonies.

CHOPSTICKS

In 1877, 16-year-old Euphemia Allen, a British girl, published "Chopsticks" under the pseudonym Arthur de Lulli. Included with the sheet music were instructions telling the pianist to play the song "with both hands turned sideways, the little fingers lowest, so that the movement of the hands imitates the chopping from which this waltz gets its name." Allen never wrote another song.

TAPS

As late as 1862, the U.S. military used a song called "Extinguish Lights" to officially end the day. General Daniel Butterfield disliked the song…so he decided to compose a new one to replace it. He couldn't play the bugle, so he composed by whistling notes to his butler, who'd play them back for Butterfield to evaluate. They went through dozens of tunes before he got one he liked.

MEET DR. SEUSS

Say hello to Dr. Seuss, a rhymer of rhymes both tight and loose. A BRI favorite he really is; the following story is really his.

VITAL STATS

Born: March 2, 1904

Died: September 25, 1991, age 87

• Although married twice, he never had any children. His slogan: "You have 'em, I'll amuse 'em."

Real Name: Theodore Seuss Geisel

• He adopted "Seuss" as his writing name during Prohibition, while attending Dartmouth College. The reason: He was caught with a half-pint of gin in his room and was told to resign as editor of the college humor magazine as punishment. Instead, he just stopped using Geisel as a byline.

• Years later, he added "Dr." to his name "to sound more scientific." He didn't officially become a doctor until 1956, when Dartmouth gave him an honorary doctorate.

CAREER STATS

Accomplishments: He wrote 48 books, selling more than 100 million copies in 20 languages. (Including four of the top 10 bestselling hardcover childrens' books of all time: *The Cat in the Hat, Green Eggs and Ham, Hop on Pop,* and *One Fish, Two Fish, Red Fish, Blue Fish.*)

• As a filmmaker, he won three Oscars—two for documentaries made in the 1940s (*Hitler Lives,* about Americans troops, and *Design for Death,* about Japanese warlords), and one in 1951 for animation (*Gerald McBoing-Boing*). By that time, he had written four kids' books and turned down Hollywood screenplay offers in order to keep writing them.

• In 1984 he won the Pulitzer Prize for his contribution to children's literature.

Flops: Only one—a novel called *The Seven Lady Godivas,* an "utterly ridiculous retelling of the story of Lady Godiva" that was first published in 1937 and republished 40 years later. He always wanted to write The Great American Novel...but the book bombed in 1977, too.

How He Got Started: He was working as a cartoonist in the late 1920s for *Judge* magazine. One of his cartoons "showed a knight using Flit insecticide to kill dragons." Someone associated with Flit's ad agency (McCann-Erikson) saw the cartoon and hired Geisel. For the next 10 years he created ads for Flit and other Standard Oil products. His greatest claim to fame at the time: a well-known ad phrase, "Quick Henry, the Flit!"

His contract with McCann-Erikson allowed him to write and publish books for kids, so he wrote *To Think That I Saw It on Mulberry Street.* It was turned down by 27 publishers. Said Seuss: "The excuse I got for all those rejections was that there was nothing on the market quite like it, so they didn't know whether it would sell." Vanguard Press finally picked it up in 1937, and it was an immediate success. So he quit the ad agency and began writing kids' books full-time.

HOW HE GOT HIS IDEAS

"The most asked question of any successful author," Seuss said in 1989, "is 'How do you get your ideas for books?' " Over the years he did reveal a number of his inspirations:

Horton Hatches the Egg

"Sometimes you have luck when you are doodling. I did one day when I was drawing some trees. Then I began drawing elephants. I had a window that was open, and the wind blew the elephant on top of the tree; I looked at it and said, 'What do you suppose that elephant is doing there?' The answer was: 'He is hatching an egg.' Then all I had to do was write a book about it. I've left that window open ever since, but it's never happened again."

Green Eggs and Ham

- Bennett Cerf, the founder and publisher of Random House, bet Geisel $50 that he couldn't write a book using just 50 words.
- Geisel won the bet. "It's the only book I ever wrote that still makes me laugh," he said 25 years later. He added: "Bennett never paid!"

Marvin K. Mooney, Will You Please Go Now?
"The puppylike creature constantly asked to 'go' is ex-President Richard M. Nixon."

The Lorax
Dr. Seuss's favorite book, he said, "is about people who raise hell in the environment and leave nothing behind." He wrote the story on a laundry list as he sat at a hotel pool in Kenya, watching a herd of elephants with his wife. "I wrote it as a piece of propaganda and disguised the fact," he told a reporter. "I was on the soapbox. I wasn't afraid of preaching—but I was afraid of being dull."

Yertle the Turtle
"Yertle the turtle is Adolf Hitler."

The 500 Hats of Bartholomew Cubbins
In 1937 Geisel was on a commuter train in Connecticut. "There was a very stiff broker sitting in front of me. I wondered what his reaction would be if I took his hat off and threw it out the window. I decided that he was so stuffy he would grow a new one."

The Cat in the Hat

- In the early 1950s, novelist John Hersey was on a panel that analyzed how reading was taught in a Connecticut school system. In May 1954, *Life* magazine published excerpts of the panel's report (called "Why Do Students Bog Down on the First R?"). In it, Hersey wrote that one of the major impediments to learning was the dull "Dick and Jane" material students were given—especially the illustrations. Kids, he said, should be inspired with "drawings like those wonderfully imaginative geniuses among children's illustrators, Tenniel, Howard Pyle, Dr. Seuss."
- A textbook publisher read the article and agreed. He contacted Dr. Seuss and asked him to create a reading book. The publisher sent Seuss a list of 400 words and told him to pick 220 to use in the book. The reason: People felt this was the maximum that "kids could absorb at one time."
- "Geisel went through the list once, twice and got nowhere," reports *Parents* magazine. "He decided to give it one more shot; if he could find two words that rhymed, they'd form the title and theme of the book. Within moments, *cat* and *hat* leaped off the page. But then it took him 9 months to write the entire book."

At least 8% of the U.S. population is the result of unwanted pregnancies.

CONDOM SENSE

Condoms used to be an embarrassing subject. Now they're advertised in the magazines that BRI members often stash in the bathroom. Here's some condom trivia.

ORIGIN

Condoms were invented in the mid-1500s by Gabriel Fallopius, an Italian doctor. (He was also the first person to describe fallopian tubes in medical literature.) His creation was made of linen and soon earned the nickname "overcoat". Fallopius believed that they prevented syphilis. They didn't.

NAME

Legend has it that condoms were named after the Earl of Condom, personal physician to King Charles II of England in the mid-1600s. The king feared catching syphilis from his dozens of mistresses and ordered the earl to devise a solution.

• Condom's invention, a sheath made of oiled sheep intestine, became popular among the king's noblemen (who were also looking for protection against venereal disease). It was the noblemen, not Condom, who called the prophylactics "condoms." Condom hated having his name associated with them.

• Condoms became known as "rubbers" in the 1850s, when they actually *were* made of vulcanized rubber. These were thick, expensive, and uncomfortable. Owners were supposed to wash them out and reuse them until they cracked or tore. Disposable, thin latex condoms did not become widely available until the 1930s.

MISCELLANY

• Four billion condoms are sold worldwide every year—enough to circle the globe 16 times.

• How does the U.S. Food and Drug Administration test the strength of condoms? By filling them with air until they pop. The average condom swells to the size of a watermelon before it bursts. Government regulators also cut condoms into rubberband-like pieces and stretch them until they snap.

• Most Muslim countries forbid the sale of green condoms, because green is a sacred color in Islam.

CONTROVERSIAL CHARACTERS

Even cartoon characters and dolls can be accused of being a bad influence on children. Here are a few who have caused major controversy.

The Character: Mighty Mouse

The Controversy: Did Mighty Mouse take cocaine on April 23, 1988, in the TV cartoon show, *Mighty Mouse: The New Adventures?*

The Fight: In 1988 a Tupelo, Mississippi, watchdog group called the American Family Association (AFA) complained to CBS about a scene in a *Mighty Mouse: The New Adventure* cartoon. Reverend Donald Wildmon, head of the AFA, described the scene as follows: "Mighty Mouse is down in the dumps, and he reaches in his cape, pulls out a substance and sniffs it through his nostrils, and from that point on in the cartoon he is his normal self." Wildmon charged that the substance Mighty Mouse "snorted" was cocaine.

The Reaction: CBS producer Ralph Bakshi, who was responsible for the cartoon, angrily rejected the accusation: "This is Nazism and McCarthyism all over again. I don't advocate drugs—that's death. I'm a cartoonist, an artist, not a pornographer. Who are these people anyway? Why does anybody listen to them?" According to Bakshi, Mighty Mouse was actually sniffing crushed flowers he had placed in his pocket during an earlier scene. According to the CBS version of the story, Mighty Mouse was sad because the female character he was attracted to did not love him. So he took out the flowers she'd given him in the earlier scene and sniffed them.

The Characters: Popeye the Sailor and Olive Oyl

The Controversy: Should Popeye and Olive take a pro-choice stand on abortion?

The Fight: In July 1992, Bobby London, the artist who wrote and drew the syndicated *Popeye* comic strip for King Features, decided "to show these old cartoon characters coping with the modern world." He submitted a strip with the following plot:

• Olive Oyl receives a baby Bluto doll in the mail and doesn't want to keep it.

• She and Popeye get into an argument about what to do with it. Olive Oyl tells Popeye that she wants to "send the baby back to its maker."

• Two priests happen to be walking by and hear the argument. They mistakenly assume that Olive Oyl is talking about having an abortion and try to persuade her not to do it. When that fails, the priests try to get passers-by to help. Olive Oyl tells them that "she can do what she wants to do, because it's her life."

The Reaction: King Features fired London and withdrew the strip before it was published.

The Character: Mattel's Barbie doll

The Controversy: Does Barbie promote the "radical agenda" of environmentalism?

The Fight: In the wake of Earth Day 1990, Mattel decided to promote its new line of Barbie dolls with the "Barbie Summit," an all-expenses-paid gathering of children who had submitted winning suggestions on how to improve the world. In the commercial announcing the contest, Barbie asked viewers how they would help make the world a better place—and offered a seemingly innocuous suggestion: "We could keep the trees from falling, keep the eagles soaring," she said.

But the Oregon Lands Commission, an anti-environmentalist lobbying group, was outraged with the ad. They claimed it was exposing children to "the preservationist's radical agenda." "We want to wake up corporate American to the fact that powerful, monied groups are at work shutting down the engines of this country and they are doing it in the name of environmentalism," the commission's spokesperson claimed. The commission organized a boycott, telling its 61,000 members that buying Barbie dolls "would help stop timber harvesting."

The Reaction: Mattel went ahead with the promotion, which was a success. "We kind of thought," explained a Mattel spokesperson, "how can anybody criticize a program that is designed to give children a voice in a world they are going to inherit?"

Forty-three thousand Americans were injured in accidents involving jewelry in 1991.

INSIDE CITIZEN KANE

Recently, Citizen Kane was voted the #1 movie of the century. Here's some info on America's most celebrated feature film, provided by BRI member Ross Owens.

BACKGROUND

On October 30, 1938, the Mercury Theater of the Air broadcast a radio dramatization of H. G. Wells's *War of the Worlds*, in which Martians invade the Earth (*Ed. note:* See "Mars Invasion," *Bathroom Reader* #3). The plot was implausible, but the performance was so realistic that thousands of Americans believed it—and actually fled their homes or prepared for a full-scale Martian war.

The man behind the radio play was 23-year-old Orson Welles (who produced and directed the broadcast). The publicity he received made him a national celebrity, and two years later RKO studios hired him to direct *Citizen Kane*, a film about a newspaper mogul who destroys his life in an endless pursuit of power.

WILLIAM RANDOLPH HEARST

• In many ways, it's amazing that *Citizen Kane* was ever made. Though its characters were supposedly fictional, the film was actually a scathing biography of real-life press baron William Randolph Hearst—head of the Hearst Newspaper chain and one of the most powerful people in America. Naturally, he wanted the movie stopped.

• When he learned that RKO was making the movie, Hearst tried to have the film destroyed. Working through the head of MGM studios, he tried to bribe RKO president George Schaefer with $800,000 (the amount *Citizen Kane* cost to make) to destroy the film's negative. Schaefer refused.

• When that attempt failed, Hearst threatened to sue the studio for libel. RKO took the threat seriously; it delayed the film's release for two months until its lawyers were convinced that the suit wouldn't stand up in court.

• Hearst kept the heat on. Before the film hit the theaters, rumors began spreading that Hearst was planning to attack the entire film industry—not just RKO—in newspaper editorials. This frightened

When asked, 38% of American kids name a movie star as their hero.

the major Hollywood studios (which also owned or controlled most U.S. moviehouses), so they refused to show *Citizen Kane* in their theaters. It had to premiere in smaller, independent theaters.

THE OUTCOME

• The film premiered in 1939. It was a commercial flop, due in large part to Hearst's attacks...plus the fact that his papers wouldn't accept advertising for it.

• Hearst's influence was felt even at the Academy Awards—where Hearst supporters in the audience booed loudly every time the picture was mentioned. Nominated in 8 different categories (including Best Picture), *Kane* won only one award—for Best Original Screenplay. It lost Best Picture to a film called *How Green Was My Valley*.

• Orson Welles never recovered from the disaster. RKO refused to give him the level of artistic freedom he had making *Kane*, and most of his later film projects either failed or were never finished.

THE SECRET WORD

The Idea. The first scene of the movie shows Charles Foster Kane crying out the mysterious name "Rosebud" on his deathbed. The name remains a secret until the last scene, when it's revealed that Rosebud was the name of Kane's childhood sled. The idea of giving Charles Foster Kane a sled was first suggested by Herman J. Mankiewicz, the film's screenwriter. As a boy, Mankiewicz had had his favorite bicycle stolen, an experience he never forgot. He thought a similar story would be useful in the film.

The Name. No one knows exactly how the sled got the name "Rosebud." Some suggestions:

• Orson Welles sometimes told interviewers that Rosebud was the pet name Hearst had given mistress Marion Davies's nose...but in other interviews, he claimed it was the nickname Hearst had given to Davies's private parts.

• Welles's biographer, Charles Higham, points out that the 1914 Kentucky Derby winner was Old Rosebud—and that a reporter in the movie suggests that Rosebud may have been a racehorse.

• Rosebud may actually have been the nickname of one of the staff's ex-girlfriends. In 1942 a woman threatened to sue Herman Mankiewicz, claiming she'd been the writer's mistress in the 1920s and that Rosebud was a nickname he'd given *her*.

The average Mother's Day gift costs about $27.

ORDER IN THE COURT!

Disorderly Conduct and *Disorder in the Court* are two books featuring amusing selections from court transcripts. They make great bathroom reading material—especially for lawyers. These quotes are taken directly from court records. People really said this stuff.

BORED IN COURT

Defendant: "Judge, I want you to appoint me another lawyer."

Judge: "And why is that?"

Defendant: "Because the public defender isn't interested in my case."

Judge (to Public Defender): "Do you have any comments on your defendant's motion?"

Public Defender: "I'm sorry, Your Honor, I wasn't listening."

JUDGE & JURY

Judge: "Is there any reason you could not serve as a juror in this case?"

Potential juror: "I don't want to be away from my job for that long."

Judge: "Can't they do without you at work?"

Potential juror: "Yes, but I don't want them to know it."

Judge to Defendant: "You have a right to a trial by jury, but you may waive that right. What do you wish to do?"

Defendant: (Hesitates.)

Lawyer to Defendant: "Waive."

Defendant: (Waves at the judge.)

UNTIL PROVEN GUILTY

Lawyer: "Have you ever been convicted of a felony?"

Defendant: "Yes."

Lawyer: "How many?"

Legal experts say: every year, about 12% of the U.S. population is arrested.

Defendant: "One, so far."

Judge: "The charge here is theft of frozen chickens. Are you the defendant, sir?"
Defendant: "No, sir, I'm the guy who stole the chickens."

Defense Attorney: "Are you sure you did not enter the Seven-Eleven on 40th and N.E. Broadway and hold up the cashier on June 17 of this year?"
Defendant: "I'm pretty sure."

ALICE IN LAWYERLAND

Lawyer: "Could you briefly describe the type of construction equipment used in your business?"
Witness: "Four tractors."
Lawyer: "What kind of tractors are they?"
Witness: "Fords."
Lawyer: "Did you say 'four?' "
Witness: "Ford. Ford. Like the Ford. It is a Ford tractor."
Lawyer: "You didn't say 'four,' you just said 'Ford?' "
Witness: "Yes, Ford. That is what you asked me, what kind of tractors."
Lawyer: "Are there four Ford tractors? Is that what there is?"
Witness: "No, no. You asked me what kind of a tractor it was and I said Ford tractors."
Lawyer: "How many tractors are there?"
Witness: "Four."

GOOD CALL

Judge: "It is the judgment of this court that you be sentenced to the state prison...for a term of ten years, the maximum penalty."
District Attorney: "Will that be dangerous or non-dangerous offender, Your Honor?"
Judge: "Well, considering the flagrant nature of his offense, the court finds that he's a dangerous offender."
Defendant: "How in the hell can you find me a dangerous offender? There's nothing in there showing any violent crime. What's

When arrested, the average shoplifter has $196 of stolen goods in their possession.

wrong with anybody anyway? You take that son-of-a-bitch and—

Judge: "That will be it; you're remanded to the custody of the sheriff."

Defendant: "You son-of-a-bitch. You bald-headed son-of-a-bitch, when I get out of there, I'll blow your f——g head away. You no-good bald-headed son-of-a-bitch."

Judge: "Get that down in the record, he's threatened to blow the judge's head off."

MISTAKEN IDENTITY?

Prosecutor: "Could you point to someone in this courtroom, or maybe yourself, to indicate exactly how close to a hair color you are referring to?"

Witness: "Well, something like hers (points at the defense attorney) except for more—the woman right here in front (points at defense attorney again). Except for more cheap bleached-blond hair."

Prosecutor: "May the record reflect, Your Honor, the witness has identified Defense Counsel as the cheap blonde."

HOT WITNESS

Prosecutor: "Did you observe anything?"

Witness: "Yes, we did. When we found the vehicle, we saw several unusual items in the car in the right front floorboard of the vehicle. There was what appeared to be a Molotov cocktail, a green bottle—"

Defense lawyer: "Objection. I'm going to object to that word, Molotov cocktail."

Judge: "What is your legal objection, Counsel?"

Defense lawyer: "It's inflammatory, Your Honor."

SPEAK OF THE DEVIL

Judge: "Mr. E., you're charged here with driving a motor vehicle under the influence of alcohol. How do you plead, guilty or not guilty?"

Defendant: "I'm guilty as hell."

Judge: "Let the record reflect the defendant is guilty as hell."

According to recent surveys, 22% of Americans are dissatisfied with their jobs.

PRESIDENTIAL TRIVIA

More unusual tidbits from the occupants of 1600 Pennsylvania Ave.

George Washington wanted Americans to address him as "His Mightiness the President."

Andrew Jackson, known for his colorful language, apparently taught his parrot to curse. When Jackson died in 1845, the parrot was brought to his funeral. It swore at him through the entire service.

Millard Fillmore was the first president to sign a treaty about bird droppings. It was a U.S.–Peru agreement dealing with bird guano, which has a high nitrate content and is useful in making explosives.

While he was president, Franklin Pierce was arrested for running down an elderly woman in his carriage. He was later found not guilty.

Dwight D. Eisenhower loved to paint but couldn't draw—so he had other artists outline on his canvas the things he wanted to paint. This led directly to the paint-by-numbers fad of the 1950s.

Grover Cleveland, 22nd president, was the first one to leave the country while in office. But he didn't really go anywhere: while on a fishing trip he sailed into international waters three miles off the U.S. coast and came right back.

Herbert Hoover was the first president to have a telephone in his office. Earlier, presidents who wanted to use a phone had to use the one in the hall.

After Thomas Jefferson took the oath of office in 1801, he left the Capitol building and walked back to his boardinghouse. Several people followed him, giving rise to the traditional inaugural parade every president has had since then.

Bad omen: It was so cold at Ulysses S. Grant's inauguration that the canaries that were supposed to sing during the inaugural ball froze to death.

President Warren G. Harding exercised regularly...by playing ping-pong.

There are 635,013,559,600 different possible hands in bridge.

AND NOW FOR SOMETHING COMPLETELY DIFFERENT

This piece about one of our favorite comedy ensembles—Monty Python—is from John Javna's book Cult TV.

HOW "MONTY PYTHON" STARTED

In the mid-1960s, David Frost—one of England's most popular TV stars—began work on a series called "The Frost Reports." The staff of young writers he hired included Michael Palin and Terry Jones (who'd performed together since college), John Cleese and Graham Chapman (who'd toured together in Cambridge University's comedy revue), and Eric Idle, a Cambridge student. It was the first time the five of them had worked together.

When Frost's show folded in 1966, they went their separate ways, but they sometimes met and discussed the possibility of doing a program together. When Terry Gilliam (an American friend of John Cleese's) moved to England, he became part of the group. Cleese helped get him a job in the BBC.

A Show Is Born. In 1969 BBC comedy producer Barry Took tried to team Palin and Cleese in their own show. But they refused to do it unless all six of the group were hired. Took decided they'd complement each other as performers and went along with it.

The BBC had been running a religious program late on Sunday nights, and no one was watching it...so the network decided to replace it with "Monty Python's Flying Circus." On October 5, 1969, anyone who tuned in for religion would have seen John Cleese instead, announcing, "And now for something completely different."

At first, Monty Python was on so late that almost no one saw it. But eventually it attracted a cult following, which meant, according to the Pythons, "it was seen by insomniacs, intellectuals, and burglars."

American audiences didn't see the "Flying Circus" until years after its British debut. In 1974, Public Broadcasting Station KERA in Dallas picked up the British series, and it became one of PBS's most popular imports.

Maryland has 325 doctors per 100,000 citizens—the most of any state.

THE NAME

The group came up with a number of names before deciding on "Monty Python's Flying Circus." They almost used:

• "A Horse, a Spoon, and a Basin"

• "The Toad Elevating Moment"

• "Bunn, Wackett, Buzzard, Stubble and Boot" (an imaginary soccer team's forward line)

• "Owl Stretching Time"

• "Gwen Dibley's Flying Circus" (Gwen was Michael Palin's music teacher when he was 11). Soon Monty Python—a name they made up—replaced Gwen Dibley. At first the BBC rejected the troupe's crazy name, but when the Pythons threatened to change their name every week, the network relented.

"I BEG YOUR PARDON?"

A few samples of Python humor.

Graham Chapman: "I think TV's killed real entertainment. In the old days we used to make our own fun. At Christmas parties I used to strike myself on the head repeatedly with blunt instruments while crooning. (sings) '*Only make believe, I love you,* (hits himself on head with bricks). *Only make believe that you love me,* (hits himself). *Others find peace of mind . . .*' "

Railroad Passenger (who thinks he's been let off at the wrong stop)**:** "I wish to make a complaint."
Porter: "I don't have to do this, you know."
Passenger: "I beg your pardon?"
Porter: "I'm a qualified brain surgeon. I only do this because I like being my own boss."
Passenger: "Er, excuse me, this is irrelevant, isn't it?"
Porter: "Oh yeah, it's not easy to pad these out to thirty minutes."

Narrator: "It was a day like any other and Mr. and Mrs. Samuel Brainsample were a perfectly ordinary couple, leading perfectly ordinary lives—the sort of people to whom nothing extraordinary ever happened, and not the kind of people to be the center of one of the most astounding incidents in the history of mankind...so let's forget about them and follow instead the destiny of this man

The U.S. had 8,915 handgun killings in 1989. Great Britain had 7.

(camera pans to businessman in bowler hat and pinstripe suit)... Harold Potter, gardener, and tax official, first victim of Creatures from another Planet."

Candy Maker: "We use only the finest baby frogs, dew picked and flown from Iraq, cleansed in finest quality spring water, lightly killed, and then sealed in succulent Swiss quintuple smooth treble cream milk chocolate envelope and lovingly frosted with glucose."

Government Hygiene Inspector: "That's as may be, but it's still a frog."

Narrator: "Dinsdale was a gentleman. And what's more, he knew how to treat a female impersonator."

* * * *

BATHROOM ETIQUETTE

In the Middle Ages, it was considered sufficient to step "an arrow's flight" distance into the gardens before doing what had to be done. Royalty apparently even thought this unnecessary—one English noble was appalled to find that the visiting king and retinue defecated wherever they chose throughout his castle—and during a conversation with a young noblewoman, he was surprised to hear tinkling water and watch a puddle spreading across his floor beneath her long dress.

Though officially banned as early as 1395 in Paris, it was a centuries-long practice throughout Europe to empty bedpans from high windows into the street. Oft-ignored etiquette demanded that they first shout the classic warning "*Gardez l'eau!*" In Edinburgh you could hire a guide to walk ahead of you and shout, "Haud your hand!" to people in the windows above.

One of history's earliest etiquette books, penned by Erasmus of Rotterdam (1465-1536), laid down several laws about behavior concerning bodily functions. "It is impolite," he wrote, "to greet someone who is urinating or defecating." He then advises the person in need of "breaking wind" to "let a cough hide the explosive sound....Follow the law: replace farts with coughs."

Sixty thousand people attended South Carolina's "World Grits Festival" in 1991.

ELVIS LIVES

Who really believes Elvis is still alive? Plenty of people. As RCA Records used to ask: Can millions of Elvis fans be wrong? BRI member John Dollison wrote this piece so you can judge for yourself.

Early in the morning on August 16, 1977, Elvis Presley and his girlfriend, Ginger Alden, returned to Graceland from a late-night dentist appointment. The two stayed up until about 7:00 a.m. Then Alden went to bed. But, according to one source, "because he had taken some 'uppers,' Elvis was still not sleepy."

So the King retired to his bathroom to read a book. That was the last time anyone saw him alive.

THE OFFICIAL STORY

• When Alden woke up at 2:00 in the afternoon, she noticed that Elvis was still in his bathroom. So she decided to check up on him.

• When she opened the door, she saw Elvis sprawled face forward on the floor. "I thought at first he might have hit his head because he had fallen," she recalls, "and his face was buried in the carpet. I slapped him a few times and it was like he breathed once when I turned his head. I lifted one eyelid and it was just blood red. But I couldn't move him." The King was dead.

• Elvis was rushed to Baptist Memorial Hospital in Memphis, but doctors could not revive him. He was pronounced dead at 3:00 p.m. The official cause of death: cardiac arrhythmia brought on by "straining at stool." (The actual cause of death: most likely a massive overdose of prescription drugs.)

• That is what is supposed to have happened. Nevertheless, Elvis aficionados across the country see a host of mysterious circumstances that suggest that the King may still be alive.

SUSPICIOUS FACTS

• The medical examiner's report stated that Elvis's body was found in the bathroom in a rigor-mortised state. But the homicide report said that Elvis was found unconscious in the bedroom. In *The Elvis Files*, Gail Brewer-Giorgio notes: "Unconsciousness and rigor mortis are at opposite ends of the physical spectrum: rigor mortis is a stiffening condition that occurs after death; unconsciousness, a state in which a living body loses awareness. Bedroom and bathroom are two different places."

• The medical examiner's report lists Elvis's weight at the time of death as 170 pounds; he actually weighed about 250 pounds.

• Elvis's relatives can't agree on how Elvis died. His stepbrother Rick claims Elvis suffocated on the shag carpet; his stepbrother David thinks Elvis committed suicide. Larry Geller, Elvis's hairdresser and spiritual adviser, claims that Elvis's doctors told Vernon Presley (Elvis's father) that the King had leukemia, which may have contributed to his death. Some theorists charge that the confusion surrounding Elvis's death proves that the star faked his death—if the King is really dead, why can't his loved ones get their stories straight?

UNANSWERED QUESTIONS

Elvis's fans want the answers to the following mysteries:

Did Elvis Foresee—or Fake—His Death?

• Elvis didn't order any new jumpsuits—his trademark outfit—in all of 1977. Why not? Did he know he wasn't going to need any?

• On his last concert tour, Elvis was overheard saying, "I may not look good tonight, but I'll look good in my coffin."

• Was Elvis imitating his manager, Colonel Tom Parker? As a young man, Parker also faked his death. An illegal immigrant from Holland whose real name was Andreas Van Kujik, Parker left Holland without telling his relatives; they thought he was dead.

Is the Corpse in Elvis's Coffin Really Elvis's?

• Country singer Tanya Tucker's sister LaCosta was at the King's funeral, and she was shocked at the body's appearance: "We went right up to his casket and stood there, and God, I couldn't believe it. He looked just like a piece of plastic laying there. He didn't look like him at all...he looked more like a dummy than a real person. You know a lot of people think it was a dummy. They don't think he was dead."

• Some observers said they thought the corpse's nose looked too "pugged" to be the King's. They speculated that even if the King had fallen forward and smashed his nose at the time of his death, it would have naturally returned to its original shape, or would at least have been fixed by the undertaker—if the body was really Elvis's. (*The Elvis Files*)

Is the Corpse in Elvis's Coffin a Wax Dummy?

• Some theorists believe that Elvis's coffin weighed more than it was supposed to. Brewer-Giorgio reports receiving a letter from an Elvis fan who claimed to have "personally" known the man who made the King's coffin. The coffin maker revealed that the casket was a "rush" order—and that "there was no way" the coffin could have weighed 900 pounds, as the press reported—even with the King in it. So what was in the coffin with Elvis that made it so heavy?

• According to Brewer-Giorgio, the discrepancy between the coffin's actual weight with Elvis in it and its weight at the funeral is about 250 to 275 pounds, "the weight of a small air-conditioner." "Was there an air-conditioner in the coffin?" Brewer-Giorgio asks, "Wax dummy? Something cool to keep the wax from beading up?"

• To many witnesses, Elvis's corpse appeared to be "sweating" at the funeral. Brewer-Giorgio says she asked Joe Esposito, Elvis's road manager, about TV reports that there were "beads of sweat" on Elvis's body. "He said that was true, that everyone was sweating because the air-conditioner had broken down. Except that dead bodies do not sweat." But wax melts.

Why Did the Mourners Act So Strange at the Funeral?

• Parker wore a loud Hawaiian shirt and a baseball cap to Elvis's funeral and never once approached the casket to say farewell to the King. Elvis's fans argue that if Elvis were really dead, Parker would probably have shown a little more respect.

• Elvis's hairdresser claims that he saw Esposito remove Elvis's TCB (Takin' Care of Business) ring from the corpse's finger during the funeral services. Why would he remove one of Elvis's favorite pieces of jewelry—Elvis would surely have wanted to have been buried with it—unless the corpse being buried wasn't the King's?

Janis Joplin was nominated "Ugliest Man on Campus" while in college.

Is Elvis in the Federal Witness Protection Program?

• In 1970 Presley—a law enforcement buff—was made an honorary Agent-at-Large of the Drug Enforcement Administration by President Nixon after a visit to the White House. According to some theorists, Presley became more than just an honorary agent—he actually got involved in undercover narcotics work.

• In addition to his DEA work, Elvis may have been an FBI agent. During the same trip to Washington D.C., Elvis also wrote a letter to J. Edgar Hoover volunteering his confidential services to the FBI. Hoover wrote back thanking Elvis for his offer, but there is no record of him ever taking it up. Still, Brewer-Giorgio and other theorists argue, the government may have been keeping the King's government service a secret.

• According to Brewer-Giorgio, Elvis was also "a bonded deputy with the Memphis Police and was known to don disguises and go out on narc busts."

• Elvis took his law-enforcement role seriously. More than one biography details the time that the King ran out onto the runway of the Las Vegas airport, flagged down a taxiing commercial airliner, and searched it for a man whom he believed had stolen something from him. Elvis looked around, realized his quarry wasn't aboard, and gave the pilot permission to take off.

• Some theorists believe that Elvis's extensive work in law enforcement made him a target for drug dealers and the Mob—and that he entered the Federal Witness Protection Program out of fear for his life. According to Brewer-Giorgio, when Elvis supplied the information that sent a major drug dealer to prison, the King and his family received death threats.

Could Elvis Be in Hiding?

Hundreds of Elvis's loyal fans think they have spotted the King since his "death." He's been sighted at a Rolling Stones concert, working at a Burger King in Kalamazoo, buying gas in Tennessee, and shopping for old Monkees records in Michigan. One woman even claims that Elvis gave her a bologna sandwich and a bag of Cheetos during a 1987 visit to the Air Force Museum in Dayton, Ohio. Could so many people be lying or mistaken?

According to zoologists, elephants love to eat licorice.

OTHER MYSTERIES COLLECTED BY ELVIS FANS

• Vernon Presley never went to the hospital the night Elvis "died." If Elvis were really dead, some theorists speculate, he probably would have.

• According to some reports, within hours of Presley's death, souvenir shops near Graceland began selling commemorative T-shirts of his death. How could they have made so many shirts in so little time—unless Graceland had let them know about the "death" in advance?

• Elvis's middle name, Aron, is misspelled "Aaron" on his tombstone. If Elvis is really dead, why don't his relatives correct the mistake?

• Elvis isn't buried next to his mother as he requested. Says Brewer-Giorgio: " 'Elvis loved his mother very much and always said he would be buried beside her,' many fans have noted. 'So why is he buried between his father and grandmother?' they ask."

• On a number of occasions after the King's death, Priscilla Presley referred to Elvis as a living legend—strange words for a woman who supposedly believes that Elvis is dead.

• Before he died, Elvis took out a multimillion-dollar life insurance policy. To date, no one in his family has tried to claim it. If Elvis's family really believes he is dead, why haven't they cashed in the policy?

PASSING ON

• The people who were in Elvis's home when he died insist that he really did die. Joe Esposito, Elvis's road manager for 17 years, was one of the first people to see the body. "Believe me, the man that I tried to revive was Elvis."

• Elvis may even have committed suicide. According to his stepbrother David Stanley, "Elvis was too intelligent to overdose [accidentally]. He knew the *Physician's Desk Reference* inside and out." Why would Elvis take his own life? He was getting old, and the strain of his stagnating career may have become too much to bear. The pressure showed: in the last years of his life, Elvis's weight ballooned to more than 250 pounds, and his addiction to prescription drugs had gotten out of control.

• The impending publication of a book chronicling the King's erratic behavior and his drug problem may have been the final straw. In August 1977, the month of his death, two of his former aides were about to publish a book revealing much of his bizarre personal life to the public for the first time. He was already depressed, and the imminent public exposure of his drug habit may have pushed him over the edge.

RECOMMENDED READING

The Elvis Files, by Gail Brewer-Giorgio (Shapolsky Publishers, 1990). *A fountain of Elvis conspiracies*.

* * *

HOLLYWOOD-ISMS

Some funny observations taken from Star Speak: Hollywood on Everything, *by Doug McClelland.*

"In Hollywood, the executives have Picassos and Chagalls on their walls and would kill to have lunch with Chuck Norris. That's why you have movies like *Howard the Duck*."

—David Steinberg

"It is not true I was born a monster. Hollywood made me one."

—Boris Karloff

"The best time I ever had with Joan Crawford was when I pushed her down the stairs in *Whatever Happened to Baby Jane?*"

—Bette Davis

"I had a dog named Duke. Every fireman in town knew that hound, because he chased all the firewagons. They knew the dog's name, but not mine, so the next thing I was Duke, too. I was named for a damn dog!"

—John Wayne

"If the scripts were as great as the sets, what a town Hollywood would be!"

—W. Somerset Maugham

A BREED APART

Ever wonder why a Dachsund is so long and skinny—or why Great Danes are so tall? The answer: They were bred with a specific purpose in mind. Here are the stories behind the names and appearances of some of the world's most popular dog breeds.

BASSET HOUNDS. The name comes from the French adjective *bas*, which means "low thing." Originally bred to hunt rabbits, raccoons, and other small mammals. Their short legs make them relatively slow runners, but they're especially adept at chasing prey through thickets.

BULLDOGS. According to legend, in 1209 A.D. Lord William Earl Warren of Stamford, England, was looking out onto his meadow and saw two dogs fighting a bull. He so admired their courage that he gave the meadow to the townspeople—on the condition that they begin holding annual dog-bull fights. Over the next 600 years, bullbaiting became a popular sport, and the bulldog breed evolved along with it. Like pit-bulls, bulldogs were originally bred to be fearless and vicious. But in 1835, bullbaiting was banned in England. Bulldog lovers used breeding techniques to eliminate their viciousness, making them acceptable house pets.

COCKER SPANIELS. A member of the Spanyell family of dogs that dates back to the 14th century. Their small size made them ideal for hunting woodcocks, earning them the name cockers, which eventually became cocking spaniels, then cocker spaniels.

FRENCH POODLES. Actually bred in 15th-century Germany as hunting dogs. The name "poodle" comes from the German word *pudeln*, which means "to splash." The reason: They're good swimmers and were often used to retrieve game from ponds, etc.

GREAT DANES. Got their name from the French, who thought they were Danish. They weren't: they were actually from Germany, where they were bred large enough to tackle and kill wild boars.

ROTTWEILERS. When soldiers of ancient Rome went into battle, they had no way of bringing enough fresh meat with them to last the entire campaign. So they brought cattle—and Rottweiler dogs to herd them. In 700 A.D., the local duke in an area of Germany the Romans had once occupied commissioned a Catholic church to be built near the ruins of some Roman baths. Because the baths had red tile roofs, the Duke issued instructions to build at "*das Rote Wil*,"—the red tiles. Later the area became known as the town of Rottweil, and the breed of dogs the Romans had left behind were called Rottweilers.

GREYHOUNDS. One of the oldest breeds of dogs; dating back as far as ancient Egypt (where they were a favorite pet of the pharoahs). Tomb paintings nearly 5,000 years old depict them hunting wild goats, deer, and other animals. According to one theory, they're actually named after the Greeks, taking their name from the word *Graius*, which means Grecian or Greek.

DACHSHUNDS. Although the name is derived from the German words *Dachs* (badger) and *Hund* (dog), dachshunds have been used to hunt animals as large as wild boars. Their long bodies make them ideal for chasing badgers and rabbits through their tunnels.

BLOODHOUNDS. The bloodhound's unrivaled sense of smell has made it one of the most popular hunting dogs in history. Dog experts believe it dates back several hundred years B.C. and was first used as a hunting dog in and around Constantinople. Its skills were so valuable that it became known as a royal, or "blooded," hound and was a favorite pet of aristocrats.

PEKINGESE. Came from imperial China, where the purest breeds were reserved for members of the royal family. The dogs were so precious that when British troops sacked the Imperial Palace in 1860, most of the pets were destroyed by their owners...who preferred killing them to surrendering them to the enemy. However one woman—the Emperor's aunt—committed suicide before she killed her dogs, and the British found five of them hiding behind a curtain in her quarters. The dogs were brought back to England, and one was presented to Queen Victoria. She fell in love with it, and the breed immediately became popular.

The busiest pay phone in the U.S.—used over 270 times a day—is in Chicago's main bus terminal.

ON THE LINE

Odds & ends of telephone trivia and lore, from the fabulous Bathroom Reader *library.*

ORIGIN OF THE PHONE NUMBER

"The early phone exchanges listed only the names of 'subscribers' to the service, and the operators had to memorize all of them in order to connect one to the other. The idea of a telephone number was vigorously resisted by customers as an indignity and loss of personal identification. However, during an epidemic of measles in Lowell, Massachusetts in 1880, a respected physician named Dr. Parker recommended the use of numbers because he feared paralysis of the town's telephone system if the four operators succumbed. He felt numbers would make it easier for substitute operators to be trained. surprisingly, no one complained...and the new system proved so practical that by 1895, official instructions to operators specified, 'Number Please?' as the proper response to a customer."

—*The Telephone Book*, by H. M. Boettinger

MESSAGE FROM A VISIONARY

The following was sent in a letter to "the organizers of the New Electric Telephone Company" by Alexander Graham Bell on March 25, 1878.

"At the present time we have a perfect network of gas pipes and water pipes throughout our large cities. We have main pipes laid under the streets [connected to] various dwellings, enabling people to draw their supplies of gas and water from a common source.

"In a similar manner it is conceivable that cables of telephone wires could be laid under ground, or suspended overhead, communicating by branch wires with private dwellings, counting houses, shops, manufactories, etc., uniting them through the main cable with a central office where the wire could be connected as desired, establishing direct communication between any two places in the city. Such a plan as this, though impracticable at the present moment, will, I firmly believe, be the outcome of the introduction of the telephone to the public....I [also] believe that in the future, wires will unite the head offices of telephone companies in different cities, and a man in one part of the country may communicate by word of mouth with another in a distant place."

THE PRESIDENT AND THE TELEPHONE

"After the invention of the telephone in 1876, one might think that the president...would be one of the first persons to have one of the new instruments. Actually, a telephone *was* installed in the White House in 1877, during the administration of Rutherford B. Hayes. But that doesn't mean that the president had a phone. The phone was not even in his office, and it was used mainly by staff members and news reporters.

"Until 1898 chief executives rarely used the telephone , and none had an instrument in his office. When the president wanted to make a phone call, he had to leave his desk and go down the hall to the phone, just like everyone else. That changed abruptly in 1898 when war broke out with Spain. With action on two fronts, in Cuba and the Philippines, the president was suddenly faced with the need for more rapid communications than could be effected by the old methods.

"Accordingly, [as technician] was brought to the White House to install a communications center...[which] provided President Mckinley with private telephone lines to the War and Navy departments...There was also a direct line to Tampa, Florida, the primary staging area for the invasion of Cuba." That was the first time the telephone was deemed absolutely essential at 1600 Pennsylvanian Avenue.

—*The Telephone and Its Several Inventors*, by Lewis Coe

EARLY TELEPHONE ETIQUETTE

"The subscriber has the right to expect the first word from the operator to be always 'Number?' to which the word 'Please' had better be added, but is not absolutely required.

"The subscriber has the right to expect the operator, if necessary, to say, 'That line is busy'; simply 'Busy' won't do.

"The operator has a right to expect that the subscriber will have the number ready when the operator answers, and that the operator will not be compelled to wait while the subscriber looks it up in the directory.

"Also that the subscriber will give the number in a a clear and distinct voice, and if the operator misunderstands a number, that she will be corrected, without evidence of anger in the tone of the subscriber"

—***Telephone Etiquette,*** **published in 1905**

OLDIES BUT GOODIES

• "New York City's first phone directory was issued in 1878. It was a small card with a printed list of 271 names. Almost a century later, 44 of the businesses listed in that first directory were still in operation, four of them at the very same address."

• Early rural telephone wires were strung across just about anything that was standing—not only telephone pulse, but windmills, silos, and even fence posts. In fact, it was fairly common for phone conversations to sputter and die out as a result of cattle rubbing against the fence lines."

• "Back n 1909, when 18,000 calls were placed daily between New York and Chicago (earning Bell $22,000, seven times a week) , a special long distance salon was opened in Manhattan. To entice Paying customers and get them into the 'long-distance habit,] the New York Telephone company sent taxis to pick them up and bring them to the salon, whereupon they were escorted over oriental carpets to a gilded booth draped with silk curtains. "

—***The What to While You're Holding the Phone Book,*** **by Gary Owens**

THE BIRTH OF THE PAY PHONE

"It started at home, where families subscribed to telephone service and paid a monthly bill to lease the company's instrument. This phone was off-limits to nonsubscribers, however. And early on, there were plenty of these. How, then, to summon the doctor? The police? The fire department? What would happen if a phoneless neighbor used another's phone? Who paid? How? How much? And what if it was three in the morning?

"With problems ranging from bookkeeping to friend keeping, it was essential that telephones be made accessible to all. Thus the first public pay station in the world went into service on June 1, 1880, in the office of the Connecticut Telephone Company in New Haven....For ten cents, paid to a uniformed attendant, anyone could talk to anyone.

"Soon, however, the coin-operated telephone was invented by William Gray. According to legend, Mr. Gray had been turned away by cold-hearted neighbors when he sought to use their telephone to call a doctor during a family emergency. Determined not to let it happen again—to himself or other 'phoneless people'—he patented and built 'the first coin-controlled apparatus for telephones.' It was installed in the Hartford Bank in 1889."

—***Once Upon a Telephone,***
by Ellen Stern and Emily Gwathmey

LEARNING TO DEAL WITH THE TELEPHONE

1917: "Another hall abomination is a telephone. Unless we want our guests to know the price of their roast, or the family to listen aghast while we tell a white lie for society's sake, or the cook to heat us asking for a new one's references, don't put your telephone in the hall closet it, or keep it upstairs, where the family alone are the bored 'listeners in.'"

—***Interior Decoration for Modern Needs,*** **by Agnes Foster Wright**

1927: "...Then the telephone. Children usually love to use it ad they should be taught to speak courteously on the pain of not being allowed to answer it. Children commit all sorts of discourtesies over the telephone if not checked and one often hears the casual 'Yep' and 'What?' and 'Wait.'"

—***Good Manners for Children,***
by Elsie C. Mead and Theordora Mead Abel

The 1940s: "When you have finished your telephone visit, and courteously said 'good-bye' or 'thank You,' replace the receiver gently. Slamming the receiver might cause a sharp crack in the ear often person with whom you have been talking. Since you would not 'slam the door' after an actual visit, be just as careful in closing you telephone door.

—***You and Your Telephone,***
distributed by the New York Telephone Company

"Hello," said a man at the phone company.

"Who is this?" asked Wanda.

"It's the phone company."

"I'm so glad you called back. What's going on?"

"Ma'am, we didn't call you. You called us."

"No, I didn't. My phone just rang. Aren't you calling about my broken phone?"

"I'm sorry, ma'am, but we have no way of knowing a phone is broken unless a customer calls us."

"But you just called me about the fellow being electrocuted."

"I'm afraid we didn't," said the man, convinced he had some loony on the phone—which was not far from the truth.

When that conversation ended, John and Alan connected Wanda back to the pizza parlor, a crisis hotline, and finally back to Professor Burns.

"Hello," said the professor.

"Hello," said Wanda.

"Adams, what is it now?"

"Professor Burns—"

"Wanda, I have not had time to grade your thesis, so you needn't call me."

"But I didn't call you. My phone rang. Something crazy is going on."

"Get some sleep, Adams."

"Professor, I didn't call you."

"Okay. Good-bye."

Finally, Wanda was connected back to the phone company. In the midst of that conversation, though, Alan let go a burst of laughter which in an instant identified him to his target.

DR. WHO?

"Dr. Who" was the longest running sci-fi show in television history, and one of the longest running dramatic programs. Here's the story of how the good Doctor came to be.

BACKGROUND. Before "Dr. Who" debuted, there had never been a family-oriented science fiction show in Britain. There had been a few radio shows, but on TV they'd all been strictly adult or strictly for children. There was no precedent for "Dr. Who." No one had any idea it would become an overnight success. But it did—literally.

How It Started. It was 1962. The BBC was expanding its line of TV programs and wanted to offer a new Saturday evening family show that would be educational as well as entertaining. They called in two people—Sydney Newman (creator of "The Avengers") and Donald Wilson (later creator of "The Forsythe Saga") to come up with it. Newman wanted to make the program science fiction. Wilson wanted history. So they compromised and came up with a time traveler.

OK. Now what was he going to travel in? They wanted 1) a space ship that didn't look like a space ship and 2) something cheap. It was originally planned for the device to have "chameleon circuits" that would enable it to blend in with its surroundings (in Greece it would like a column, in a field it would like a rock, etc.) Since the first story took place in London, the time machine started off looking like a telephone booth. An immediate problem: the budget didn't allow them to keep changing it. So the time machine remained a telephone booth.

"Dr. Who" was an immediate sensation. For six years the writers got away without saying anything specific about the doctor's origin. There were vague hints that he was fleeing from something, but that was it. Finally the producers needed an explanation. So they finally "revealed" that Dr. Who was a time lord from the planet Gallifrey.

INSIDE FACTS

In The Beginning. H.G. Wells' *The Time Machine* was the source that inspired Sydney Newman, "Dr.Who's" co-creator, to come up with his time-traveler.

Bad Timing. The first episode of "Dr. Who" was aired in England on Nov. 23, 1963, the day after John F. Kennedy's assassination. Because of the assassination, the BBC figured a lot of people had missed the first show (good guess), so the following week they showed the first episode again, right before the second one.

It Seemed Like a Good Idea. The original idea behind "Dr. Who" was serious. By having contemporary characters travel back in time and witness important historical events, the show could make the past seem alive to its young audience. Ratings of the historical episodes were poor, while the fantastic adventures in outer space attracted huge numbers of viewers.

Calling Dr. Who. The Doctor's time machine, which looks like a police telephone booth, is called a TARDIS. The name is an acronym invented by Dr. Who's companion, Susan. It stands for Time and Relative Dimension in Space.

Successful Transplant. "Dr. Who" was first sold to American TV in 1973. It never really caught on and it wasn't until Lionheart Television syndicated it through PBS in the early 1980s with a different star, that the show really took off. All the PBS channels started carrying it. Then they started ordering newer episodes, with yet *another* star. That led to the resyndication of the earlier series.

DR. WHO'S ENEMIES

The Daleks. Mutated organisms living in mobile war machines, they have a "dislike for the unlike." Anything that isn't a Dalek shouldn't be allowed to exist, so they kill everything in sight.

The Cybermen. Were human once, but all their bodies have been replaced by mechanical parts. Have no emotions and believe that, logically, they should control the universe.

The Yeti. Robots controlled by the Great Intelligence, an extradimensional entity attempting to enter our universe.

The Sontarans. Cloned warriors who live for combat. They're fighting "an interminable war against the Rutans."

The Ice Warriors. The only villains in "Dr. Who" who ever reformed. They're Martians who left home and have returned.

WHO KILLED MALCOLM X?

The film version of Malcolm X's autobiography put this controversial leader in the spotlight again, 27 years after his assassination. But it also raised some interesting questions about how and why he was killed. Was it a government plot? Read this excerpt from It's a Conspiracy!, *by the National Insecurity Council, and judge for yourself.*

On February 21, 1965, Malcolm X rose to address a largely black crowd in the Audubon Ballroom in New York City. But before he could begin speaking, a scuffle broke out in the audience.

In his book *Seven Days*, Alan Berger describes what happened next: "All heads turned to see what was happening...Malcolm's bodyguards moved down from the stage toward the disturbance. Malcolm himself stepped out from behind the podium and toward the front of the stage.

"There was a muffled explosion at the rear of the hall and smoke...a woman screamed. A man in one of the front rows held up a sawed-off shotgun and fired into Malcolm's chest. As Malcolm keeled over, two or three men were seen standing in the front row, 'like a firing squad,' pumping bullets into him. After he had fallen, the gunmen emptied their revolvers into the inert body."

According to a 1967 article in *The Realist*, "All eyewitness reports of the assassination indicated a total of five gunmen had been involved, but only one, Thomas Hagan, was caught after he was slowed by a thrown chair and shot in the leg." Hagan was a member of a militant religious sect—the Black Muslims—from which Malcolm had recently broken off. The following week, two more suspects (both Black Muslim "enforcers") were arrested. All three were convicted and sentenced to life in prison.

BACKGROUND

• Malcolm X's pilgrimage from street tough to international figure began in prison when he discovered the writings of Elijah Mohammed. This Black Muslim philosophy of racial separation and black self-reliance appealed to Malcolm, and when he was released from jail in 1952, he joined the group. He quickly became their most effective evangelist...and their most prominent spokesman. He was often quoted in the national press.

• In 1963, while the country was still grieving the death of President Kennedy, he remarked that the murder was just a case of "the chickens coming home to roost." His remark so incensed the public that the Black Muslims suspended him.

• Unrepentant, he quit the church in March 1964 and started his own group, taking so many Black Muslims with him that Elijah Mohammed's followers vowed revenge. Malcolm repeatedly told aides that he had been "marked for death."

• From the beginning of the investigation, the police and FBI assumed the killing had been ordered by the Black Muslims. The media echoed that official story. The *New York Herald Tribune*'s report was typical: "Now the hatred and violence that he preached has overwhelmed him, and he has fallen at the hand of Negroes."

WAS IT A CONSPIRACY?

Many prominent blacks saw a different reason for Malcolm X to have been killed. Some suspected the U.S. government. Said CORE National Director James Foreman in The New York Times: *"The killing of Malcolm X was a political act, with international implications and not necessarily connected with black nationalism."*

A THORN IN THE GOVERNMENT'S SIDE

• In 1964 Malcolm X visited Mecca and Africa. He was greeted as the roving ambassador of an American black nation; he met with presidents, prime ministers, and kings. In Ghana, for example, he addressed a joint session of the Ghanian parliament—the first American to do so. Wherever he went, he encouraged African governments to speak out against American racism. He also reported that wherever he went in Africa, he was followed by CIA agents.

• In July 1964, he traveled to Cairo to address the Summit Conference of African prime minsters. There he introduced a program to "bring the American racial problem before the U.N. under the Human Rights provision of its charter, as South Africa had been." (*The Realist*)

• A few weeks later, the State and Justice departments acknowledged that they considered Malcolm a threat. A spokesman told

Elizabeth Taylor appeared on the cover of *Life* magazine more than any other actress.

The New York Times: "If [Malcolm X] succeeds in convincing just one African government to bring up the charge at the United Nations, the United States government would be faced with a touchy problem."

• After returning to the U.S., Malcolm X continued to push for his U.N. program. In the fall of 1964, he spent most of his time at the U.N., lobbying African delegates to support his efforts. In November 1964 the U.S. intervened in the Congo Civil War. Malcolm X warned African leaders that if they didn't speak out, "the same thing can happen to you."

• They took his advice. During a U.N. General Assembly debate on the Congo, African delegates condemned the U.S. as being indifferent to the fate of blacks everywhere, citing as evidence the U.S. government's attitude toward the civil rights struggle in Mississippi. The State Department reportedly blamed Malcolm X for its embarrassment.

• Friends and family were concerned that Malcolm X was taking a great risk by interfering in American foreign policy. He was under constant surveillance. His half sister, Ella Collins, said she had heard from reliable sources that there were even CIA agents in the group Malcolm X had founded, the Organization of Afro-American Unity. "Malcolm knew the dangers, but he said he had to go ahead." (*Seven Days*)

• Just before he was killed, Malcolm X told his biographer, Alex Haley, that he no longer believed that the biggest threat to his life was the Black Muslim organization. "I know what they can do, and what they can't, and they can't do some of the stuff recently going on." (ibid.)

SUSPICIOUS FACTS

In Cairo

• The U.S. State Department didn't want Malcolm X to attend the summit in Cairo. The U.S. embassy in Cairo tried, and failed, to get the Egyptian government to bar his appearance. (*The New York Times*)

• The day before Malcolm X was scheduled to speak at the summit, he ate dinner at the Hilton Hotel in Cairo. Shortly after the meal, he collapsed with severe stomach pains. He was rushed to a hospital.

• "His stomach was pumped out, cleaned thoroughly, and that saved him," said an associate. "Malcolm said afterwards he would have died if he had not got immediate treatment." Reportedly, a "toxic substance" was found, and natural food poisoning was ruled out. Malcolm suspected the CIA. (*The Realist*)

In France

• Two weeks before he was killed, Malcolm X was scheduled to address a conference in France, as he had on other occasions. But when his plane landed, he was told he could not disembark—the French Government had branded him "an undesirable person." He was ordered to leave the country immediately.

• Three months earlier, Malcolm X had visited France without incident, so he was baffled by the expulsion order: "I was surprised when I arrived in Paris and was prohibited from landing. I thought that if there were any country in Europe that was liberal in its approach to the problem it was France."

• After the assassination, a prominent North African diplomat approached an American journalist with information about the incident. "This official, who insists on anonymity, said that the French Department of Alien Documentation and Counter Espionage had been quietly informed that the CIA planned to murder Malcolm, and France feared he might be liquidated on its soil." (*Seven Days*)

Firebombing

• Ten hours after Malcolm X's return from France, four firebombs were hurled into his home in Queens, New York. It looked like a professional hit job, with bombs positioned to block all possible escapes. Fortunately the fourth bomb glanced off a windowpane and exploded harmlessly on the front lawn, allowing Malcolm, his wife, and their four children to narrowly escape. The house was destroyed.

• To Malcolm X, the timing of the attack could not be chalked up to coincidence: "It was no accident that I was barred from France,

The first words ever recorded on a film soundtrack were, "You ain't heard nothing yet, folks!"

and ten hours after I arrived home my home was bombed," he declared at a February 17, 1965, press conference.

• Malcolm X announced, "We are demanding an immediate investigation by the FBI of the bombing. We feel a conspiracy has been entered into at the local level, with some local police, firemen and press. Neither I, nor my wife and child have insurance, and we stand in no way to gain from the bombing....My attorney has instructed me and my wife to submit to a lie detector test and will ask that the same test be given to police and firemen at the scene." But Malcolm X's hopes of pursuing this investigation were cut short eight days later.

THE ASSASSINATION

Police Protection

• Malcolm X had held meetings in the Audubon Ballroom many times before. Usually, there was a large contingent of uniformed police to prevent violence from followers of Elijah Mohammad. But on the day he was murdered, there were only two uniformed police officers—posted at the exit. (*Seven Days*)

• After the murder, New York Deputy Police Commissioner Walter Arm claimed that protection had been offered to Malcolm X, but that he had refused it. According to Alex Haley, however, Malcolm X had made repeated requests for increased protection, but the police had ignored him. (*Seven Days*)

Gene Roberts

• The police certainly knew about the threats against Malcolm X. His chief bodyguard, Gene Roberts—who was with him when he was assassinated—was an undercover New York City policeman.

• Roberts actually did his best to save Malcolm X. He attacked one of the armed assailants with a chair and chased him into a crowd. When the assailant was captured by the crowd, Roberts returned to give Malcolm mouth-to-mouth resuscitation.

• According to *Newsday*, later in the evening, Roberts was called by his supervisors and questioned extensively. Why had he, for example, given Malcolm mouth-to-mouth resuscitation and tried to stop the gunman? "Isn't that what I'm supposed to do?" Roberts responded. "I'm a cop. It's my job to save people's lives. What was I supposed to do...let him bleed to death?"

• Years after the assassination, Roberts voiced his doubts about the integrity of the police and raised questions about a larger conspiracy. Certain events at that meeting seemed particularly suspicious to Roberts:

✓ After the shooting, "people were trying to get medical help from Columbia-Presbyterian Hospital," which was across the street from the hall. "It damn near took them a half an hour."

✓ No other policemen came to Gene's assistance. "The cops were outside. None of them came inside."

The Patsies

• Although eyewitness accounts suggest there were as many as five gunmen, only three were captured, and only one of those was actually apprehended in the ballroom.

• Gunman Thomas Hagan was shot in the leg as he fled the ballroom and was quickly trapped by the crowd and arrested by police. But it was only after an "intensive investigation" that two others, Norman Butler and Thomas Johnson, were arrested weeks later. Both were "enforcers" for the Black Muslims who were awaiting trial for the shooting of a Muslim defector.

• When Hagan stood trial he confessed to the murder, but he told the court that the other two suspects were innocent: "I just want the truth to be known—that Butler and Johnson didn't have anything to do with this crime. Because I was there. I know what happened and I know the people who were there." (*Seven Days*)

• On March 1, 1966, *The New York Times* reported that Hagan "said that he had three accomplices, but he declined to name them. He said he had been approached early in the month of the murder and offered money for the job, but he declined to say by whom....One thing he did know, he said, was that no one involved in the murder was a Black Muslim."

• Regardless, on April 16, 1966, Hagan, Johnson, and Butler were each sentenced to life imprisonment for Malcolm X's murder.

Legendary lawmaker Wyatt Earp was kicked out of California for horse-stealing.

The One That Got Away

• There may have been another suspect caught at the scene who mysteriously disappeared. The first edition of *The New York Times* the next day reported that one of the two police officers at the exit "said he 'grabbed a suspect' whom people were chasing. 'As I brought him to the front of the ballroom, the crowd began beating me and the suspect,' Patrolman Hoy said. He said he put this man—not otherwise identified later for newsmen—into a police car to be taken to the Wadsworth Avenue station." (*The Realist*)

• That second suspect was never heard from again, and the press did not pursue the issue. In later editions of the *Times*, the story had been changed and the earlier subhead, "Police Hold Two For Question," had been changed to "One Is Held In Killing." (ibid.)

• What makes the case of this mystery suspect even more intriguing is that his appearance—"a thin-lipped, olive-skinned Latin-looking man"—matches the description of a man whom Malcolm X had noticed trailing him through London and on the plane to New York one week before his death. (ibid.)

BURYING THE TRUTH

The Films

• According to a February 25, 1965, article in *The New York Times:* "the police were in possession of motion pictures that had been taken at the Audubon Ballroom...where the killing took place." These films would have been invaluable evidence—but there was no further mention of them by press or police. (*The Realist*)

The Mysterious Death of Leon Ameer

• Leon Ameer was the New England representative of Malcolm X's group, the Organization of Afro-American Unity—and many believed him to be Malcolm X's hand-picked successor. On March 13, 1965, he announced, "I have facts in my possession as to who *really* killed Malcolm X. The killers aren't from Chicago [Muslim headquarters]. They're from Washington." (*The Realist*)

• Ameer promised to hold a press conference to reveal evidence proving the "power structure's" involvement in the killing, including documents and a tape recording Malcolm X had given him.

#1 jukebox song of all time, according to industry sources: "Crazy," by Patsy Cline.

• The next morning, Ameer's body was discovered by a maid in Boston's Sherry Biltmore Hotel. The police announced that he had died of an epileptic fit, but Ameer's wife contended that her husband had had a complete medical checkup just one month before—"and there was no hint of epilepsy." (ibid.)

RECOMMENDED READING

• "The Murder of Malcolm X" by Eric Norden (*The Realist*, February 1967)

• "Who Killed Malcolm X?" by Alan Berger (*Seven Days*, March 24 and April 7, 1978)

* * * *

TALES OF THE CIA

• As the Cold War ended, the CIA decided it needed to project "a greater openness and sense of public responsibility." So it commissioned a task force. On December 20, 1991, the committee submitted a 15-page "Task Force Report on Greater Openness." It is stamped SECRET, and agency officials refuse to disclose any of the contents.

• In its war against Fidel Castro during the 1960s, the CIA literally tried to play hardball politics. "The CIA tried to cut off the supply of baseballs to Cuba. Agents persuaded suppliers in other countries not to ship them. (U.S. baseballs were already banned by the trade embargo the U.S. had declared.)" The bizarre embar go was effective. Some balls got through, "but the supply was so limited that the government had to ask fans to throw foul balls and home runs back onto the field for continued play."

—Jonathan Kwitny, *Endless Enemies*

• *Quiz:* What motto is inscribed on the wall of the CIA headquarters in Langley, Virginia?

A) "Keep the Faith" **B)** "And Ye Shall Know Truth and the Truth Shall Make You Free" **C)**"A Secret Kept Is a Secret Saved"

Answer: B

Four percent of California automobiles have personalized license plates.

THE TV SPEECH THAT MADE A PRESIDENT

Richard Nixon's "Checkers Speech" was a trademark mixture of self-pity, pathos, paranoia, sentimentality, and attack. It was the most important speech of his life, because it saved his career and made him a national figure. But it was also one of the most important speeches ever made on TV because it established the power of the medium to influence the political process.

BACKGROUND

In the summer of 1952, the Republican party nominated General Dwight D. Eisenhower for president and Senator Richard M. Nixon of California for vice president.

Nixon, who'd only been in politics for six years, was clearly the rising star of the Republican party. But in the middle of September, his political career suddenly became endangered. Investigative reporters revealed that for two years, a group of wealthy Californians had contributed $18,000 to a secret Nixon slush fund. Nixon insisted he'd done nothing wrong—the money was simply "to help defray political expenses." But polls showed that most Americans thought he was a crook, and should give up the VP nomination.

Right or Wrong?

Eisenhower wasn't sure. He declared in a formal statement he believed "Dick Nixon to be an honest man." But behind the scenes, his advisors were hotly debating the issue. Was it worse strategy to dump Nixon...or to keep him on and let him drag the whole ticket down?

Eventually, even Republicans began to clamor for Nixon's resignation. At that point, Ike made it clear that unless Nixon could prove he was "clean as a hound's tooth," the veep-to-be would be off the ticket.

After a private meeting with Eisenhower, Nixon announced he would make a nationwide radio and TV address. People wondered whether he would defend himself or resign from the campaign. Nixon wouldn't even tell his own aides what he planned.

Holy Mackerel: A tuna can swim 100 miles a day.

THE CHECKERS SPEECH

Immediately following the "Milton Berle Show" on September 23, 1952, Senator Richard Nixon took to the airwaves to defend himself. The program began with a shot of Nixon's calling card. Then the camera focused on the senator, who was sitting behind a desk. Here are some excerpts of what Nixon said:

"My Fellow Americans: I come before you tonight as a candidate for the vice presidency and as a man whose honesty and integrity have been questioned....I am sure that you have read the charge and you've heard that I, Senator Nixon, took $18,000 from a group of my supporters. Now, was that wrong? Because it isn't a question of whether it was legal or illegal, that isn't enough. The question is, was it morally wrong?...

"Let me say this: Not one cent of the $18,000 ever went to me for my personal use. Every penny of it was used to pay for political expenses that I did not think should be charged to the taxpayers of the United States."

Paying Political Expenses

"The question arises, you say, 'Well, how do you pay for these and how can you do it legally?' There are several ways that it can be done. The first way is to be a rich man. I don't happen to be a rich man so I couldn't use that. Another way that is used is to put your wife on the payroll. Let me say, incidentally, my opponent, my opposite number for the vice presidency on the Democratic ticket, does have his wife on the payroll. And has had her on his payroll for the past ten years....

"Now just let me say this. That's his business and I'm not critical of him for doing that. You will have to pass judgment on that particular point. But I have never done that for this reason. I have found that there are so many deserving stenographers and secretaries in Washington that needed the work that I just didn't feel it was right to put my wife on the payroll.

"My wife's sitting over here. She's a wonderful stenographer. She used to teach stenography and she used to teach shorthand in high school. That was when I met her. And I'm proud to say tonight that in the six years I've been in the House and the Senate of the U. S., Pat Nixon has never been on the government payroll."

Here's What I'll Do

"Now what I am going to do—and incidentally this is unprecedented in the history of American politics—I am going at this time to give to this television and radio audience a complete financial history; everything I've earned; everything I've spent; everything I owe. I want you to know the facts. I'll have to start early.

"I was born in 1913. Our family was one of modest circumstances and most of my early life was spent in a store out in East Whittier. It was a grocery store—one of those family enterprises....I worked my way through college and to a great extent through law school. And then, in 1940, probably the best thing that ever happened to me happened, I married Pat—sitting over here. We had a rather difficult time after we were married, like so many of the young couples who may be listening to us. I practiced law; she continued to teach school. I went into the service."

The Respectable Cloth Coat

"Now what have I earned since I went into politics? Well, here it is—I jotted it down, let me read the notes. First of all I've had my salary as a Congressman and as a Senator....I have made an average of approximately $1,500 a year from nonpolitical speaking engagements and lectures. And then, fortunately, we've inherited a little money....

"What did we do with this money? What do we have today to show for it? This will surprise you, because it is so little, I suppose, as standards generally go, of people in public life. First of all, we've got a house in Washington, which cost $41,000 and on which we owe $20,000.

"We have a house in Whittier, California, which cost $13,000 and on which we owe $10,000....I have just $4,000 in life insurance, plus my G. I. policy which I've never been able to convert...I have no life insurance whatever on Pat. I have no life insurance on our two youngsters, Patricia and Julie. I own a 1950 Oldsmobile car. We have our furniture. We have no stocks and bonds of any type. We have no interest of any kind, direct or indirect, in any business."

"It isn't very much but Pat and I have the satisfaction that every dime that we've got is honestly ours. Pat doesn't have a mink coat.

But she does have a respectable Republican cloth coat. And I always tell her that she'd look good in anything."

I'm Keeping Checkers

"One other thing I probably should tell you because if I don't they'll probably be saying this about me, too, we did get something—a gift—after the election. A man down in Texas heard Pat on the radio mention the fact that our two youngsters would like to have a dog. And, believe it or not, the day before we left on this campaign trip we got a message from Union Station in Baltimore saying they had a package for us. We went down to get it. You know what it was?

"It was a little cocker spaniel dog in a crate that he sent all the way from Texas. Black and white spotted. And our little girl—Trisha, the six-year-old—named it Checkers. And you know, the kids love the dog and I just want say this right now, that regardless of what they say about it, we're gonna keep it."

Just a Common Fellow

"It's fine that a man like Governor Stevenson who inherited a fortune from his father can run for president. But I also feel that it's essential in this country of ours that a man of modest means can also run for president. Because, you know, remember Abraham Lincoln, you remember what he said: "God must have loved the common people—he made so many of them."

I'm a Fighter, Not a Quitter

"Now, let me say this: I know that this is not the last of the smears. In spite of my explanation tonight other smears will be made; others have been made in the past. And the purpose of the smears, I know, is this—to silence me, to make me let up.

"Well, they just don't know who they're dealing with....And as far as this is concerned, I intend to continue the fight....because, you see, I love my country. And I think my country is in danger."

Help Me Decide

"And, now, finally, I know that you wonder whether or not I am going to stay on the Republican ticket or resign. Let me say this: I don't believe that I ought to quit because I'm not a quitter. And, incidentally, Pat's not a quitter. After all, her name was Patricia

Financial whiz: Rock star Mick Jagger went to the London School of Economics for 2 years.

Ryan and she was born on St. Patrick's Day, and you know the Irish never quit.

"But the decision, my friends, is not mine....I am submitting to the Republican National Committee tonight through this television broadcast, the decision which it is theirs to make.

"Let them decide whether my position on the ticket will help or hurt. And I am going to ask you to help them decide. Wire and write the Republican National Committee whether you think I should stay on or whether I should get off. And whatever their decision is, I will abide by it.

"But just let me say this last word. Regardless of what happens I'm going to continue this fight. I'm going to campaign up and down America until we drive the crooks and the Communists and those that defend them out of Washington. And remember, folks, Eisenhower is a great man. Believe me. He's a great man. And a vote for Eisenhower is a vote for what's good for America."

THE REACTION

When the speech was over, Nixon was depressed—he was sure his political career was over. "I loused it up and I'm sorry," he told his aides. "It was a flop."

But when he arrived at his hotel, the phones were going crazy with pro-Nixon calls. Telegrams supporting him poured into Republican headquarters all over the country. Ike wired Nixon: "Your presentation was magnificent." Even movie mogul Darryl F. Zanuck (who knew good acting when he saw it) called to tell Nixon, "It was the most tremendous performance I've ever seen." Hundreds of thousands of cards and telegrams were received; Nixon flew to Wheeling, West Virginia, to meet Ike and officially rejoin the ticket. Eisenhower rushed to Nixon's plane, and the VP candidate burst into tears, "the most poignant photo of the campaign."

The success of the speech, says one historian, "sent the Republican campaign soaring, establishing Nixon as a national figure and the best-known, largest-crowd-drawing vice presidential candidate in history." Nixon's career was saved, making his election to the presidency—and Watergate—possible two decades later.

The average American spends less than two hours a day with his or her family.

SPACED OUT

Some people who claim to have seen UFOs seem completely off their rockers. Others seem more credible. Here are five real-life "sightings." Did they really see UFOs...or are they just making it up? You decide.

The Place: Gulf Breeze, Florida, November 1987

The Sighting: "Four-foot-tall gray aliens who sometimes speak Spanish."

Background: Ed Walters (a Gulf Breeze developer) and his wife, Frances (president of the local PTA), claim to have had repeated encounters with the Spanish-speaking space aliens over several months in 1987. In March 1990, the couple wrote a book, *The Gulf Breeze Sightings*, that chronicles their experiences.

The Place: Greece, 1979

The Sighting: Space aliens that "looked like fetuses wearing wrap-around sunglasses."

Background: Joseph Ostrom, an advertising executive, was honeymooning with his wife in Greece. One evening, he says, their hotel room "filled with an orangish-red light," and a large alien (wearing a silver suit) led him to the roof of the hotel. His wife stayed behind. Suddenly, a turquoise ray-beam pulled him into the space ship that was hovering overhead. The aliens on the ship examined him, but he didn't mind. "When they did their exam, I felt love and support. It was as if we knew each other." The aliens hypnotized Ostrom to forget the experience, and he did. But several years later he visited an Earthling hypnotist, and the memories came flooding back, changing his life forever.

After a second hypnosis, Ostrom quit his job and moved to Colorado. Today he makes his living conducting New Age workshops and writing. He is the author of the book *You and Your Aura.*

The Place: Mundrabilla, Australia, 1988

The Sighting: A "huge bright glowing object."

Background: Fay Knowles and her three sons were driving along Eyre Highway when their car was sucked into the air. One of the sons told reporters, "we were doing about 68 miles per hour when it came over us and suddenly lifted the car off the road. We felt the thump on the roof and then it started lifting us. We were frightened and began to yell, but our voices had changed." Then the car was violently dropped back to earth. The shock of the landing blew out one of the rear tires; police officers who later inspected the car said the roof had been damaged and that the car was covered inside and out with "a thick layer of black ash."

Several other UFO sightings were reported the same night—some more than 100 miles away. An airplane flying overhead saw a bright light hovering nearby; a truck driver on the same highway also reported being followed; and a fishing trawler spotted a UFO from offshore. Police officials told reporters they were taking the multiple sightings "seriously."

The Place: Somewhere near the Martian moon Phobos, 1989

The Sighting: A "mysterious...long, faintly aerodynamic shaped pencil-like object with round ends."

Background: On March 25, 1989, the unmanned Soviet space probe Phobos transmitted a photograph to Earth of a strange object that appeared to have darted into the range of the probe's camera. According to news reports, immediately after transmitting the photograph, the Soviet probe stopped transmitting signals back to Earth and "inexplicably disappeared." It has been missing ever since. Marina Popovich, a top Soviet test pilot, displayed the photograph at a UFO convention and explained that the probe's "encounter" and last photograph could be explained either as a legitimate UFO sighting, or the last, faulty transmission of a malfunctioning camera system.

The Place: Mount Vernon, Missouri, 1984

The Sighting: Aliens kidnapping cows.

Background: One morning Paula Watson, a Mount Vernon resident, witnessed space aliens kidnapping cows near her house. Later in the day while canning vegetables in her basement, she noticed a "silvery alien with large eyes" peeking at her through the basement window. She tried to speak to the alien, but it backed away and she fell asleep. The next thing Watson knew she was inside the alien's spaceship being examined. "I was standing up on a white table and the...alien was running his hands down my body, scanning my body." Watson was later returned to Earth unharmed.

THE SEARCH FOR AMELIA EARHART

Was she the victim of a fuel shortage, a bad navigator, or the Japanese military? America's most famous aviatrix vanished on July 2, 1937. Now, over 60 years later, we may be close to finding out what really happened to her.

BACKGROUND

She was the best-known—and perhaps the greatest—female aviator in American history...which is all the more remarkable because of the age in which she lived. Born in 1897, Amelia Mary Earhart began her flying career in 1921, at a time when few women had careers of any kind and had only won the right to vote a few years earlier.

She took her first flying lessons at the age of 24, and, after 2½ hours of instruction, told her teacher, "Life will be incomplete unless I own my own plane." By her 25th birthday she'd saved enough money working at her father's law firm, as a telephone company clerk, and hauling gravel, to buy one. Within another year she set her first world record, becoming the first pilot to fly at 14,000 feet.

In 1928 Earhart became the first woman to fly across the Atlantic Ocean when she flew with pilot Wilmer Stultz. Ironically, she was asked to make the flight merely because she was a woman, not because of her flying talent. Charles Lindbergh had already made the first solo transatlantic flight in 1927, and Stultz was looking for a way of attracting attention to his flight. So he brought Earhart along...as a passenger.

That was the first—and last—frivolous flying record she would ever set. In 1930 she set the speed record for women (181 mph); in 1932 she became the first woman to fly solo across the Atlantic; on another flight became the first woman to fly solo across the continental United States; and in 1935 became the first pilot of either gender to fly from Hawaii to the U.S. mainland. (She also set several speed and distance records during her career.) By the mid-1930s, "Lady Lindy" was as famous as Charles Lindbergh. But her greatest flying attempt lay ahead of her. In 1937 she tried to circumnavigate the globe along the equator.

She never made it.

THE FINAL FLIGHT

Earhart described her round-the-world flight as "the one last big trip in her." Taking off from Oakland, California, on May 21, 1937, she and her navigator, Frederick Noonan, flew more than 3/4 of the way around the world, making stops in South America, Africa, the Middle East, Asia, and the South Pacific. But when they landed in New Guinea on June 28, the most difficult part of the journey lay ahead: the 2,556-mile flight from New Guinea to Howland Island, a "tiny speck" of an island in the middle of the Pacific. It would be difficult to find even in the best conditions.

Monitoring the flight from Howland Island was the Coast Guard cutter *Itasca*. The *Lady Lindy*, Amelia's airplane, rolled off the runway at 10:22 a.m. on July 2. She remained in contact with the radio operator in New Guinea for seven hours, then was out of contact until well after midnight.

- Finally, at 2:45 a.m., the Itasca picked up her first radio transmission. Another short message was picked up at 3:45 a.m.: "Earhart. Overcast."
- At 4:00 a.m., the *Itasca* radioed back: "What is your position? Please acknowledge." There was no response.
- At 4:43 a.m., she radioed in again, but her voice was too faint to pick up anything other than "partly cloudy."
- The next signal was heard at 6:14 a.m., 15 minutes before the plane's scheduled landing at Howland. She asked the *Itasca* to take a bearing on the signal, so that Noonan could plot their position. The signal was too short and faint to take a bearing. At 6:45 a.m., Earhart radioed a second time to ask for a bearing, but the signal again was too short.
- A more ominous message was received at 7:42 a.m.: "We must be on you but cannot see you but gas is running low. Been unable to reach you by radio. We are flying at altitude one thousand feet. Only one half hour gas left." One radio operator described Earhart's voice as "a quick drawl like from a rain barrel." She was lost, panicking, and nearly out of fuel. She would radio two more times before 8:00 a.m. asking the Itasca to take a bearing, but each time her signals were too weak.

The average person sweats 2½ quarts of water a day.

• Her next message was received at 8:44 a.m.—a half hour past the time she predicted her fuel would run out: "We are on the line of position 156-157. Will repeat message....We are running north and south." Operators described her voice as "shrill and breathless, her words tumbling over one another." That was the last confirmed message she would broadcast.

Then Amelia Earhart vanished.

UNANSWERED QUESTION: WHAT WENT WRONG?

Theory #1: Noonan's erratic behavior and faulty navigation sent the plane off course, dooming it.

Suspicious Facts

• Noonan was an alcoholic. A former Pan Am pilot, he'd been fired from the airline because of his drinking problem. He claimed to have gotten his drinking under control, but during a stopover in Hawaii he'd gotten drunk in his hotel room. According to one reporter in Hawaii, Earhart didn't want him to continue with the flight.

• The episode in Hawaii may not have been the only one. During a stopover in Calcutta, Earhart reported to her husband that she was "starting to have personnel trouble," but that she could "handle the situation." Paul Collins, a friend of Earhart's, overheard the conversation. He took this to mean that Noonan had gotten drunk again. Whatever it meant, Earhart was still having "personnel trouble" when she phoned from New Guinea, the last stopover before she disappeared.

• Why would Earhart have used Noonan as her navigator in the first place? According to one theory, the reason was financial: unlike other navigators, "the reputed alcoholic would work for very little money."

Theory #2: Earhart herself was to blame. Despite her fame as America's premier aviatrix, according to many pilots who knew her, she was actually a poor pilot—and an even worse navigator—who was unfamiliar with the plane she was flying.

Suspicious Facts

• Earhart had very little experience flying the Lockheed Electra she used on the trip. It was her first twin-engine plane, "a powerful, complicated aircraft loaded with special equipment" that was different from any other plane she had owned. Even so, in the eyes of the pilots who trained her to fly it, she didn't spend enough time getting to know it.

• In fact, her round-the-world flight was delayed after she crashed the plane during takeoff on March 20. Paul Mantz, her mentor and trainer, blamed the accident on her, claiming she had "jockeyed" the throttle. Paul Capp, another pilot who knew her, described her as "an inept pilot who would not take the advice of experts."

• Earhart's skills as a Morse code operator were atrocious—even though Morse code, which could be transmitted in the worst of conditions, was the most reliable form of communication. Earhart preferred to transmit by voice, which required a much more powerful signal and was harder to intercept. (In fact, she preferred voice communication so much that partway through the flight she abandoned some of her Morse code radios and flew the rest of the trip without them. She also dumped a 250-foot-long trailing antenna, which made the remaining radios far less powerful.)

• Earhart was also a poor navigator. During the flight to the African coast her miscalculations set her 163 miles off course—a mistake that would have been deadly if the plane had been low on fuel. Some theorists speculate that if her navigation and Morse code skills had been better, she might have survived.

UNANSWERED QUESTION: WHAT HAPPENED?

Theory #1: Earhart ran out of fuel before sighting land, ditched her plane in the sea, and drowned.

Suspicious Facts

• This is the most popular theory...and it's supported by the fact that no conclusive proof has ever been found indicating what really happened. According to one newspaper report, "nothing has been found that can be traced irrefutably to the plane or its crew: nothing bearing a serial number, for example, such as the plane's engines or propellers, nor any numbered equipment known to belong to the aviators."

• However, the islands in many areas of the South Pacific are scattered with the wreckage of 1930s-era planes. A lot of the major sea battles of World War II were fought in the Pacific; many fighter

Esquire **magazine nominated Billy Carter "Primate of the Decade" in 1980.**

pilots ditched on nearby islands. This makes it next to impossible to confirm that any given piece of wreckage belonged to Earhart's plane, unless it contains a serial number or includes a personal effect of some kind.

Theory #2: Earhart was captured by the Japanese.

• According to this theory, Earhart and Noonan were using their flight as a cover for a number of reconnaissance flights over Japanese-held islands in the South Pacific. The Roosevelt administration believed that war with Japan was inevitable and may have asked Earhart to help gather intelligence information. Some theorists suggest that after one such flight over the Truck Islands, they got lost in a storm, ran out of fuel, and were forced to land on an atoll in the Marshall Islands (which at the time were controlled by Japan). Earhart and Noonan were captured, imprisoned, and eventually died in captivity.

Suspicious Facts

• In 1967 CBS reporter Fred Goerner met a California woman who claimed to have seen two captured Americans—one man and one woman, matching the descriptions of Noonan and Earhart—on the Japanese island of Saipan in 1937. Acting on the tip, Groener went to Saipan, where he found more than a dozen island natives who told similar stories about "American fliers who had been captured as spies," including one man who claimed to have been imprisoned in a cell next to an "American woman flyer."

• Fleet Admiral Chester W. Nimitz, commander of U.S. naval forces in the Pacific during the war, reportedly also believed that Earhart and Noonan had been captured and killed by the Japanese; in one statement in 1966 he said, "I want to tell you Earhart and her navigator did go down in the Marshalls and were picked up by the Japanese." The Japanese government denies the charge.

• Goerner believes that when the Marines recaptured Saipan in 1944, they unearthed Earhart and Noonan's bones and returned them to the United States. He thinks the bones were secretly turned over to the National Archives, which has kept them hidden away ever since. Why? The reason is as mysterious as the disappearance.

• Alternate theory: Joe Klass, author of *Amelia Earhart Lives*, also believes that Earhart was captured by the Japanese. But he argues that Earhart survived the war and may have even returned to the United States to live under an assumed name. According to his theory, the Japanese cut a deal with the United States to return Earhart safely after the war if the U.S. promised not to try Emperor Hirohito as a war criminal. The U.S. kept its promise, and Earhart was allowed to return home. She may have lived as long as the 1970s, protecting her privacy by living under an assumed name.

Theory #3: Earhart and Noonan crash-landed on a deserted island in the South Pacific, hundreds of miles off course from their original destination, where they died from exposure and thirst a few days later.

Suspicious Facts

• For three days after Earhart and Noonan disappeared, mysterious radio signals were picked up by ships looking for Earhart's plane. The signals were transmitted in English in a female voice; some radio operators familiar with Earhart's voice recognized it as hers. They were misunderstood at the time, but if they were indeed broadcast by Earhart, they gave several clues to her whereabouts.

• One signal said, "We are on the line of position 156–157"; another said, "Don't hold—with us—much longer—above water—shut off." Others had similar messages. At the end of the three days, the signals abruptly stopped.

• If those signals were indeed sent by Earhart, she must have landed *somewhere* to have been able to broadcast them. Nikumaroro Island, 350 miles north of Howland Island, is a likely candidate for the crash site. The mysterious broadcasts offer several clues:

✓ Nikumaroro is one of the few islands within range of Earhart's plane—and it was in their "line of position 156–157."

✓ One of the last transmissions described a "ship on a reef south of equator." For years afterward researchers assumed that the "ship" being described in the transmission was Earhart's plane. But perhaps it wasn't: one of Nikumaroro's most prominent landmarks is a large shipwreck off the south shore of the island—four degrees south of the equator.

✓ Why were those final broadcasts separated by hours of silence? For more than 40 years it was assumed that they were broadcast at random intervals. But in the late 1980s, Thomas Gannon and Thomas Willi, two retired military navigators, proposed a theory: Nearly out of fuel, Earhart and Noonan landed on a part of the island's coral reef that was above sea level only during low tide. This meant that they could only broadcast during low tide, when the radio's batteries weren't flooded and the plane's engine could be used to recharge them.

✓ To test their theory, Gannon and Willi compared the times the signals were broadcast to a chart listing high and low tides on Nikumaroro Island on the week of the disappearance. All but one of the signals were broadcast during Nikumaroro's low tide.

Other Evidence

• In 1960 Floyd Kilts, a retired Coast Guard carpenter, told the *San Diego Tribune* that while assigned to the island in 1946, one of the island's natives told him about a female skeleton that had been found on the island in the late 1930s. According to the story, the skeleton was found alongside a pair of American shoes and a bottle of cognac—at a time when no Americans lived on the island.

When the island's magistrate learned of the skeleton, he remembered the story about Earhart and decided to turn the bones over to U.S. authorities. So he put the bones in a gunnysack and set sail with a group of native islanders for Fiji. But he died mysteriously en route—and the natives, fearing the bones, threw them overboard.

• Many aspects of this story were later confirmed; in 1938 Gerald Gallagher, the island's magistrate, *did* fall ill while en route to Fiji and died shortly after landing. But it is not known whether or not he had any bones with him when he died.

UPDATE

To date, Nikumaroro Island and nearby McKean Island (thought to be another possible crash site) have been searched extensively. In March 1992, a search team on Nikumaroro found a sheet of aircraft aluminum that they believed was from Earhart's plane...but that theory was later disproved. Other artifacts recovered include a cigarette lighter manufactured in the 1930s (Noonan was a smoker) and pieces from a size-9 shoe (Earhart wore size 9). But no conclusive evidence has been found. The search continues.

Uncle John's

SIXTH BATHROOM READER

First published October 1993

UNCLE JOHN'S NOTES:

This is my favorite of the three books.

While we were working on it, my brother Gordon commented that the articles ought to be edited better. I challenged him to do it himself... and to my surprise, he did. Then he taught *us* how to edit.

The result, from my point of view, is that we made a transition from trivia to stories. Sure, there are still plenty of bits o' information. But take a look at the piece on the Salem witches...or the Mona Lisa. They're very different from anything found in the previous book. Pages on subjects like Sibling Rivalry and Three Memorable Promotions are tighter and better-organized than before, too.

We added new formats and regular features in this book. Our "Q&A: Ask the Experts" is something we now include in every new edition. So is "Oops."

Some of our favorite pieces (we like a lot of this book, though):

- Henry Ford vs. the Chicago Tribune
- Myth-America: The U.S. Constitution
- Barnum's History Lesson
- The King of Farts
- Start Your Own Country

YOU'RE MY INSPIRATION

It's fascinating to see how many pop characters—real and fictional—are inspired by other characters. Here's a a handful of examples.

TINKER BELL. Walt Disney's animators reputedly gave her Marilyn Monroe's measurements. (Some say it was Betty Grable's.)

JAFAR, the Grand Vizier. The villain in the 1993 animated film *Aladdin*—described by the director as a "treacherous vizier...who seeks the power of the enchanted lamp to claim the throne for his own greedy purposes"—was inspired by Nancy Reagan. The Sultan, a doddering, kindly leader, was inspired by Nancy's husband.

THE EMPEROR in the *Star Wars* movies. In early drafts of the *Star Wars* scripts, George Lucas portrayed the emperor as "an elected official who is corrupted by power and subverts the democratic process." Lucas modeled him after Richard Nixon.

MICK JAGGER. Studied the way Marilyn Monroe moved, and learned to mimic her onstage.

THE STATUE OF LIBERTY. The face of Miss Liberty, sculpted by Frederic Auguste Bartholdi, was inspired by his mother. Ironically, although the statue has welcomed immigrants to New York City since 1886, Madame Bartholdi was "a domineering bigot."

DR. STRANGELOVE. Dr. Kissinger, I presume? According to Penny Stallings in *Flesh & Fantasy*, "[Director] Stanley Kubrick... made a special trip to Harvard to meet Dr. Henry Kissinger while researching the title role for his screen adaptation of *Dr. Strangelove*."

DR. JEKYL & MR. HYDE. Inspired by Dr. Horace Wells, celebrated inventor of modern anesthetics. He got hooked on ether and went mad; he was jailed for throwing acid in a woman's face while under its effects.

William Moulton Marston, creator of Wonder Woman, also invented the polygraph.

FAMILIAR PHRASES

Here are the origins of some well-known sayings.

A LOOSE CANNON

Meaning: Dangerously out of control.

Origin: On old-time warships, cannons were mounted on "wheeled carriages." When they weren't being used, they were tied down. "Now imagine a warship rolling and pitching in a violent gale." A gun breaks loose and starts rolling around the ship—"a ton or so of metal on wheels rolling unpredictably about the deck, crippling or killing any sailor unlucky enough to get in the way and perhaps smashing through the ship's side. Human loose cannons are equally dangerous to their associates and to bystanders." (From *Loose Cannons and Red Herrings*, by Robert Claiborne)

DYED IN THE WOOL

Meaning: Dedicated, committed, uncompromising.

Origin: From the textile trade. "It was discovered that yarn that's dyed 'in the wool'—before being woven—retained its color better than yarn that was dyed 'in the piece,' i.e. after being woven." So if something's dyed-in-the-wool, it's unlikely to change. (From *Getting to the Roots*, by Martin Manser)

GET YOUR DUCKS LINED UP IN A ROW

Meaning: Get organized, ready for action.

Origin: Refers to setting up bowling pins—which were called *duck-pins* in early America, because people thought they looked like ducks.

FIRST RATE

Meaning: The very best.

Origin: "In the 1600s a system for rating British naval ships according to their size and strength was developed. There were six different ratings, with a warship of the first rate being the largest and most heavily armed and one of the sixth rate being considerably smaller and having far fewer guns." The general public picked up the phrase right away, using it for anything topnotch. (From *Why You Say It*, by Webb Garrison)

Unemployment stat: Nevada has more out-of-work dancers than any other state.

START YOUR OWN COUNTRY

Ever wondered what it'd be like to be king—or president—of your own country? Here are some people who found out.

ATLANTIS

Founding Father: J. L. Mott, a Danish sea captain

History: In 930 A.D., Leif Ericson, a Viking explorer, discovered some Caribbean islands he mistook for remnants of the lost continent of Atlantis. In 1934, claiming to be Ericson's descendant, Mott declared himself the rightful heir to the islands, which he could not locate but believed "were somewhere near Panama." He drafted a one-page constitution and began issuing passports and triangle-shaped postage stamps.

What Happened: The International Postal Union refused to recognize Mott's postage stamps. Then, in 1936, Mott was almost arrested for trying to enter the United States using an Atlantis passport. By 1954 the elusive country had been renamed the Empire of Atlantis and Lemuria. Despite the country's fancy new name, however, all attempts to actually *locate* it have failed.

GRANBIA

Founding Father: Andrew Richardson, a Liverpool postal worker

History: In the 1970s, Richardson declared his semi-detached flat to be the independent nation of Granbia (the rest of the building remained a part of the United Kingdom).

What Happened: He lost interest, and the apartment reverted to England by default.

NEW ATLANTIS

Founding Father: Leicester Hemingway, little brother of author Ernest Hemingway

History: In 1964 he built an 8-by-30-foot floating bamboo platform seven miles off the coast of Jamaica, anchoring it to the ocean floor with a Ford engine block. "I can stand on the platform, walk around on it, and salute the flag, all of which I do periodically,"

Hemingway bragged to reporters. "There are no taxes here, because taxes are for people not smart enough to start their own countries."

What Happened: Part of the country was destroyed by fishermen in search of scrap wood; the rest sank in a storm.

HUTT RIVER PROVINCE PRINCIPALITY

Founding Father: "Prince" Leonard George Casely, an Australian wheat farmer

History: When the Western Australia Wheat Quota Board limited the amount of wheat he could grow in 1969, Casely and his 18,500-acre farm seceded. He designed his own national flag and motto, printed his own money, and set up his own parliament.

What Happened: Australia refused to recognize his sovereignty, so in 1977 he declared war. Nothing came of it—he backed down two days later and re-established diplomatic relations. Casely claims he pays no Australian taxes, but admits he makes payments to the Australian government as an "international courtesy."

ISLE OF THE ROSES

Founding Father: Giorgio Rosa, an Italian engineering professor

History: Rosa built a tower in the Adriatic Sea large enough to contain a bar, restaurant, and post office, and declared independence from Italy.

What Happened: The Italian government ignored him at first—but after a while they invaded the tower and blew it up.

SOLAR ATLANTIC EMPIRE

Founding Father: David Owen, a writer for the *Atlantic Monthly*

History: Owen wanted to form his own country but couldn't find any available land. So he took possession of the sun, one of the last unclaimed territories in the solar system. He backed up his claim by writing a letter to the U.S. State Department asking for official recognition. "The sun should now be referred to as the Solar Atlantic Empire," he wrote, "and I, henceforth, will be known as Lord High Suzerain of Outer Space."

What Happened: The State Department wrote back saying that it was unable to consider his application.

The Columbia University football team's mascot, Leo the Lion, inspired the MGM lion.

FAMOUS FOR 15 MINUTES

Here it is again—our feature based on Andy Warhol's prophetic comment that "in the future, everyone will be famous for 15 minutes." Here's how a few people are using up their allotted quarter-hour.

THE STAR: Angelyne (she won't tell anyone her real name)
THE HEADLINE: *Blonde Bimbo's Billboards Bring Big Bonus*
WHAT HAPPENED: In 1981 Angelyne—an out-of-work busty blonde—began posting billboards of herself all over L.A. (they simply said *Angelyne*, and listed a phone number) and distributing hot-pink press releases (describing her as "a living icon, Hollywood billboard queen, the new Love Goddess of the Future!") from her pink Corvette. Later she had an 85-foot-high likeness of herself painted on the side of a building at Hollywood and Vine.

The result: She made more than 250 media appearances, including bit parts in films like *Earth Girls Are Easy* and *L.A. Story*. Her billboard appeared in the opening montage of "Moonlighting" and in an issue of *National Geographic*.

THE AFTERMATH: She never made it as a sex symbol, but has come to represent, as one writer put it, "raw fame, unsullied by any known talent, charm, or accomplishments." She doesn't mind. "I'm the first person in the history of Hollywood to be famous for doing nothing," she says, and adds: "I really don't want to be famous for being an actress. I just want to be famous for the magic I possess."

THE STAR: Larry Villella
THE HEADLINE: *14-Year-Old Chips in to Cut Deficit*
WHAT HAPPENED: In February 1993, President Clinton was trying to drum up support for his "deficit-reduction plan." So Larry Villella, a 14-year-old from Fargo, North Dakota, sent the White House $1,000 (money he earned watering trees) to help pay it off.

Somehow, the media found out about Larry's check *before* it got to Washington—and every U.S. news service reported it as a major story. Larry was an instant celebrity. He was invited to appear on network TV talk shows, where he told interviewers his story—and

General Douglas MacArthur's mother dressed him in skirts until he was eight years old.

got a chance to plug a tree-watering gizmo he'd invented.

THE AFTERMATH: He inspired people all over the U.S. One San Francisco man even sent the White House 375 lbs. of coins (about $500) he'd been saving. As for Larry's check: Clinton sent it back with a note that said: "I am very impressed with your concern...but I cannot accept your money." (Bonus: Bill Cosby sent Larry $2,000 as "a thank-you on behalf of the American people.")

THE STAR: Keron Thomas, a 16-year-old New York student

THE HEADLINE: *New York Youth Takes A-Train on Joyride*

WHAT HAPPENED: On May 8, 1993, a man carrying a set of motorman's tools and a Transit Authority identification signed in at New York City's subway trainyard. "I'm the substitute man," he said. "Got anything for me?" They did—an A train.

The only problem: he wasn't the substitute man—and wasn't even a transit employee. He was Keron Thomas, a high school sophomore.

Thomas drove his train the length of Manhattan and all the way to Queens, carrying an estimated 2,000 passengers and making 85 stops along the way (he was even on *schedule*). The trip was so uneventful that he probably would have gotten away with it...until he took a turn too fast and set off the emergency brakes. He escaped before they learned his true identity, but investigators arrested him two days later.

THE AFTERMATH: He pled guilty to three misdemeanors and was sentenced to three years' probation. Why such a light sentence? As *The New York Times* said, authorities were "wary of punishing a folk hero." As he left the courtroom, he declared: "I'm going to be a train engineer."

THE STAR: Don Calhoun

THE HEADLINE: *Lucky Fan Hits $1 Million Shot in Chicago*

WHAT HAPPENED: On April 14, 1993, a 23-year-old office supply salesman named Don Calhoun got a free ticket to an NBA game between the Miami Heat and the Chicago Bulls.

As Calhoun headed for his seat at the game, someone told him he'd been picked to take the "Million Dollar Shot" (a promotion sponsored by Coca-Cola and a local restaurant chain). He'd get to

A married man is four times more likely to die during sex if his partner isn't his wife.

shoot a basket. The prize: $1 million. Eighteen people had already tried and failed. (Why was he picked? *His shoes:* the Bulls marketing representative loved his yellow suede hiking boots.)

At first he didn't want to do it—he even suggested that his friend make the shot instead. But the Bulls representative insisted. "I thought she was crazy," Calhoun told reporters. "But she ran after me, so I shrugged and said 'Okay.' " During a time-out early in the third period, he was brought to the floor. He took one dribble, launched the ball, and...basket!

THE AFTERMATH: Just about every sportscaster in the country carried Calhoun's Cinderella story on the news that night. He also did radio interviews, TV shows, even NBC's "Today" show. But a few days later, the bubble burst: It turned out Calhoun had played 11 games of college basketball, and the rules stipulated that no one who'd played in college could participate. But the ensuing publicity was so bad that Coke, the owner of the Bulls, and the restaurant all assured him he'd get his money anyway.

THE STAR: Holden Hollom

THE HEADLINE: *Frisco Cabbie Nabs Runaway Crook*

WHAT HAPPENED: On a June night in 1989, Hollom, a 51-year-old San Francisco cabbie (and former stunt driver) was driving a fare up Market Street, when he saw someone knock down a woman and steal her purse. He gave chase, yelling to his surprised passenger, "You're riding for free!"

He cornered the purse snatcher (a 212-lb. ex-convict) in an alley. To keep him from running away, he pinned him to the wall with his cab bumper. Newspapers all over the country reported the citizen's arrest as an example of what's *right* about America, and lauded Hollom for getting involved. He appeared on every major talk show, including "Larry King" and "Donahue."

AFTERMATH: The crook had to undergo three operations on his legs, and in 1992 sued Hollom for using excessive force. When he won, and was awarded $24,500 by a jury, the verdict got as much attention as the original incident. It generated more than $100,000 from outraged sympathizers who felt the cabbie had been shafted. (The verdict was later overturned.) Fleeting fame: Hollom later ran for the S.F. Board of Supervisors, but came in 19th in a field of 26 candidates.

New Hampshire allows boys to be married at 14 and girls at 13—with parental permission.

WHAT DOES IT SAY?

Here's a game where the position *of words and letters is part of the sentence. See if you can figure out what these say. If you need a sample answer, check out the Hints at the end of the last column. Answers on page 661.*

1. A letter was addressed to:
WOOD
JOHN
MASS
Who got it; where did they live?

2. I thought I heard a noise outside, but it was
ALL 0

3. Let's have STANDING
AN

4. LOOK
LOOK U LOOK
LOOK

5. "Remember," she said to the group,
WE WESTAND FALL

6. "Why'd he do that?" Jesse asked. "Well, son," I said, he's a DKI

7. Texas? I love
S P A C E S

8. "Drat! My watch broke." Time to get it RE-RE

9. "I remember the 1960s," she said, GNIKOOL

10. No, we're not living together anymore. It's a
L E G A L

11. Haven't seen him in a while. He's
FAR HOME

12. Careful, I warned my sister. He's a WOWOLFOL

13. "How do I get out of here?" he asked. I said, "Just calm down and put the
RAC

14. I tried to teach her, but no luck. I guess she's a
DLIHC

15. When it's raining...
AN UMBRELLA
SHEME

HINTS (if you need them):

- The answer to #1 is John Underwood, Andover Mass (JOHN under WOOD and over MASS)
- Answer to #14: I guess she's a *backward child.* (DLIHC is child spelled backward.)

A FOOD IS BORN

These foods are fairly common, but you've probably never wondered where they come from, have you? Doesn't matter. We'll tell you anyway.

CAMPBELL SOUP. Arthur Dorrance and his nephew, Dr. John Thompson Dorrance, took over the Campbell canning company when its founder, Joseph Campbell, retired in 1894. A few years later they perfected a method of condensing tomato soup—which made it cheaper to package and ship—but they couldn't decide on a design for the label. That Thanksgiving, company employee Herberton L. Williams went to a football game between Cornell and the University of Pennsylvania. He was impressed with Cornell's new red and white uniforms—and suggested to his bosses that they use those colors on the label. They did.

WHEATIES. Invented in 1921 by a Minneapolis health spa owner who fed his patients homemade bran gruel to keep them regular and help them lose weight. One day he spilled some on the stove, and it hardened into a crust. He was going to throw it out, but decided to eat it instead. To his surprise, the flakes he scraped off the stove tasted better than the stuff in the pot...so he made more and showed them to a friend at the Washburn Crosby Company (predecessor to General Mills). People at the company liked the flakes too, but didn't like the way they crumbled. So they came up with a better one using wheat. Once they had a flake they were satisfied with, they held a company-wide contest to name the product. Jane Bausman, the wife of a company executive, suggested *Wheaties*.

PEPPERIDGE FARM. One of Margaret Rudkin's sons suffered from severe asthma, a condition that became worse when he ate processed food. She couldn't find any bread that didn't make him ill, so in 1935 she started baking him stone-ground whole wheat bread. One day she brought a loaf to the boy's doctor; he liked it so much he began recommending it to other patients. After building up a small mail-order business to local asthmatics and allergy-sufferers, she expanded her customer base to include people who *weren't* sick—and named her company after the family's 125-acre farm in Connecticut, *Pepperidge Farm*.

That's progress: Jimmy Carter was the first president born in a hospital.

LOG CABIN SYRUP. Invented in 1887 by P. J. Towle, a St. Paul, Minnesota, grocer who wanted to combine the flavor of maple syrup with the affordability of sugar syrup. He planned to name his creation after his boyhood hero, Abraham Lincoln, but there were already so many Lincoln products that he named it after the president's birthplace instead. It sold in tin containers shaped like log cabins until World War II, when metal shortages forced the company to switch to glass bottles.

BROWN 'N SERVE ROLLS. Invented accidentally by Joe Gregor, a Florida baker and volunteer firefighter. One morning the fire alarm sounded while Gregor was baking some rolls, and he had to pull them out of the oven half-baked to go fight the fire. He was about to throw them out when he got back, but he decided to finish baking them, to see if they were still good. They were.

SANKA. Dr. Ludwig Roselius was a turn-of-the-century European coffee merchant looking for a way to decaffeinate coffee beans without harming the aroma and flavor. He wasn't having much luck—until someone gave him a "ruined" consignment of coffee beans that had been swamped with seawater while in transit. The damaged beans behaved differently than regular beans, and inspired Roselius to begin a new round of experiments with them. He eventually succeeded in removing 97% of the caffeine while keeping the natural coffee flavor. He named his new product *Sanka*, a contraction of the French "*sans caffeine*."

FOLGER'S COFFEE. James Folger and his older brothers, Edward and Harry, planned on joining the California Gold Rush in 1849—but when they got to San Francisco, they only had enough money for two of them to continue on to the Gold Country. James had to stay behind; he eventually decided to go into the coffee business. Today people take roasted coffee for granted—but in the 1840s most people roasted coffee themselves in their own homes. When Folger thought of his brothers in the Gold Country and how difficult it was for them to roast their own beans, he decided to roast his beans before selling them.

Random thought: "History is a set of lies agreed upon."

—*Napoleon Bonaparte*

ACCORDING TO SHAW...

A few thoughts from George Bernard Shaw, the curmudgeon who was considered the greatest English playwright since Shakespeare.

"I often quote myself; it adds spice to my conversation."

"Youth is a wonderful thing. What a crime to waste it on children."

"When a stupid man is doing something he is ashamed of, he always declares that it is his duty."

"A perpetual holiday is a good working definition of hell."

"A government which robs Peter to pay Paul can always count on the support of Paul."

"I am a gentleman; I live by robbing the poor."

"England and America are two countries separated by the same language."

"If all economists were laid end to end they would not reach a conclusion."

"Life does not cease to be funny when people die any more than it ceases to be serious when people laugh."

"No man can be a pure specialist without being, in a strict sense, an idiot."

"There may be some doubt as to who are the best people to have in charge of children, but there can be no doubt that parents are the worst."

"We should all be obliged to appear before a board every five years and justify our existence...on pain of liquidation."

"The fickleness of the women whom I love is only equaled by the infernal constancy of the women who love me."

"The power of accurate observation is commonly called cynicism by those who have not got it."

"The trouble with her is that she lacks the power of conversation but not the power of speech."

"There is no satisfaction in hanging a man who does not object to it."

They have more to say: 29% of 18 to 24-year-olds talk in their sleep; 9% of people over 50 do.

APRIL FOOLS!

Why is April 1 a "fools' day"? The most plausible explanation is one we wrote in the first Bathroom Reader: *"Until 1564 it was a tradition to begin the New Year with a week of celebration, ending with a big party. But the calendar was different then; the New Year began on March 25, and the biggest party fell on April 1. In 1564 a new calendar made January 1 the New Year. People who forgot—or didn't realize—what had happened, and still showed up to celebrate on April 1, were called 'April fools.' "*

These days, most of the memorable April Fools' jokes are played by radio and TV stations. Here are a few recent classics.

PASTA FARMING

On April 1, 1966, the BBC broadcast a TV documentary on spaghetti-growing in Italy. Among the film's highlights: footage of Italian farmers picking market-ready spaghetti from "spaghetti plants." To the BBC's astonishment, British viewers accepted the news that Italy's "pasta farmers" had been able to fight off the "spaghetti weevil, which has been especially destructive recently."

HE'S BA-A-ACK

In 1992 National Public Radio's "Talk of the Nation" news show announced on April 1 that Richard Nixon had entered the race for president. They actually interviewed the "former president" (played by impressionist Rich Little) on the air. "I never did anything wrong," he announced, "and I won't ever do it again." Listeners actually called the show to comment. "Nixon is more trustworthy than Clinton," one remarked. "Nixon never screwed around with anyone's wife except his own. And according to some accounts, not even with her."

GRAVITATIONAL PULL

On April 1, 1976, a famous British astronomer told BBC radio audiences that since the planet Pluto would be passing close to Jupiter on April 1, the Earth's gravitational pull would decrease slightly for about 24 hours. He explained that listeners would feel the effect most if they jumped into the air at precisely 9:47 a.m. that morning. The BBC switchboard was jammed with listeners calling to say that the experiment had worked.

Gail Borden, inventor of condensed milk, also coined the phrase "Remember the Alamo!"

COLORFUL BROADCAST

In the 1970s, Britain's Radio Norwich announced on April 1 that it was experimenting with "color radio," and that the tests would affect the brilliance of tuning lights on radios at home. Some listeners actually reported seeing results: one complained that the experiment had affected the traffic lights in his area; another asked the station managers how much longer the bright colors he saw would be streaming out of his radio.

ANIMAL BEHAVIOR

On April 1, 1992, TV's Discovery Channel ran a "nature documentary" called "Pet Hates," actually a spoof of nature films by a British humorist posing as an animal expert. In the film the humorist criticized the animals for their "sexual excesses, appalling sense of hygiene and all-around stupidity"—and denounced them as "sex-crazed, bug-awful, foul-breathed, all-fornicating, all-urinating, disease-ridden, half-wit, furry, four-legged perverts."

DRIVING PRANK

One year a Paris radio station announced that from April 1 on, all Europe would begin driving on the left. Some drivers actually started driving on the left side of the road. A number of accidents resulted (no fatalities, though).

NEEDLING PEOPLE

In 1989 a Seattle TV station interrupted its regular April 1 broadcast with a report that the city's famous Space Needle had collapsed, destroying nearby buildings in the fall. The report included fake eyewitness accounts from the scene, which were punctuated with bogus updates from the studio newsroom. The "live" footage was so realistic that viewers jammed 911 lines trying to find out if their loved ones were safe. The station later apologized.

THE JOKE IS RED

Even the media of the former Soviet Union celebrates April Fools' Day. In 1992 the Moscow press printed stories claiming that gay rights activists had crossed the Atlantic Ocean in condoms, and that the Moscow City Council was planning a second subway system "in the interest of competition."

Model citizen: President Zachary Taylor never voted in a presidential election.

MYTH AMERICA

A few things you probably didn't know about the founding fathers who wrote the U.S. Constitution.

THE MYTH: The men who attended the Constitutional Convention in 1787 were a sober, well-behaved group. They showed up on time, stuck it out 'til the end, and were all business when it came to the important task at hand.

THE TRUTH: Not quite. According to historical documents found by researchers at the National Constitution Center in 1992:

• Nineteen of the 74 people chosen to attend the convention never even showed up. (At least one of them had a good excuse, though—William Blount of New York refused to make the horseback ride to Philadelphia because of hemorrhoids.)

• Of the 55 who *did* show up, only 39 signed the document. Twelve people left early, and 4 others refused to sign. "A lot of them ran out of money and had to leave because they were doing a lot of price gouging here," observes researcher Terry Brent. Besides, he adds, the hot weather and high humidity must have been murder on the delegates, who wore wool breeches and coats. "They must have felt like dying. Independence Hall must have smelled like a cattle barn."

• And how did the Founding Fathers unwind during this pivotal moment in our nation's history? By getting drunk as skunks. One document that survived is the booze bill for a celebration party thrown two days before the Constitution was signed on September 17, 1787. According to the bill, the 55 people at the party drank 54 bottles of Madeira, 60 bottles of claret, 8 bottles of whiskey, 22 bottles of port, 8 bottles of cider, 12 bottles of beer, and 7 large bowls of alcoholic punch. "These were really huge punch bowls that ducks could swim in," Brent reports. "The partiers were also serenaded by 16 musicians. They had to be royally drunk—they signed the Constitution on the 17th. On the 16th, they were probably lying somewhere in the streets of Philadelphia."

Important first: Dwight D. Eisenhower was the first president to make a hole-in-one in golf.

Q & A: ASK THE EXPERTS

Everyone's got a question or two they'd like answered—basic stuff, like "Why is the sky blue?" Here are a few of those questions, with answers from books by some of the nation's top trivia experts.

HOLY QUESTION

Q: *Why are manhole covers round?*

A: "So they can't be dropped *through* the manhole itself. Squares, rectangles, ovals, and other shapes could be positioned so they'd slip into the manhole. Round manhole covers rest on a lip that's smaller than the cover. So the size and shape keeps the manhole cover from falling in." (From *The Book of Answers*, by Barbara Berliner)

SHOE TIME

Q: *How and why did people start shining their shoes?*

A: "A high polish on shoes is a tradition passed down from the Spanish caballero (gentleman on horseback), whose shiny boots served notice that he rode his own horse and didn't walk along dusty roads with lesser men." (From *Do Elephants Swim?*, compiled by Robert M. Jones)

NIPPED IN THE BUD

Q: *Why do men have nipples?*

A: "Males actually have the anatomical equipment in place to provide milk, but it lies dormant unless stimulated by estrogen, the female hormone. Might men have suckled babies in the distant past? No one knows." (From *Why Do Men Have Nipples*, by Katherine Dunn)

PRUNY SKIN

Q: *Why does your skin get wrinkled when you soak for a long time in water?*

A: Normally, skin is water-resistant because of a "protective barrier of keratin," a protein made by the epidermis to keep moisture, bacteria, and other unwanted stuff out. But if skin is immersed in water for a long time, moisture gets through and "the cells in the epidermal layer…absorb water and swell. The enlarged cells cause the skin to pucker and wrinkle."

Luckily, they don't stay that way. "Several minutes after toweling off, the water in the skin cells evaporates, and the cells return to their normal shape and size. Otherwise, we would all be walking around looking like the California raisins." (From *The Book of Totally Useless Information*, by Don Voorhees)

EGGS-ACTLY!

Q: *Why don't people ever eat turkey eggs?*

A: "They don't taste good. More precisely, they don't have as much water in them as chicken eggs. The next time you eat a couple of chicken eggs, think about how wet they are. But a turkey egg, if exposed to high heat, turns rubbery." (From *Why Things Are, Volume II*, by Joel Achenbach)

HALF-WIT?

Q: *Is the old saying true that "we only use 10% of our brains?"*

A: "No—you use every part of your brain. Not every area at the same time, of course; they all do different things at different times. At any given moment, only about 5% of your brain cells are actually firing—that is, working. So in one sense this is actually true. But as far as we know, there are no parts that never do *any*thing." (From *Know It All!*, by Ed Zotti)

EAT LIKE A BIRD

Q: *How do birds find worms underground?*

A: "When a bird stands on the ground near a worm that is crawling underneath, it can feel the earth's vibrations with its very sensitive feet. It will also cock its head to put into operation the low-frequency apparatus of its ears. Then, when it zeroes in on the victim, it pierces the earth with a sudden stab of its beak, grabs the worm, and pulls it out." (From *How Do Flies Walk Upside Down?*, by Martin M. Goldwyn)

The biggest state? Alaska is bigger than Texas and California *combined*.

PEOPLE-WATCHING

It's scary what behavior experts can predict about us. All it takes is a few studies...and they know more about what we'll to do in a situation than we *do. Following are the results from a few of those studies, including some from* The Book of You *by Bernard Asbell. Here's lookin' at you, kid!*

ON NONVERBAL COMMUNICATION...

A variety of factors affect the way we silently communicate with each other.

• For instance, one study shows that if you've been told that a person you're about to meet has a lot in common with you, you'll actually position yourself physically closer to that person than if you've been informed you're "opposites."

• According to another study, your nationality plays a role in how "touchy-feely" you are. For instance, over an hour long coffee break in a cafe...

—American friends will touch each other in conversation about twice.

—British friends generally won't touch each other at all.

—By comparison, the French can't keep their hands off each other; they average about 110 touches an hour.

—But Puerto Ricans were the most tactile in the study, with about 180 "touches" in the same period.

• Something else to remember, next time you find yourself chatting with someone you don't know: According to Asbell...

—"If you're a man, the farther you sit from the other person, (within a range of 2-10 feet), the more willing you are to talk intimately about yourself."

—"If you're a woman, the closer you sit together (within a range of 2-10 feet) the more willing you are to tell intimate details about yourself. "

—"Within that range of 2-10 feet (whether you're a man or a woman), you'll talk with a stranger longer and volunteer the most about intimate topics at a distance of 5 feet."

ON GIVING & LIVING...

• Want long life? A recent study of about 2,700 individuals found lower death rates among those who volunteered their time to a favorite charity or cause.

• Another interesting study in behavior had students watch a movie on Mother Teresa. The film depicted her administering to the needy and sick, bringing comfort and solace. Immediately following the film, researchers found in the students, a significant increase in immunoglobulin, an antibody that helps the body fight respiratory infections.

ON ROMANCE & DATING...

• The most common thing we all do when we want to be romantic is say "I love you" to our partner. Sweet...but not as effective as you might think. When people were asked "How you'd want your lover to treat you to romance" in a study, the most common answer was "lying around in front of a fire."

• Other choices included: "Taking a shower together" and "Walking on the beach." Ironically, hearing "I love you" came in twelfth.

Other people-watching facts:

• If you're a man and you get anxious about dating, chances are that male friendships are also cause for anxiety.

• First-date anxiety for a guy almost never centers around sex. It's usually worry about what to talk about, how to behave, and what to expect.

• First dates are tough for everyone, but if you're a guy, you're probably going to be a lot more uptight about the situation than the woman is.

• If it's any consolation, however, the chances are that if you're a man—even if you're uptight about an encounter—you probably like your body more than your date does hers. Studies show that men are generally more likely to see their bodies as attractive to women than woman are to see their bodies as attractive to men.

* * *

Thank goodness: "Things are more like they are now than they ever have been." —*President Gerald Ford*

COLORS

Colors have a lot more impact on our daily lives than you might think. Here are some things researchers have found out about people and color.

BLUE

• Blue has a tranquilizing effect. Bridges are often painted blue to discourage suicide attempts. And according to one report: "When schoolroom walls were changed from orange and white to blue, students' blood pressure levels dropped and their behavior and learning comprehension soared."

• Researchers say blue is the #1 color for women's sweaters, because women think men like it. (They're right; it's U.S. men's favorite color.)

RED

• Red is a stimulant that can cause "restlessness and insomnia" if it's used in bedrooms.

• According to marketing studies, red makes people oblivious to how much time is passing. That's why it's "the color of choice for bars and casinos."

• Women tend to prefer blue-toned reds, while men like yellowish reds. Businesses keep this in mind. For example: the Ford Mustang, which is targeted to men, is orange-red (called "Arrest-me" red at Ford); the Probe, targeted to women, is offered in more blue-red shades.

GREEN

• Because it reminds people of fields and foliage, green makes us feel secure. Researchers say it's a good color for bedrooms; and green kitchens reportedly make cooks more creative.

• Studies show that "people working in green environments get less stomachaches than people in areas where other colors predominate."

YELLOW

• It's the color most likely to stop traffic...or sell a house.

• But yellow also represents "caution or temporariness—so car rental agencies and taxis use it, but not banks."

• Too much yellow makes people anxious. "Babies cry more and temperamental people explode more in yellow rooms."

America's favorite colors: #1 is blue. Then red, green, white, pink, purple, and orange.

MISS PIGGY

Porcine words of wisdom from one of America's favorite pigs.

DIET TIPS

"Never eat anything at one sitting that you can't lift."

"Always use one of the new—and far more reliable—elastic measuring tapes to check on your waistline."

ARTICHOKES

"These things are just plain annoying...after all the trouble you go to, you get about as much actual 'food' out of eating an artichoke as you would from licking thirty or forty postage stamps. Have the shrimp cocktail instead."

PERFUME

"Perfume is a subject dear to my heart. I have so many favourites: Arome de Grenouille, Okéfénokée, Eau Contraire, Fume de Ma Tante, Blast du Past, Kermes, Je suis Swell, and Attention S'il Vous Plait, to name but a few."

TIPPING

"There are several ways of calculating the tip after a meal. I find that the best is to divide the bill by the height of the waiter. Thus, a bill of $12.00 brought by a six foot waiter calls for a $2.00 tip."

TRAVEL TIPS

"If you're traveling alone, beware of seatmates who, by way of starting a conversation, make remarks like, 'I just have to talk to someone—my teeth are spying on me' or 'Did you know that squirrels are the devil's oven mitts?' "

"Public telephones in Europe are like our pinball machines. They are primarily a form of entertainment and a test of skill rather than a means of communication."

HOTELS

"Generally speaking, the length and grandness of a hotel's name are an exact opposite reflection of its quality. Thus the Hotel Central will prove to be a clean, pleasant place in a good part of town, and the Hotel Royal Majestic-Fantastic will be a fleabag next to a topless bowling alley."

HATS

"Someone you like is wearing an ugly hat, and she asks you to give her your honest opinion of it: 'What a lovely chapeau! But if I may make one teensy suggestion? If it blows off, don't chase it.' "

Pigs killed off the dodo bird.

STRANGE LAWSUITS

These days, it seems that people will sue each other over practically anything. Here are a few real-life examples of unusual legal battles.

THE PLAINTIFF: Frank Zaffere, a 44-year-old Chicago lawyer

THE DEFENDANT: Maria Dillon, his 21-year-old ex-fiance

THE LAWSUIT: In June 1992—about two months before they were supposed to get married—Dillon broke off the engagement. Zaffere responded by suing her for $40,310.48 to cover his "lost courting expenses." In a letter sent to Dillon, he wrote, "I am still willing to marry you on the conditions herein below set forth: 1) We proceed with our marriage within 45 days of the date of this letter; 2) You confirm [that you]...will forever be faithful to me; 3) You promise...that you will never lie to me again about anything." He closed with: "Please feel free to call me if you have any questions or would like to discuss any of the matters discussed herein. Sincerely, Frank."

"He's trying to...make me say, 'OK Frank, I'll marry you,' " said Dillon. "But...I can't imagine telling my children as a bedtime story that Mommy and Daddy got married because of a lawsuit."

THE VERDICT: The case was dismissed.

THE PLAINTIFF: 27-year-old Scott Abrams

THE DEFENDANTS: The owners and managers of his apartment building

THE LAWSUIT: During an electrical storm in 1991, Abrams was sitting on the ledge of the apartment-building roof with his feet in a puddle of water. He was hit by lightning and suffered a cardiac arrest; fortunately, he was revived by a rescue squad. But in 1993 he filed a $2 million lawsuit charging the defendants with negligence. His reason: "They should have provided signs and brighter paint."

THE VERDICT: Pending.

Talk-talk: Americans make more than 350 billion phone calls a year.

THE PLAINTIFF: Ronald Askew, a 50-year-old banker from Santa Ana, California

THE DEFENDANT: His ex-wife, Bonnette

THE LAWSUIT: In 1991, after more than a decade of marriage, Bonnette admitted to her husband that although she loved him, she'd never really found him sexually attractive. He sued her for fraud, saying he "wouldn't have married her had he known her feelings."

THE VERDICT: Incredibly, he won. The jury awarded him $242,000 in damages.

THE PLAINTIFF: The family of 89-year-old Mimi Goldberg, a Jewish woman who died in 1991

THE DEFENDANT: The Associated Memorial Group, a Hawaiian firm that ran nine funeral homes

THE LAWSUIT: In 1993 Goldberg's body was shipped from the Nuuanu Mortuary in Hawaii to California. When the casket was opened at an Oakland synagogue, "the remains of a dissected fetal pig in a plastic bag" were found resting next to the body. A mortuary representative said the pig had been put there accidentally by an employee "whose wife was taking a class requiring the dissection of fetal pigs." The woman's family, horrified because Jewish religious law specifically bans pork, sued.

THE VERDICT: The family won $750,000. In addition, the funeral home was ordered to make a donation to the U.S. Holocaust Memorial, and print an apology in leading West Coast newspapers.

THE PLAINTIFF: Dimitri K. Sleem, a 38-year-old Yale graduate

THE DEFENDANT: Yale University

THE LAWSUIT: In April 1993, an old college friend called Sleem to read him the entry listed under his name in the 1993 Yale alumni directory. It said: "I have come to terms with my homosexuality and the reality of AIDS in my life. I am at peace." Sleem—who didn't have AIDS, wasn't gay, and was married with four children—filed a $5 million libel suit against Yale.

THE VERDICT: Still pending. Meanwhile, Yale hired a handwriting expert to find out who submitted the false statement.

In New Orleans, the soil is too wet for regular burials—so the dead are buried above ground.

PRIMETIME PROVERBS

TV comments about everyday life. From PrimeTime Proverbs, *by Jack Mingo and John Javna.*

ON GROWING UP

Robin [gazing at a female criminal's legs]: "Her legs sort of remind me of Catwoman's."

Batman: "You're growing up Robin, but remember: In crimefighting, always keep your sights high."

—*"Batman"*

ON LIFE

[As she folds her son's clothes] "There's got to be more to life that sittin' here watchin' 'Days of Our Lives' and foldin' your Fruit of the Looms."

—Mama, *"Mama's Family"*

Coach Ernie Pantusso: "How's life, Norm?"

Norm Peterson: "Ask somebody who's got one."

—*"Cheers"*

ON PSYCHIATRY

TV interviewer: "You mean, you ask forty dollars an hour and you guarantee nothing?"

Bob Hartley: "Well, I validate."

—*"The Bob Newhart Show"*

ON MENTAL HEALTH

Bob Hartley: "Howard, what do you do when you're upset?"

Howard Borden: "Well, I've got a method—it always works. I go into a dark room, open up all the windows, take off all my clothes, and eat something cold. No, wait a minute, I do that when I'm overheated. When I have a problem I just go to pieces."

—*"The Bob Newhart Show"*

[To an old flame] "Someday your Mr. Right will come along. And when he does, he's gonna be wearing a white coat and a butterfly net."

—Louie DePalma, *"Taxi"*

ON MASCULINITY

Ward Cleaver: "You know, Wally, shaving is just one of the outward signs of being a man. It's more important to try to be a man inside first."

Wally Cleaver: "Yeah sure, Dad."

—*"Leave It to Beaver"*

THE CURSE OF KING TUT

After Tutankhamen's tomb was unearthed in 1922, a number of people associated with the discovery died mysterious deaths. Was it coincidence...or was it a curse?

BACKGROUND King Tutankhamen reigned from about 1334 to 1325 B.C., at the height of ancient Egypt's glory. The "boy king" was only about 9 when he was crowned, and died mysteriously at the age of 18 or 19. He was buried beside other pharaohs in the Valley of the Kings, near the Nile River at Luxor, the capital of ancient Egypt.

THE DISCOVERY

King Tutankhamen's tomb remained undisturbed for more than 3,000 years until it was unearthed in November 1922 by Howard Carter, an amateur archeologist commissioned by the English nobleman Lord Carnarvon to find it. Carter's discovery was due largely to luck; having exhausted a number of other leads, he finally decided to dig in a rocky patch of ground between the tombs of three other pharaohs. Three feet under the soil he found the first of a series of 16 steps, which led down to a sealed stone door. Markings on the door confirmed that it was a royal tomb. Realizing what he had discovered, Carter ordered the steps buried again, and wired Lord Carnarvon in London to join him.

Three weeks later, Carnarvon arrived and digging resumed. The first stone door was opened, revealing a 30-foot-long passageway leading to a second stone door. Carter opened the second door and, peeking into the darkness with the light of a single candle, was greeted by an amazing sight—two entire rooms stuffed with priceless gold artifacts that had not seen the light of day for more than 30 centuries. The room was so crammed with statues, chariots, furniture, and other objects that it took two full months to catalog and remove items in the first room alone. Tutankhamen's body lay in a solid gold coffin in the next room; the gold coffin was itself encased inside three other coffins, which rested inside a huge golden shrine that took up nearly the entire room.

Beer wasn't sold in cans until 1935.

The discovery of the site was hailed as "the greatest find in the annals of archeology." Unlike other tombs, Tutankhamen's was almost completely undisturbed by graverobbers; its hundreds of artifacts provided a glimpse of ancient Egyptian cultural life that had never been seen before.

THE CURSE

But unearthing the treasures may have been a dangerous move—soon after the Tut discovery was announced, rumors about a curse on his tomb's defilers began to circulate. They weren't taken seriously—until Lord Carnarvon came down with a mysterious fever and died.

The curse gained credibility when word came from Lord Carnarvon's home in England at 1:50 a.m.—the exact moment of Lord Carnarvon's death—that his favorite dog had suddenly collapsed and died. And at *precisely* the same moment, Cairo was plunged into darkness, due to an unexplainable power failure.

Other Deaths: Over the next several years, a series of people associated with the Tut excavation died unexpectedly, often under mysterious circumstances. The dead in 1923 alone included Lord Carnarvon's brother, Col. Aubrey Herbert; Cairo archaeologist Achmed Kamal, and American Egyptologist William Henry Goodyear.

• The following year, British radiologist Archibald Reed died on his way to Luxor, where he planned to X-ray Tut's still-unopened coffin. Oxford archeologist Hugh Eveyln-White, who had dug in the necropolis at Thebes, also died in 1924.

• Edouard Neville, Carter's teacher, as well as George Jay-Gould, Carnarvon's friend, papyrus expert Bernard Greenfell, American Egyptologist Aaron Ember, and the nurse who attended to Lord Carnarvon all died in 1926. Ember's death was particularly spooky—he was attempting to rescue from his burning house a manuscript he had worked on for years: *The Egyptian Book of the Dead.*

• In 1929 Lord Carnarvon's wife, Lady Almina, died, as did John Maxwell, the Earl's friend and executor, and Carter's secretary, Richard Bethell, who was found dead in bed, apparently from circulatory failure, at the age of 35.

THE AFTERMATH

Fallout from the rumors of the curse continued for years, as did the string of mysterious deaths.

• As accounts of the deaths circulated, hysteria spread. In England, hundreds of people shipped everything they had that was even remotely Egyptian to the British Museum—including an arm from a mummy.

• The popularity of the curse legend led to a series of classic horror films: "The Mummy" (1932), starring Boris Karloff, and "The Mummy's Hand" (1940) and three sequels starring Lon Chaney, Jr.—"The Mummy's Tomb" (1942), "The Mummy's Ghost" and "The Mummy's Curse" (both 1944).

LAST WORDS

• Was the curse for real? Many prominent people insisted that it wasn't; they argued that the mortality rates of people associated with the Tutankhamen discovery and other finds were no higher than that of the general public. Dr. Gamal Mehrez, Director-General of the Egyptian Museum in Cairo, disputed the curse in an interview made several years after the discovery of Tut's tomb. "All my life," he said, "I have had to deal with pharaonic tombs and mummies. I am surely the best proof that it is all coincidence." Four weeks later he dropped dead of circulatory failure, as workers were moving Tutankhamen's gold mask for transport to London.

• For what it's worth, Lord Carnarvon's son, the sixth Earl of Carnarvon, accepts the curse at face value. Shortly after the fifth earl's burial, a woman claiming psychic powers appeared at Highclere Castle and warned the sixth earl, "Don't go near your father's grave! It will bring you bad luck!" The wary earl heeded her advice and never visited the grave. In 1977 he told an NBC interviewer that he "neither believed nor disbelieved" the curse—but added that he would "not accept a million pounds to enter the tomb of Tutankhamen."

* * *

Profound thought: "It's a question of whether we're going to go forward with the future, or past to the back." —*Dan Quayle*

(JUNK) FOOD FOR THOUGHT

Background info on some of the foods you love—and some you love to hate.

CHEEZ WHIZ. Invented by Kraft laboratory technicians in 1951. According to *The Encyclopedia of Pop Culture*, they were looking for a cheese product that wouldn't clump or "disintegrate into ugly, oily wads of dairy fat glop," like real cheese did when heated. It was first test-marketed to housewives in 1952; they found 1,304 different uses for it.

TANG. Fresh from the success of its decade-long struggle to get consumers to give instant coffee a try, in 1955 General Foods decided to try the same tactic with orange juice. Its goal: To make a "fruit-flavored breakfast companion to Instant Maxwell House coffee." It took 10 years to perfect the recipe, but one advantage of the delay was that three months after it made its nationwide debut in 1965, NASA announced that Tang would be used to feed the *Gemini* astronauts in space. General Foods played the endorsement for all it was worth. The orangy powder never bit into orange juice sales, but it was still a hit—at least until Americans lost their taste for both the space program and artificial foods in the 1980s.

PRETZELS. According to legend, pretzels were invented by an Italian monk during the Middle Ages because he wanted something he could give to children who memorized their prayers. He rolled dough into a long rope and shaped it so it looked like arms folded in prayer. He called his salty treats *pretioles*, Latin for "little gift."

MACARONI & CHEESE. During the Depression, the Kraft company tried to market a low-priced cheddar cheese powder to the American public—but the public wouldn't buy it. One St. Louis salesman, looking for a way to unload his allotment of the stuff, tied individual packages to macaroni boxes and talked grocers on his route into selling them as one item, which he called "Kraft Dinners." When the company found out how well they were selling, it made the Dinners an official part of its product line.

Bathroom news: Franklin Roosevelt thought up the name "United Nations" in the shower.

THE GODZILLA QUIZ

Here's a multiple-choice quiz to find out how much you really know about filmdom's most famous dinosaur. Answers are on page 662.

1. Godzilla first lumbered out of the ocean in a 1954 film titled *Gojira.* The dino-monster was awakened from a million-year slumber by A-bomb testing underseas and went on a rampage, destroying Tokyo, wreaking havoc with his radioactive breath. In 1956, the movie was brought to the U.S. as *Godzilla, King of Monsters* ("Makes King Kong Look Like a Midget!"). How did they adapt it for American audiences?

A) They made it seem as though Godzilla was fighting for the U.S. during World War II.

B) They inserted footage of Godzilla destroying New York City and Washington, D.C. as well.

C) They added Raymond Burr, casting him as a hospitalized reporter who remembers the whole incident as a flashback.

2. The first Japanese sequel to *Gojira* was made in 1955. But when this flick finally made it to the U.S. in 1959, it didn't mention Godzilla in the title. What was it called, and why?

A) *The Monster vs. the Maiden*; the studio tried to make it sexier.

B) *The Rockin' Monster*; rock 'n' roll movies were hot.

C) *Gigantis*; it was illegal to use the name Godzilla.

3. In the 1964 flick, *Godzilla vs. Megalon*, Godzilla saves the world from the Seatopians, an evil alien race that plans to take over using two secret weapons—Gaigan and Megalon. How would you describe this evil pair?

A) A King Kong-like ape and a giant poisonous frog.

B) A giant cockroach and a robot with a buzz saw in his stomach.

C) A giant pickle and a Richard Nixon look-alike.

4. *Godzilla vs. the Thing* was released in 1964. What Thing did Godzilla fight?

A) A giant rabbit.

B) A giant moth.

C) A giant spider.

5. How did Godzilla celebrate his 20th anniversary in 1974?

A) He fought a Godzilla robot from outer space.

B) He saved the world from a giant alien grasshopper.

C) He made an appearance on the "The Tonight Show."

6. *Godzilla on Monster Island* was released in 1971. The plot: Earth is invaded again. This time it's giant cockroaches from outer space, using monsters to do their dirty work. They've got Gaigan (the monster in *Godzilla vs. Megalon*) and Ghidrah. Who's Ghidrah?

A) Godzilla's mother-in-law.

B) A giant anteater.

C) A three-headed dragon.

7. In 1972 a scientist discovers a growing mass in a polluted lake. He wonders if it's a giant tadpole...but no! It's a new monster named Hedora. What will Godzilla be fighting this time?

A) The Smog Monster—a 400-foot blob of garbage.

B) The Phlegm Monster—a 2-ton ball of mucus.

C) The Sludge Monster—A 60-foot-wide hunk of waste.

8. In *Godzilla's Revenge*, released in 1969, Godzilla returns for what purpose?

A) To settle a score with another monster named Gorgo.

B) To show a little kid how to fight bullies.

C) To get revenge on Raymond Burr.

9. In the 1966 epic, *Godzilla vs. the Sea Monster*, Godzilla fights for the Free World against Red Bamboo, an evil totalitarian group. Their secret weapon is Ebirah. Who is he?

A) A hypnotist who can brainwash Godzilla.

B) A mechanical jellyfish.

C) A giant lobster.

10. In 1969 Godzilla reappeared with Minya. What was special about this new monster?

A) It was Godzilla's mother.

B) It was Godzilla's cousin.

C) It was Godzilla's son.

Strange legacy: Marietta, Ohio, is named after Marie Antoinette.

SILLY BRITISH VILLAGE NAMES

People often ask how we find the material for our Bathroom Readers. *This one was easy—Uncle John was doing some leisurely bathroom reading one morning, checking out the six newspapers he gets, when he found himself laughing at an article in the* Wall Street Journal. *That led to more research... and now we've got enough silly English names to last a lifetime—or at least a sitting. Here are a few dozen of our favorites.*

ROADMAP AS COMIC BOOK

"New York has Flushing. Maryland has Boring. Pennsylvania, of course, has Intercourse," the *Wall Street Journal* reports. "But probably no territory in the English-speaking world can match Britain's wealth of ludicrous place names: Crackpot, Dorking, Fattahead, Goonbell, Giggleswick, Nether Poppleton, Wormelow Tump, Yornder Bognie. The litany, which swells with each page of the atlas, sounds like a Monty Python gag."

For example: According to Chris Longhurst, in *Daft Place Names*, you might already have visited...

- Foulbog
- Dull
- Muck
- Mold
- Moss of Barmuckity
- Belchford
- Burpham
- Lickey End
- Spital in the Street
- Bug's Bottom
- Pratts Botttom
- Slack Bottom
- Iron's Bottom
- Horsey
- Bunny
- Corney
- Swine Sty
- Pig Street
- Dog Village
- Donkey Town
- Toad's Mouth
- Maggots End
- Ufton Nervet
- Crazies Hill
- Shootup Hill
- Bat and Ball
- Pity Me
- No Place
- Haltwhistle
- Slaggyford
- Nether Wallop
- Weeford
- Limpley Stoke
- Nempnett
- Thrubwell
- Butcombe
- Bell End
- Great Bulging
- Eggborough
- Ham
- Pill
- Christmas Pie
- Furzedown
- World's End

UPPER AND LOWER

"Over time," the *Wall Street Journal* continues, "many villages also have subdivided, with silly consequences: Great Snoring and Little Snoring, Middle Wallop and Nether Wallop, Helions Bumpstead and Steeple Bumpstead, Sheepy Magna (Latin for 'big') and Sheepy Parva (Latin for 'small'). Then there is the English habit of designating 'upper' and 'lower' ends of villages, which may grow into communities of their own. Optimists, for instance, will feel at home in the hamlet of Upperup—which is reached, appropriately, via High Street.

"'If the hamlet grows any more, we'll have to call one end of it Upper Upperup,' jokes Charles Hadfield, a local historian."

Other pairs:

* Fetcham and Bookham (too bad there's no Jail'am)
* Downham and Turnham Green (in West London)
* "Piddles and Puddles, leading to Poole. (Or away from Poole, depending which side you start)," writes Longhurst
* Upper and Lower Peover

HERE AND THERE...

• There's a river in the south somewhere (Dorset) called the River Piddle," Longhurst notes in *Daft Place Names*. "Around it are placed called 'Puddletown' and 'Piddlehampton.' Don't know why they get puddle from piddle." He adds: "And there's a village by the name of Nasty, to the southeast 272 of Leighton Buzzard. I've only been past it (never to it) but the idea of the Nasty Village Pub, Nasty Inn, Nasty Bakery, etc. somehow appeal to me."

• "Goon" is Cornish for "pasture." As a result, there are plenty of Goons dotting the English countryside. For example: Goonbell, Goongumpus, Goonearl, Goonown and Gooninnis. "It's true we have a lot of goons here," says one resident. "but I've never thought of that as funny.

• Regarding the village of Piddle: A funny name? "Not if you live there," writes the *WSJ*. "Ian Curthoy's, a pig farmer in North Piddle, gripes that passersby often pose for snapshots beside signs for the village—usually while piddling. Other travelers steal the signs, a common nuisance in villages with silly names. Asked about the origin of Piddle's name, Mr. Curthoys replies: 'It's a wet place, isn't it?' Sloshing through the mud to feed his sows, he smiles, adding: 'There was a South Piddle once, but it dried up.'"

• And finally, the town called Ugley. Its most famous civic group: The Ugley Women's Institute, "a group that meets every month in the Ugley Village Hall and "holds scholarly lectures and afternoon teas." Members have tried to rename it the Women's Institute of Ugley, but no one pays attention. When the members have to identify their affiliation at conventions, they wind up announcing: "We're Ugley."

* * *

SILLY NAMES AROUND THE WORLD

From *Daft Name Places:*

• In Newfoundland, Canada, you can find: Heart's Content, Heart's Desire, Heart's Delight, Tickle Harbour, Come By Chance, Goobies, Little Heart's Ease, Seldom, St. Jones Within, Sop's Arm, Sheshatsheits and Toogood Arm.

• "There is a village about half an hour's train ride north of Tromsoe, Norway, on the way to Bodo, called Hell."

• In Germany, there are two towns near Munich called Grub and Poing.

• There's a Bavarian mountain (near Garmisch-Partenkirchen to be precise) known as the Wank. You can even take the Wankbahn to the top.

• In Texas, there's apparently a place called Myass.

• Reportedly, there's a road near Tucson, Arizona called the Superchicken Highway.

...And two useful phrases to learn for your next trip to France:

1. "Excuse me, waiter, but there's a German Shepherd in my soup."
Pardon, garçon, mais il y a un berger allemand dans mon potage

2. "May I have a manicure with my toast, please?"
Est-ce que je peux faire une manicure avec mon pain grillé, s'il vous plaît?

Camel's hair brushes are made with squirrel hair. They got their name

THE WORLD'S MOST POPULAR TWINS

To most people, all twins are fascinating. Here are three sets of twins who are famous as well.

CHANG AND ENG BUNKER

Claim to Fame: The original "Siamese twins."

Background: Chang and Eng—"left" and "right" in Thai—were born at Meklong, Siam (Thailand) on May 11, 1811, permanently attached at the chest by a band of skin. They were discovered by an American sea captain who put them on display in Europe and America—where P. T. Barnum bought out their contract.

The Bunkers became world-famous as "Siamese twins." They managed to live relatively normal lives, becoming American citizens, marrying (unattached) sisters Adelaide and Sarah Yates in 1864, and somehow fathering 22 children between them. They spent their entire lives looking for a doctor who'd guarantee they'd both survive an operation to separate them, but never found one. They died hours apart in 1874.

Gossip: Chang and Eng hated each other—and fought constantly. According to an 1874 article in the *Philadelphia Medical Times*, "Eng was very good-natured, Chang cross and irritable....Chang drank pretty heavily—at times getting drunk; but Eng never drank. They often quarrelled; and, of course, under the circumstances their quarrels were bitter. They sometimes came to blows, and on one occasion came under the jurisdiction of the courts."

ESTHER PAULINE AND PAULINE FRIEDMAN

Claim to Fame: The most popular advice columnists in America.

Background: Esther Pauline (Eppie) and Pauline Esther (Popo) Friedman were born 17 minutes apart on July 4, 1918, in Sioux City, Iowa. They were inseparable throughout their youth; they dressed identically, double-dated, slept in the same bed until their wedding nights, and married on the same day in a double wedding.

Eppie got her start as Ann Landers in 1955 when she entered and won a *Chicago Sun-Times* contest to succeed the original Ann Landers. In the first weeks of the column, Eppie mailed some of the Landers column's letters to California, where Popo apparently helped answer them. But when the *Sun-Times* editors found out about it, they prohibited her from sending any more letters out of the office. The twins had to stop working together.

A few weeks later, Popo walked into the office of the *San Francisco Chronicle* and complained about the paper's advice columnist. The editor gave her a stack of past columns and told her to fill in her own answers. She did—and the editor hired her the next day. Popo chose Abigail Van Buren as her pen name (from President Martin Van Buren), and her column became Dear Abby.

Gossip: When Eppie found out about her sister's column, she was furious. "I got into this work first," she told a reporter. "She saw what a great time I was having. And she got into it. I felt it was mine, something that I did. It was a serious problem." They didn't speak to each other for 8 years, but eventually buried the hatchet.

JOAN AND JANE BOYD

Claim to Fame: TV's first "Doublemint Twins."

Background: In 1959, the 21-year-old sisters were singing advertising jingles on CBS radio. One day they were asked if they wanted to audition to be the first live Doublemint twins. (Wrigley's Gum had used illustrated twins since the 1920s.) They were taken to meet the boss—P. K. Wrigley—who hired them on the spot. That was the only time they ever saw him.

The girls became American icons and made Doublemint the #1 gum. But the magic ended in 1963, when Wrigley learned that Joan—recently married—was pregnant…and fired them. (Their contract prohibited pregnancy, even within marriage.) Since then there have been more than 20 different sets of Doublemint twins—but none as popular as the originals.

Gossip: Wrigley never gave the twins free gum—even though fans were always walking up to them and asking for it. "We never got a free pack of chewing gum in our lives," Jane remembers. "So we'd buy our own gum to give to people on the street." They were also never allowed to chew gum in their commercials. According to Joan, "We were told that Mr. Wrigley had said, 'I never want to see gum in the mouths of the Doublemint Twins. My girls do not chew gum on-camera.' "

The write stuff: Famous storyteller Hans Christian Anderson couldn't spell.

FAMILIAR NAMES

Some people become famous because their names become commonly associated with an item or activity. You know the names, now here are the people.

Andre Marie Ampere. A 19th-century French physicist. His work on electricity and magnetism "laid the groundwork for modern electrodynamics." The standard unit of electrical current—the *ampere*, or *amp*—was named after him.

Fitzherbert Batty. A Jamaican lawyer. "In 1839," writes an English etymologist, "he was certified as insane, which attracted considerable interest in London." His surname became "an affectionate euphemism to describe someone who is harmlessly insane."

William Beukel. A 14th-century Dutchman. Invented the process "by which we shrink and sour cucumbers." The result was originally called a *beckel* or *pekel*, after him. It eventually became known as a *pickle*.

Mr. Doily (or Doyley). A 17th-century London merchant whose first name has been forgotten. "He became prosperous," says *Webster's Dictionary*, "by selling various summer fabrics trimmed with embroidery or crochet work, and, being a good businessman, used up the remnants by making ornamental mats for the table called *doilies*."

Hans Geiger. German physicist. In 1920 he perfected a device for measuring radioactivity—the *Geiger counter*.

John McIntosh. A Canadian farmer. In 1796 he found a wild apple tree on his Ontario property and cultivated it. The *McIntosh apple* is now America's favorite variety.

Col. E. G. Booz (or Booze). An 18th-century Philadelphia distiller who sold his Booz Whiskey in log cabin-shaped bottles. His product helped make the Old English term *booze* (from *bouse*, "to drink") slang for alcohol.

Sotheby's auction house sold a 200-year-old piece of Tibetan cheese for $1,513 in 1993.

Archibald Campbell, the third Duke of Argyll. Powerful Scottish noble in the early 1700s. Had the Campbell clan tartan woven into his *argyle* socks.

Enoch Bartlett. A 19th-century businessman. Distributed a new kind of pear developed by a Massachusetts farmer. Eventually bought the farm and named the pear after himself.

Brandley, Voorhis, and Day. Owners of an underwear manufacturing company. Known by their initials: BVD's.

Robert Wilhelm Bunsen. German chemist in the mid-1800s. Invented the gas burner used in chemistry labs.

Lambert de Begue. A monk whose 12th-century followers were wandering mendicants. His name—pronounced *beg*—became synonymous with his followers' activities.

Rudolph Boysen. California botanist. In 1923, he successfully crossed blackberries and raspberries to create *boysenberries*.

Charles F. Richter. A 20th-century American seismologist. In 1935 he came up with a scale for measuring the "amplitude of the seismic waves radiating from the epicenter of an earthquake." The *Richter scale* is now used worldwide to understand the magnitude of shock waves.

Thomas "Jim Crow" Rice. A white "blackface" comedian. In 1835 he came up with a typically racist song-and-dance routine that went: "Wheel about, turn about / Do just so / Every time I wheel about / I jump 'Jim Crow." For some reason, this phrase came to refer to all discrimination by whites against blacks.

* * *

TOTALLY IRRELEVANT FACT

The faces on today's U.S. banknotes have been unchanged since 1929. No one knows for sure why each coin or banknote ended up with the face it did: according to the Bureau of Engraving and Printing, "Records do not reveal the reasons that portraits of certain statesmen were chosen in preference to those of other persons of equal importance and prominence."

THE GOODYEAR BLIMP

No major sporting event is complete without it. In fact, it's probably the best-known lighter-than-air ship ever (except maybe the Hindenburg, *which is famous for blowing up). Here's the story of the Goodyear blimp.*

In 1809 Charles Goodyear, a hardware merchant from Connecticut, saw that rubber had tremendous commercial potential—but only if it could be made less sticky and would hold a shape better than it already did.

So he obtained a large quantity of latex, and tried mixing it with everything in his desk, cellar, and pantry—including witch hazel, ink, and cream cheese—with no luck. One day he tried mixing rubber with sulfur. Then, while working on something else, he accidentally knocked the sulfurized rubber mixture onto a hot stove. He found that the rubber had changed form: it was no longer sticky and it snapped back to its original shape when stretched. He named the process *Vulcanizing* after Vulcan, the Roman god of fire.

THE GOODYEAR COMPANY

Goodyear didn't get rich from his discovery—he died penniless in 1860. But when Frank A. Seiberling started a rubber company in Akron, Ohio, in 1898, he decided to name it after the inventor. It's likely he hoped to profit from the confusion created by having a name similar to another Akron rubber company, B.F. Goodrich.

Goodyear's first products were bicycle and horse carriage tires, rubber pads for horseshoes, rubber bands, and poker chips. The company produced its first auto tires in 1901, airplane tires in 1909, and, using a Scottish process for rubberized fabric, the skins for airplanes in 1910. (This was back when airplanes were based on kite designs and made mostly of wood and cloth.)

The same rubberized fabric turned out to be useful for lighter-than-air craft, and Goodyear flew its first dirigible in 1922.

THE MILITARY CONNECTION

The military used Goodyear blimps for observation and reconnaissance during World War I and World War II. After World War II,

The distance between a Boeing 747's wingtips is longer than the Wright Brothers' first flight.

Goodyear bought five of its blimps back from the armed forces. It painted them and began using them for promotional purposes. But the company's executives didn't see the value of having blimps. In 1958 they tried to ground the airships permanently, to save the operating and maintenance expenses.

The plan was stalled at the last minute by a plea from Goodyear's publicity director, Robert Lane. To demonstrate the blimps' worth to the company, he scheduled a six-month marathon tour that sent the airship *Mayflower* barnstorming the Eastern Seaboard. It generated so much favorable press that the executives were convinced to keep it.

The blimps' first TV coverage was an Orange Bowl game in the mid-1960s. Now they're used in about 90 televised events a year. Goodyear doesn't charge TV networks; the publicity generated makes the free service worthwhile.

BLIMP FACTS

• Each blimp is equipped with a crew of 23, consisting of 5 pilots, 17 support members who work on rotating schedules, and 1 public relations representative. The blimps cruise at a speed of 45 to 50 mph (maximum 65 mph unless there's a really good wind).

• Each blimp can carry 9 passengers along with the crew. The seats have no seatbelts.

• The camera operator shoots from the passenger compartment through an open window from about 1,200 feet up, from which you can see everything, read a scoreboard, and hear the roar of a crowd. The hardest sport to film is golf, because the pilots have to be careful not to disturb a golfer's shot with engine noise or by casting a sudden shadow over the green.

• If punctured, the worst that will happen is that the blimp will slowly lose altitude. Good thing, too, since the company reports that a blimp is shot at about 20 times a year.

• Each blimp is 192 feet long, 59 feet high, and holds 202,700 cubic feet of helium. The helium does leak out, like a balloon's air, and has to be "topped off" every four months or so.

• The word *blimp* is credited to Lt. A. D. Cunningham of Britain's Royal Navy Air Service. In 1915 he whimsically flicked his thumb against the inflated wall of an airship and imitated the sound it made: "Blimp!"

Creative naming: "Booker" T. Washington got the nickname Booker because he loved books.

GO ASK ALICE

Alice in Wonderland and Through the Looking Glass aren't just for kids. They're great reading for grown-ups, too. Especially in the bathroom. Here are some sample quotes.

"Dear, dear! How queer everything is today! I wonder if I've been changed in the night? Let me think: was I the same when I got up this morning? I almost think I can remember feeling a little different. But if I'm not the same, the next questions is, 'Who *am* I?' Ah, that's the puzzle!"

—Alice, *Alice in Wonderland*

"Cheshire Puss," began Alice, "would you tell me, please, which way I ought to go from here?"

"That depends a good deal on where you want to get to," said the Cat.

"I don't much care where—" said Alice.

"Then it doesn't matter which way you go," said the Cat.

"—so long as I get *somewhere*," Alice added as an explanation.

"Oh, you're sure to do that," said the Cat, "if only you walk long enough."

—Alice in Wonderland

Alice laughed. "There's no use in trying," she said. "One can't believe impossible things."

"I daresay you haven't had much practice," said the Queen. "When I was your age, I always did it for half-an-hour a day. Why, sometimes I've believed as many as six impossible things before breakfast."

—Through the Looking Glass

"You should say what you mean," said the March Hare.

"I do," Alice hastily replied; "at least—I mean what I say—that's the same thing, you know."

"Not the same thing a bit!" said the Hatter. "Why, you might just as well say that 'I see what I eat' is the same as 'I eat what I see'!"

"You might as well say," added the March Hare, "that 'I like what I get' is the same thing as 'I get what I like'!"

"You might just as well say," added the Dormouse, "that 'I breathe when I sleep' is the same thing as 'I sleep when I breathe'!"

"It *is* the same thing with you," said the Hatter.

—Alice in Wonderland

"It's no use going back to yesterday, because I was a different person then."

—Alice, *Alice in Wonderland*

"Be what you would seem to be—or, if you would like it put more simply—Never imagine yourself not to be otherwise than what it might appear to others that what you were or might have been was not otherwise than what you had been would have appeared to them to be otherwise."

—The Duchess, *Alice in Wonderland*

"Take some more tea," the March Hare said to Alice, very earnestly.

"I've had nothing yet," Alice replied in an offended tone: "So I can't take more."

"You mean you can't take less," said the hatter: "It's very easy to take *more* than nothing."

—Alice in Wonderland

"If everybody minded their own business," the Duchess said in a hoarse growl, "the world would go round a deal faster than it does."

"Which would not be an advantage," said Alice. "Just think what work it would make with the day and night! You see, the earth takes twenty-four hours to turn round on its axis—"

"Talking of axes," said the Duchess, "chop off her head!"

—Alice in Wonderland

Believe it or not: The U.S. Congress was so unpopular during the American Revolution that its

WEDDING SUPERSTITIONS

If this book was Modern Bride, *we'd probably call these "wedding traditions" rather than superstitions. But think about it—most of them were started by people who believed in evil spirits and witches and talismans.*

BRIDAL VEIL. The veil has served a number of purposes throughout history, including: 1) protecting the bride from the "evil eye;" 2) protecting her from jealous spinsters (who might also be witches); and 3) protecting the groom, his family, and other wedding guests from the bride's psychic powers—just in case she has any.

WEDDING KISS. A toned-down but direct throwback to the days when the couple was required to consummate their marriage in the presence of several witnesses, to insure that the consummation actually took place.

BRIDE'S GARTER AND BOUQUET OF FLOWERS. Originally the groomsmen fought with each other to see who would get the bride's garter, which was supposed to bring good luck to the person who possessed it. But the Catholic Church frowned on the rowdy practice, and it was eventually replaced by a milder custom: the bride throwing a bouquet of flowers to her bridesmaids. Today the customs exist side by side.

WEDDING RINGS. One of the oldest wedding practices. Ancient Egyptians, Romans, and Greeks all exchanged rings during their wedding ceremonies. Because a circle is a round, unending shape, it came to symbolize the ideal love that was supposed to come from marriage: it flowed from one person to the other and back again, forever. The ring has always been worn on the left hand—and was originally worn on the thumb. It was later moved to the index finger and then to the middle finger, and eventually ended up on the third, or "medical," finger. Reason: The third finger was believed to lead straight to the heart, via a single nerve.

detractors named it "King Congress." The name was later shortened to "King Cong."

HONEYMOON. This European tradition dates back hundreds of years and gets its name from the fact that newlyweds were expected to drink honey (believed to be an aphrodisiac) during the period of one full cycle of the moon (about a month).

THROWING RICE OR CONFETTI. Originally a fertility ritual. Wedding guests threw wheat at the bride only, in the hope that she would bear children the same way that wheat produced bread.

WEDDING CAKE. Guests originally gave "bride-cakes" to a just-married woman to encourage fertility.

JUNE WEDDING. It was customary for Romans to marry in June to honor the queen of the gods, Juno—who was also the goddess of women. They hoped to win her favor to make the marriage last, and make childbirth easier.

CARRYING THE BRIDE OVER THE THRESHOLD. Romans thought good and evil spirits hung around the entrance of a home. They also believed that if you walked into your house left foot first, the evil spirits won. So to be sure the bride—whom Romans figured was "in a highly enotional state and very apt to be careless"—didn't accidentally step into her new home with the wrong foot, the groom just picked her up and carried her.

RECEPTION SPEECH. In pre-Christian Rome, newlyweds hired an "official joker" to tell dirty stories to guests during the reception. The Romans believed that "unclean" thoughts in the minds of guests turned the attention of vengeful gods away from the newlyweds, which helped protect them from evil.

DECORATING THE WEDDING CAR. In medieval France, when a couple was unpopular, people derided them publicly by banging on pots, kettles, etc. This was a *charivari*, or "rough serenade." In America it became a *shivaree*, and people got the treatment from friends. This gave way to a new custom—trying to keep a couple from consummating their marriage by making noise at their window. When newlyweds began leaving weddings by car, the only way to harass them was to deface the vehicle.

Most popular sheet-music song of all time: "Yes, We Have No Bananas."

LIMERICKS

Limericks have been around since the 1700s. Here are some that readers have sent us over the years.

There once was a spinster
from Wheeling,
Endowed with such
delicate feeling,
That she thought any chair
Should not have its legs bare,
So, she kept her eyes fixed
on the ceiling.

There was a young lady
of Kent,
Who always said just what
she meant;
People said, "she's a dear—
So unique—so sincere—"
But they shunned her by
common consent.

There once was a pious
young priest,
Who lived almost wholly
on yeast;
"For," he said, "it is plain
We must all rise again,
And I want to get started
at least."

I sat next to the Duchess
at tea,
Distressed as a person
could be.
Her rumblings abdominal
Were simply phenomenal—
And everyone thought
it was me!

A rocket explorer
named Wright
Once traveled much faster
than light.
He set out one day
In a relative way,
And returned
on the previous night.

There once was an old man
of Boolong
Who frightened the birds
with his song.
It wasn't the words
Which astonished the birds
But the horrible
dooble ontong.

A classical scholar
from Flint
Developed a
curious squint.
With her left-handed eye
She could scan the whole sky
While the other was reading
small print.

There was a young girl
from Detroit
Who at kissing was
very adroit;
She could pucker her lips
Into total eclipse,
Or open them out
like a quoit.

Size of the smallest man alive, in inches: 26.

FAMILIAR PHRASES

Here are the origins of a few common phrases.

TO CLOSE RANKS

Meaning: To present a united front.

Origin: "In the old-time European armies, the soldiers were aligned side by side, in neat rows, or ranks, on the battlefield. When the enemy attacked, officers would order the troops to close ranks; that is, to move the rows close together, so that the enemy faced a seemingly impregnable mass of men." (From *Fighting Words*, by Christine Ammer)

FOR THE BIRDS

Meaning: Worthless.

Origin: According to Robert Claiborne in *Loose Cannons and Red Herrings*, it refers to city streets before cars. "When I was a youngster on the streets of New York, one could both see and smell the emissions of horse-drawn wagons. Since there was no way of controlling these emissions, they, or the undigested oats in them, served to nourish a large population of English sparrows. If you say something's for the birds, you're politely saying that it's horseshit."

BEYOND THE PALE

Meaning: Socially unacceptable.

Origin: "The pale in this expression has nothing to do with the whitish color, but comes originally from Latin *palus*, meaning a pole or stake. Since stakes are used to mark boundaries, a pale was a particular area within certain limits." The pale that inspired this expression was the area around Dublin in Ireland. Until the 1500s, that area was subject to British law. "Those who lived beyond the pale were outside English jurisdiction and were thought to be uncivilized." (From *Getting to the Roots*, by Martin Manser)

I'VE GOT A FROG IN MY THROAT

Meaning: I'm hoarse from a cold.

Origin: Surprisingly, this wasn't inspired by the croaking sound of a cold-sufferer's voice, but a weird medical practice. "In the Middle Ages," says Christine Ammer in *It's Raining Cats and Dogs*, "throat infections such as thrush were sometimes treated by putting a live frog head first into the patient's mouth; by inhaling, the frog was believed to draw out the patient's infection into its own body. The treatment is happily obsolete, but its memory survives in the 19th-century term *frog in one's throat*."

KEEPING UP WITH THE JONESES

Meaning: Trying to do as well as your neighbors.

Origin: "Keeping Up with the Joneses" was the name of a comic strip by Arthur R. "Pop" Momand that ran in the *New York Globe* from 1913 to 1931. At first, Momand planned to call it "Keeping Up with the Smiths," but his real-life neighbors were named Smith, and a lot of his material came from observing them. So he picked another common surname. (From *Why Do We Say It?*, by Nigel Rees)

XXX

Meaning: A kiss, at the end of a letter.

Origin: In medieval times, when most people were illiterate, "contracts were not considered legal until each signer included St. Andrew's cross after his name." (Or instead of a signature, if the signer couldn't write.) To prove his sincerity, the signer was then required to kiss the X. "Through the centuries this custom faded out, but the letter X [became associated] with a kiss." This is also probably where the phrase "sealed with a kiss" comes from. (From *I've Got Goose Pimples*, by Martin Vanoni)

TO READ BETWEEN THE LINES

Meaning: To perceive or understand a hidden meaning.

Origin: In the 16th century, it became common for politicians, soldiers, and businessmen to write in code. "To a person ignorant of the code, a secret paper was meaningless. Ordinary folk fascinated with this mystery concluded that the meaning was not in lines of gibberish, but in the space between them." (From *Why You Say It*, by Webb Garrison)

Q. Who was the first person to put *Frankenstein* on film? A. Thomas Edison.

CAFFEINE FACTS

What's America's favorite drug? You guessed it—caffeine. We use more caffeine than all other drugs—legal or illegal—combined. Want to know what the stuff is doing to you? Here's a quick overview.

BACKGROUND

If you start the day with a strong cup of coffee or tea, you're not alone. Americans ingest the caffeine equivalent of 530 million cups of coffee *every day*. Caffeine is the world's most popular mood-altering drug. It's also one of the oldest: according to archaeologists, man has been brewing beverages from caffeine-based plants since the Stone Age.

HOW IT PICKS YOU UP

Caffeine doesn't keep you awake by supplying extra energy; rather, it fools your body into thinking it isn't tired.

• When your brain is tired and wants to slow down, it releases a chemical called *adenosine*.

• Adenosine travels to special cells called *receptors*, where it goes to work counteracting the chemicals that stimulate your brain.

• Caffeine mimics adenosine; so it can "plug up" your receptors and prevent adenosine from getting through. Result: Your brain never gets the signal to slow down, and keeps building up stimulants.

JAVA JUNKIES

• After a while, your brain figures out what's going on, and increases the number of receptor cells so it has enough for both caffeine *and* adenosine.

• When that happens, caffeine can't keep you awake anymore... unless you *increase* the amount you drink so it can "plug up" the new receptor cells as well.

• This whole process only takes about a week. In that time, you essentially become a caffeine addict. Your brain is literally restructuring itself to run on caffeine; take the caffeine away and your brain has too many receptor cells to operate properly.

• If you quit ingesting caffeine "cold turkey," your brain begins to reduce the number of receptors right away. But the process takes about two weeks, and during that time your body sends out mild "distress signals" in the form of headaches, lethargy, fatigue, muscle pain, nausea, and sometimes even stiffness and flu-like symptoms. As a result, most doctors recommend cutting out caffeine gradually.

CAFFEINE'S EFFECTS

• **Good:** Caffeine has been scientifically proven to temporarily increase alertness, comprehension, memory, reflexes, and even the rate of learning. It also helps increase clarity of thought.

• **Bad:** Too much caffeine can cause hand tremors, loss of coordination or appetite, insomnia, and in extreme cases, trembling, nausea, heart palpitations, and diarrhea.

• Widely varying the amount of caffeine you ingest can put a strain on your liver, pancreas, heart, and nervous system. And if you're prone to ulcers, caffeine can make your situation worse.

• If you manage to consume the equivalent of 70-100 cups of coffee in one sitting, you'll experience convulsions, and may even die.

CAFFEINE FACTS

• The average American drinks 210 milligrams of caffeine a day. That's equal to 2-3 cups of coffee, depending on how strong it is.

• How you make your coffee has a lot to do with how much caffeine you get. Instant coffee contains 65 milligrams of caffeine per serving; coffee brewed in a percolator has 80 milligrams; and coffee made using the "drip method" has 155 milligrams.

• Top four sources of caffeine in the American diet: coffee, soft drinks, tea, and chocolate, in that order. The average American gets 75% of their caffeine from coffee. Other sources include over-the-counter pain killers, appetite suppressants, cold remedies, and some prescription drugs.

• What happens to the caffeine that's removed from decaf coffee? Most of it is sold to soda companies and put into soft drinks. (Cola contains some caffeine naturally, but they like to add even more.)

• Do you drink more caffeine than your kids do? If you correct for body weight, probably not. Pound for pound, kids often get as much caffeine from chocolate and soft drinks as their parents get from coffee, tea, and other sources.

Read all about it: 28% of Americans go to a library at least once a month; 27% never go at all.

J. EDGAR HOOVER AND THE RED MENACE

Was there really a Red menace in the 1950s?...And did FBI director J. Edgar Hoover really know how to deal with it? Or was the whole thing just a PR scam, devised to make Hoover look good (as some historians now suggest)? We may never know. But the controversy makes this article, from It's A Conspiracy, *interesting to ponder.*

J. Edgar Hoover was considered an expert on Communist infiltration. Here are excerpts from different interviews he gave from 1947 to 1950 telling Americans how to protect themselves against the Red Menace.

INTERVIEWER: "How can you tell a Communist?"

HOOVER: "A Communist is not always easy to identify. It is possible that a concealed Communist may hide in the most unsuspected and unlikely place. He is trained in deceit and uses cleverly camouflaged movements to conceal his real purposes. But he may frequently be detected by certain characteristics. He will always espouse the cause of Soviet Russia over that of the United States. His viewpoint and position will shift with each change in the Communist Party 'line.' He will utilize a language of 'double talk'—referring to the Soviet-dominated countries as 'democracies' and complain that the United States is 'imperialistic.' He will attempt to infiltrate and gain control of organizations and subvert them to the use of the party.

"My advice to the public is this: Be alert to the dangers of Communism. Report your information immediately and fully to the FBI."

INTERVIEWER: "Where do you find Communists?"

HOOVER: "Communists may be found in most sections of the United States. Of course, in some areas, the Communists are more thickly located than others. As a general rule, the Communists are less strong in agricultural areas. The Communists are strongest today in the industrial areas. The Communists, as a basic principle of infiltration, are interested in possessing strength in heavy industry, that is coal, steel, rubber, automobile, etc. It is here that, in event of an emergency, they can do their greatest harm to the country. That is one of the potential sabotage dangers facing America today."

INTERVIEWER: "Is the FBI interested in any Communist, or only those connected with espionage rings or possible sabotage?"

HOOVER: "The FBI is interested in knowing the identity of all Communists in the United States, as any Communist, properly qualified, might be recruited into espionage. He may today be circulating peace petitions or selling Communist literature. Tomorrow he may be sabotaging American industry or serving as an espionage courier. Every member of this international conspiracy is a potential saboteur and espionage agent."

INTERVIEWER: "Don't you draw a distinction between philosophical Communists and those who are tools of spy rings?"

HOOVER: "Any person who subscribes to these teachings, regardless of his reason, is working against American democracy and for the benefit of Soviet Russia. Stalin is his omnipotent oracle from whom all wisdom flows. The Communist party is today a Trojan horse of disloyalty, coiled like a serpent in the very heart of America.

"It may mouth sweet words of 'peace,' 'democracy,' 'equality,' and flourish gay slogans of 'international solidarity' and 'brotherhood of men,' but its body and feet are from the Russian bear."

INTERVIEWER: "Are Communists trained to lie?"

HOOVER: "The concept of morality and fair play, as practiced in our democracy, is alien and repugnant to him. Moreover, the Communists employ a purposeful double-talk, roundabout style, known as 'Aesopian language,' in their literature and speeches, designed to deceive and evade, to clothe their true thoughts. This technique, utilized by Lenin, is the very epitome of deceit."

INTERVIEWER: "Would you say it was a favorite Communist technique to belittle the amount of Communist activity here?"

HOOVER: "Very definitely. As an illustration, a few years ago

The fox uses its tail to balance when it runs.

there was a Communist Action group which was hard pressed in a given area, primarily through the energetic efforts of a few individuals. So, to counteract these few anti-Communists, the Communists developed a technique: Whenever anybody would denounce Communists, they would say, 'What's wrong with being a Communist?' And the average person had given little thought to the subject. They knew they didn't like Communism, but were at a disadvantage with a trained Communist agitator."

INTERVIEWER: "Do you have many Communists whom you are actually watching from day to day? "

HOOVER: "We have a relatively small force when you take into consideration that there is approximately one special agent to every 29,000 inhabitants in this country. With some 43,217 members of the Communist Party and only 5,200 agents—it's a physical impossibility to keep all of them under surveillance."

INTERVIEWER: "What would you say to the charge often made that we are engaging in 'thought control' with our constant watching of Communists?"

HOOVER: "The FBI is concerned not with what Communists think, but with what they do—their actions, just as in any other field of its investigative activity. There is no scintilla of evidence to substantiate the charge that the FBI is engaged in 'thought control' activities."

INTERVIEWER: "Isn't it possible that by asking citizens to report subversive activities, some may be encouraged to circulate gossip and rumor and engage in 'witch hunts'?"

HOOVER: "I think that citizens cooperating with the FBI provide the greatest barrier you could possibly have against 'witch hunts' and hysteria; because, if the citizen has a suspicion, it is his duty to turn it over to the FBI and from that time on do nothing unless he receives a request. A 'Gestapo' under the American system would be an impossibility. In addition to the protection of our courts and Congress, we have a free press, which would quickly spot injustices or any excesses on the part of any government agency."

Q. Who invented swim fins? A. Benjamin Franklin.

ENGLISH / JAPANESE WORDS

Purists in the Land of the Rising Sun don't like it, but the Japanese language is becoming more Westernized. A number of words that commonly appear in Japanese pop culture have been loosely adapted from English. Here are some of them, written phonetically. See if you can tell what they mean. Answers are at the bottom of the page.

1. Biiru
2. Terebi
3. Nyusu
4. Supotsu
5. Basu
6. Rajio
7. Gasu
8. Hoteru
9. Resutoran
10. Sabisu
11. Memba
12. Peji
13. Kappu
14. Bata
15. Sekkusu
16. Bitami
17. Dezain
18. Pantsu
19. Supu
20. Dorama
21. Sosu
22. Burausu
23. Sutecchi
24. Bonasu
25. Kado
26. Pointo
27. Makudonarudo
28. Sungurasu
29. Sunobbari
30. Caresu
31. Weta
32. Tawa
33. Sumato
34. Boru
35. Gorufu
36. Sumoggu

ANSWERS

1. beer; 2. TV; 3. news; 4. sports; 5. bus; 6. radio; 7. gas; 8. hotel; 9. restaurant; 10. service; 11. member; 12. page; 13. cup; 14. butter; 15. sex; 16. vitamin; 17. design; 18. pants; 19. soup; 20. drama; 21. sauce; 22. blouse; 23. stitch; 24. bonus; 25. card; 26. point; 27. McDonald's; 28. sunglasses; 29. snobbery; 30. caress; 31. waiter; 32. tower; 33. smart; 34. ball; 35. golf; 36. smog

Malaysians wash their babies in beer to protect them from disease.

BASKETBALL NAMES

In the Second Bathroom Reader, *we did the origins of baseball and football names. Here's what we could dig up about origins of pro basketball names.*

Seattle Supersonics. Named after a supersonic jet proposed by Seattle-based Boeing in the late '60s. (The jet was never built.)

Los Angeles Lakers. There are no lakes in L.A. The team was originally the Minneapolis Lakers; Minnesota is the "Land of 1,000 Lakes."

Detroit Pistons. Not named for that city's auto industry. The team's founder, Fred Zollner, owned a piston factory in Fort Wayne, Indiana. In 1957 the Zollner Pistons moved to Detroit.

New Jersey Nets. Originally called the New York Nets to rhyme with N.Y. Mets (baseball) and N.Y. Jets (football).

Houston Rockets. Ironically, it has nothing to do with NASA. They began as the San Diego Rockets—a name inspired by the theme of a "city in motion" and its "space age industries."

Orlando Magic. Inspired by Disney's Magic Kingdom.

New York Knicks. Short for knickerbockers, the pants that Dutch settlers in New York wore in the 1600s.

Indiana Pacers. Owners wanted to "set the pace" in the NBA.

Los Angeles Clippers. Started out in San Diego, where great sailing boats known as clipper ships used to land 100 years ago.

Sacramento Kings. When the Cincinnati Royals moved to the Kansas City-Omaha area in 1972, they realized b*oth* cities already had a Royals baseball team. They became the K.C. Kings, then Sacramento Kings.

Atlanta Hawks. Started in 1948 as the Tri-Cities Blackhawks (Moline and Rock Island, Illinois, and Davenport, Iowa), they were named after Sauk Indian chief Black Hawk, who fought settlers of the area in the 1831 Black Hawk Wars. In 1951 the team moved to Milwaukee and shortened the name to Hawks.

In case you were wondering: In general, frogs hop faster than toads.

OOPS!

Everyone's amused by tales of outrageous blunders—probably because it's comforting to know that someone's screwing up even worse that we are. So here's an ego-building page from the BRI. Go ahead and feel superior for a few minutes.

A PUBLISHING BOMB

"In 1978 Random House issued a cookbook that contained a potentially lethal mistake. *Woman's Day Crockery Cuisine* offered a recipe for caramel slices that inadvertently left out one simple ingredient—water. It was soon discovered that if the recipe was followed exactly, a can of condensed milk called for in the book could explode. Random House had to recall 10,000 copies of the book" to correct the potentially lethal recipe.

—From *The Blunder Book,* by M. L. Ginsberg

TAKE THAT!

"In 1941 the British warship *Trinidad* sighted a German destroyer and fired a torpedo at it. The icy Arctic waters apparently affected the torpedo's steering mechanism—it began to curve in a slow arc. As the crew watched in horror, it continued curving slowly around until it was speeding right back at them at forty knots. The *Trinidad*'s torpedo slammed into the *Trinidad* and caused so much damage that it put the warship out of action for the rest of the war."

—From *The Emperor Who Ate the Bible,* by Scott Morris

SOLID PLANNING

"In 1974 the Nigerian government decided to initiate a 'Third National Nigerian Development Plan,' intended to bring the country in a single leap into line with most developed Western nations.

"The planners calculated that to build the new roads, airfields, and military buildings which the plan required would call for some 20 million tons of cement. This was duly ordered and shipped by freighters from all over the world, to be unloaded at Lagos docks.

"Unfortunately, the Nigerian planners had not considered the fact that the docks were only capable of handling two thousand tons a day. Working every day, it would have taken 27 years to unload just the ships that were at one point waiting at sea off Lagos. These contained a third of the world's supply of cement—much of it showing its fine quality by setting in the hold of the freighters."

—From *David Frost's Book of the World's Worst Decisions*

CALLING ALL CARS

In 1977 American carmakers actually recalled more vehicles than they produced: 9.3 million cars were made in the United States that year; 10.4 million were recalled.

RAISING THE DEAD

"A mixup at a company that makes compact disks resulted in rock music with lines like 'God told me to skin you alive' being shipped to radio stations labeled as religious music.

"The Southern Baptist Radio-TV Commission, which markets a weekly religious radio program called "Powerline," is calling more than 1,200 radio stations across the country to warn them that some CDs it sent out for religious broadcasts are mislabeled.

"The CDs are supposed to contain inspirational talks and music. They are actually the alternative rock band Dead Kennedys' album, 'Fresh Fruit for Rotting Vegetables.' "

—Reported in the *Chicago Tribune*, June 22, 1993

HAPPY BIRTHDAY

"Festivities marking the centennial of organized soccer in Hereford, England, were canceled abruptly when officials discovered the league was only 90 years old."

—From *News of the Weird*

USING HIS HEAD

"On May 26, 1993, Texas Rangers outfielder Jose Canseco went back for a fly ball hit by Carlos Martinez of the Cleveland Indians. It missed his glove, bounced off his head, and ricocheted into the stands for a home run. 'I thought I had it,' Canseco explained later. 'Now I'll be on ESPN for a month.' "

—From the *San Francisco Chronicle*

A restaurant in Mississippi called *Hello, I'm...Jello* served over 400 dishes made from Jell-O.

FABULOUS FLOPS

Next time you see the hype for some amazing "can't miss" phenomenon, hold on to a healthy sense of skepticism by remembering these duds.

ESPERANTO

Glorious Prediction: "Where will Esperanto be tomorrow as a world language? 1) Everyone will *learn* Esperanto; 2) Everyone will *use* Esperanto; 3) It will be the international *neutral* language; and 4) It will be a major step toward *world peace and prosperity.*"

Background: Esperanto was created in 1887 by Lazarus Ludwig Zamenhof, an idealistic 28-year-old Polish ophthalmologist. According to one account, "Zamenhof's neighbors—Poles, Russians, Estonians, Latvians, and Germans—profoundly misunderstood and mistrusted each other in a multitude of tongues. It was his dream to fashion a new language they could share, and through which they could learn to coexist." Drawing on nearly all the romance languages, Zamenhof created a simplified, hybrid version with only 16 rules of grammar, no irregular verbs (English has 728), and words that could be changed from nouns to adjectives, adverbs, or verbs by changing the vowel at the end of the word. He published his language under the pseudonym Dr. Esperanto, which translates as "one who hopes."

What Happened: Despite more than 100 years of lobbying by Esperanto devotees, the language has never taken hold. Still, today there are thousands of Esperanto speakers organized into clubs in 100 countries around the world—including special-interest chapters for vegetarians and nudists.

THE COMET KAHOUTEK

Glorious Prediction: "Kahoutek will be the greatest sky show of the century, with a brilliance fifty times that of Halley's comet and a tail extending across a sixth of the sky." One Harvard astronomer even predicted that the comet's tail length "might reach 36 times the apparent diameter of the full moon."

Poll results: Twelve percent of American boat owners name their boats "Serenity."

Background: The comet, "a grimy lump of chemical ice some three miles in diameter" was discovered by German astronomer Lubos Kahoutek in 1973.

What Happened: Nothing. On January 15, 1974, the comet came as close to the earth as it would get in 80,000 years—and no one on Earth could see it. One astronomer described the spectacle as "a thrown egg, that missed." Where was Dr. Kahoutek? He and 1,692 other passengers were on the Queen Elizabeth 2, which had been specially chartered for the event. As *Newsweek* magazine put it, "The weather turned out rough and overcast, and Dr. Kahoutek spent much of the voyage too seasick to leave his cabin." Two weeks later the comet did emit a burst of explosive color—but by then it was so close to the sun that only three people saw it—the astronauts aboard Skylab.

THE WORLD FOOTBALL LEAGUE

Glorious Prediction: The WFL would become a successful alternative to the NFL by 1978. "The National Football League has grown arrogant and complacent," announced the WFL's founder in 1973. "The doors are open to a rival....The war is on!"

Background: In October 1973, Gary Davidson, a Newport Beach lawyer, announced he had formed the World Football League. The league started with 12 domestic teams but predicted it would become the first international football league, with franchises in Tokyo, Madrid, London, Paris, and other cities within five years.

What Happened: The WFL went broke in its first season, and collapsed 12 weeks into its second season more than $20 million in debt. Nearly all the teams in the league were bankrupt. The Florida franchise was so broke that the coach had to pay for the team's toilet paper out of his own pocket, and the Philadelphia team had to fire its cheerleaders because it couldn't come up with enough cash to pay them their $10-per-game salary.

But perhaps the worst embarrassment came after the 1974 championship "World Bowl" game between the Birmingham Americans and the Florida Blazers. Americans owner Bill Putnam owed the IRS money, and according to *Sports Illustrated,* "After the game, sheriff's deputies moved right into the locker room to repossess the uniforms as soon as the champions took them off."

WHAT REALLY HAPPENED IN 1000 A.D.? (Part II)

On page 118, we told you the dramatic tale of the "panic-terror" of 1000. Here's the rest of the story.

WAS THERE REALLY A PANIC?

To put it simply, many historians think the story we quoted on page 118 is nonsense. Here's why:

MAYBE YES, MAYBE NO

☞ There's no mention of millennial fears in any official documents of A.D. 1000—or in connection with any important events, such as the eruption of Mt. Vesuvius in 993 or Pope Gregory's death in 999.

☞ "The year 1000 sounds impressive," says *The Book of Predictions*, but in the Middle Ages, people used Roman numerals. It would simply have been "M" with no magic properties attached to it. Furthermore, numerical dates had little meaning to medieval people. Their lives were guided by the feast and fast days of the church, not calendars."

☞ The "panic-terror" story implies that Europeans all used the Common Calendar and celebrated New Year's on the same day. They didn't. There were dozens of different systems in use.

On top of that, there were no printed calendars, and no mechanical clocks. Given these conditions, the idea that the masses rose as one and embraced the terror is a little hard to swallow.

ORIGIN OF THE MYTH

So where did the tale come from? Probably a book called *Five Histories*, written in 1044 A.D. by a monk named Raoul Glaber. His account of the panic-terror is compelling enough to be believable...but it was written after the fact, and there's little evidence to support it.

The story really took hold in 18th-century France. According to *The Book of Predictions:* "Wishing to discredit the [values of] the Middle Ages, many writers such as Voltaire and Gibbon exaggerated the superstitions and credulous nature of medieval Christians." Anti-Catholic politicians also used it for their own purposes, "spreading the rumor that priests had used the millennium to defraud people of their land and money." Since then, it has been embellished and retold by dozens of modern authors.

THE MIDDLE GROUND

If there *was* a panic, it was probably confined to a few local areas. Henri Foucillon, a respected scholar, suggests that there were "stirrings in France, Lorraine, and Thuringia, toward the middle of the 10th century."

And maybe there were. But the interesting question is: Why do some people believe the story today?

HIGH ANXIETY

According to Peter N. Stearns in his book *Millennium III*, the reason is simple: anxiety about the millennium...which may not be a bad thing, if it "pushes people toward soul-searching." He writes:

> The effect [of the tale of the "panic-terror" of 1000 A.D.] may be rather like a good Halloween story. If told with relish, even an audience that doesn't believe in ghosts may wonder a bit about some coming fright; a few will buy into the full terror package. In the process, books or magazine articles will be sold, the public will have another kind of sensation to distract them, and maybe some useful chastening of modern pride and superficiality will occur.

But he insists:

> whether or not we want or need a good scare, as we approach the year 2000 we should at least get the facts about the past right and be properly suspicious of those who try to dish up demonstrable nonsense....
>
> If we want to be afraid of the year 2000 or 2001, fine, but let's not pretend it's because of a clear medieval precedent. If we choose to be scared, fine, but let's recognize that our medieval ancestors weren't.

BARNUM'S HISTORY LESSON

P. T. Barnum said, "There's a sucker born every minute"...then he proved it with his sideshows and circuses. He also wrote about it. In a book called Humbugs of the World, *published in 1866, he delightedly catalogued some of the great hoaxes in history. This excerpt was one of his favorites. It took place in 1667 in France, when an ambassador from Persia arrived at the pampered court of Louis XIV.*

THE AMBASSADOR ARRIVES

It was announced formally, one morning, to Louis XIV, that His Most Serene Excellency, Riza Bey, with an interminable tail of titles, hangers-on and equipages, had reached the port of Marseilles to lay before the great "King of the Franks" brotherly congratulations and gorgeous presents from his own illustrious master, the Shah of Persia.

The ambassador and his suite were lodged in sumptuous apartments in the Tuileries, under the care and guidance of King Louis's own assistant majordomo and a guard of courtiers and regiments of Royal Swiss. Banqueting and music filled up the first evening; and the next day His Majesty sent the Duc de Richelieu to announce that he would receive them on the third evening at Versailles.

THE AMBASSADOR IS WELCOMED

Meanwhile the most extensive preparations were made for the audience; when the time arrived, the entire Gallery of Mirrors was crowded with the beauty, the chivalry, the wit, taste, and intellect of France at that dazzling period. Louis the Great himself never appeared to finer advantage. His royal countenance was lighted up with pride and satisfaction as the Envoy of the haughty Oriental king approached the splendid throne on which he sat. As he descended a step to meet him, the Persian envoy bent the knee, and with uncovered head presented the credentials of his mission.

A grand ball and supper concluded this night of splendour, and Riza Bey was launched at the French court; every member of the illustrious court tried to outdo his peers with the value of the books, pictures, gems, etc. which they heaped upon the illustrious Persian.

"The more outrageous a subject can get, the more I like it." —Alfred Hitchcock

The latter gentleman very quietly smoked his pipe and lounged on his divan before company—and diligently packed up the goods when he and his jolly companions were left alone. The presents of the Shah had not yet arrived, but were daily expected, and from time to time the olive-coloured suite was diminished by the departure of one of the number with his chest on a special mission to England, Austria, or other European powers. In the meantime, the Bey was feted in all directions...and it was whispered that the fair ones of the court were, from the first, eager to bestow their favours.

THE AMBASSADOR'S PLANS

The King favoured his Persian pet with numerous personal interviews, at which, in broken French, the Envoy unfolded the most imposing of schemes of conquest and commerce that his master was willing to share with his great brother of France. At one of these tête-à-têtes, the magnificent Riza Bey, upon whom the King had already conferred his own portrait set in diamonds, and other gifts worth several millions of francs, placed in the Royal hand several fragments of opal and turquoise said to have been found near the Caspian sea, which teemed with limitless treasures of the same kind, and which the Shah of Persia proposed to divide with France for the honour of her alliance. The King was enchanted.

THE AMBASSADOR DISAPPEARS

At length, word was sent to Versailles that the gifts from the Shah had come, and a day was appointed for their presentation. The day arrived, and the Hall of Audience was again thrown open. All was jubilee; the King and the court waited, but no Persian—no Riza Bey—and no presents from the Shah!

That morning three men had left the Tuileries at daylight with a bag and a bundle, never to return. They were Riza Bey and his last bodyguards; the bag and the bundle were the smallest in bulk but the most precious in value of a month's plunder. The turquoises and opals bestowed upon the King turned out, on close inspection, to be a new and very ingenious variety of coloured glass.

Of course, a hue and cry was raised—but totally in vain. It was afterward believed that a noted barber and suspected bandit, who had once really travelled in Persia, was the perpetrator of this pretty joke. But no one was sure—no one ever heard from him again.

White House meals were cooked over a fireplace until 1850.

WORD ORIGINS

We use them, and we understand them. But where do familiar words come from? Probably not where you'd guess. Here are a few examples.

Debonair
French for "of good air." In the Middle Ages, people's health was judged partly by how they smelled. A person who gave off "good air" was presumed healthier and happier.

Gymnasium
Meant "to train naked" in ancient Greece, where athletes wore little or nothing.

Carnival
Literal meaning: "Flesh, farewell." Refers to traditional pre-Lenten feast (like Mardi Gras) after which people usually fasted.

Daisy
Comes from "day's eye." When the sun comes out, it opens its yellow eye.

Ukelele
In the 1800s, an English sailor gave such enthusiastic performances with this instrument that he was nicknamed *Ukelele*—"little jumping flea" in Hawaiian. He went on to popularize it around the world.

Gung Ho
Means "work together" in Chinese. After a group called Carlson's Raiders used it as their motto in WWII, it became a term to describe an enthusiastic soldier.

Ballot
Italian term for "small ball or pebble." Origin: Italian citizens once voted by casting a small pebble or ball into one of several boxes.

Jiggle
Refers to the jig (a dance).

Genuine
Originally meant "placed on the knees." In ancient Rome, a father legally claimed his newborn child by sitting in front of his family and placing the child on his knee.

Cab
Old Italian term for goat. The first carriages for public hire bounced so much they reminded people of goats romping on a hillside.

Spectator sports: 38% of Americans say they enjoy football on TV; only 16% like baseball.

THE WHOLE TOOTH

Some info to give you a little historical perspective when you're brushing your teeth.

TOOTHBRUSHES. People have been cleaning their teeth for thousands of years, but the implements they used weren't much like toothbrushes. Many cultures used "chew sticks," pencil-sized twigs with one end frayed into soft bristles; they've been found in Egyptian tombs dating back to 3000 B.C.

The first toothbrush to resemble modern ones originated in China around 1498. The bristles were plucked from hogs and set into handles of bone or bamboo. But animal hair is porous and water-absorbent, which makes it a breeding ground for bacteria; so brushing often did more harm than good. Nevertheless, by the 19th century, hogs-hair brushes were the standard for people who brushed.

Toothbrushing didn't become widely popular in the U.S. until the late 1930s. Two reasons for its spread: with the invention of nylon bristles by DuPont chemists in 1938, Americans finally had a hygienic substitute for hogs-hair; and every soldier who fought in World War II was instructed in oral hygiene and issued a brush—when the war ended they brought the habit home to their families.

TOOTHPASTE. History's first recorded toothpaste was an Egyptian mixture of ground pumice and strong wine. But the early Romans brushed their teeth with human urine...and also used it as a mouthwash. Actually, urine was an active component in toothpastes and mouthwashes until well into the 18th century—the ammonia it contains gave them strong cleansing power.

Fluoridated toothpaste came about as the result of a discovery made in Naples, Italy, in 1802, when local dentists noticed yellowish-brown spots on their patients' teeth—but no cavities. Subsequent examination revealed that high levels of fluoride in the water caused the spots *and* prevented tooth decay, and that less fluoride protected teeth without causing the spots. It took a while for the discovery to be implemented; the first U.S. fluoridated water tests didn't take place until 1915, and Crest, the first toothpaste with fluoride in it ("Look, Ma...") didn't hit stores until 1956

Poll results: U.S. bartenders say they hear more complaints about work than any other subject.

SANDBURGERS

Thoughts from Carl Sandburg, one of America's most celebrated poets and authors.

"Even those who have read books on manners are sometimes a pain in the neck."

"Put all your eggs in one basket and watch the basket."

"Everybody talks about the weather and nobody does anything about it."

"Blessed are they who expect nothing for they shall not be disappointed."

"Those who fear they may cast pearls before swine are often lacking in pearls."

"May you live to eat the hen that scratches on your grave."

"A lawyer is a man who gets two other men to take off their clothes and then he runs away with them."

"Six feet of earth make us all one size."

"I want money in order to buy the time to get the things that money will not buy."

"Many kiss the hands they wish to see cut off."

"Time is the storyteller you can't shut up."

"We asked the cyclone to go around our barn but it didn't hear us."

"Someday they'll give a war and nobody will come."

"Who swindles himself more deeply than the one saying, 'I am holier than thou?' "

"There are dreams stronger than death. Men and women die holding these dreams."

"If there is a bedbug in a hotel when I arrive he looks at the register for my room number."

"Why is the bribe-taker convicted so often and the bribe-giver so seldom?"

"Liberty is when you are free to do what you want to do and the police never arrest you if they know who you are and you got the right ticket."

After the birth: New parents spend about 50% more on health care and 34% less on alcohol.

TWISTED TITLES

California Monthly, *the magazine for alumni of the University of California at Berkeley, features a game called* Twisted Titles. *They ask readers to send the title of a book, film, play, etc., with just one letter changed—and include a brief description of the new work they envision. Here are excerpts from* Twisted Titles XII.

LITTLE RED HIDING HOOD
Marxist midget shelters Hoffa.

DON'T FIT UNDER THE APPLE TREE
The Andrews Sisters experience middle-age spread.

JUNE THE OBSCURE
Wally and the Beaver's reclusive mom tells all.

THE CAT IN THE CAT
Dr. Seuss introduces toddlers to the facts of life.

MY LIFE AS A LOG
Pinocchio reflects on his childhood.

THE NOW TESTAMENT
Bible of the "Me" generation.

DUNCES WITH WOLVES
Western epic starring the Three Stooges.

PATRIOT DAMES
The DAR does the IRA.

'TIL DEATH DO US PARK
Vows exchanged in New York City gridlock.

NEVER THE TWAIN SHALL MEAT
Sam Clemens becomes a vegetarian.

CANTERBURY TALKS
Phil, Oprah, Geraldo, and now, GEOFF!

CLUB TED
High jinks at Hyannisport.

MY LEFT FOOD
Politically correct chow.

GOYZ 'N THE HOOD
Jews and blacks unite to drive the KKK out of Beverly Hills.

THE WINNER OF OUR DISCONTENT
I'm more dysfunctional than you are.

SLEEPING WITH THE ENEMA
A tragedy in one act.

World record: In 1993, Japan became the first country with 1/5 of its population age 65 or older.

GIVE YOURSELF SOME CREDIT

Did you use a credit card to buy this book? Credit cards are a way of life to Americans. In fact, you could argue that those little pieces of plastic are actually the backbone of the American economy. How's that for a scary thought?...And they haven't even been around that long. Here is a brief history.

BACKGROUND By the 1950s, gasoline companies, department stores, and major hotels had developed their own credit cards—small pieces of cardboard or metal plates they gave their best customers to use instead of cash (allowing holders to pay for purchases at the end of the month). But these early cards were different than the ones we use today—they were only accepted at the business that had issued them.

THE FIRST SUPPER

According to legend, that all changed in one night in 1950, when businessman Robert X. McNamara finished his dinner in a posh New York restaurant—and realized that he didn't have enough cash to pay for the meal. His wife had to drive across town to pay for it, which embarrassed him deeply. But it also gave him an idea: why not issue a "diners card" that people could use to pay for meals when they were short of cash?

McNamara proposed his idea to a number of restaurants around town. In exchange for honoring his new "Diners Club" card, he would pay for the meal of anyone who presented the card. Diners Club would absorb the risk of non-payment; the restaurant got the money even if the cardholder was a deadbeat. How the card made its money: it paid the restaurants 90¢ to 95¢ on the dollar, billed the cardholder $1.00, and kept the difference in the form of a "discount." The restaurants balked at this arrangement at first, but McNamara convinced them that people with cards would spend more money—and more often—than people without them. By the end of the year, he had signed up 27 New York restaurants and 200 cardholders. The age of the credit card as we know it had begun.

The Danish flag, used since the 13th century, is the oldest unchanged national flag in existence.

CREDIT CARD FACTS

• The average American holds 2.9 Visas or MasterCards; even so, credit card companies send out more than 1 billion new credit card offers every year.

• Why do merchants like credit cards? On average, consumers spend 23% more money when they pay with credit cards than when they pay cash.

• Had you signed up for Sears' Discover card when it premiered in 1986, you would have been entitled to meal discounts at Denny's restaurants and 50% off psychiatric exams.

• In 1993, more than 31 million of the 211 million MasterCard and Visa cards in circulation were "affinity cards"—cards that donated a portion of each purchase to the charity shown on the card. One of the least popular: the Muscular Dystrophy Association Card, which has a picture of Jerry Lewis on it. It bombed so badly that it was taken off the market.

• It's illegal now, but credit card companies used to mail credit cards to people who hadn't even applied for them. It wasn't always good business: In 1966, five Chicago banks banded together and mailed five million credit cards to people who hadn't asked for them. But "the banks had been less than cautious in assembling their mailing lists. Some families received 15 cards. Dead people and babies got cards. A dachshund named Alice was sent not one but four cards, one of which arrived with the promise that Alice would be welcomed as a 'preferred customer' at many of Chicago's finest restaurants."

• In 1972 Walter Cavanagh and a friend bet a dinner to see who could accumulate the most credit cards. Eight years later he won the bet—and broke the world record—by applying for and getting 1,003 credit cards, weighing 34 pounds and entitling him to $1.25 million in credit. He's still applying for credit cards, and has set a goal of 10,000 cards.

• In 1987 aspiring moviemaker Robert Townsend paid for his first film, *Hollywood Shuffle*, by charging $100,000 on his 15 personal credit cards. Luckily, the movie made enough money for him to pay back the money.

According to one study, the "average American" is a 32.7-year-old woman who likes potato

SCRATCH 'N' SNIFF

No, this is not a scratch 'n' sniff page—it's about the scratch 'n' sniff phenomenon.

BACKGROUND

For years advertisers understood that scents help sell products, but they couldn't find a way to include smells in printed advertisements. The first attempt came in the 1950s, when newspaper companies tried printing with scented ink. The experiment flopped—either the smells dissipated rapidly, or they mixed with the newspaper's smell, spoiling the effect.

In 1969 the 3M Corp. and National Cash Register Co. (NCR) each developed a way to impregnate printed advertisements with fragrances. They called the technique "microencapsulation," because it literally sealed the smells in the surface of the ad until the consumer released them by scratching the page. For the first time in history, products as diverse as bananas, bourbon, shaving cream, dill pickles, pine trees—and, of course, perfume, could be advertised using their scents.

HOW IT WORKS

- The printing company takes a product like perfume or food, and extracts its aromatic oils.
- The oils are mixed with water, which breaks them up into tiny droplets—an average of one million drops per square inch.
- The droplets are sprayed onto paper or some other surface, and are covered with a layer of plastic resin or gum arabic.
- The scent remains fresh beneath the resin until someone scratches the surface. This bursts the layer of resin or gum that holds the droplets, and the smell escapes.

SCRATCH 'N' SNIFF FACTS

- Scratch 'n' sniff pages and scented pages aren't just novelties; they're big business. According to a study commissioned by Ralph Lauren Fragrances, 76% of women who buy new perfumes are introduced to the fragrances through scented inserts in magazines.
- On average, scented pages cost twice as much as scent-free ads.

chips, weighs 134 pounds, believes in the devil, and has sex about five times a month.

• A lot of people hate perfume strips, despite their popularity with perfume and ad companies. In fact, they can actually make sensitive people ill. In June 1991, a man wrote to *The New Yorker* complaining that "A very noxious and pervacious [sic] odor invaded this house with the mail today. Much to our surprise, it came from the arriving copy of *The New Yorker*....I am an elderly asthmatic, allergic to perfume, and although I have retched occasionally at some material in *The New Yorker*, I have never vomited on it before." As a result of his and other complaints, many magazines now offer scented and unscented editions.

• Another problem was that magazines were running more and more ads with perfume strips. Magazines got so smelly that perfume companies had to limit the number that could appear—and the post office itself began regulating scented inserts.

WEIRD USES

• In 1989 the English National Opera produced a scratch 'n' sniff version of Prokofiev's "Love for Three Oranges." Audience members received a special "fragrance panel" at the beginning of the play, along with instructions telling them when to sniff. The card even contained a scent for an unpleasant character named Farfarello, who has "bad breath and emits gasses." His smell was supposed to be "a cross between bad eggs and body odor," but the stench was so overpowering that it made the entire fragrance panel stink. In later performances of the play, his scent was left out.

• In 1990 the rock group Swamp Zombies released *Scratch and Sniff Car Crash*, an album whose cover smelled like burnt rubber. Weird inspiration: The band members got the idea after two of them narrowly escaped serious injury in automobile accidents.

• In 1989 the RJ Reynolds Tobacco company test-marketed Chelsea cigarettes, a brand targeted at women. Its major selling point: the smokes were rolled in a paper that gave off a sweet smell when it burned. They promoted the brand with scratch 'n' sniff newspaper ads showing off the scented papers. The ads smelled great—but cigarette sales stank, and the brand was dropped.

• In 1989 BEI Defense Systems, a Dallas missile manufacturer, ran a scratch 'n' sniff ad in *Armed Forces Journal* touting the company's "extraordinarily lethal" Flechette rocket. The ad smelled like cordite (the explosive contained in the warhead), an aroma the company called "the smell of victory."

According to most pollsters, it's easier to get a person to disclose intimate details about

FAMILIAR PHRASES

Here are more origins of common phrases.

BORN WITH A SILVER SPOON IN ONE'S MOUTH

Meaning: Pampered; lucky; born into wealth or prosperous circumstances.

Origin: At one time, it was customary for godparents to give their godchild a silver spoon at the baby's christening. These people were usually well-off, so the spoon came to represent the child's good fortune.

BITE THE BULLET

Meaning: Get on with a difficult or unpleasant task.

Origin: "Although one can find other explanations, it seems most plausible that the term originated in battlefield surgery before the days of anesthesia. A surgeon about to operate on a wounded soldier would urge him to bite on a bullet of soft lead to distract him from the pain; at least it would minimize his ability to scream and thus divert the surgeon." (From *The Dictionary of Clichés*, by James Rogers)

SOMETHING FITS TO A "T"

Meaning: It fits perfectly.

Origin: Commonly thought of as a reference to the T-square, which is used to draw parallel lines and angles. But this phrase was used in the 1600s, before anyone called the tool a T-square. "A more likely explanation is that the expression was originally 'to a tittle.' A tittle was the dot over the "i", so the phrase meant 'to a dot' or 'fine point.' " (From *Why Do We Say It*, by Nigel Rees)

THINGS WILL PAN OUT/ HAVEN'T PANNED OUT

Meaning: Optimistic view that things will work out / things haven't worked out.

Origin: When prospectors look for gold, they kneel by a river or stream and wash dirt from the bed in a shallow pan. This is called *panning*. Traditionally, when prospectors were sure they'd find gold,

their private life than it is to get them to tell you how much money they make.

they said things "would pan out." When they didn't find it, they said things "didn't pan out." (From *Gold!*, by Gordon Javna)

YOU'RE NO SPRING CHICKEN

Meaning: You're not young anymore; you're past your prime.

Origin: "Until recent generations, there were no incubators and few warm hen houses. That meant chicks couldn't be raised during winter. New England growers found that those born in the spring brought premium prices in the summer market places." When these Yankee traders tried to pass off old birds as part of the spring crop, smart buyers would protest that the bird was 'no spring chicken.' " (From *Why You Say It*, by Webb Garrison)

CLEAR THE DECKS

Meaning: Prepare for action; take care of minor matters, so you can focus on important ones.

Origin: A battle order in the days of sailing ships. "A crew prepared for battle by removing or fastening down all loose objects on deck that might otherwise get in the way of the guns or be knocked down and injure a sailor." (From *Fighting Words*, by Christine Ammer)

TRYING TO MAKE BOTH ENDS MEET

Meaning: Trying to stretch your income to live within your means.

Origin: On sailing ships of the 1400s and 1500s, sails "were raised and lowered separately, and the rigging involved hundreds of ropes. Some were permanently fixed. When such a rope broke, most preferred to replace it rather than attempt a repair job." But ship owners who were low on cash often told their captains "to pull broken rope ends together and splice them." So "a piece of rigging was stretched to the limit in order for both ends to meet." Gradually, the term moved from ship to shore, and came to mean stretching things to the limit because of a shortage of funds. (From *I've Got Goose Pimples*, by Martin Vanoni)

* * *

Important thought: "If you're killed, you've lost a very important part of your life." —***Brooke Shields***

BY GEORGE!

Wisdom from our first president, George Washington.

"Associate with men of good quality if you esteem your own reputation; for it is better to be alone than in bad company."

"Discipline is the soul of an army. It makes small numbers formidable, procures success to the weak, and esteem to all."

"Cursing and swearing is a vice so mean and low that every person of sense and character detests and despises it."

"Let us rise to a standard to which the wise and honest can repair."

"I have always given it as my decided opinion that...everyone had a right to form and adopt whatever government they liked best to live under themselves."

"It is only after time has been given for cool and deliberate reflection that the real voice of the people can be known."

"To be prepared for war is one of the most effectual means of preserving peace."

"A great and lasting war can never be supported on [patriotism] alone. It must be aided by a prospect of interest, or some reward."

"Few men have virtue to withstand the highest bidder."

"Do not conceive that fine clothes make fine men, any more that fine feathers make fine birds."

"In a free and republican government, you cannot restrain the voice of the multitude."

"The preservation of the sacred fire of liberty, and the destiny of the republican model of government, are...staked, on the experiment entrusted to the hands of the American people."

"Our cruel and unrelenting enemy leaves us only the choice of brave resistance, or the most abject submission. We have, therefore, to resolve to conquer or die."

"It is well I die hard, but I am not afraid to go."

Poll results: 59% of married men and 61% of married women say sex gets better after marriage.

BY GEORGE, TOO

Words of wisdom from George Carlin, one of America's most popular wise guys.

"Energy experts have announced the development of a new fuel made from human brain tissue. It's called assohol."

"I think I am. Therefore, I am...I think."

"The only good thing to come from religion is the music."

"When I was real small I heard about this thing called the decline of civilization... and I decided that it was something I would like to become involved in."

"I hope that someday a pope chooses the name Shorty."

"If God really made everything, I'd say he had a quality control problem."

"People are okay taken two or three at a time. Beyond that number they tend to choose up sides and wear armbands."

"I am not a complete vegetarian. I eat only animals that have died in their sleep."

"If you want to really test a faith healer, tell him you want a smaller shoe size."

"Remember: Dishonesty is the second best policy."

"I wonder why prostitution is illegal. Why should it be illegal to sell something that's perfectly legal to give away?"

"I say live and let live. Anyone who can't accept that should be executed."

"Just when I found the meaning of life, they changed it."

"I never thought I'd grow old. I always thought it was something that would happen to the other guy."

"Scientists announced today that they have discovered a cure for apathy. However, they claim no one has shown the slightest bit of interest in it."

"I don't mind a little government regulation, but requiring people to wear helmets during intercourse is going too far."

Estimated number of one room schoolhouses in Nebraska: 300.

FAMOUS TRIALS: THE WITCHES OF SALEM

Here's a bit of American history we're all familiar with...but know almost nothing about. The BRI wants to change that, because we don't want witch trials—or witch hunts—in our era. After all, someone just might decide that reading in the bathroom is a sign of demonic possession.

BACKGROUND The trouble at Salem, Massachusetts, began with two young girls acting oddly. It exploded into one of the strangest cases of mass hysteria in American history. In the six-month period between March and September 1692, 27 people were convicted on witchcraft charges; 20 were executed, and more than 100 other people were in prison awaiting trial.

CHILD'S PLAY

In March 1692, nine-year-old Betty Parris and her cousin Abigail Williams, 12, were experimenting with a fortune-telling trick they'd learned from Tituba, the Parris family's West Indian slave. To find out what kind of men they'd marry when they grew up, they put an egg white in a glass...and then studied the shape it made in the glass.

But instead of glimpsing their future husbands, the girls saw an image that appeared to be "in the likeness of a coffin." The apparition shocked them...and over the next few days they exhibited behavior that witnesses described as "foolish, ridiculous speeches," "odd postures," "distempers," and "fits."

Reverend Samuel Parris was startled by his daughter's condition and took her to see William Griggs, the family doctor. Griggs couldn't find out what was wrong with the girl, but he suspected the problem had supernatural origins. He told Rev. Parris that he thought the girl had fallen victim to "the Evil Hand"—witchcraft.

The family tried to keep Betty's condition a secret, but rumors began spreading almost immediately—and within two months at least eight other girls began exhibiting similar forms of bizarre behavior.

THE PARANOIA GROWS

The citizens of Salem Village demanded that the authorities take action. The local officials subjected the young girls to intense questioning, and soon the girls began naming names. The first three women they accused of witchcraft were Tituba and two other women from Salem Village, Sarah Good and Sarah Osborne.

The three women were arrested and held for questioning. A few weeks later two more suspects, Martha Cory and Rebecca Nurse, were arrested on similar charges. And at the end of April a sixth person—the Reverend George Burroughs, a minister that Abigail Williams identified as the leader of the witches—was arrested and imprisoned. The girls continued to name names. By the middle of May, more than 100 people had been arrested for witchcraft.

THE TRIALS

On May 14, 1692, the newly appointed governor, Sir William Phips, arrived from England. He immediately set up a special court, the Court of Oyer and Terminer, to hear the witchcraft trials that were clogging the colonial legal system.

• The first case heard was that against Bridget Bishop. She was quickly found guilty of witchcraft, sentenced to death, and then hung on June 10.

• On June 19 the court met a second time, and in a single day heard the cases of five accused women, found them all guilty, and sentenced them to death. They were hung on July 19.

• On August 5 the court heard six more cases, and sentenced all six women to death. One woman, Elizabeth Proctor, was spared because she was pregnant—and the authorities didn't want to kill an innocent life along with a guilty one. The remaining five women were executed on August 19.

• Six more people were sentenced to death in early September. (Only four were executed: one person was reprieved, and another woman managed to escape from prison with the help of friends.) The remaining sentences were carried out on September 22.

• On September 17, the court handed down nine more death sentences. (This time five of the accused "confessed" in exchange for a commutation of the death sentence and were not hung.) The remaining four were hung on September 22.

• Two days later, the trials claimed their last victim when Giles Cory, an accused wizard, was executed by "pressing" (he was slowly crushed to death under heavy weights) after he refused to enter a plea.

REVERSAL OF FORTUNE

By now the hysteria surrounding the witch trials was at its peak: 19 accused "witches" had been hung, about 50 had "confessed" in exchange for lenient treatment, more than 100 people accused of witchcraft were under arrest and awaiting trial—and another 200 people had been accused of witchcraft but had not yet been arrested. Despite all this, the afflicted girls were still exhibiting bizarre behavior. But public opinion began to turn against the trials. Community leaders began to publicly question the methods that the courts used to convict suspected witches. The accused were denied access to defense counsel, and were tried in chains before jurors who had been chosen from church membership lists.

The integrity of the girls then came under question. Some of the adults even charged that they were faking their illnesses and accusing innocent people for the fun of it. One colonist even testified later that one of the bewitched girls had bragged to him that "she did it for sport."

As the number of accused persons grew into the hundreds, fears of falling victim to witchcraft were replaced by an even greater fear: that of being falsely accused of witchcraft. The growing opposition to the proceedings came from all segments of society: common people, ministers—even from the court itself.

THE AFTERMATH

Once the tide had turned against the Salem witchcraft trials, many of the participants themselves began having second thoughts. Many of the jurors admitted their errors, witnesses recanted their testimony, and one judge on the Court of Oyer and Terminer, Samuel Sewall, publicly admitted his error on the steps of the Old South Church in 1697. The Massachusetts legislature made amends as well: in 1711 it reversed all of the convictions issued by the Court of Oyer and Terminer (and did it a second time in 1957), and it made financial restitution to the relatives of the executed, "the whole amounting unto five hundred seventy eight pounds and twelve shillings."

What's an ermine? A weasel whose coat has turned white for the winter.

THE COOLEST MOVIE LINES EVER

Here's an entry inspired by the Captain of Cool, Gene Sculatti, and his book Too Cool.

THE WILD ONE
Girl to Brando: "Hey Johnny, what are you rebelling against?"
Brando: "Whaddaya got?"

THE KILLERS
Claude Akens: "You said Johnny North died. How'd he die?"
Clu Gulager: "Questions...he asked one too many."

HIGH SCHOOL CONFIDENTIAL
(*Teenage interpretation of Queen Isabella's reaction to Columbus*) "Christy, what is this jazz you puttin' down 'bout our planet being round? Everybody's hip that it's square!"

THE COURT JESTER
Mildred Natwick: "The pellet with the poison's in the flagon with the dragon. The chalice from the palace holds the brew that is true."
Danny Kaye: "What about the vessel with the pestle?"

OCEANS 11 (*to doc examining X-rays*) "So tell me, doc. Is it the big casino?"

I WAS A TEENAGE FRANKENSTEIN
"I know you have a civil tongue in your head. I sewed it there myself."

THE BIG CARNIVAL
"I've met some hard-boiled eggs in my time, but you—you're 20 minutes."

MIDNIGHT RUN
Dennis Farina (*to henchman*)**:** "I want this guy taken out and I want him taken out fast. You and that other dummy better start gettin' more personally involved in your work, or I'm gonna stab you through the heart with a f—— pencil. You understand?"
Henchman: "You got it, Jimmy."

THE SWEET SMELL OF SUCCESS
(*Hustler Tony Curtis, about to go into action*) "Watch me make a hundred-yard run with no legs."

GOODFELLAS
"I'm an average nobody. I get to live the rest of my life like a schnook."

5 most persuasive words in the English language: *discover, easy, guarantee, health,* and *results.*

THREE MEMORABLE SALES PROMOTIONS

Companies are always trying to get our attention—and our money—with catchy slogans, free stuff, discounts, and so on. But occasionally a promotion stands out for ineptitude...or cleverness. Here are three examples.

A PENNY SAVED

The Company: *Reader's Digest*

The Promotion: For years the *Digest* solicited subscriptions with a letter that began, "An ancient Persian poet once said, 'If thou hast two pennies, spend one for bread and the other to buy hyacinths for the soul...' " In 1956 someone decided to give it a new twist by including two pennies with each letter. The point: People could keep one, and send the other back with their subscription order to get the "soul-satisfying" *Digest.*

What Happened: The magazine planned to send out 50 million letters, which meant they needed 100 million coins—enough to deplete the entire New York area of pennies. The U.S. Mint intervened, forcing *Reader's Digest* to make quick arrangements to ship in 60 million more pennies from all over the country. Then, when the company finally got all the pennies it needed, it stored them all in one room—and the floor collapsed under the weight. In the end, though, it was worth the effort—the promo drew a record number of responses.

HOOVERGATE

The Company: Hoover Europe, England's most prestigious manufacturer of vacuum cleaners

The Promotion: In 1992 Hoover tried to put a little life into the British vacuum market by offering an incredible deal: Any customer who bought at least 100 British pounds' (about $150) worth of Hoover merchandise got two free round-trip plane tickets to a European destination. Customers who bought 250 pounds' worth ($375) qualified for two tickets to either New York or Orlando, Florida.

What Happened: It was one of the biggest marketing fiascos in history. Customers realized the obvious—vacuum cleaners are cheaper than airline tickets—and snapped up every available Hoover. An estimated 200,000 customers—roughly 1 in every 300 people in Great Britain and Ireland—claimed they qualified for free flights.

The company sold so many vacuums that the factory switched to a seven-day work week to meet the demand—which made it, as one obeserver noted, "a classic case of mispricing a promotion so that the more products the company sold, the more money it lost." The promotion caused such a run on airline tickets that Hoover had to charter entire planes to meet the demand.

The promotion cost the company $48.8 million more than it expected—and cost 3 top executives their jobs. The parent company, Maytag, had to take a $10.5 million loss in the first quarter of 1993.

NORTH TO ALASKA

The Company: Quaker Oats

The Promotion: Quaker was the long-time sponsor of "Sergeant Preston of the Yukon," a popular kids' TV series. In 1955 they decided to create a tie-in between the show and some cereals that weren't selling too well—Quaker Puffed Rice and Quaker Puffed Wheat. Their ad agency came up with an unusual plan: Buy up a parcel of land on the Yukon River in Alaska, then subdivide it into 21 million one-inch-square parcels and give away a real deed to one of the parcels in each box of cereal.

What Happened: According to *Getting It Right the Second Time*, "[Quaker's ad exec] and a company lawyer flew to Dawson, Alaska, selected a 19.11-acre plot of ice on the Yukon River from the air, and bought it for $10,000. [The ad man] wanted to go home, but the Quaker lawyer insisted on investigating the land close up by boat. As it turned out, the boat developed a leak in the middle of the half-frozen river, and the passengers were forced to jump overboard. They paddled back to shore, only to find they'd missed their dogsled connection back to the airstrip. As darkness fell, the Quaker contingent was forced to walk six miles in subzero weather to meet the aircraft and go home."

Was it worth the aggravation? Quaker thought so. They sold more than 21 million boxes of Puffed Rice / Wheat; it has been cited as one of the three most successful cereal promotions ever.

Immediately after the last episode of "M*A*S*H*", New York City's sewer flow increased by

LEFT-HANDED FACTS

We've considered doing something about left-handedness for several years, but the question always comes up—are there enough left-handed bathroom readers to make it worthwhile? After six years, we finally don't care; we just want to use the information. So here's a section for southpaws.

Are you left-handed? If so, you're not alone—but you're definitely outnumbered; lefties make up only 5% to 15% of the general population. If you're a female southpaw, you're even more unusual—there are roughly 50% more left-handed males than females. For centuries scientists have tried to figure out what makes people left- or right-handed, and they still aren't sure why. (They're not even sure if all lefties are that way for the same reason.) Here are some theories:

WHAT MAKES A LEFTIE?

- Scientists used to think that left- and right-handedness was purely a genetic trait, but now they have doubts. Reason: In 20% of all sets of identical twins, one sibling is left-handed, and the other is right-handed.

- Some scientists think the hand you prefer is determined by whether you're a "right-brained" person or a "left-brained" person. The right half of the brain controls the left side of the body, as well as spatial / musical / aesthetic judgement and perception; the left half controls the right side of the body, plus communication skills. Lefties are generally right-brained.

- Support for this theory: Most children begin demonstrating a preference for one hand over the other at the same time their central nervous system is growing and maturing. This leads some scientists to believe the two processes are linked.

- According to another theory, before birth all babies are right-handed—which means that the left side of their brain is dominant. But during a stressful or difficult birth, oxygen deficiency can cause damage to the left side of the brain, making it weaker and enabling the right side to compete against it for dominance. If the right side wins out, the baby will become left-handed.

320 million gallons—the equivalent of 1 million toilets flushing simultaneously.

• This theory also explains, researchers claim, why twins, any child born to a smoker, or children born to a mother more than 30 years old are more likely to be left-handed: they are more prone to stressful births. Children of stressful births are also more likely to stammer and suffer dyslexia, traits that are more common in lefties.

LEFT-HANDED HISTORY

No matter what makes southpaws what they are, they've been discriminated against for thousands of years—in nearly every culture on Earth. Some examples:

• The artwork found in ancient Egyptian tombs portrays most Egyptians as right-handed. But their enemies are portrayed as left-handers, a sign they saw left-handedness as an undesirable trait.

• Ancient Greeks never crossed their left leg over their right, and believed a person's sex was determined by their position in the womb—with the female, or "lesser sex," sitting on the left side of the womb.

• The Romans placed special significance on right-handedness as well. Custom dictated that they enter friends' homes "with the right foot forward"...and turn their heads to the right to sneeze. Their language showed the same bias: the Latin word for left was *sinister* (which also meant "evil" or "ominous"), the word for right was *dexter* (which came to mean "skillful," or "adroit"). Even the word ambidextrous literally means "right-handed with both hands."

• The Ango-Saxon root for left is *lyft*, which means "weak," "broken," or "worthless." *Riht* means "straight," "just," or "erect."

BIBLICAL BIAS

• The Bible is biased in favor of right-handed people. Both the Old and New Testament refer to "the right hand of God." One Old Testament town, Nineveh, is so wicked that its citizens "cannot discern between their right hand and their left hand."

• The saints also followed the right-hand rule; according to early Christian legend, they were so pious even as infants that they refused to nurse from their mother's left breast.

• The distinction is made even in religious art: Jesus and God are nearly always drawn giving blessings with their right hand, and the Devil is usually portrayed doing evil with his left hand.

Close encounters: 10% of Americans swear they've "been in the presence of a ghost."

MTV FACTS

These pages were contributed by Larry Kelp, whose picture has been on the back cover since the first Bathroom Reader. *He's a music writer in the San Francisco Bay Area, and was Uncle John's neighbor.*

I WANT MY MTV!

In 1981 Robert Pittman, a 27-year-old vice president in charge of new programming at Warner-Amex, came up with an idea for Music Television, an all-music channel that would play almost nothing but rock videos. The gimmick: free programming— the videos would be supplied by record companies at no charge. "The explicit aim," explains one critic, "was to deliver the notoriously difficult-to-reach 14 to 34 demographic segment to the record companies, beer manufacturers, and pimple cream makers."

Based on that appeal, Pittman talked Warner into investing $30 million in the idea. Four years later, Warner-Amex sold MTV to Viacom for $550 million. In 1992 its estimated worth was $2 billion. Today it broadcasts in more than 50 different countries.

GETTING STARTED

• Pittman planned to call the channel TV-1, but immediately ran into a problem: "Our legal department found another business with that name. The best we could get was TV-M...and TV-M it was, until our head of music programming said, "Don't you think MTV sounds a little better than TV-M?"

• The design for the logo was another fluke. "Originally," Pittman recalls, "We thought MTV would be three equal-size letters like ABC, NBC and CBS. But...three 'kids' in a loft downtown, Manhattan Design, came up with the idea for a big M, with TV spray-painted over it. We just cut the paint drips off the TV, and that's the logo. We paid about $1,000 for one of the decade's best-known logos."

• MTV originally planned to use astronaut Neil Armstrong's words, "One small step for man, one giant leap for mankind," with its now-famous "Moon Man" station identification. "But a few days before we launched," Pittman says, "an executive came flying into my office. We had just received a letter from Armstrong's lawyer threatening to sue us if we used his client's voice. We had no time and,

Long live the King: 13 countries around the world have issued Elvis Presley postage stamps.

worse, no money to redo this on-air ID. So we took his voice off and used the ID with just music. Not at all what we had envisioned, yet, fortunately, it worked fine."

MTV DATA

• MTV went on air at midnight, August 1, 1981. Its first video was the Buggles' prophetic "Video Killed the Radio Star."

• The average MTV viewer tunes in for 16 minutes at a time.

• MTV's VJs have a short shelf life. Once they start looking old, they're retired.

• Not all of the music channel's fans are teenagers. One unusual audience: medical offices. *Prevention* magazine says MTV in the doctor's office helps relieve women's tension before medical exams.

• MTV reaches 75% of those households inhabited by people 18 to 34 years old and 85% of the households with one teenager.

• While many countries served by MTV Europe have local programming with their own VJs, most are in English, the global language of rock. In Holland, a Flemish language show was dropped because viewers complained that it wasn't in English.

YO, MTV!

It took constant badgering by 25-year-old former intern Ted Demme (nephew of film director Jonathan) to get MTV to air a rap show, "Yo! MTV Raps," in 1989. He argued that white suburban kids wanted rap. The execs gave him one shot at it. "Yo!" was aired on a Saturday. By Monday the ratings and calls were so impressive that "Yo!" got a daily slot, and quickly became MTV's top-rated show.

UNPLUGGED

In 1990 MTV first aired "Unplugged," which went against everything music videos had stood for. Instead of stars lip-synching to prerecorded tracks, "Unplugged" taped them live in front of a studio audience, and forced them to use acoustic instruments, making music and talent the focus. What could have been a gimmick turned into a trend when Paul McCartney released his "Unplugged" appearance as an album, and it became one of his bestselling albums. Two years later, Eric Clapton did the same, which made "Layla" a hit song all over again and earned him Grammy Awards as well as platinum records.

More than 50% of Americans believe in the devil; 1 in 10 say they've talked to him personally.

PRIMETIME PROVERBS

TV comments about everyday life. From Primetime Proverbs, *by Jack Mingo and John Javna.*

ON AMBITION

"I'm tired of being an object of ridicule. I wanna be a figure of fear, respect, and SEX!"

—Radar O'Reilly,
M*A*S*H

ON AMERICA

George Jefferson: "It's the American dream come true. Ten years ago, I was this little guy with one store. And now look at me—"

Louise Jefferson: "Now your're the little guy with seven stores."

—The Jeffersons

ON THE ARTS

"You know, if Michelangelo had used me as a model, there's no telling how far he could have gone."

—Herman Munster,
The Munsters

ON DATING

"Randy, there are three reasons why I won't go out with you: one, you're obnoxious; two, you're repulsive; and three, you haven't asked me yet."

—Julianne,
Van Dyke

ON MEN

"A good man doesn't happen. They have to be created by us women. A guy is a lump like a doughnut. So, first you gotta get rid of all the stuff his mom did to him. And then you gotta get rid of all that macho crap that they pick up from the beer commercials. And then there's my personal favorite, the male ego."

—Roseanne,
Roseanne

ON COURAGE

"Wanna do something courageous? Come to my house and say to my mother-in-law, 'You're wrong, fatso!' "

—Buddy Sorrell,
The Dick Van Dyke Show

ON BANKERS

"Why do they call them tellers? They never tell you anything. They just ask questions. And why do they call it interest? It's boring. And another thing—how come the Trust Department has all their pens chained to the table?"

—Coach Ernie Pantusso,
Cheers

Claim to fame: Grand Rapids, Michigan, was the first city to fluoridate its water supply.

AUNT LENNA'S PUZZLES

Some adventures with my favorite aunt. Answers are on p. 663.

MURDER AT THE BIG HOTEL

My Aunt Lenna loves puzzles. Not complicated ones—just the kind people call *brain teasers*. "I don't like those puzzles where you have to be a genius at math," she often says. "I want simple puzzles of logic."

One day she was reading a mystery, and she began musing out loud: "It was a very large, fancy hotel. The hotel detective was making his rounds, walking in the hallway…when suddenly he heard a woman cry, 'Please! Don't shoot me, Steve!' And a shot rang out!"

"Sounds original, Aunt Lenna."

"Well now, hold on, Nephew. The detective ran as fast as he could to the room the shot came from, and pushed his way in. The body of a woman who'd been shot lay in a corner of the room; the gun that had been used to kill her was on the floor near her. On the opposite side of the room stood a postman, an accountant, and a lawyer. For a moment, the detective hesitated as he looked at them. Then he strode up to the postman and said—'You're under arrest for murder.'

"A little hasty, wasn't he? Or was there some evidence you're not mentioning?"

"He wasn't hasty, and there was no other evidence…and the detective made the right choice."

"Well, how did he know?"

How did he?

Aunt Lenna likes word games, too. Some are real groaners. Like she once asked me, "What word is it that when you take away the whole, you still have some left?" Another time she asked, "Can you make one word out of the letters D R E N O O W?"

Got the answers?

Owls are the only birds that can see the color blue.

THE DEATH OF VICKI MORGAN

Was Vicki Morgan murdered by her mentally disturbed housemate—or by her powerful enemies in the Republican establishment?

Suspicious Death: Vicki Morgan, model and longtime mistress of Alfred Bloomingdale, one of the wealthiest men in America. (He was heir to the Bloomingdale department store fortune, and a member of Ronald Reagan's Kitchen Cabinet.)

How she died: On July 7, 1983, Morgan was found dead in her apartment, beaten to death with a baseball bat. The man who shared her Studio City condo, Marvin Pancoast, confessed.

BACKGROUND

• Morgan was Bloomingdale's mistress for twelve years—from 1970 to 1982, when Bloomingdale contracted terminal throat cancer. Once Alfred was hospitalized, his wife, Betsy, long furious about the affair, cut off Morgan's income—which was reportedly between $10,000 and $18,000 a month.

• In response, Morgan decided to go public about the affair. She first tried to place her memoirs, *Alfred's Mistress*, with the William Morris Agency. When that attempt fizzled—allegedly because of White House pressure—she filed a $10 million palimony suit against Bloomingdale in which she revealed all of Bloomingdale's indiscretions, from his taste for kinky sex—she once described him as "a drooling sadist" with a fondness for bondage and beatings—to his loose talk about "secret and delicate matters such as campaign contributions for Mr. Reagan."

• The case was thrown out, but the trial was an enormous embarrassment to Betsy Bloomingdale—Nancy Reagan's close friend—as well as to Bloomingdale's highly placed Republican cronies.

Not just for kids: Nintendo estimates that 42% of the people who use its games are over 18.

SUSPICIOUS FACTS

Marvin Pancoast

• Pancoast had a history of mental illness. (In fact, Morgan had met him four years earlier when they were both patients in a mental institution.) He had previously confessed to crimes he hadn't committed. At one point he even confessed to the Tate-LaBianca murders committed by the Manson family.

• The room in which Morgan was killed was spattered with blood—but, according to John Austin, author of *Hollywood's Unsolved Mysteries*, when Pancoast turned himself in, he did not have a spot of blood on him anywhere. No bloodstained clothes of his were ever found.

Kissing and Telling

• Morgan may have been more than just Bloomingdale's mistress—Bloomingdale may have used her to gather dirt on top-level Republican officials. According to Austin, Bloomingdale had his Hollywood house wired with "state-of-the-art video cameras in every room and hidden behind false walls. Even the three johns were 'wired' behind two-way mirrors.... Vicki and Pancoast would often 'share' a high ranking member of the [Reagan] Administration....Anyone who was important in the pre-Administration and the Administration of Ronald Reagan and who wanted *divertissement* called on Alfred, regardless of what his or her fetish might be." And Bloomingdale allegedly got it all on tape.

• If the tapes existed, what happened to them? Five days after Morgan's death, attorney Robert Steinberg held a press conference in Los Angeles announcing that he had received three videotapes showing "Bloomingdale and Miss Morgan engaging in group and sadomasochistic sex with top government officials." The sex tapes, Steinberg asserted, could "bring down the Reagan government." But when a court ordered Steinberg to turn them over to police, he suddenly declared that they had been stolen from a bag in his office during the press conference. The media denounced the whole thing as a hoax.

• Morgan's apartment wasn't sealed by the L.A. Police Department until more than 24 hours after the murder. According to author Anne Louise Bardach, "This is really a story of police negligence.

McDonalds hired 45 Ph.D. scientists to help it develop "carrot sticks" in 1991.

People could just walk in and walk out. And they did. If there were any 'sex tapes' in the condo, then they could easily have disappeared during those 24 hours."

• Morgan may have sensed that the end was near. The night before she was killed, according to her friend Gordon Basichis, "Vicki confided in me that she was afraid of being murdered. I have a feeling that someone with knowledge of the Bloomingdale 'tapes' had approached her, possibly through Pancoast, with a proposal for blackmail."

POSSIBLE CONCLUSIONS

• **Pancoast killed her.** After all, he confessed and was sentenced in the case.

• **Someone in power had Morgan killed.** She could have been killed to silence her. If the videotapes did exist, they would have been severely damaging to the Reagan administration. Bloomingdale was a close personal friend of the president and an appointee to the Foreign Intelligence Advisory Board.

RECOMMENDED READING

• *Encyclopedia of American Scandal*, by George C. Kohn (Facts On File, 1989)

• *Hollywood's Unsolved Mysteries*, by John Austin (Shapolsky Publishers, Inc., 1990)

TALES OF THE CIA

The ultimate in insider trading was described in Warren Hinkle and William Turner's book *Deadly Secrets*: "When the White House gave the green light for the [Bay of Pigs invasion of Cuba in 1961], a number of CIA insiders began buying the stocks of Francisco and other sugar companies, the earnings of which had been depressed by the loss of Cuban plantations. Stockbrokers became curious about the sudden influx of orders as friends were cut in on the tip that cheap sugar shares might prove a sweet gamble."

Hooters, a Las Vegas company, charges $57 an hour to have topless women clean your home.

SHAKESPEARE SAYETH...

Here's the "high culture" section of the Bathroom Reader.

"The first thing we do, let's kill all the lawyers."

"Neither a borrower, nor a lender be; For oft loses both itself and friend."

"He is well paid that is well satisfied."

"What's in a name? That which we call a rose / By any other name would smell as sweet."

"Some are born great, some achieve greatness, and some have greatness thrust upon them."

"Though this be madness, yet there is method in it."

"When Fortune means to men most good, she looks upon them with a threatening eye."

"Remuneration! O! that's the Latin word for three farthings."

"Words pay no debts."

"You taught me language; and my profit on't is, I know how to curse."

"Talkers are not good doers."

"The saying is true, the empty vessel makes the loudest sound."

"My words fly up, my thoughts remain below: Words without thoughts never to heaven go."

"If all the year were playing holidays / To sport would be as tedious as to work."

"The fault, dear Brutus, is not in our stars / But in ourselves."

"A politician....One that would circumvent God."

"When my love swears that she is made of truth / I do believe her, though I know she lies."

"Let me have no lying; it becomes none but tradesmen."

"If it be a sin to covet honor, I am the most offending soul."

"One may smile, and smile, and be a villan."

"Time is come round, and where I did begin, there shall I end."

In the average film, male actors utter 10 times as many profanities as female actors.

EVERYDAY ORIGINS

Some quick stories about the origins of everyday objects.

SCOTCH TAPE. Believe it or not, the sticky stuff gets its name from an ethnic slur. When two-toned paint jobs became popular in the 1920s, Detroit carmakers asked the 3M Company for an alternative to masking tape that would provide a smooth, sharp edge where the two colors met. 3M came up with 2-inch wide cellophane tape, but auto companies said it was too expensive. So 3M lowered the price by only applying adhesive along the sides of the strip. That caused a problem: the new tape didn't stick—and company painters complained to the 3M salesman, "Take this tape back to your stingy 'Scotch' bosses and tell them to put more adhesive on it!" The name—and the new tape—stuck.

BRASSIERES. Mary Phelps Jacob, a teenage debutante in 1913, wanted to wear a rose-garlanded dress to a party one evening. But, as she later explained, her corset cover "kept peeping through the roses around my bosom." So she took it off, pinned two handkerchiefs together, and tied them behind her back with some ribbon. "The result was delicious," she later recalled. "I could move much more freely, a nearly naked feeling." The contraption eventually became known as a *brassière*—a name borrowed from the corset cover it replaced. (Jacob later became famous for riding naked through the streets of Paris on an elephant.)

DINNER KNIVES. Regular knives first had their points rounded and their sharp edges dulled for use at the dinner table in 1669. According to Margaret Visser, author of *The Rituals of Dinner*, this was done "apparently to prevent their use as 'toothpicks,' but probably also to discourage assassinations at meals."

WRISTWATCHES. Several Swiss watchmakers began attaching small watches to bracelets in 1790. Those early watches weren't considered serious timepieces, and they remained strictly a women's item until World War I, when armies recognized their usefulness in battle and began issuing them to servicemen instead of the traditional pocket watch.

"Smut" gets its name from a fungus that lives on corn kernels.

FORKS. Before forks became popular, the difference between refined and common people was the number of fingers they ate with. The upper classes used three; everyone else used five. This began to change in the 11th century, when tiny, two-pronged forks became fashionable in Italian high society. But they didn't catch on; the Catholic Church opposed them as unnatural (it was an insult to imply that the fingers God gave us weren't good enough for food), and people who used them were ridiculed as effeminate or pretentious. Forks weren't generally considered polite until the 18th century—some 800 years after they were first introduced.

PULL-TOP BEER CANS. In 1959 a mechanical engineer named Ermal Cleon Fraze was at a picnic when he realized he'd forgotten a can opener. No one else had one either, so he had to use the bumper guard of his car to open a can of soda. It took half an hour, and he vowed he'd never get stuck like that again. He patented the world's first practical pull-top can later that year, and three years later, the Pittsburgh Brewing Company tried using it on its Iron City Beer. Now every beer company does.

REFRIGERATOR MAGNETS. Mass-produced magnets *designed* for refrigerators didn't appear until 1964. They were invented by John Arnasto and his wife Arlene, who sold a line of decorative wall hooks. Arlene thought it would be cute to have a hook for refrigerator doors, so John made one with a magnet backing. The first one had a small bell and was shaped like a tea kettle. It sold well, so the Arnastos added dozens of other versions to their lines. Believe it or not, some of the rare originals are worth more than $100.

TOOTHPASTE TUBES. Toothpaste wasn't packaged in collapsible tubes until 1892, when Dr. Washington Wentworth Sheffield, a Connecticut dentist, copied the idea from a tube of oil-based paint. Increasing interest in sanitation and hygiene made the new invention more popular than jars of toothpaste, which mingled germs from different brushes. Toothpaste tubes became the standard almost overnight.

Believable Quote: "I was not lying. I said things that later on seemed to be untrue."

—***Richard Nixon***

Top 4 presidential religions: Episcopal (12), Presbyterian (9), Baptist and Unitarian (tied at 4).

REEFER MADNESS

After being widely cultivated for 10,000 years, marijuana was suddenly outlawed in America in 1937. Was it because it was a threat to the American public—or only to certain business interests?

For thousands of years, hemp (*cannabis sativa*) has been one of the most useful plants known to man. Its strong, stringy fibers make durable rope and can be woven into anything from sails to shirts; its pithy centers, or "hurds," make excellent paper; its seeds, high in protein and oil, have been pressed for lighting and lubricating oils and pulped into animal feed; and extracts of its leaves have provided a wide range of medicines and tonics.

HEMP & AMERICA

• Hemp also has a notable place in American history:

✓ Washington and Jefferson grew it.

✓ Our first flags were likely made of hemp cloth.

✓ The first and second drafts of the Declaration of Independence were written on paper made from Dutch hemp.

✓ When the pioneers went West, their wagons were covered with hemp canvas (the word "canvas" comes from *canabacius*, hemp cloth).

✓ The first Levi's sold to prospectors were sturdy hemp coveralls.

✓ Abraham Lincoln's wife, Mary Todd, came from the richest hemp-growing family in Kentucky.

• After the Civil War, hemp production in the States declined steeply. Without slave labor, hemp became too expensive to process. Besides, cotton ginned by machines was cheaper. Still, hemp fabric remained the second most common cloth in America.

• The plant's by-products remained popular well into this century. Maple sugar combined with hashish (a resin from hemp leaves) was sold over the counter and in Sears Roebuck catalogs as a harmless candy. Hemp rope was a mainstay of the navy. Two thousand tons of hemp seed were sold annually as bird feed. The pharmaceutical industry used hemp extracts in hundreds of potions and vigorously

Which George Washington portrait is more accurate, the $1 bill or the quarter? The quarter.

fought attempts to restrict hemp production. And virtually all good paints and varnishes were made from hemp-seed oil and/or linseed oil.

WHAT HAPPENED

• In the 1920s and 1930s, the American public became increasingly concerned about drug addiction—especially to morphine and a "miracle drug" that had been introduced by the Bayer Company in 1898 under the brand name "Heroin." By the mid-1920s, there were 200,000 heroin addicts in the United States alone.

• Most Americans were unaware that smoking hemp leaves was intoxicating, however, until William Randolph Hearst launched a campaign of sensational stories that linked "the killer weed" to jazz musicians, "crazed minorities," and unspeakable crimes. Hearst's papers featured headlines like:

✓ MARIJUANA MAKES FIENDS OF BOYS IN 30 DAYS: HASHEESH [SIC] GOADS USERS TO BLOOD-LUST

✓ NEW DOPE LURE, MARIJUANA, HAS MANY VICTIMS

• In 1930, Hearst was joined in his crusade against hemp by Harry J. Anslinger, commissioner of the newly organized Federal Bureau of Narcotics (FBN). Hearst often quoted Anslinger in his newspaper stories, printing sensational comments like "If the hideous monster Frankenstein came face to face with the monster marijuana he would drop dead of fright."

• Not everyone shared their opinion. In 1930, the U.S. government formed the Siler Commission to study marijuana smoking by off-duty servicemen in Panama. The commission found no lasting effects and recommended that no criminal penalties apply to its use.

• Nonetheless, Hearst and Anslinger's anti-hemp campaign got results. By 1931, twenty-nine states had prohibited marijuana use for nonmedical purposes. In 1937, after two years of secret hearings—and based largely on Anslinger's testimony—Congress passed the Marijuana Tax Act, which essentially outlawed marijuana in America.

• Because Congress wasn't sure that it was constitutional to ban hemp outright, it taxed the plant prohibitively instead. Hemp growers had to register with the government, sellers and buyers had

The original Gotham City was a mythical English town whose residents were extremely stupid.

to fill out cumbersome paperwork, and, of course, it was a federal crime not to comply.

• For selling an ounce or less of marijuana to an unregistered person, the federal tax was $100. (To give some sense of how prohibitive the tax was, "legitimate" marijuana was selling for $2 a pound at the time. In 1992 dollars, the federal tax would be roughly $2,000 per ounce.)

• The Marijuana Tax Act effectively destroyed all legitimate commercial cultivation of hemp. Limited medical use was permitted, but as hemp derivatives became prohibitively expensive for doctors and pharmacists, they turned to chemically derived drugs instead. All other nonmedical uses, from rope to industrial lubricants, were taxed out of existence.

• With most of their markets gone, farmers stopped growing hemp, and the legitimate industry disappeared. Ironically, though, hemp continued to grow wild all over the country, and its "illegitimate" use was little affected by Congress.

WAS IT A CONSPIRACY?

Was a viable hemp industry forced out of existence because it was a threat to people's health or because it was a threat to a few large businesses that would profit from banning it?

THE HEARST CONSPIRACY

• Hemp was outlawed just as a new technology would have made hemp paper far cheaper than wood-pulp paper.

• Traditionally, hemp fiber had to be separated from the stalk by hand, and the cost of labor made this method uncompetitive. But in 1937—the year that hemp was outlawed, the *decorticator* machine was invented; it could process as much as three tons of hemp per hour and produced higher-quality fibers with less loss of fiber than wood-based pulp. According to some scientists, hemp would have been able to undercut competing products overnight. Enthusiastic about the new technology, *Popular Mechanics* predicted that hemp would become America's first "billion-dollar crop." The magazine pointed out that "10,000 acres devoted to hemp will produce as much paper as 40,000 acres of average [forest] pulp land."

• According to Jack Herer, an expert on the "hemp conspiracy,"

Coney Island was once full of rabbits, which New York's colonists called "coneys."

Hearst, the Du Ponts, and other "industrial barons and financiers knew that machinery to cut, bale, decorticate (separate fiber from the stalk) and process hemp into paper was becoming available in the mid-1930s." (*The Emperor Wears No Clothes*)

• Hearst, one of the promoters of the anti-hemp hysteria, had a vested interest in protecting the pulp industry. Hearst owned enormous timber acreage; competition from hemp paper might have driven the Hearst paper-manufacturing division out of business and caused the value of his acreage to plummet. (ibid.)

• Herer suggests that Hearst slanted the news in his papers to protect his pulp investments. "In the 1920s and '30s," he writes, "Hearst's newspaper chain led the deliberate...yellow journalism campaign to have marijuana outlawed. From 1916 to 1937, as an example, the story of a car accident in which a marijuana cigarette was found would dominate the headlines for weeks, while alcohol-related car accidents (which outnumbered marijuana-related accidents by more than 1,000 to 1) made only the back pages." (ibid.)

• Herer says that Hearst was even responsible for popularizing the term "marijuana" in American culture. In fact, he suggests, popularizing the word was a key strategy of Hearst's efforts: "The first step [in creating hysteria] was to introduce the element of fear of the unknown by using a word that no one had ever heard of before...'marijuana.' " (ibid.)

THE DU PONT CONSPIRACY

• The Du Pont Company also had an interest in the pulp industry. At this time, it was in the process of patenting a new sulfuric acid process for producing wood-pulp paper. According to the company's own records, wood-pulp products ultimately accounted for more than 80% of all of Du Pont's railroad car loadings for the next 50 years. (ibid.)

• But Du Pont had even more reasons to be concerned about hemp. In the 1930s, the company was making drastic changes in its business strategy. Traditionally a manufacturer of military explosives, Du Pont realized after the end of World War I that developing peacetime uses for artificial fibers and plastics would be more profitable in the long run. So it began pouring millions of dollars into research—which resulted in the development of such synthetic fibers as rayon and nylon.

Los Angeles' full name is *El Pueblo de Nuestra Señora la Reina de los Angeles de Porciuncula.*

✓ Two years before the prohibitive hemp tax, Du Pont developed a new synthetic fiber, nylon, that was an ideal substitute for hemp rope.

✓ The year after the hemp tax, Du Pont was able to bring another "miracle" synthetic fabric onto the market—rayon. Rayon, which became widely used for clothing, was a direct competitor to hemp cloth.

✓ "Congress and the Treasury Department were assured, through secret testimony given by Du Pont, that hemp-seed oil could be replaced with synthetic petrochemical oils made principally by Du Pont." These oils were used in paints and other products. (ibid.)

• The millions spent on these products, as well as the hundreds of millions in expected profits from them, could have been wiped out if the newly affordable hemp products were allowed onto the market. So, according to Herer, Du Pont worked with Hearst to eliminate hemp.

• Du Pont's pointman was none other than Harry Anslinger, the commissioner of the FBN. Anslinger was appointed to the FBN by Treasury Secretary Andrew Mellon, who was also chairman of the Mellon Bank, Du Pont's chief financial backer. But Anslinger's relationship to Mellon wasn't just political—he was also married to Mellon's niece.

• Anslinger apparently used his political clout to sway congressional opinion on the hemp tax. According to Herer, the American Medical Association (AMA) tried to argue for the medical benefits of hemp. But after AMA officials testified to Congress, "they were quickly denounced by Anslinger and the entire congressional committee, and curtly excused."

FOOTNOTES

• Five years after the hemp tax was imposed, when Japanese seizure of Philippine hemp caused a wartime shortage of rope, the government reversed itself. Overnight, the U.S. government urged hemp cultivation once again and created a stirring movie called "Hemp for Victory"—then, just as quickly, it recriminalized hemp after the shortage had passed.

• While U.S. hemp was temporarily legal, however, it saved the life of a young pilot named George Bush, who was forced to bail

Cincinnati was so famous for its hog industry in the 1830s that it was nicknamed "Porkopolis."

out of his burning airplane after a battle over the Pacific. At the time, he didn't know that:

✓ Parts of his aircraft engine were lubricated with hemp-seed oil.

✓ His life-saving parachute webbing was made entirely from U.S.-grown cannabis hemp.

✓ Virtually all the rigging and ropes of the ship that rescued him were made of cannabis hemp.

✓ The fire hoses on the ship were woven from cannabis hemp.

Ironically, President Bush consistently opposed decriminalizing hemp grown in the United States.

• Does the hemp conspiracy continue? In March 1992, Robert Bonner, the chief of the Drug Enforcement Agency, effectively rejected a petition to permit doctors to prescribe marijuana for patients as a medication for chronic pain. Bonner said: "Beyond doubt the claims that marijuana is medicine are false, dangerous and cruel." But, according to a federal administrative law judge Francis Young, "the record clearly shows that marijuana has been accepted as capable of relieving the distress of great numbers of very ill people and doing so with safety under medical supervision." (*The New York Times*)

RECOMMENDED READING

• This article was excerpted from *It's a Conspiracy!*, by the National Insecurity Council. It's highly recommended by the BRI for your bathroom reading.

• If you'd like a copy (and we know you would), send a check for $10 to EarthWorks Press, P.O. Box 1117, Ashland, OR 97520. Or ask for it at your local bookstore.

AND NOW, A COUPLE OF BAD JOKES...

A mushroom walks into a bar and says, "Drinks are on me."
The bartender asks, "Why are you buying everybody drinks?"
The mushroom says "Because I'm just a Fungi."

Q: Why was the idiot staring at a carton of orange juice?

A: Because it said concentrate.

Q & A: ASK THE EXPERTS

More random questions and answers from America's trivia experts.

ON THE SPOT

Q: *What causes freckles?*

A: "Except in the case of albinos, every person's skin has cells called *melanocytes*, which produce a certain amount of melanin, a dark pigment that absorbs ultraviolet light. These cells produce melanin at increasing rates when the skin is exposed to sunlight—hence the sunbather's tan. Some melanocytes are more active than others. Thus when groups of active melanocytes are surrounded by groups of less active melanocytes, the results are islands of pigment known as freckles." (From *Do Elephants Swim?* compiled by Robert M. Jones)

INFLATED WITH PRIDE

Q: *Why is Chicago called the Windy City?*

A: Chicago is pretty windy (with a 10.3-mph-wind average), but that's not where the nickname comes from. It comes from the 1893 Chicago World's Columbia Exposition—which was supposed to commemorate the 400th anniversary of Columbus's discovery of the New World, but ended up being used by city politicos to hype Chicago. "So boastful and overblown were the local politicians' claims about the exposition and the city that a New York City newspaper editor, Charles A. Dana, nicknamed Chicago 'the windy city.' "(From *The Book of Totally Useless Information*, by Don Voorhees)

EVERYTHING'S RELATIVE

Q: *Is it true that Einstein's parents once thought he was retarded?*

A: Believe it or not, yes. "It took Einstein so long to learn to speak (he didn't become fluent in his mother tongue of German until age nine) that his parents suspected he was 'subnormal.' His teachers agreed: according to legend, when Einstein's father ask his schoolmaster which profession young Albert should adopt, the schoolmaster replied, 'It doesn't matter; he'll never make a success of anything.' Actually, though, historians don't know all that much about his childhood. The reason: Einstein's memory for personal things was so bad that even *he* couldn't remember what happened to him as a kid. 'You are quite right,' he said when a friend commented this was hard to believe. 'My bad memory for personal things [is] really quite astounding.'

"Interesting note: Even as an adult, Einstein's genius was not immediately recognized. As late as 1910, more than five years after he published his famous papers on statistical mechanics, quantum mechanics, and the special theory of relativity, he was still only an associate professor at the University of Zurich earning just 4,500 francs a year. The meager salary wasn't enough to live on; he was forced to supplement his income with lecture fees and by taking in student boarders. He once told a colleague: 'In my relativity theory, I set up a clock at every point in space, but in reality I find it difficult to provide even one clock in my room.'" (From *Late Night Entertainment*, by John Dollison)

HAIRY THOUGHTS

Q: *Why do people get goose bumps?*

A: "Goose bumps are a vestige from the days when humans were covered with hair. When it got cold, the hairs were stood on end, creating a trap for air and providing insulation. The hairs have long since disappeared, but in the places where they used to be, the skin still bristles, trying to get warm." (From *The Book of Answers*, by Barbara Berliner)

SLICK QUESTION

Q: *Why is ice so slippery?*

A: "Ice has several unusual properties, one of them being that it melts when subjected to pressure. Your foot on ice is such pressure, and a film of melted ice—water—reduces the amount of friction and thus sliding can occur." (From *Science Trivia*, by Charles Cazeau)

See for yourself: Sitcom characters on TV rarely say goodbye when they hang up the phone.

FIRST REPORTS

Over the years, we've collected "First Reports," newspaper articles that gave readers their first glimpse of something that eventually became important in some way. Here are a few examples.

SPACED OUT

Most people don't know it was one incident—and one short newspaper story—that started the UFO craze. Here's the story, sent out over the AP wire from the Pendleton East Oregonian *on June 25, 1947.*

Pendleton, Ore. June 25 (AP)—"Nine bright saucer-like objects flying at 'incredible speed' at 10,000 feet altitude were reported here today by Kenneth Arnold, a Boise, Idaho, pilot who said he could not hazard a guess as to what they were.

"Arnold, a United States Forest Service employee engaged in searching for a missing plane, said he sighted the mysterious objects yesterday at three p.m. They were flying between Mount Rainier and Mount Adams, in Washington State, he said, and appeared to weave in and out of formation. Arnold said that he clocked and estimated their speed at 1,200 miles an hour.

"Enquiries at Yakima last night brought only blank stares, he said, but he added he talked today with an unidentified man from Ukiah, south of here, who said he had seen similar objects over the mountains near Ukiah yesterday.

" 'It seems impossible,' Arnold said, 'but there it is.' "

This story was picked up by papers all over the world. At that moment, according to the UFO Encyclopedia, *"the age of flying saucers began."*

THE XEROX MACHINE

When this article appeared in 1948, Xerox was still known as the Haloid Company.

Rochester, N.Y. Oct. 23—"A revolutionary process of inkless printing has been developed that might completely change all the operations of the printing and publishing industry. This was announced yesterday by Joseph C. Wilson, presidential the Haloid Company of Rochester, New York.

"Known as 'Xerography,' this basic addition to the graphic arts reproduces pictures and text at the speed of 1,200 feet a minute, on any kind of surface.

"Although there is no immediate prospect of applying the method to general photography, the process will be available within about six months for copying uses. Wilson said it will be in the form of a compact Xerocopying machine for reproducing letters, documents, and line work...

"Looking farther ahead, he said he foresaw incorporating the entire process in a portable Xerocamera. 'With such a camera, the picture taker can snap the shutter and within a few seconds pull out a finished Xeroprint. If he doesn't like the picture, he can discard it and try again, using the same Xeroplate.' "

DEAR ABBY

Dear Abby's first column appeared in the San Francisco Chronicle *on January 9, 1956. She answered four letters. Here's one of them.*

"Dear Abby: Maybe you can suggest something to help my sister. She is married to a real heel. He is 6'3" and weighs 240 and she is 5' and weighs 106. He has a terrible temper and frequently knocks the daylights out of her. —L.L.

"Dear L.L.: I admit your sister is no physical match for her heavyweight husband, but I've seen smaller gals flatten out bigger guys than this with just one look. If your sister has been letting this walrus slap her around frequently, maybe she likes it. Stay out of their family battles, Chum."

INTRODUCING THE CD

This article appeared in the New York Times, *March 18, 1983.*

"Five years ago, the electronics industry brought out the videodisk, heralded as the future of home entertainment systems. This month, the digital compact disk audio system will make its way into American homes, making similar promises. But marketers of the audiodisk play down the kinship, with good cause; sales of videodisks have been dismal. The compact audiodisk system, meanwhile, is expected to replace stereo turntables and albums as the industry standard within the decade.

"Some question whether the audiodisk will succeed. Players now cost $800-$900, and disks are $16-20 each, far too expensive for a popular market.

"Even if prices come down ...some analysts doubt whether consumers will be willing to sacrifice substantial investments in turntables and stacks of traditional recordings."

Women have Adam's apples, too. Men's are larger to accommodate their longer vocal cords.

FAMOUS TRIALS: THE CADAVER SYNOD

Here's the story of a trial that's stranger than anything you'll ever see on "Court TV" or "Judge Judy."

BACKGROUND. The late ninth century was a difficult period in the history of the Catholic Church. The Holy Roman Empire was disintegrating and as the empire's power slipped away, so did the authority of the Church; not strong enough militarily to survive on its own, it had to depend on powerful European nobles for protection.

HERE COMES GUIDO

In 891, Pope Stephen V turned to Duke Guido III of Spoleto for protection. To cement the relationship, Stephen adopted him as his son and crowned him Holy Roman Emperor.

...AND POPE FORMOSUS

That relationship didn't last long. Pope Stephen V died a few months later and a new pope, Formosus I, was elected to head the Church. Guido was suspicious of the new pope's loyalty. So in 892, he forced Formosus to crown him emperor a second time. He also insited that Formosus name his son Lambert "heir apparent."

When Guido died in 894, Formosus backed out of the deal. Rather than crown Lambert emperor, he called on King Arnulf of the East Franks to liberate Rome from Guido's family.

...AND ARNULF

A year later Arnulf conquered Rome...and Formosus made him emperor. This relationship didn't last long either: within a few months, Arnulf had suffered paralysis and had to be carried back to Germany; a few months after *that*, Pope Formosus died.

...AND LAMBERT AGAIN

Lambert, who had retreated back to Spoleto, used the crisis to rally his troops and march on Rome. He reconquered the city in 897.

Who's the St. Pauli Girl? Hint: The German beer is named for Hamburg's red-light district.

The new pope, Stephen VI, quickly switched sides and crowned Lambert emperor.

THE TRIAL

What followed was one of the most peculiar episodes in the history of the Catholic Church. Eager to prove his loyalty to the Spoletos, Pope Stephen convened the "cadaver synod," in which he literally had Pope Formosus's nine-month-old, rotting corpse put on trial for perjury, "coveting the papacy," and a variety of other crimes. On Stephen's orders the cadaver was disinterred, dressed in papal robes, and propped up on a throne for the trial. Since the body was in no condition to answer the charges made against it, a deacon was appointed to stand next to it during the proceedings and answer questions on its behalf.

Not surprisingly, the cadaver was found guilty on all counts. As punishment, all of Formosus's papal acts were declared null and void. The corpse itself was also desecrated: The three fingers on the right hand used to confer blessings were hacked off, and the body was stripped naked and dumped in a cemetery for foreigners. Shortly afterwards it was tossed in Tiber River, where a hermit fished it out and gave it a proper burial.

WHAT GOES AROUND...

Stephen VI himself survived the cadaver synod by only a few months. While the gruesome synod was still in session, a strong earthquake struck Rome and destroyed the papal basilica. Taking this as a sign of God's anger with the upstart pope, and encouraged by rumors that Formosus's corpse had begun performing miracles, Formosus's supporters arrested Stephen and threw him into the papal prison, where he was later strangled.

TIME FLIES

According to recent studies, in a lifetime the average American spends...

- ✓ 8 months opening mail
- ✓ 5 years waiting on line
- ✓ 2 years returning phone calls
- ✓ 1 year looking for misplaced items

DAVE BARRY'S EMBARRASSING MOMENTS

The inspiration for this section was a column written by humorist Dave Barry. Why put his name in the title? Strategic planning. If we mention his name, maybe he'll put us in his column. Clever, huh? On the other hand, what if it backfires on us? Boy, that would be an embarrassing mess...

THE UNFORGETTABLE EMBARRASSMENT

Ever embarrassed yourself so badly that you're still suffering from it? Of course you have. And of course, Dave Barry writes, "you've probably noticed that your brain never lets you forget it." Doesn't matter who you are or what you've become in life—certain moments will haunt you forever.

Barry's "special moment": "My own personal brain is forever dredging up the time in 11th grade when I took a girl, a very attractive girl on whom I had a life-threatening crush, to a dance. I was standing in the gym next to her, holding her hand, thinking what a sharp couple we made—Steve Suave and His Gorgeous Date—when one of my friends sidled up to me and observed that, over on the other side, my date was using her spare hand to hold hands with another guy....I thought: What am I supposed to do here?" Finally I turned to my date, dropped her hand, looked her square in the eye, and said: "Um." Just like that: "Um."

"My brain absolutely loves to remember this. "Way to go, Dave!" it shrieks to me, when I'm stopped at red lights, 23-1/2 years later. Talk about eloquent! My brain can't get over what a jerk I was."

Sound familiar? Well, things could be worse. Imagine screwing up like that in front of *millions* of people were watching. A few examples:

MOST EMBARRASSING MOMENT AT THE OSCARS

"Frank Capra is one of Hollywood's most famous directors. Among his achievements: *It's a Wonderful Life*, *Mr. Smith goes to Washington*, *It Happened One Night*. In 1933, Capra was so sure he was going to win the Best Director Oscar for his film *Lady for a Day* that even before the presenter, Will Rogers, finished announcing the winner, he stood up headed for the podium.

"He kept saying, 'Over here, over here,' says Hollywood historian Stephen Schochet, "because the spotlight was thrown on the other side of the room and he wanted to bask in his triumph.

"Capra was even more confused on his way up to the dais when Rogers opened the envelope and said, 'Come on up and get it, Frank.'

"But he wasn't referring to the humiliated Capra. 'It turns out the winner was another Frank—Frank Lloyd, for the film *Cavalcade*. Capra called his return to his seat 'the longest, saddest, most shattering walk in my life.'"

—*The Wolf Files*, ABC *News*

MOST EMBARRASSING FAST FOOD PROMOTION

"Back in 1964, Colonel Sanders sold Kentucky Fried Chicken to some Louisville entrepreneurs; they, in turn, sold it to Heublein, Inc., in 1971. Through it all, the Colonel was expected to remain a well-paid living legend, with no direct control over the product. One July day in 1975, however, the living legend told a Bowling Green, Kentucky newspaper that the new, 'extra-crispy' KFC was a 'damn fried doughball stuck on some chicken," and referred to the gravy as 'pure wallpaper paste.'

"A year later, the Colonel visited a New York City outlet and declared its food 'the worst fried chicken I've ever seen.' Embarrassed parent company execs called Sanders 'a purist.'"

—Ira Simmons, in *Junk Food*

MOST EMBARRASSING NEWSPAPER HEADLINE

Or maybe the 2nd-most embarrassing. You may have seen the 1948 photo of President-elect Harry Truman holding up a *Chicago Tribune* emblazoned with the headline: "Dewey Defeats Truman!" But have you heard about the *Baltimore Sun* on April 15, 1912? It said: "All *Titanic* Passengers Are Safe; Transferred In Lifeboats At Sea."

"It's heartwarming to know that the famous headline is still giving assurance to *Sun* readers," writes John Leo. "Certain editors have been known to send the headline to people who complain that the paper doesn't carry enough positive news."

He continues: "The *Sun's* famous mistake, repeated by the *Los Angeles Express*, had many authors—a White Star spokesman who kept explaining that the *Titanic* was unsinkable, radiomen who garbled emergency messages and the usual mix of reporters eager to beat the competition with news almost certain to be correct, since everybody already knew the ship couldn't possibly sink.

"One confident [section] of the *Sun's* erroneous headline said 'Towing Great Disabled Liner Into Halifax.' This phrase had some basis in real-world confusion: a message sent from ship to ship in Morse code confused *Titanic* with a no-name oil tanker, which in fact was being towed to Halifax because of engine trouble. A few frantic radio operators who came upon the message in the middle of transmission assumed the report referred to *Titanic* and passed the word on. The moral for modern days: assume nothing."

MOST EMBARRASSING TV GASOLINE AD

Hard to imagine a "most embarrassing" oil company ad—but this one fits because the company got caught.

From 1962 through 1968, Shell Oil claimed that its gas provided superior gas mileage. Why? Because it contained the special ingredient, *Platformate*. To prove it, in TV ads they showed two cars driving down a road. One was filled with "Shell with Platformate"; the other contained an unidentified gas with no Platformate. Of course he Platformate-less car ran out of gas while the other kept on running, breaking through a paper barrier to show it had "won."

Then the government stepped in and stopped the farce. Turns out that *all* gasolines available at the time contained Platformate... or equivalent chemicals known as "reformates," which were used to produce higher octane gas, reduce knocking, and improve mileage. (Shell used platinum as a reformate, which is how it came up with the name "platformate.") For that matter, Shell admitted that both of the cars in the commercial contained Shell gasoline. The only difference was that Shell chemists removed the Platformate from the "unidentified" gasoline so it would run out of gas first.

Howard Judson, Shell's embarrassed advertising manager, defended the ads as technically accurate. "Our advertising has never claimed that Platformate, or any equivalent, is Shell's exclusively," he insisted. The government insisted, too—that Shell withdraw the commercials and stop advertising the "secret" ingredient.

—John Dollison

Read my lips: 13% of women reapply their lipstick more than eight times a day.

COLORS

Colors have a lot more impact on our daily lives than you might think. Here are some things researchers have found out about people and color.

PINK

• Studies show that people almost always believe "pastries from a pink box taste better than from any other color box."

• People are willing to pay more for personal services (e.g., haircuts) performed by people wearing pink.

• Men believe pink products do the best job, but don't want to be seen buying them. If they think someone's watching, they'll choose something brown or blue.

ORANGE

• A quick attention-getter, it communicates informality.

• When it's used on a product, it "loudly proclaims that the product is for everyone."

PALE BLUE

• Pale blue can actually make people feel cooler. Designers often use it in places where men work, "because men feel 5° warmer than a woman in the same room temperature."

•Blue inhibits the desire to eat; in fact, researchers say "people tend to eat less from blue plates."

• Because blue is associated with eating less, marketers use it to sell products like club soda, skim milk, and cottage cheese.

BROWN

• Researchers say a brown suit "a symbol of informality that invites people to open up." It's recommended for reporters and marriage counselors.

GRAY

• Your eye processes gray more easily than any other color.

• Even so, people often become prejudiced against it, especially in areas with a bleak climate.

BRONZE

• This metallic hue gets a negative response. Researchers say it's "useful when rejection is desired."

GREEN

It's used to sell vegetables and chewing gum. But people avoid using it to sell meat, because it reminds consumers of mold.

Red is rarely used on ice cream packages because it reminds people of heat.

FIRST FILMS

Stars like Madonna would probably just as soon you forgot about what they were doing before they hit it big. You'd never guess they started out this way.

TOM SELLECK

First Film: *Myra Breckinridge* (1970)

The Role: In his 17 seconds onscreen, Selleck plays an unnamed talent agent (listed as "The Stud" in the credits) opposite Mae West, the star of the film, who wants to help him find "a position." West discovered Selleck in a Pepsi commercial and had him cast in the bit part.

HARRISON FORD

First Film: *Dead Heat on a Merry-Go-Round* (1966)

The Role: The 24-year old Ford plays an unnamed bellhop who appears in only one scene, in which con man James Coburn gets some information from him and then refuses to give him a tip. The part is so small that Ford is not even listed in the credits.

Memorable Line: "Paging Mr. Ellis..."

MADONNA

First Film: *A Certain Sacrifice* (1979)

The Role: In this Super 8 student film, Madonna plays a minor character named Bruna, who shows her breasts, has "simulated" group sex, and gets smeared with a dead man's blood. The film is so bad that the home video version opens with a disclaimer warning the viewer of the film's "technical inconsistancies."

Memorable Line: "I'm a do-do girl, and I'm looking for my do-do boy."

JEFF GOLDBLUM

First Film: *Death Wish* (1974)

The Role: Goldblum plays "Freak #1," one of three unnamed punks who break into Charles Bronson's house, kill his wife, and rape his daughter. Bronson spends the rest of the film (and three

sequels) gunning down punks on the streets of New York.
Memorable Line: "Don't jive, mother, you know what we want!"

KEVIN COSTNER

First Film: *Sizzle Beach, USA* (1974)
The Role: Costner is John Logan, a wealthy rancher, in this film about three big-breasted women who share a house in Malibu. The girls exercise and perform household chores while topless, and one of them, Dit, falls in love with Costner's character. (Incidentally, Costner also played a corpse in *The Big Chill*, but all of his scenes were cut out.)
Memorable Line: "L.A. women seem to be very impressed with money."

TOM CRUISE

First Film: *Endless Love* (1981)
The Role: Cruise plays Billy, a teen arsonist who gives the film's costar, Martin Hewitt, the idea of burning down Brooke Shields's house in order to act as a hero and win the respect of her parents.
Memorable Line: "When I was eight years old I was into arson."

SYLVESTER STALLONE

First Film: *A Party at Kitty and Stud's*, (1970). Later renamed "The Italian Stallion" to cash in on Stallone's fame.
The Role: In this pre-*Rocky* soft-core porno flick, Stallone plays Stud, a frisky playboy with big hair (and small muscles) who spends much of the film entirely nude except for a medallion around his neck and a wristwatch...though he never actually engages in intercourse.
Memorable Line: "Mmmmm."

Can't Get No Respect

Stallone never lived his blue movie down. According to *Esquire* magazine, "Even when *Rocky* won the Oscar for best picture of 1976...the [only] Stallone movie in demand for the private screening rooms of Bel Air and Beverly Hills was the soft-core porn film he'd made when it was the only work he could get."

MYTH-PRONUNCIATION

It's surprising how many of our words are references to gods that we've never heard of. Here are some of the characters in Greek and Roman mythology we refer to daily.

Cereal: Named after Ceres, the Roman goddess of grain and agriculture.

Atlas: One of the Greek Titans banished by Zeus when they sided with his son against him. Atlas was condemned to carry the world on his shoulders. That scene was popular with early map-makers, who regularly put it on the covers of their books of maps. The books themselves eventually became known as atlases.

Panic: Named after the Greek god Pan, who was believed to howl and shriek in the middle of the night. Greeks who heard these noises often *panicked*.

Hygiene: Inspired by Hygeia, the Greek goddess who brings good health.

Panacea: The Roman goddess who cures diseases.

Tantalize: Tantalus was a Greek king who was punished by the other gods for trying to deceive them. He was forced to stand in a pool of water up to his chin, but when he lowered his head to drink, the water receded just out of reach. The same was true with food: Whenever he reached to pick a piece of fruit from a tree, the wind blew it just out of his reach. The *tantalizing* food filled him with desire, but was completely unobtainable.

Siren: The Greeks believed the Sirens were women who called to passing sailors with their beautiful singing voices. Sailors couldn't resist them; in fact, men were driven mad by the songs and dashed their ships on the nearby rocks in their frenzy to get closer.

Helium: This element, found in the gaseous atmosphere of the sun, is named after Helios, the Greek god of the sun.

Iridescent: Named after Iris, the Greek goddess of the rainbow.

Slow Learner: President Woodrow Wilson couldn't read until he was 11 years old.

Erotic: Named after Eros, the Greek god of...you guessed it: love.

Brownie: These cousins of the Girl Scouts are named after the Celtic *brownies*, small, brown-cloaked fairies that perform household chores while the family sleeps.

Aphrodisiac: Named after Aphrodite, the Greek goddess of love. Her specialty: stirring up feelings of desire among the other gods.

Ghouls: From the Arabic word *ghul*, which was an evil spirit that robbed tombs and ate corpses. Today the name is given to anyone with an unhealthy interest in the deceased.

Lethargy: Named after the mythical Greek river of forgetfulness, *Lethe*.

Aegis: Originally the name of the shield of Zeus; today anything that's protected by something else is said to be under its aegis.

Money: Named after Juno Moneta, the Roman goddess of money.

SPACE-FILLER: MONEY FACTS

• Ancient Sparta had a creative way of preventing capital flight: They made their coins so large and heavy that it was almost impossible to take them out of the country.

• The British Pound Sterling, originally composed of 240 silver pennies, really did weigh a pound.

• The Greek word *drachma* originally meant "handful."

• Why were gold and silver so widely used in coins? They were rare, valuable, and didn't deteriorate or rust. They were also pretty to look at—which historians say was no small consideration.

• U.S. law requires that the words "liberty," "United States of America," "E Pluribus Unum," and "In God We Trust" be inscribed on all coins.

• Biggest and smallest coins in history: the 1644 Swedish *ten-daler* coin (43.4 pounds), and the 1740 Nepalese silver *quarter-dam* (1/14,000 of an ounce).

• Biggest and smallest bills in history: the 14th-century Chinese *one-kwan* note (9 x 13 inches) and the 1917 Rumanian *ten-bani* note (1 1/2 square inches).

THREE WEIRD MEDICAL CONDITIONS

You never know what's going to happen to you, right? Like, you might get stuck on that seat, have to call 911 and wind up in the next edition of the Bathroom Reader*...or you might find you've got one of these conditions. Don't laugh—it could happen to YOU!*

FOREIGN ACCENT SYNDROME

When: April 1993

Where: Worcester, Mass.

Headline: *Car Wreck Leaves American Speaking Like a Frenchman*

News Report: "A 46-year-old Massachusetts man walked away from a car accident with an unexpected problem: he spoke with a French accent.

" 'At first it bothered me very much because I can't make myself well understood,' said the man, who asked not to be identified, in a phone interview. He said he had no experience with a foreign language and had never even traveled farther than New Jersey from his home in Worcester."

MARY HART DISEASE

When: July 11, 1992

Where: New York City

Headline: *TV Co-Host's Voice Triggers Seizures*

News Report: "A neurologist reports in today's *New England Journal of Medicine* that a woman got epileptic seizures by hearing the voice of 'Entertainment Tonight' co-host Mary Hart.

"Symptoms included an upset feeling in the pit of her stomach, a sense of pressure in her head, and mental confusion. 'It was very dramatic,' said her doctor, who studied the seizures. 'She would rub her stomach, hold her head, and then she would look confused and out of it.'

"The woman has not had any major seizures of this type since she stopped watching the syndicated TV show."

VGE—VIDEO GAME EPILEPSY

When: April 1991

Where: America and Japan

Headline: A *Case of Nintendo Epilepsy*

News Report: "On screen the aliens get zapped and enemy helicopters crash and burn. But people playing video games do not expect to get hurt. Most do not, but a few wind up with a case of video game epilepsy (VGE).

"A team of Japanese neurologists recently described the problem in an issue of *Developmental Medicine and Child Neurology*. They looked at five boys and two girls, ages 4 to 13, who suffered from headaches, convulsions and blurred vision while playing games. The convulsive responses lasted only a few minutes and, in some cases, happened only during a particular scene in a particular game.

"Parents can prevent VGE. A letter in the *New England Jounral of Medicine* reports a similar incident of 'Nintendo epilepsy' in a 13-year-old girl. The doctor discussed the options with her and the parents: abstention from Nintendo or anti-convulsion drugs.

"The family chose the drugs, since they felt she would not be able to resist Nintendo's lure."

...AND NOW FOR SOME "STRANGE DEATHS"

February 30. When Augustus Caesar became emperor, February had 29 days in regular years and 30 days in leap years. Though the calendar had 365 days, leap years came every three years—which gradually threw the calendar out of sync with the movement of the sun. Augustus fixed this, ordering that leap years come every four years instead. While he was at it, he decided to add a day to August, the month named after him. So he shortened February to 28 days, and lengthened August to 31 days.

Mauch Chunk, Pennsylvania. Jim Thorpe was one of the world's most famous athletes. But he was penniless when he died in 1953. His estate couldn't pay for the memorial his widow felt he deserved, so she asked his home state, Oklahoma, to foot the bill. When they refused, she offered to bury him in any U.S. town that would change its name to Jim Thorpe. The people of Mauch Chunk accepted the offer, and the town became Jim Thorpe, PA.

Q. What's the only animal on Earth with only one ear? A. The praying mantis.

DOROTHY PARKER SEZ...

Wisecracks from one of America's all-time sharpest female wits.

"Hollywood money isn't money. It's congealed snow, melts in your hand, and there you are."

"You can lead a horticulture ...but you can't make her think."

"If all the girls who attended the Yale prom were laid end to end—I wouldn't be a bit surprised."

"Wit has truth in it. Wisecracking is simply calisthenics with words."

"The only *ism* Hollywood believes in is plagiarism."

"The two most beautiful words in the English language are 'check enclosed.' "

"That would be a good thing for them to cut on my tombstone: 'Wherever she went, including here, it was against her better judgement.' "

"This is not a novel to be tossed aside lightly; it should be thrown with great force."

"Most good women are hidden treasures who are safe because nobody looks for them."

"I misremember who first was cruel enough to nurture the cocktail party into life. But perhaps it would be not too much to say, in fact it would be not enough to say, that it was not worth the trouble."

"Excuse me, everybody, I have to go to the bathroom. I really have to telephone, but I'm too embarrassed to say so."

"One more drink and I'd have been under the host."

"You can't teach an old dogma new tricks."

"The best way to keep children at home is to make the home atmosphere pleasant and let the air out of the tires."

"His voice was as intimate as the rustle of sheets."

"These young writers...are worth watching. Not reading; just watching."

The Swiss spend more money per capita on insurance than any other nation.

CANDY BITS

It occurs to us that reading this stuff is sort of like getting a sugar rush from candy, only you're consuming empty calories of addictive information, which fill you up quick but leave you still craving more. An "info-rush."

REESE'S PEANUT BUTTER CUPS. H. B. Reese was an employee of the Hershey Chocolate Company. In 1923 he quit and opened his own candy factory in the same town.

KRAFT CARAMELS. During the Depression, Joseph Kraft started making caramels. He didn't particularly like candy; he just needed another dairy product for cheese salesmen to carry on their routes. The product succeeded becasuse grocers needed a summer substitute for chocolate, which melted in the heat.

JUJUBES. Named after the jujube berry, which grows in the tropics. It isn't clear why—the jujube *isn't* an ingredient in the candy.

PEZ. Invented in 1927 by Eduard Haas, an Austrian antismoking fanatic who marketed peppermint-flavored PEZ as a cigarette substitute. The candy gets its name from the German word for peppermint, *Pfefferminz*. Haas brought the candy to the U.S. in 1952. It bombed, so he reintroduced it as a children's toy, complete with cartoon heads and fruity flavors that kids liked. One of the most secretive companies in the United States, PEZ doesn't have a company archivist or historian—and won't even disclose who currently owns the company.

POP ROCKS. In 1956, a General Foods chemist named William Mitchell was looking for a way to make instant carbonated soda pop by trapping carbon dioxide in hard candy tablets. One afternoon he popped some nuggets he was experimenting with into his mouth...and felt them pop. No one at General Foods could think of a use for the substance, so it was shelved for almost 20 years. But in 1975 it was introduced as Pop Rocks—and became the hottest selling candy in history. Between 1975 and 1980, more than *500 million* packets were sold... and then in 1980 they were suddenly withdrawn from the market. Reason: A pervasive urban myth—that "Mikey" of Life Cereal fame had washed down a handful of pop rocks with a bottle of soda and exploded—turned concerned parents against the product. Pop Rocks were re-introduced in 1987, but sales never recovered.

21,203 Japanese citizens were arrested for "the illegal sale or abuse of paint thinner" in 1993.

EAT YOUR VITAMINS!

You've heard about vitamins since you were a little kid—but how much do you really know about them (besides the fact that they come in little pills)? Here's some food for thought, from BRI member John Dollison.

BACKGROUND: The cells in your body are constantly converting digested fats, proteins, and carbohydrates into energy, new tissue, and bone cells. Unfortunately, they can't perform this task alone—they need help from certain catalyst chemicals that your body can't produce (or can't produce in sufficient quantities). You have to get these chemicals—called *vitamins*—from food.

VITAMIN HISTORY

• Long before scientists unlocked the chemical code of vitamins, it was generally understood that eating certain foods would prevent specific diseases. One example: In the 18th century people discovered that adding citrus fruits to their diet could prevent scurvy, a disease whose symptoms included internal hemorrhaging and extreme weakness. In the 19th century, it was proven that substituting unpolished rice for polished rice would prevent beriberi, whose symptoms include paralysis and anemia.

• No one understood the relationship between these foods and the diseases they prevented until 1906, when the British biochemist Frederick Hopkins proved that in addition to proteins, carbohydrates, fats, minerals, and water, foods also contained what he called "accessory factors"—substances that the body needed to convert food into chemical forms that the body could use.

• In 1911 Casimir Funk, a Polish chemist, discovered that the beriberi-preventing substance in unpolished rice was an *amine*, a type of nitrogen-containing compound. Funk understood that the amine was vital to proper body function, so he named it "vitamine" (for "vital amine").

• A year later he and Hopkins proposed the Vitamin Hypothesis of Deficiency, which theorized that the absence of a particular vitamin in the diet could lead to certain diseases. By depriving animals of different types of foods in strictly controlled experiments, scientists identified a number of these substances.

48% of Americans say they'd donate the organs of deceased relatives *without* their permission.

• But they still didn't understand their chemical makeup, so they couldn't give them proper scientific names. Instead, they just called them all vitamines, and kept them separate by assigning a different letter of the alphabet to each new substance they discovered. They soon realized that many of the vitamins weren't amines at all—but by that time, the word "vitamine" had become so popular that they couldn't change it. So they just dropped the "e."

VITAMIN BASICS

• Scientists divide vitamins into two different types: water-soluble (the B-complex vitamins and vitamin C), and fat-soluble (A, D, E, and K).

• Your body can't store water-soluble vitamins very well, so if you eat more than your RDA, or Recommended Dietary Allowance, most of them pass out of your body in your urine. That's why it's important to eat them every day.

• Fat-soluble vitamins are more easily stored: Your liver tissue can store large amounts of vitamins A and D, and vitamin E is stored in body fat and reproductive organs.

KNOW YOUR VITAMINS

Vitamin A (retinol).

Sources: Animal fats and dairy products, green leafy vegetables, and carrots.

Why it's needed: Because it is a component of the pigment in the retinas of your eyes, vitamin A is necessary for good vision. It also helps keep the immune system healthy, and is necessary for the proper functioning of most organs.

Vitamin B complex (B1 [thiamine], B2 [riboflavin], B3 [niacin and niacinamide], B5 [pantothenic acid], biotin, folacin, and B12 [cobalamin]).

Sources: All meats, cereals, grains, green vegetables, dairy products, and brewer's yeast.

Why they're needed: B vitamins are necessary for healthy skin and for the normal operation of a number of cell processes, including digestion, respiration, blood cell and bone marrow production, and metabolism. They're also needed by the nervous system.

That's slow: The average drop of Heinz ketchup leaves the bottle travelling at 25 miles *per year*.

Vitamin C (ascorbic acid).

Sources: Fresh fruit and vegetables, especially citrus fruit and tomatoes.

Why it's needed: Vitamin C helps your body heal wounds and bone fractures, build tendons and other tissues, and absorb iron. It's also needed for healthy teeth, gums, and blood.

Vitamin D.

Sources: Your skin produces it when exposed to sunlight; also found in eggs, butter, and fish that have fat distributed through their tissue (salmon, tuna, sardines, oysters, etc).

Why it's needed: Your body uses Vitamin D to regulate its absorption of calcium and phosphorus, which makes it essential for proper bone and cartilage formation.

Vitamin E.

Sources: Green, leafy vegetables, wheat germ oil, margarine, rice.

Why it's needed: Vitamin E is one of the least understood vitamins, but it is known to be necessary for proper reproduction and prevention of muscular dystrophy in laboratory rats. It may also affect neuromuscular functions.

Vitamin K.

Sources: This vitamin is not made by the body itself, but by organisms that live in your intestinal tract. Also found in yogurt, egg yolks, leafy green vegetables, and fish liver oils.

Why it's needed: It enables your body to synthesize the proteins required for the proper clotting of blood. Also helps reduce excessive menstrual flow in women.

HEALTHY HINTS

- It's a good idea to wash your vegetables before you eat them—but don't soak them. You'll lose a lot of the water-soluable vitamins (B and C) if you do.
- If you don't eat fresh vegetables within a week of buying them, you're better off buying frozen vegetables. Fresh vegetables lose their vitamins over time, and after about a week in your refrigerator they have fewer vitamins than frozen ones. And frozen veggies almost always have more vitamins than canned vegetables.

Male moths can smell female moths from as far as seven miles away.

MYTH AMERICA

Some of the stories we recognize today as American myths were taught as history for many years. This one, about the "father of our country," was reverentially passed down for more than 150 years.

MYTH: Young George Washington chopped down a cherry tree. When his father found the demolished tree and asked who was responsible, George stepped forward and said, "I cannot tell a lie, father—I did." The elder Washington was so moved by George's honesty that he didn't punish his son.

BACKGROUND: It's hard to believe today, but as late as the 1950s, this tale was still being taught in school as fact. It first appeared in a biography of Washington written by Parson Mason Locke Weems, called *The Life of George Washington with Curious Anecdotes: Equally Honorable to Himself and Exemplary to His Young Countrymen*. Here's the original version of the story:

> "George," cried his father, "do you know who killed this beautiful little cherry tree yonder in the garden?" This was a tough question: and George staggered under it for a moment; but quickly recovered himself: and looking at his father, with the sweet face of youth brightened with the inexpressible charm of all-conquering truth, he bravely cried out, "I can't tell a lie, Pa; you know I can't tell a lie, I did it with my hatchet." — "Run to my arms, you dearest boy," cried his father in transports, "run to my arms; glad am I, George, that you killed my tree: for you have paid me for it a thousand fold. Such an act of heroism in my son is more worth than a thousand trees, though blossomed with silver, and their fruits of purest gold."

THE TRUTH: Weems made it up. The book was first published in 1800—and was a huge best-seller in its time—but the story about the cherry tree didn't show up until the fifth edition, in 1806. Weems's only supporting documentation was his own statement that the tale was "too true to be doubted."

Weems didn't claim to be much of a historian to begin with; he was just capitalizing on an obvious market. "There's a great deal of money lying in the bones of old George," he reportedly told his publisher.

SIBLING RIVALRY

Brothers who go into business together don't always stay close. In fact, going into business with a relative might be the best way to lose a family. Here are four classic cases.

ADIDAS / Adolf & Rudolf Dassler

Background: According to *Everybody's Business*, "Adolf and Rudolf Dassler were the sons of a poor laundress who grew up in the tiny Bavarian milltown of Herzogenerauch, near Nuremburg. Before World War II, they started a factory there to make house slippers, then branched to track shoes and soccer boots."

Rivalry: "They had a violent falling out and after the war went their separate ways. Rudolf left Adidas and started a rival athletic shoe company, Puma. Before long Adidas and Puma—both headquartered in Herzogenerauch—were battling head-to-head all over the world. When Adolf died in 1978, the two brothers hadn't spoken to each other in 29 years."

GALLO WINE / Ernest, Julio & Joseph Gallo

Background: Ernest, Julio, and Joseph Gallo inherited the family vineyard in 1933 when their father murdered their mother and then committed suicide. Twenty-four-year-old Ernest and 23-year-old Julio used their inheritance to start the Gallo Winery. At the same time, they raised their teenage brother, Joseph, who went to work for them as a vineyard manager when he was old enough. After toiling for his brothers for 18 years, Joseph bought a nearby ranch. He grew grapes (which he sold to the Gallo Winery) and raised cattle.

Rivalry: In 1983, Joseph expanded his dairy operation to include Gallo cheese...but his brothers said he was infringing on their trademark, and in 1986 they sued him. Joseph retaliated with a countersuit, claiming that his 1/3 share of his father's inheritance entitled him to 1/3 of the winery. The fight was nasty. During the trial, the winemakers accused Joseph of "running a rat-infested cheese plant"; Joseph shot back that his brothers specialized in making cheap wine for drunks. Ernest and Julio won both suits.

The average American kid aged 5-17 has three cavities—down from 11 during the 1940s.

REVLON / Charles, Joseph & Martin Revson

Background: According to *Everybody's Business*, "The cosmetics giant was founded in 1932 by Charles Revson, his older brother Joseph, and Charles Lachman. A younger brother, Martin, joined the firm later. But it was Charles who led the company's drive to the top."

Rivalry: "Joseph left the company in 1955 because he didn't agree with Charles that Revlon should go public. He sold all his stock to the company for $2.5 million. (If he'd waited four years, the stock would have been worth $35 million.) Martin left in 1959 after bitter fights with his older brother. He sued the company, charging that his brother Charles 'engaged in a practice of mistreating executives and abusing them personally.' The brothers didn't speak to each other for 13 years. 'What brother?' Charles once said. 'I don't have a brother.' "

KELLOGG'S / John & William Kellogg

Background: In 1876, 25-year-old Dr. John Harvey Kellogg became head of the Battle Creek Sanitarium. His first official act was to hire his younger brother, William, as "chief clerk." To make the institution's vegetarian food more palatable, the brothers invented a number of foods—including Corn Flakes. Then they set up a company on the side, manufacturing and distributing their cereal around the country.

Rivalry: John, a world-famous doctor by 1900, insisted that Kellogg's cereals be "health foods." So he forbade the use of white sugar. William just wanted something that would sell...and when he added sugar to the flakes while John was out of the country, the partnership fell apart. "Will set out on his own...in 1906," writes William Poundstone in *Bigger Secrets*. "By 1909 the brothers weren't on speaking terms. Both spent much of the next decade suing each other. These legal actions resulted in the ruling that only Will's company could market cereal under the Kellogg's name, and in lifelong mutual enmity for the two brothers." When John Harvey died in 1942, the two hadn't spoken in 33 years.

Quickie: Robert, James, and Edward Mead Johnson started *Johnson & Johnson* in an old wallpaper factory. Edward left and started Mead Johnson, which now competes with Johnson & Johnson.

We love our freedom: Americans buy 12 million cordless phones every year.

Q & A: ASK THE EXPERTS

More random questions and answers from America's trivia experts.

CRACKING THE CODE

Q: *How did phone companies assign area codes?*

A: It seems strange that 212 is for New York City, and 213 is for Los Angeles, across the country. But in 1948, assigning area codes had nothing to do with geography; it had to do with how fast people could dial them (not punch them on a touchtone phone, but *dial* them on a rotary phone). The faster numbers—1, 2, and 3—were called "low dial-pull" numbers. They were given to large cities for one simple reason: it saved the phone company money.

"Millions of people called those cities every day. The faster each caller was able to dial his number, the less time the phone company's switching machines would be tied up making the connection...[and] the fewer machines the phone company had to buy.

"Today, the only concern when assigning new area codes is to make them as different as possible form neighboring codes, so people won't confuse the numbers." (From *Know It All!*, by Ed Zotti)

BUG OFF!

Q: *How do flies walk upside down?*

A: A fly has six legs. On each leg there are two little claws that look sort of like a lobster's claws. "Underneath the claws [are] a pair of small weblike fuzzy pads called *pulvilli*. These are functional suction pads which the fly presses to the surface to squeeze out the air and create enough suction to hold itself up. Thus, with its claws and suction pads, the little pest can walk majestically upside down." (From *How Do Flies Walk Upside Down?*, by Martin M. Goldwyn)

STUMPED

Q: *Can you tell a tree's age by counting the rings on a stump?*

A: Not necessarily. "In temperate climates, a single ring of light and dark wood is usually added each year—but sometimes more than one ring is produced in a growing season, or sometimes no ring at all. If a tree loses most of its leaves from a severe insect attack or drought, it begins producing dense wood and thus completes a ring. Then if a new crop of leaves grows again that same season, another ring will be formed. In a very dry year the tree might not grow at all, and no ring would be added that year." (From *Do Elephants Swim?*, compiled by Robert M. Jones)

LOVE MATCH

Q: *Why is zero called* Love *in tennis?*

A: It has nothing to do with affairs of the heart. "Love is really a distortion of the French word *oeuf*, which means egg, as in goose egg." (From *The Book of Totally Useless Information*, by Don Voorhees)

ILLOGICAL

Q: *Where did the people who created "Star Trek" come up with the name of Spock's home planet, Vulcan?*

A: Believe it or not, astronomers were sure there actually *was* a planet called Vulcan somewhere between the planet Mercury and the sun. "Its existence—first proposed by French astronomer Urbain Jean Joseph Leverrier in 1845—was hypothesized to explain a discrepancy in Mercury's orbit. Vulcan was even reported to have been observed once, but the observation was never confirmed. Einstein's general theory of relativity explained Mercury's odd orbit, and the existence of Vulcan was discredited." (From *The Book of Answers*, by Barbara Berliner)

DARK SECRETS

Q: *What is espresso?*

A: "Espresso is Italian for 'quick,' and it refers to a particular way of brewing coffee. Various espresso machines have been devised, but the basic idea always is to heat water under pressure above the boiling point and then force it rapidly through the ground coffee. The hotter the water, the more flavor is extracted from the coffee. The shorter the brewing time, the less bitter the coffee." Espresso also refers to dark-roasted types of coffee that make the best espresso brew. (From *Why Do Men Have Nipples*, by Katherine Dunn)

Crowd control: Purse-snatching is punishable by death in Haiti.

AUNT LENNA'S PUZZLES

More conversations with my puzzle-loving auntie.
Answers are on page 663.

My Aunt Lenna is quite talkative. One day she took a cab and chattered on at the driver incessantly. Finally, the man apologetically explained that his hearing aid was off, and without it he wasn't able to make out a word she said. She stopped talking for the rest of the trip, but when she got to her destination, she realized she'd been tricked.

How did she realize this?

Aunt Lenna was chuckling.

"What's so funny?" I asked her.

"Just a silly little puzzle," she said.

"Tell me."

"Okay. See if you can write the number *one hundred* using six 9's."

"You mean, 9-9-9-9-9-9?"

"That's not how you do it, but those are the numbers."

How can I do it?

"Such a pity," said Aunt Lenna.

"What?" I asked.

"Oh, my friend's wife passed away. It was quite sudden. He kissed her before he left for work, shut the apartment door, walked to the elevator and pressed the ground-floor button. He immediately knew his wife had died. Very sad."

"Wait a minute," I stopped her. "How did he know she was dead? Is he psychic?"

Aunt Lenna shook her head.

"Well, then what happened?"

What did happen?

Physics isn't my strong suit, so I was stumped when Aunt Lenna asked me this question: "Suppose there are three men on one side of a river, and someone fires a gun on the other side. One man sees the smoke from the gun; another hears the gunfire; and the third sees the bullet hit the water by his feet. Which of them knows the gun was fired first?"

Do you know the answer?

Aunt Lenna went for a walk by the water, and came back quite upset.

"What's the matter?" I asked.

"Oh, it was terrible! There was a woman standing on the pier. There were tears in her eyes. She was very angry, and she seemed indignant over some injury that had been inflicted upon her.

"I heard her cry, 'You monster of cruelty! I've stayed with you too long. You've hurt the very foundations of my being! I've endured your tortures day after day. The first time we met, your ease and polish attracted me to you... and when you became my own, my friends were quite envious. But now...take a look at what I've suffered for your sake! You keep me from advancing myself! My standing in society has been ruined by you! If we'd never met, I might have walked in peace...but now...now we part forever!'

"And I declare, nephew, she threw something in the water. I rushed over and ..."

"Aunt Lenna! Did you call the police?!"

"Don't be silly."

"But I don't understand. Who...or what did she throw off the pier?"

Do you know?

"I went to a family reunion the other day," Aunt Lenna told me. There were 2 grandfathers, 2 grandmothers, 3 mothers, 3 fathers, 3 daughters, 3 sons, 2 mothers-in-law, 2 fathers-in-law, 1 son-in-law, 1 daughter-in-law, 2 brothers, and 2 sisters. Can you guess how many people there were?"

I thought for a moment. "Mm-m-m...I'd say, 10."

"That's right!" Lenna said, amazed. "How did you know?"

How did I get that number?

Fleas jump 130 times their own height—the equivalent of a human jumping a 65-story building.

FAMILIAR PHRASES

More origins of common phrases.

TO UNDERMINE

Meaning: To weaken, usually secretly and gradually.

Origin: "The term dates from the 14th century, when it was common practice for besiegers to tunnel under the foundations of a castle, either to enter it or to weaken the walls." The tunnels were called "mines," and the damaged walls were considered "undermined." By the 15th century, any underhanded method used to defeat an enemy had become known as "undermining." (From *Fighting Words*, by Christine Ammer)

TO THROW SOMEONE TO THE WOLVES

Meaning: Abandon someone; sacrifice someone to save yourself.

Origin: The term comes from the Victorian age, when it was popular for printmakers to depict sleighs, drawn by horses at full gallop, being chased by packs of wolves. "Traditionally, if the wolves got too close, one of the passengers was thrown out to lighten the sleigh, in hopes that the rest of the company could escape while the animals were devouring the victim." No one's sure if this really happened, but it resulted in a "durable metaphor." (From *Loose Cannons and Red Herrings*, by Robert Claiborne)

TO TURN OVER A NEW LEAF

Meaning: Get a fresh start; change your ways.

Origin: Believe it or not, the expression has nothing to do with leaves from a plant; it refers to the "leaves" (pages) in a *book*—"the turning to a blank page in a [journal or] exercise book where one can start one's work anew. Figuratively, such a fresh start gives the possibility of learning a new lesson in the book of life's principles: a chance to begin again and mend one's ways." (From *Getting to the Roots*, by Martin Manser)

Pigs and humans are the only animals that get sunburned.

PRIMETIME PROVERBS

TV comments about everyday life. From Primetime Proverbs, *by Jack Mingo and John Javna.*

ON RAISING KIDS:

Fred Sanford: "Didn't you learn anything being my son? Who do you think I'm doing this all for?"

Lamont Sanford: "Yourself."

Fred: "Yeah, you learned something."

—*"Sanford and Son"*

Sophia: "She's always tellin' me what to do!"

Rocco: "Don't worry. My daughter treats me the same way."

Sophia: "Kids. Once they're over fifty, they think they know everything."

—*"The Golden Girls"*

ON PETS:

"He who lies down with dogs gets up with fleas."

—Herman Munster, *"The Munsters"*

Morticia Addams: "Now Pugsley darling, who could be closer than a boy and his mother?"

Pugsley Addams: "A boy and his octopus?"

Morticia [smiling]: "Hmmm... Perhaps."

—*"The Addams Family"*

ON MAKEUP:

"City women is spoiled rotten. All they think about is smearin' themselves with beauty grease. Fancy smellin' renderin's. Why, if you was to hug one of 'em, she'd squirt out of yore arms like a prune pit!"

—Granny, *"The Beverly Hillbillies"*

"I haven't worn makeup in years. It takes away that unnatural look that we girls like."

—Lily Munster, *"The Munsters"*

ON SCIENCE:

"The roots of physical aggression found in the male species are in the DNA molecule itself. In fact, the very letters, D-N-A, are an acronym for 'Dames Are Not Agressors.' "

—Cliff Claven, *"Cheers"*

Aesop, Jr.: "There's no fuel like an old fuel!"

Aesop, Sr.: "Hmmm...I *gas* you're right."

—*"The Bullwinkle Show"*

FUN WITH ELVIS

Imagine what a kick it would have been to hang out with the King at Graceland. Well, it's too late now—but here are some of the exciting moments you missed.

AT THE POOL

Want to go for a dip? According to David Adler in *The Life and Cuisine of Elvis Presley*, "Elvis enjoyed sitting around the pool eating watermelon hearts. For entertainment while he ate, he would float flashbulbs in the pool. Then he would take out a .22 and shoot at them. When they were hit, they would flash, and then sink to the bottom."

ON THE FOURTH OF JULY

Every Independence Day at Graceland, Elvis had a "fireworks display." His Memphis Mafia split into two teams, put on gloves and football helmets, and shot fireworks at one another. "They would level arsenals of rockets and Roman candles at each other and blast away at point-blank range for hours," says Steve Dunleavy in *Elvis: What Happened.*

It was all laughs: "I've backed into burning rockets and had my ass burned half off," laughs Elvis aide Red West. "I've seen Elvis bending over a giant rocket and watched the thing go off while he is leaning over it, nearly blowing his fool head off. [My brother] Sonny carries a scar on his chest to this day where one of us tried to blow a rocket through him. Roman candles would blow up in our hands. The house caught fire twice."

DEMOLITION DERBY

You never knew what might happen when the King was bored. There was a beautiful little cottage in the corner of the Graceland property. One day, Elvis decided to demolish it…so he put on a football helmet and revved up his bulldozer. The only problem: His father, Vernon Presley, was sitting on the cottage porch.

According to Red West, "[He yelled] 'You better move, Daddy.' Vernon asks why and Elvis says, 'Because I'm gonna knock the goddamn house down.' …Vernon gives one of those looks like 'Oh, Lordie,' but he doesn't say anything…he just gets up and Elvis starts roaring away." To make it more interesting, Elvis and Red set the house on fire while they battered it with heavy machinery.

AT THE MOVIES

The King couldn't just go out to the movies whenever he felt like it—he would have been mobbed. So he rented the whole theater instead. "Elvis had private midnight screenings at the Memphian Theater," writes David Adler. "They were attended by about a hundred of his friends. Admission was free, and so was the popcorn, but you had to watch the movie on Elvis's terms. Elvis made the projectionist repeat his favorite scenes. If the action got slow, such as during a love scene, the projectionist would have to skip to the next good part. Elvis once saw *Dr. Strangelove* three times straight, with a number of scenes repeated so he could figure out exactly what was going on."

"Elvis liked James Bond and *Patton*, and any movie with Peter Sellers. His favorite movie of all time was *The Party*."

WATCHING TV

And, of course, you could always stay home and spend a quiet evening watching TV...as long as Elvis liked the programs. If not, there was a good chance he'd pull out a gun and shoot out the screen. "Honestly," Red West says, "I can't tell you how many television sets went to their death at the hands of Elvis....He would shoot out television sets in hotel rooms and in any one of the houses he had. He shot out a great big one at Graceland, in Memphis, the one he had in his bedroom."

A classic example: One afternoon in 1974, the TV was blaring while Elvis was eating his breakfast. His least favorite singer, Robert Goulet, came on. As Red related: "Very slowly, Elvis finishes what he has in his mouth, puts down his knife and fork, picks up this big mother of a .22 and—boom—blasts old Robert clean off the screen and the television set to pieces....He then puts down the .22, picks up his knife and fork and says, 'That will be enough of that s—,' and then he goes on eating."

Elvis Trivia: On his way to meet Richard Nixon in 1970 (to pose for the famous photo), the King suddenly had a craving. He insisted that his driver pull over to buy a dozen honey-glazed donuts; then he polished them off as they drove to the White House.

There are three colors of blood: red, blue (lobsters), and yellow (insects).

MONEY FACTS

A few odds and ends about almost everyone's favorite subject.

THE FDR DIME

Here's how FDR wound up on our 10¢ coin:

• Franklin D. Roosevelt, who was crippled by polio in 1921, escaped from his disability by swimming whenever he could. One of his favorite swimming holes was Warm Springs, Georgia, a natural spring. In 1926 the future president donated enough money to start a polio foundation at the site, so that other polio sufferers could enjoy the waters too.

• Despite the large donation, the foundation was always running out of money.

• Singer Eddie Cantor (a popular radio personality) knew about Roosevelt's concern for the foundation, and in 1937 he proposed to the president that he ask every American to send a dime to the White House to be used for polio research. Cantor suggested a name for the promotion: The March of Dimes.

• Roosevelt took his suggestion and made the appeal. The public response was enormous: on some days the White House was flooded with as many 150,000 letters containing dimes.

• The president became so closely associated with the March of Dimes that after his death in 1945, Congress voted to create the Roosevelt dime in his honor. The first ones were released to the public on January 30, 1946, Roosevelt's birthday—and the traditional start of the March of Dimes annual fund-raising campaign.

• The vaccine for polio was announced on April 12, 1955, on the 10-year anniversary of Roosevelt's death.

CATTLE CALL

• In about 2000 B.C., man began trading bronze ingots shaped like cows (which had about the same value as a real cow). The value of these "coins" was measured by weighing them—which meant that any time a transaction was made, someone had to get out a scale to measure the value of the money.

• Around 800 B.C., the Lydians of Anatolia—who traded bean-shaped ingots made of a gold-silver alloy called *electrum*—began stamping the ingot's value onto its face. This eliminated the need for a scale and made transactions much easier.

• But switching to countable coins from weighed ones increased the chances of fraud—precious metals could be chipped or shaved off the edges of the coins. One of the techniques designed to prevent this is still evident on modern U.S. coins, even though they no longer contain precious metals. What is it? Feel the edges of a dime or a quarter. Those grooves were originally a way to tell if any metal had been shaved off.

ARE YOUR BILLS REAL?

Here are some anticounterfeit features of U.S. paper currency you probably didn't know about:

✓ The currency paper is fluorescent under ultraviolet light.

✓ The ink is slightly magnetic—not enough for household magnets to detect, but enough for special machines to notice.

✓ The paper has thousands of tiny microscopic holes "drilled" into it. Reason: when the money is examined under a microscope, tiny points of light shine through.

COIN FACTS

• The Director of the Mint gets to decide who appears on our coins, but the decisions have to be approved by the Treasury Secretary—and changes on any coin can't be made more than once every 25 years.

• Prior to the assassination of President Lincoln, it was a long-standing tradition *not* to have portraits on U.S. coins. Symbols of liberty were used instead. The only reason Lincoln's face got the nod: he was considered a human embodiment of liberty.

• If you design a portrait that gets used on a coin, you get to have your initials stamped in the coin alongside it. That's normally an innocuous addition to the coin, but there have been exceptions: When the Roosevelt dime was released in 1946, some concerned anticommunists thought the initials "JS" (for designer John Sinnock) stood for Joseph Stalin. And when the John F. Kennedy memorial half-dollar was issued in 1964, some conspiracy theorists thought the letters "GR" (for Gilroy Roberts) were a tiny rendition of the communist hammer and sickle.

OOPS!

More blunders to make you feel superior.

A SLIGHT MISUNDERSTANDING

"At the end of World War II, the Allies issued the Potsdam telegram demanding that the Imperial Japanese armies surrender forthwith. The Japanese government responded with an announcement that it was withholding immediate comment on the ultimatum, pending 'deliberations' by the Imperial government.

"Unfortunately, the official Japanese government news agency, in the heat of issuing this critical statement in English, decided to translate the Japanese word that means 'withholding comment for the time being' as 'deliberately ignore.'

"A number of scholars have suggested that if the ultimatum had not been so decisively rejected, President Truman might never have authorized the A-bomb attacks on Hiroshima and Nagasaki."

—From *David Frost's Book of the World's Worst Decisions*

CONTROL FREAKS

"The March 21, 1983, issue of *Time* magazine featured Lee Iacocca on the cover, along with a tease for Henry Kissinger's 'New Plan for Arms Contol.' After two hundred thousand of the covers had been printed, someone noticed a typographical error—the 'r' had been left out of 'Control.' It was printed as *Contol.*

"There had never been a misspelling on a *Time* cover in the history of the magazine. They stopped the presses, corrected the error, and withdrew all the *Contol* covers. The goof cost *Time* $100,000, and 40% of the newsstand copies went on sale a day late."

—From *The Emperor Who Ate the Bible,* by Scott Morris

THE WICKED BIBLE

In 1631, two London printers left one word out of an official edition of the Bible. The mistake cost them 3,000 pounds and nearly led to their imprisonment. The word was "not;" they left it out of the Seventh Commandment, which then told readers, "Thou shalt commit adultery." The book became known as "the Wicked Bible."

Mark Twain coined the phrase "gossip column" in 1893.

TRICK-OR-TREAT

"Two Illinois skydivers, Brian Voss, 30, and Alfred McInturff, 50, were tossing a pumpkin back and forth on their 1987 Halloween skydive when they accidentally dropped it from 2,200 feet. It crashed through the roof of Becky Farrar's home, leaving orange goo all over her kitchen walls and breaking the kichen table. Said Farrar, 'If this had happened an hour earlier, we would have been sitting at the table having lunch.' "

—From *News of the Weird*

NAKED TRUTH

PORTLAND, OR. "Amtrak apologized and issued refunds to dozens of junior high students who took a train trip with a group of rowdy grown-ups playing strip poker.

"About half the 93 members of Portland's Robert Gray Middle School band and choir said they had to ride in a car with a smoking section and were subjected to rude comments from adults who took their clothes off in a poker game. The students were returning from a music competition in San Jose, California. Amtrak has promised to send the group a refund check for $4,830."

—AP, June 23, 1993

BACKFIRE

On August 7, 1979, a jet plane in the Spanish Air Force shot itself down when its own gunfire ricocheted off a hillside target, flew back, and hit the plane during field maneuvers.

GOOD LUCK?

"At a dinner party in the late 19th century, French playwright Victolen Sardou spilled a glass of wine. The woman sitting next to him poured salt on the stain, and Sardou picked up some of the salt and threw it over his shoulder for luck. The salt went into the eye of a waiter about to serve him some chicken. The waiter dropped the platter, and the family dog pounced on the chicken. A bone lodged in the dog's throat, and when the son of the host tried to pull it out, the dog bit him. His finger had to be amputated."

—John Berendt, *Esquire* magazine

President John Adams regularly referred to George Washington as "an old muttonhead."

READER'S ARTICLE OF THE YEAR

We get all kinds of articles and suggestions from readers, of course...some are very interesting, some are pretty weird...but this one is special. It's got a little bit of everything we look for in a Bathroom Reader *piece: an "origin" story, some gossip, pop history, the "gee whiz" factor, and so on. It was written by humorist Leo Rosten, and it's from his book* The Power of Positive Nonsense.

A MISCONCEPTION

"Any man who hates dogs and babies can't be all bad."

Sure, sure, I know: Umpteen anthologies of quotations credit this to W. C. Fields. But he did not say it. He may have said, "A woman drove me to drink, and I never even wrote to thank her," or "How do I like children? Boiled," or "Never give a sucker an even break." But he did not come up with "Any man who hates dogs and babies can't be all bad." The line was uttered *about* Fields.

ROSTEN IN HOLLYWOOD

The place was Hollywood. The time: 1939. I was working on a solemn sociological...study of the movie colony. One day, to my surprise, I received a telegram from the Masquers' Club, inviting me to be their guest at a banquet in honor of W. C. Fields.

I was delighted. I was transported. I revered Mr. Fields as the funniest misanthrope our land ever produced. And I knew that the Masquer dinners of homage were in fact "roasts" in which celebrated wits eviscerated the guest of honor with sparkling insults... and steamy boudoir revelations which, if uttered on any other occasion, could provide an airtight case for a lawsuit worth millions in damages for character assassination. I accepted the invitation.

THE MASQUERS' CLUB

I appeared at the Masquers' with a wide grin and anticipatory chuckles. The lobby was packed with moviedom elite: stars, producers, directors, writers. All male, all famous, all treating me, as I circulated amongst them, the way princes of the blood treat a peasant with anemia. I might have been made of glass, so easily did the

Q. What's the #1 reason welfare recipients give for going on welfare? A. Divorce.

glances of the celebrated go right through me. But I did not mind. I was very young, and felt lucky to be a guest on Parnassus. My heart thumped faster as I recognized noble Spencer Tracy, great Goldwyn, wonderful William Wyler, incomparable Ben Hecht. And was that Errol Flynn holding court in the corner?...I do not know. I was not sure, to tell you the truth, because I was so excited that my vision and my imagination were playing leapfrog.

TO THE STAGE

Suddenly I heard my name blaring, over and over, from loudspeakers, and an agitated voice pleading that I report to the desk "at once!"...I ploughed through the glittering assemblage to the distant desk, where I was told...that I was "damn late" for one who would be seated "on the dais!" A majordomo swiftly (and sourly) led me backstage. There I beheld Mr. Fields, already red-nosed from fiery waters, surrounded by illustrious roasters: Groucho Marx, Bob Hope, Jack Benny, George Burns, Edgar Bergen, Milton Berle....It was they, I assure you, in the flesh.

"Time to line up!" called a praetorian guard.

A hotel Hannibal began to recite name after hallowed name. Mine, unhallowed, was last.

"Proceed to the dais!" blared another....Someone flung heavy red draperies aside.

As we marched through the opening and across the stage, the glittering audience rose to its feet...applauding Marx, Benny, Hope, reaching a crescendo for Fields, hailing Berle, Bergen, Burns—until I appeared, last, certainly least, pale, brave, anonymous. The applause seeped away like sand in a net of gauze.... Amidst the anticlimax of my reception, we all sat down to break bread.

THE NIGHTMARE

The dinner was excellent, the wines ambrosial, the brandy and cigars sublime. Then William Collier, Sr., rose to conduct the festivities. He received an ovation, which he deserved. A renowned M.C. and wit, he orated a barrage of dazzling, scathing yet affectionate ribs about our...guest of honor. The audience roared in counterpoint. And to each barbed line, Mr. Fields responded with an evil grin, a leering grunt and another sip of alcoholic disdain.

Jesse James, Jr. played his famous father in two Hollywood films.

Mr. Collier completed his backhanded eulogy. A tornado of applause. Then the masterful M.C. proclaimed: "Our first speaker to 'honor' Bill Fields is..." (he consulted his prep sheet and, there is no denying it, winced) "Dr. Leo Boston—no, I guess it's Rosten." It would be wrong to say that I could not believe my ears; the full measure of my horror lay in the fact that I did. I sat paralyzed. This could not be. It was a dream. It was a nightmare....It took the elbow of Red Skelton, jabbing into my ribs, to propel me to my feet.

"SAY SOMETHIN!"

The "applause" which had greeted Mr. Collier's garbled recitation of my name would not have awakened a mouse. Now, my erectness and visibility compounded my shame, for the faces of that auditorium broke into frowns of confusion and the many mouths uttered murmurs seeking enlightenment....I prayed for a trapdoor to open beneath me, or for lightning to strike me dead. Neither happened. Instead, I heard George Burns's hoarse sotto voice: "Say somethin'!" with unmistakable disgust. I gulped—then someone who was hiding in my throat uttered these words: "The only thing I can say about Mr. W. C. Fields, whom I have admired since the day he advanced upon Baby LeRoy with an icepick, is this: Any man who hates dogs and babies can't be all bad."

The appearance of Mae West in a G-string would not have produced a more explosive cachinnation. The laughter was so uproarious, the ovation so deafening, the belly-heavings and table-slapping and shoulder-punchings so vigorous, that I cleverly collapsed onto my chair.

I scarcely remember the rest of that historic night—except that the jokes and gags and needlings of Mr. Fields (who by now resembled a benign Caligula) put all previous celebrity "roasts" to shame. The next morning, the local papers led off their stories about the banquet with my ad lib. The AP and UP flung my remark around the world. CBS and BBC featured the quip on radio. Overnight, I was an international wit.

Alas, God put bitters in the wine of my enflatterment; for ever since then, "Any man who hates dogs and babies can't be all bad" has been credited to—W. C. Fields. Hardly a week passes in which I do not run across some reference to "Fields's immortal crack." But it was mine. Mine, I tell you, mine!

Casanova spent the last 13 years of his life working as a librarian.

OH NO, IT'S MR. BILL!

Comments from William F. Buckley, one of America's best-known conservatives:

"I get satisfaction of three kinds. One is creating something, one is being paid for it, and one is the feeling that I haven't just been sitting on my ass all afternoon."

"I would like to take you seriously, but to do so would affront your intelligence."

"Idealism is fine, but as it approaches reality the cost becomes prohibitive."

"I'd rather entrust the government of the United States to the first 400 people listed in the Boston telephone directory than to the faculty of Harvard University."

"Life can't be all bad when for ten dollars you can buy all the Beethoven sonatas and listen to them for ten years."

"I, for one, yearn for the days of the Cold War."

"One must bear in mind that the expansion of federal activity is a form of eating for politicians."

"Kennedy, after all, has lots of glamour. Gregory Peck with an atom bomb in his holster."

"Any sign of weakness by the Free World increases the appetite of the enemy for more war and more conquest as surely as the progressive revelations of the stripteaser increase the appetite of the lecher."

"All civilized men want peace. And all truly civilized men must despise pacifism."

"In the wake of yet another disappearance of a teenager into the mortal coils of the flower world in Greenwich Village, where love is exercised through rape made tolerable by drugs and abstract declarations of fellowship with the North Vietnamese, one wonders anew about the pretensions of progress."

"What has détente done for us except provide a backdrop for the exchange of toasts between American presidents and Communist tyrants?"

Dolly Parton once *lost* a Dolly Parton look-alike contest.

THE LATEST THING

Nothing is sacred in the bathroom—go ahead and admit that you owned a pet rock or a mood ring...we understand...confession is good for the soul. And while you're pondering your follies, we'll tell you where they came from.

PAC-MAN. A Japanese import that hit American shores in late 1980, Pac-Man got its name from the word *paku*, which means "eat" in Japanese. The video game was so popular that Pac-Man was named *Time* magazine's "man" of the year in 1982. That year, Americans pumped $6 *billion* in quarters into Pac-Man's mouth, more than they spent in Las Vegas casinos and movie theatres combined.

MOOD RINGS. The temperature-sensitive jewelry that supposedly read your emotions, Mood Rings were the brainchild of Joshua Reynolds, a New Age heir to the R. J. Reynolds tobacco fortune. Reynolds envisioned them as "portable biofeedback aids" and managed to sell $1 million worth of them in a three-month period in 1975. Even so, the company went bankrupt—but not before it inspired a hoard of imitators, including "mood panties" (underwear studded with temperature-sensitive plastic hearts).

PET ROCKS. One night in 1975, an out-of-work advertising executive named Gary Dahl was hanging out in a bar listening to his friends complain about their pets. It gave him an idea for the perfect "pet": a rock. He spent the next two weeks writing the *Pet Rock Training Manual*, which included instructions for house-training the rock. ("Place it on some old newspapers. The rock will know what the paper is for and will require no further instructions.") He had a friend design a box shaped like a pet carrying case—complete with air holes and a bed of straw—and then filled them with rocks he bought from a builder's supply store for a penny apiece. The rock debuted in August 1975 and sold for $3.95; by the end of October Dahl was shipping 10,000 a day. The fad encouraged a host of imitations as well as an entire Pet Rock "service industry," including dude ranches, "hair-care" products, and burials-at-sea. The fad died out in 1976.

According to recent estimates, 99% of the universe is nothing.

EARTH SHOES. Earth Shoes were one of the best-selling shoes of the 1970s. Invented by a Danish shoe designer named Anne Kalsø, they were brought to the United States in 1969 by a woman who discovered them on a trip to Europe. She claimed they cured her back pains, but foot experts argued that the shoes—which forced wearers to walk on the backs of their feet—were actually pretty bad for you. One study found that most wearers suffered "severe pain and cramping for the first two weeks of wear"; another expert predicted that the shoes would "cripple everyone who wears them." Still, they were a counterculture hit and sold thousands of pairs a year in their peak. The original Earth Shoes company went bankrupt in 1977, the victim of cheap knockoffs and changing times.

COATS OF ARMS. In the '60s, anyone with $20 could send away for a crest corresponding to their last name. At the fad's peak in 1969, status-seeking Americans spent $5 million a year displaying them on sport coats, ashtrays, bank checks, etc. Elitists were outraged. "People of good taste," one blueblood sniffed, "don't use a coat of arms they're not entitled to." But by the early 1970s, just about everyone had a crest—which defeated the purpose of having one in the first place. The fad died out soon afterwards.

SMILEY FACES. Introduced in 1969 by N. G. Slater, a New York button manufacturer. At first sales were slow, but by the spring of 1971 more than 20 million buttons had been sold—enough for one in every 10 Americans—making it a craze as popular as the Hula Hoop of the 1950s. Pop-culture pundits called it the "peace symbol of the seventies," and presidential candidate George McGovern adopted it as his campaign logo. The fad died out after about a year, but in the mid-1970s made a comeback—this time colored yellow and bearing the cheerful message, "Have a Happy Day!" By the late 1970s, however, Americans were completely sick of it.

Smiley Face Update

"Attorneys for a convicted killer asked yesterday that his death sentence be overturned because a judge signed the July 15, 1993 execution order with a 'happy face' sketch....The judge has said that he always signs his name that way as a symbol of his faith in God and that he does not plan to change it." ***—The Associated Press***

WESTERN NICKNAMES

Wild Bill...Black Bart...Billy the Kid...Butch and Sundance. Western heroes had colorful nicknames—but they weren't all as complimentary as they sound. Here's some info on a few of the names.

James Butler "Wild Bill" Hickok. Had a long nose and a protruding lip, and was originally nicknamed "Duck Bill."

William "Bat" Masterson. The famous sheriff of Ford County, Kansas, hit more lawbreakers over the head with his cane than he shot with his gun, and thus earned the nickname "Bat."

Robert LeRoy "Butch Cassidy" Parker. As a teenager, Parker idolized a criminal named Mike Cassidy, and eventually began using his friend's last name as an alias. He picked up the name "Butch" while working in a Rock Springs, Wyoming, butcher shop.

Harry "The Sundance Kid" Longabaugh. As a teenager during the 1880s, Longabaugh spent 1 1/2 years in the Sundance Jail in Wyoming, serving out a sentence for horse stealing.

William "Billy the Kid" Bonney. Looked like a kid.

Henry "Billy the Kid" McCarty. Looked like a goat.

John "Doc" Holliday. A professional dentist by trade, he became a gunslinger and professional gambler after a bout with tuberculosis forced him to move West in search of a drier climate. Even at the height of his criminal career, he practiced dentistry part-time. Holliday's girlfriend was a prostitute named "Big Nose" Kate Elder.

Charles E. "Black Bart" Boles. Came up with the name himself after he became a stagecoach robber by accident. Originally a schoolteacher in northern California's gold country, Boles had a friend who was a Wells Fargo stagecoach driver and decided to play a trick on him. One day in 1875, he covered his face with a scarf, found a stick about the size of a pistol, and jumped out in front of the coach hoping to scare his friend. To his surprise, the driver threw down the strongbox and rode off before Boles could tell him it was only a joke. Opening the strongbox, Boles discovered a for-

It's against the law to play rock music on a Venitian gondola.

tune in gold coins and bullion. Realizing there was more money in stickups than there was in education, Boles quit his teaching job and began holding up stagecoaches full time. He robbed 28 stagecoaches between 1875 and 1883.

After each robbery, he penned a short poem and left it behind in the empty strongbox where he knew investigators would find it. He always signed it "Black Bart, Po-8." One read: "Blame me not for what I've done, I don't deserve your curses/and if for some cause I must be hung/Let it be for my verses." Boles was eventually caught and sentenced to four years in San Quentin prison, but returned to stagecoach robbing within a few weeks of his release. This time Wells Fargo detectives cut a deal with Boles behind the scene: According to legend, they offered Boles a lifelong pension of $200 a month in exchange for his agreement to give up crime. Whether or not the story is true, the robberies stopped immediately.

...and now, folks, we'd like you to meet the dumbest train robber in the West.

Al Jennings, a successful Oklahoma lawyer in the early 1890s, and his brother Frank, also a lawyer, gave up their chosen profession and began second career: sticking up trains—or at least trying to.

In 1897 they tried to rob a mail car on a Santa Fe train, but the conductor chased them away. Two weeks later the brothers tried to stop another train by blocking the track with railroad ties, but the train steamed right through the barrier. In another robbery attempt, they tried to dynamite open two safes, but succeeded only in blowing up the boxcar the safes were on.

The law eventually caught up with them. Frank got five years in prison and Al was sentenced to life in prison, but President Theodore Roosevelt granted him a "full citizenship" pardon in 1907.

Jennings returned to his law practice and eventually ran for county attorney under the slogan, "When I was a train robber I was a good train robber, and if you choose me, I will be a good prosecuting attorney." He lost. In 1914 he ran for governor of Oklahoma (this time his slogan was "It takes the same sort of nerve to be an honest governor as to rob a train or bank") and lost that too.

Born conformists: Ostriches yawn in groups before they go to sleep.

HERE'S JOHNNY...

Quips from the archetypal late-night talk show host, Johnny Carson.

"I now believe in reincarnation. Tonight's monologue is going to come back as a dog."

"The only absolute rule is: Never lose control of the show."

On Jimmy Carter: "I think he rented his family. I don't believe Lillian is his mother. I don't believe Billy is his brother. They're all from Central Casting."

"[Rona Barrett] doesn't need a steak knife. Rona cuts her food with her tongue."

"I like my work and I hope you do, too—but if you don't, I really couldn't care less. Take me or leave me—but don't bug me."

"The difference between divorce and legal separation is that a legal separation gives a husband time to hide his money."

"Never use a big word when a little filthy one will do."

"I don't know where my creativity comes from, and I don't want to know."

"The best things in life are free. And the cheesiest things in life are free with a paid subscription to *Sports Illustrated*."

"The worst gift is a fruitcake. There is only one fruitcake in the entire world, and people keep sending it to each other."

"The difference between love and lust is that lust never costs over two hundred dollars."

"Married men live longer than single men. But married men are a lot more willing to die."

"Anytime four New Yorkers get into a cab together without arguing, a bank robbery has just taken place."

"Thanksgiving is an emotional holiday. People travel thousands of miles to be with people they only see once a year. And then discover once a year is way too often."

20% of French women say being asked to undress during a job interview isn't sexual harassment.

THE AVENGERS

If there was ever one television show that could be described as both "stylish" and "English," it would be "The Avengers." This secret agent send-up of the mid-'60s gave us a taste of "swinging England"—the team of the veddy British Steed (played by Patrick Macnee), and one of the coolest, sexiest women ever to star on the small screen—Emma Peel (played by Shakespearian actress Diana Rigg).

HOW IT STARTED

"The Avengers" immediate inspiration was a show called *Police Surgeon*. It wasn't popular with British viewers, but its star, Ian Hendry, was. So Sydney Newman, the head of programming at ABC-TV in England, decided to feature him on a new show in 1961.

Newman's plan: team Hendry with a secret-agent character in a crusade against crime. Hendry would still play a surgeon, but he wouldn't practice medicine. His fiancé would be killed by a gang of criminals, and he'd become obsessed with vengeance! He would make it his life's work, as he and Steed (the agent) formed "The Avengers." That's how they came up with the name of the show. "Also," admitted Newman, "it's a great title."

The "cult" Avengers—featuring Steed, played by Patrick Macnee, and a macho female partner—evolved a little later. During the first season, an actors' strike forced a layoff in the show; Hendry, with a film career in mind, walked out. The producer decided to replace him with a woman. She'd be a new kind of heroine. Beautiful, but tough; a fighter...but a fashion plate. After a 6-month search for the "right woman," Honor Blackman was selected to play Cathy Gale...and the approach worked so well that the co-ed team became an instant cult phenomenon, one of Europe's most popular series. When Blackman left for films three years later, Diana Rigg stepped ably into her boots as Emma Peel and kept the show a favorite.

The show first aired in England in 1961. It debuted in America in 1966 and ran until 1969. It was resurrected again 1976 as *The New Avengers*.

President Andrew Jackson thought the world was flat.

MILESTONES

"The Avengers" was the first British show ever to air in a U.S. networks fall TV schedule. It was also the groundbreaker in portraying women as tough, capable fighters—predating today's female cops by 20 years.

KUNG FU FIGHTING

Diana Rigg was the first person ever to do Kung Fu on the small screen. In 1965, stuntman Ray Austin went to his producers and said, "listen, I want to do this thing called Kung Fu." They said, "Kung *what?*" and insisted that Emma, like her predecessor, stick to judo. Instead, Austin secretly taught Diana Kung Fu.

If the fight scenes look choreographed...well, they are. Every move in them was created by Austin.

NAME GAME

Emma Peel's name was taken from the British film industry expression "M-Appeal," or "Man Appeal," which is what the show's producers were looking for in her character.

THE LEATHER LOOK

The show helped create the "mod" fashion boom in the '60s. But the most famous of Cathy Gale's clothing, the "kinky" leather look, was created by accident when she split her pants doing karate. Clearly, something more durable was needed, and Patrick Macnee suggested a leather outfit. It became a fad–and "The Avengers" became instant fashion trendsetters.

MERRIE OLDE ENGLAND

If you think about while you're watching, you'll notice how "veddy English" everything is in *The Avengers*, from the scenery to the slang (they don't say "truck," they say "lorry"). Quaint? Not quite. It was an international ploy. The producers figured their only shot at selling the show in America was to offer something that Hollywood couldn't—England. So they hammed it up with the British stuff.

The world population increases by the equivalent of the population of Mexico every year.

THE STARS

Patrick Macnee

• Was an assistant producer in English TV when he was offered the lead role in the new adventure series, "The Avengers." He saw his future in production, not acting, so he asked for a ridiculously high salary to discourage the offer. To his shock, they accepted.

• "They told me to make up a character, so I did," he explained later. Inspired by Leslie Howard in *The Scarlet Pimpernel*, his father, and his C.O. in the navy, Macnee made Steed very British—a cool, upper-class dandy dressed in Edwardian clothes. Predating "Swinging London" by three years, Steed was a major influence on international fashion.

• "Steed is pretty much me," he said. "I feel I'm satirizing my own class—hunting, shooting, fishing, and Eton."

Honor Blackman

Played Steed's first sidekick, and TV's first "superwoman—an anthropologist and judo expert—from 1962 to 1965. She quit to become a movie star when she was offered the role of Pussy Galore in *Goldfinger*.

Diana Rigg

• By the time she appeared as Emma in 1965, she was already a 5-year veteran of the Royal Shakespeare Company. She'd toured Europe and America in a 1964 production of *King Lear* and appeared on United States. TV in *A Comedy of Errors*. However, she had decided to take more commercial roles to avoid being typecast as "a lady actress."

• Meanwhile, "The Avengers" producers were having a rough time replacing Honor Blackman. They'd already hired and fired one actress (Elizabeth Shepard) and had tested dozens more. Then the casting director suggested an actress she'd recently used in a TV drama—Diana Rigg.

• A screen test followed, and Diana was awarded the most coveted female TV role in Britain. The only other regular role she had on a TV series (besides emceeing *Mystery* for PBS) was a short-lived sitcom called "Diana," which aired in 1973. It bombed.

GREETINGS FROM OZ

The Wizard of Oz, by Frank Baum, is on the BRI's list of recommended bathroom reading for adults. Here are a few random quotes taken from it.

ON COURAGE

"There is no living thing that is not afraid when it faces danger. True courage is in facing danger when you are afraid."

—The Wizard

ON MONEY

"Money in Oz!...Did you suppose we are so vulgar as to use money here? If we used money to buy things, instead of love and kindness and the desires to please one another, then we should be no better than the rest of the world....Fortunately, money is not known in the Land of Oz at all. We have no rich, no poor: for what one wishes, the others all try to give him in order to make him happy, and no one in all of Oz cares to have more than he can use."

—The Tin Woodsman

ON EXPERIENCE

"Can't you give me brains?" asked the Scarecrow.

"You don't need them. You are learning something every day. A baby has brains, but it doesn't know much. Experience is the only thing that brings knowledge, and the longer you are on Earth, the more experience you are sure to get."

ON THE VALUE OF BRAINS

"I realize at present that I'm only an imitation of a man, and I assure you that it is an uncomfortable feeling to know that one is a fool. It seems to me that a body is only a machine for brains to direct, and those who have no brains themselves are liable to be directed by the brains of others."

THE BEST THING IN THE WORLD

"Brains are not the best thing in the world," said the Tin Woodsman.

"Have you any?" enquired the Scarecrow.

Expensive hobby: The British monarchy costs taxpayers $85 million a year.

"No, my head is quite empty," answered the Tin Woodsman. "But once I had brains, and a heart also; so, having tried them both, I should much rather have a heart...for brains do not make one happy, and happiness is the best thing in the world."

* * *

...And Now, Back to the World of Facts & Stats

• There are an estimated 5,000 foreign languages spoken throughout the world today—and nearly all of them have a dictionary translating them into English.

• The largest encylopedia of all time was a 16th-century Chinese encyclopedia; it was 22,937 volumes.

• Do you know what "unabridged" means when it refers to English dictionaries? It doesn't mean the work contains all the words in the English language; it just means that it contains all the words listed in earlier editions.

• The world's first Mongolian-English dictionary was published in 1953.

• What language has the most words? Mandarin Chinese, which has an estimated 800,000 words. English is believed to rank second.

• In English dictionaries, the letter "T" has the most entries.

• Few English dictionaries agree on which word is the longest in the language. Two contenders:

✓ *floccinaucinihilipilification* (Oxford English Dictionary), "the action of estimating as worthless."

✓ *pneumonoultramicroscopicsilicovolcanoconiosis* (Webster's Third International), "a lung disease common to miners."

• Many dictionaries do agree on the longest word *in common use:* it's *disproportionableness*.

• The oldest word in the English language that still resembles its earliest form is *land*, which is descended from *landa*, the Old Celtic word for "heath." It predates the Roman Empire (founded in 200 B.C.) by many hundreds of years.

UNEXPECTED ENCOUNTERS

"East is east, and west is west, and never the twain shall meet." When we were kids, that seemed to make sense—except the 'twain' part. That wasn't even a word, as far as we knew. Anyway, here are some examples of people you'd never expect to see together:

CHARLIE CHAPLIN & MAHATMA GANDHI

When: 1931, in London

Who: Chaplin, the "Little Tramp," was the world's most famous comedian. Gandhi, a tiny figure in a loincloth, was one of the world most revered political and religious leaders.

What Happened: As they posed for photographers, Chaplin tried to figure out what to say. In his autobiography, he writes about his terror: "The room was suddenly attacked by flashbulbs from the camera as we sat on the sofa. Now came that uneasy, terrifying moment when I should say something astutely intelligent upon a subject I know little about...I knew I had to start the ball rolling, that it was not up to the Mahatma to tell me how much he enjoyed my last film...I doubted he had ever even seen a film." He finally got up the courage, and the two men politely exchanged political views. Then Chaplin stayed and watched Gandhi at his prayers.

GORGEOUS GEORGE & MUHAMMAD ALI

When: 1961, at a radio studio in Las Vegas

Who: Gorgeous George, with his permed blonde hair and purple robes, was one of TV wrestling's original superstars. He sold out arenas wherever he played, and was named Mr. Televison in 1949; but by 1961 his career was almost over. Cassius Clay (aka Muhammad Ali) was a young boxer who'd just turned pro.

What Happened: In 1961 George made a wrestling appearance in Las Vegas. To promote it, he went on a local radio show, shouting, "I am the greatest!" As it happened, the other guest on the program was a young Cassius Clay, who was so impressed with George's theatrics that he went to the wrestling match that evening. The place was packed. "That's when I decided I'd never been shy about talking," Ali remembers, "but if I talked even more, there was no

Americans say microwave ovens are the best recent change in their lives, infomercials the worst.

telling how much money people would pay to see me."

NICHELLE NICHOLS & MARTIN LUTHER KING, JR.

When: 1967, at a party

Who: King was America's greatest civil rights leader, and the recipient of the Nobel Peace Prize. Nichols was playing Lt. Uhura in *Star Trek*'s first (low-rated) season. She was considering quitting the show because Paramount wouldn't give her a contract.

What Happened: According to one source: "A friend came up to Nichols at a party and said someone wanted to meet her. She expected a gushing Trekkie...but when she turned around, she was looking at Martin Luther King...who actually *was* a fan. He said he'd heard she was considering leaving *Star Trek*, and urged her not to; she was too important a role model for blacks—and the only black woman on TV with real authority. 'Do you realize that you're fourth in command on the *Enterprise*?' he asked. Nichols didn't. The next day she checked and found he was right....She stayed with the show and finally got her contract the next season."

HARPO MARX & GEORGE BERNARD SHAW

When: 1931, at the Villa Gallanon in the south of France

Who: Shaw was "the most important British playright since Shakespeare." Marx was part of the world's most popular slapstick team.

What Happened: Here's how Harpo described the meeting in his autobiography: "I went down the cliff to the little sheltered cove we used for nude bathing, took off my clothes, and went for a swim. I came out of the water and stretched out on a towel to sunbathe. ...I was startled out of my doze in the sun by a man's voice, blaring from the top of the cliff. 'Halloo! Halloo! Is there nobody home?'

"I wrapped the towel around myself and scrambled up the cliff to see who it was. It was a tall, skinny, red-faced old geezer with a beard, decked out in a sporty cap and knicker suit. There was a lady with him. 'Who the devil are you?' I told him I was Harpo Marx. 'Ah, yes, of course,' he said. He held out his hand. 'I'm Bernard Shaw,' he said. Instead of shaking hands with me, he made a sudden lunge for my towel and snatched it away, and exposed me naked to the world. 'And this,' he said, 'is Mrs. Shaw.' From the moment I met him, I had nothing to hide from George Bernard Shaw." They became good friends.

Teenage boys use more shampoo—and less deodorant—than teenage girls.

ORIGIN OF THE "BIG THREE" NETWORKS

They're a big part of your life...but we'll bet you don't know how they got there. Let's correct that.

THE NATIONAL BROADCASTING COMPANY (NBC)

NBC is the oldest of the "Big three" American broadcasting networks. It was founded on September 13, 1926, by the Radio Corporation of America (RCA), the world's largest radio manufacturer, because they feared poor-quality radio broadcasting was hurting sales.

Spurred on by RCA president David Sarnoff, NBC quickly became the most potent force in radio. The demand for programming was so high that within a year NBC split its radio operations into two divisions—the Red and Blue networks. The two continued broadcasting side by side until 1943, when the U.S. government forced NBC to sell off the Blue network in an antitrust suit.

Meanwhile, RCA was experimenting with television (which Sarnoff called "the art of distant seeing"). In 1931 NBC built its first television transmitter, on top of the Empire State Building. Although development of TV was subsequently slowed by the Depression, regular TV service was started by NBC in 1939...and the first TV network broadcast ever was on January 11, 1940, from NBC in New York City to a General Electric-owned station in Schenectady, New York.

Because America was putting its resources into the war effort from 1941 to 1945, NBC couldn't begin regular network TV broadcasts until 1945. RCA was the sole owner of NBC until 1985, when GE—an original partner in 1926—bought RCA for $6.8 billion.

THE COLUMBIA BROADCASTING SYSTEM (CBS)

In the 1920s, Arthur Judson was a talent agent whose clients included the New York Philharmonic. When NBC pioneered TV broadcasting in 1926, Judson cut a deal with them to broadcast several of his clients—but NBC reneged on its promise. Judson was so angry that he started his own radio broadcasting network. He called it the United Independent Broadcasters and began signing up independent radio stations around the country.

Judson was too broke to run the company alone, so he joined forces with the Columbia Phonograph and Records Co. and changed the network's name to the Columbia Phonograph Broadcasting System. It initially provided 10 hours of programming per week to 16 affiliates. But CPBS was losing money, and Columbia Phonograph pulled out. They sold their shares to Jerome Louchheim, a wealthy Philidelphia builder, who renamed CPBS the Columbia Broadcasting System. He, in turn, sold out to William S. Paley for $400,000 in 1929. Paley (whose father, owner of the Congress Cigar Co., was one of CBS's largest advertisers) turned the ailing network around almost overnight. By 1932 CBS was earning more than $3 million a year in profits—and in 1939 it was doing so well that it bought its former owner, Columbia Phonograph and Records.

THE AMERICAN BROADCASTING SYSTEM (ABC)

When the U.S. government forced NBC to sell off its Blue network in 1943, Lifesaver candy manufacturer Edward J. Noble bought it for $8 million and renamed it the American Broadcasting Company. Ten years later, ABC merged with United Paramont Theaters—a chain of movie theaters the government had forced Paramount Pictures to sell—and went into TV broadcasting.

A perpetual "weak sister" to its larger rivals, ABC remained a second-rate network until 1954, when its gavel-to-gavel coverage of the U.S. Senate's Army-McCarthy hearings made broadcasting history...and gave them newfound respectability.

ABC remained much smaller than its rivals, but made up for its lack of money and affiliate stations by producing more innovative TV shows than CBS and NBC. Some of its groundbreaking shows: "Disneyland," "The Mickey Mouse Club," and "Batman." ABC also revolutionized sports coverage with shows like "Monday Night Football," "Wide World of Sports," and its coverage of the Olympics. The network used the profits generated from sports and miniseries shows to strengthen its news and prime-time programming—and in 1975 its overall ratings shot ahead of its rivals for the first time. It has been on equal footing ever since.

America has 1,103 drive-in movie theaters, more than any other nation on Earth.

THE GENUINE ARTICLE

A random sampling of authentic articles, dialogue, commentary. You are there.

OUTRAGE OVER ELVIS

In 1956, Elvis Presley appeared on the "Ed Sullivan Show." We think of it as a great moment in TV history, but at the time, critics (and other grown-ups) didn't. These comments appeared in the New York Times:

"Last Sunday on the "Ed Sullivan Show," Mr. Presley made another of his appearances and attracted a record audience. In some ways, it was the most unpleasant of his recent three performances. Mr. Presley initially disturbed adult viewers with his strip-tease behavior on last spring's Milton Berle's program....On the Sullivan program he injected movements of the tongue and indulged in wordless singing that were singularly distasteful....

"Some parents are puzzled or confused by Mr. Presley's almost hypnotic power; some are concerned; [but] most are a shade disgusted and [will be] content to let the Presley fad play itself out."

CHARLIE CHAPLIN'S FAVORITE JOKE

At lunch one afternoon, Charlie Chaplin was asked to relate the funniest joke he'd ever heard. You'd think that "the world's greatest comic genius" would tell something hilarious. But...well...you decide.

"A man in a tea shop orders a cup of coffee and a piece of shortbread. On paying the bill, he compliments the manager on the quality of the shortbread and asks if it could be custom-made in any shape. 'Why, certainly.'

" 'Well, if I come back tomorrow, could you make me a piece shaped like the letter "e"?'

" 'No trouble,' says the manager. Next day, on returning to the shop, the man looks aghast.

" 'But you've made it a capital "E"!' He arranges to come back another day, and this time expresses himself completely satisfied.

" 'Where would you like me to send it?' asks the manager.

" 'Oh, I won't give you the trouble to send it anywhere,' says the

According to *Family Circle* magazine, each American averages one greasy-food stain per month.

customer. 'I'll sit down here, if I may, and eat it now.' And he does."

No one at lunch thought it was funny, either. (Neither do we.)

HISTORIC RECIPE

In 1770, American revolutionaries published these detailed directions for tarring and feathering, which was, at the time "a mob ritual."

How to Tar and Feather Someone

"First, strip a person naked, then heat the Tar until it is thin & pour it upon naked Flesh, or rub it over with a Tar brush.

"After which, sprinkle decently upon the Tar, whilst it is yet warm, as many Feathers as will stick to it.

"Then hold a lighted Candle to the Feathers, & try to set it all on Fire."

GREAT MOMENTS IN CENSORSHIP

In 1937, Mae West was barred from radio after she engaged in a slightly risqué dialogue on NBC's Edgar Bergen/Charlie McCarthy Show. The conversation was with McCarthy, a ventriloquist's dummy!

Mae West: "Why don't you come home with me now honey? I'll let you play in my woodpile."

Charlie McCarthy: "Well, I don't feel so well tonight. I've been feeling nervous lately...."

West: "You can't kid me. You're afraid of women. Your Casanova stuff is just a front, a false front."

McCarthy: "Not so loud, Mae, not so loud! All my girlfriends are listening...."

West: "You weren't so nervous when you came up to see me at my apartment. In fact, you didn't need any encouragement to kiss me."

McCarthy: "Did I do that?"

West: "You certainly did. I got marks to prove it. And splinters, too."

Protests poured in from church groups, ostensibly because the show had aired on a Sunday (more likely reason: they objected to West's general "promiscuity"). The sponsor agreed it was "inappropriate," and apologized on the air; Hollywood disavowed both the skit and *West; NBC declared she would never appear on radio again.*

Most popular book genre: mysteries and thrillers; 25% of American readers read them to relax.

IMMACULATE CONCEPTION

On Nov. 4, 1874, this article allegedly appeared in The American Weekly. *It was quoted in an 1896 book,* Anomalies and Curiosities of Medicine, but it's really just an early urban legend.

"During the fray [between Union and Confederate troops], a soldier staggered and fell to earth; at the same time a piercing cry was heard in the house nearby. Examination showed that a bullet had passed through the scrotum and carried away the left testicle. The same bullet had apparently penetrated the left side of the abdomen of a young lady...and become lost in the abdomen. The daughter suffered an attack of peritonitis, but recovered.

"Two hundred and seventy-eight days after the reception of the minie ball, she was delivered of a fine boy weighing eight pounds, to the surprise of herself, and the mortification of her parents and friends.

"The doctor concluded that...the same ball that had carried away the testicle of his young friend...had penetrated the ovary of the young lady and, with some spermatozoa upon it, had impregnated her. With this conviction, he approached the young man and told him of the circumstances. The soldier appeared skeptical at first, but consented to visit the young mother; a friendship ensued, which soon ripened into a happy marriage."

NIXONIA

You think Richard Nixon was "a little" stiff and formal? Here's a memo he sent to his wife on January 25, 1969.

To: Mrs. Nixon

From: The President

With regard to RN's room, what would be the most desirable is an end table like the one on the right side of the bed, which will accomodate two dictaphones as well as a telephone. RN has to use one dictaphone for current matters and another for memoranda for the file, which he will not want transcribed at this time. In addition, he needs a bigger table on which he can work at night. The table which is presently in the room does not allow enough room for him to get his knees under it.

Only 33% of people in the United Arab Emirates are women—the lowest percentage on Earth.

CARTOON NAMES

How did our favorite cartoon characters get their unusual names? Here are a few answers.

Bugs Bunny: Warner Brothers cartoonist Bugs Hardaway submitted preliminary sketches for "a tall, lanky, mean rabbit" for a cartoon called "Hare-um Scare-um"—and someone labeled the drawings "Bugs's Bunny." Hardaway's mean rabbit was never used—but the name was given to the bunny in the cartoon "A Wild Hare."

Casper the Friendly Ghost: Cartoonist Joe Oriolo's daughter was afraid of ghosts—so he invented one that wouldn't scare her. "We were looking for a name that didn't sound threatening," he says.

Chip 'n' Dale: Disney animator Jack Hannah was meeting with colleagues to pick names for his two new chipmunk characters. His assistant director happened to mention Thomas Chippendale, the famous furniture designer. "Immediately," Hannah remembers, "I said 'That's it! That's their names!' "

Mickey Mouse: Walt Disney wanted to name the character *Mortimer* Mouse—but his wife hated the name. "Mother couldn't explain why the name grated; it just did," Disney's daughter Diane remembers. Disney wanted the character's name to begin with the letter M (to go with Mouse)—and eventually decided on Mickey.

Porky Pig: According to creator Bob Clampett: "Someone thought of two puppies named Ham and Ex, and that started me thinking. So after dinner one night, I came up with Porky and Beans. I made a drawing of this fat little pig, which I named Porky, and a little black cat named Beans."

Rocky & Bullwinkle: Rocky was picked because it was "just a square-sounding kid's name"; Bullwinkle was named after Clarence Bulwinkel, a used-car dealer from Berkeley, California.

Elmer Fudd: Inspired by a line in a 1920s song called "Mississippi Mud." The line: "It's a treat to meet you on the Mississippi Mud—Uncle Fudd."

Foghorn Leghorn: Modeled after Senator Claghorn, a fictional politician in comedian Fred Allen's radio show.

MORE LEFT-HANDED FACTS

Here's more info for lefties. Why devote two more pages to the subject? Okay, okay. We admit it—Uncle John is left-handed.

LEFT-HANDED STATS

• Lefties make up about 5% to 15% of the general population—but 15% to 30% of all patients in mental institutions.

• They're more prone to allergies, insomnia, migranes, schizophrenia and a host of other things than right-handers. They're also three times more likely than righties to become alcoholics. Why? Some scientists speculate the right hemisphere of the brain—the side left-handers use the most—has a lower tolerance for alcohol than the left side. Others think the stress of living in a right-handed world is responsible.

• Lefties are also more likely to be on the extreme ends of the intelligence scale than the general population: a higher proportion of mentally retarded people *and* people with IQs over 140 are lefties.

LEFT OUT OF SCIENCE

• For centuries science was biased against southpaws. In the 1870s, for example, Italian psychiatrist Cesare Lombroso published *The Delinquent Male*, in which he asserted that left-handed men were psychological "degenerates" and prone to violence. (A few years later he published *The Delinquent Female*, in which he made the same claims about women.)

• This theory existed even as late as the 1940s, when psychiatrist Abram Blau wrote that left-handedness "is nothing more than an expression of infantile negativism and falls into the same category as...general perverseness." He speculated that lefties didn't get enough attention from their mothers.

LEFT-HANDED TRADITIONS

• Why do we throw salt over our left shoulders for good luck? To throw it into the eyes of the Devil, who, of course, lurks behind us to our left.

Hmm: 61% of college women, but only 28% of college men, say they're in a "steady relationship."

• In many traditional Muslim cultures, it is extremely impolite to touch food with your left hand. Reason: Muslims eat from communal bowls using their right hand; their left hand is used to perform "unclean" tasks such as wiping themselves after going the bathroom. Hindus have a similar custom: they use their right hand exclusively when touching themselves above the waist, and use only the left hand to touch themselves below the waist.

• What did traditional Christians believe was going to happen on Judgement Day? According to custom, God blesses the saved with his right hand—and casts sinners out of Heaven with his left.

• Other traditional mis-beliefs:

✓ If you have a ringing in your left ear, someone is cursing you. If your right ear rings, someone is praising you.

✓ If your left eye twitches, you're going to see an enemy. If the right twitches, you're going to see a friend.

✓ If you get out of bed with your left foot first, you're going to have a bad day.

✓ If your left palm itches, you're going to owe someone money. If your right palm does, you're going to make some money.

LEFT-HANDED MISCELLANY

• Why are lefties called "southpaws"? In the late 1890s, most baseball parks were laid out with the pitcher facing west and the batter facing east (so the sun wouldn't be in his eyes). That meant left-handed pitchers threw with the arm that faced south. So Chicago sportswriter Charles Seymour began calling them "southpaws."

• Right-handed bias: Some Native American tribes strapped their children's left arms to the mother's cradleboard, which caused most infants to become predominantly right-handed. The Kaffirs of South Africa acheived similar results by burying the left hands of left-handed children in the burning desert sand.

• The next time you see a coat of arms, check to see if it has a stripe running diagonally across it. Most stripes are called *bends* and run from the top left to the bottom right. A stripe that runs from the bottom left to the top right, is called a "left-handed" bend or a *bend sinister*—and means the bearer was a bastard.

MORE STRANGE LAWSUITS

More bizarre doings in the halls of justice, from news reports.

THE PLAINTIFF: James Hooper, a 25-year-old student at Oklahoma State University.

THE DEFENDANT: The Pizza Shuttle, a Stillwater, Oklahoma, pizza restaurant.

THE LAWSUIT: Hooper ordered an "extra cheese, pepperoni, sausage, black olive and mushroom pizza." Instead, he said, the Pizza Shuttle delivered "a pizza with something green on it, maybe peppers." He sued the restaurant for $7.00 in damages ($5.50 for the pizza and $1.50 for the delivery boy's tip).

VERDICT: The court found in favor of the Pizza Shuttle—and ordered Hooper to pay $57 in court costs.

THE PLAINTIFF: Widow of Walter Hughes, who died in 1991.

THE DEFENDANTS: McVicker's Chapel on the Hill and Kevin Robinson, Hughes's son-in-law and former director of the Longview, Washington, funeral home.

THE LAWSUIT: Mrs. Hughes sued the funeral home when she learned that it had buried her husband without his favorite cowboy hat.

VERDICT: She was awarded $101,000 in damages.

THE PLAINTIFF: Seven patrons of Charley Brown's, a Concord, California, restaurant.

THE DEFENDANT: The restaurant.

THE LAWSUIT: In 1992, the restaurant hired an actor to stage a mock robbery as part of a dinner show called "The Suspect's Dinner Theater." The actor, dressed as a masked gunman, burst into the restaurant shouting "All you m——, hit the floor!" Dinner guests, thinking the robbery was real, cowered under their tables while the man shouted threats and fired several blank rounds from his .45-caliber pistol. (One patron, an investigator with the county

district attorney's office, fought with the gunman until restaurant employees told him the robbery was part of the show.) "When the hostess said it was all just an episode of Mystery Theater," another diner told reporters, "I said, 'Mystery Theater, my a—. You're going to hear from my lawyer.' " He and six others sued the restaurant, claiming assault and intentional infliction of emotional distress.
VERDICT: The restaurant offered to settle the case by paying $3,000 to each of the plaintiffs—and later went out of business.

THE PLAINTIFF: Andrea Pizzo, a 23-year-old former University of Maine student.
THE DEFENDANT: The University of Maine.
THE LAWSUIT: Apparently, Pizzo was attending a class in livestock management one afternoon in 1991, when a cow attacked her. (It butted her into a fence.) She sued, claiming the school "should have known that the heifer had a personality problem."
VERDICT: Unknown.

THE PLAINTIFF: William and Tonya P., who booked a room at a Michigan Holiday Inn during their honeymoon in 1992.
THE DEFENDANT: The Holiday Inn.
THE LAWSUIT: William and Tonya claim that a hotel employee walked into their room on their wedding night while they were having sex. They filed a $10,000 lawsuit against the hotel, claiming the unannounced visit ruined their sex life. Holiday Inn does not dispute the charge but says they should have hung up a "Do Not Disturb" sign.
VERDICT: Unknown.

THE PLAINTIFF: John M., a 50-year-old Philadelphia teacher.
THE DEFENDANT: His wife, Maryann K., a 46-year-old receptionist.
THE LAWSUIT: One day after her divorce from John became final, Ms. K. turned in a lottery ticket that was about to expire and won $10.2 million. Her lawyer claims that "Lady Luck" led her to find the ticket and turn it in two weeks before it expired—but Mr. M. thinks she deliberately waited until after the divorce was finalized to turn it in. He sued to get his share.
VERDICT: Pending.

Q. What's the most-played song in history? A. Paul McCartney's "Yesterday."

BLOTTO, LOOPED, FRIED

Most people know what sloshed, loaded and looped mean: being drunk, of course. But there are plenty of other words that mean the same thing. Here's a list of America's favorites that appear in I Hear America Talking.

(The words are followed by the years they came into use.)

Stiff (1737)
Fuzzy (1770)
Half Shaved (1818)
Bent (1833)
Slewed (1834)
Stinking (1837)
Screwed (1838)
Lushy (1840)
Pixilated (1850)
Swizzled (1850)
Whipped (1851)
Tanglefooted (1860)
Spiffed (1860)
Frazzled (1870)
Squiffy (1874)
Boiled (1886)
Paralyzed (1888)
Pickled (1890)
Woozy (1897)
Pifflicated (1900)
Ginned (1900)
Ossified (1901)
Petrified (1903)
Tanked (1905)
Blotto (1905)

Shellacked (1905)
Jingled (1908)
Piped (1912)
Plastered (1912)
Gassed (1915)
Hooted (1915)
Have a Snoot Full (1918)
Jugged (1919)
Canned (1920)
Juiced (1920)
Fried (1920)
Buried (1920)
Potted (1922)
Dead to the World (1926)
Crocked (1927)
Busted (1928)
Rum-dum (1931)
Bombed (1940)
Feeling No Pain (1940)
Swacked (1941)
Sloshed (1950)
Boxed (1950)
Clobbered (1951)
Crashed (1950s)
Zonked (1950s)

HELLMAN'S LAWS

Wisdom from Lillian Hellman, one of America's greatest playwrights.

"Nothing, of course, begins at the time you think it did."

"Nobody can argue any longer about the rights of women. It's like arguing about the rights of earthquakes."

"I like people who refuse to speak until they are *ready* to speak."

"Nothing you write, if you hope to be any good, will ever come out as you first hoped."

"Cynicism is an unpleasant way of saying the truth."

"I cannot, and will not, cut my conscience to fit this year's fashions."

"God forgives those who invent what they need."

"People change...and forget to tell each other."

"Fashions in sin change."

"The convictions of Hollywood and television are made of boiled money."

"There are people who eat the earth and eat all the people on it, like in the Bible with the locusts. And [there are] other people who stand around and watch them eat it."

"It is a mark of many famous people that they cannot part with their brightest hour: what once worked must *always* work."

"It doesn't pay well to fight for what we believe in."

"Since when do you have to agree with people to defend them with justice?"

"Callous greed grows pious very fast."

"We are a people who do not want to keep much of the past in our heads. It is considered unhealthy in America to remember mistakes, neurotic to think about them, psychotic to dwell upon them."

"If I had to give young writers advice, I would say don't listen to writers talk about writing...or themselves."

Older and wiser: The average Ph.D. candidate spends seven years on their dissertation.

AUNT LENNA'S PUZZLES

More conversations with my favorite aunt. Answers are on page 664.

MONEY MINDED

My Aunt Lenna is a little unreliable when it comes to money. So I wasn't surprised when she came to me and asked, "Nephew, why are 1993 dollar bills worth more than 1992 dollar bills?"

"Aunt Lenna, don't be silly, they—"

"Tut, tut, Nephew. Think before you answer."

What's the answer to her question?

TRAIN OF THOUGHT

Aunt Lenna and I went down to the train station to pick up a friend. On the way, she came up with a little puzzle for me.

"Let's say that two sets of train tracks run right alongside one another...until they get to a narrow tunnel. Both tracks won't fit, so they merge into one track for the whole length of the tunnel... then go back to being parallel tracks. One morning a train goes into the tunnel from the east end...and another goes into the tunnel from the west end. They're traveling as fast as they can go, in opposite directions, but they don't crash. Can you tell me why not?"

"Really, Aunt Lenna. I know I'm not the brightest guy in the world, but even I can figure this one out."

What's the story?

GREETINGS

"What have you got there, Aunt Lenna?"

"Oh, it's just the card I'm sending this year."

"Let's see." I looked at the card. It read:

ABCDEFGHIJKMNOPQRSTUVWXYZ

"Very cute, Aunt Lenna."

What did it say?

THE BLACK STONES

Aunt Lenna had a puzzle for me:

"Once there was a beautiful woman whose family owed money to an evil moneylender. 'I'll give you a chance to rid yourself of the debt,' the evil guy told her. 'How?' 'I'll put two stones in this bag,' he said—'one white, one black. You reach in and take one. If you pick the white one, your debt is wiped out. If you pick the black one, you marry me.' "

"I suppose he laughed maniacally at that point."

"Why, yes, how did you know? Where was I? Oh, yes—the girl agreed, and watched as the man put two stones in the bag. But she realized he had put two black stones in, and there was no chance of picking a white stone. How could she win the bet?"

How did she win?

QUICK CUT

Aunt Lenna loves to bake. One day she was busy rolling out dough for a cake when she turned to me and said, "Nephew, I've got a little puzzle for you. How is it possible to cut a cake into eight equal parts…with just three straight cuts with a knife?"

I thought for a minute. "It's not."

"Oh yes it is. Think about it awhile."

How can it be done?

TIME TO GO

Aunt Lenna was reminiscing. "When I was a teenager, there was a boy who kept coming around, asking me to the movies and such. I didn't want to hurt his feelings, but finally one day, I had to do something. So I asked him if he'd heard about the nine O's. He said no, so I drew nine O's, like this: O O O O O O O O O.

Then I added five vertical lines to the Os…and he got the message and stopped bothering me."

What did Aunt Lenna do with the lines?

Q & A: ASK THE EXPERTS

More random questions...and answers from America's trivia experts.

VISIONARIES

Q: *Can animals see in color?*

A: "Apes and some monkeys [see] the full spectrum of color, as may some fish and birds. But most mammals see color only as shades of grey." (From *The Book of Answers*, by Barbara Berliner)

YOURS, MINE, AND HOURS

Q: *Why are there 24 hours in a day?*

A: "To the ancients, 12 was a mystical number. It could be evenly divided by 2, 3, 4, and 6 (that's one of the reasons we still use dozens today). Twenty-four hours is made up of two 12s—12 hours before noon, and 12 hours after." (From *Know It All!*, by Ed Zotti)

GR-R-R

Q: *Why does your stomach rumble when you're hungry?*

A: "Every 75-115 minutes, your stomach's muscles contract. When no food is present, their rhythm is a wave-like stretching and contracting that molds the air, mostly digestive gases, in the stomach cavity. No one understands exactly why this makes the tummy-rumble noise, but it surely does." (From *Why Can't You Tickle Yourself?* by Ingrid Johnson)

FAR A-FIELDS

Q: *Did W. C. Fields actually say, "Anyone who hates dogs and children can't be all bad?"*

A: Nope, it was Leo Rosten. See page 369 for more info.

GOLD DISC

Q: *What was the first gold record?*

A: Glenn Miller got it for "Chattanooga Choo-Choo." The first certified million-selling album was the soundtrack from *Oklahoma*.

Lobbyist's leverage: The average freshman U.S. senator enters office $266,073 in debt.

ROCKIN' ROBIN

Q: *Why do birds sing?*

A: No, it's not because they're happy. "The vast majority of bird songs are produced by males and break down to two kinds: first, a call from male to male, proclaiming territory and warning other males away, and second, a call to females, advertising the singer's maleness...if he's not already committed." (From *Do Elephants Swim?*, compiled by Robert M. Jones)

OVER THE HUMP

Q: *How long can a camel go without water?*

A: "A camel can go for 17 days without drinking any water.... There is a secret to this: The camel carries a great deal of fat in its hump and has the ability to manufacture water out of this hump by oxidation. This is not to say that the camel doesn't get thirsty. When it gets the chance to drink after a long drought, it can suck down 25 gallons of water." (From *Science Trivia*, by Charles Cazeau)

BOXED RAISINS

Q: *Why don't the raisins in Raisin Bran fall to the bottom of the box?*

A: "Raisins are added to boxes only after more than half of the cereal has already been packed. The cereal thus has a chance to settle and condense. During average shipping conditions, boxes get jostled a bit...so the raisins actually sift and become evenly distributed throughout the box." (From *Why Do Clocks Run Clockwise, and Other Imponderables*, by David Feldman)

CHOCOLATE

Q: *Who brought chocolate from the New World to Europe?*

A: When the Spanish conquistador Hernan Cortés wrote to Emperor Charles V of Spain from the New World, he described a "divine drink...which builds up resistance and fights fatigue." Cortés was speaking of *chocolatl*, a drink the Aztecs brewed from the native *cacao* bean, which was valued so highly that it was used as currency. He brought some home to Spain and it became popular instantly.

Ants stretch—and possibly even yawn—when they wake up in the morning.

OTHER PRESIDENTIAL FIRSTS

We all know the first president (Washington), the first president to serve more than two terms (FDR), and so on. But who was the first to get stuck in a bathtub? Here's another BRI list of presidential firsts, with thanks to Bruce Fowler's book One of a Kind.

THE PRESIDENT: Grover Cleveland (1885-89; 1893-97)
NOTABLE FIRST: First president to have hanged a man.
BACKGROUND: From 1871 to 1873, he was sheriff of Erie County, New York. When two men were sentenced to death there, Cleveland put the hoods over their heads, tightened the noose, and sprung the trap door himself. He explained later that he couldn't ask his deputies to do it just because he didn't want to. The experience affected him so deeply that he didn't run for re-election.

THE PRESIDENT: James Garfield (1881)
NOTABLE FIRST: First president who could write in two languages at once.
BACKGROUND: Garfield was ambidextrous; he could write in Greek with one hand while writing in Latin with the other.

THE PRESIDENT: William Howard Taft (1909-1913)
NOTABLE FIRST: First president entrapped by a White House plumbing fixture.
BACKGROUND: Taft weighed in at between 300 and 350 lbs. while he was president. He was so big that one morning he got stuck in the White House tub—and had to call his aides to help him get out. Taft subsequently ordered a tub large enough to hold four men. He never got stuck again.

THE PRESIDENT: James Madison (1809-1817)
NOTABLE FIRST: First president to weigh less than his IQ.
BACKGROUND: Madison, the unofficial "Father of the U.S.

More Americans die in January than in any other month.

Constitution," was only 5'4" tall and never weighed more than 98 lbs. as president. One historian has called him "a dried-up, wizened little man"—and observed that when he went walking with his friend Thomas Jefferson, the two looked "as if they were on their way to a father-and-son banquet."

THE PRESIDENT: John Tyler (1841-1845)

NOTABLE FIRST: First president to elope while in office.

BACKGROUND: On June 26, 1844, the 54-year-old Tyler sneaked off to New York City with 24-year-old Julia Gardiner to tie the knot. They decided on a secret wedding because supporters were worried about the public's reaction to their 30-year age difference. It didn't matter—the press found out about it almost at once. Ironically, Julia turned out to be just about the most popular part of Tyler's presidency. (P.S.: They had seven kids—the last one when Tyler was 70.)

THE PRESIDENT: Herbert Hoover (1929-1933)

NOTABLE FIRST: First president to have an asteroid named after him.

BACKGROUND: No, it's not in honor of his presidency. In 1920, Austrian astronomer Johann Palisa discovered an asteroid and named it *Hooveria*, to honor Hoover's humanitarian work as chairman of the Interallied Food Council, which was helping to feed starving people in post–World War I Europe. Said Palisa, "It is a pity we have only a middle-magnitude asteroid to give to this great man. He is worthy of at least a planet."

THE PRESIDENT: Jimmy Carter (1976-1980)

NOTABLE FIRST: First president to see a UFO.

BACKGROUND: One evening in 1969, Carter and a few companions saw a "bluish...then reddish" saucer-shaped object moving across the sky. "It seemed to move toward us from a distance," Carter later told UFO researchers, "then it stopped and moved partially away. It returned and departed. It came close...maybe three hundred to one thousand yards away...moved away, came close, and then moved away." He added: "I don't laugh at people anymore when they say they've seen UFOs."

The U.S. government spends $79 million a day on "intelligence."

COLD FOODS

The title doesn't really mean anything. We had a bunch of stories about food we wanted to use, and "cold" was the only thing we could think of that the foods had in common.

SWANSON TV DINNERS. When Carl Swanson stepped off the boat from Sweden in 1896, the only thing he owned was the sign around his neck that read, "Carl Swanson, Swedish. Send me to Omaha. I speak no English." Someone sent him to Omaha, where he started a grocery wholesale business that grew into the largest turkey processor in the United States. When his sons took over the company after his death, they began expanding their product line beyond turkeys. Two of their first additions: frozen turkey and fried-chicken meals they called "TV dinners," packaged in wood-grain boxes that simulated televisions. (Swanson didn't only intend that the meals be eaten in front of the TV—it also wanted to associate its "heat-and-eat miracle" with the magic of television.)

Swanson's first TV dinners bombed. The sweet potatoes in the turkey dinner were too watery, and customers complained that the fried chicken tasted like bananas—a problem caused by slow-drying, banana-scented yellow dye that leached from the cardboard box onto the chicken. Swanson fixed the first problem by switching to regular potatoes; it solved the chicken problem by giving the boxes a longer time to dry. (What did it do with the chicken that had already been contaminated? It sold it to a Florida food chain that said its customers preferred the "new" banana taste.)

ESKIMO PIES. Christian Nelson owned a candy and ice cream store in Onawa, Iowa. One day in 1920, a kid came into the store and ordered a candy bar...and then changed his mind and asked for an ice cream sandwich...and then changed his mind again and asked for a marshmallow-nut bar. Nelson wondered for a minute why there wasn't any one candy-and-ice-cream bar to satisfy all of the kid's cravings—and then decided to make one himself: a vanilla bar coated with a chocolate shell. Once he figured out how to make the chocolate stick to the ice cream, he had to think of a name for his product. At a dinner party, someone suggested

What professionals are most likely to become alcoholics? Barbers, say drug treatment experts.

"Eskimo," because it sounded cold. But other people thought it sounded too exotic—so Nelson added the word "pie."

MINUTE MAID ORANGE JUICE. In 1942 the U.S. Army announced that it would award a $750,000 contract to any company that could produce an orange juice "powder" cheap enough to send to troops overseas. After three years of intense research, the National Research Corporation (NRC) developed a way to concentrate and freeze orange juice, and was working out the bugs in the drying process. It won the contract—but just as it was lining up the financing for an orange juice plant, the U.S. dropped the A-bomb on Hiroshima and World War II came to an end.

Convinced that powdered orange juice had a future, the NRC decided to forge ahead with its efforts to perfect the drying process. To raise money for the research, the company decided to unload some of its backlog of frozen concentrated orange juice. Marketed under the name Minute Maid, the stuff sold so well that NRC went into the frozen orange juice business instead.

ICE CREAM MISCELLANY

Ice Cream Sodas. In 1874, soda-fountain operator Robert M. Green sold a drink he made out of sweet cream, syrup, and carbonated water soda. One day he ran out of cream...so he used vanilla ice cream instead.

Ice Cream Sundaes. It seems ridiculous now, but in the 1890s, many religious leaders objected to people drinking ice cream sodas on Sunday. It was too frivolous. When "blue laws" were passed prohibiting the sale of ice cream sodas on Sunday, ice cream parlor owners fought back—they created the "Sunday," which was only sold on the Sabbath; it contained all of the ingredients of a soda *except* the soda water. A few years later the dish was being sold all week, so the name was changed to *sundae*.

Baskin-Robbins 31 Flavors. After World War II, Irvine Robbins and Burton Baskin built a chain of ice cream stores in southern California. One day in 1953, Robbins says, "we told our advertising agency about our great variety of flavors and we said, almost in jest, that we had a flavor for every day of the month—thirty-one. They hit the table and said that was it, the thirty-one. So we changed the name of the company to Baskin Robbins 31. Like Heinz 57."

The White House receives an average of 75,850 pieces of correspondence *every day*.

RUMORS

Why do people believe wild, unsubstantiated stories? According to some psychologists, "rumors make things simpler than they really are." And while people won't believe just anything, it's suprising what stories have flourished in the past. Many of these tales are stll in circulation today...

RUMOR: Wint-O-Green Lifesavers can kill you.

HOW IT SPREAD: In 1968 Dr. Howard Edward and Dr. Donald Edward wrote a letter to the *New England Journal of Medicine* warning that the eerie green sparks given off when you chomp on the Lifesavers could—under certain conditions—start a fire. Some possible conditions in which the Lifesavers could kill you: if you ate them in an oxygen tent, a space capsule, or in a room filled with flammable gas. (No word on whether anyone as ever actually *chewed* Wint-O-Greens under such conditions.)

WHAT HAPPENED: The letter inspired a number of researchers around the country to experiment with Wint-O-Green Lifesavers to see what made them spark, and to see if the sparks were indeed dangerous. Their findings: The sparks are caused by *methyl salicylate*, the synthetic crystalline substance that's used for flavoring instead of real wintergreen oil. The sparking effect is known scientifically as "triboluminescence," which is what happens when a crystalline substance is crushed. And since the spark is a "cold luminescence" and not a real spark, it can't cause an explosion. (Even so, researchers advise, if you are still nervous, just chew on them with your mouth closed.)

THE RUMOR: Silent-screen starlet Clara Bow slept with the entire starting lineup of the 1927 USC football team.

HOW IT SPREAD: The story was started by Bow's private secretary, Daisy DeVoe, whom Bow fired after DeVoe tried to blackmail her. DeVoe got back at her by selling an "inside story" account of Bow's private life to *Graphic*, a notorious New York tabloid. The USC rumor was only part of the story; DeVoe also claimed that Bow had had affairs with Eddie Cantor, Gary Cooper, Bela Lugosi, and other celebrities.

Home video sales and rentals are the biggest source of income for movie studios.

WHAT HAPPENED: The surviving members of the 1927 team deny the story is true. Author David Stenn tracked them down while researching his biography *Clara Bow: Runnin' Wild.* They admit that Bow often invited them to her parties, but they were entirely innocent—Bow didn't even serve alcohol. Even so, the tabloid story destroyed her career: Paramont Studios refused to renew her contract, and Bow "spent the greater part of the rest of her life suffering a series of nervous breakdowns in sanitariums."

THE RUMOR: Sesame Street is planning to "kill off" Ernie, the famous muppet of "Ernie and Bert" fame.

HOW IT SPREAD: The Children's Television Workshop believes the rumor started somewhere in New England after the 1990 death of muppet creator Jim Henson, who was Ernie's voice. CTW denied the rumor, but it quickly gained strength; according to Ellen Morgenstern, CTW's spokeswoman, "We've also heard that Ernie was going to die of AIDS, leukemia, a car crash....Someone in New Hampshire even started a letter-writing campaign to save him. "

WHAT HAPPENED: Sesame Street, the Children's Television Workshop, and PBS have repeatedly denied the story. As Morgenstern puts it, "Ernie's not dying of AIDS, he's not dying of leukemia. Ernie is a puppet."

THE RUMOR: Corona Extra beer, imported from Mexico, is contaminated by workers at the brewery who regularly urinate into the beer vats.

HOW IT SPREAD: Corona Extra beer was introduced into the United States in 1981. It immediately became the brew of choice for southern California surfers. The fad quickly spread—and despite almost no advertising, by 1986 Corona had become the #2 imported beer in the nation. Less than a year later, however, the brand's importer, Barton Beers of Chicago, was inundated with rumors that Corona was contaminated with urine. Barton traced the rumor back to a competing wholesaler in Reno, Nevada.

WHAT HAPPENED: Barton Beers sued. In July 1987, the wholesaler settled out of court, and agreed to declare publicly that Corona "was free of any contamination."

What's the biggest dating turn-off for American women? 74% say foul language.

THE RUMOR: Newspaper baron William Randolph Hearst started the war in Cuba. The legend goes like this: In 1898, Hearst sent the famous artist Frederic Remington to sketch the war for the Hearst newspapers. The only problem: There was no war in Cuba—and Remington didn't think it would ever start. He cabled to Hearst, "Everything is quiet. There is no trouble here. there will be no war. I wish to return." Hearst cabled back, "Please remain. You furnish the pictures and I'll furnish the war"—and then single-handedly used his newspapers to generate enough pro-war public opinion to actually start the war.

HOW IT SPREAD: James Creelman, a Hearst reporter, first published the story in his memoirs.

WHAT HAPPENED: He never produced any evidence to support his charge, and Hearst denied the story in private. Many historians question whether the exchange ever took place...but no one knows for sure.

THE RUMOR: Cellular phones can give you brain tumors.

HOW IT SPREAD: In February 1993, according to a news report, "A Florida widower alleged on the CNN show 'Larry King Live' that the brain tumor which killed his wife in May, 1992 was caused by radio waves emitted by the cellular phone she used. His wife's monthly cellular bill was $150, roughly twice the national average....He contends the tumor was near the place the antenna of the phone pointed."

WHAT HAPPENED: Stock in some cellular phone companies dropped 6% overnight...but later recovered. Motorola, one of the country's largest cellular phone manufacturers, called a news conference to cite "thousands of studies" that showed the phones do not cause cancer. The Food and Drug Administration found that "there is no proof that there is a cancer threat from these phones." But the FDA conducted no independent tests before issuing the statement; instead it relied on information submitted by cellular phone manufacturers. All cellular phones on the market in 1993 tested well below federal guidelines for radio-frequency protection; nevertheless, Motorola advised customers "not to press body parts against the antennas of cellular phones."

Poll results: 17% of "Entertainment Tonight" viewers believe Elvis is still alive.

THE TOUGHEST TOWN IN THE WEST

Think of a typical Western town in the 1870s. Saloons with swinging doors...horse manure all over the street...painted ladies waving at passersby...and gunfights. Lots of gunfights. It was such a popular image that Palisade, Nevada, decided to preserve it. Here's the story, with thanks to the People's Almanac.

A LEGEND IS BORN

By the late 1870s, the "Wild West" era was winding down. But it was such an entrenched part of American lore that many people hated to see it go.

One town, Palisade, Nevada, decided to keep it alive for as long as possible—by staging fake gunfights for unsuspecting train passengers on the Union Pacific and Central Pacific railroads, which regularly pulled into town for brief rest stops.

The idea got started when a train conductor suggested to a citizen of Palisade that "as long as so many easterners were travelling west hoping to see the Old West, why not give it to them?"

COMMUNITY ACTIVITY

The townspeople took the idea and ran with it: one week later they staged the first gunbattle in Palisade's history. The good guy was played by Frank West, a tall, handsome cowhand from a nearby ranch; Alvin "Dandy" Kittleby, a popular, deeply religious man (who also happened to look like a villain), played the bad guy.

Just as the noon train pulled into town for a 10-minute stop, Kittleby began walking down Main Street toward the town saloon. West, who was standing near a corral about 60 feet away, stepped out into the street and shouted at the top of his lungs, "There ya are, ya low-down polecat. Ah bin waitin' fer ya. Ah'm goin' to kill ya b'cause of what ya did ta mah sister. Mah pore, pore little sister." Then he drew his revolver and fired it over Kittleby's head. Kittleby fell to the ground kicking and screaming as if he had been shot, and the passengers immediatly dove for cover; several of the women fainted and some of the men may have too.

Q. What's the world's largest office building? A. The Pentagon. It holds 25,000 workers.

Ten minutes later when the train pulled out of the station, nearly every passenger was still crouched on the floor of the passenger compartment.

A MILESTONE

That was probably the first faked gunfight in the history of the Wild West, but it wasn't the last. Over the next three years, the Palisadians staged more than 1,000 gunfights—sometimes several a day.

To keep the townspeople interested and the train passengers fooled, the town regularly changed the theme of the gunfight, sometimes staging a duel, sometimes an Indian raid (in which real Shoshone Indians on horseback "massacred" innocent women and children before being gunned down themselves), and bank robberies involving more than a dozen robbers and sheriff's deputies.

Those who didn't directly participate in the gun battles helped out by manufacturing blank cartridges by the thousands and collecting beef blood from the town slaughterhouse. Nearly everyone within a 100-mile radius was in on the joke—including railroad workers, who probably thought the battles sold train tickets and were good for business. Somehow they all managed to keep the secret; for more than three years, nearly every passenger caught in the crossfire of a staged fight thought he was witnessing the real thing. The truth is, the town during these years was so safe that it didn't even have a sheriff.

NATIONAL OUTRAGE

One group of onlookers that weren't in on the joke were the metropolitan daily newspapers in towns like San Francisco, Chicago, and New York, which regularly reported the shocking news of the massacres on the front pages. Editorials were written by the dozens denouncing the senseless waste of human life and calling on local officials to get the situation under control. They even called on the U.S. Army to occupy the town and restore order...but since the Army itself was in on the joke, it never took action.

Over time Palisade developed a reputation as one of the toughest towns in the history of the West—a reputation that it probably deserved more than any other town, since it worked so hard to earn it.

FABULOUS FLOPS

These products cost millions to invent. Their legacy is a few bathroom laughs.

The Studebaker Dictator. Not exactly "the heartbeat of America" when it was introduced in 1934. According to one auto industry analyst, "after Hitler and Mussolini came to power, a name like Dictator was downright un-American." Yet incredibly, the nation's #5 automaker stuck with it for three years.

Bic Perfume. The snazzy $5.00 perfume that looked like a cigarette lighter. Why wasn't it a hit with women? According to one industry expert, "It looked like a cigarette lighter." Bic lost $11 million.

Chilly Bang! Bang! Juice. The kiddie drink in a pistol-shaped package. Kids drank it by putting the barrel in their mouths and squeezing the trigger. Outraged parents—and complaints from officials in at least two states—got it yanked from the shelves.

Hop 'N' Gator. The inventor of Gatorade sold his original drink to a major corporation in 1966. Then, in 1969, he used the money to create another can't-miss product: a mixture of beer and Gatorade. The Pittsburg Brewing Company tried it out for a couple of years. Unfortunately, people didn't want Gatorade in their beer.

Zartan the Enemy action figures. Hasbro promoted the soldier doll as a "paranoid schizophrenic" that becomes violent under pressure. They pulled the product after mental health organizations complained.

Pepsi A.M. Why not get your morning caffeine from cola instead of coffee? The world's first breakfast soft drink didn't get far. Pepsi found out most consumers didn't *want* a breakfast soft drink—and people who *did* "still preferred the taste of plain old Pepsi."

Hands Up! Kids' soap in an aerosol can, introduced in 1962. Instead of a nozzle, there was a plastic gun mounted on top. You got soap out of the can by pointing the gun at a kid and squeezing the trigger. The Hands Up! slogan: "Gets kids clean and makes them like it."

EVERYDAY PHRASES

More origins of common phrases.

TOO MANY IRONS IN THE FIRE

Meaning: Working on too many projects at once.

Origin: "Refers to the blacksmith's forge, where if the smith had too many irons heating in the fire at the same time he couldn't do his job properly, as he was unable to use them all before some had cooled off." (From *Everyday Phrases*, by Neil Ewart)

THE NAKED TRUTH

Meaning: The absolute truth.

Origin: Comes from this old fable: "Truth and Falsehood went swimming. Falsehood stole the clothes that Truth had left on the river bank, but Truth refused to wear Falsehood's clothes and went naked." (From *Now I Get It!*, by Douglas Ottati)

TO GIVE SOMEONE THE COLD SHOULDER

Meaning: Reject, or act unfriendly toward, someone.

Origin: Actually refers to food. In England, a welcome or important visitor would be served a delicious hot meal. A guest "who had outstayed his welcome, or an ordinary traveler" would get a cold shoulder of mutton. (From *Rejected!* by Steve Gorlick)

READ SOMEONE THE RIOT ACT

Meaning: Deliver an ultimatum.

Origin: Comes from an actual Riot Act, passed by the British Parliament in 1714, that made it unlawful for a dozen or more people to gather for "riotous or illegal purposes." An authority would literally stand up and read out the terms of the Act, so that the rioters knew what law they were breaking: "Our Sovereign Lord the King chargeth and commandeth all persons assembled immediately to disperse themselves and peacefully to depart to their habitations or to their lawful business." If the crowd didn't disperse, they were arrested. (From *Why Do We Say It?*, by Nigel Rees)

Poll results: 40% of U.S. couples say they first discussed marriage in the back seat of a car.

PASS THE BUCK

Meaning: Blame someone else; avoid accepting responsibility.

Origin: "The original buck was a buckhorn knife passed around the table in certain card games. It was placed in front of the player whose turn it was to deal the cards and see that the stakes for all the players were placed in the pool." Someone who "passed the buck" literally passed that responsibility to the person next to him. (From *Everyday Phrases*, by Neil Ewart)

A BITTER PILL TO SWALLOW

Meaning: An experience that's difficult or painful to accept.

Origin: Refers to taking medicine in the time before doctors had any way to make pills more palatable. "The bark of a New World tree, the cinchona, was effective in fighting malaria. But the quinine it contains is extremely bitter. Widely employed in the era before medications were coated, cinchona pellets caused any disagreeable thing to be termed a bitter pill to swallow." (From *Why You Say It*, by Webb Garris)

HE'S TIED TO HER APRON STRINGS

Meaning: A man is dominated by his wife.

Origin: In England several hundred years ago, if a man married a woman with property, he didn't get title to it, but could use it while she was alive. This was popularly called *apron-string* tenure. A man tied to his wife's apron strings was in no position to argue; hence, the phrase came to stand for any abnormal submission to a wife or mother." (From *I've Got Goose Pimples*, by Marvin Vanoni)

Credit Where Credit Is Due

The name "credit card" was coined in 1888 by futurist author Edward Bellamy, who wrote a fictional account of a young man who wakes up in the year 2000 and discovers that cash has been dumped in favor of "a credit corresponding to his share of the annual product of the nation...and a credit card is issued to him with which he procures at the public storehouses...whatever he desires, whenever he desires it." Sixty years later, his vision (in slightly altered form) came true.

PRIMETIME PROVERBS

TV comments about everyday life. From Primetime Proverbs, *by Jack Mingo and John Javna.*

ON DOCTORS

Henry Blake: "I was never very good with my hands."

Radar O'Reilly: "Guess that's why you became a surgeon, huh, Sir?"

—M*A*S*H

Sophia: "How come so many doctors are Jewish?"

Jewish Doctor: "Because their mothers are."

—*The Golden Girls*

ON GOD

"It's funny the way some people's name just suits the business they're in. Like God's name is just *perfect* for God."

—Edith Bunker,
All in the Family

ON FRIENDS

"I've never felt closer to a group of people. Not even in the portable johns of Woodstock."

—Rev. Jim Ignatowski,
Taxi

"A friend, I am told, is worth more than pure gold."

—*Popeye*
The Popeye Cartoon Show

ON GREED

"Oh, yes indeedy, it doesn't pay to be greedy."

—Popeye,
The Popeye Cartoon Show

Robin [*anguished*]**:** "The Bat-diamond!"

Batman: "What about it, Robin?"

Robin: "To think it's the cause of all this trouble!"

Batman: "People call it many things, old chum: passion, lust, desire, avarice....But the simplest and most understandable word is greed."

—*Batman*

ON SEX

Sam Malone: "I thought you weren't going to call me stupid now that we're being intimate."

Diane Chambers: "No, I said I wasn't going to call you stupid *while* we were being intimate."

—*Cheers*

ON DEATH

"Death is just nature's way of telling you, 'Hey, you're not alive anymore.' "

—Bull,
Night Court

The Canadian Mounties haven't mounted horses since 1938.

A WILD & CRAZY GUY

Observations from Steve Martin, one of America's biggest hams.

"Sex is one of the most beautiful-natural things that money can buy."

"I gave my cat a bath the other day....He sat there, he enjoyed it, it was fun for me. The fur would stick to my tongue, but other than that...."

"What? You been keeping records on me? I wasn't so bad! How many times did I take the Lord's name in vain? One million and six? Jesus CH—!"

"A celebrity is any well-known TV or movie star who looks like he spends more than two hours working on his hair."

"In talking to girls I could never remember the right sequence of things to say. I'd meet a girl and say, 'Hi was it good for you too?' If a girl spent the night, I'd wake up in the morning and then try to get her drunk..."

"I learned about sex watching neighborhood dogs. The most important thing I learned was: Never let go of the girl's leg no matter how hard she tries to shake you off."

"Boy, those French, they have a different word for *everything*."

"I believe you should place a woman on a pedestal, high enough so you can look up her dress."

"I like a woman with a head on her shoulders. I hate necks."

"What is comedy? Comedy is the art of making people laugh without making them puke."

"There is something going on now in Mexico that I happen to think is cruelty to animals. What I'm talking about, of course, is cat juggling."

"I believe that Ronald Reagan can make this country what it once was—an arctic region covered with ice."

"I started a grease fire at McDonald's—threw a match in the cook's hair."

"I have a new book coming out. It's one of those self-help deals. It's called *How to Get Along with Everyone*. I wrote it with this other asshole."

Q. What's the most common language spoken by New York City cabdrivers? A. Urdu.

GONE, BUT NOT FORGOTTEN

You can see them in museums or in books—but you won't see them on the road, because no one makes them anymore. Here's some info about five automobile legends.

THE PIERCE-ARROW (1901-1938). One of the most prestigious cars of its day, the Pierce-Arrow set the standard for luxury and performance. According to one auto critic, "Even a massive limousine could whisper along at 100 mph—uniformed chauffeur up front; tycoon, cigar, and *Wall St. Journal* in the rear. (Some cars had speedometers back there so the owner could keep an eye on the chauffer's lead-foot tendencies.)" Pierce-Arrow was the car of choice for rumrunners—who liked its quiet engine and reliability—and presidents: Woodrow Wilson rode in a customized Pierce-Arrow limousine; so did FDR and J. Edgar Hoover (theirs were bulletproof).

Fate: When the Depression hit, the company kept building expensive cars, thinking the business downturn was temporary. Sales dropped from a high of 10,000 cars in 1929 to only 167 in 1937. The company was sold at auction a year later.

THE REO (1905-1936). In 1904, Ransom Eli Olds left the Olds Motor Vehicle Co. and began a new one. The Olds Motor Vehicle Company wouldn't let him use his last name—but couldn't stop him from using his initials, so he called it the REO Motor Car Co. By 1907 it had become the third largest auto manufacturer, after Ford and Buick. Five years later Olds announced his retirement and introduced his last car, REO the Fifth (the company's fifth model).

Fate: Olds retired from day-to-day operations, but retained enough veto power to make himself a nuisance. As a result, REO began to lag behind its competitors. Olds finally gave up control in 1934, but it was too late: Two years later the company became yet another victim of the Great Depression.

THE STUTZ BEARCAT (1911-1935). Grandfather of the American muscle car, it was built for speed. According to legend, founder Harry Stutz designed his clutches with "springs so stiff that a woman couldn't operate them." It was a teenager's dream car in the 'teens and 'twenties, because it won so many races. In 1912 it won 25 of the 30 national races it entered, and in 1915 Cannonball Baker drove a 4-cylinder Bearcat from San Diego to New York in less than 12 days, shattering the transcontinental record.

Fate: Another casualty of the Depression. Stutz couldn't slash costs and prices fast enough to stay competitive. In January 1935 it got out of the passenger-car business, and went bankrupt two years later.

THE DUESENBERG (1920-1937). To the driver of the 1920s, the name Duesenberg meant the top of the line: "The Duesenberg was more than a status symbol; it was status pure and simple, whether the owner was a maharajah, movie star, politician, robber baron, gangster, or evangelist....'He drives a Duesenberg' was the only copy in many company advertisements." The first passenger cars rolled off the assembly line in 1920; for the next 17 years the phrase "It's a Duesy" meant the very best.

Fate: Duesenberg was the best carmaker of its day—but it was probably also the worst run. The Duesenberg brothers were notoriously bad administrators. Chronic mismanagement, combined with the stock market crash of 1929, pushed the ailing company permanently into the red. It collapsed in 1937.

KAISER (1946-55). When World War II ended in 1945, shipbuilding magnate Henry J. Kaiser decided to start his own car company. The U.S. government wasn't buying ships anymore, and the auto industry hadn't released new models since the beginning of the war. Kaiser thought he could beat existing carmakers to market with flashy new models and change the Big Three to the Big Four.

Kaiser's 1946 models *did* make the Big Three's cars look dowdy and old-fashioned in comparison. The company's sales hit 70,000 in 1947—but it soon ran into trouble.

Fate: Ford, GM, and Chrysler shed their prewar image in 1947–48, and began beating Kaiser on price. The situation became desperate: some years Kaiser's sales were so bad that rather than introduce a new model, the company just changed the serial numbers on unsold cars and introduced *them* as the new models. In 1954 the company merged with the Willys-Overland (forerunner of the Jeep company); one year later the Kaiser model line was discontinued.

Explosive fact: 12,000 Americans are injured by fireworks every year.

CHILDHOOD WISDOM

Quotes from classic children's books.

"We are all made of the same stuff, remember, we of the Jungle, and you of the City. The same substance composes us—the tree overhead, the stone beneath us, the bird, the beast, the star—we are all one, all moving to the same end....Bird and beast and stone and star—we are all one, all one—Child and serpent, star and stone—all one."

—The Hamadryad, *Mary Poppins*

"If I can fool a bug, I can fool a man. People are not as smart as bugs."

—Charlotte, *Charlotte's Web*

"Money is a nuisance. We'd all be much better off if it had never been invented. What does money matter, as long as we all are happy?"

—Dr. Doolittle, *Dr. Doolittle*

"Winter will pass, the days will lengthen, the ice will melt in the pasture pond. The song sparrow will return and sing, the frogs will awake, the warm wind will blow again. All these sights and sounds and smells will be yours to enjoy, Wilbur—this lovely world, these precious days."

—Charlotte, *Charlotte's Web*

"Don't be angry after you've been afraid. That's the worst kind of cowardice."

—Billy the Troophorse, *The Jungle Book*

"Time flies, and one begins to grow old. This autumn I'll be ten, and then I guess I'll have seen my best days."

—Pippi Longstocking, *Pippi Goes on Board*

Are you lonesome tonight? In a recent survey, 1% of Americans said they have no friends.

LOOK IT UP!

Every bathroom reader knows the value of a good record book, or a volume of quotes, in a pinch. Here are the stories of the originals.

BARTLETT'S FAMILIAR QUOTATIONS.
John Bartlett was 16 years old when he left school in 1836 and got a job as a clerk at the University Bookstore across the street from Harvard.

Over the next 13 years he saved enough money to buy the store—and in that time managed to read nearly every book it contained. He became so well-known as a "quotation freak" that whenever someone asked where a familiar saying came from, or needed a quote to dress up a term paper, the answer would be, "Ask John Bartlett." By the mid-1850s, his reputation had grown beyond even his own remarkable abilities; no longer able to recite everything from memory, he began writing things down.

In 1855 he printed up 1,000 copies of his 258-page list of quotes, and began selling them at the store. "Should this be favorably received," he wrote in the preface, "endeavors will be made to make it more worthy of the public in a future edition." Sixteen editions and nearly 140 years later, *Bartlett's Familiar Quotations* is the most frequently consulted reference work of its kind.

THE GUINNESS BOOK OF WORLD RECORDS.
In 1954 Sir Hugh Beaver, an avid sportsman and managing director of Arthur Guinness, Son and Company (brewers of Guinness Stout beer), shot at some game birds in the Irish countryside...but they all got away. Looking for an excuse, he exclaimed that he'd missed because the breed of birds—plovers—were "the fastest game bird we've got" in the British Isles. But were they? He had no idea, and no reference he consulted could tell him.

He never found out for sure about the plovers. But the experience *did* give him the idea for a book of world records. He commissioned two researchers, Norris and Ross McWhirter, to write it for Guinness. Four months later, they were finished, and four months after that the first *Guinness Book of World Records* was #1 on the British best seller list.

More collect calls are made on Father's Day than on any other day.

A HANDY GUIDE TO THE END OF THE WORLD (Part II)

Here are more "end-time" predictions from Uncle John's Indispensable Guide to the Year 2000*—this time from three Native American sources.*

HOPI

Background: A Pueblo tribe that today occupies several mesa villages in northeast Arizona. Their stories are passed on orally. Frankly, if they are really from ancient times, and not "backdated" by someone to make them sound more accurate, they're pretty amazing.

Signs the End Is Near: According to many Hopi tribal elders (such as Dan Evehama, Thomas Banyacya, and Martin Gashwaseoma), the coming of "white-skinned men" and "a strange beast, like a buffalo but with great long horns" that would "overrun the land" (cattle) were predicted as precursors to the end of time. They also say their prophecies include:

- "The land will be crossed by snakes of iron and rivers of stone. The land shall be criss-crossed by a giant spider's web. Seas will turn black."
- "A great dwelling-place in the heavens shall fall with a great crash. It will appear as a blue star. The world will rock to and fro."
- "The white man will battle people in other lands, with those who possess the first light of wisdom. Terrible will be the result. There will be many columns of smoke in the deserts. These are the signs that great destruction is here."

When the World Ends: Many will die, but those "who understand the prophecies...and stay and live in the places of my people (Hopi) shall also be safe."

- Pahana, the True White Brother will return to plant the seeds of wisdom in people's hearts and usher in the dawn of the Fifth World.

For More On the Hopi: www.timesoft.com/hopi/

Dollar bills last an average of 17 months; coins last at least 30 years.

MAYANS

Background: An ancient Meso-American civilization with a highly developed, extraordinarily accurate system of mathematics and astronomy. Many people think the Mayan calendar ends at around 2012 or 2013, and assume that's the scheduled date for the end of the world.

Signs the End Is Near: According to *The Mayan Prophecies*, the earth will be destroyed by environmental disasters—earthquakes, tidal waves, you name it. Civilization will collapse; then Kulkulcan (Quetzalcoatl)—a feathered serpent deity who represents the forces of good and light—will arrive.

When the World Ends: Again, according to *The Mayan Prophecies*: "The end of artificial time signals…the return to natural time, a time in harmony with the Earth and with the natural cycles.…It holds within it the potential to reinstate a balanced, positive love and unity."

For More On the Mayans: www.halfmoon.org/

SIOUX

Background: A confederation of several Native American Plains tribes. They also have an oral tradition.

Signs the End Is Near: According to an Ogalala (Sioux) medicine man, a "darkness descends over the tribe...the world is out of balance. There are floods, fires and earthquakes. There is a great drought." A White Buffalo will be born and the White Buffalo Calf Woman (according to legend, a representative of the spirit world) will return.

When the World Ends: White Buffalo Calf Woman will purify the world. "She will bring back harmony again, and balance, spiritually."

Note: A white buffalo was born in 1994…and another in 1995. Many tribal elders feel these are clear signs that their prophecy is being fulfilled. "Yes indeed, it is a sign," says one. "The important ones are the last two. These were created with the influence of the Masters."

For More On the Sioux: www.blackhills-info.com/lakota_sioux/

Pet lovers: 21% of cat owners and 27% of dog owners include their pets in their wills.

MORE PEOPLE-WATCHING

Here are more findings about human behavior, gleaned from Bernard Asbell's The Book of You *and* People Watching: Downtown Los Angeles, *by Bob Herman.*

ON MARRIAGE...

• According to a University of Michigan researcher, if you think you're starting to look like your spouse, you might be right.

• His study went something like this: Wedding photos of couples that were now in their 50s and 60s were collected, along with current pictures of the same couples. Students were then asked to match pictures of individuals with pictures of their spouses.

• In the younger wedding pictures, students weren't able to match the couples any better than chance. However, with the contemporary pictures, the students did significantly better.

• Conclusion: Apparently, married individuals are good at mimicking their partners. This can produce similar laugh or frown lines around the eyes and mouth as we age, changing our expressions and making us appear more like our spouses.

Another hint about what's going on in your marriage: Research shows that the less comfortable you are with your spouse, the more you'll look at one another. If you're comfortable in your marriage, you'll talk more frequently without glancing at one another. Why? Apparently, people who aren't relaxed in their marriage tend to monitor their spouses for reactions to what they say and do.

ON JOGGING...

• Research tells us that if you're a guy out running for exercise, and you pass a woman—any woman—you'll actually speed up significantly as you pass her...*if* she's facing your direction. Even if she's buried in a book, or completely preoccupied and looking through you, your performance will increase as you pass.

• But if her back's towards you, you won't change your pace.

Clear priorities: More than 50% of teenage boys say they'd "rather be rich than smart."

ON PORNOGRAPHY...

• Whether you're male or female, looking at *Playboy*, *Penthouse*, or similar magazines won't improve your sex life.

• Studies find that after eyeing nude photos, people of *both* sexes will rate their partners as less sexually appealing.

• According to research, people also report that they feel less in love with their partners after reading a nudie rag.

ON LOITERING...

• Loitering's not as easy to do as it may seem—security is pretty tight in some places. But people-watching has proven time and again that some people get away with it more often than others.

• One trick—If you carry something, or if you're standing in an entranceway, you're less likely to be hassled by authorities.

• You're also less likely to attract attention if you're holding an umbrella or a briefcase rather than standing around empty-handed. Reading, working on something, or at least pretending to do either, while using a library or park bench will buy you a lot more resting time than if you simply reclined for a nap in the same spot.

ON "PERSONAL SPACE"...

• According to Asbell's *The Book of You*, personal space can be a vertical issue: "If you observe a stranger in a room gradually moving closer to you, you'll show symptoms of alertness or anxiety sooner if the ceiling is low than if it's high."

• When the "room" is an elevator, however, there are special rules:

—If you're male, you'll stand closer to a female on an elevator than to another man.

—If you're female, either a man or woman stranger can stand close to you on an elevator, but they stand a better chance of squeezing in if they're to your sides, than in front of you.

—Whether male or female, if a stranger on an elevator smiles at you, you're much more likely to stand closer than if they don't smile.

The War Between the Sexes continues: You have a 5-to-1 chance of winning the elbow-rest between the seats on an airplane if you're male.

Seventy-six percent of teenagers say they believe in angels. That's up from 64% in 1978.

THE MONA LISA

It's the most famous painting in the world—even Uncle John has heard of it. But what else do you know about this mysterious lady?

BACKGROUND. Sometime between 1501 and 1506—no one is sure exactly when—Leonardo da Vinci, the great Renaissance artist, scientist, and thinker, painted his masterpiece *La Joconde*, better known as the Mona Lisa. Hardly anything is known about the painting. Da Vinci kept extensive records on many of his *other* paintings, but none on the Mona Lisa. He never once mentioned it in any of his notebooks, and never made any preliminary studies of it.

However, historians believe the painting was one of Leonardo's favorites. Unlike most of his other paintings, which he painted on commission and turned over to their owners as soon as they were finished, da Vinci kept the Mona Lisa for more than 10 years—and still had it in his possession when he died in 1519.

WHO'S THAT GIRL?

No one knows who really modeled for the Mona Lisa—but some of the popular candidates are:

- **Mona Lisa Gherardini,** wife of Francesco del Giocondo, a Florentine silk merchant. After da Vinci's death, Gherardini was so widely believed to have been the model for the painting that it was named after her. But art historians now doubt she was the model, because the source of this rumor was Giorgio Vasari, da Vinci's biographer—who never even saw the painting in person.
- **Another noblewoman** da Vinci knew—or perhaps a composite painting of two or more of them.
- **No one.** Some historians think the painting was a *finzione* or "feigning"—a fictional woman not based on any particular person.
- **Himself.** The painting is a feminine self-portrait. This theory is strange but surprisingly plausible. In 1987, computer scientists at AT&T Bell Laboratories took da Vinci's 1518 *Self-Portrait*, reversed the image (it faces right, not left like the Mona Lisa), enlarged it to the same scale, and juxtaposed it against the Mona Lisa, the similarities were too striking to be accidental...or so they say.

MONA LISA FACTS

• The Mona Lisa is considered one of the most important paintings of the Renaissance period—but King Francis I of France, who took possession of the painting after da Vinci died, hung it in the palace bathroom.

• Napoleon, on the other hand, was a big fan of the painting; he called it "The Sphinx of the Occident" and kept it in his bedroom.

• Why is Mona Lisa wearing such a strange smile? Some art historians suspect that this most famous feature may actually be the work of clumsy restorers who tried to touch up the painting centuries ago. Da Vinci may have intended her to wear a much more ordinary expression. Dozens of other theories have been proposed to explain the strange grin, including that Mona Lisa has just lost a child, has asthma or bad teeth, or is really a young man. Sigmund Freud theorized that da Vinci painted the smile that way because it reminded him of his mother.

• Mona Lisa may be "in the family way." According to writer Seymour Reit, "the lady is definitely pregnant, as shown by the slightly swollen hands and face, and her 'self-satisfied' expression." Other historians disagree—they think that Mona Lisa is just chubby.

THE THEFT

• According to a 1952 Paris study, there are at least 72 excellent 16th- and 17th-century replicas and reproductions of the Mona Lisa in existence—leading conspiracy theorists to speculate that the painting in the Louvre is itself a replica.

• One of the most interesting forgery theories has to do with a theft of the painting that occurred in 1911. On August 21 of that year, the Mona Lisa vanished from the Louvre in what was probably the biggest art heist of the century. French authorities conducted a massive investigation, but were unable to locate the painting. Two years later, an Italian carpenter named Vincenzo Perugia was caught trying to sell the masterpiece to an Italian museum.

The official story is that Perugia wanted to return the work to Italy, da Vinci's (and his) birthplace. But Seymour Reit, author of *The Day They Stole The Mona Lisa*, theorizes that the plot was the work of Marqués Eduardo de Valfierno, a nobleman who made his living selling forged masterpieces to unsuspecting millionaires. He wanted to do the same with the Mona Lisa—but knew that no one

European country with the most auto-related fatalities: Portugal. Great Britain has the least.

would buy a forgery of such a famous painting unless the original were stolen from the Louvre first. So de Valfierno paid a forger to paint half a dozen fakes, and then hired Perugia to steal the real Mona Lisa.

Reit argues that de Valfierno had no plans for the original masterpiece—he didn't want to sell it or even own it himself—and was only interested in selling his forgeries. He never even bothered to collect the original from Perugia, who hid it in the false bottom of a dirty steamer trunk for more than two years waiting for de Valfierno to come and get it. But he never did, so Perugia finally gave up and tried to sell the Mona Lisa to an Italian museum. As soon as he handed over the painting, he was arrested and the painting was returned to France. Perugia was tried and convicted, but spent only 7 months in prison for his crime. De Valfierno was never tried.

PROTECTING THE PAINTING

• The Mona Lisa isn't painted on canvas—it's painted on a wood panel made from poplar. This makes it extremely fragile, since changes in the moisture content of the wood can cause it to expand and shrink, which cracks the paint.

• Because of this, the Louvre goes to great lengths to protect the Mona Lisa from the elements—and from vandals. Since 1974, the painting has been stored in a bulletproof, climate-controlled box called a *vitrine* that keeps the painting permanently at 68° Fahrenheit and at 50-55% humidity.

• Once a year, the painting is removed from its protective case and given a checkup. The process takes about an hour and requires almost 30 curators, restorers, laboratory technicians, and maintenance workers.

• Despite nearly 500 years of accumulated dust, dirt, and grime, the risks associated with cleaning the masterpiece are so great that the museum refuses to do it—even though the filth has changed the appearance of the painting dramatically. Pierre Rosenberg, the Louvre's curator, says: "If we saw the Mona Lisa as da Vinci painted it, we would not recognize it....Da Vinci actually painted with bright, vivid colors, not the subdued tones that are visible today." But he's adamant about leaving the painting in its present state. "The Mona Lisa is such a sacrosanct image that to touch it would create a national scandal."

How about you? 64% of women sleep on the left side of the bed.

WHAT IS HYPNOTISM?

You are getting sleepy...sleepy...you will do anything we tell you. Now listen carefully: When you leave the bathroom, you will experience an irresistible urge to give everyone you know copies of Uncle John's Legendary Lost Bathroom Reader. *Do you understand? Good. When you emerge from the bathroom, you won't remember anything we've said. Now resume reading.*

BACKGROUND. The history of hypnotism—drawing someone into an "altered state of consciousness" in which they are more susceptible to suggestion than when fully conscious—dates back thousands of years and is as old as sorcery, medicine, and witchcraft. The first person in modern times to study it was Franz Mesmer, an 18th-century Viennese physician. In 1775 he devised the theory that a person could transmit "universal forces," known as *animal magnetism*, to other people.

Critics derisively named this practice "Mesmerism," and chased him out of Vienna for practicing witchcraft. He then resettled in Paris, where a royal commission dismissed Mesmerism's "cures" as the product of his patients' imaginations.

Viewed as a crackpot science by the entire medical establishment, mesmerism might have died out, except for one thing: Anesthesia hadn't been invented yet, and physicians were desperately looking for something to kill pain during surgical procedures. Mesmer himself had performed surgery using mesmerism as anesthesia as early as 1778, and other doctors soon began trying it.

One of the most successful was John Elliotson, a London surgeon who used it successfully on thousands of patients—but at great personal cost: he was booted out of his professorship and became a laughingstock of English medical society. John Elsdaile, a medical officer with the East India Company, had better luck: He performed hundreds of operations, including amputations, "painlessly and with few fatalities" using mesmerism. At about the same time, James Braid, another English physician experimenting with the procedure renamed it "hypnosis," after Hypnos, the Greco-Roman god of sleep.

In the 1880s Sigmund Freud visited France and decided to experiment with hypnosis in the fledgling field of psychology. He used it to treat neurotic disorders by helping patients remember events in their past that they had either forgotten or repressed. But as he developed his method of psychoanalysis, he lost interest in hypnosis and eventually dumped it entirely.

Despite Freud's rejection, hypnotism continued to grow in popularity. By the mid-1950s the British and American Medical Associations had approved its use. Although hypnotism is seldom used as an anesthetic in surgery today—except in combination with pain-killing drugs—it is widely used to prepare patients for anesthesia, ease the pain of childbirth, lower blood pressure, combat headaches; and ease the fear associated with dental appointments, and has a variety of other applications. More than 15,000 physicians, dentists, and psychologists currently incorporate hypnotherapy into their practices.

BENEFITS

According to *U.S. News and World Report*, as many as 94% of hospital patients who are hypnotized as part of their therapy "get some benefit" from it. Some examples cited by the magazine:

- "Cancer patients can undergo chemotherapy without the usual nausea if they are first hypnotized."
- "Burn patients recover faster and with less medication if they are hypnotized within two hours of receiving their burns and told they will heal quickly and painlessly. Researchers think hypnotherapy gives them the ability to will the release of anti-inflammatory substances that limit the damage."
- "J. Michael Drever, a cosmetic surgeon, finds that postsurgical hypnotic suggestions can see his patients through breast reconstructions and tummy tucks with less bleeding, fewer complications and quicker recovery."

NONBELIEVERS

One of hypnotism's most outspoken critics is Las Vegas performer "The Amazing Kreskin," who dismisses it as "just a figment of the imagination." Kreskin worked as a hypnotherapist under the supervision of a New Jersey psychologist in the 1960s. But he ultimately became a skeptic: "Anything I ever did with a patient who was supposedly under hypnosis I was able to do without putting them in the slightest trance—by persuading them, encouraging them, threatening them, browbeating them or just giving them an awful lot of confidence....All that's happening is what Alfred Hitchcock does every time he terrifies you and changes the surface of your skin with goosebumps. You're using your imagination."

HYPNOSIS FACTS

- It is impossible to hypnotize someone against their wishes.
- A hypnotized person, even when they appear to be asleep or in a trance, is physiologically awake at all times. Unlike sleepwalkers, their brain waves are identical to those of a person who's fully awake.
- A hypnotized person is always completely aware of his or her surroundings—although they can be instructed to ignore surrounding events, which creates the appearance of being unaware of them.

ANOTHER FORM OF HYPNOSIS?

Here's some background on America's most pervasive credit cards.

American Express. Formed by American Express in 1958 to complement its lucrative travelers-check business. According to *American Heritage* magazine, "American Express came to dominate the field partly because it could cover the credit it was extending with the float from its traveler's checks, which are, after all, a form of interest-free loan from consumers to American Express."

Visa. California's Bank of America began issuing its BankAmericard in 1958. At first it was intended to be used at stores near Bank of America branches, but it was so profitable that the bank licensed banks all over the country to issue it. However, other banks hated issuing a card with B of A's name on it. So in 1977 the card's name was changed to Visa.

MasterCard. Originally named Master Charge, the card was formed in 1968 by Wells Fargo Bank and 77 other banks, who wanted to end BankAmericard's dominance of the credit card business. They succeeded: Thanks to mergers with other credit cards, it became the biggest bank card within one year. Can you remember why it changed its name to MasterCard in 1979? According to company president Russell Hogg, they wanted to shed the card's "blue collar" image.

JFK's PRESIDENTIAL AFFAIRS

You've heard about his liaison with Marilyn Monroe. But there's more. A lot more. Here's some of the gossip you probably haven't heard.

BACKGROUND

Rumors of marital infidelity have plagued a number of Presidents, but perhaps none as much as John F. Kennedy.

According to books like *JFK: A Question of Character*, many of the rumors are true. While he was president, Kennedy's youth and charisma proved irresistible to scores of attractive young women who found themselves in his company—and JFK made the most of the opportunity. One member of the administration remembers: "It was a revolving door over there. A woman had to fight to get into that line."

As Traphes Bryant, a White House employee who served under the Kennedys and other first families, says, "Despite all the stories I've heard about other past presidents, I doubt we will ever have another one like Kennedy."

Here are a few of the *tamer* details that have surfaced since JFK's infidelities became public in 1977.

A LITTLE HELP FROM HIS FRIENDS

• The White House staff were directly involved in Kennedy's womanizing. Top aides such as Evelyn Lincoln, the President's personal secretary, were responsible for sneaking women in and out of the White House unobserved by Mrs. Kennedy or the press.

• According to Bryant, "there was a conspiracy of silence to protect his secrets from Jacqueline and to keep her from finding out. The newspapers would tell how First Lady Jacqueline was off on a trip, but what they didn't report was how anxious the President sometimes was to see her go. And what consternation there sometimes was when she returned unexpectedly."

• The Secret Service was also in on the act. They helped remove traces of JFK's affairs from White House bedrooms, and were responsible for ferrying Kennedy to and from "love nests" undetected during presidential trips. Charles Spaulding, one of Kennedy's closest friends, remembers one such trip when the president was staying at the Carlyle Hotel in New York. He and Kennedy traveled to their mistresses' nearby apartments via a network of underground tunnels beneath the hotel. "It was kind of a weird sight," Spaulding remembers. "Jack and I and two Secret Service men walking in these huge tunnels underneath the city streets alongside those enormous pipes, each of us carrying a flashlight. One of the Secret Service men also had this underground map and every once in a while he would say, 'We turn this way, Mr. President.' "

• On occasions when Kennedy felt he couldn't trust his Secret Service detachment with his affairs—or simply didn't want them around—he just ditched them. Once he even became separated from the army officer carrying the "football," the briefcase containing the nation's nuclear launch codes—and went to a party unescorted. "The Russians could have bombed us to hell and back," one aide remembered, "and there would have been nothing we could have done about it."

JFK's THOUSAND POINTS OF LIGHT

• JFK liked to sleep with famous women—Marilyn Monroe and actor David Niven's wife among them. According to one story, a White House staffer once asked Kennedy what he wanted for his birthday. According to another staffer's diary entry, the President "named a TV actress from California....His wish was granted."

• In addition to actresses and models, Kennedy had relationships with numerous female employees on the White House staff. He also slept with female reporters in the White House Press Pool. He even had an affair with Judith Campbell Exner, the girlfriend of a reputed mob boss Sam Giancana. And according to some accounts, the Mafia recorded the President's lovemaking sessions and used the tapes to blackmail the White House into going easy on them.

• Kennedy loved to frolic nude with girlfriends in the White House pool and let his mistresses streak through the White House corridors. Once Bryant was riding in an elevator when it stopped on the President's floor. "Just as the elevator door opened, a naked blonde office girl ran through the hall. There was nothing for me to do but get out fast, and push the button for the basement."

Michael Landon played the title role of *I Was a Teenage Werewolf* in 1957.

DANGEROUS LIAISONS

On at least one occasion, Kennedy's romances came close to destroying his presidency. Not long after being elected president, he talked his wife into hiring Pamela Turnur, a striking 23-year-old brunette with whom he was having an affair, as her press secretary. "That way [Pamela would] be right there close at hand when he wanted her," one friend remembers.

Although Jacqueline apparently knew about their relationship from the beginning and seemed to grudgingly accept it, Turnur's landlady, Mrs. Leonard Kater, did not. She waited and snapped a picture of Kennedy leaving Turnur's apartment early one morning. Determined to expose the president as a "debaucher of a girl young enough to be his daughter," Kater contacted the media and told them her story.

But luckily for JFK, the photo she took didn't actually show Kennedy's face (he was covering it with his hands)—so nobody could be sure it was really the president. When the reporters refused to cover the story, Mrs. Kater wrote a letter to the Attorney General (Bobby Kennedy)—and when that failed, she marched up and down Pennsylvania Avenue carrying a sign that said, "Do you want an adulterer in the White House?" and gave away copies of her photograph. Kater was dismissed as a crackpot.

KEEPING SECRETS

No matter how hard he and the White House staff tried, Kennedy couldn't prevent his wife from finding out about his numerous affairs. Mrs. Kennedy apparently became aware of JFK's extracurricular activities soon after their marriage in 1953. And according to one close friend, she took the discovery hard. "After the first year they were together, Jackie was wandering around looking like the survivor of an airplane crash."

But as time went on she became resigned to Jack's womanizing, and even a bit cynical. Once when she discovered a pair of panties stuffed into a pillowcase on their bed, she confronted him with the evidence. One witness remembers, "She delicately held it out to her husband between thumb and forefinger—about the way you hold a worm—saying, 'Would you please shop around and see who these belong to? They're not my size.' "

Edgar Allen Poe's *The Murders in the Rue Morgue* was the first detective story ever written.

STAR WARS

"There's a whole generation growing up without any kind of fairy tales. And kids need fairy tales—it's an important thing for society to have for kids." —George Lucas

BACKGROUND. In July 1973, George Lucas was an unknown director working on a low-budget 1960s nostalgia film called *American Graffiti*. He approached Universal Studios to see if they were interested in a film idea he called *Star Wars*. Universal turned him down.

It was the biggest mistake the studio ever made.

Six months later, Lucas was the hottest director in Hollywood. *American Graffiti*, which cost $750,000 to make, was a smash. It went on to earn more than $117 million, making it the most profitable film in Hollywood history.

While Universal was stonewalling Lucas, an executive at 20th Century-Fox, Alan Ladd, Jr., watched a smuggled print of *American Graffiti* before it premièred and loved it. He was so determined to work with Lucas that he agreed to finance the director's new science fiction film.

Star Wars opened on May 25, 1977, and by the end of August it had grossed $100 million—faster than any other film in history. By 1983 the film had sold more than $524 million in tickets worldwide—making it one of the 10 best-selling films in history.

MAKING THE FILM

• It took Lucas more than two years to write the script. He spent 40 hours a week writing, and devoted much of his free time to reading comic books and watching old Buck Rogers and other serials looking for film ideas.

• Lucas insisted on casting unknown actors and actresses in all the important parts of the film—which made the studio uneasy. Mark Hamill had made more than 100 TV appearances, and Carrie Fisher had studied acting, but neither had had much experience in films. Harrison Ford's biggest role had been as the drag racer in *American Graffiti*, and when he read for the part of Han Solo he was working as a carpenter.

The first hot airplane meals were served on a Pan Am flight in 1935.

THE CHARACTERS

Luke Skywalker. At first Lucas planned to portray him as an elderly general, but decided that making him a teenager gave him more potential for character development. Lucas originally named the character Luke Starkiller, but on the first day of shooting he changed it to the less violent Skywalker.

Obi-Wan Kenobi. Lucas got his idea for Obi-Wan Kenobi and "the Force" after reading Carlos Castaneda's *Tales of Power*, an account of Don Juan, a Mexican-Indian sorcerer and his experiences with what he calls "the life force."

Darth Vader. David Prowse, a 6'7" Welsh weightlifter, played the part of Darth Vader. But Lucas didn't want his villain to have a Welsh accent, so he dubbed James Earl Jones's voice over Prowse's. Still, Prowse loved the part. "He took the whole thing very seriously," Lucas remembers. "He began to believe he really was Darth Vader."

Han Solo. In the early stages of development, Han Solo was a green-skinned, gilled monster with a girlfriend named Boma who was a cross between a guinea pig and a brown bear. Solo was supposed to make only a few appearances in the film, but Lucas later made him into a swashbuckling, reckless human (allegedly modeled after film director Francis Ford Coppola).

Chewbacca. Lucas got the idea for Chewbacca one morning in the ealy 1970s while watching his wife Marcia drive off in her car. She had their Alaskan malamute, Indiana, in the car (the namesake for Indiana Jones in *Raiders of the Lost Ark*), and Lucas liked the way the large shaggy mutt looked in the passenger seat. So he decided to create a character in the film that was a cross between Indiana, a bear, and a monkey.

Princess Leia. Carrie Fisher was a beautiful 19-year-old actress when she was cast to play Princess Leia, but Lucas did everything he could to tone down her femininity. At one point, he even ordered that her breasts be strapped to her chest with electrical tape. "There's no jiggling in the Empire," Fisher later joked.

First words typed on a "practical" typewriter: "C. LATHAM SHOLES, SEPTEMBER 1867."

R2-D2. Lucas got the name R2-D2 while filming *American Graffiti*. During a sound-mixing session for the film, editor Walter Murch asked him for R2, D2 (Reel 2, Dialogue 2) of the film. Lucas liked the name so much that he made a note of it, and eventually found the right character for it.

C-3P0. This droid's name was inspired by a robot character in Alex Raymond's science-fiction novel, *Iron Men of Mongo*. Raymond's robot was a polite, copper-colored, robot who was shaped like a man and who worked as a servant. Lucas intended that C-3P0 and R2-D2 be a space-age Laurel and Hardy team.

SPECIAL EFFECTS

• The spaceship battles were inspired by World War II films. Before filming of the special effects began, Lucas watched dozens of war movies like *Battle of Britain* and *The Bridges of Toko-Ri*, taping his favorite air battle scenes as he went along. Later he edited them down to a 10 minute black-and-white film, and gave it to the special effects team—which re-shot the scenes using X-wing and TIE fighter models.

• None of the spaceship models ever moved an inch during filming of the flight sequences. The motion was an optical illusion created by moving the cameras around motionless models. The models were so detailed that one of them even had Playboy pinups in its cockpit.

MISCELLANEOUS FACTS

• The executives at 20th Century-Fox hated the film the first time they saw it. Some of the company's board of directors fell asleep during the first screening; others didn't understand the film at all. One executive's wife even suggested that C-3PO be given a moving mouth, because no one would understand how he could talk without moving his lips.

• The underwater monster in the trash compactor was one of Lucas's biggest disappointments in the film. He had planned to have an elaborate "alien jellyfish" in the scene, but the monster created by the special-effects department was so poorly constructed that it reminded him of "a big, wide, brown turd." Result: The monster was filmed underwater during most of the scene—so that moviegoers wouldn't see it.

Some names rejected for Disney's seven dwarfs: Gaspy, Doleful, Awful, Gabby, and Helpful.

Q & A: ASK THE EXPERTS

More random questions...and answers from America's trivia experts.

HIC!

Q: *What are hiccups...and why do we have them?*

A: "Hiccups...involve an involuntary contraction of the diaphragm, the muscle separating the abdomen and chest. When the diaphragm contracts, the vocal chords close quickly, which is what makes the funny 'hiccuping' sound." Hiccups seem to be induced by many different factors. No one's sure *why* people hiccup, but in some circumstances, hiccups are predictable: for example, eating or drinking too fast, nervousness, pregnancy, or alcoholism.

"Most of the time hiccups...stop in a few minutes whether you do anything about them or not....There was, however, one case of hiccups listed in the *Guinness Book of World Records* that lasted for 60 years. Charles Osborne of Anthon, Iowa, started hiccuping in 1922 after slaughtering a hog, and he must have hiccuped at least 430 million times. He said he was able to live a fairly normal life, during which he had two wives and eight children. He did have some difficulty keeping his false teeth in his mouth." (From *Why Doesn't My Funny Bone Make Me Laugh?*, by Alan Xanakis, M.D.)

BIRD POOP

Q: *What's the black dot in the middle of bird droppings?*

A: "The black dot is fecal matter. The white stuff is urine. They come out together, at the same time, out of the same orifice. The white stuff, which is slightly sticky, clings to the black stuff." (From *Why Do Clocks Run Clockwise, and Other Imponderables*, by David Feldman)

ONCE IN A BLUE MOON

Q: Is there really such a thing as a blue moon?

A: Yes, occasionally it *looks* blue "because of dust conditions in the atmosphere. The most famous widely observed blue moon of recent times occurred on September 26, 1950, owing to dust raised by Canadian forest fires." (From *The Book of Answers*, by Barbara Berliner)

A BIRD ON THE WIRE

Q: *Why don't birds get electrocuted when they perch on electric wires?*

A: Because they're not grounded. "There must be a completed circuit in order for the current to go through its body. If the bird could stand with one leg on the wire, and one on the ground, the circuit would be completed. In all cases where a person has been electrocuted, part of the body touched the wire and another part touched an uninsulated object, such as the ground, or something touching the ground." (From *How Do Flies Walk Upside Down?*, by Martin M. Goldwyn)

GRIN AND BEAR IT

Q: *Do bears really hibernate?*

A: Some bugs, reptiles, amphibians, and mammals do hibernate, but though the bear is known for it, it's not a "true" hibernator. "It does gain fat and, when winter arrives, sleeps for long periods, but not continuously. At irregular intervals, it arouses and wanders about, but doesn't eat much." (From *Science Trivia*, by Charles Cazeau)

ABOUT FIBER

Q: *What is fiber, and why is it good for you?*

A: Fiber—the 'roughage' found in fruits, vegetables, grains and beans—helps food move through the body. It's been credited with a long list of preventive health benefits, including lowering blood cholesterol levels and reducing the risk of colon cancer.

There are two types of fiber: Insoluble fiber is found mainly in whole grains and the outside, or skin, of seeds, fruits, and beans. Studies show that this fiber may help prevent colorectal cancer. It absorbs food like a sponge and moves it through the bowel, decreasing the amount of cancer-causing substances that come in contact with the bowel wall. Soluble fiber is found in fruits, vegetables, seeds, brown rice, barley, and oats. It may lower cholesterol by adhering to fatty acids and reducing the amount of fat absorbed into the bloodstream.

At any one time, there are 1,800 thunderstorms taking place somewhere in the world.

THE KING OF FARTS

Just when you think you've heard it all...someone comes up with something like this. It's from a little book called It's a Gas, *by Eugene Silverman, M.D., and Eric Rabkin, Ph.D. It's required reading for BRI history buffs.*

In all fairness to the farters of the world, the greatest of them all was not by his passing of gas also passing a judgment. His completely conscious control of his abilities was confirmed by numerous chemical examinations, including two in published form. This man, a hero at bottom, was a gentle and loving father, a noble and steadfast friend, a successful and generous businessman, and a great stage entertainer. This unique individual, a phenomenon among phenomena, this explosive personality and credit to our subject, was christened Joseph Pujol, but invented for himself the name by which all history knows him: Le Petomane!

THE ART OF THE FART

Le Petomane could fart as often and as frequently as he wished. His farts were odorless. As other people use their mouths, Le Petomane had learned to use his anus. Furthermore, by constricting or loosening his anus he could vary the pitch of the air he expelled and by controlling the force of abdominal contraction he could control its loudness. With these two fundamental tools, simple enough but rarely seen, Le Petomane contrived not only to imitate a variety of farts, but also to make music.

He headlined at the Moulin Rouge in Paris, the most famous nightclub in the world at that time, and brought in box office receipts more than twice as high as those of the angelic Sarah Bernhardt. He was one of the greatest comedians of the turn of the century. The manager of the Moulin Rouge kept nurses in the theater to tend to female customers whose uncontrolled laughter in tight corsets often caused them to pass out as Le Petomane passed gas. Here was not a court fool at all, but the toast of civilized society.

DISCOVERING HIS GIFT

As a boy, Joseph had had a frightening experience in the sea. Holding his breath and ducking under water, he suddenly felt a rush of cold water enter his bowels. He went to find his mother but was embarrassed to see water running out of himself. Although he recounted this in later years, apparently as a child he tried to keep his terrifying experience a secret.

Early in his married life he was called to military service and in the all-male atmosphere of the barracks he recounted for the first time his strange experience in the sea. When asked for a demonstration, he agreed to try again. On their next furlough, he and his unit went to the sea. He did succeed in taking water in and then letting it out. This might have been viewed as mere freakishness, but combined with Joseph's gentleness and good humor, it struck the soldiers as a delightful feat.

Pujol, using a basin, practiced this art in private with water and, once able to control the intake and outflow by combined exertions of his anal and abdominal muscles, he soon began to practice with air as well. This, of course, was only for his own amusement and the occasional amusement of his fellow soldiers.

A STAR IS BORN

When he returned home, he resumed his life as a baker and father but added to it his newfound love of entertainment. He began to work part-time in music halls as an ordinary singer, as a trombone player, and soon as a quick-change artist with a different costume for each song. He added comic routines of his own writing to his singing and playing acts, and became quite popular locally.

At the same time, he began to turn his special ability into an act, learning to give farts as imitations. Soon his friends urged him to add this to his act but he was diffident about the propriety of such a thing. In order to give it a try, he rented a theater of his own. He was an almost instant success. He left the bakery in care of his family and went to a number of provincial capitals, and at each stop Le Petomane played to packed houses. Finally, in 1892, he blew into Paris.

HIS FART'S DESIRE

The Moulin Rouge was his aim—and he went right for it. The manager of the Moulin Rouge, one Oller, on hearing of Le Petomane's specialty, was astounded at Pujol's audacity but agreed to give him an audition. In Paris as in Marseilles, the act was an instant success.

Like to fish? You're not alone: Fishermen spend $24 billion a year on their hobby.

HIS ACT

Le Petomane would begin by walking out dressed quite elegantly in silks and starched white linen, a thorough swell.

After his opening monologue Le Petomane leaned forward, hands on knees, turned his back to the audience, and began his imitations. "This one is a little girl," he would say and emit a delicate, tiny fart. "This one is a mother-in-law," he'd say, and there would be a slide. "This is a bride on her wedding night," very demure indeed, "and this the morning after," a long, loud one. Then he would do a dressmaker tearing two yards of calico, letting out a cracking, staccato fart that lasted at least ten seconds, and then cannonfire, thunder and so on. The public loved the act and the Moulin Rouge gave him an immediate contract. In a short time, he was their headliner.

A PATRON OF THE FARTS

His act grew with his popularity. Among other feats he could mix into the performance were tricks dependent upon inserting a rubber tube in his rectum (very decorously passed through his pocket). With this tube he could amiably chat away while at the same time smoking a cigarette. Sometimes he would insert a six-stop flute into the tube and accompany his own singing. A few simple nursery tunes he could play without recourse to the tube at all. And finally, he would almost always end his acts by blowing out a few of the gas-fired footlights. All that was left, before rising and bowing out, was to invite the audience to join him—and they did with gusto, their own convulsed abdomens insuring that many of the patrons could indeed participate in the group farting at the appropriate moment.

SPECIAL PERFORMANCES

The management of the Moulin Rouge wanted Le Petomane to submit to a medical examination so that his authenticity would be even more accepted, and this he did. For similar reasons of believability, Oller allowed Pujol to give private performances for all-male audiences at which he could perform wearing pants with an appropriate cut-out.

Before these events, and before his regular performances as well, he thoroughly washed himself by drawing water in and then shooting it out. In the smaller groups he would extinguish a candle at the distance of a foot and demonstrate his water jet over a range of four or five yards. These distances are also corroborated by medical observation.

FARTING IN EUROPE

The Moulin Rouge, acting as Le Petomane's agent, also encouraged him to travel abroad. In other European countries, and especially in Belgium, he was a star attraction. At his private performances in France, where no admission was charged, Pujol would finish by passing the hat. At one of these gatherings a man leaned forward and put a 20 louis gold piece in the hat and told him to keep it, that the show was worth it although he had had to travel from Brussels to see it. He had heard so much about Le Petomane but could not see him in Belgium because his own movements were so closely watched there. So he had come to Paris that night incognito to see and hear the great Le Petomane. He was King Leopold II of Belgium.

FINAL PASSING

The Medical Faculty at the Sorbonne offered Pujol 25,000 francs for the right to examine his body after his death. He was a vigorous man, a proud patriarch, and, knowing what such a sum could mean to his children and grandchildren, he accepted. But, despite the fact that he had distinguished himself by publicly displaying himself for so many years, he was held in such regard by those around him that, on his peaceful demise in 1945 at the age of 88, the family refused the offer. And so, having made flatulence a subject not for aggression but for pleasantry, Joseph Pujol, the greatest farter in history, came to his proper end.

A PAUSE FOR POETRY

A profound poem by Sir John Suckling, 17th-century cavalier poet:

Love is the fart
of every heart
For when held in,
doth pain the host,
But when released,
Pains others most.

FAMOUS TRIALS: HENRY FORD VS. THE *TRIBUNE*

Here's an episode that's been forgotten by most historians: In 1916 Henry Ford sued the Chicago Tribune *for libel after it called him "ignorant" in an editorial.*

BACKGROUND

On march 9, 1916, just before World War I, the United States was "invaded" by Mexican revolutionary Pancho Villa. He led a 1,500-man raid on Columbus, New Mexico, and killed 17 people—including eight U.S. soldiers.

President Woodrow Wilson's response: He mobilized the National Guard to patrol the Mexican-American border. As a part of its coverage of the story, the *Chicago Tribune* asked the Ford Motor Company whether employees called up for the Guard would be paid by Ford while they served on the Mexican border. The *Tribune* wanted to talk to Henry Ford himself, but he wasn't available, so they talked to company treasurer Frank Klingensmith instead.

THE CONFLICT

Without checking with his superiors, Klingensmith told the reporters that not only was Ford not going to pay employees who left their jobs to fulfill their reserve duties, it was also not going to reinstate them when they returned from patrolling the border.

Actually, Ford employees who were called up to serve in the National Guard were given special badges that guaranteed them their jobs back when they returned, and the company set up a special program to assist the families of reservists while they were away. But the *Tribune* ran the story without double-checking the information, and on June 23, 1916, it printed a scathing editorial titled *Ford Is An Anarchist*, attacking Ford for being "not merely an ignorant idealist, but an anarchistic enemy of the nation which protects him in his wealth"—and suggested that "a man so ignorant as Henry Ford may not understand the fundamentals of the government under which he lives."

World's largest toy company: Hasbro. Second largest: Mattel.

THE LAWSUIT

Ford, no stranger to criticism, initially dismissed the *Tribune's* assault on his character. But his lawyer, Alfred Lucking, wanted him to sue the paper for libel. Ford reconsidered the matter, and agreed.

It would have been easy to prove the libel charge against the *Tribune* if Ford's legal team had sued the newspaper specifically for using the word "anarchistic"—which in earlier cases had been proven to be a libelous term. But instead the lawyers made their complaint against the entire editorial, which gave the *Tribune* more room in which to maneuver: Instead of having to prove that Ford was an anarchist, they had only to prove that he was "ignorant." And they set out to do just that.

EDUCATING HENRY

The son of a farmer, Henry Ford had left school at the age of 15. To make matters worse, he rarely if ever found time to read the newspaper, and had only a superficial understanding of what was going on in the world. So Ford's lawyers tried to give him a crash course on U.S. history, current events, and other topics, but Ford was a less-than-perfect student.

In the end the task proved too great; try as they might, Ford's lawyers couldn't fill his head with facts quickly enough, and when he arrived to testify at the trial on July 16, 1919, he was forced to admit "ignorance of 'most things.' " Here are some quotes from the transcript of the *Tribune's* lawyer, Elliot G. Stevenson, questioning Henry Ford:

On Ignorance

Q: Mr. Ford, have you ever read history?

A: I admit I am ignorant about most things.

Q: You admit it?

A: About most things.

On the Military

Q: Did you understand what a mobile army was?

A: A large army mobilized.

Q: A large army mobilized. Is that your notion of a mobile army?

A. An army ready to be mobilized.

Q: What is your understanding about a mobile army?

A: I don't know.

27% of men and 61% of women agree: "The way to a partner's heart is through their stomach."

On History

Q: Have you ever heard of a revolution in this country?
A: There was, I understand.
Q: When?
A: In 1813.
Q: In 1813, the revolution?
A: Yes.
Q: Any other time?
A: I don't know.
Q: You don't know of any other?
A: No.
Q: Don't you know there wasn't any revolution in 1813?
A: I don't know that; I didn't pay much attention to it.
Q: Don't you know that this country was born out of a revolution—in 1776—did you forget that?
A: I guess I did.

Q: Do you know when the United States was created?
A: I could find it in a few minutes.
Q: Do you know?
A: I don't know as I do, right offhand.

Q: Did you ever hear of Benedict Arnold?
A: I have heard the name.
Q: Who was he?
A: I have forgotten just who he is. He is a writer, I think.
Q: What subjects do you recall he wrote on?
A: I don't remember.
Q: Did you ever read anything that he wrote?
A. Possibly I have, but I don't know.
Q. Would you be surprised to be informed that Benedict Arnold was a general in the American army who was a traitor and betrayed his country?
A: I don't know much about him.

On Government

Q: Mr. Ford, have you heard of the Declaration of Independence?
A: Oh, yes. That is based on justice.
Q: Did you ever read it?
A: Yes, I have read it.
Q: Have you in mind any of the significant things in that?
A: No, I have not.

U.S. city with the most skyscrapers: New York, with 130. Chicago is second with 53.

On Reading

Q: Mr. Ford, I think the impression has been created by your failure to read one of these that have been presented to you that you could not read; do you want to leave it that way?

A: Yes, you can leave it that way. I am not a fast reader, and I have the hay fever, and I would make a botch of it.

Q: Are you willing to have that impression left here?

A: I am not willing to have that impression, but I am not a fast reader.

Q: Can you read at all?

A: I can read.

Q: Do you want to try it?

A: No, sir.

THE VERDICT

After hearing testimony from dozens of witnesses on both sides of the case for more than 14 weeks, the jury—composed of 11 local farmers and one public roads inspector—met to decide on a verdict. A short time later, they found the *Chicago Tribune* guilty of libeling Henry Ford. But Ford's own testimony had damaged his case severely—the jury agreed that he was not an anarchist, but they weren't convinced he wasn't ignorant—and in the end they awarded the automaker a whopping 6¢ in damages.

THE PUBLIC RESPONSE

The public and the press began taking sides on the issue almost immediately. The *Nation* dismissed Ford as a "Yankee mechanic… with a mind unable to 'bite' into any proposition outside of his automobile business"; the *New York Times* editorialized that Ford had not "received a pass degree" in the case.

But the general public was more forgiving. According to Robert Lacey in *Ford: The Men and the Machine*, "His very nakedness when subjected to the city-slicker cleverness of the *Tribune* attorneys struck a chord with thousands who were equally hazy on their knowledge of the American Revolution, and who would have been even more reluctant to read aloud in public."

The trial was big news in its day, but in the long run—like Ford's isolationism, his anti-Semitism, and his early admiration of Adolf Hitler—it had almost no impact on the way he is remembered.

WHO KILLED MARILYN?

Ever wondered what really *happened to Marilyn Monroe? You're not alone. Here's a version that appeared in* It's A Conspiracy, *by the National Insecurity Council. It's great bathroom reading; be sure to pick up a copy for yourself.*

At 4:25 a.m. on August 5, 1962, Sergeant Jack Clemmons of the West Los Angeles Police Department received a call from Dr. Hyman Engelberg. "I am calling from the house of Marilyn Monroe," he said. "She is dead."

When Clemmons arrived at 12305 Helena Drive, he found Marilyn's body lying face down on the bed. The coroner investigating the case ruled that Monroe, 36, had died from "acute barbiturate poisoning due to ingestion of overdose...a probable suicide."

THE OFFICIAL STORY

• The night before, Monroe had gone to bed at about 8:00 p.m., too tired to attend a dinner party at actor Peter Lawford's beach house. A few hours later, Monroe's housekeeper, Eunice Murray, knocked on the star's bedroom door when she noticed a light was on inside, but got no response. Assuming that Monroe had fallen asleep, Murray turned in.

• When Murray awoke at about 3:30 a.m. and noticed the light still on in Monroe's room, she went outside to peek into the window. She saw Monroe lying nude on the bed in an "unnatural" position. Alarmed, Murray called Dr. Ralph Greenson, Monroe's psychiatrist, who came over immediately and broke into the bedroom. She also called Dr. Engelberg, Monroe's personal physician. After Engelberg pronounced her dead, they called the police.

SUSPICIOUS FACTS

From the start, there were conflicting versions of what had happened.

When Did Monroe Die?

Although Murray told the police she'd found the body after 3:30 a.m., there's evidence that Monroe died much earlier.

• Murray first told the police that she'd called Dr. Greenson at midnight; she later changed her story and said she'd call at

3:30 a.m. Sgt. Clemmons claims that when he first arrived on the scene, Engelberg and Greenson agreed that Murray had called them at about midnight. But in their official police statements, the doctors said they were called at 3:30 a.m.

• According to Anthony Summers in his book *Goddess*, Monroe's press agent, Arthur Jacobs, may have been notified of Monroe's death as early as 11:00 p.m., when he and his wife were at a Hollywood Bowl concert. According to Jacob's wife, Natalie, "We got the news long before it broke. We left the concert at once."

• In 1982, Peter Lawford admitted in a sworn statement that he learned of Monroe's death at 1:30 a.m., when her lawyer, Milton Rudin, called from the house to tell him about it.

• The ambulance crew summoned by the police noticed that Monroe's body was in "advanced rigor mortis," suggesting that she had been dead for 4 to 6 hours. That would mean she died about midnight.

Where Did Monroe Die?

Monroe supposedly died in her bedroom. But did she?

• Monroe's body was stretched out flat on the bed, with the legs straight—not typical for a person who had overdosed on barbiturates. According to Sgt. Clemmons, barbiturate overdoses often cause a body to go into convulsions, leaving it contorted. "You never see a body with the legs straight. And I've seen hundreds of suicides by drug overdose." He speculated that she had been moved. (*The Marilyn Conspiracy*, by Milo Speriglio)

• William Shaefer, president of the Shaefer Ambulance Service, insists that "in the very early morning hours"—well before 3:00 a.m.—one of his ambulances was called to Monroe's house. She was comatose; the ambulance took her to Santa Monica Hospital, where she died. "She passed away at the hospital. She did not die at home." And he was certain it was Monroe. "We'd hauled her before because of [earlier overdoses of] barbiturates. We'd hauled her when she was comatose." (ibid.)

How Did Monroe Die?

• Though Deputy Medical Examiner Thomas Noguchi speculated that Monroe had swallowed roughly 50 Nembutal pills, a common barbiturate, he found "no visual evidence of pills in the stomach or the small intestine. No residue. No refractile crystals." Yet, as

Yecch! 3% of American households keep a supply of anchovy paste in the kitchen.

Noguchi recounted in his book *Coroner*, toxicological reports of Monroe's blood confirmed his suspicions of an overdose.

• Why was there no pill residue in Monroe's body? Noguchi said that some "murder theorists" have suggested that an injection of barbiturates would have killed her without leaving pill residue. Other theorists have suggested that a suppository with a fatal dose of barbiturates would also leave no residue in her stomach. Or, at some point after the overdose, Monroe's stomach may have been pumped.

MISSING EVIDENCE

Why has so much evidence pertaining to Marilyn Monroe's case disappeared or been destroyed?

Phone Records

• Did Monroe try to call anyone the night she died? When a reporter for the *Los Angeles Herald Tribune* tried to get her phone records and find out, a phone company contact told him, "All hell is breaking loose down here! Apparently you're not the only one interested in Marilyn's calls. But the tape [of her calls] has disappeared. I'm told it was impounded by the Secret Service....Obviously somebody high up ordered it." (*Goddess*)

• In 1985, a former FBI agent claimed, "The FBI did remove certain Monroe records. I was on a visit to California when Monroe died, and became aware of the removal of the records from my Los Angeles colleagues. I knew there were some people there, Bureau personnel, who normally wouldn't have been there—agents from out of town. They were there on the scene immediately, as soon as she died, before anyone realized what had happened. It had to be on the instruction of somebody high up, higher even than Hoover...either the Attorney General or the President." (ibid.)

Monroe's Diary

• Monroe supposedly kept a detailed diary. According to Robert Slatzer, a longtime friend of the actress, "For years, Marilyn kept scribbled notes of conversations to help her remember things." What things? Slatzer said the diary included her intimate discussions with people like Robert Kennedy. Monroe supposedly told Slatzer, "Bobby liked to talk about political things. He got mad at me one day because he said I didn't remember the things he told me." (*The Marilyn Conspiracy*)

Americans buy 129 million eggs per week on average—and 206 million the week before Easter.

• After Monroe's death, Coroner's Aide Lionel Grandison claimed that the diary "came into my office with the rest of Miss Monroe's personal effects" during the investigation. But by the next day the diary had vanished—and, according to Grandison, someone had removed it from the list of items that had been brought in for investigation. (ibid.)

The Original Police Files

• In 1974, Captain Kenneth McCauley of the Los Angeles Police Department contacted the Homicide Department to ask about the files. They wrote back that the department had no crime reports in its files pertaining to Monroe's death. Even the death report had vanished.

• The files on Monroe may have disappeared as early as 1966. That year, Los Angeles Mayor Sam Yorty requested a copy of the files from the police department. The police declined, saying that the file "isn't here."

• What happened to the files? Lieutenant Marion Phillips of the Los Angeles Police Department claimed that he was told in 1962 that a high-ranking police official "had taken the file to show someone in Washington. That was the last we heard of it."

MONROE AND THE KENNEDYS

• As part of his research for *Goddess*, the most authoritative book on Marilyn Monroe, Anthony Summers interviewed more than 600 people linked to her. He quotes friends, acquaintances, reporters, and politicians who confirm what many Americans already suspected—that Monroe had affairs with both John and Robert Kennedy.

• Apparently, John Kennedy met her through his brother-in-law, Peter Lawford. According to Lawford's third wife, Deborah Gould, "Peter told me that Jack...had always wanted to meet Marilyn Monroe. It was one of his fantasies." Quoting Lawford, Gould says "Monroe's affair with John Kennedy began before he became president and continued for several years." (*Goddess*)

• According to Gould, JFK decided to end his affair with Monroe early in 1962. He sent his brother Robert to California to give her the news. "Marilyn took it quite badly," says Gould, "and Bobby went away with a feeling of wanting to get to know her better. At the beginning it was just to help and console, but then it led into

Top six juices in the U.S.: orange, apple, "blends," grape, grapefruit, prune.

an affair between Marilyn and Bobby." (ibid.)

• It didn't last long. By the summer of 1962, RFK began having second thoughts and decided to break off the affair. Monroe, already severely depressed, began acting erratically after being dumped by Bobby. She began calling him at home; when he changed his unlisted phone number to avoid her, she began calling him at the Justice Department, the White House, and even at the Kennedy compound in Hyannisport. When Bobby still refused to take her calls, Monroe threatened to go public with both affairs.

WAS IT A CONSPIRACY?

THEORY #1: Monroe was distraught about her affairs and committed suicide. To protect the Kennedys from scandal, someone tried to cover up the suicide and cleaned up Monroe's house.

• Monroe may have become frantic when Robert Kennedy cut her off, perhaps—as some theorists guess—because she was pregnant.

• Fred Otash, a Hollywood private detective, claimed that a "police source" told him that weeks before her death Monroe had gone to Mexico to have an abortion. According to Otash, "An American doctor went down to Tijuana to do it, which made Monroe safe medically, and made the doctor safe from U.S. law," since at that time abortion was illegal in the United States. But author Summers disagrees, noting: "There was no medical evidence to support the theory that Monroe had been pregnant." (*Goddess*)

• In any event, if Monroe was threatening to embarrass the Kennedys by going public about their affairs, it was cause for alarm. According to several reports, Robert Kennedy—who was vacationing with his family near San Francisco—flew to Los Angeles on August 4 to meet with Monroe and try to calm her down. It didn't work.

• Terribly depressed, Monroe took a massive dose of sleeping pills, but not before calling Peter Lawford and saying, in a slurred voice, "Say goodbye to Pat [Lawford's wife], say goodbye to Jack [JFK], and say goodbye to yourself, because you're such a nice guy."

• The call may have frightened Lawford so badly that he—and perhaps RFK—drove to Monroe's home. There he may have found her comatose and called an ambulance. (This would explain the Shaefer Ambulance claim of having taken Monroe to the hospital that night.) If Monroe had been taken to a hospital emergency room

On Mother's Day, Americans spend $329 million per year on candy, and $75 million on phone calls.

because of an overdose, her stomach would almost certainly have been pumped—which would account for the coroner's finding no "pill residue" in her stomach. When even the hospital's best attempts could not save Monroe, perhaps her body was returned to her bedroom in an effort to avoid controversy.

The Cleanup

• No suicide note was ever found, nor was Monroe's personal phone book. Someone had probably "sanitized" her bedroom before the police came. The most likely person was Peter Lawford. His second wife claimed, "He went there and tidied up the place, and did what he could, before the police and the press arrived." She also claimed Lawford had found a suicide note and destroyed it.

• Lawford may also have hired detective Fred Otash to finish the cleanup. According to a security consultant who worked with Otash, Lawford hired him on the night of the death to "check her house, especially for papers or letters, that might give away her affairs with the Kennedys."

THEORY #2: The Mob killed Monroe to embarrass—or even frame—Attorney General Robert Kennedy.

• The Mob almost certainly knew of Monroe's affairs with the Kennedys: In fact, several reputable accounts claim that the star's house had been bugged by the Mob. By recording intimate moments between Monroe and Robert Kennedy, the syndicate may have hoped to blackmail the attorney general and thus end his prosecution of Teamsters boss Jimmy Hoffa and other gangsters.

• In their book *Double Cross*, Chuck and Sam Giancana—the brother and godson of Mob godfather Sam "Mooney" Giancana—allege that the Mafia eventually decided to kill Monroe and make with RFK, they figured, the public would decide that Monroe had killed herself over him. They figured a sex and suicide scandal would force him to resign. So the Mob waited for Kennedy to visit Monroe in response to her desperate phone calls.

• Finally, Kennedy took the bait. According to the authors of *Double Cross*, when Sam Giancana learned that Bobby would be in California the weekend of August 4, he arranged the hit on Marilyn. The authors allege he chose Needles Gianola, an experienced killer, for the mission. Needles selected three men of his own to help him. Together they traveled to California "under Mooney's orders, to murder Marilyn Monroe."

• According to *Double Cross*, the mob had already bugged Marilyn's home, and the hit men were waiting at their secret listening post nearby when Kennedy arrived late Saturday night. They heard Bobby and another man enter the home and begin talking to Marilyn, who was extremely upset. Marilyn, the authors report, "became agitated—hysterical, in fact—and in response, they heard Kennedy instruct the man with him, evidently a doctor, to give her a shot to 'calm her down.' Shortly afterwards, RFK and the doctor left."

• *Double Cross* claims that the four killers waited until nightfall and then sneaked into Monroe's home to make the hit. Marilyn resisted, but was easily subdued because of the sedatives: "Camly, and with all the efficiency of a team of surgeons, they taped her mouth shut and proceeded to insert a specially 'doctored' Nembutal suppository into her anus. According to the authors, the killers waited for the lethal combination of barbiturates and chloral hydrate to take effect. Once she was totally unconscious, the men carefully removed the tape, wiped her mouth clean, and placed her across the bed. Their job completed, they left as quietly as they had come."

• Unfortunately for the conspirators, however, Kennedy's close friends and the FBI so thoroughly cleaned up Monroe's house and commandeered her phone records that any proof of the romance was eliminated. The Giancanas say that J. Edgar Hoover protected the Kennedys because, after keeping their secrets, he knew that they'd never fire him. *Double Cross* also alleges that the CIA was also in on the hit, but its reasoning is not convincing.

FOOTNOTE

In 1982, after reinvestigating Marilyn Monroe's death, the Los Angeles District Attorney's Office released the following statement: "Marilyn Monroe's murder would have required a massive, in-place conspiracy covering all of the principals at the death scene on August 4 and 5, 1962; the actual killer or killers; the Chief Medical Examiner-Coroner; the autopsy surgeon to whom the case was fortuitously assigned; and almost all of the police officers assigned to the case, as well as their superiors in the LAPD....Our inquiries and document examination uncovered no credible evidence supporting a murder theory."

Good for business: The Boston pub that inspired the "Cheers" TV show served 1,484 beers a day.

Uncle John's

SEVENTH BATHROOM READER

First published October 1994

UNCLE JOHN'S NOTES:

It strikes me, rereading this, that by 1994 we'd finally developed a sense of the mix of material that works in a *Bathroom Reader*.

We've got articles on fingerprinting and the Dodo bird mixed in with histories of the Jeep and the pencil. We've got Barney...and Joseph McCarthy. We've got Lloyds of London...and bad hair days. We've got the Flying Nun...and Elvis.

One of the reasons this worked so well was a BRI alumus named John Dollison—a natural storyteller who loves history. He took many of our ideas and made them even more interesting than we'd imagined. And of course, Gordon was always in the background, reminding us to concentrate on the story and not the extraneous details.

Some of our favorites in this volume: (There are a lot)

- Mama Mia!
- Pirate Lore
- What Is SPAM?
- Accidentally X-Rated
- Monumental Mistakes
- Knitting with Dog Hair
- Sweetened with Fruit Juice?
- Mummy's the Word
- The Strange Fate of the Dodo Bird

RUMORS

Why do people believe wild, unsubstantiated stories? According to some psychologists, "rumors make things simpler than they really are." And while people won't believe just anything, *it's surprising what outrageous stories we* do *seem willing to swallow.*

RUMOR: A leper was working at the Chesterfield cigarette factory in Richmond, Virginia.
HOW IT SPREAD: Unknown
WHAT HAPPENED: One of the all-time classic rumors to afflict an American product, the "Chesterfield Leper" rumor spread across the U.S. in the fall of 1934, costing Chesterfield thousands of dollars in sales as panicky puffers, fearful of catching leprosy themselves, switched brands overnight. The company fought the rumor hard—it invited Richmond officials to visit the plant and offered $1,000 for information on who had started the rumor. They never found out who was behind the rumor, but believed it was a competitor.

RUMOR: The Ku Klux Klan, to encourage a "a kinder, gentler attitude" toward its members and upgrade its image as a "historic American institution," is forming a multiracial "KKK Symphony" to travel around the country and spread music, good cheer, and white supremacy. The band will be an equal-opportunity employer: All races are invited to apply for positions, including blacks, Jews, and Catholics—although everyone will be expected to wear white robes during performances.
HOW IT SPREAD: Through a widely circulated fake press release, which boasted that the KKK Symphony would "tour the country, bring culture to various underprivileged areas, and work to modify mainstream attitudes" towards the Klan...all without the Klan changing its racist views. The release, which surfaced in 1990, stated that orchestra members would be paid $1,500 a week and $60 per diem, and would be covered by Blue Cross health insurance.
WHAT HAPPENED: Both the Klan and a number of Klan-watch organizations denied the story. Klansmen and other garden-

variety bigots took the story in stride: "I wouldn't be surprised if [an individual] Klansman was behind this. We're jokesters," Richard Ford, the National Wizard of the Fraternal White Knights of the Ku Klux Klan, told *Esquire* magazine, adding that "Klansmen don't appreciate classical [music]. And about that equal-opportunity thing. Well, there wouldn't be much point to being in the Klan if there was equal opportunity, would there?"

RUMOR: Nine months after a massive power failure hit New York City in November 1965, the birthrate rose dramatically.

HOW IT SPREAD: It started as a joke about what people would do when the lights were out for a long time. Then an article in the *New York Times* on August 8, 1966, reporting an increase in births at the city's Mt. Sinai Hospital seemed to prove it was true.

WHAT HAPPENED: It turned out that the newspaper had only compared births that occurred on August 8, 1965, with the births of August 8, 1966. In other words, they were reporting a one-day variation in one hospital. Not exactly conclusive evidence. In 1970, J. Richard Udry, director of the Carolina Population Center at the University of North Carolina, went back and studied birthrates from several New York hospitals between July 27 and August 14, 1966. His finding: The birthrate nine months after the blackout was actually slightly *below* the five-year average.

RUMOR: The Snapple Beverage Corp. supports Operation Rescue and the Ku Klux Klan.

HOW IT SPREAD: Unknown. One theory: The maritime graphic on the label—taken from a historic drawing of the Boston Tea Party—may have been misinterpreted as a slave ship. There is also a small letter K inside a circle on the label that signifies that the drinks are *Kosher*—not Klannish. But the main source may have been the company's sponsorship of Rush Limbaugh's program.

WHAT HAPPENED: The company launched a $100,000 print and radio advertising campaign targeted specifically at dispelling the rumor. "It is hurting us as human beings," one of the company's founders said in September 1993. "The Ku Klux Klan is a horrible organization. I mean, three Jewish boys from Brooklyn supporting the Ku Klux Klan?"

A handful of countries have been kicked out of the U.N., but only Switzerland *refuses to join.*

WORDPLAY

Here are the origins of some familiar phrases.

CASH ON THE BARRELHEAD
Meaning: "Paying up front or before a delivery."
Background: Frontier saloons often consisted of little more than a lean-to shed, a couple of barrels of whiskey, and a wooden plank across them that served as the bar. And when you didn't have a plank, you just stood one of the barrels up on its end and used it as a bar. Drinks were paid for in advance—by putting your *cash on the barrelhead.*

GET THE SACK/GET SACKED
Meaning: "Get fired / lose your job."
Background: When you worked on assembly lines in the old days., you had to bring your own tools—which most people carried in *sacks*—to work with you. If your boss fired you, he literally *gave you the sack*—handed you your tool bag and told you to get lost.

OUT OF TOUCH
Meaning: "A person is out of physical or mental contact with others."
Background: In the 18th century it became fashionable among European military leaders to have their soldiers march as close together as possible. "As a practical way of regulationg his space," one observer notes, "the soldier in the ranks had to be sure that his swinging elbows would touch those of comrades on each side." When gaps in the line formed, it was a sure sign that somewhere a soldier was—literally—*out of touch.*

BEHIND THE SCENES
Meaning: "In the background; out of view."
Background: It was common in Elizabethan theater to leave important actions and events out of plays entirely, and instead just report to the audience that the event had taken place between acts. Audience members joked that the actions had taken place *behind the scenes*—behind the props and backdrops on the stage—where no one could see them.

For the first federal income tax (1914), the "normal" tax rate was 1%; five years later, it was 77%.

THE SINGING NUN

She's mostly forgotten now, but the "Singing Nun" was one of the most famous nuns in American history. Here's a look at her unusual career.

POP NUN

Remember the *Ed Sullivan Show*? If you had tuned in to watch it one particular evening in 1963, you would have seen a peculiar sight: a Belgian nun in full habit, playing a guitar and singing a song called "Dominique." The nun's name was Sister Luc-Gabrielle, but she was better known as Soeur Sourire ("Sister Smile")—and her song was fast becoming a pop-music hit all over the world.

Hardly anyone who tuned in that night had any idea what Soeur Sourire was singing—"Dominique's" lyrics were entirely in French. But the tune's light melody was so catchy that the song went all the way to #1 on U.S. pop-music charts and ultimately sold more than 1.5 million copies.

The song was a critical success as well, winning the 1963 Grammy for the best religious song and numerous other awards. Soeur Sourire became a star in her own right. In 1966, Debbie Reynolds portrayed her in the film *The Singing Nun*.

IN THE BEGINNING

Soeur Sourire got her start singing songs during religious retreats. As one nun told *Time* magazine in 1963, "We have these retreats for young girls at our Fichermont monastery, and in the evenings we sing songs composed by Sister Luc-Gabrielle. The songs are such a hit with our girls that they asked us to transcribe them." One of the catchiest tunes was "Dominique," a song that honors St. Dominic Guzman, founder of Soeur Sourire's Dominican order (and the man credited with introducing rosary beads to the Roman Catholic faith).

In 1961, the nuns decided to record some of Soeur Sourire's songs and give them away during the retreats...but they couldn't afford to rent a recording studio or manufacture their own records, so they asked the Philips record company to lend them one of its studios. After a few months of prodding, the company agreed. Philips initially planned to issue a few dozen pressings of the album and donate them to the nuns for their own use, but company executives liked the album so much they contracted with the convent to sell it all over Europe.

Philips issued Sister Luc-Gabrielle's album in Europe under the name *Soeur Sourire*, and it took the continent by storm. But when it was released in the United States a few months later under the name *The Singing Nun*, no one bought it. So Philips issued "Dominique" as a 45-rpm single and sold more than 400,000 copies in three weeks.

FROM BAD TO VERSE

Soeur Sourire seemed to adjust quite well to her celebrity status at first...but it didn't last long: She left her convent in 1966 before taking her final vows, telling the press that she wanted to continue her missionary work while pursuing a recording career. (She did, however, turn all of her song royalties over to her religious order before she left.)

For her next single, she chose a song called "Glory be to God for the Golden Pill," a tribute to artificial birth control. It didn't have quite the same ring to it that "Dominique" had. Nobody bought it, nor did they buy the updated synthesizer version of "Dominique" that she issued in 1983.

A Sad Note: Soeur Sourire lived to regret her decision to give up all of her royalties. The Belgian government hounded her for $63,000 in back taxes for the next 20 years, and in 1983 the center for autistic children that she and a friend (also an ex-nun) founded closed its doors due to lack of funds. Her life ended tragically in 1985 when she and the friend were found dead in their apartment, the victims of an apparent double suicide brought on by their financial problems. She was 51.

* * *

THE SPIRIT OF 2000

In November 1997, Hair of the Dog Brewing Co. in Portland, Oregon, created *Fred*—a beer designed to get better as it ages. "Meet *Fred*, the beer you're not even supposed to crack open until the millennium," wrote the *Wall Street Journal* in 1998. The first batch sold out in an hour.

ACRONYMANIA

The AHD (American Heritage Dictionary, *in case you were wondering) says an acronym is "a word formed from the initial letters of a name." Here are some acronyms you may have heard—without realizing they were acronyms. See if you know (or can guess) what they stand for.*

(Answers are on page 665.)

1. ZIP code
2. DNA
3. DOA
4. EST (there are two)
5. HUD (a govt. agency)
6. INTERPOL
7. KISS (a business axiom)
8. LASER
9. UNIVAC (the 1950s computer)
10. NABISCO
11. NASA
12. NECCO (the candy company)
13. NIMBY
14. NOW (women's group)
15. OPEC
16. OSHA
17. QUASAR
18. RAND Corp.
19. RBI (sometimes pronounced "ribbie")
20. REM
21. SCUBA tank or diver
22. SWAK
23. TNT
24. UNESCO
25. UNICEF
26. CAT scan
27. AWACS
28. AWOL
29. CD-ROM
30. M*A*S*H
31. WILCO (as in "Roger-wilco, over and out")
32. SONAR
33. SNAFU
34. NATO
35. SALT (as in "SALT agreement")
36. RADAR
37. SCUD
38. SAC
39. WYSIWYG (computer term)
40. WAC
41. SEALS
42. MS-DOS (computer term)
43. NORAD
44. TASER
45. RAM (computer term)
46. WOMBAT
47. AKA
48. CANOLA (the oil)

What's so special about Elvis's 1957 film *Loving You?* Both of his parents were extras in it.

CAVEAT EMPTOR

Here's a look at some advertising claims that prove the old adage caveat emptor*—"let the buyer beware"—is still good advice.*

TRIUMPH CIGARETTES

The Claim: *"Triumph Beats Merit! In a recent taste test, an amazing 60 percent said Triumph cigarettes taste as good or better than Merit!"*

The Truth: Actually, Merit beat Triumph. The results: 36% of the people surveyed said Triumph was better than Merit, but 40% said that Merit was better than Triumph. Triumph pulled ahead of Merit only when the 24% who said the two brands were equal were added to the total. That's why the ad used the words "*as good* or better than Merit."

USAIR

The Claim: *"USAir had the best on-time record of any of the seven largest airlines!"*

The Truth: USAir conveniently forgot that Pan Am, the *eighth*-largest airline, was actually rated first.

ITT CONTINENTAL BAKERIES

The Claim: *"Fresh Horizons bread contains five times as much fiber as whole wheat bread!"*

The Truth: The bread did indeed contain five times as much fiber, but the extra fiber came from *wood*...which the Federal Trade Commission dryly called "an ingredient not commonly used, nor anticipated by consumers to be commonly used, in bread."

ANACIN-3

The Claim: *"Hospitals recommend acetaminophen, the aspirin-free pain reliever in Anacin-3, more than any other pain relievers!"*

The Truth: They neglected to mention that Tylenol also contains acetaminophen...and hospitals recommend that product more than they recommend Anacin-3.

Meow! Number of muscles in a cat's ear: 32.

LEVI'S 501 JEANS

The Claim: *"Ninety percent of college students say Levi's 501 jeans are 'in' on campus!"*

The Truth: Levi's cited a fall fashion survey conducted annually on 100 U.S. college campuses. What they *didn't* say was that Levi's 501 jeans were the *only* blue jeans listed in the survey. Other entries included T-shirts, 1960s-style clothing, overalls, beach pants, and neon-colored clothing. So anyone who wanted to choose any type of jeans had no choice but to pick 501s.

LITTON MICROWAVE OVENS

The Claim: *"76% of independent microwave oven technicians surveyed recommended Litton!"*

The Truth: The survey included only Litton-authorized technicians "who worked on Littons and at least one other brand of microwaves. Technicians who serviced other brands, but not Littons, were excluded from the study."

* * * * *

CAR COMMERCIALS

The Claim: In 1990, Volvo aired a commercial showing a monster truck driving over several cars, including one Volvo. The roofs of the other cars were crushed; the Volvo's roof withstood the abuse.

The Truth: An onlooker videotaping the making of the commercial observed workers reinforcing the Volvo's roof with wooden planks and welded steel rods...and *cutting* the roof supports on the other cars. The man turned over his evidence to the Texas state attorney general's office; they alerted the media and threatened to sue Volvo. The company, embarrassed by the negative publicity, removed the ad from the airwaves.

The Claim: In a commercial showing Chrysler chairman Lee Iacocca speaking to the company's board of directors, Iacocca lectures, "Some things you wait for, some you don't. Minivans with air bags? You don't wait."

The Truth: Iacocca fought for years to keep the federal government from mandating airbags, even claiming that a safety engineer had once told him airbags were so dangerous that they should be used for executions.

Vincent Van Gogh was able to sell only one painting (*The Red Vineyard*) during his lifetime.

CLOUDMASTER ELVIS

So you thought Elvis was just a rock'n'roll singer? Maybe not. Maybe he had special powers over nature...and was an expert on embalming. Here are two bizarre stories told in Elvis, What Happened? *by Steve Dunleavy.*

CONTROLLING THE CLOUDS

As Elvis got more famous, he came to believe that he was no ordinary human being. How did he know? Well, for one thing, he believed he could move clouds.

"I remember one day in Palm Springs," says former aide Dave Hebler. "It was hotter than hell, over a hundred degrees, and Elvis wanted to go shopping. So we all jam into this car....Elvis was talking about the power of metaphysics, although I'm not quite sure he knew the real definition of the word."

The sky in the desert was cloudless, except for one small, far-off cloud. "Suddenly Elvis yells out, 'Stop the car. I want to show you want I mean, Dave. Now see that cloud? I will show you what my powers really are. Now I want you all to watch. All of you, look at that cloud.'

"Well, we all look at the damn little cloud up there like a bunch of goats. Elvis is staring a hole through the damn thing. Well, the perspiration is dripping off us. Not a sound in the car, just a whole bunch of dummies dying of heat stroke looking up at the cloud.

"I'm near dying and I am praying that the sonofabitch would blow away. At the same time, I'm really having a problem not to burst out laughing. After about ten minutes, thank God, the damn thing dissipated a little. I saved the day by noticing it first....I said, 'Gee, Elvis, you're right. Look, it's moving away.' [He] gave me one of those sly little smiles that told me he had done it again. 'I know, I moved it,' he says. Then we drive off."

COMMUNING WITH THE DEAD

"You never knew where a night out with Elvis would end up," says Sonny West, Elvis's bodyguard. "Worst of all were the trips to the funeral home." Elvis had a particular fondness for visiting the Memphis funeral home where his mother's body had been "laid out."

One night, Elvis and some of his troupe went to the funeral home. Elvis began wandering around, trying doors and poking his head into various rooms. He seemed to be looking for something.

Meanwhile, Sonny had his gun out, expecting a security guard to come charging in, thinking "we're grave robbers or something and start blazing away." But no one else seemed to be around.

West recalls: "Then I get the shock of my life. We come into this big room with heads sticking from under the sheets. They were bodies, and they were sort of tilted upward, feet first. This was the damn embalming room. I'm horrified. But this was apparently what Elvis was looking for. He is happy he has found this room."

Elvis started checking out the bodies, explaining to his companions how people get embalmed. "He is walking around and lifting up sheets looking at the bodies, and he is telling us all the cosmetic things the morticians do when people are in accidents. He is showing us the various veins....How a body is bled. Then he shows us where the bodies were cut, and because the cuts don't heal, there is only the stitches holding the body together."

"[Some of us] hated those trips, but that's what Elvis wanted and you just went along with it."

* * * *

Strange Lawsuits: *Japanese Version*

THE PLAINTIFF: Reiko Sekiguchi, 56, a Japanese sociology professor.

THE DEFENDANT: The University of Library and Information Science in Tsukuba, Japan

THE LAWSUIT: In 1988, the university stopped paying Sekiguchi's research expenses and travel allowances because she signed official documents using her maiden name instead of her married name. So she sued the university, arguing that "women should have the right to use their maiden names in professional activities and in daily life."

THE VERDICT: She lost.

The average U.S. family spends $3,900 a year on travel.

PRIMETIME PROVERBS

TV wisdom from Primetime Proverbs: The Book of TV Quotes, *by Jack Mingo and John Javna.*

ON AGING
"Those little lines around your mouth, those crow's feet around your eyes, the millimeter your derriere has slipped in the last decade—they're just nature's way of telling you that you've got nine holes left to play, so get out there and have a good time."

—**David Addison,**
Moonlighting

ON BALDNESS
"I cried for the man who had no hair until I met the man with no head."

—**Bud Lutz,**
Eisenhower and Lutz

Buddy Sorrell [to Mel Cooley]: "I wish you'd kept your hair and lost the rest of you."
Sally Rogers: "Watch it Buddy, he'll turn on you."
Buddy: "What's the difference? He's the same on both sides."

—***The Dick Van Dyke Show***

ON DEATH
"Abracadabra, the guy's a cadaver."

—**David Addison,**
Moonlighting

"I'd rather live in vain than die *any* way."

—**Bret Maverick,**
Maverick

ON COWARDICE
"My Pappy always said, 'A coward dies a thousand deaths, a hero dies but one.' A thousand to one is pretty good odds."

—**Bret Maverick,**
Maverick

"He who chickens out and runs away will chicken out another day."

—**Robot,**
Lost in Space

ON CULTURE
"Culture is like spinach. Once you forget it's good for you, you can relax and enjoy it."

—**Uncle Martin,**
My Favorite Martian

"You can't let a job stifle your mind, buddy boy. You've got to keep yourself free for cultural pursuits, you know....Good reading, good music...bowling."

—**Mike Stone,**
The Streets of San Francisco

Famous but forgotten superstition: People with dimpled chins never commit murder.

FAMOUS FOR 15 MINUTES

Here it is again—our feature based on Andy Warhol's prophetic comment that "In the future, everyone will be famous for 15 minutes." Here's how a few people have been using up their allotted quarter hour.

THE STAR: Joe "Mule" Sprinz, a professional baseball player from 1922 to 1948

THE HEADLINE: "Ouch! Blimp Ball Takes Bad Bounce"

WHAT HAPPENED: In 1939, Sprinz, 37-year-old catcher for the San Francisco Seals, caught five baseballs dropped from the Tower of the Sun (450 feet) at the San Francisco World's Fair. The Seals' publicity agent was impressed and asked Sprinz if he'd catch a ball dropped 1,200 feet from a Goodyear Blimp, which would break the world record of 555 feet, 5 1/8 inches. "You'll become famous!" the agent promised.

Two teammates stood alongside Sprinz as the first baseball was dropped, but when they saw it break a bleacher seat...and then saw the second ball "bury itself in the ground," they backed off and let him make the third attempt by himself. "So the third one came down and I saw that one all the way. But nobody told me how fast it would be coming down," Sprinz later recalled. Traveling at a speed of 150 miles per hour, the ball bounced off Sprinz's glove and slammed into his face just below the nose, smashing his upper jaw, tearing his lips, and knocking out four teeth.

THE AFTERMATH: Sprinz spent three months in the hospital (and suffered headaches for more than five years), but recovered fully and continued his baseball career, retiring in 1948. He never made it into the Hall of Fame...but did earn a place in the *Guinness Book of World Records* for the highest baseball catch "ever attempted." Sprinz passed away in January 1994 at the age of 91.

THE STARS: Officer Bob Geary of the San Francisco Police Department and his sidekick, Officer Brendan O'Smarty

THE HEADLINE: "Ventriloquist Vindicated in Vote"

WHAT HAPPENED: In 1992, Geary, an amateur ventriloquist, began taking "Officer Brendan O'Smarty"—a dummy dressed as a police officer—on his rounds in the city's North Beach area.

When the popular O'Smarty started to get some publicity, Geary's captain told him to leave the dummy at home; he said it made the department "look stupid."

Geary not only refused, he used $10,000 of his own money to finance an "initiative" that put the "O'Smarty issue" on the ballot in San Francisco's 1993 municipal elections. The result: Voters overwhelmingly supported O'Smarty.

THE AFTERMATH: The pro-dummy election was reported in newspapers all over the country. O'Smarty kept his "job"...and Geary made his money back when he sold the movie rights to his story.

THE STAR: Dallas Malloy, a 16-year-old girl from Bellingham, Washington

THE HEADLINE: "Woman TKOs Boxing Association in Court ...and Opponent in Ring"

WHAT HAPPENED: In 1992, Malloy set out on an amateur boxing career...but learned that the U.S. Amateur Boxing Association had a bylaw banning females from boxing in sanctioned bouts. She contacted the ACLU and together they sued, claiming that the bylaw violated Washington State's antidiscrimination laws.

Malloy won the suit, and on October 30, 1993, she squared off in the ring against 21-year-old Heather Poyner. A crowd of about 1,200 turned out to watch Malloy batter Poyner for three two-minute rounds. Malloy won in a unanimous decision. "It was great to get in the ring," she told reporters afterward. "The only thing I would change is that I would knock her out the next time. I really wanted to knock her out."

THE AFTERMATH: Malloy abandoned her career two months later. "After [the fight] I kind of lost interest," she told the Associated Press. Her boxing career had lasted 14 months.

THE STAR: Andrew Martinez, a University of California, Berkeley, college sophomore

THE HEADLINE: "No Nudes Is Good Nudes? Naked Guy Nixed"

WHAT HAPPENED: In September 1992, Martinez began attending classes completely in the buff, calling his nudity a form of free speech. The university did nothing until they received numerous complaints from students and employees.

But what could they do? There weren't any university regulations banning public nudity, so the school updated its student conduct regulations to forbid indecent exposure, public nakedness, and "sexually offensive conduct." Martinez was then suspended for two weeks when he gave a nude interview to a (clothed) reporter. When he showed up nude at an administrative hearing to protest the charges, he was permanently expelled from school for failing to wear "proper attire." "I didn't think this was so controversial," Martinez told the *San Francisco Chronicle*. "I was surprised they gave me the boot."

THE AFTERMATH: Martinez became a mini-celebrity, featured in magazine and newspaper stories all over the world and appearing on several TV talk shows. His expulsion didn't stop him from waging his lone crusade. In March 1993, he was arrested near the campus for distributing free beer to the homeless while shouting the slogan, "Drink for the Revolution." He was, course, nude, and was quickly arrested on suspicion of drinking in public, for being a minor in possession of alcohol, and for resisting an officer.

THE STAR: Charlie Shaw, owner of a London, Ohio, deli shop

THE HEADLINE: "Clinton Burger Bites Back"

WHAT HAPPENED: When President Bill Clinton visited Shaw's deli in February 1994, Shaw served him a "Clinton Burger"—a beef pattie with bacon, cheese, mushrooms, onions, and a secret "Clinton sauce." Shaw and his Clinton Burger made headlines across the nation.

THE AFTERMATH: Unfortunately for Shaw, he also caught the attention of state government officials. They discovered he was operating his business while collecting disability benefits from a previous job-injury claim, a violation of state law. Authorities also discovered that he didn't have a food-service permit—which is also illegal. He was indicted on state fraud charges.

MAMA MIA!

Here's a look at five famous American mothers. You'll never guess who gave Uncle John the idea for this page.

ELIZABETH FOSTER GOOSE

Known as: Mother Goose

Background: In the 1750s, Boston printer Thomas Fleet heard his mother-in-law, Elizabeth Goose, singing nursery rhymes to her grandson—including "Hickory Dickory Dock," "Humpty Dumpty," and "Little Bo-peep." Fleet began writing them down, and in 1765 published them in a book called *Mother Goose's Melodies for Children*.

MARY HARRIS JONES

Known as: Mother Jones

Background: Mary Harris was a schoolteacher in Monroe, Michigan, in the 1850s. She married George Jones in 1861, moved to Chicago, and started a dressmaking business. But the great Chicago fire of 1871 wiped her out. Soon afterward she became active in the U.S. labor movement, and for the next 50 years traveled all over the country organizing workers in steel mills, railroads, coal mines, and the garment industry. She remained an active organizer until shortly before her death in 1930 at the age of 100.

FREDERIKA MANDELBAUM

Known as: "Marm" Mandelbaum (aka "Ma Crime")

Background: She's almost forgotten now, but Frederika Mandelbaum was one of the earliest, most famous, and most successful organized crime figures in American history. She was nicknamed "Marm," but if she were alive today, she might be known as "the Godmother." The *Encyclopedia of American Crime* describes her as "the leading criminal in America during the latter part of the 19th century."

Marm got her start as the wife of an honest dry goods store owner in New York City. She eventually took over the business and began fencing stolen property. Operating from warehouses scattered all over town, Mandelbaum bought and sold stolen property from heists up and down the East Coast. In little more than a decade she built her enterprise into one of the largest criminal organizations in the city's

Just a kid at heart: George Washington loved to play marbles.

history, an empire she kept afloat by paying tens of thousands of dollars in bribes to the police. She retained Howe and Hummel, one of New York's most prestigious criminal law firms, to keep her and her friends out of jail.

She was finally caught in possession of stolen property that had been secretly marked by Pinkerton detectives (the New York D.A. thought the police were too corrupt to be trusted for the job) and was thrown in jail. A reporter later described what the detectives found when they stormed Marm's house to put her under arrest:

> It did not seem possible that so much wealth could be assembled in one spot. There seemed to be enough clothes to supply an army. There were trunks filled with precious gems and silverware. Antique furniture was stacked against a wall and bars of gold from melted jewelry settings were stacked under newspapers.

Mandelbaum and her son Julius posted $21,000 in bail the next day...and escaped to Canada with an estimated $1 million in cash. She died a free, very wealthy woman 10 years later at the age of 76.

ANNA WHISTLER

Known as: Whistler's Mother

Background: In October 1871, James Whistler decided to paint a portrait of his mother. "I want you to stand for a picture," he said. Mrs. Whistler agreed. "I stood bravely two or three days—I stood still as a statue!" she told a friend. But in the end she was too frail to stand for the long hours the portrait required. So Whistler painted her sitting down instead. Today the painting, officially called *Arrangement in Grey and Black: Portrait of the Painter's Mother*, is the 2nd most recognizable portrait in the world...after the Mona Lisa.

KATE BARKER

Known as: "Ma" Barker

Background: She was the mother of Freddy, Herman, Lloyd, and "Doc"—"the Barker Brothers," four of the most famous gangsters of the 1930s. She not only *encouraged* her boys to become criminals, she actually masterminded many of their bank heists, post-office robberies, and other crimes—including the kidnapping and $100,000 ransom of Brewery magnate William A. Hamm, Jr. in 1933. She and Freddy were killed in a shootout with the FBI at their Florida hideout in 1935.

THE PENCIL

Ever wonder how the pencil got its lead? We did too.

IS THERE REALLY LEAD IN A PENCIL?

Not anymore. The ancient Greeks, Romans and Egyptians used small lead disks for drawing guidelines on papyrus before writing with brushes and ink, and artists in Europe used metallic rods of lead, silver, and zinc to make very light drawings centuries ago. But all that changed in 1564, when a graphite deposit was unearthed in Borrowdlae, England.

Using graphite for writing wasn't new; the Aztecs did it long before the arrival of Columbus. But it was new to the Europeans. They discovered that the soft graphite—a form of carbon—made rich, dark lines. They began carving pointed "marking stones" out of it and using the stones to write with.

The problem was that the stones marked the writer's hands as much as the paper. Eventually, people figured out that they could wrap a string around the stick to keep their hands clean, unwinding the string as the graphite wore down. That was the first version of the modern pencil.

HOW THEY GET THE "LEAD" INTO THE PENCIL

Now, of course, the graphite comes in a wood casing. But how does it get in there?

- First the graphite is ground up and mixed with fine clay. The more clay added, the harder the lead.
- Then the mixture is forced through an "extruder" to make a long, thin rod.
- The rod is fired at a temperature of 2200° F to harden it and then treated with wax for smooth writing.
- The wood is sawed into small boards that are the length of one pencil, the width of seven pencils, and the thickness of half a pencil.
- Seven tiny grooves are cut lengthwise. Then the lead is laid into each of them, and an identical board is glued on top. A machine cuts the boards into seven individual pencils.
- Last step: They're painted with nontoxic paint.

An adult crocodile exerts a force of 1,540 lbs. between its jaws. Humans exert 40 to 80 lbs.

THE FINGERPRINT FILE

It seems like law enforcement agencies have been catching criminals using fingerprints for ages...but actually the practice is less than a century old. Here's a little background on one of the most important crimefighting techniques of the 20th century.

WHERE THERE'S A WILL...

In 1903 a convicted criminal named Will West was being processed for entry into Leavenworth penitentiary when prison officials realized that they already had a man matching his name and description at the prison. After double-checking their records (including a photograph of the inmate), they confirmed that the man being processed was the same Will West who was supposedly already behind bars. What was he doing on the outside?

Prison officials assumed he had escaped without anyone noticing . . . until they checked Will West's cell and found he was still in it. The men looked like twins.

At the time, the standard method for criminal identification was the "Bertillon System," a system based on physical descriptions and anatomical measurements. Robert Liston describes the theory behind it in his book, *Great Detectives:*

> If one measurement was taken of a man, his height, for example, the chance of another man having exactly the same height was four to one. If a second measurement was added, his head circumference, say, the chances increased to 16 to 1. If eleven meausurements were taken, the odds against a duplication were 4,191,304 to 1. If fourteen measurements were kept, the odds were 286,435,456 to 1.

It seemed foolproof. But now the Wests had proved it fallible. They resembled each other so closely that the system concluded they were the *same individual.*

WHAT HAPPENED

Left with no alternative, prison officials turned to a new system being developed by England's Scotland Yard. They *fingerprinted* the men and discovered that, although the men appeared to be identical, their fingerprints had almost nothing in common.

FINGERPRINT HISTORY

In 1858 William Herschel, an English civil servant working in India, began collecting his friends' fingerprints as a hobby. Carefully studying the prints over the years, he made two discoveries: No two fingerprints were the same, and each subject's fingerprints remained identical throughout their life. He brought his hobby to work with him: Put in charge of paying out pensions to Indian subjects, Herschel—a bigot who thought all Indians looked alike—required each Indian to place their thumbprint on the payroll next to their signature. He figured he could more easily spot fraudulent claimants if he took their fingerprints.

In 1880 Dr. Henry Faulds, a Scottish missionary in Japan, published an article describing how the Japanese had been signing legal documents with their fingerprints for generations. He reported another important discovery: Even when their fingers were perfectly clean, people left fingerprints on every surface they touched. Faulds called on British law enforcement agencies to make fingerprint searches a standard part of police investigations; Scotland Yard finally took his advice in 1901.

FINGERPRINT FACTS

- The FBI didn't begin fingerprinting until the 1920s; but by the late 1980s it had more than 140 million sets of prints on file, including those of every government employee and member of the military. An estimated 2,700 criminals per month are identified using the FBI's files.
- It is possible to have your fingerprints removed, but it's painful and pretty pointless. Even if you do burn or slice off your prints, the scars that are left behind are as unique as the prints they replaced. There is no known case of a criminal successfully concealing his identity by mutilating their fingertips.
- It's just about impossible to get a set of fingerprints from a handgun; experts place the odds as low as 1 in 1,000. All that stuff you see in movies about cops picking up guns by inserting a pencil under a trigger guard are hooey—there simply aren't enough smooth, flat surfaces on most handguns to get a good print.
- No one fingerprint is *necessarily* unique; scientists figure there's a 1 in 2 quadrillion (about 1 million times the Earth's population) chance that someone on Earth has the same fingerprint you do.

DEMOCRACY IN ACTION

"It's the worst form of government," said Mark Twain, "except for every other form of government." Or something like that. Or maybe it wasn't Twain. In any case, it was a good point. So here's the BRI election news.

ABSENTEE BALLOTS

"What if they held an election and no one voted? It happened in Centerville, Miss.…Denny James looked like a sure thing for the board of aldermen—he was the only candidate. But no one voted for him. State law says a candidate must get at least one vote before being declared the winner of an election.

"The moral of the story: Don't take anything for granted. Everyone in town assumed the neighbors would be voting. When the polls closed early, even James—who worked late that day—was shut out. But another election was held, and James got 45 votes."

—*Parade* magazine, January 2, 1994

MAKING AN ASS OF VOTERS

In 1936, Kenneth Simmons, mayor of Milton, Washington, placed a candidate named Boston Curtis on the ballot for the Republican precinct committee. Curtis ran as a "dark horse"…and although he gave no speeches and made no promises, he won.

The victory made national news, because Curtis was a mule; his hoof prints were even imprinted on the filing notice. Simmons later claimed he'd sponsored the mule's candidacy "to show how careless many voters are."

MAN STOPS FOR BURRITO—ALTERS HISTORY

ASHFORD, CONN.— "Robert Brady was driving through town last month and decided to stop at a convenience store for a burrito. Next door, in front of Town Hall, he saw a sign that read, 'Vote Today.'

"For a lark, the former Ashford resident—who was still registered to vote here—strolled into the Town Hall and voted 'Yes' in what turned out to be a referendum on the town budget. He later learned that the $5 million budget had passed by a single vote. 'Hey, I changed the course of history, all for a burrito,' Brady said, laughing."

—*Hartford Courant*, July 15, 1991

PLANNED OBSOLESCENCE

"In 1978, William Smith, of Waukegan, Illinois, was elected Lake County auditor. But in a referendum on the same ballot, voters abolished the position of auditor altogether. 'I feel like I've gone off a diving board and suddenly found the pool was empty,' Smith said."

—*The Emperor Who Ate the Bible*

HEADS, YOU SERVE

In 1975, Lib Tufarolo and Miles Nelson ran for mayor of Clyde Hill, Washington. Tufarolo got 576 votes; so did Nelson.

"The law says that in case of a tie you decide the election by lot," the local superintendent of elections informed them. Then he suggested they flip a coin. Tufarolo was outraged. "It's just ridiculous. I don't think that's how the people would want it done," he said. But Nelson, who'd spent a total of $5 on his campaign (which was $5 more than Tufarolo had spent), disagreed. He called it "the least offensive method" of settling the issue.

Tufarolo won the toss and became mayor. The Associated Press noted that "the community of 3,200 appears indifferent."

—Fenton and Fowler's
More Best & Worst & Most Unusual

DEAD MEN CAST NO VOTES

U.S. voters have occasionally elected dead men to office. Usually the candidate dies after being nominated, and it's too late to remove the name from the ballot and nominate someone who's alive. But at least once—in 1868—a corpse was actually nominated... and elected. The "elected official" was the last remains of Rep. Thaddeus Stevens of Lancaster County, Pennsylvania. His supporters did it as a tribute.

TIPS FOR TEENS

Here are some classic "how-to" tips for teenagers from the 1950s. We're sure you'll find the information as "valuable" now as it was then.

BOYS' DATING DO'S AND DON'T'S

How to Ask a Girl for a Date

When a boy wants to ask a girl for a date, there are several rules to follow and pitfalls to avoid.

First of all, he invites her specifically for a particular occasion, giving her the time, the place, and the nature of the affair. He says, for example, "May I take you to the game in Hometown Gym at two next Saturday afternoon?" Knowing all the relevant facts, she has a basis upon which to refuse or to accept.

In the second place, he is friendly and acts as though he really wants her to accept his invitation. He looks at her with a smile while he waits for her reply.

If she accepts, he seems pleased and arranges definitely for the time at which he will call for her. If she refuses, he says that he is sorry and suggests that perhaps another time she will go with him.

How Not to Ask Her

Boys find that girls do not like the indirect approach that starts, "What are you doing next Friday night?" That puts the girl "on a spot."

Boys should not act as though they expect to be refused, as Amos does when he says, "I don't suppose you'd like to go on a date with me, would you?" This can make the girl feel uncomfortable and is a mark of the boy's feeling of insecurity, too.

Girls do not like to be asked for dates at the last minute. It is no compliment to call a girl up the very evening of an affair.

Since asking a girl for a date is both a compliment and an invitation, a boy needs have no fear of using the simplest, most direct approach he can muster. He might be surprised to know how eager the girl has been to hear the words he is struggling to say!

The Navajo symbol for the sun is the *swastika*.

LOONEY LAWS

Believe it or not, these laws are real.

In Las Vegas, Nevada, it's against the law to pawn your dentures.

In Natoma, Kansas, it's illegal to throw knives at men wearing striped suits.

It's illegal to sleep with your boots on in Tulsa, Oklahoma.

Michigan law forbids pet owners from tying their crocodiles to fire hydrants.

If you're 88 years of age or older, it's illegal for you to ride your motorcycle in Idaho Falls, Idaho.

It's against the law in Tuscumbia, Alabama, to have more than eight rabbits per city block.

It's against the law (not to mention impossible) to whistle under water in Vermont.

In Alabama, it's illegal to play dominoes on Sunday.

It's illegal to eat snakes in Kansas.

In Barber, North Carolina, it's illegal for a cat to fight a dog (or vice versa).

It's illegal to sleep with chickens in Clawson City, Michigan ...and illegal to walk your elephant without a leash in Wisconsin.

The law prohibits barbers in Omaha, Nebraska, from shaving the chests of customers.

In California, it's illegal to hunt whales from your automobile. It's also against the law to use your dirty underwear as a dust rag.

In St. Louis, Missouri, it's illegal for you to drink beer out of a bucket while you're sitting on a curb.

Cotton Valley, Louisiana, law forbids cows and horses from sleeping in a bakery.

The maximum penalty for double parking in Minneapolis, Minnesota, is working on a chain gang with nothing to eat but bread and water.

For the past 150 years, Bolivia has averaged about one new government a year.

A FOOD IS BORN

Sure, you've eaten the foods...but at the BRI we know that you can't really *enjoy them unless you know their origins, too.*

CHEX CEREALS

When William Danforth was a child, the mother of a classmate bought a bolt of gingham cloth and made checkered pants, shirts, and dresses for every member of the family. The odd clothing made such an impression that townsfolk were still talking about it decades later.

That's why, when he wanted a distinctive trademark for his Ralston Purina products, Danforth adopted a checkerboard pattern. He became so obsessed with it that he wore red-check ties, jackets, and socks to work, and even changed the company's address to Checkerboard Square. Then, in 1937, he commissioned a checkerboard breakfast cereal, Wheat Chex. Rice Chex followed in 1950, Corn Chex in 1958, and Bran Chex in 1987.

KOOL-AID

Edwin E. Perkins, a prodigious entrepreneur of the 1920s, was the president of a company called Onor-Maid that sold more than 125 different household products—including spices, food flavorings, toiletries, and medicines, many of which Perkins had invented himself. One of his products was Fruit Smack, a fruit-flavored soft drink syrup that was popular with people who couldn't afford the new drink Coca-Cola. But Fruit Smack was shipped in glass bottles, which were expensive and frequently broke in transit. So when Perkins saw how successful the new powdered gelatin product, called Jell-O, was becoming, he decided to convert his syrup into powder form and sell it that way. (He also renamed the product Kool-Aid, modeling it loosely after the company name, Onor-Maid.)

RAGU SPAGHETTI SAUCE

When Giovanni and Assunta Cantisano stepped off the boat at Ellis Island at the turn of the century, they brought with them a few belongings...and the family recipe for spaghetti sauce. Giovanni opened a store selling Italian wine and foods. He thought he might be able to make a little extra money selling the family's spaghetti sauce there, too; so in 1937 he put some in mason jars and stocked his shelves with it. He never bothered to name it—he just called it *Ragú*, the Italian word for "sauce."

Today Ragú controls about 60% of the $550 million spaghetti sauce market.

GOLD MEDAL FLOUR

In 1856, Cadwallader C. Washburn built an enormous new flour mill in Minneapolis, Minnesota. However, flour from harsh Minnesota wheat was dark and not very popular. So Washburn hired an engineer to design a system for separating the bran from the rest of the wheat. The result: a whiter, more desirable flour. To help shake consumer bias against Minnesota wheat flour, in 1880 Washburn entered his flour in the first Millers' International Exhibition... and won the gold medal.

CELESTIAL SEASONINGS

In the 1960s, four hippies spent their time roaming the Rocky Mountains gathering herbs for their own homemade tea. They got so good at it that they decided to sell herbs to local health food stores. They bankrolled the operation by selling an old Volkswagen and named the company after one of the women, whose "cosmic" 1960s name was *Celestial*. Today, Celestial Seasonings is the largest herbal tea company on Earth.

HAWAIIAN PUNCH

"Hawaiian Punch was not invented in Hawaii," writes Vince Staten in *Can You Trust a Tomato in January?* "Nor was it invented by Hawaiians. It was invented in 1936 by a couple of Southern Californians, A. W. Leo and Tom Yates."

"It actually began as a soda fountain syrup. Mixed with water it was a drink, but it could also be used as an ice cream topping. By 1944, department stores were selling it in their gourmet food sections, so Leo began bottling it for consumers....At first it was only available as a syrup. [Then] Leo brought it out in a premixed 46-oz. bottle.... It owes a large part of its national popularity to its late-fifties TV commercials with a guy in a Hawaiian shirt offering a friend a Hawaiian Punch and giving him a sock in the puss."

Heavy thought: Hailstones can weigh as much as 1½ lbs.

THE GRIMM PHILOSOPHY

The Brothers Grimm are among the most famous storytellers in history. During the 1800s, they collected such classic folk tales as Rumpelstiltskin *and* Cinderella. *But these weren't the Disney versions—the view of life portrayed in Grimm tales was...well...grim. Here's an example.*

THE CAT AND THE MOUSE

A **certain cat made** the acquaintance of a mouse, and said so much about the great love and friendship she felt for her, that the mouse agreed that they should live and keep house together. "But we must put some food aside for winter, or we'll go hungry," said the cat; "And you, little mouse, can't venture out alone, or you'll be caught in a trap some day."

This good advice was followed, and a pot of fat was bought—but they didn't know where to put it. The cat gave it a lot of thought, and said: "I know no place where it will be safer than in the church, for no one dares take anything from there. We'll set it beneath the altar, and not touch it until we really need it."

So the pot was placed in safety, but it wasn't long before the cat had a great yearning for it, and said: "Little mouse; my cousin has brought a little son into the world, and has asked me to be godmother; he is white with brown spots, and I am to hold him over the font at the christening. Let me go out today, and you look after the house by yourself." "Yes," answered the mouse, "by all means go, and if you get anything very good to eat, think of me, I should like a drop of sweet red christening wine myself."

All this, however, was untrue; the cat had no cousin, and had not been asked to be godmother. She went straight to the church, stole to the pot of fat, began to lick at it, and licked the top of the fat off. Then she stretched herself in the sun. She didn't get home until evening. "Well, here you are again," said the mouse. "No doubt you've had a merry day." "All went well," answered the cat. "What name did they give the child?" "Top off!" said the cat quite coolly. "Top off!" cried the mouse, "What an unusual name. Is it a family name?" "What does that matter," said the cat, 'it's no worse than Crumb-stealer, as your god-children are called."

Before long the cat was seized by another fit of yearning. She said to the mouse: "You must do me a favor, and once more manage the house for a day alone. I am again asked to be godmother, and, as the child has a white ring round its neck, I cannot refuse." The good mouse consented, but the cat crept to the church and devoured half the pot of fat. When she went home the mouse inquired: "And what was this child named?" "Half-done," answered the cat. "Half-done?" replied the mouse, "Why, I never heard such a name in all my life!"

The cat's mouth soon began to water again. "All good things go in threes," said she, "I am asked to stand godmother again. The child is quite black, except for its paws. This only happens once every few years; you will let me go, won't you?" "Top-off! Half-done!" mused the mouse, "they are such odd names, they make me very thoughtful." "You sit at home," said the cat, "in your dark-gray fur coat and long tail, and are filled with fancies, that's because you do not go out in the daytime."

During the cat's absence the mouse cleaned the house and put it in order, but the greedy cat entirely emptied the pot of fat. She did not return home till night. The mouse at once asked what name had been given to the third child. "It will not please you more than the others," said the cat. "He is called All-gone." "All-gone!" cried the mouse, "That's the most suspicious name of all! I have never seen it in print. All-gone; what can that mean?" She shook her head, curled up, and lay down to sleep.

After this, no one invited the cat to be godmother, but when the winter came and there was no longer any food to be found outside, the mouse said: "Come, cat, let's go to the pot of fat which we've stored up for ourselves—we shall enjoy that." "Yes," answered the cat, "you'll enjoy it as much as you'd enjoy sticking that dainty tongue of yours out of the window." They set out on their way, but when they arrived, they found that the pot of fat was empty. "Alas!" said the mouse, "now I see what has happened! You a true friend! You have devoured all when you were standing godmother. First top off, then half done, then—" "Hold your tongue," cried the cat. "One word more, and I'll eat you too." "All gone" was already on the poor mouse's lips; scarcely had she spoken it before the cat sprang on her, seized her, and swallowed her down.

Verily, that is the way of the world.

ZAP!

Frank Zappa was one of the first rock musicians to admit publicly that he could think. Here are a few of his thoughts.

"In the fight between you and the world, back the world."

"One of my favorite philosophical tenets is that people will agree with you only if they already agree with you. You do not change people's minds."

"Without deviation, progress is not possible."

"In the old days your old man would say 'Be home by midnight' and you'd be home by midnight. Today parents daren't tell you what time to be in. They're frightened you won't come back."

"Most rock journalism is people who can't write interviewing people who can't talk for people who can't read."

"Everyone has the right to be comfortable on his own terms."

"Most people wouldn't know good music if it came up and bit them in the ass."

"Pop is the new politics. There is more truth in pop music than in most political statements rendered by our leaders, even when you get down to the level of really simplified pop records. What I'm saying is that's how bad politics is."

"If your children ever found out how lame you are, they'd kill you in your sleep."

"Politics is a valid concept but what we do is not really politics...it's a popularity contest. It has nothing to do with politics. What it is, is mass merchandising."

"I can't understand why anybody would want to devote their life to a cause like dope. It's the most boring pastime I can think of. It ranks a close second to television."

"I think cynicism is a positive value. You have to be cynical. You can't not be cynical. The more people that I have encouraged to be cynical, the better job I've done."

THE TV DINNER

We mentioned Swanson's TV dinners briefly in Uncle John's Sixth Bathroom Reader. *Here's the rest of the story, submitted by BRI correspondent Jack Mingo.*

IN THE BEGINNING

Credit the Swanson brothers, Gilbert and Clarke, with inventing the TV dinner in 1951. The Swansons owned the nation's largest turkey plant in Omaha, Nebraska, and were frustrated that most Americans ate turkey only on Thanksgiving. They wanted to make turkey an everyday part of the American diet.

GONE TO POT

Their first attempt was the Swanson turkey pot pie. It was extremely popular. In fact, people started demanding more variety. The Swansons tried another approach: Inspired by popular diner "blue plate specials" in which an entire meal was served on a segmented plate, the Swansons began putting individual meal courses on segmented aluminum trays.

BALANCING ACT

In the early 1950s, television was taking over America's living rooms, and Swanson decided to sponsor its own show, "Ted Mack's Family Hour." On the night of the show's premiere, Gilbert Swanson invited some friends over for a buffet dinner to celebrate. One of the guests looked around and pointed out how funny it looked for everybody to be balancing trays on their laps in front of the TV.

Swanson suddenly thought about the product his company was working on. It would be perfect for eating in front of television—and tying it into the TV craze couldn't hurt. Why not call it a TV dinner? Gilbert mentioned the idea to his brother, who suggested putting a picture of a TV on the box, with the dinner coming off the screen. In January 1952, the first Swanson's TV Dinner rolled off the line. It contained turkey with cornbread stuffing and gravy, buttered peas, and sweet potatoes in orange and butter sauce, and cost only 98¢.

When TV lost its novelty in the 1960s, Swanson redesigned the package, got rid of the picture of the TV, and downplayed the TV Dinner brand name. By 1984 it was completely off the package.

First vehicle to use inflatable rubber tires: Queen Victoria's carriage, in 1846.

Q & A: ASK THE EXPERTS

Everyone's got a question or two they want answered—basic stuff like "Why is the sky blue?" Here are a few of those questions, with answers from books by some top trivia experts.

NAVEL ENCOUNTER

Q: *Where does belly-button lint come from?*

A: "Your navel is one of the few places on your body where perspiration has a chance to accumulate before evaporating. Lint from your clothing, cottons especially, adheres to the wet area and remains after the moisture departs." (From *The Straight Dope*, by Cecil Adams)

MYTH-INFORMATION

Q: *Why do the symbols ♂ and ♀ represent male and female?*

A: "They're related to Greek mythology. The female symbol ♀ is supposed to represent a woman holding a hand mirror, and is associated with Aphrodite, the Greek goddess of beauty. The male symbol ♂ represents a spear and a shield and is associated with the Greek god of war, Ares. The male and female symbols also represent the planets Mars (the Roman god of war) and Venus (the Roman goddess of beauty)." (From *The Book of Totally Useless Information*, by Don Voorhees)

CIRCULAR LOGIC

Q: *Why do clocks run clockwise?*

A: No one knows for sure, but here's one answer: "Before the advent of clocks, we used sundials. In the Northern Hemisphere, the shadows rotated in the direction we now call 'clockwise.' The clock hands were built to mimic the natural movements of the sun. If clocks had been invented in the Southern Hemisphere, [perhaps] 'clockwise' would be in the opposite direction." (From *Why Do Clocks Run Clockwise? and Other Imponderables*, by David Feldman)

First U.S. novel, by W. Brown, 1789, was about "seduction, incest, abduction, rape, suicide."

DON'T WORRY, BEE HAPPY

Q: *We've all heard the phrase "busy as a bee." Are bees really busy?*

A: Judge for yourself: "In order to fill its honey sac, the average worker bee has to visit between 1,000 and 1,500 individual florets of clover. About 60 full loads of nectar are necessary to produce a mere thimbleful of honey. Nevertheless, during a favorable season, a single hive might store two pounds of honey *a day*—representing approximately five million individual bee journeys." (From *Can Elephants Swim?* compiled by Robert M. Jones)

STAYING COOL

Q: *Does iced tea or iced coffee really cool you off?*

A: "Contrary to popular belief, neither iced tea nor iced coffee will really cool you off much because they contain caffeine, which constricts the blood vessels. Because of this effect, coffee or tea, either iced or hot, can cause you to become overheated...so it's best to avoid these drinks on hot days. But don't substitute a cola drink for them; colas also contain caffeine. Instead, drink water or juice." (From *FYI, For Your Information*, by Hal Linden)

GONE TO THE DOGS

Q: *Is a dog year really the equivalent of seven human years?*

A: "No—it is actually five to six years. The average life expectancy of a dog is 12-14 years. However, most dogs mature sexually within six to nine months, so in a sense there is no strict correspondence to human years." (From *The Book of Answers*, by Barbara Berliner)

TO PEE OR NOT TO PEE?

Q: *Why does people's pee smell funny after eating asparagus?*

A: "The odor is caused by an acid present in the vegetable, and it doesn't happen to everybody. Whether you produce the odor or not is determined genetically." In a British study using 800 volunteers, only 43% of the people "had the characteristic ability to excrete the six sulfur alkyl compounds that combine to produce the odor in urine. This inherited ability is a dominant trait. If one of your parents had it, so will you." (From *Why Do Men Have Nipples?* by Katherine Dunn)

IT LOSES SOMETHING IN TRANSLATION...

Have you ever thought that you were communicating brilliantly, only to find out other people thought you were speaking nonsense? That's a particularly easy mistake when you're speaking a foreign language. A few classic examples:

BUT HE'S NOT SQUEEZING THEM

When President Jimmy Carter arrived in Poland in 1977, he made a brief speech to press and officials. But his interpreter delivered a slightly different speech. Carter said he had "left the United States that day." His interpreter said he'd "abandoned" it. Carter referred to the Poles' "desires for the future." His interpreter translated this as "lusts for the future." And, finally, the interpreter explained to the crowd: "The president says he is pleased to be here in Poland grasping your private parts."

LOOKING FOR PROTECTION

Shannon, Ireland (UPI) — "A young Russian couple caused an embarrassing mix-up at Shannon Airport when they were mistaken for political defectors.

"The pair, on a technical stopover on the Havana-Moscow Aeroflot route, approached a counter at the big Shannon duty-free store Monday. In halting English, the man asked for "protection," according to an airport spokesman.

"He was quickly whisked away for questioning by immigration authorities. But after 20 minutes, officials determined it was not political protection he was after, but sexual protection. He just wanted to buy some condoms."

MORE BIRTH CONTROL

In one campaign to introduce its ballpoint pens to Mexico, the Parker Pen Co. used the slogan "It won't leak in your pocket and embarrass you." The company's translators mistakenly used the verb *embarazar*, which sounds like "to embarrass" but actually means "to become pregnant." The ad appeared to suggest that the pen could prevent unwanted pregnancies.

New Mexico is the only state named after a country.

CULTURAL THAI'S

"Thais still talk about President Lyndon Johnson's visit in the mid-'60s, when, seated next to King Bhumibol Adulyadej on national television, the lanky Texan hitched his foot up over his thigh and pointed his shoe directly at the king—a common obscene gesture in that country. It didn't relieve tensions when, on the same telecast, the American president gave the Thai queen a big "hi, honey" hug. Solemn tradition in Thailand demands that nobody touches the queen."

—***The Washington Post***

COMIC DELIVERY

According to Roger Axtell, in his book *Do's and Taboos of Hosting International Visitors*, a high-ranking insurance company executive visiting Japan in the 1980s delivered a speech that began with a joke. It went over well...but later on he learned that it was translated something like this:

> American businessman is beginning speech with thing called joke. I am not certain why, but all American businessmen believe it necessary to start speech with joke. [Pause] He is telling joke now, but frankly you would not understand it, so I won't translate it. He thinks I am telling you joke now. [Pause] Polite thing to do when he finishes is to laugh. [Pause] He is getting close. [Pause] Now!

"The audience not only laughed," Axtell says, "but in typical generous Japanese style, they stood and applauded as well. After the speech, not realizing what had transpired, the American remembered going to the translator and saying, 'I've been giving speeches in this country for several years and you are the first translator who knows how to tell a good joke.' "

WHAT A GUY!

When the Perdue Chicken Co. translated its slogan—"It takes a tough man to make a tender chicken" —into Spanish, they ended up with "It takes a hard [sexually aroused] man to make a chicken affectionate."

STRANGE LAWSUITS

We've been including this section in the Bathroom Reader *for years, and we've never run out of material. In fact, we've got a bulging folder of articles we haven't even used. It seems that people are getting weirder and weirder.*

THE PLAINTIFF: J. R. Costigan

THE DEFENDANT: Bobby Mackey's Music World, a country music bar in Wilder, Kentucky

THE LAWSUIT: In papers filed in small claims court, Costigan claimed a ghost "punched and kicked him" while he was using the bar's restroom one night in 1993. He sued the bar, asking for $1,000 in damages and demanding that a sign be put up in the restroom warning of the ghost's presence.

The club's lawyer filed a motion to dismiss the case, citing the difficulty of getting the ghost into court to testify for the defense.

THE VERDICT: The case was dismissed.

THE PLAINTIFF: Frederick Newhall Woods IV, serving a life sentence for the infamous Chowchilla, California, school bus kidnapping.

THE DEFENDANT: The American Broadcasting Company

THE LAWSUIT: In 1976, Woods and two accomplices kidnapped a bus driver and 26 elementary school students and buried them underground. When ABC aired a TV movie docudrama about the kidnapping in 1994, Woods was offended. He sued the network, claiming that the show "portrayed (him) as being callous, vicious, hardened, wild-eyed, diabolical, and uncaring."

THE VERDICT: Unknown.

THE PLAINTIFF: Carl Sagan, world-famous astronomer

THE DEFENDANT: Apple Computer, Inc.

THE LAWSUIT: Late in 1993, computer designers at Apple code-named a new computer model *Sagan*. Traditionally, this is an honor—"You pick a name of someone you respect," explained one employee. "And the code is only used while the computer is being developed. It never makes it out of the company." Nonetheless, Sagan's lawyers complained that the code was "an illegal usurption of his name for commercial purposes" and demanded that it be changed. So Apple designers changed it to BHA. When Sagan heard that it stood for "Butt-Head Astronomer, " he sued, contending that "Butt-Head" is "defamatory on its face."

THE VERDICT: Pending (in 1994).

THE PLAINTIFF: Barry Manilow

THE DEFENDANT: K-BIG FM, a Los Angeles radio station

THE LAWSUIT: In 1994, the station ran a TV ad campaign saying what they *wouldn't* play—namely Barry Manilow songs. Manilow sued, claiming "irreparable damage to his reputation"

THE VERDICT: Settled out of court for an undisclosed amount.

THE PLAINTIFF: Saul Lapidus, a New York City landlord

THE DEFENDANT: Empire Szechuan Gourmet

THE LAWSUIT: When the local Chinese restaurant left takeout menus at his building, Lapidus billed them for cleanup costs. When they refused to pay, he took them to court.

THE VERDICT: Lapidus won; Empire paid the bill.

THE PLAINTIFF: David Pelzman, owner of David's on Main, a Columbus, Ohio, restaurant

THE DEFENDANT: Jeff Burrey, 24, a (former) customer

THE LAWSUIT: In 1993, Burrey made a reservation for four at the restaurant but didn't show up. So Pelzman sued him for $440 ($60 per person, and $200 for the private detective he hired to track Burrey down). Incredulous, Burrey filed a $10,000 countersuit, alleging defamation, fraud, and misrepresentation.

"If they can sue a customer for not showing up for a reservation," Burrey said, "then a customer can sue the restaurant for having to wait 15 minutes to be seated."

THE VERDICT: Pending (in 1994).

Man of the world: Both China and Russia have their own "Tarzan" legends.

WHAT IS SPAM?

Everybody's tried it and hardly anyone says they like it...but 30% of all American households have a can on hand. So how much do you know about SPAM? How much do you want *to know? Not much, probably. Too bad—we're going to tell you about it anyway.*

MAKING A SILK PURSE OUT OF A SOW'S EAR

It's a question as timeless as the pork-packing industry itself: Once you've removed all the choice meat from the carcass of a pig, what do you do with all the pig parts nobody wants?

That's the question the folks at the George A. Hormel Company faced in 1937. Their solution: Take the *parts* that nobody wants and make them into a *loaf* nobody wants. Jack Mingo describes the historic moment in his book *How the Cadillac Got Its Fins:*

> Seeing thousands of pounds of pork shoulders piling up in the Hormel coolers in 1937 gave one of the company's executives an idea: Why not chop the meat up, add some spices and meat from other parts of the pig, and form it into small, hamlike loaves? Put it in a can and fill the excess space with gelatin from the pig's leftover skin and bones—you could probably keep the meat edible for months without refrigeration. They tried it. It worked. Hormel's Spiced Ham quickly found a niche in the market. It was inexpensive, savory, and convenient, and it didn't need refrigeration.

PORCINE PLAGIARISM

But pig parts were piling up just as high at other pork packers, and as soon as they saw Hormel's solution they began selling their own pig loafs. Afraid of being lost in the sow shuffle, Hormel offered a $100 prize to anyone who could come up with a brand name that would make its pork product stand out from imitators. The winner: A brother of one of the Hormel employees, who suggested turning "*Sp*iced H*am*" into *SPAM*.

PIGS AT WAR

Described by one writer as "a pink brick of meat encased in a gelatinous coating," SPAM seems pretty gross to folks who aren't used to it (and even to plenty who are). It probably wouldn't have become popular if it hadn't been for World War II.

Because it was cheap, portable, and didn't need refrigeration, SPAM was an ideal product to send into battle with U.S. GIs. It became such a common sight in mess halls (where it earned the nickname "the ham that didn't pass its physical") that many GIs swore they'd never eat the stuff again. Even General Dwight Eisenhower complained about too much SPAM in army messes.

THEIR SECRET SHAME

American G.I.s *said* they hated SPAM, but evidence suggests otherwise. Forced to eat canned pork over a period of several years, millions of soldiers developed a taste for it, and when they returned home they brought it with them. SPAM sales shot up in supermarkets after the war.

Laugh if you want (even Hormel calls it "the Rodney Dangerfield of luncheon meat—it don't get no respect"), but SPAM is still immensely popular: Americans consume 3.8 cans of it every second, or 122 million cans a year. That gives SPAM a 75% share of the canned-meat market.

SPAM FACTS

• More than five billion cans of SPAM have been sold around the world since the product was invented in 1937. "Nowhere," says Carolyn Wyman in her book *I'm a SPAM Fan,*"is SPAM more prized than in South Korea, where black-market SPAM regularly flows from U.S. military bases and locally produced knockoffs, such as Lospam, abound. In fact, young Korean men are just as likely to show up at the house of a woman they are courting with a nine-can gift pack of SPAM as wine or chocolate."

• SPAM may have helped defeat Hitler. Nikita Khruschev, himself a war veteran, credited a U.S. Army shipment of SPAM with keeping Russian troops alive during World War II. "We had lost our most fertile, food-bearing lands," he wrote in *Khruschev Remembers*, "Without SPAM, we wouldn't have been able to feed our army."

• SPAM isn't as gross as legend would have you believe. There aren't any lips, eyes, or other pig nasties in it—just pork shoulder, ham, salt, sugar, and sodium nitrate.

Built-in bias? 96.1% of all television writers are white.

TEST YOUR "BEVERLY HILLBILLIES" IQ

What do you know about one of the most popular shows in TV history? Take this quiz and see. (*Answers on page* 666.)

1. How did Paul Henning, the creator of "The Beverly Hillbillies," get the idea for the show?

A) He based the story on his own experience of moving from the Ozarks to California with his hillbilly uncle. (The character Jethro is loosely autobiographical.)

B) He was touring a Civil War site while on vacation with his wife and mother-in-law.

C) Someone told him the story of Ned Klamper, a Texas sharecropper who struck oil blowing up a tree stump, and moved to Las Vegas with his family. Henning changed the names and locations so that he wouldn't have to pay for the story.

2. What was planned as the original location for the show?

A) New York

B) Beverly Hills—Henning wanted a wealthy town with the word "hills" in it...and Beverly Hills fit the bill perfectly.

C) Riyadh, Saudi Arabia—Henning originally conceived of the show as the "Arabian Hillbillies." According to the original storyline, Jed strikes it rich and moves to the Middle East so that he can learn the oil business from a greedy Saudi prince. He brings Granny (originally conceived as a Bible-thumping, anti-Arab bigot) with him; she would have had run-ins with merchants, camel dealers, etc. But protests from the Saudi royal family forced Henning to move the location to California and remake the greedy prince into Milburn Drysdale, head of the Commerce Bank.

3. Granny was the last character cast, and Irene Ryan was a long shot for the part from the get-go. Who almost got her part?

A) A real live hillbilly—but she was illiterate and couldn't read the script.

From 1950 to 1971, buying or displaying a Chinese stamp was considered "trading with the enemy."

B) Actress Bea Benaderet—but her boobs were too big for the part. She went on to play Cousin Pearl in *The Beverly Hillbillies* and later had her own show, *Petticoat Junction*.

C) Both of the above.

D) None of the above—There was no "Granny" character called for in the original story, but Irene Ryan, wife of Filmways chairman Jack Ryan, had just completed an acting class and was itching to try out her training. She badgered her husband for a full nine months for a part in one of his shows, but he refused to give her one...until she threatened him with divorce, that is. He finally gave in and ordered that the character be created for *The Beverly Hillbillies*. Why that show? He was convinced the series would bomb.

4. Why was Raymond Bailey so believable in his role as Milburn Drysdale, the Clampett's banker (and a complete jerk) who lives next door to them and manages their family fortune?

A) He really was a banker.

B) He really was a jerk.

C) Trained as a classical Shakespearean performer by Lawrence Olivier, Bailey was one of the greatest actors of his time. The other members of the *Hillbillies* called him "the human chameleon" and boasted that he could have played Granny if he had wanted to.

5. Donna Douglas, who played Elly May, was as friendly in real life as she was on the show, but she was downcast and moody when she returned from vacation to film the 1966 season. Why?

A) She was bitten by a wild racoon during a camping trip and had to endure more than a dozen painful rabies shots into her abdomen. The experience traumatized her so much so that she didn't want to work with animals anymore. But studio officials insisted...and for a while she was depressed because she had to work with them.

B) She fell in love with Elvis Presley while filming a movie with him in the off-season...but he didn't return her feelings.

C) Eager to cash in on her affinity with "critters," Douglas wanted to form her own "Elly May" pet food company...but studio officials vetoed the idea and she spent the entire 1966 season in a funk.

Playing football was outlawed at Yale University in 1822. Maximum fine: 50¢.

6. How well did the show fare with critics and the public?

A) The critics loved the show's traditional family values (Jed took care of Granny, and Elly May and Jethro lived at home until they married)...but the public hated it.

B) The critics hated it—even so, the public loved it.

C) The critics *and* the public loved it, especially Ryan's portrayal of Grannie—she became known as "the backwoods Bette Davis."

7. At first, Buddy Ebsen didn't want the part of Jed. Why?

A) He'd already played too many hillbillies and was afraid of being typecast as a hayseed.

B) He hated hats, especially the ratty old one he wore on the show.

C) He'd lost the part of the Tin Woodsman in the 1939 film *The Wizard of Oz* (and almost lost his life after the poisonous silver makeup infected his eyes and lungs and forced him to drop out of the film), and never got over it. He was trying to drum up support for a sequel. He took the part of Jed after the Oz project collapsed.

8. What did the owners of the Bel-Air mansion used in the series think of the show?

A) They loved it—after the show became popular they sold the estate for 10 times what they had paid for it.

B) They hated it—the house became a sort of West Coast Graceland, with fans of the show hounding them day and night.

C) They never saw it—the house was owned by Ravi Shankar, the famous guru and mentor to the Beatles. He didn't own a TV.

9. What ill-fated celebrity had a part in the show as a typist in the Commerce Bank's secretarial pool?

A) Janis Joplin

B) Sharon Tate

C) Christine Jorgenson

10. What was Granny Clampett's real name on the show?

A) Elvira Clampett

B) Daisy May Moses

C) Nadene Peckinpah

Brazilian fans are so rowdy that many of the country's sports fields are surrounded by moats.

I WAS A TEENAGE MONSTER MOVIE

In the late 1950s, teenage culture was big business—Elvis, James Dean, and rock 'n' roll were bringing in the bucks. That's when (not so coincidentally) a brand new kind of exploitation film appeared—the teenage monster movie. Today it's just a cliche, but "I Was a Teenage...(fill in the blank)" was hot stuff for awhile. Here's Uncle John's salute to the best (and worst) of them.

I WAS A TEENAGE WEREWOLF (1957)

Starring: Michael Landon, Whit Bissell, Yvonne Lime, Barney Phillips, Joseph Mell. Director: Gene Fowler Jr.

The Plot: Tony Rivers—played by Michael Landon in his first feature film—is a hot-tempered teenager who's always getting into fights. (In fact, the first scene is a fist thrown right at the audience.) But when he accidentally hits his girlfriend, Arlene, he realizes things are out of control. So he decides to see Dr. Brandon, a local psychiatrist.

Bad move. Brandon doesn't want to cure Tony...he wants to experiment on him. Using "retrogression therapy," he injects Tony with a serum and hypnotizes the teenager to bring out his "primitive" side. Now whenever Tony gets startled, he grows body hair and fangs and suddenly gets the urge to kill. After killing at least one person and scaring the hell out of everyone in town, the creature is gunned down by the cops. Of course, he kills the crazy shrink just before he dies. Inevitable final line (delivered by the cop): "It is not for man to interfere in the ways of God."

Commentary: Not a bad film, as '50s schlock goes. Legend has it that after seeing the poster, American International Pictures' (AIP) head Samuel Z. Arkoff declared it "A million dollar title in a hundred thousand dollar movie." AIP knew how to exploit teenagers, but by today's standards, they kept it pretty tame. In her website, "And You Call Yourself a Scientist!," Liz writes:

> Astonishingly, *I Was A Teenage Werewolf* provoked the ire of politicians and moral crusaders alike, who accused the film of "promoting juvenile delinquency." One can only assume that—as is often the case with politicians and moral crusaders—they hadn't actually seen

Legal logic: In 19th-century England, attempting suicide was a crime punishable by death.

the film they were attacking.

It is quite clear that at first AIP underestimated the cash crop their adolescent audiences represented. Later, when the money began pouring in, the executives pitched their films more and more to the teenagers, and cared less and less about upsetting the adults; but this early effort is not only a moral little film, it is populated with some of the best behaved teenagers and the most caring adults ever put on screen. Cops, teachers, parents—they only want what's best for the kids. There's even a subplot about the perils of parental neglect. As for the kids themselves, well, you should see what constitutes their idea of a hot party. *Warning*: before you get to the good part of this film, you have to sit through some of the most painfully embarrassing teenage party scenes ever committed to film, which cause Tony's girlfriend to announce that "I've never had so much fun!"—sad, but probably true.

IMMORTAL LINES

They don't write 'em like this anymore:

Dr. Brandon (the Mad psychiatrist): "At last, after years of searching, I've found a suitable person for my experiment! His record at school, what the principal told me, and what I learned through Dt-Sgt Donovan gives him the proper disturbed emotional background. And with what I found out from the physical examination, this boy's my perfect subject! There were certain tell-tale marks on his body only I would recognize..."
Assistant: "But you know what might happen!"
Brandon: "'Might'? In science, one must be sure!"

Brandon: "Mankind is on the brink of destroying itself! The only hope for the human race is to hurl it back to its primitive dawn, to start all over again. What's one life compared to such a triumph?"

Brandon: "Through hypnosis, I'm going to regress this boy back... back into the primitive past that lurks within him! I'm going to transform him, and unleash the savage instincts that lie hidden within!"

Janitor: "I know what killed him. He was killed by...by a werewolf!"
Policeman: "A what?"
Janitor: "In the old country, in my little village in the Carpathian mountains, there was a story...."

Japan has only half the population of the U.S., but buys 10 times as many comic books.

Assistant: "Alfred, you read the paper! You know what happened!"
Brandon: "There's a difference between a newspaper story and a scientific report!"
Assistant: "Aren't you wasting your time? Or do you have a second victim in view?"
Brandon: "I'm not wasting my time, and I don't like to hear the subject of a world-shaking experiment referred to as a 'victim'!"

Brandon: "We'll have it all on film, from the time I give him the injection through the transformation! And then no one will doubt my word! Even the most exacting, the most sceptical of scientists will be convinced that I have penetrated the deepest secrets of creation!"

MORE TEENAGE MONSTER-MANIA

***I Was A Teenage Frankenstein* (1957)** "Herman Cohen's sequel to *I Was a Teenage Werewolf*, with Whit Bissell reappearing as a mad doctor—a relative of the infamous Baron. Ludicrous as its title, with severed limbs graphically offered up for their shock value (and severed limbs in 1957 were an onscreen rarity)....You, too, will be a teenage zombie if you sit through this."

—***Creature Features,* John Stanley**

***Teenage Caveman* (1958)** "After...*I Was a Teenage Frankenstein*, American International Pictures further mined the youth market with–what else—*Teenage Caveman*. Robert Vaughn stars as the boy (he would later become the man...From U.N.C.L.E., that is), who defies his elders by venturing...into the forbidden land...where he finds 'the monster who kills with a touch.' Directed by Roger Corman in ten days on a $70,000 budget."

—Cult Flicks and Trash Pics

***Teenagers from Outer Space* (1959)** "'They blast the Flesh off humans!' claimed the ads. A young alien falls for a teenage earth girl and ruins the plans of his invading cohorts by blowing them up. The invaders, who arrived in a flying saucer, carry deadly ray guns and breed giant lobster monsters for food. Only the shadow of one of the creatures is shown in this extremely low-budget feature."

—***The Psychotronic Encyclopedia of Film,* Michael Weldon**

DISASTER FILMS

Some films, like The Poseidon Adventure *and* The Towering Inferno, *are* about *disasters. Other films* are *disasters. Take these losers, for example:*

ISHTAR (1987)

Description: Dustin Hoffman and Warren Beatty starred as inept singer-songwriters who travel to the Middle East looking for work.

Dollars and Sense: Budgeted at $27.5 million, *Ishtar* wound up costing $45 million...and losing $37.3 million.

Wretched Excess: Director Elaine May decided the desert's natural sand dunes didn't look authentic—so workers spent nearly 10 days scraping away the dunes to make the desert flat. *Ishtar's* crew spent days looking for a suitable animal to play a blind camel. They found the perfect camel, but when they came back to pick it up, the owner had eaten it. Dustin Hoffman and Warren Beatty each received $6 million—roughly the cost for filming the entire film *Platoon*.

The Critics Speak: "It's interesting only in the way that a traffic accident is interesting." —Roger Ebert

INCHON (1982)

Description: A 140-minute epic about General Douglas MacArthur's military excursion into Korea. Bankrolled by Reverend Sun Myung Moon, who shipped the entire cast and crew to South Korea to film on location.

Dollars and Sense: "They wasted tremendous amounts of money in every way imaginable," said one crew member. "Always in cash. I got the feeling they were trying to make the film cost as much as possible." The film ultimately cost $48 million...and *lost* $48 million, making it the biggest bomb of the 1980s.

Wretched Excess: At first *Inchon* was dismissed as just another weirdo cult project, but then Moon began to sign big names to the project, including Jacqueline Bisset, Ben Gazzara...and Sir Laurence Olivier as General Douglas MacArthur. "People ask me why I'm playing in this picture," Olivier told a critic. "The answer is simple: Money, dear boy." He was paid $1.25 million for the part

From the age of 20 to his death, Winston Churchill smoked an estimated 300,000 cigars.

...and later sued for an additional $1 million in overtime when the film ran months behind schedule. Terence Young received $1.8 million to direct.

Cast and crew waited for two months for their equipment to clear customs—at a cost of $200,000 a day!

A typical day of shooting featured a fleet of ships, six fighter bombers, and a bagpipe marching band. The film's opening was hyped with "The *Inchon* Million Dollar Sweepstakes." Prizes included a Rolls Royce, paid vacations to Korea, MacArthur-style sunglasses and "50,000 beautifully illustrated *Inchon* souvenir books."

The Critics Speak: "Quite possibly the worst movie ever made... stupefyingly incompetent." —Peter Rainer, L.A. *Herald Examiner*

"A larger bomb than any dropped during the Korean police action."—*Variety*

HEAVEN'S GATE (1981)

Description: Written and directed by Michael Cimino, whose *Deer Hunter* had won Oscars for best director and best film the previous year. Kris Kristofferson starred as an idealistic Harvard graduate who became a U.S. marshall in the Wyoming territory.

Dollars and Sense: Studio executives put Cimino's girlfriend in charge of controlling expenses; he wound up spending nearly $200,000 a day. Originally budgeted at $7.8 million, the film cost $44 million to make. It lost over $34.5 million.

Wretched Excess: Harvard refused to let Cimino shoot the film's prologue on their campus, so for an additional $4 million, the director took his crew and cast to England and shot the scene at Oxford. In the final version, it was less than 10 minutes of the film.

They picked Glacier National Park as their ideal location, then painted acres of unspoiled grassland there with green and yellow paint to make it look more "natural." Two hundred extras were hired for a roller skating scene, given a cassette with their skating music, and sent home for six months to practice.

The Critics Speak: "*Heaven's Gate* fails so completely," Vincent Canby wrote in The *New York Times*, "that you might suspect Mr. Cimino sold his soul to the Devil to obtain the success of *The Deer Hunter*, and the Devil has just come around to collect."

MYTH AMERICA

More of the stories we now recognize as American myth, but were taught as history for many years. These might surprise you.

MANHATTAN ISLAND

The Myth: In 1626, Peter Minuit bought Manhattan Island from the Canarsee Indians for $24 worth of beads and other trinkets.

The Truth: Minuit did give 60 guilders (roughly $24) worth of beads, knives, axes, clothes, and rum to Chief Seyseys of the Canarsee tribe "to let us live amongst them" on Manhattan Island—but the Canarsee actually got the best of the deal...because they didn't own the island in the first place. They lived on the other side of the East River, in *Brooklyn*, and only visited the southern tip of Manhattan to fish and hunt. The Weckquaesgeeks tribe, which lived on the upper three-fourths of the island, had a much stronger claim to the island, and were furious when they learned they'd been left out of the deal. They fought with the Dutch settlers for years until the Dutch finally paid them, too.

THE LIBERTY BELL

The Myth: The Liberty Bell, which rang at the first public reading of the Declaration of Independence, has always been a precious symbol of our nation's heritage.

The Truth: The bell, installed in the Pennsylvania State House in Philadelphia in 1753, was almost bartered off as scrap metal in 1828 when the building was being refurbished. According to one account, "The Philadelphia city fathers...contracted John Wilbank, a bell maker from Germantown, Pennsylvania, to cast a replacement for the Liberty Bell. He agreed to knock $400 off his bill in exchange for the 2,000-pound relic. When Wilbank went to collect it, however, he decided it wasn't worth the trouble. 'Drayage costs more than the bell's worth,' he said." The city of Philadelphia actually sued to force him to take it. But Wilbank just gave it back to them as a gift, "unaware that he'd just bartered away what would become the most venerated symbol of American independence."

WASHINGTON CROSSING THE DELAWARE

The Myth: Emanuel Leutze's famous painting is a dramatically accurate portrayal of General Washington's famous crossing.

The Truth: According to Scott Morris, there are inaccuracies.

• "The crossing was in 1776, but the Stars and Stripes flag shown wasn't adopted until the next year."

• "The real boats were forty to sixty feet long, larger than the rather insubstantial ones shown."

• The soldiers wouldn't have pointed their guns in the air, because it was snowing.

• "Washington certainly knew not to stand—a pose that would have made the boat unstable, and put him in danger of falling overboard."

• The river in the painting isn't the Delaware. Leutze worked in Dusseldorf, Germany, and used the Rhine River as his model.

HAMILTON WAS AN INNOCENT VICTIM

The Myth: Alexander Hamilton, who was was killed in a duel with Vice President Aaron Burr in 1804, was too decent a man to shoot his rival. So he shot in the air instead...and died when Burr paid him back by shooting to kill.

The Truth: "For nearly two centuries," Steve Talley writes in *Bland Ambition,*"history saw Hamilton as something of a martyr who...never meant to harm Burr. But it now appears that he lost the duel...*because he tried to use an unfair advantage* to kill the vice president." Talley continues:

> As part of the U.S. bicentennial celebration, the Smithsonian Institution decided to have the pistols used in the Burr-Hamilton duel restored. What they found was that the guns—which had been provided for the duel by Hamilton—had several features that were not allowed on dueling pistols...most significantly, a special hair-trigger feature. By surreptitiously setting the trigger so that only a half pound of pressure—instead of the normal ten to twelve pounds—was needed to fire the gun, a duelist could gain an incredible advantage, since both men were to fire at the same time. Instead of displaying nearly godlike mercy, Hamilton planned to kill Burr before Burr had a chance to fire. But in his nervousness, Hamilton apparently held the gun too tightly, firing it too soon, and the shot struck the leaves over Burr's head.

BOW-WOW...OR WANG-WANG?

It's a truism we all learn as kids: A dog goes bow-wow...a cat goes meow...etc. A universal language, right? Nope. Believe it or not, animal sounds vary from language to language. Here are some examples.

PIGS
English: Oink Oink!
Russian: Kroo!
French: Groin Groin!
German: Grunz!

ROOSTERS
English: Cock-a-doodle-doo!
Arabic: Ku-ku-ku-ku!
Russian: Ku-ka-rzhi-ku!
Japanese: Ko-ki-koko!
Greek: Ki-ki-ri-koo!
Hebrew: Ku-ku-ri-ku!

DUCKS
English: Quack Quack!
Swedish: Kvack Kvack!
Arabic: Kack-kack-kack!
Chinese: Ga-ga!
French: Guahn Quahn!

FROGS
English: Croak!
Spanish: Croack!
German: Quak-quak!
Swedish: Kouack!
Russian: Kva-kva!

TWEETY-BIRDS
English: Tweet Tweet!
French: Kwi-kwi!
Hebrew: Tsef Tsef!
Chinese: Chu-chu!
German: Tschiep Tschiep!

GEESE
English: Honk Honk!
Arabic: Wack Wack!
German: Schnatter-schnatter!
Japanese: Boo Boo!

OWLS
English: Who-whoo!
Japanese: Ho-ho!
German: Koh-koh-a-oh!
Russian: Ookh!

CATS
English: Meow!
Hebrew: Miyau!
German: Miau!
French: Miaou!
Spanish (and Portuguese and German): Miau!

DOGS
English: Bow-wow!
Swedish: Voff Voff!
Hebrew: Hav Hav!
Chinese: Wang-wang!
Japanese: Won-won!
Swahili: Hu Hu Hu Huuu!

CHICKENS
English: Cluck-cluck!
French: Cot-cot-cot-codet!
German: Gak-gak!
Hebrew: Pak-pak-pak!
Arabic: Kakakakakakakakaka!

The average person laughs seven to eight times a day.

BOMBECKISMS

Thoughts from Erma Bombeck, one of America's wittiest dispensers of common sense.

"A child develops individuality long before he develops taste."

"Never go to a doctor whose office plants have died."

"The bad times I can handle. It's the good times that drive me crazy. When is the other shoe going to drop?"

"My mother phones daily to ask, 'Did you just try to reach me?' When I reply 'No,' she adds, 'So, if you're not too busy, call me while I'm still alive,' and hangs up."

"There are few certainties when you travel. One of them is that the moment you arrive in a foreign country, the American dollar will fall like a stone."

"I firmly believe kids don't want your understanding. They want your trust, your compassion, your blinding love and your car keys, but you try to understand them and you're in big trouble."

"To my way of thinking, the American family started to decline when parents began to communicate with their children. When we began to 'rap,' 'feed into one another,' and encourage our kids to 'let things hang out' that mother didn't know about and would rather not."

"If a man watches three football games in a row, he should be declared legally dead."

"It seems rather incongruous that in a society of supersophisticated communication, we often suffer from a shortage of listeners."

"I will never engage in a winter sport with an ambulance parked at the bottom of the hill."

"When you look like your passport photo, it's time to go home."

"Guilt is a gift that keeps on giving."

"LET ME WRITE SIGN—I SPEAK ENGLISH"

When signs in a foreign country are written in English, any combination of words is possible. Here are some real-life examples.

"It is forbidden to steal hotel towels please. If you are not person to do such thing is please not to read notis."

—Japanese hotel

"You are invited to take advantage of the chambermaid."

—Japanese hotel

"Do not enter the lift backwards, and only when lit up."

—Leipzig hotel elevator

"To move the cabin, push button for wishing floor. If the cabin should enter more persons, each one should press a number of wishing floor. Driving is then going alphabetically by national order."

—Belgrade hotel elevator

"Please leave your values at the front desk."

—Paris hotel elevator

"Our wines leave you nothing to hope for."

—Swiss restaurant menu

"Visitors are expected to complain at the office between the hours of 9 and 11 a.m. daily."

—Athens hotel

"The flattening of underwear with pleasure is the job of the chambermaid."

—Yugoslavia hotel

"The lift is being fixed for the next day. During that time we regret that you will be unbearable."

—Bucharest hotel lobby

"Not to perambulate corridors in the hours of repose in the boots of ascension."

—Austrian hotel for skiers

"Salad a firm's own make; limpid red beet soup with cheesy dumplings in the form of a finger; roasted duck let loose; beef rashers beaten up in the country people's fashion."

—Menu at a Polish hotel

According to many psychologists, fingernail biting is a sign of stubbornness.

PHRASE ORIGINS

Here are the origins of some more famous phrases.

THE HANDWRITING IS ON THE WALL

Meaning: The outcome (usually negative) is obvious.

Background: The expression comes from a Babylonian legend in which the evil King Belshazzar drank from a sacred vessel looted from the Temple in Jerusalem. According to one version of the legend, "A mysterious hand appeared after this act of sacrilege and to the astonishment of the king wrote four strange words on the wall of the banquet room. Only the Hebrew prophet, Daniel, could interpret the mysterious message. He boldly told the ruler that they spelled disaster for him and for his nation. Soon afterward, Belshazzar was defeated and slain, just as Daniel said." The scene was a popular subject for tapestries and paintings during the Middle Ages.

OLD STOMPING GROUND

Meaning: Places where you spent a lot of time in your youth or in years past.

Background: The prairie chicken, which is found in Indiana and Illinois, is famous for the courtship dance it performs when looking for a mate. Large groups of males gather together in the morning to strut about, stamp their feet, and make booming noises with their throats. The original settlers used to get up early just to watch them; and the well-worn patches of earth became known as *stomping grounds*.

JIMINY CRICKET

Meaning: The name of the cricket character in the Walt Disney film *Pinocchio*; also a mild expletive.

Background: The name Jiminy Cricket predates *Pinnochio*...and has nothing to do with crickets. It is believed to have originated in the American colonies as "a roundabout way of invoking Jesus Christ." (Since the Puritans strictly forbade taking the Lord's name in vain, an entire new set of kinder, gentler swear words—darn, dang, heck, etc.—were invented to replace them.

More shoplifters are arrested on Wednesdays in January than at any other time of the year.

THE BITTER END

Meaning: The very end—often an unpleasant one.

Background: Has nothing to do with bitterness. It's a sailing term that refers to end of a mooring line or anchor line that is attached to the *bitts*, sturdy wooden or metal posts that are mounted to the ship's deck.

HAVE A SCREW LOOSE

Meaning: Something is wrong with a person or mechanism.

Background: The phrase comes from the cotton industry and dates back as far as the 1780s, when the industrial revolution made mass production of textiles possible for the first time. Huge mills sprang up to take advantage of the new technology (and the cheap labor), but it was difficult to keep all the machines running properly; any machine that broke down or produced defective cloth was said to have "a screw loose" somewhere.

MAKE THINGS HUM

Meaning: Make things run properly, smoothly, quickly, and efficiently.

Background: Another cotton term: the guy who fixed the loose screws on the broken—and thus *silent*—machines was known as the person who *made them hum* again.

IF THE SHOE FITS, WEAR IT

Meaning: "If something applies to you, accept it."

Background: The term is a direct descendant of the early 18th-century term "if the cap fits, put it on," which referred specifically to *fool's caps*.

PLEASED AS PUNCH

Meaning: Delighted.

Background: Believe it or not, the expression has nothing to do with party beverages—it has to do with the rascally puppet character Punch (of Punch and Judy fame), who derived enormous sadistic pleasure from his many evil deeds. The phrase was so popular that even Charles Dickens used it in his 1854 book, *Hard Times*.

There's enough salt in the world's oceans to cover the entire U.S. with a layer 1½ miles deep.

DIAMOND VOODOO

Uncle John has a lot of bathroom superstitions. He won't use soap if it's already wet; he always wears a baseball cap while brushing his teeth; he'll only sing in the shower if the fan is on. Maybe that's why he likes this article by Jack Connelly.

A BASEBALL TRADITION

If you pay close attention when you're watching your favorite baseball team, you may notice that the so-called boys of summer engage in some pretty odd behavior. [For example,] you might see a coach kick dirt at first base while spitting toward second base four times. This supposedly prevents a runner from being picked off or thrown out while trying to steal.

Even the most sophisticated athletes have been known to give in to the power of superstition as an aid to winning or avoiding injury. Most are quick to deny it, claiming they only follow a certain routine, but a routine becomes a superstition when you feel it must be followed to ensure good luck.

Pitcher Frank "Lefty" O'Doul, who played for the New York Yankees from 1919 to 1922, explained: "It's not that if I stepped on the foul line it would really lose the game, but why take a chance? It's just become part of the game for me."

THE GREAT SUPERSTITIONS

Here are some of baseball's most famous rituals and the players who put stock in them.

Al Simmons, who played for seven teams from 1924 to 1944, would step out of the shower, stand dripping wet in front of his locker, and put on his baseball cap before drying off. Then he'd continue dressing.

Frank "Wildfire" Schulte, who played for the Chicago Cubs, Pittsburgh Pirates, Philadelphia Phillies, and Washington Senators between 1904 and 1918, was sure that success depended on finding hairpins. One hairpin equaled one hit that day; two hairpins equaled two hits. If he found a handful, he'd be a hitting star for a week or more.

Joaquin Andujar, a pitcher who played for the Houston Astros,

St. Louis Cardinals, and Oakland A's between 1976 and 1988, knew how to break a losing streak on the mound: Shower with your uniform on to "wash the bad out of it."

Frank Chance, who played for the Cubs and the Yankees from 1898 to 1914, would only occupy a lower berth on a train and always No. 13. If that berth wasn't available, he would accept another and paint a 13 on it.

Arthur "Six O'clock" Weaver. During his playing days in the early 1900s, Weaver felt it was tempting fate to keep playing baseball after 6 p.m. He'd abruptly leave the field and head home if the game was still in progress when the clock struck six.

Luis Tiant, a pitcher who played for six teams between 1964 and 1982, had a penchant for smoking cigars in the postgame shower, but his fans never saw the strands of beads and the special loincloth he wrapped around his waist under his uniform, "to ward off evil."

Leo Durocher, among many others, would not change his clothes—underclothes included—during a winning streak. He would also ride in the back of the bus to break a losing streak. If his team was leading in the ninth inning, he'd walk the length of the dugout for a drink of water after each out recorded against the opposition.

Jackie Robinson, of the Brooklyn Dodgers, never stepped into the batter's box until the catcher took his position; then Robinson walked in front of him.

George Stallings, when he was the Boston Braves' manager, would "freeze" in whatever position he was in when a Brave got a hit and stay in that position until one failed to hit.

Phil Rizzuto, New York Yankee shortstop in the 1940s and 1950s, put a wad of gum on the button of his cap, removing it only when his team lost.

Forrest "Spook" Jacobs, who played from 1954 to 1956 for the Philadelphia Athletics and Kansas City Athletics, always squirted a mysterious liquid on his bat before a game. When pressed for an explanation, Jacobs said he was applying Murine so that he'd have a "seeing eye" bat.

Austin, Dallas, and Houston are all Scottish surnames.

Vic Davalillo, who played for six teams from 1963 to 1980, believed in petting chickens before a game.

Lou Skizas, who played for four teams between 1956 and 1959, had to step between the catcher and the umpire when getting into the [batter's] box. He always took a practice swing with one arm (his left), keeping his right hand in his back pocket (which held his lucky Greek medal) until the instant before the ball was delivered.

Mike Cuellar, a pitcher who played on five teams from 1959 to 1977, never looked at home plate while he was warming up to pitch. Also, he would allow only that game's catcher to warm him up. Cuellar would not take the field until all his teammates were in position, and he expected the ball to be sitting on the mound, not thrown to him, when he arrived there.

Tito Fuentes, who played on four teams from 1965 to 1978, wore as many as 17 chains under his uniform and each had to be in perfect alignment. Fuentes feared being touched at second base by anybody trying to break up a double play, and he would coat his body with grease and chalk before games.

The Chicago Cubs, as a team, once believed that it was bad luck to hit solid line drives during batting practice, on the theory that a bat contained just so many hits and they weren't to be wasted.

George Herman "Babe" Ruth never failed to touch second base on his way to the dugout at the end of each inning; Giants player **Willie Mays** thought along the same lines but *kicked* the bag instead. Ruth, former Boston Red Sox greats **Ted Williams** and **Carl Yastremski**, and former Pittsburgh Pirate **Willie Stargell** believed that bats with knots held the most hits.

Billy Williams, former Cubs and A's outfielder, had to sharpen his batting eye at least once a game by walking toward the plate, spitting, and swinging his bat through the spit before it hit the ground.

Mark Fidrych, of the Detroit Tigers made no secret of talking to the ball while on the mound, so there was no misunderstanding about the route it was to take.

Al Lopez, a Hall of Fame catcher who played from 1928 to 1947, would repeat the meals of the previous day—or days—when his team was on a winning streak, which is why he once breakfasted on kippered herring and eggs 17 days in a row.

THE FIRST LADIES OF POLITICS

Mrs. Uncle John insists that women don't read in the bathroom—and we might believe her, if we didn't get letters from women who do. In their honor, here's a bit of political history about women.

FIRST WOMAN ELECTED TO THE U.S. HOUSE OF REPRESENTATIVES: 1917

In 1913, Montana granted women the right to vote. Three years later, Jeanette Rankin, who'd spearheaded the suffrage movement there, ran for the House...and won. She ran for the Senate two years later, but was defeated—not because she was a woman, but because as a dedicated pacifist, she had opposed America's entry into World War I. Ironically, Rankin was also serving in the House when the vote to enter World War II was taken. She voted no again.

FIRST WOMAN TO SERVE IN THE U.S. SENATE: 1922

When Senator Thomas Watson died in 1922, Georgia's governor appointed 87-year-old Rebecca Felton to fill the seat...until a special election could be held seven days later. It was a purely political move: Congress wasn't in session, and Felton had no duties. But she convinced Senator-elect Walter George to let her serve one day in Washington before he officially took office. She made national headlines when she was sworn in on November 21.

FIRST WOMAN ELECTED GOVERNOR: 1924

In 1917, "Farmer Jim" Ferguson, governor of Texas, was impeached and booted out of office. Seven years later his wife, M. A. "Ma" Ferguson, ran as Farmer Jim's surrogate. She won, and was elected again in 1932.

FIRST WOMAN ELECTED TO THE U.S. SENATE: 1932

When Senator Thaddeus Caraway died in 1931, the governor of Arkansas appointed Caraway's wife, Hattie, to the seat...after making her promise she wouldn't seek reelection. She changed her mind, ran for the office on her own, and won two full terms.

California was the first state to send two women to the U.S. Senate at the same time.

THE FIRST WOMAN CABINET MEMBER: 1933

When FDR was governor of New York, Frances Perkins—a reformer committed to improving working conditions—was his state industrial commissioner. When Roosevelt became president, he appointed her Secretary of Labor. Perkins's legacy includes social security, unemployment insurance, and minimum wages.

FIRST WOMAN TO SERVE IN BOTH HOUSES OF CONGRESS: 1949

When Rep. Clyde Smith died in 1940, his wife Margaret won a special election to take his place. She won three full terms on her own, then ran successfully for the Senate in 1948. This made her only the second woman elected to a full term in the Senate...and the first elected to the Senate *without* following her husband. She served four terms. She also became the first woman to stage a serious run for the presidential nomination of a major political party (Republican, in 1964).

FIRST WOMAN TO HAVE AN ELECTORAL VOTE CAST FOR HER: 1973

Theodora Nathan, Libertarian Party VP candidate, got it.

FIRST WOMAN GOVERNOR ELECTED WITHOUT SUCCEEDING HER HUSBAND: 1974

A former Connecticut state legislator and the secretary of state, Rep. Ella Grasso was elected to two terms. She resigned in 1981, a few months before dying of cancer.

FIRST WOMAN ON THE U.S. SUPREME COURT: 1981

Although Sandra Day O'Connor graduated third in her class at Stanford Law School in 1952, she was only offered a job as a *legal secretary*. By the mid-'70s she'd been an Arizona state senator (R), a state deputy attorney general, and a Superior Court judge. In 1975 she was appointed to the Arizona Court of Appeals, and in 1981 President Reagan picked her for the Supreme Court.

FIRST WOMAN VICE PRESIDENTIAL CANDIDATE FOR A MAJOR POLITICAL PARTY: 1984

Rep. Geraldine A. Ferraro (D-New York) was chosen by Walter Mondale as his running mate.

America has three times as many animal shelters as shelters for victims of domestic violence.

IF HEARTACHES WERE WINE

Are you a fan of country-western music? Here are some toe-tappin' titles picked by the Pittsburgh Post-Gazette *for their "Annual All Time Best of the Worst Country Song Titles."*

"Get Your Tongue Outta My Mouth 'Cause I'm Kissing You Goodbye"

"You're a Cross I Can't Bear"

"Mama Get the Hammer (There's a Fly On Papa's Head)"

"She Made Toothpicks Out of the Timber of My Heart"

"You're the Reason Our Kids Are So Ugly"

"If Fingerprints Showed Up on Skin, Wonder Whose I'd Find on You"

"It Ain't Love, but It Ain't Bad"

"I've Been Flushed from the Bathroom of Your Heart"

"I'm the Only Hell Mama Ever Raised"

"I Got in at 2 with a 10 and Woke Up at 10 with a 2"

"I Don't Know Whether to Come Home or Go Crazy " (*Not to be confused with* "I Don't Know Whether to Kill Myself or Go Bowling")

"If You See Me Gettin' Smaller, It's Cause I'm Leavin' You."

"If Heartaches Were Wine (I'd Be Drunk All the Time)"

"If You Can't Feel It (It Ain't There)"

"Touch Me with More than Your Hands"

"I've Got the Hungries for Your Love and I'm Waiting in Your Welfare Line"

"The Last Word in Lonesome Is 'Me'"

"I'll Marry You Tomorrow but Let's Honeymoon Tonite"

"When We Get Back to the Farm (That's When We Really Go to Town)"

"You Stuck My Heart in an Old Tin Can and Shot It Off a Log"

"Why Do You Believe Me When I Tell You That I Love You, When You Know I've Been a Liar All My Life?"

"He's Been Drunk Since His Wife's Gone Punk"

When George Washington died in 1799, Napoleon ordered 10 days of mourning in France.

MUMMY'S THE WORD

Mummies are as much a part of American pop culture as they are a part of Ancient Egyptian culture. But how much do you know about them?

RAG TIME

As long as there have been people in Egypt, there have been mummies—not necessarily *man-made* mummies, but mummies nonetheless. The extreme conditions of the desert environment guaranteed that any corpse exposed to the elements for more than a day or two dried out completely, a process that halted decomposition in its tracks.

The ancient Egyptian culture that arose on the banks of the Nile River believed very strongly in preserving human bodies, which they believed were as necessary a part of the afterlife as they were a part of daily life. The formula was simple: no body, no afterlife—you couldn't have one without the other. The only problem: As Egyptian civilization advanced and burial tombs became increasingly elaborate, bodies also became more insulated from the very elements—high temperatures and dry air—that made natural preservation possible in the first place.

The result was that a new science emerged: artificial mummification. From 3100 B.C. to 649 A.D., the ancient Egyptians deliberately mummified the bodies of their dead, using methods that became more sophisticated and successful over time.

MUMMY SECRETS

Scientists have yet to unlock all of the secrets of Egyptian mummification, but they have a pretty good idea of how the process worked:

- When a king or other high official died, the embalmers slit open the body and removed nearly all the organs, which they preserved separately in special ceremonial jars. A few of the important organs, like the heart and kidneys, were left in place. The Egyptians apparently thought the brain was useless and in most cases they shredded it with small hooks inserted through the nostrils, pulled it out the nose using tiny spoons, and then threw it away.)

Some Egyptian mummies wore dentures.

• Next, the embalmers packed the body in oil of cedar (similar to turpentine) and natron, a special mineral with a high salt content. The chemicals slowly dried the body out, a process that took from 40 to 70 days.

• The body was now compeletely dried out and "preserved," but the process invariably left it shrunken and wrinkled like a prune, so the next step was to stuff the mouth, nose, chest cavities, etc., with sawdust, pottery, cloth, and other items to fill it out and make it look more human. In many cases the eyes were removed and artificial ones put in their place.

• Then the embalmers doused the body with a waterproofing substance similar to tar, which protected the dried body from moisture. In fact, the word mummy comes from the Persian word *mumiai*, which means "pitch" or "asphalt," and was originally used to describe the preservatives themselves, not the corpse that had been preserved.

• Finally, the body was carefully wrapped in narrow strips of linen and a funerary mask resembling the deceased was placed on the head. Afterwards it was placed in a large coffin that was also carved and painted to look like the deceased, and the coffin was placed in a tomb outfitted with the everyday items that the deceased would need in the afterlife.

THE MUMMY GLUT

Pharaohs weren't the only ancient Egyptians who were mummified—nearly anyone in Egyptian society who could afford it had it done. The result: By the end of the Late Period of Ancient Egypt in the seventh century A.D., the country contained an estimated 500 million mummies, far more than anyone knew what to do with. They were too numerous to count, too disconnected from modern Egyptian life to have any sacred spiritual value, and in most cases were thought to be too insignificant to be worthy of study. Egyptians from the 1100s onward thought of them as more of a natural resource than as the bodies of distant relatives, and treated them as such.

Well into the 19th century, mummies were used as a major fuel source for locomotives of the Egyptian railroad, which bought them by the ton (or by the graveyard). They were cheaper than wood and burned very well.

What country do Americans look up most often in the *World Book Encyclopedia?* Canada.

For more than 400 years, mummies were one of Egypt's largest export industries, and the supply was so plentiful that by 1600 you could buy a pound of mummy powder in Scotland for about 8 shillings. As early as 1100 A.D., Arabs and Christians ground them up for use as medicine, which was often rubbed into wounds, mixed into food, or stirred into tea.

By the 1600s, the medicinal use of mummies began to decline, as many doctors began to question the practice. "Not only does this wretched drug do no good to the sick," the French surgeon Ambrose Paré wrote in his medical journal, "...but it causes them great pain in their stomach, gives them evil smelling breath, and brings on serious vomiting which is more likely to stir up the blood and worsen hemorrhaging than to stop it." He recommended using mummies as fish bait.

By the 1800s, mummies were imported only as curiosities, where it was fashionable to unwrap them during dinner parties.

Mummies were also one of the first sources of recycled paper: During one 19th-century rag shortage (in the days when paper was made from *cloth* fibers, not wood fibers), one Canadian paper manufacturer literally imported Egyptian mummies as a source of raw materials: he unwrapped the cloth and made it into sturdy brown paper, which he sold to butchers and grocers for use as a food wrap. The scheme died out after only a few months, when employees in charge of unwrapping them began coming down with with cholera.

Note: What happened when the supply of mummies became scarce? A grisly "instant mummy" industry sprang up in which fresh corpses of criminals and beggars were hastily embalmed and sold as real mummies.)

MUMMY FACTS

• Scientists in South America have discovered mummies from the ancient civilization of Chinchorros that are more than 7,800 years old—nearly twice as old as the oldest Egyptian mummy. And, just as in Egypt, the mummies are plentiful there. "Every time we dug in the garden or dug to add a section to our house, we found bodies," one elderly South American woman told *Discover* magazine. "But I got used to it. We'd throw their bones out on a hill, and the dogs would take them away."

• The average Egyptian mummy contains more than 20 layers of cloth that, laid end-to-end, would be more than four football fields long.

• In 1977, an Egyptian scientist discovered that the mummy of Pharaoh Ramses II, more than 3,000 years old, was infested with beetles. So they sent it to France for treatment, complete with an Egyptian passport describing his occupation as "King, deceased."

• What's the quickest way to tell if an Egyptian mummy still has its brains? Shake the skull—if it rattles, the brain is still in there.

• The Egyptians were also fond of mummifying animals. To date, scientists have discovered the preserved remains of bulls, cats, baboons, birds, crocodiles, fish, scorpions, insects...even wild dogs. One tomb contained the remains of more than one *million* mummified birds.

• Some mummies have been discovered in coffins containing chicken bones. Some scientists believe the bones have special religious meaning, but (no kidding) other experts theorize that the bones are actually leftover garbage from the embalmer's lunch.

* * * *

CELEBRITY MUMMIES

Jeremy Bentham and his "Auto Icon." Bentham was a famous 19th-century English philosopher. When he died in 1832, he left instructions with a surgeon friend that his body be beheaded, mummified, dressed in his everyday clothes, and propped up in a chair, and that a wax head be placed on his neck to give the corpse a more realistic appearance. He further instructed that his real head also be mummified and placed at his feet, and that the whole arrangement be put on public display. The corpse and its head(s) can still be seen at University College in London, where they sit in a glass case specially built for that purpose.

Vladimir Lenin. When the Soviet leader died on January 21, 1924, the Communist Party assembled a team of top embalmers to preserve his corpse for all eternity. Unlike the embalming processes of the ancient Egyptians, which prevented decomposition by removing body fluids, the Soviets *replaced* cell fluids with liquids that inhibited deterioration.

WHY YOUR FEET SMELL

This is dedicated to our good friend Pete McCracken. It originally appeared as an article in Health *magazine. It's written by Teo Furtado.*

My wife and I sat crosslegged beside a litter of puppies. I knew what she was thinking. "We're not taking one, no matter how cute he is," I told her.

"That's fine," she said. "I don't want one either. Just another animal in the house to train."

And without another word, she selected a furrowed, sad-eyed, seven-week-old yellow Labrador retriever and placed him at my bare feet. The pup sniffed my toes excitedly and began to lick them. I was smitten. How could I resist a dog that actually liked the way my feet smelled? Ten years later, Boris still takes to my toes without the least hint of repugnance.

TRUE CONFESSIONS

Like lots of other people I've always been self-conscious about the bouquet of my feet. No wonder books on hygiene refer to smelly feet—*bromidrosis*, in medical jargon—as "the social disease" or "the unmentionable." Funny, when I was growing up, no one in my family ever had trouble mentioning it.

My brothers and I were in a no-win situation. While watching TV, we weren't allowed to put our feet up on the cocktail table with our shoes on. But taking our shoes off raised a loud...protest from my sisters. As they pinched their noses and gagged dramatically, they wiggled their toes in smug, odorless condescension.

IT'S THE SHOES!

Fortunately, we can take some comfort in the knowledge that the source of all this social angst isn't our feet; it's the shoes we wear. "There's no such thing as foot odor," says William Rossi, a podiatrist who's written extensively on foot problems. "There's only *shoe* odor. Just look at societies in which people go unshod. You never hear of foot odor problems."

Yes, it's civilization that's to blame—never mind the fact that there are more than a quarter of a million sweat glands in a pair of feet. That's more than in any other part of the human body, including the underarms.

The glands release about one gallon of moisture every week, but there's no problem so long as you're roaming around barefoot, says Rossi: Most of the sweat simply evaporates when your feet go through the world au naturel.

IF THE SHOE FITS...

All that changes when you confine a foot in a shoe. The buildup of sweat creates a nearly unlimited food supply for hungry bacteria, with salt, vitamins, glucose, fatty acids and lactic acid—nutritious stuff for the nearly six trillion bacteria that thrive on our feet.

With so much food and housing available, the organisms are fruitful and multiply. The food is digested; what's not used is broken down and excreted.

"You mean that the smell is bacterial poop?" I asked Rossi.

"Something like that," he responded.

THE CULPRITS

Researchers recently discovered that the main culprits in shoe odor are *micrococci*, bacteria that break sweat down into sulfur compounds that smell like rotten eggs or Limburger cheese.

How to attack them?

ODOR EATERS

There are plenty of over-the-counter remedies, but University of Pennsylvania microbiologist Ken McGinley advises some skepticism. It's true that foot powders absorb sweat and antiperspirant sprays cut down on its production. But, says McGinley…neither product adequately reduces the offending microbe's numbers because micrococci don't need as much moisture as other bacteria to survive.

Before you make that trip to the drugstore, there are some simpler—and usually more effective—solutions to try. First, the Imelda Marcos approach.

"Avoid wearing the same shoes over and over again," Rossi says.

Even if you don't have a roomful of shoes to choose from, rotate the ones you do wear. Each pair should air out for at least twenty-four hours between uses, says Rossi.

That advice, I figure, partly explains why my sisters didn't have bromidrosis: They simply changed shoes more often to match different outfits. The boys wore the same clodhoppers over and over again. Yet researchers say it's particularly important for men to rotate their shoes, because—silly as it sounds—they have larger toes that often stick together, making it harder for sweat to evaporate.

PLAYING HARDBALL

If a favorite pair of shoes is excessively odoriferous, Rossi offers a tip to try before you toss them out: sterilization. Roll some blotting paper into a cylinder to make a wick, and insert it partway into a small jar of formaldehyde (available at any pharmacy). Then place the jar and the shoes inside a cardboard box, tape the box shut, and put it into a closet or garage for a day or two. After taking the shoes out, be sure to let them dry overnight before you wear them again.

* * * *

Here's a special list of dating tips from the 1950s, just for girls!

THE TEN COMMANDMENTS OF GOOD CONDUCT

1. Be a teen with taste, dressing appropriately for the occasion.
2. Act like a lady and he will treat you as such.
3. Be able to enjoy an everyday date as well as the glamour occasions.
4. Don't hang on him too possessively.
5. Don't have him fetch and carry just to create an impression.
6. Make up if you like, but do not try to make over what you are.
7. Be popular with girls as well as boys.
8. Learn to like sports—it's an all-American topic in which boys are interested.
9. Don't be too self-sufficient; boys like to feel needed.
10. Be natural.

The average cat brain is as big as a marble; the average ostrich's eyes are as big as tennis balls.

MYTH AMERICA

Do you think all cowboys in the Old West looked like John Wayne? Here's some info about at least one important difference.

THE MYTH

All the cowboys in the American West were white.

BACKGROUND

Most of what Americans "know" about the Wild West comes from movies, TV, and popular authors. For years, these media have portrayed the Old West as virtually lily-white.

For example: Seven of the top 10 television shows of the 1958-1959 season were Westerns: *Gunsmoke*, *Wagon Train*, *Have Gun Will Travel*, *The Rifleman*, *Maverick*, *Tales of Wells Fargo*, and *Wyatt Earp*. All of them featured all-white regular casts.

Hollywood even went so far as to cast white actors to play the parts of real-life black cowboys, as in the 1951 film *Tomahawk*. The film featured Jim Beckwourth, a legendary black frontiersman... but the part was played by Jack Oakie, a white actor.

THE TRUTH

Nearly one in three cowboys in the American West were black, with the ratio higher in some states. Oklahoma, for example, saw 30 all-black towns spring up between 1890 and 1910, and 26 of the first 44 settlers of Los Angeles were black.

In fact, many of the most celebrated American cowboys were black, including:

- **Bill Pickett,** a rodeo star who toured under the name Will Pickett the Dusty Demon. He was a huge rodeo star in the early 1900s (Will Rogers was one of his early assistants) and starred in several silent films. He also invented the sport of "bulldogging"—wrestling a bull to the ground by its horns—although his preferred method, biting the bull's lip as he threw it to the ground, never caught on with other rodeo stars.
- **Nat Love,** also known as "Deadwood Dick," was a unique character who got his start as a cowboy in Dodge City at the age of 15

and went on to become a rodeo star. A friend of the famous lawman Bat Masterson, Love boasted of having 14 bullet wounds, and was famous for an incident in a Mexican bar in which he ordered drinks for his horse.

• **Cherokee Bill,** an Indian scout and notorious outlaw who in his day was as well known as Billy the Kid. His luck was just about as bad as Kid's was, too: His run-ins with the law resulted in his being hanged one month shy of his 20th birthday.

• **Mary Fields,** better known as Stagecoach Mary, a "strapping 6-footer who never shied from a shootout. A fearless mail carrier while in her 60s, she spent much of her final years in a Cascade, Montana, saloon playing cards with the boys."

• **Isom Dart,** a former slave who became famous as a rodeo clown, cattle rustler, prospector, and broncobuster.

*   *   *

BLACK WESTERNS

Hollywood has, on occasion, featured blacks in Westerns, but the depictions have rarely been historically accurate. The '30s and '40s saw a spate of cowboy 'race' films, including *Bronze Buckaroo* and *Harlem Rides the Range;* the '60s saw some racially relevant Westerns like *Major Dundee* and *The Professionals*...and the "blaxploitation" wave of the '70s even resulted in some patronizing black Westerns, the worst of which was probably *The Legend of Nigger Charlie*.

In the 1980s it became common to cast blacks in Westerns without referring to their race in the film, but it wasn't until the 1990s—when independent black filmmakers began directing their own Westerns—that films like Mario Van Peebles's *Posse* (1993) began to feature blacks as they really were in the West, a development that has been lauded by filmmakers, historians, and sociologists alike. "It's so important that the West be pictured as it was, not some lily-white John Wayne adventure story," says William Loren Katz, author of *The Black West* and *Black People Who Made the Old West*. "Books make it seem like, after the Civil War, blacks went home and went to sleep and didn't wake up until Martin Luther King. A whole heritage has been lost to generation after generation of schoolchildren, black and white."

American tables are set with salt and pepper; in Hungary it's salt and paprika.

ROBIN'S RAVINGS

Crazy comments from comedian Robin Williams.

On Princess Di: "She is exquisite. She is porcelain. She has that look, like some incredible cocker spaniel."

"I love San Francisco. It's a human game preserve."

When asked if he had a political consciousness during the Vietnam War: "I had only a genital consciousness during those years."

"The French are going the Americans one better with their Michelin bomb: it destroys only restaurants under four stars."

"Cocaine is God's way of saying you're making too much money."

"Why do they call it rush hour when nothing moves?"

WILLIAMS: Next thing I knew, I was in New York.
INTERVIEWER: Was that a heavy adjustment for you to make?
WILLIAMS: I was the walking epitome of fur*shirrr* meets yo'ass. On my first day in New York, I went to school dressed like a typical California kid: I wore tie-up yoga pants and a Hawaiian shirt, and I kept stepping in dog shit with my thongs."

On Ronald Reagan: "I still think Nancy does most of his talking; you'll notice that she *never* drinks water when Ronnie speaks."

"The first time I tried organic wheat bread, I thought I was chewing on roofing material."

On birth: "She's screaming like crazy.... You have this myth you're sharing the birth experience. Unless you're passing a bowling ball, I don't think so. Unless you're circumcising yourself with a chainsaw, I don't think so. Unless you're opening an umbrella up your ass, I don't think so."

"What's right is what's left if you do everything else wrong."

"Death is nature's way of saying 'Your table is ready.' "

Uneven stats: There are about 10,700 births and 5,700 deaths every day in the United States.

KNITTING WITH DOG HAIR

When we heard about this "hobby," we couldn't believe it. But sure enough, it's real. First we found a book called Knitting with Dog Hair, *by Kendall Crolius...then several web pages on the subject. All are apparently serious, so here are some ideas if you're interested in "Putting on the dog."*

MY DOG HAS FLEECE

"Let's be honest," writes Kendall Crolius in her book *Knitting with Dog Hair.* "Everything in your house is probably covered with a fine coat of pet hair. Now all that fuzz that used to clog up your vacuum cleaner can be put to good use. In fact, you'll probably want to brush your dog more often—you'll not only have gorgeous new clothes but a better-groomed pet and a cleaner house."

Gorgeous new clothes? Is she really suggesting we make clothes out of dog hair? You bet. And why not? After all, before there were sheep in Scandanavia and on the American content, there were canines. While other animals were killed for their fur, prehistoric natives on both continents considered dogs too valuable as hunters and companions for that. So, she informs us, they saved dog hair and knitted it into fabrics.

PUBLIC OPINION

Dedicated dog hair knitters have learned from experience that other people think they're weird.

"When you first tell your friends that the garment you're wearing was previously worn by your dog, you're bound to get some raised eyebrows, not to mention a few shrieks of horror," Crolius writes. That's why most of them have learned that it's a better idea not to say "dog hair" at all when showing off a new hand-knitted sweater. After all, most people immediately think of fleas, itching and doggy smells when they think of canine fur.

Some even ask,with eyes wide, "How many dogs have to be killed to make a sweater?"

Q: What kind of wood is used to make Scrabble letters? A: Vermont Maple.

DOG HAIR BY ANY OTHER NAME SMELLS AS SWEET?

• Faced with such reactions from friends, family and neighbors, knitters have dealt with the issue…by avoiding it—they've come up with a new name.

• Combining the French word for "dog" with the name of another natural hair fiber, angora, they've coined a fashion euphemism that's nearly as good as the day that furriers discovered that "ermine" sounds more luxurious than "white weasel." The new name for dog-hair creations…"Chiengora."

• In fact, in her *Merry Spinster* web page, Patty Lee Dranchak insists that dog hair should be considered a luxury fiber, like all the others that come from humble origins including cashmere and angora (goat) and mohair (rabbit).

Reasons to Bark

• The hardcore dog-lovers who practice the art have created sweaters, hats, mittens and pantsuits from the hair of their beloved pets.
• They report that chiengora is—to quote Dranchak—"soft and fluffy, lovely and lustrous, incredibly warm and it sheds water. This furry look just seems to invite touching. Wearing it invites comments, questions and even an occasional pat on the back to see if it is really as soft as it looks."

• Besides that, Dranchak says, dog lovers have sentimental reasons: "By having a pet's hair spun, dog lovers will always have a part of their treasured companion with them—a reminder of the love, loyalty and good times they shared together."

• Jerilyn Monroe, who makes yarn out of her half-wolf dogs, agrees: "Having a scarf, blanket or hat made from a special pet can be a lovely way to remember them."

A SHAGGY DOG YARN

• The key to knitting with dog hair is its length. "Rule number one is that you should never shear, cut, or shave fur from your pet," says Crolius. "Not only would such a radical approach seriously humiliate your companion and render him exceedingly unattractive, it is counterproductive. To spin a really nice yarn, you need the longest, softest fibers your pet can grow. It's best if the hair is two inches or longer if you want a pure chiengora yarn, so collies, Afghans, poodles, samoyeds, golden retrievers, sheepdogs and huskies work better than basset hounds or chihuahuas."

• Shorter hair has to be blended with wool, silk or other fibers to hold it together. "Properly blended and spun, it's difficult to tell that the resulting yarn isn't all dog hair," observes Dranchak.

THE HARVEST

However, unlike sheep, you don't shear your dog—you merely collect hair from brushes and combs. So even with the hairiest dog, it can take several years to collect enough hair for a major project like a sweater or a blanket.

• After you gather it, you should store it dry in a paper bag—never plastic, say some dog hair experts.

• However, other experts disagree, saying it should be stored tightly sealed in a plastic bag to keep out fleas and moths. "Moths love dog hair," says one, who recommends zip-lock bags.

• Regardless, paper grocery bags make a good standard of measure: a knitted sweater takes about two bags, a vest about one and a hat about 1/3 of a bag. Crocheting adds another 33% for each garment; weaving about 33% less.

WARP AND WOOF...WOOF...WOOF

• Once you have your big bags of hair, how do you turn it into yarn? Dog hair requires gently hand-spindling with a weighted drop spindle—none of these newfangled machines like the spinning wheel. The result comes from twisting the hairs around each other.

• The good thing about fibers like dog hair is that if the yarn breaks, you just fluff up the end and begin again, adding fibers. "This is a craft that the whole family can participate in," suggests Crolius. "The younger kids can help brush the dog, and the older kids can help prepare the fiber for spinning. It's a terrific way to spend time together."

ODDS & ODDS

• If you have a multi-colored dog, experts suggest keeping the colors somewhat separate to give an interesting graduated color effect.

• Mixing the hair together yields a uniform gray-beige color

• Like the dogs it came from, dog-hair garments should be handwashed—not thrown into a washing machine. Unlike the dogs, the fabrics can be dry-cleaned. Dog-hair garments can last 20 years.

The automobile "population" of Seoul, South Korea, increases by 800 cars *every day*.

IT SEEMED LIKE A GOOD IDEA AT THE TIME

What if they minted a coin and no one would use it? That's what happened with the Susan B. Anthony dollar.

BACKGROUND

In the mid-1970s, the demand for dollar bills was increasing at a rate of about 10% a year. Each bill cost the government 2¢ to make...but lasted only about 18 months. Treasury officials figured they could save taxpayers about $50 million a year if they replaced the $1 bill with a $1 coin—which would last about 14 years and cost only 3¢ to make. They were confident that the American public would make the change.

BEAUTY AND THE BEAST

Responding to the political currents of the mid-'70s, U.S. Mint officials told chief designer Frank Gasparro to draw a portrait of a woman for the proposed new dollar coin. "I decided to draw Miss Liberty," he says, "but they told me they didn't want Miss Liberty. It had to be Susan B. Anthony." Gasparro had no idea what Anthony, an activist for women's rights in the late 1800s, looked like. So he went down to the local newspaper and looked at the photograph files. They contained two portraits of Anthony: one taken at the age of 28, and the other at age 84. "I chose the younger one," he recalls. "She was a very attractive woman at 28."

But feminists complained that it was "too pretty." So Gasparro drew a new portrait of Anthony, trying to approximate what she looked like in middle age. He gave her a square jaw, a hooked nose, a heavy browline, and a drooping right eye. Though he succeeded at his task (hardly anyone accuses the Susan B. Anthony dollar of being "too pretty" anymore), he had reservations about the final design. But the U.S. Treasury approved it.

DAMSEL IN DISTRESS

Introduced on July 2, 1979, the Susan B. Anthony dollar was an instant failure. Everybody hated it—people said it was too small to be

Twenty-five percent of U.S. prescription drugs contain compounds from plants.

a dollar and too ugly to represent the United States.

But the biggest problem with the coin was that it looked and felt like a quarter. Many businesses refused to accept them, fearing that cashiers would mistake them for quarters and give them away as change.

STOPGAP MEASURES

Government officials fought hard to keep the coin alive, spending more than $600,000 on a nationwide campaign to increase public acceptance. Then they brought in a New York public relations firm to help—the first time in history that a coin had to be *promoted.* But it was hopeless. "Our job was to get the good story out about the coin," said a spokesman for the PR firm,

> But we made a false assumption. We assumed that there would be good stories to get out. There weren't. We were looking for any little piece of good news about the coin, so we could feed it to the networks and the wire services. The stories didn't have to come from big cities; we were looking for the little town that decided to pay everyone in Susan B. Anthony coins—that kind of thing. We'd take *anything*. Spokane, San Luis Obispo, Dover-Foxcroft, Mobile...our feeling was that as soon as something good happened, we could start to build a success. But nothing good ever happened. Anywhere.

FEMME FATAL

By the time production was halted in the spring of 1980, more than 840 million coins had been minted...but only 315 million had made it into circulation. "There is an extraordinary amount of resistance to this coin," a U.S. Mint official admitted. "As far as I can tell, it isn't being accepted anywhere."

Esquire magazine reported in April 1981 that, "Most Americans refuse to carry the coins. Bank tellers and cashiers in stores have learned not to even try to give them out as change; people won't take them. People...don't even like to touch them."

The Treasury department suspended production in 1981, estimating they had enough of them on hand to last 40 to 50 years.

"I think we will just let sleeping dogs lie," the Secretary of the Treasury said.

The world's five smallest countries would easily fit inside of Walt Disney World.

PIRATE LORE

We've all got an idea of what it was like to be a pirate in the 1700s—but a lot of it is pure Hollywood hooey. Here are a few of our most common misconceptions about pirates...and the truth about them.

NICKNAMES

Why did so many pirates have colorful nicknames like "Blackbeard" and "Half Bottom"? The main reason was to prevent government officials from identifying and persecuting their relatives back home. (How did "Half Bottom" get his nickname? A cannonball shot half his bottom off.)

WALKING THE PLANK

Few (if any) pirate ships ever used "the plank." When pirates took over a ship, they usually let the captured crewmembers choose between joining the pirate crew or jumping overboard. Why go to all the trouble of setting up a plank to walk off? As historian Hugh Rankin put it: "The formality of a plank seems a bit absurd when it was so much easier just to toss a prisoner overboard."

BURIED TREASURE

Another myth. No pirate would have trusted his captain to bury treasure for him. According to pirate expert Robert Ritchie, "The men who turned to piracy did so because they wanted money. As soon as possible after capturing a prize they insisted on dividing the loot, which they could then gamble with or carry home. The idea of burying booty on a tropical island would have struck them as insane."

BOARDING A SHIP BY FORCE

It's a scene from the movies: A pirate ship pulls up alongside another ship, and then the pirates swing across on ropes and storm the ship. But how realisitic is this scene? Not very, experts say. Most ship captains owned their cargos, which were usually fully insured. They preferred to surrender the minute they were approached by a pirate ship, seeing piracy as one of the costs of doing business.

At one English bed-and-breakfast, visitors get to take home "a free bootload of manure."

THE JOLLY ROGER (SKULL AND CROSSBONES)

Pirates used a variety of flags to communicate. The Jolly Roger was used to coerce nearby ships into allowing the pirates to board. But it wasn't the only flag of choice—some pirate ships preferred flags with hourglasses on them (to let would-be victims know that time was running out); others used black or red flags. How did the Jolly Roger get its name? Nobody knows for sure—although some historians believe it comes from the English pronunciation of *Ali Raja*, the Arabic words for "King of the Sea."

PIRATE SHIPS

In the movies they're huge—but in real life they were much smaller. "Real pirates," one expert writes, "relied on small, swift vessels and hit-and-run attacks."

ROWDINESS

Not all pirate ships were rough-and-tumble. Pirates often operated under a document that had some similarity to a constitution. Here are a few of the articles from an agreement drawn up by the crew of Captain John Phillips in 1723.

> 1. Every man shall obey civil Command; the Captain shall have one full Share and a half in all prizes; the Master, Carpenter, Boatswain, and Gunner shall have one share and a quarter.
>
> 2. If any man shall offer to run away, or keep any Secret from the Company, he shall be maroon'd with one Bottle of Powder, one Bottle of Water, one small Arm, and Shot.
>
> 3. If any Man shall steal any Thing in the Company, or game, to the Value of a Piece of Eight, he shall be maroon'd or shot.
>
> 4. That Man that shall strike another whilst those Articles are in force, shall receive Moses's Law (that is 40 stripes lacking one) on the bare Back.
>
> 5. That Man that shall not keep his Arms clean, fit for an Engagement, or neglect his Business, shall be cut off from his Share, and suffer such other Punishment as the Captain and the Company shall think fit.
>
> 6. If any Man shall lose a Joint in time of an Engagement, shall have 400 Pieces of Eight; if a limb 800.
>
> 7. If at any time you meet with a prudent Woman, that Man that offers to meddle with her, without her Consent, shall suffer Death.

The average office Christmas party is attended by 75% of a company's employees.

PRIMETIME PROVERBS

More TV wisdom from Primetime Proverbs: A Book of TV Quotes, *by Jack Mingo and John Javna.*

ON FATHERS

Ben Cartwright: "I'm not in the habit of giving lectures, and if I do, it's because they're needed. Might have been a good idea if your father had given you a few."
Candy Canaday: "Oh, he did."
Ben: "Obviously they didn't have much effect."
Candy: "Oh, yes they did: I left home."

—*Bonanza*

"I am your father. I brought you into this world and I can take you out."

—**Cliff Huxtable,**
The Cosby Show

ON DREAMS

"The only thing I ever dream is that I just won every beauty contest in the world and all the people I don't like are forced to build me a castle in France."

—**Stephanie Vanderkellen,**
Newhart

ON FEAR

"Some people are afraid of the dark and some are afraid to leave it."

—**Beau Maverick,**
Maverick

Caine: "Of all things, to live in darkness must be the worst."
Master Po: "Fear is the only darkness."

—***Kung Fu***

"The subject: fear. The cure: a little more faith. An Rx off the shelf—in the Twilight Zone."

—**Rod Sterling,**
The Twilight Zone

ON LEARNING

"What a wonderful day we've had. You have learned something, and I have learned something. Too bad we didn't learn it sooner. We could have gone to the movies instead."

—**Balki Bartokomous,**
Perfect Strangers

Boy: "Teach me what you know, Jim."
Reverend Jim Ignatowski: "That would take hours, Terry. Ah, what the heck! We've all got a little Obi-Wan Kenobi in us."

—***Taxi***

ON LIFE

"God forbid anything should be easy."

—***Hawkeye,* M*A*S*H**

TIPS FOR TEENS

More advice from a teen guidebook of the 1950s.

GOOD GROOMING FOR GIRLS

YOU'RE YOUR OWN SHOW!

Rest, relaxation, and good food all help *keep a clear skin, shiny hair, good teeth and bones, but they aren't the* whole *story...*

Let's start with posture. Think about walking tall; it's surprising how much better clothes look! There'll be fewer backaches, or even headaches, too. Don't slouch as you walk, nor slump as you sit. Relax! Lift your head and shoulders, then walk as if you're going *somewhere.*

Look at yourself in the mirror! Have you a regular nighttime, morning and weekly cleanliness program? Soon you'll be at college or on your own; no family to remind you of the toothbrush, nail file, comb, or soap and water. Yet regular attention to teeth, nails and hair is a habit just as important to good health as food.

Give that room of yours the "once-over." Of course you meant to hang things up after last night's party, but did you *do* it? It's only smart to hang clothes in your closet immediately—they need less pressing and laundry care that way. And tidy, wrinkle-free clothing is an important part of the shined-and-polished look!

In actuality, beauty is lots more than skin deep. Beauty is as deep as you are. Beauty is all of you, your face, your figure, your skin. More than any other part, though, your skin will be the barometer of your beauty weather. It will tell you how well you are keeping to a beauty schedule. A broken-out complexion is a sure sign that you have slipped up somewhere. It is an indication that you have eaten too many sweets or skimped on cleanliness. Be diligent in your daily habits, and your reward will be a smooth, silken complexion (and, not incidentally, a fine face and figure).

Just remember, most of us wouldn't take the first prize in a beauty contest. Yet it's possible, with some time and attention, to improve the looks we have. So form good grooming habits *now*—for the rest of your life.

BRAND NAMES

You've used the products...now here are the people behind the names.

RALSTON-PURINA

In the 1890s, it was common for grain millers to separate wheat germ from the whole-wheat cereals of the day, because the germ tended to spoil rapidly. Then, in 1898, a Kansas miller discovered a way to keep it from rotting. But the stuff was still removed from the wheat, and no one knew what to do with it —at least until William Danforth, an animal-feed manufacturer and inventor of "health cereals," decided to sell it as a breakfast food. Borrowing from his company's slogan, "Where purity is paramount," he gave his new product the name *Purina* and marketed it with the endorsement of Dr. Albert Webster Edgerly, who had written a popular health-and-fitness book called *Life Building* under the pen name Dr. *Ralston*.

BLACK & DECKER

In 1910, twentysomethings S. Duncan Black and Alonzo Decker quit their jobs at the Rowland Telegraph Company and founded the Black & Decker company. They built and sold bottlecap machines, auto shock absorbers, candy-dipping machines, and other specialty equipment for industry.

They probably would have stuck with industry sales forever had they not seen a news item during World War II reporting a record wave of employee thefts of portable power tools from U.S. defense plants. Realizing that the workers in the plants had become hooked on portable power tools and would be hungry for them after the war, Black & Decker's Post-War Planning Committee began designing a line of *home* power tools that premiered in 1946.

PARKER PENS

The modern fountain pen was perfected by L. E. Waterman, an American inventor, in 1884. But even *his* pens leaked once in a while, creating a cottage industry for "pen repairmen" like George

The Mona Lisa has no eyebrows.

S. Parker, of Janesville, Wisconsin. Parker got to know fountain pens so well that he designed an improved model and founded the Parker Pen Company in 1892. Business was slow until World War I, when the company invented the Parker Trench Pen and sent them overseas with U.S. soldiers so they could write home. The doughboys were so sold on the pens that Parker went on to become one of the best-known brand names in America.

SPALDING SPORTING GOODS

Have you ever heard of Albert Goodwill Spalding? One of the greatest pitchers in history, Spalding played for the Boston Red Stockings and the Chicago White Sox in the 1870s. Between 1871 and 1875, he pitched 301 games and won 241, becoming baseball's first 200-game winner. But he was unique for another reason as well: The baseballs he pitched were ones he made himself. When he retired in 1876, he opened his own sporting goods company and began selling them to the public. The National Baseball League was founded a year later and made the Spalding ball the official ball of the league.

BISSELL CARPET SWEEPERS

Melville and Anna Bissell owned a crockery shop in Grand Rapids, Michigan, in the 1870s. One of Anna's least favorite chores was sweeping the sawdust used as packing material off of the shop's carpet at the end of the day. So in 1876, Melville went out and bought Anna a newly invented "carpet sweeper." But while it worked pretty well on ordinary dirt, it was useless on the sappy, fibery sawdust that literally stuck to the carpet. Undaunted, Melville took apart the carpet sweeper and built an improved model for his wife.

Note: Melville Bissell built the *sweeper*, but it was Anna who built the *company:* when Melville died from pneumonia in 1889, Anna took over the business, streamlining procedures and selling the sweeper in foreign markets for the first time—including to Queen Victoria of England, who authorized their use on the priceless rugs of Buckingham Palace. Anna Bissell is one of the earliest and most successful female CEOs in the history of American business.

ROSEANNE SEZ...

A few choice thoughts from Roseanne.

"Men read maps better than women because only men can understand the concept of an inch equaling a hundred miles."

"Women are cursed and men are the proof."

"Women complain about premenstrual syndrome, but I think of it as the only time of the month I can be myself."

"My husband said he needed more space, so I locked him outside."

"You marry the man of your dreams, but fifteen years later you're married to a reclining chair that burps."

"When Sears comes out with a riding vacuum cleaner, then I'll clean house."

"As a housewife, I feel that if the kids are still alive when my husband gets home from work, then hey, I've done my job."

"My children love me. I'm like the mother they never had."

"I asked the clothing store clerk if she had anything to make me look thinner, and she said, 'How about a week in Bangladesh?' "

"It's okay to be fat. So you're fat. Just be fat and shut up about it."

"I think the sexiest thing a woman could do is be as fat as me—or fatter."

"Husbands think we should know where everything is: like the uterus is a tracking device. He asks me, 'Roseanne, do we have any Cheetos left?' Like he can't go over to that sofa cushion and lift it himself."

"Excuse the mess but we live here."

On tabloids: "They say this comes with the territory but ...it's like a hand from hell that continually reaches up to grab my ankles."

To the staff of her TV show: "This is not a democracy, this is queendom."

You're born with 300 bones, but have only 206 as an adult. The others fuse together.

SOUND EFFECTS

Jurassic Park and Star Wars—two of the most popular and profitable films of all time—got a big boost from their unusual sound effects. Here are a few of the secrets behind them.

STAR WARS

Ben Burtt, a talented USC college student, recorded most of the sounds needed for the film. Some of his secrets:

- Chewbacca's voice was created from a combination of walrus, badger, sea lion, three different bears, and bear cub recordings. After mixing the sounds together, Burtt changed the pitch and slowed them down to "match" a Wookie photo Lucas had sent him.
- The light sabers were a combination of humming film projectors and static from Burtt's TV set.
- The Jawas spoke a mixture of sped-up Swahili and Zulu dialects.
- R2-D2's "voice" was Burtt's own voice combined with sounds of bending pipes and metal scraping around in dry ice.

JURASSIC PARK

- The *Tyrannosaurus rex*'s voice is an assortment of animal noises—elephants, tigers, dogs, penguins, and alligators, etc.—and the thudding sound of his feet are recordings of trees falling in a forest.
- The sound of a sick *Triceratops* was recorded at a farm for "retired" performing lions. Sound designers went to the farm looking for sounds for the t-rex, but they found that the "wheezy, pained breathing" of the old lions was perfect for the triceratops.
- The *Velociraptors* used 25 different animals sounds...but not all at once: a "very old" horse was used to provide the breathing sounds they make when stalking prey; dolphin sounds were used to make the "attack" screeches; and mating tortoises provided the hooting call that raptors make to each other.
- The sound designers wanted to use whale sounds for the *Brachiosaurus* (the veggie-munching, long-necked dinosaur)—but they couldn't get the right recording...so they recorded a donkey braying, slowed it down, and played it backwards. The end result was practically indistinguishable from a whale.

THE TRUTH ABOUT PEARL HARBOR

Japan's attack on Pearl Harbor was one of the most dramatic incidents in U.S. history—and the source of persistent questions. Did President Roosevelt know the attack was coming? If so, why didn't he defend against it? Here's some insight from It's a Conspiracy!

Shortly after dawn on Sunday, December 7, 1941, Japanese warplanes launched an all-out attack on Pearl Harbor, the major U.S. military base in Hawaii. Within two hours, they had damaged or destroyed 18 warships and more than 200 aircraft, killing 2,403 American soldiers, sailors, and marines, and wounding 1,178. Americans were stunned and outraged.

The next day, FDR delivered a stirring speech to Congress in which he referred to the day of the attack as "a date which will live on in infamy." In response, Congress declared war, and the country closed ranks behind the president.

Despite America's commitment to the war, however, questions arose about Pearl Harbor that were not easily dismissed: How were we caught so completely by surprise? Why were losses so high? Who was to blame? Did the president know an attack was coming? Did he purposely do nothing so America would be drawn into the war? Although there were seven full inquiries before the war ended, the questions persist to this day.

UNANSWERED QUESTION #1

Did the United States intercept Japanese messages long before the attack, but fail to warn the Hawaiian base?

Suspicious Facts

- By the summer of 1940, the United States had cracked Japan's top-secret diplomatic code, nicknamed "Purple." This enabled U.S. intelligence agencies to monitor messages to and from Tokyo.
- Although several U.S. command posts received machines for decoding "Purple," Pearl Harbor was never given one.
- Messages intercepted in the autumn of 1941 suggested what the

Japanese were planning:

✓ On October 9, 1941, Tokyo told its consul in Honolulu to "divide the water around Pearl Harbor into five sub-areas and report on the types and numbers of American war craft."

✓ The Japanese foreign minister urged negotiators to resolve issues with the U.S. by November 29, after which "things are automatically going to happen."

✓ On December 1, after negotiations had failed, the navy intercepted a request that the Japanese ambassador in Berlin inform Hitler of an extreme danger of war...coming "quicker than anyone dreams."

On the Other Hand

• Although the United States had cracked top-secret Japanese codes several years earlier, "the fact is that code-breaking intelligence did not prevent and could not have prevented Pearl Harbor, because Japan never sent any message to anybody saying anything like 'We shall attack Pearl Harbor,'" writes military historian David Kahn in the autumn 1991 issue of *Military History Quarterly*.

• "The [Japanese] Ambassador in Washington was never told of the plan," Kahn says, "Nor were other Japanese diplomats or consular officials. The ships of the strike force were never radioed any message mentioning Pearl Harbor. It was therefore impossible for cryptoanalysts to have discovered the plan. Despite the American code breakers, Japan kept her secret."

• Actually, Washington *had* issued a warning to commanders at Pearl Harbor a few weeks earlier. On November 27, 1941, General George Marshall sent the following message: "Hostile action possible at any moment. If hostilities cannot, repeat CANNOT, be avoided, the United States desires that Japan commit the first overt act. This policy should not, repeat NOT, be construed as restricting you to a course of action that might jeopardize your defense."

• But the commanders at Pearl Harbor were apparently negligent. The base should have at least been on alert, but the antiaircraft guns were unmanned and most people on the base were asleep when the attack came.

UNANSWERED QUESTION #2

Did a sailor pick up signals from the approaching Japanese fleet and pass the information on to the White House—which ignored it?

Suspicious Facts

• This theory is promoted in John Toland's bestselling book, *Infamy*. He asserts that in early December, an electronics expert in the 12th Naval District in San Francisco (whom Toland refers to as "Seaman Z") identified "queer signals" in the Pacific. Using cross-bearings, he identified them as originating from a "missing" Japanese carrier fleet which had not been heard from in months. He determined that the fleet was heading directly for Hawaii.

• Toland says that although Seaman Z and his superior officer allegedly reported their findings to the Office of Naval Intelligence, whose chief was a close friend of the president, Pearl Harbor never got the warning.

On the Other Hand

• Gordon Prange, author of *Pearl Harbor: The Verdict of History*, refutes many of Toland's assertions. Although he concedes that there may have been unusual Japanese signals that night, Prange says that they were almost certainly signals *to* the carriers from Tokyo—and thus would have been useless in locating the carriers.

• To prove his point, Prange quotes reports written by Mitsuo Fuchida, who led the air attack on Pearl Harbor: "The Force maintained the strictest silence throughout the cruise....[Admiral] Genda stressed that radio silence was so important that the pilots agreed not to go on the air even if their lives depended upon it." The chief of staff for Fleet Admiral Nagumo adds, "All transmitters were sealed, and all hands were ordered to be kept away from any key of the machine."

• Prange notes, "It would be interesting to know how the 12th Naval District in San Francisco could pick up information that the 14th Naval District, much nearer the action in Honolulu, missed."

• Finally, Prange reports that years after the war, "Seaman Z" was identified as Robert D. Ogg, a retired California businessman. Ogg flatly denied that he had said the unusual signals were "the missing carrier force," nor was he even sure that the transmissions were in Japanese—"I never questioned them at the time."

UNANSWERED QUESTION #3

Even if FDR didn't specifically know about an impending attack on Pearl Harbor, did he try to provoke the Japanese into attacking the U.S. to gain the support of the American public for his war plans?

Suspicious Facts

• FDR told close aides that if the Allies were to be victorious, the U.S. had to enter the war before Japan overran the Pacific and Germany destroyed England.

• FDR told a British emissary that the United States "would declare war on Japan if the latter attacked American possessions... [but] public opinion would be unlikely to approve of a declaration of war if the Japanese attack were directed only against British or Dutch territories."

• Earlier that year, on July 25, 1941, Roosevelt froze Japanese assets in the United States.

• In 1937, Japan sank a U.S. warship in China's Yangtze River, and relations between America and Japan began deteriorating. Both countries made a public effort to negotiate, but FDR presented a series of impossible ultimatums to the Japanese negotiators and openly loaned money to the Nationalist Chinese, whom the Japanese were fighting at the time.

• According to columnist Pat Buchanan, Roosevelt also committed an act of war against Japan in August 1941, when he secretly approved sending a crack U.S. Air Force squadron, the "Flying Tigers," to fight alongside the Chinese Nationalists. Although these fliers were officially "volunteers," Buchanan claims that they were "recruited at U.S. bases, offered five times normal pay [and] sent off to fight Japan months before Pearl Harbor, in a covert operation run out of FDR's White House....Though their planes carried the insignia of the Chinese army, [they] were on active duty for the United States."

On the Other Hand

• No evidence *proving* a conspiracy to goad the Japanese into attacking has come to light in the 50-plus years since Pearl Harbor. If there had been one, it would have surfaced by now...wouldn't it have? We'll probably never know.

Most popular pizza topping in South Korea: Tuna.

HOW TO TAKE A SHOWER-BATH

Showers are so commonplace today that it's hard to think of them as a novelty. But this article by W. Beach, M.D., printed in an 1848 magazine, shows that 150 years ago, dripping water on your head was still a weird and exotic practice.

***Reprinted from* The American Practice of Medicine, 1848.**

The shower bath is a species of cold bath, an invention by which water falls from a height through numerous holes or apertures, on the head and body. It may be conveniently made by boring numerous small holes through a tub or half barrel, which must be fastened a few feet above the head of the person.

Another tub, of a sufficient size to contain two pails of water, must be suspended over the other, and made to turn upon an axis. A rope or cord must be fastened to this, so that it can be inverted or turned downward at pleasure.

The person taking the shower bath must place himself beneath, uncovered; and, having filled the tub with water, he will suddenly pull upon the cord, when almost instantaneously the contents of the upper tub or bath will fall into the lower one containing the holes, and the water will thus be conveyed in numerous and copious streams upon the head and body.

The apparatus should be enclosed, as well as the body, in a box or frame a few feet square, or large enough to enable the person to stand or turn round with convenience. A few boards or planks enclosed in a small frame is sufficient for the purpose. Rub the body well with a dry towel after the bathing.

This bath may be used in all diseases of the head, epilepsy, nervous complaints, headache, melancholy, hypochondriasis, obstruction of the menses, and such complaints as arise therefrom, delirium, general debility, &c.

Dr. Sylvester Graham,* who has become very celebrated on account of his lectures on temperance and diet, recommends, I am told,

***The Graham cracker was named after Dr. Sylvester Graham.**

the shower bath for numerous complaints.

A writer in *Zion's Herald*, over the appropriate signature "Comfort," has the following interesting remarks on the shower bath, and his own experience in applying the same:

> I had a shower bath made at the expense of ten dollars, and it makes a neat article of furniture in one corner of my chamber. On the top a box, that holds about a pail of water, swings on a pivot, and a string from it communicates inside; and underneath, to catch the water, is a snug-fitting drawer.
>
> Immediately on rising in the morning I shut myself in this enclosure, and receive the contents of the box at the top, let it drip off a moment, and then apply briskly a crash towel, and immediately a fine healthy glow is produced all over the body.
>
> The time occupied does not exceed five minutes: I have often done it conveniently in three or four minutes, particularly when the wind has been in a cold corner, and all cheerless out of doors; but in these melting times it is too great a luxury to be hurried through with.
>
> I hope all will be induced to try this plan who can possibly raise ten dollars to pay for the bath. I can assure them they will never put this article aside as useless, or sell it for less than cost. I certainly would not part with mine for ten times its cost, if another could not be procured.

The portable shower bath may be constructed at a small expense, and placed in a bedroom or other place. Both the bath and the water may be drawn to the desired height by means of a cord or rope running over the pulleys, and fastened to the ceiling.

The person taking the shower bath is placed within, surrounded partially or wholly by curtains, when he pulls a wire or cord which inverts the vessel overhead containing the water, and lets it fall in copious streams over the whole body.

"The warm, tepid, cold, or shower bath," says Dr. Combe, "as a means of preserving health, ought to be in as common use as a change of apparel, for it is equally a measure of necessary cleanliness." A bath on the above plan can be purchased for eight dollars.

Doctors in ancient China were paid when patients were healthy, not sick.

MISSED IT BY *THAT* MUCH

It's bizarre to think that the outcome of some of the most momentous events in Western history have hinged on one detail. But that's the case. Here are four examples of what we mean.

THE AMERICAN REVOLUTION

Near Miss: If, in 1776, a pro-British soldier had read a note instead of sticking it in his pocket, America might have lost the Revolutionary War.

What Happened: The British had captured New York and sent the rebels scattering across New Jersey. Now winter set in, and while British troops quartered in towns and villages, George Washington and his men camped in the wilderness without sufficient shoes or blankets for everyone. Morale was low; Washington badly needed a victory to rally his troops or, he said, "I think the game will be pretty near up." Just in time, Washington learned that the Hessian troops (pro-British German mercenaries) stationed at Trenton were vulnerable to a surprise attack. So around midnight, December 26, he and his men secretly crossed the Delaware river to strike.

A British spy found out their plans. But when the spy arrived at the Hessian camp, he was told to leave a note for the German-speaking colonel in charge. The colonel was busy "drinking apple-jack and playing cards"...and when he was handed the note, he ignored it. "It was late, he was groggy, and the note was in English, which he couldn't read. He put it in his pocket."

"Washington attacked at dawn and took one thousand prisoners in a much-needed victory. The colonel was wounded in the battlefield. As he lay dying, the note was found and translated into German. Had he read it earlier, he admitted, 'I would not be here.' "

THE TITANIC

Near Miss: With an extra pair of binoculars, the *Titanic* might have been saved.

What Happened: After the *Titanic* was launched, but before it left on its maiden voyage in 1912, one of the ship's lookouts reported that two pairs of binoculars—used by the deck crew to spot icebergs—were missing. He put in a request for a new pair, but the request was denied. So the deck crew kept watch for icebergs with their naked eyes. On April 1912, the *Titanic* struck an iceberg and sank, drowning more than 1,500 people. Lookout Frederick Fleet, one of only 705 survivors, told investigators that the binoculars would have allowed the crew to see the iceberg in time to avoid it.

PEARL HARBOR

Near Miss: The U.S. almost learned of the attack on Pearl Harbor in time to defend against it.

What Happened: At 7 a.m. on the morning of December 7, 1941, radar operators Joseph Lockhard and George Elliott had just finished their shift at a radar station on the island of Oahu, Hawaii. But the truck that was supposed to pick them up was late, so they stayed at their consoles a few minutes longer, and at 7:02 Elliott picked up the biggest blip either man had ever seen. They tried to call the control room, but according to the John and Claire Whitcomb in their book *Oh Say Can You See*, "the line was dead—the men in the control room had gone to breakfast."

> Elliott tried the regular phone circuit and got through to Lieutenant Kermit Tyler, a pilot who was the only person on duty. "There's a large number of planes coming in from the north, three degrees east." Lieutenant Tyler was unimpressed. Lockard got on the line and tried to convince the lieutenant that it was important—he had never seen so many planes on the screen. "Well, don't worry about it," Tyler finally said. At 7:45 a.m. the truck came and the two privates shut down the station and left. At 7:55 a.m. the first bombs fell on Pearl Harbor.

A PRESIDENT'S LIFE

Near Miss: President Franklin Delano Roosevelt was almost assassinated in 1943, during World War II...by the *U.S. Navy*.

What Happened: On November 14, 1943, the battleship *Iowa* was carrying FDR and his joint chiefs of staff to Cairo for a secret conference with Winston Churchill and Chiang Kai-shek. According to one account, "In one of the U.S. Navy's most embarrassing moments, the destroyer *William D. Porter*, making a simulated torpedo attack during defensive exercises, inadvertently fired a live 'fish' directly at the *Iowa*. Five minutes of pure panic ensued. The *Iowa*'s skipper desperately executed a high-speed turn, trying to get his ship out of the line of fire. However, as the torpedo entered the *Iowa*'s churning wake, it exploded, set off by the extreme turbulence of the sea."

Yuck! 70% of the dust in your house is skin your family members (including pets) have shed.

TWISTED TITLES

California Monthly, the magazine for alumni of the University of California at Berkeley, features a game called Twisted Titles. They ask readers to send the title of a book, film, play, etc., with just one letter changed—and include a brief description of the new work they envision. Here are some that were submitted way back in 1994.

WHAT KIND OF FOOD AM I?
The Donner Party's marching song.

IN THE BIGINNING
God created baseball.

THE COLD RUSH
Limbaugh is shipped to Alaska.

PREPARATION "I"
To reduce the swelling of an inflated ego.

A FRIDGE TOO FAR
Couch potato dies of thirst.

SHORTS ILLUSTRATED
Playboy *for pygmies.*

TOP NUN
Hollywood does the biography of Mother Teresa.

WHEN I SAY HO I FEEL GUILTY
Self-help book for Santas who laugh too much.

WAA AND PEACE
The baby's finally asleep.

MRS. DOUBTTIRE
AAA gets a new automotive critic.

IN THE LINE OF TIRE
The reason behind road kills.

BORN FRED
Marilyn shocks her classmates at their 25th reunion.

NAIR
The original, unsightly Broadway cast is removed only to appear again in 3 to 4 days.

CAR AND DRIVEL
Magazine features automotive nonsense.

FIFTY WAYS TO LEASE YOUR LOVER
Innovative ways to beat the recession.

I GET A KINK OUT OF YOU
Chiropractic anthem.

I CHUNG
Connie tries a new greeting on TV.

Scientists say: An average person gives off about as much heat in an hour as a 100-watt lightbulb.

PRESIDENTIAL QUIZ

How much obscure stuff about the presidents do you know? Here's a multiple-choice quiz by Jerome Agel to help you find out. Answers on page 669.

1. Before Congress decided that the responsibility was the nation's and not an individual's, ____________ personally paid pensions to the widows of former presidents.

(a) Babe Ruth
(b) William S. Paley
(c) Andrew Carnegie
(d) Oliver Wendell Holmes, Jr.

2. The term "First Lady" was first used to describe the wife of

(a) President John F. Kennedy
(b) President Martin Van Buren
(c) President George Washington
(d) President Rutherford B. Hayes

3. The first president to be born in the United States rather than in an English colony was

(a) Martin Van Buren
(b) James K. Polk
(c) John Quincy Adams
(d) Zachary Taylor

4. No president and only one vice president, ____________, has been sworn in outside the United States.

(a) Alben Barclay
(b) Thomas Jefferson
(c) William Rufus De Vane King
(d) Harry S. Truman

5. After his presidency, William H. Taft (1857-1930) became

(a) the owner of a health farm in Ludlow, Vermont
(b) chief justice of the Supreme Court
(c) commissioner of major league baseball
(d) president of the International Red Cross

6. No president has been

(a) An alcoholic
(b) An only child
(c) A driven man
(d) Close to his father

1960s music trivia: The Byrds say they wrote "Eight Miles High" about an airplane ride.

7. President Theodore Roosevelt (1858-1919) was awarded the Nobel Peace Prize in 1906 for

(a) putting down his "big stick" diplomacy
(b) warning Czar Nicholas that his Baltic fleet would be ambushed by the Japanese in Tsushima Strait
(c) mediating the Russo-Japanese War, in a treaty conclave in Portsmouth, New Hampshire
(d) keeping U.S. marines out of the French-German war over the future of Morocco

8. The first president to accept in person the nomination of his party's convention rather than follow tradition and acknowledge it weeks later was

(a) Thomas Jefferson
(b) Zachary Taylor
(c) Grover Cleveland (the third time)
(d) Franklin D. Roosevelt

9. The first president to visit a foreign country was ________ and he visited __________.

(a) Grover Cleveland, Canada
(b) Theodore Roosevelt, Panama
(c) Zachary Taylor, Mexico
(d) Thomas Jefferson, France

10. _________ presidents were professional soldiers.

(a) Two
(b) Six
(c) Nine
(d) Twelve

11. _________ was defeated for the legislature, failed in business, suffered a nervous breakdown, was defeated for nomination for Congress, lost renomination to Congress, was rejected for land office, was defeated for the Senate, was defeated for nomination for vice president, was defeated for the Senate, then became president.

(a) Abraham Lincoln
(b) William McKinley
(c) James Madison
(d) Jimmy Carter

Did you see it? A 1966 movie was called *Jesse James Meets Frankenstein's Daughter*.

THE BIRTH OF THE COMIC BOOK

A story for people who read comics in the bathroom.

The modern comic book was born at the Eastern Color Printing Company in Waterbury, Connecticut.

In the late 1920s, Eastern printed the Sunday comic sections for a number of East Coast newspapers. Eastern's sales manager, Harry Wildenberg, was looking for ways to increase the company's profits and keep the printing presses busy. He came up with a clever idea: bind some of the comics into a "tabloid-sized book," and sell them as a premium.

He convinced the Gulf Oil Company to give it a shot. They bought the books, gave them to customers...and were pleased with the results. Eastern had a new product to sell.

Meanwhile, Wildenberg was trying to make the package more practical. He noticed that if he shrank the comic strips to half-size, he could fit two complete strips on each tabloid-sized page. He played with the idea, and figured out how to produce a 64-page book of comics on Eastern's presses.

A NEW PRODUCT

This new creation was a big hit with companies whose products were geared to kids. Procter & Gamble, Kinney Shoes, Canada Dry, and other businesses gave away anywhere from 100,000 to 250,000 copies at a time.

Then it occurred to people at Eastern that if the product was so popular as a premium, maybe it could be sold directly to kids. So in 1934, they printed 200,000 copies of a "comic book" called *Famous Funnies*, put a price on them (10¢), and got them onto newsstands around the country.

Famous Funnies was an instant hit. Eastern sold 180,000 copies—90% of the first print run. And by the 12th issue, they were making as much as $30,000 a month from it.

The comic book was established as a profitable part of American pop culture.

Three most profitable sections in a supermarket: meat, fresh produce, pet food.

GROUNDS FOR DIVORCE

Think you're in a bad relationship? Take a look at these folks.

In Loving, New Mexico, a woman divorced her husband because he made her salute him and address him as "Major" whenever he walked by.

One Tarittville, Connecticut, man filed for divorce after his wife left him a note on the refrigerator. It read, "I won't be home when you return from work. Have gone to the bridge club. There'll be a recipe for your dinner at 7 o'clock on Channel 2."

In Lynch Heights, Delaware, a woman filed for divorce because her husband "regularly put itching powder in her underwear when she wasn't looking."

In Honolulu, Hawaii, a man filed for divorce from his wife, because she "served pea soup for breakfast and dinner...and packed his lunch with pea sandwiches."

In Hazard, Kentucky, a man divorced his wife because she "beat him whenever he removed onions from his hamburger without first asking for permission."

In Frackville, Pennsylvania, a woman filed for divorce because her husband insisted on "shooting tin cans off of her head with a slingshot."

One Winthrop, Maine, man divorced his wife because she "wore earplugs whenever his mother came to visit."

A Smelterville, Idaho, man won divorce from his wife on similar grounds. "His wife dressed up as a ghost and tried to scare his elderly mother out of the house."

In Canon City, Colorado, a woman divorced her husband because he made her "duck under the dashboard whenever they drove past his girlfriend's house."

No escape: In Bennettsville, South Carolina, a deaf man filed for divorce from his wife because "she was always nagging him in sign language."

The Last Straw: In Hardwick, Georgia, a woman actually divorced her husband because he "stayed home too much and was much too affectionate."

Ayatollah Ruhollah Khomeini had a weakness for cologne.

OOPS!

Everyone's amused by tales of outrageous blunders—probably because it's comforting to know that someone's screwing up even worse than we are. So here's an ego-building page from BRI. Go ahead and feel superior for a few minutes.

STAMP OF DISAPPROVAL

In January 1994, the Postal Service unveiled a new set of commemorative stamps called *Legends of the West*. One of them honored rodeo star Bill Pickett, "the nation's foremost black cowboy." The portrait on the stamp was copied from a photo that Pickett's biographer had pulled from a folder marked "B. Pickett" years earlier. However, the face on the stamp wasn't Bill Pickett's. It was that of Bill's brother, Ben. The Postal Service had to recall the 100 million stamps they'd sent out. The cost: $1 million.

HE'S GOT A GUN!

In June 1993, a security officer patrolling the parking lot at Rochester General Hospital noticed a mustachioed figure sitting in the back seat of a car, with a rifle propped between his knees. The guard yelled to the man, got no response, then called the police. First, they sealed the back entrance to the hospital. Then, sharpshooters surrounded the car and tried to negotiate with the armed man. Then they realized the figure was a mannequin.

A BAD REVIEW

"In 1987 the *San Francisco Chronicle* published a review of the San Francisco ballet's performance of *Bizet pas de Deux*. The review, headlined 'S.F. Ballet Misses a Step at Stern Grove,' slammed the performance. It nicknamed the principal dancer, Ludmila Lupokhova 'Lumpy,' and referred to her 'potato-drenched Russian training.' However, it turned out that the program had been changed at the last minute to *Ballet d'Isoline*, performed by five male dancers; Lupokhova had not even appeared.

Critic Heuwell Tircuit blamed poor health. He said he had been so sick during the performance that he hadn't noticed the change in program and dancers.

1994 news report: Taco Bell had 3 restaurants in downtown Mexico City.

His editors said his story was "hardly credible" and fired him.

—From *If No News, Send Rumors*

A DATE TO REMEMBER

On November 7, 1918, Admiral Henry B. Wilson, director of U.S. naval operations in France, received a telegram from Paris informing him that World War I was finally over. Wilson leaked the information to Roy Howard, president of the United Press wire service, and the news quickly crossed the Atlantic. It made headlines in afternoon papers all over the U.S., bringing business to a halt, causing joyous celebrations, and prompting a mammoth tickertape parade through the streets of New York City.

Later that evening, Howard discovered the message had been a fake. The war actually ended four days later.

MISSED HIM BY *THAT* MUCH

"In April 1993, just after Steve Morrow scored the goal that gave the Arsenal team England's League Cup soccer championship, his teammates tossed him into the air in ritual celebration of their victory. However, they failed to catch him when he came down and Morrow was carried off the field on a stretcher and oxygen mask over his face. It was later determined he had a broken arm."

—From *News of the Weird*

EATING CROW

"During the Reagan era, a mother of four wrote to the White House saying she couldn't feed her family on the reduced-food-stamps program. Someone apparently thought it was a request for a recipe and forwarded it to the First Lady's office...which sent the woman a copy of Mrs. Reagan's crab and asparagus recipe, costing about $20 to prepare.

"The Reagan administration was in the midst of trying to declare ketchup a vegetable and lines of the hungry were forming to pick up surplus cheese," writes *The New York Times*, and the news media had a field day with the incident. "Thereafter, when the White House was asked for a recipe, it sent out one of Ronald Reagan's favorites: macaroni and cheese."

—From *But Not That Subject*

Mark Twain tried to convince children that Santa Claus lived on the moon. He couldn't.

THE NATURAL HISTORY OF THE UNICORN

Today we know that there's no such thing as unicorns. But back in the 1500s, they were a sort of respectable version of Bigfoot. Although only a few people had ever "seen" them, it was widely believed that they existed. So when Topsell's Historie of Four-footed Beastes, *the first illustrated natural history in English, was published in 1607, unicorns were included. Here are some excerpts from the original version of the book. Remember, as you read, that these descriptions were considered science, not fantasy.*

ABOUT THE HORN

• "We will now relate the true history of the horn of the unicorn. The horn grows out of the forehead between the eyelids. It is neither light nor hollow, nor yet smooth like other horns, but hard as iron, rough as a file. It is wreathed about with divers spires. It is sharper than any dart, and it is straight and not crooked, and everywhere black except at the point."

• "The horn of the unicorn has a wonderful power of dissolving and expelling all venom or poison. If the unicorn puts his horn into water from which any venomous beast has drunk, the horn drives away poison, so that the unicorn can drink without harm. It is said that the horn being put upon the tables of kings and set among their junkets and banquets reveals any venom if there be any such therein, by a certain sweat which comes over the horn."

• "The horn of a unicorn being beaten and boiled in wine has a wonderful effect in making the teeth white or clear. And thus much shall suffice for the medicines and virtues arising from the unicorn."

THE WILD CREATURE

• "Unicorns are very swift. They keep for the most part in the deserts and live solitary in the tops of mountains. There is nothing more horrible than the voice or braying of the unicorn, for his voice is strained above measure."

• "The unicorn fights with both the mouth and his heels, with the mouth biting like a lion's and with the heels kicking like a horse's.

He is a beast of an untamable nature. He fears not iron nor any iron instrument."

• "What is most strange of all other is that he fights with his own kind (yea, even with females unto death, except when he burns in lust for procreation), but unto stranger-beasts, with whom he has no affinity in nature, he is more sociable and familiar, delighting in their company when they come willingly unto him, never rising against them, but proud of their dependence and retinue, keeps with them all quarters of league and truce."

• "With his female, when once his flesh is tickled with lust, he grows tame, gregarious, and loving, and so continues till she is filled and great with young, and then returns to his former hostility."

NATURAL ENEMIES

• "The unicorn is an enemy to the lion, wherefore, as soon as ever a lion sees a unicorn, he runs to a tree for succor, so that, when the unicorn makes force at him, he may not only avoid his horn but also destroy the unicorn, for, in the swiftness of his course, the unicorn runs against the tree wherein his sharp horn sticks fast."

• "Then, when the lion sees the unicorn fastened by his horn, he falls upon him and kills him."

CAPTURING THE UNICORN

• "It is said that unicorns above all other creatures do reverence virgins and young maids, and that many times at the sight of them, unicorns grow tame, and come and sleep beside them, for there is in their nature a certain savor by which the unicorns are allured and delighted."

• "The Indian and Ethiopian hunters are said to use a stratagem to take the beast. They take a goodly strong and beautiful young man, whom they dress in the apparel of a woman, besetting him with divers odoriferous flowers and spices."

• "The man so adorned, they set him in the mountains or the woods where the unicorn hunts, so as the wind may carry the savor to the beast, and in the mean season, the other hunters hide themselves."

As a person ages, the first sense to go is the sense of smell.

• "Deceived by the outward shape of a woman and the sweet smells, the unicorn comes unto the young man without fear and so suffers his head to be covered and wrapped within his large sleeves, never stirring but lying still and asleep, as in his most acceptable repose."

• "Then when the hunters by the sign of the young man perceive the unicorn fast and secure, they come upon him and by force cut off his horn and send him away alive."

PROOF THAT UNICORNS EXIST

Why was Edward Topsell so sure that unicorns roamed the earth? A matter of faith. Although he'd never seen a unicorn, Topsell believed that to doubt its existence was to deny the very existence of God:

• "That there is such a beast Scripture itself witnesses, for David thus speaks in Psalm 92: 'My horn shall be lifted up like the horn of a unicorn.'"

• "All divines that have ever written have not only concluded that there is a unicorn, but also affirm the similitude between the kingdom of David and the horn of the unicorn, for as the horn of the unicorn is wholesome to all beasts and creatures, so should the kingdom of David be in the generation of Christ."

• "Do we think that David would compare the virtue of his kingdom and the powerful redemption of the world unto a thing that is not or is uncertain and fantastical? Likewise, in many other places of Scripture, we will have to traduce God, Himself, if there is no unicorn in the world."

* * *

MISC. BATHROOM NEWS

Denver, Sept. 29, 1993—"Portable potties at the construction site at Denver International Airport stink so much that someone has been setting them on fire. Five have been burned in the last month.

"One of the two burned on Monday bore a graffiti warning: 'If you don't fix the toilet paper dispenser, I'll burn down another one. Signed, The Flame Man.'

"Last week, a similar message on a charred toilet warned officials to 'Keep the toilets clean or they'll get burned.'"

Fifty-four percent of U.S. women say they'd rather "get run over by a truck" than gain 150 lbs.

WELCOME TO... "THE OUTER LIMITS"

Monsters have always been hits with moviemakers and their audiences, but "The Outer Limits" (which aired from 1963 to 1965) marked the first time TV viewers got a "monster of the week." The show was more than that, though; the lighting and cinematography gave the show an offbeat, intensely atmospheric look—and the writing was impressively literate. Despite its lukewarm ratings in its first run it remains one of TV's most memorable shows.

HOW IT STARTED

In 1961, Leslie Stevens came up with an idea for a science-fiction show about "the awe and mystery of the universe." He brought it up in a conversation with "packager programmer" Dan Melnick, who agreed it would make a good show—as long as it had monsters in it to make it commercial. And "The Outer Limits" was born.

Well, actually *Please Stand By* was born, because that was the title of the proposed pilot that Stevens sold to ABC in 1962. Filming began December 2, with Joe Stefano producing. Early on, ABC requested the addition of a Rod Sterling-like host to speak directly to the audience. Stefano didn't want one, so he compromised: he created an unseen presence called "the Control Voice" which introduced and commented on each episode. It was Stefano's excuse to editorialize. However, 1962 was a bad time to be flashing "Please Stand By" on screen while an "ominous voice" took control of viewers' TV sets. Only a few months earlier, the Cuban missile crisis had brought us to the brink of World War III. ABC guessed that an already frightened public might mistake the show for an official announcement and create an Orson Welles-type panic.

So the name was changed to Beyond Control and then to "The Outer Limits." The series finally began shooting on May 22, 1963, and premiered 3½ months later. The show only ran until January 16, 1965.

71% of college-educated women—but only 44% of non-college-educated women—breastfeed.

SPECIAL EFFECTS

To the producers of *The Outer Limits*, the monsters were metaphors; it was the contemporary themes of the stories that mattered, not the costumes and special effects. This was convenient, because their "creature budget" was only $10,000 to $40,000 per episode. They had to be very creative when it came to the scary stuff. For example:

• The Andromedan from the episode "Galaxy Being" was a guy in a brown wetsuit coated with glycerin and oil, and negative-reversed to produce a shimmering *white* monster.

• In one scary episode, poisonous alien plants take root on the earth and shoot deadly spores into the air. But the audience wouldn't have been too frightened if they had known the "spores" were actually puffed wheat cereal!

• By consensus, the most ridiculous *Outer Limits* monster ever created was the Megasoid. It consisted of "a floppy velour gorilla suit (through which the actor's T-shirt could frequently be seen), a dubbed-in German shepherd growl, and a "recycled bird mask" from a previous episode.

CAN YOU BEAR IT?

Although Stevens and Stefano had lofty ideas about what they were trying to accomplish in their stories, ABC only cared about the monsters, which Stefano always referred to as "the bears." He explained: "In the old vaudeville days, when things were going wrong and the audience was getting bored, out would come a comic in a bear outfit. That's what we do in each of our shows—'Bring on the bear!'"

HOT PROP-ERTY

Eleven years after "The Outer Limits" last showing, Robin Williams appeared as Mork from Ork, wearing a helmet used in an "Outer Limits" episode called "The Specimen."

CENSORED

"The Cats," an episode in which aliens "take possession of the bodies of household pets to invade the Earth," was never shown. ABC feared that viewers who had cats at home might become scared of them."

IRS fact: 20 million taxpayers a year wait until April to begin filling out their tax returns.

REALLY SCARY

"The Outer Limits'" producer Joseph Stefano also wrote the screenplay for Alfred Hitchcock's classic film, *Psycho*.

TRUE CONFESSIONS

Instructions given to Outer Limits writers: "Each play should have one splendid, staggering, shuddering effect that induces awe, wonder, tolerable terror, or even merely conversation and argument."

THE CONTROL VOICE

An announcer named Vic Perrin supplied the narrator's voice ("There is nothing wrong with your television set...Do not attempt to adjust the picture...) Here's the sort of thing viewers heard him say every week:

> Here, in the bright, clustered loneliness of thebillion, billion stars, loneliness can be an exciting, voluntary thing, unlike the loneliness man suffers on earth. Here, deep in the starry nowhere, a man can be as one with space and time; preoccupied, yet not indifferent; anxious, yet at peace. His name is Joseph Reardon. He is, in this present year, thirty years old. This is the first time he has made this journey alone..."

OUR FAVORITE EPISODES

"The Architects of Fear." Robert Culp, a scientist, is selected by idealistic cronies to frighten the nations of Earth into unite against a common enemy. the plan: He'll be transformed into a monster, land a flying saucer at the U.N, and threateningly announce he is from the planet Theta. Instead, the saucer crashes off course, and he's shot by a bunch of hunters.

"The Man Who Never Was Born." Reardon, a time traveler, discovers that in the year 2148 the human population has been wiped out by an alien germ which was nurtured by a man named Cabot. So he and a disfigured humanoid from the future travel back in time to prevent Cabot's birth.

* * *

"In the year 2000, Twinkies from 1973 will still be fresh."

—***Conan O'Brien***

PROMOTIONS THAT BACKFIRED

When companies want to drum up some new business to get favorable publicity, they sponsor promotions. But sometimes things don't work out as planned. The businesses wind up with angry customers and egg on their face. Here are three promos that companies wish they could take back.

RADIO DAZE

The Promotion: On April 6, 1994, KYNG-FM radio in Fort Worth, Texas, announced that it had hidden $100 worth of $5 and $10 bills in books in the fiction section of the Fort Worth Central Library. The station said it organized the publicity stunt "to boost public interest in the library."

What Happened: The station expected only about 30 people to show up and look for the cash, but when a rumor surfaced that there was $10,000 hidden in the books, more than 500 people descended on the library looking for the loot, sparking a near riot in the fiction section.

Backfire! "Books were sailing, and elbows were flying, and people were climbing the shelves," the library's spokesperson told reporters. "To a librarian, that's sacrilege." More than 3,500 books were knocked off the shelves in the process, and hundreds were damaged. KYNG apologized for the incident, agreed to pay for the damaged books, and reimbursed the library for the time the librarians spent putting them back on the shelves.

PEPSI HITS THE SPOT

The Promotion: In 1993, Pepsi launched their "Number Fever" contest promotion in the Philippines. It promised instant cash of up to 1 million pesos ($37,000) to contestants who held bottle caps with the correct 3-digit winning number.

What Happened: Thanks to a "computer software glitch," the company accidentally printed and circulated 800,000 caps bearing the number 349...and on May 25, 1992, that number was selected at random as the winning number. Thousands of winners came forward to collect their prizes. Pepsi admitted its mistake, but agreed to pay only $18 to anyone holding one of the caps. They called it a "goodwill" gesture.

Backfire! Pepsi spent about $10 million paying off more than 500,000 people...but many of the winners refused to cooperate. They were *really* angry. The *Chicago Tribune* reported in August 1993:

> Irate winners rioted at some of the plants. Others attacked bottling plants and delivery trucks with grenades and firebombs. At least 37 trucks have been burned in such attacks and a bottling plant stopped operation because of grenade damage. A teacher and a 5-year-old girl died when a grenade bounced off a truck and exploded near a crowd on a street.

THE REAL THING

The Promotion: In the summer of 1990, Coca-Cola launched the largest consumer promotion in its history—a $100 million ad campaign featuring 750,000 high-tech "MagiCans." These seemingly ordinary 12-ounce cans of Coke actually contained millions of dollars in cash and prizes. "When a buyer pops the top," the *Wall Street Journal* wrote, "a device rises through the opening in the can and displays legal tender—anywhere from $1 to $100—or a scroll of paper, redeemable for prizes. To give the cans the feel of the real product, Coke has partially filled them with chlorinated water."

What Happened: In May, an 11-year-old Massachusetts boy opened a defective MagiCan and drank the water. His mother thought the can had been tampered with because it was filled with "a clear liquid...tasting and smelling like cleaning solution." She called the police...who found the malfunctioning prize-delivery mechanism and a soggy $5 bill.

Backfire! Coke—trying to save the promotion—ran full-page ads in newspapers, warning consumers not to drink the contents of prize-filled cans. They included a toll-free number, so people could report defective cans. But the bad publicity (and potential for lawsuits) spread. By the end of May, more than 20 malfunctioning cans had been reported. Then experts pointed out that "the labeling on some Coke cans could be illegal, because the cans contain prizes instead of the real article." On June 1, citing adverse publicity, Coke cancelled the campaign.

Most effective deterrent to house break-ins: "A noisy dog," thieves say.

JOE McCARTHY'S JOKE

In the early 1950s, Senator Joseph McCarthy had Americans believing that Red Agents were infiltrating the U.S. government. The result was one of the biggest witch-hunts in American history. But according to It's a Conspiracy! *by The National Insecurity Council, McCarthy lied. Here's the part of the story you may not have heard.*

On February 9, 1950, Joe McCarthy, a rumpled, ill-shaven junior senator from Wisconsin, made a Lincoln's Birthday speech to a Republican women's club in Wheeling, West Virginia. No one—not even McCarthy—considered it an important appearance. Yet that speech made Senator Joseph McCarthy the most feared man in America.

Waving a piece of paper before the group, McCarthy declared, "I have here in my hand a list of 205 names made known to the Secretary of State as being members of the Communist party, who are nevertheless still working and shaping policy in the State Department."

Republicans had been calling Democrats Communists for years. But before this, it had just been political name-calling—no one had claimed to know exactly how many Communists were supposedly in the government. This was a paranoid nation's worst nightmare come true; McCarthy's speech made headlines. By the time he had given a similar speech in Salt Lake City and returned to Washington, D.C., newspapers from coast to coast had repeated his charges as fact and the country was in an uproar.

The McCarthy Era—an American inquisition that ruined the lives of thousands of innocent citizens accused of being Communists, Communist dupes, or Communist sympathizers—had begun.

THE McCARTHY ERA

• Although he never substantiated his charges, McCarthy's influence grew rapidly. As chair of the Permanent Investigations Sub-Committee of the Senate Committee on Government Operations, he presided over a witch-hunt for Communists. Americans from all walks of life were challenged to prove their loyalty in an atmosphere of panic and paranoia.

How do they count them? There are one trillion atoms in a grain of salt.

• Fear became his most potent weapon. "Many of those who came before McCarthy, as well as many who testified before the powerful House Un-American Activities Committee (HUAC), were willing to point fingers at others to save their own careers and reputations," writes Kenneth Davis in *Don't Know Much About History*. "To fight back was to be tarred with McCarthy's 'Communist sympathizer' brush....In this cynical atmosphere, laws of evidence and constitutional guarantees didn't apply."

• For four years, McCarthy was as powerful as anyone in Washington. He forced President Eisenhower to clear appointments through him; the president even instituted loyalty programs for people in government, to prove that he, too, was tough on Communism.

THE TRUTH ABOUT MCCARTHY

But did McCarthy and his cronies really believe there was a Communist conspiracy...or was it just an attempt to gain power? There are plenty of suspicious facts to consider:

• Early in 1950, McCarthy told friends he needed a gimmick to get reelected. He was in political hot water with voters because he had introduced no major legislation and had been assigned to no important committees. Newspaper correspondents in the capital had voted him "the worst in the Senate."

• According to Frederick Woltman, a friend of the senator's, McCarthy had made up the number of Communists on the spur of the moment during his Lincoln's Birthday speech—and had just as promptly forgotten it. Caught off-guard by the outcry, McCarthy and his advisors wracked their brains for some lead as to what he had said in the Wheeling speech. "He had no copy...he could not find the notes....The Senator's staff could find no one who could recall what he'd said precisely."

• That may be why every time McCarthy counted Communists, he came up with a different number. The day after the Wheeling speech, he changed the number from 205 to 57 "card-carrying Communists." A week later, he stated before a Senate Foreign Relations subcommittee that he knew of "81 known Communists." The number changed to 10 in open committee hearings, 116 in an executive session, 121 at the end of a four-month investigation, and 106 in a June 6 Senate speech.

When asked, "Joe, just what did you have in your hand down there in Wheeling?" McCarthy gave his characteristic roguish grin and replied, "An old laundry list."

• He was able to keep up the charade for so long because he would attack anybody who questioned his accuracy. For example: When the majority leader of the Senate asked if the newspaper accounts of his Wheeling speech were accurate, McCarthy replied indignantly, "I may say if the Senator is going to make a farce of this, I will not yield to him. I shall not answer any more silly questions of the Senator. This is too important, too serious a matter for that."

J. EDGAR HOOVER IN THE BACKGROUND

• According to Curt Gentry in *J. Edgar Hoover: The Man and the Secrets*: "On returning home from his speaking tour, McCarthy called J. Edgar Hoover and told him he was getting a lot of attention on the Communist issue. But, he admitted, he had made up the numbers as he talked...and he asked if the FBI could give him the information to back him up." William Sullivan, who later became third in command at the FBI, protested that the Bureau didn't have sufficient evidence to prove there was even *one* Communist in the State Department.

• Hoover—completely ignoring the FBI's charter—assigned FBI agents to gather domestic intelligence on his ideological enemies, poring over hundreds of Bureau security files to help support McCarthy's charges. According to Gentry, Hoover did even more: "He supplied speechwriters for McCarthy...and instructed him how to release a story just before press deadline, so reporters wouldn't have time to ask for rebuttals. Even more important, he advised him to avoid the phrase 'card-carrying Communist,' which usually couldn't be proven, substituting 'Communist sympathizer' or 'loyalty risk,' which required only some affiliation, however slight."

McCARTHY'S DOWNFALL

When McCarthy began attacking Eisenhower and the army in 1954, Hoover sensed that his own job might be in danger and ordered FBI aides not to help the senator further. Poorly prepared, McCarthy tried to bluff his way through the televised army hearings, but this time he failed. Americans saw him as a bully and a liar, and the press turned on him. In Dec. 1954, McCarthy became the fourth member in history to be censured by the U.S. Senate.

There really is an insect called the love bug. It spends 56 hours—more than 1/2 its life—mating.

DOUBLE-CROSS IN THE DESERT?

Was Jimmy Carter just unlucky, or was his plan to rescue the Iranian hostages sabotaged?

On November 4, 1979, mobs in revolutionary Iran stormed the U.S. Embassy in Teheran and took 53 Americans hostage. For the next six months, President Jimmy Carter tried to gain the hostages' release by negotiating with the Iranian government. Finally, frustrated with the lack of progress and concerned about deteriorating political conditions in Iran, Carter ordered a military rescue of the hostages on the night of April 24, 1980.

THE RESCUE PLAN

• The mission, code-named Operation Eagle Claw, was spearheaded by roughly 100 members of Delta Force, a crack team chosen from all four U.S. military services.

• It was a complicated plan:

✓ Four C-130 cargo planes with most of the Delta Force flew from a military base in Egypt to Desert One, a remote area in eastern Iran. There, they were to rendezvous with eight helicopters coming from an aircraft carrier stationed near the mouth of the Persian Gulf.

✓ The commandos were to board the helicopters and fly to Desert Two, located fifty miles from Teheran. There they would meet with U.S. and Iranian operatives, then be transported by truck into the capital city.

✓ At the embassy the team would storm the walled compound and free the hostages.

PROBLEMS

• From the first, things went wrong. "Two of the helicopters experienced problems en route...and at the desert landing a third experienced a severe hydraulic malfunction." (The *New York Times*)

• Other sources claim that two other helicopters became "clogged

F. Scott Fitzgerald wrote nine books in 1939. He was paid a total of $33 for them.

with desert sand." (*Covert Action*)

• Since there weren't enough choppers to get the troops to Desert Two, the mission was aborted. But then, even more disaster struck: one of the helicopters collided with a cargo plane and exploded. The Americans fled, leaving behind wrecked aircraft and top-secret documents. There were eight American casualties.

• Carter was forced to admit failure. "The President has ordered the cancellation of an operation in Iran that was under way to prepare for a rescue of our hostages," the White House announced. "The mission was terminated because of equipment failure....The President accepts full responsibility."

SUSPICIOUS FACTS

• According to The *New York Times*, "the breakdown of three of eight helicopters in a single operation is disturbing. Aircraft industry experts said they could not account for the high percentage of breakdowns and estimated the actuarial figures at 1 in 10,000."

• The manufacturer, Sikorsky, was also baffled: A company spokesperson said the helicopters were "routinely fitted with engine air-particle separators designed to exclude sand." Had the filters been removed?

• Many analysts thought the mission ill-conceived. "Ninety men, no matter how well trained and armed, could not storm a fortress, which is what the embassy has become, against a determined garrison of militants." (The *New York Times*)

• One of the support crew at Desert Two was a marine officer, Oliver North. He was later assigned to work with Major General Richard Secord on a second rescue mission.

WAS IT A CONSPIRACY?

Was the hostage rescue mission sabotaged?

Some people suspect it was—possibly in a plot by Reagan supporters to discredit Carter. Conspiracy theorists point out that the helicopters could have been sabotaged by a single person removing engine filters or puncturing a hydraulic line. But as intriguing as it would be to link Oliver North to another conspiracy, so far there's no evidence either way. In fact, it's probably fortunate that the rescue failed where it did. Had Delta Force besieged the embassy, the hostages might well have been executed by their captors.

The "first electronic computer" was built in 1889 for the U.S. Census Bureau.

SHEER SHANDLING

A few thoughts from the man with the original "bad hair day," comedian Garry Shandling.

"The mirror over my bed reads, 'Objects appear larger than they are.'"

"I'm dating a women who, evidently, is unaware of it."

"I'm not kinky, but occasionally I like to put on a robe and stand in front of a tennis ball machine."

"I once made love for an hour and fifteen minutes, but it was the night the clocks were set ahead."

"Oysters are supposed to enhance your sexual performance, but they don't work for me. Maybe I put them on too soon."

"After making love I said to my girl, 'Was it good for you, too?' And she said, 'I don't think this was good for anybody.'"

"They should put expiration dates on clothes so we would know when they go out of style."

"I'm not thrilled about flying.... We don't know how old the airplanes are and there's really no way for us to tell, 'cause we're laymen. But I figure if the plane smells like your grandmother's house, get out. That's where I draw the line."

"I'm dating a homeless woman. It was easier to talk her into staying over."

"I can't believe I actually own my own house. I'm looking at a house and it's two hundred grand. The realtor says, 'It's got a great view.' For two hundred grand I better open up the curtains and see breasts against the window."

"I'm very loyal in relationships. Even when I go out with my mom I don't look at other moms."

"The last girl I made love to, it was not going well. Anytime you make love and have to give her the Heimlich maneuver at the same time, it's not a good thing."

Sure, blame the kids: 9% of women and 4% of men say their divorce is the kids' fault.

FOOD FIGHT!

This title probably conjures up visions of leftover vegetables being hurled across a school cafeteria. But in at least two instances, people actually used food as a weapon in real wars. Here are the stories.

TAKE THAT!

"The Uraguayan army once fought a sea battle using cheeses as cannonballs.

"It happened in the 1840s. The aggressive Argentine dictator Juan Manual de Rosas, in an attempt to annex Uraguay, ordered his navy to blockade Montevideo, the capital. The besieged Uraguayans held their own in battle until they ran out of conventional ammunition. In desperation, they raided the galleys of their ships and loaded their cannons with very old, hard Edam cheeses and fired them at the enemy.

"Contemporary chronicles record that the Uraguayans won the skirmish."

—From *Significa,* by Irving Wallace, David Wallechinsky, and Amy Wallace

YOU SAY POTATO...

"A World War II destroyer once defeated a submarine with the help of a seldom-used weapon of destruction: potatoes.

"The *USS O'Bannon* was on patrol off the Solomon Islands in April 1943 when it encountered a Japanese sub. The crew shot off the sub's conning tower, preventing it from diving, but the captain of the sub brought it so close to the destroyer that the *O'Bannon*'s big guns couldn't be aimed at it....When the Japanese came topside, the gallant *O'Bannon* crewmen pelted them with potatoes. The Japanese thought they were being showered with grenades, threw their guns overboard, then panicked, submerged the sub and sank it.

"When the *O'Bannon* was decommissioned in the early 1970s, a plaque was made to commemorate the event, and donated to the ship, by the Maine potato growers."

— From *Beyond Belief!*, by Ron Lyon and Jenny Pacshall

Q: Which country drinks more Coke than any other nation on earth? A: Mexico.

LLOYD'S OF LONDON

Insurance companies are probably the last subject you'd expect to read about in the Bathroom Reader. *But Lloyd's of London is special. They insure stuff like people's legs and performing insects and floating bathtubs. Here's the story of Lloyd's, courtesy of BRI alum Jack Mingo, author of* How the Cadillac Got Its Fins *and numerous other books.*

ORIGIN. Today most business is conducted over the phone or in company offices, but in the 17th century the most popular place for businesses and their clients to meet was in coffeehouses—many of which were built specifically to the business trade. Lloyd's Coffee House, opened by Edward Lloyd in London in 1688, was just such a place. Lloyd wanted to take advantage for the maritime insurance trade, so he built his coffeehouse near the London docks.

Lloyd never personally got involved in the insurance business, but he provided a congenial business atmosphere, semi-enclosed booths, and even writing materials for his patrons. The cafe developed a reputation as a source of accurate shipping news and quickly became the hub of London's maritime insurance industry.

Long after Lloyd's death in 1723, his coffeehouse remained an important business meeting place.

A GROWING BUSINESS

In the 17th and 18th centuries, merchants with a ship or cargo to insure didn't buy insurance from companies—they hired a broker to go from one wealthy person to another, selling a share of the risk in exchange for a share of the insurance premium.

This was considered a respectable profession. But covering wagers on things like who would win a particular sports contest or war, or when the current king would die, was not. These less respectable brokers began frequenting Lloyd's, too.

In 1769, a number of "high-class" brokers decided they didn't want to be associated with their seamier brethren anymore. So they set up their own coffee house and called it the "New Lloyd's Coffee House." They allowed business dealings in maritime insurance only. The new building soon proved too small, so 79 brokers, underwriters, and merchants each chipped in £100 to finance new headquarters. When they moved this time, they left the coffee business behind. Over the following century, the Lloyd's society of underwriters evolved into its modern incarnation, expanding to all forms of insurance except life insurance. As one broker put it, "Everybody dies, so what's the fun of writing life insurance?"

RISKY BUSINESS

Lloyd's will insure just about anything. Here are some of the weirder items:

• **Celebrity anatomy.** Bruce Springsteen has insured his voice for £3.5 million; Marlene Dietrich had a $500,000 policy on her legs; and supermodel Suzanne Mizzi was insured for £10 million against any "serious injury" that left her unable to model underwear. During filming of the movie *Superman*, man of steel Christopher Reeves was insured for $20 million.

• **Whiskers.** Forty members of the Derbyshire, England, "Whiskers Club" insured their facial hair "against fire and theft." Cost: £20 a head.

• **Laughter.** One theater group took out a policy "against the risk of a member of their audience dying from laughter."

• **Space debris.** Before Skylab, the space laboratory, crashed to earth, Lloyd's offered coverage of up to £2.5 million for property damage and £500,000 for death coverage to anyone who wanted it. (No takers.)

• **The weather.** Lloyd's insures the opera festival of Verona, Italy, for £1 million against bad weather. Reason: When outdoor performances get cancelled due to rain, the festival has to refund ticket holders.

• **Souvenirs.** When Charles and Diana announced they were tying the knot, Lloyd's insured commemorative souvenir makers...just in case the wedding got called off.

• **A floating bathtub.** When a 20-year-old merchant navy officer sailed from Dover, England, to Cap Gris Nez, France, in a bathtub, Lloyd's insured it for £100,000 on one condition: that the tub's drain plug "remain in position at all times."

• **Dead rats.** Lloyd's once insured an entire boatload of dead rats (which were en route to a Greek research lab) for £110,000 against their condition deteriorating any further.

• **A tiny portrait.** A grain of rice with a portrait of Queen Elizabeth and Prince Philip engraved on it was insured for £20,000.

• **Nessie.** Cutty Sark Whiskey once offered £1 million to anyone who could capture the Loch Ness monster alive, and took out two £1 million policies with Lloyd's...just in case.

• **The King.** When a Memphis radio station offered $1 million to anyone who could prove Elvis was really alive, Lloyd's backed them up 100 percent.

THE NAME GAME

How Lloyd's works. Lloyd's of London isn't a company at all: It's a "society" of thousands of members (called Names because they put their "name," or full reputation and worth, behind the risk), who underwrite insurance policies with their personal assets. As was the case three centuries ago, each Name is personally liable for claims. The Name never has to turn over the money he "invests" with Lloyd's—he just has to prove that he *has* it and can surrender it on demand to pay claims.

HARD TIMES

The system worked great for hundreds of years, but disaster struck in the late 1980s, after more than a decade of excessive policy writing in which Lloyd's Names insured asbestos manufacturers, the Exxon *Valdez*, and the San Francisco earthquake of 1989. Between 1988 and 1990 the company had to pay out more than $10 billion in claims, which meant that by 1991 each of the company's 32,000 Names owed more than $312,500 to policyholders, with the total expected to climb still further. More than 21,000 of the Names sued Lloyd's, claiming that Lloyd's underwriters were negligent in writing insurance contracts. Lloyd's admitted as much in 1994, and offered a $1.3 billion settlement to the Names, but, at the time this was written, the lawsuits were still pending.

Family attachment: eight times more women than men buy Father's Day cards.

THE NUMBERS GAME

This is a tough game—very few people can solve more than a few of these equations on the first try. But don't look at the answers in the back of the book right away. People often come up with them later, when their minds are relaxed. And you can work on this page for a number of "sittings." It was sent to us by BRI member Peter Wing. Answers are on page 670.

INSTRUCTIONS

Each equation contains the initials of words that will make it a correct statement. Your job is to finish the missing words. For example: *26 = L. of the A.* would be *26 = Letters of the Alphabet*. Good luck.

1. 7 = W. of the A. W.
2. 1001 = A. N.
3. 12 = S. of the Z.
4. 54 = C. in a D. (with the J.)
5. 9 = P. in the S. S.
6. 88 = P. K.
7. 13 = S. on the A. F.
8. 32 = D. F. at which W. F.
9. 90 = D. in a R. A.
10. 99 = B. of B. on the W.
11. 18 = H. on a G. C.
12. 8 = S. on a S. S.
13. 3 = B. M. (S. H. T. R.)
14. 4 = Q. in a G.
15. 1 = W. on a U.
16. 5 = D. in a Z. C.
17. 24 = H. in a D.
18. 57 = H. V.
19. 11 = P. on a F. T.
20. 1000 = W. that a P. is W.
21. 29 = D. in F. in a L. Y.
22. 64 = S. on a C.
23. 40 = D. and N. of the G. F.
24. 2 = T. T.
25. 76 = T. in a B. P.
26. 8 = G. T. in a L. B. C.
27. 101 = D.
28. 23 = S.
29. 4 = H. a J. G. F.
30. 16 = M. on a D. M. C.
31. 12 = D. of C.
32. 5 = G. L.
33. 7 = D. S.
34. 2.5 = C. in a T. A. F.
35. 1, 2, 3 = S. Y. O. at the O. B. G.
36. 3 = M. in a T.
37. 13 = B. D.

Thirty-three percent of Americans say being an hour late still counts as being "fashionably late."

IT LOSES SOMETHING IN TRANSLATION...

Mongo teep robinek. Pargo meep, kiga lorb. Squarp? Neegah! Sheerik sot morbo. Pid rintu...guira—gop fibge. More nonsense that seems perfectly understandable to the person who's speaking. *For the first batch see page 483.*

PARDON ME...

"I once observed a foreign gentleman with halting English at a subway station asking for the correct time," author Roger Axtell recalls in his book *Do's and Taboos of Hosting International Visitors*. "He was repeatedly rebuffed by brusque New Yorkers. Edging closer, I heard the patient but tiring visitor finally say to the fifth or sixth passerby, 'Pardon me, sir, but do *you* have the correct time...or should I go screw myself, as the others have suggested?'"

ADVENTURES IN THE EAST

• In China, Kentucky Fried Chicken's slogan "finger-lickin' good" was translated as "eat your fingers off" and a phonetic adaptation of Coca-Cola came out as "Bite the Wax Tadpole."

• In Taiwan, Pepsi's "Come Alive with Pepsi" came out as "Pepsi Will Bring Your Ancestors Back from the Dead."

• Japan's second-largest tourist agency, Kinki Nippon Tourist Co., had to change the name of its overseas division because the word "Kinki" was too close to the English word "kinky." The company was worried about attracting the "wrong kind of customer."

NO HABLO ESPANOL

• Many of the T-shirts made for Pope John Paul II's visit to Miami were in Spanish. They were supposed to say "I saw the Pope." Instead, they said, "I saw the potato."

• Braniff Airlines once wanted to promote the fact that its leather seats were comfortable. According to reporters, when they did ads for Hispanic customers, they "used a slang term for leather which means a person's hide as well as a cowhide. Rather than asking people to fly Braniff on leather seats, the airline asked them to fly in the nude."

The average U.S. family redeems 81 coupons a year, compared to 33 in Canada.

• A frozen foods manufacturer used the word *burruda* to describe its burrito line. They didn't realize that the word is slang for "huge mistake."

JUST DO WHAT?

In one of its shoe commercials, Nike showed a Kenyan Samburu looking into the camera and speaking Maa, his native language. The subtitle read "Just do it," Nike's advertising slogan...but it wasn't until after the commercial hit the airwaves that company officials realized he was saying, "I don't want these. Give me big shoes."

NO SEX, PLEASE

• The Swedish company that makes Electrolux vacuum cleaners once tried to market their products in the United States using the slogan "Nothing sucks like an Electrolux." (The company's translators talked them out of it at the last minute.)

• What Brazilian would have admitted to driving a Ford Pinto? Pinto, it turns out, is slang in Portuguese for "small male genitals." Ford changed the name in Brazil to "Corcel," which means *horse*.

* * * * *

AND FUNNY MONEY, TOO

WELLINGTON, New Zealand — March 4, 1992.
Lance Aukett, a 13-year-old boy, found a 10,000-yen note in a box of schoolbooks while he was cleaning his bedroom. Unsure of its value, he decided to check with some banks. One bank said it that it might be worth $8 in American money; another valued it at $26. But the best deal came from the National Bank of New Zealand, which accepted the note and gave Aukett $78 for it.

Two weeks later the bank realized they had purchased a piece of Monopoly money (from a Japanese version of the game).

"Since 1971, any money lost through bribery has been tax deductible. According to the IRS's official taxpayers' guide, "bribes and kickbacks to governmental officials *are* deductible unless the individual has been convicted of making the bribe or has entered a plea of not guilty or *nolo contendere*."

—*2201 Fascinating Facts*, by David Louis

A GAGGLE OF GEESE

You've used the terms a "pack" of wolves and a "flock" of sheep... here are some animal terms you probably haven't even heard *of:*

MAMMALS

A shrewdness or troop of apes (also monkeys)

A pace of asses

A cete of badgers

A sloth of bears

A colony of beavers

A singular of boars

A clouder of cats

A brood of chickens

A rag of colts

A cowardice of curs

A gang of elk

A business of ferrets

A skulk or troop of foxes

A trip of goats

A drift of hogs

A troop of kangaroos

A kindle of kittens

A leap of leopards

A nest of mice

A barren of mules

A string of ponies

A nest of rabbits

A crash of rhinoceroses

A bevy of roebucks

A dray of squirrels

A sounder of swine

A pod or gam of whales

BIRDS

A murder of crows

A dole or piteousness of doves

A paddling of duck (swimming)

A raft of duck (in the water, but *not* swimming)

A team of ducks (in the air)

A charm of finches

A gaggle of geese (on the ground)

A skein of geese (in the air)

A siege of herons

A deceit of lapwings

An exaltation or bevy of larks

A parliament of owls

A covey of quail

An ostentation of peacocks

A nye or covey of pheasants (on the ground)

A bouquet of pheasants (taking to the air)

An unkindness of ravens

A murmuration of sandpipers

A rafter of turkeys

A descent of woodpeckers

INSECTS

An army of caterpillars

A business of flies

A cluster of grasshoppers

A plague or swarm of locusts

OTHER

A shoal of bass

A clutch of eggs

A bed of snakes

A knot of toads

A bale of turtles

A nest of vipers

PRIMETIME PROVERBS

TV wisdom from Primetime Proverbs: The Book of TV Quotes *by Jack Mingo and John Javna.*

ON LAWYERS
"Lawyers and tarts are the two oldest professions in the world. And we always aim to please."

—Horace Rumpole,
Rumpole of the Bailey

ON CROOKS
"All the laws in the world won't stop one man with a gun."

—Det. Lt. Mike Stone,
The Streets of San Francisco

Friend of a suspect: "I just know she isn't guilty. She's just too nice."
Sgt. Joe Friday: "Well, if she's nice, she isn't guilty...and if she's guilty, she's not that nice."

—Dragnet

ON LYING
"That's not a lie, it's a terminological inexactitude."

—Alexander Haig,
1983 television news interview

"Virgins don't lie."

—Fonzie,
Happy Days

ON TOUGH COPS
Crook [explaining herself]**:** "You can understand, can't you?"
Sgt. Joe Friday: "No, lady, we can't. You're under arrest."

—Dragnet

"Would you like to sit down, hairball, or do you prefer internal bleeding?"

—Mick Belker,
Hill Street Blues

"Another outburst like this and I'm gonna handcuff your lips together."

—Sgt. Wojohowicz,
Barney Miller

ON POLICE PROCEDURE
"If you really want to study police methods, do what I do: watch television."

—Officer Gunther Toody,
Car 54, Where Are You?

ON STEALING
"If you're gonna steal, steal from kin—at least they're less likely to put the law on you."

—Bret Maverick,
Maverick

The average person has 1,460 dreams a year. That's four a night.

DISASTER FILMS II

Here are more of the worst losers Hollywood has ever produced.

CLEOPATRA (1963)

Description: It started out as a low-budget "tits-and-togas" epic, but became a high-cost extravaganza when studio executives offered Liz Taylor the lead. "Sure," she supposedly replied, "I'll do it for a million dollars." She was joking—no one had *ever* been paid that much for a single film role before—but 20th Century-Fox took the bait and made her the first million-dollar star in Hollywood history.

Dollars and Sense: Adjusted for inflation, *Cleopatra* is believed to be the biggest money loser in the history of film. It had a $6 million budget when Taylor was signed, but cost $44 million—the equivalent of $110.6 million in 1980 dollars. Twenty years after it was released, the film was still an estimated $46.2 million in the hole.

Wretched Excess: More than eight acres of sets were built near London, and the Thames River was diverted to create a "mini Nile" for the film. But the fog made filming impossible. "On a good day," said the director, "whenever a word was spoken, you could see the vapor coming from the actors' mouths. It was like a tobacco commercial." Taylor almost died of pneumonia during the filming and couldn't return to the damp London sets for more than six months. Overhead costs piled up at $45,000 a day. Finally the studio gave up and shut the London studios down. Total cost: $6 million for 12 minutes of usable film.

The Critics Speak: "After [the London premiere], I raced back to the Dorchester and just made it to the downstairs lavatory and vomited." —Elizabeth Taylor

THE GREATEST STORY EVER TOLD (1965)

Description: In 1954, 20th Century-Fox paid $100,000 for the film rights to *The Greatest Story Ever Told*, a novel about the life of Jesus Christ. The studio set out to make a big-budget Bible epic along the lines of *Samson and Delilah* (1949) and *The Ten Commandments* (1956).

Dollars and Sense: The film cost more than $20 million to make;

five years later it had still only earned $8 million worldwide.

Wretched Excess: Director George Stevens insisted on building a fake Holy Land in Arizona, arguing that the *real* Holy Land wasn't good enough. "I wanted to get an effect of grandeur as a background to Christ," he explained, "and none of the Holy Land areas shape up with the excitement of the American Southwest." Six months into the film, a blizzard pounded the 22-acre Jerusalem set and buried it in snow. Stevens just moved to Los Angeles, where he built a whole *new* Jerusalem.

Filming fell so far behind schedule that two members of the cast and crew died, and the actress who played Mary Magdalene became pregnant (forcing Stevens to film her standing behind furniture and in other odd angles). Stevens handed out so many cameo roles to Hollywood celebrities that "it made the road to Calvary look like the Hollywood Walk of Stars." In one scene, John Wayne played a centurion who barked out the now-famous line, "Truly, this man *wuz* the Son of Gawd!!"

MOHAMMED: MESSENGER OF GOD (1977)

Description: A cinematic biography of the prophet Mohammed, *Mohammed: Messenger of God* was intended by the producer to be Islam's *The Ten Commandments*.

Dollars and Sense: Two different versions of the film were made: one with Islamic actors for the Islamic world, and one with Western actors. Both versions bombed; in fact, every Islamic country except Turkey banned the Islamic version. The film(s) cost $17 million and earned less than $5 million.

Wretched Excess: When rumors spread that Peter O'Toole—and then Charleton Heston—had been signed to play Mohammed, angry protests broke out all over the Middle East. Saudi Arabia's King Faisal had granted permission to film on location in Mecca, but changed his mind and kicked the director out of the country. The director then moved to the desert outside of Marrakesh, Morocco, and spent hundreds of thousands of dollars building a detailed replica of Mecca. Six months after filming began, King Faisal "communicated his displeasure" over the film to King Hassan of Morocco by threatening to cut off oil shipments to the kingdom and banning all Moroccan pilgrims from entering Saudi Arabia. The director had to move to the Libyan desert and build *a third* Mecca.

G.I. blues: Elvis received 10,000 letters a week during his stint in the U.S. Army.

BAD HAIR DAYS

Think you've ever had a bad hair day? Just be glad you never had one like these folks.

BACKGROUND

"One kind of day that everyone dreads is the widely known and feared *bad hair day*," wrote columnist William Safire when a reader asked him about the term. Safire speculated that it started with comedian Gary Shandling. "Irritated with his coverage in *Us* magazine, Shandling (who used to begin his routine with 'Is my hair all right?') told the *Seattle Times* in January 1991: 'I was at a celebrity screening of *Misery* and they made up a quote for me. They said I told them I was having a *bad hair* day. They didn't even talk to me.'"

A month later the phrase appeared in the *L.A.Times*, then the *Toronto Star* ("Was Robert DeNiro caught in a crosswind, or was he just having a bad hair day?"), and now it's a part of our lexicon.

SIX *REAL* BAD HAIR DAYS

1. Michael Jackson

In February 1984, Jackson and his brothers were filming a $1.5 million commercial for Pepsi-Cola in which he walked down a staircase as a pyrotechnic display went off behind him. They shot the scene four times, but according to *Time* magazine, "The effect was not quite right for Director Bob Giraldi....He asked the singer to move more slowly and ordered the fireworks 'heated up' a bit. The combination proved volatile: On the fiery fifth take...sparks from a smoke bomb ignited Jackson's hair, sending the singer to the hospital with second- and third-degree burns on his scalp.

2. Albert Anastasia

Anastasia was head of the Mangano crime family, one of the infamous "five families" of the New York mafia. On the morning of October 25, 1957, he went for a haircut at the Park Sheraton Hotel. While his bodyguard parked the car, Anastasia sat down in the barber chair and fell asleep. Minutes later, two men wearing scarves over their faces walked up to him, drew their guns, and opened fire. Anastasia jumped out of the chair and tried to attack the gunmen, but he was too badly wounded and collapsed dead on the floor.

A blue whale's sound can be heard from more than 500 miles away.

3. Hans Steininger

Steineger was a 16th-century Austrian man famous for having the longest beard in the world. In September 1567, he tripped on his beard as he was climbing the stairs to the council chamber of Brunn, Austria. He fell down the stairs and died.

4. Hans Hoffman

In 1993, Hoffman, a 31-year-old vagrant, robbed a Rotterdam (Netherlands) bank of $15,000, telling the teller he needed the money to get a haircut and buy a piece of cheese. A few hours later he showed up at the Rotterdam police department, surrendered, and handed over a bag full of cash. Police counted the money and it was all there—minus the price of a haircut and a piece of cheese.

5. King Louis VII of France

King Louis had a beard when he married Eleanor of Aquitaine in 1137, but when he shaved it off, Eleanor thought he looked ugly without it and insisted he grow it back. Louis refused—so she left him and married King Henry II of England. However, Louis refused to give back Aquitaine, Eleanor's ancestral lands, which had became part of France when the couple got married. King Henry declared war. "The War of the Whiskers" lasted 301 years, until peace was finally signed in 1453.

6. President Bill Clinton

In May 1993, President Clinton received a $200 haircut on Air Force One. The only problem: At the time, Air Force One was parked on the tarmac, and according to a Federal Aviation Administration official, the trim shut down two of LAX's four runways for 56 minutes. The scene generated so much bad publicity that the hair stylist, Christophe, held a press conference to deny that Clinton was as smug, self-important, or stylish as the incident suggested.

"I am not saying this in a negative way," he told reporters, "but from what you can see, do you really think that Hillary or Bill Clinton, are very concerned about their appearance?"

The whole thing may have been the work of a political trickster. Subsequent checks of the records at LAX showed that the haircut had actually caused no problems. Runways were not shut down, and no planes were kept waiting.

William Shakespeare invented more than 1,700 words.

LIMERICKS

Limericks have been around since the 1700s. And our readers have been sending them in since 1988. Here are few of their favorites.

There was a faith-healer
of Deal,
Who said, "Although pain
isn't real,
If I sit on a pin,
And it punctures my skin,
I dislike what I fancy I feel."

There were once two young
people of taste
Who were beautiful, down to
the waist.
So they limited love
To the regions above,
And thus remained perfectly
chaste.

There was an old man
of Blackheath,
Who sat on his set of false
teeth;
Said he, with a start,
"O Lord, bless my heart!
I've bitten myself
underneath!"

There was a young man
of Montrose,
Who had pockets in none of
his clothes.
When asked by his lass
Where he carried his brass,
He said: "Darling, I pay
through the nose."

There was a young student
called Fred,
Who was questioned on
Descartes and said:
"It's perfectly clear
That I'm not really here,
For I haven't a thought in my
head."

Dr. Johnson, when sober
or pissed,
Could be frequently heard
to insist,
Letting out a great fart:
"Yes, I follow Descartes—
I stink, and I therefore exist."

A cute secretary,
none cuter,
Was replaced by a clicking
computer.
T'was the wife of her boss
Who put the deal across;
You see, the computer
was neuter.

There was a young lady
named Jeanie,
Who wore an outrageous
bikini,
Two wisps light as air,
One here and one there,
With nothing but Jeanie
betweenie.

President Clinton's feet (size 13C) are the biggest presidential feet since Woodrow Wilson's.

DEAR ABBY

A few thoughts from one of America's all-time favorite advisors, Abigail Van Buren.

"If you want a place in the sun, you have to put up with a few blisters."

"Some people are more turned on by money than they are by love. In one respect they are alike. They're both wonderful as long as they last."

"If you are looking for a kindly, well-to-do older gentleman who is no longer interested in sex, take out an ad in the *Wall Street Journal*."

Dear Abby: My wife sleeps nude. Then she showers, goes into the kitchen and fixes breakfast—still in the nude. We're newlyweds and have no kids, so I suppose there's nothing wrong with it. What do you think?
Dear Rex: It's all right with me, but tell her to put on an apron when she's frying bacon.

"The best index to a person's character is how he treats people who can't do him any good, and how he treats people who can't fight back."

Dear Abby: I have always wanted to have my family history traced, but I can't afford to spend a lot of money on it. Any suggestions?
Dear Sam: Yes. Run for public office.

"Wisdom doesn't automatically come with old age. Nothing does—except wrinkles. It's true, some wines improve with age. But only if the grapes were good in the first place."

"It is almost impossible to throw dirt on someone without getting a little on yourself."

Dear Abby: What factor do you think is the most essential if a woman is to have a lasting marriage?
Dear Dotty: A lasting husband.

"I have long suspected that more people are sleeping apart because of snoring than are sleeping together for all the other reasons combined."

"People who fight fire with fire usually end up with ashes."

Mr. Potatohead was the first toy advertised on TV.

THE FLYING NUN

If you had to pick the most ridiculous sitcom premise in history, what would it be? Our choice is "The Flying Nun." How did they come up with such a stupid idea? And why did Sally Field take the role? Here are the answers.

NUN-SENSE

It was one of the most improbable sitcom plots in American television history: Elsie Ethrington, an American teenager, gives up her life as a beach bunny and enters a Puerto Rican nunnery called the Convent San Tanco, where she is ordained as Sister Bertrille. Weighing only 90 pounds, she discovers that wearing her order's bulky coronet (nun's hat) on windy days enables her to fly, a skill she uses to get into and out of trouble (and fight crime).

Sure, the concept was ridiculous, but the show was one of the surprise hits of the 1967 TV season. More important, it gave a needed boost to the acting career of 19-year-old actress Sally Field, who had just finished work on the "Gidget" TV series.

YOU'RE MY INSPIRATION(S)

• Believe it or not, "The Flying Nun" was inspired by a real-life incident involving a small nun, a big hat, and high winds.

• In 1955, author Tere Rios recalled a trip she had made to France. "I saw a little Sister of Charity in her big white bonnet nearly blown off her feet in Paris," she recalls. It gave her the idea for *The Fifteenth Pelican*, a book about a flying nun that became the inspiration for the TV series.

• The show was also inspired by "Bewitched," a successful TV series about a friendly witch with magic powers, and "I Dream of Jeanie," a show about a magical genie who marries an astronaut. "Bewitched" creator Harry Ackerman thought a similar show about a nun would be a hit, but he worried that giving a nun magical powers would be too controversial. So he stuck with *The Fifteenth Pelican*'s original premise and gave the nun special powers, brought on by high winds, her coronet, and the laws of aerodynamics, instead of magic ones.

You burn 50% more calories watching TV than you do when you sleep.

SHE'D HAVE NUN OF IT

• The show might never have made it onto the air if "Gidget," another of Ackerman's shows, hadn't bitten the dust in 1965. Ackerman knew that Sally Field, the show's 19-year-old star, had talent, and he wanted to find another series for her.

• The only problem: Field wanted to quit TV. When "Gidget" failed, she took it to heart. As *TV Guide* put it, "Sally came away with the feeling that she was somehow responsible for Gidget's flop and no one would tell her why....She left the studio 'feeling defeated'... and embarked on a movie career, determined that TV should never darken her door again."

• Field's first stab at a movie career bombed as badly as "Gidget." She tried out for the part of daughter Elaine Robinson in *The Graduate*...but Katherine Ross got the part. Then she tried out for the role of Neely in *Valley of the Dolls*...but lost it to Patty Duke.

• All of a sudden, another TV series didn't look so bad. "It was presumptuous to think I could step into movies," Field later recalled. "'Idiot,' I told myself, 'you're not Liz Taylor!' 'The Flying Nun' would give me time to learn and still keep me in the public eye. So—I changed my mind." (Studio executives cemented the deal by raising her $450-a-week "Gidget" salary to $4,000 a week.)

CATHOLIC CONTROVERSIES

• Studio executives were worried about potential Catholic objections to "The Flying Nun" and went to great lengths to see that the Church was not offended. They gave special sneak previews of the pilot episode to high Church officials all over the country, hoping to enlist their support for the show. "We just wanted to be sure the Catholic community dug it," one of the show's promoters told *TV Guide* in 1968.

But their concerns were unfounded: Catholic Church officials loved the show. They saw it as a much-needed recruiting film for nuns, whose numbers had been in decline since Vatican II.

"The show is positioning nuns as human beings," an official with the National Catholic Office for Radio and Television said. "Only the studio, the agencies and the sponsors were worried. I guess they thought Catholics might stop buying toothpaste."

FIVE PET FADS

An informal study by the BRI has shown that many bathroom readers are also pet aficionados. Uncle John himself keeps a piranha in his bathtub. And he's trying to convince Mrs. Uncle John to keep a fainting goat in the bedroom.

AQUARIUMS

Fish tanks were popular in the United States as far back as the early 1800s, but for the most part only the wealthy had them. The reason: Water quickly became deprived of oxygen, and fish died unless the water was constantly changed. No one wanted to take on that responsibility...unless they could afford to pay someone to do it for them.

It wasn't until 1850 that Robert Warington, a chemist, announced to the world that he'd kept a pet fish alive for a year in a tank without changing the water. His secret: He added plants to the tank, which replenished the oxygen supply. His contribution was so significant that the first aquariums were known as Warrington [sic] cases.

Not long afterward, British naturalist Philip Gosse published *The Aquarium*, a how-to book that quickly became a bestseller. Soon, American and British fish lovers had made aquarium-keeping one of the largest and most popular pet fads in the world.

COLLIES

For centuries, collies were common in the Scottish Lowlands, but virtually unknown everywhere else in the world. A working dog used to guard the large flocks of sheep that roamed the area, the collie might still be uncommon today if it hadn't been for Queen Victoria. She happened to notice some of the dogs outside of Balmoral Castle and was so charmed by them that she brought a few back to London. The British upper classes, quick to take a royal hint, made the collie one of the most popular breeds in the country...and eventually in the world.

THE MAKECH BEETLE

A short-lived fad of the 1960s, the "makech" was a gilded and stone-encrusted living beetle that was attached to a pin by a thin gold chain. The wearer attached the pin to their shirt, and let the beetle walk over their shoulder and neck. Phyllis Diller wore a makech emblazoned with gold lace and white seed pearls. "How else," she asked at the time, "am I going to get ten men standing around looking at my chest?" Not everyone liked the fad. "A makech's appeal is primarily to the screwball fringe," said a customs agent in charge of breaking up illegal beetle-smuggling rings. "It takes some kind of nut to wear a bug."

PIRANHAS

Another weird pet craze of the 1960s was the piranha. Enterprising pet store owners skirted laws banning importation and possession of the meat-eating fishes, claiming they were actually friendly pets, not the flesh-eating meanies they were reputed to be. "We got very attached to ours," one owner told reporters about her aquatic carnivore. "He had a personality that most tropical fish don't seem to have." But state and federal officials held the line—to date it is still illegal to import or own a piranha. According to one biologist with the California Fish and Game Department, "Piranhas eat people."

FAINTING GOATS

Fainting goats aren't much different from normal goats…except that they have a genetic trait that causes them to stiffen up and fall over when someone (usually the owner or the owner's friends) frightens them. Fainting faddists rank their pets' "skill" on a scale of one to six, with "six being the highest, meaning they lock up most of the time and fall over," says Kathy Majewski, founder of The American Tennessee Fainting Goat Association (TATFGA).

First observed in Tennessee in the 1800s, the goats were nearly driven extinct by coyotes, who (for obvious reasons) preferred them to regular goats. But TATFGA was formed to save them.

The group boasts more than 200 members, but not everyone thinks their motives are pure. "To raise animals with an abnormality for use as entertainment is sick," says Lisa Landres of the Tennessee Humane Society. "The whole phenomenon is mind-boggling." She may not have to worry, though—the fad may die out on its own because it gets increasingly harder to scare the goats once they get to know you…which defeats the purpose of owning them in the first place.

SWEETENED WITH FRUIT JUICE?

If a label says "100% fruit juice," it's a healthy food, right? Not necessarily; someone may be lying to you. This article is adapted from the Nutrition Action Healthletter, *published by the Center for Science in the Public Interest.*

BACKGROUND

The first fruit juice listed on the label of After the Fall's Georgia Peach 100% Fruit Juice Blend isn't peach.

Raspberries aren't the first fruit ingredient listed in Polaner's Raspberry All Fruit Spreadable Fruit, either....And apple isn't first in Frookie's Fat Free Apple Spice Cookies.

Nope. It's "grape juice concentrate."

Some—nobody knows how much—of the "grape" (and "pear" and "apple") juice concentrate in foods like juices, spreads, and cookies is little more than sugar water. It's been "stripped" of the flavor, color, and nutrients that were in the fruit. As a result, unsuspecting shoppers end up paying premium prices for "100% fruit juice" or "fruit-juice sweetened" or "no sugar added" foods that are anything but.

HOW SWEET IT IS

"Sugar is a great ingredient," says Rich Worth, president of the cookie maker R. W. Frookies. "It's white, tasteless, and performs the same every time." But sugar's empty calories and unsavory reputation aren't so great, say many consumers, who refuse to buy foods that contain it. Enter fruit-juice concentrate.

Fruits contain fructose, glucose, sucrose, and other sugars. So if you crush the fruit and then remove most of the water, you end up with a sweetener that contains many of the nutrients that were in the fruit to begin with.

But fruit juice concentrate isn't uniform. A Rome apple, for example, tastes different from a Red Delicious. Concentrate has another unfortunate characteristic: It tastes like the fruit from which it came. And that can be a problem for companies looking for a "natural" sweetener.

The *Pinta* was pint-sized: Columbus's third ship was only 50 feet long.

"Real fruit-juice concentrate is a pain in the butt," says Frookies' Rich Worth. But, he adds, he uses it to sweeten his cookies. Most other companies that make "fruit-juice sweetened" or "100% fruit juice" products told us the same.

Some of them are lying.

LIFE ALONG THE STRIP

"Its lack of color and flavor makes it the ideal blending ingredient where no grape flavor or color is desired, but when the application requires an all-natural sweetener."

That's the way Daystar International describes its "deionized white grape juice concentrate," which "has been stripped of most acids and minerals characteristic of grape juice, leaving a totally clear concentrate that is practically void of flavor and color."

The laboratory director for a concentrate maker, who asked not to be identified, explained that juices are typically "stripped" by passing them through two "ion-exchange" columns.

In one column the juice's positively charged minerals are replaced with hydrogen (H) atoms. In the other column the negatively charged acids (and flavor and color compounds) are replaced with molecules of oxygen and hydrogen bound together (OH). The Hs then combine with the OHs to form (you guessed it) [H_2O].

"It's an expensive way to make sugar water," said the lab director. But to many food companies it's worth the extra cost, since it allows them to label products "100% juice" or "no sugar added."

None of the "strippers" would tell us which companies use their products, and many companies that use fruit juice concentrate either didn't return our calls or refused to say much of anything when they did. Among them: After the Fall, Apple & Eve, Dole, Tree Top, and Tropicana.

HIDE AND SEEK

"There is no methodology to detect modified juices in foods," explains Joe Soeroni, director of food research at Ocean Spray. "And if you can't detect it, you can't say who is and isn't doing it."

Jim Tillotson, director of the Food Policy Institute at Tufts University, offers this tip: "In the supermarket, if I saw white grape, apple, or pear juice concentrate, I'd be suspicious."

Only 14% of Americans go to at least one play a year; only 3% go to the opera.

FAMILIAR PHRASES

More inside info on the origins of phrases we use every day.

THE SEAMY SIDE

Meaning: "The unsavory or worst part."

Background: Originally referred to the inside part of a sewed garment: If the garment was turned inside out so that the *wrong* side was showing, the stitched *seams* were clearly visible.

TOP DRAWER

Meaning: "The best quality."

Background: Traditionally, the top drawer of a dresser is the place where jewelry and other valuables are kept.

ALL OVER BUT THE SHOUTING

Meaning: "Any situation in which victory is clear before a final decision is reached."

Background: Rather than hold formal elections to decide local issues, for centuries in England it was common practice to call an assembly of townspeople and decide matters with a simple voice vote. The assemblies themselves were known as "shoutings," and when the outcome of an issue was known before the meeting, the situation was described as *all over but the shouting*.

GUM UP THE WORKS

Meaning: "Screw something up."

Background: Believe it or not, the phrase has a pre-industrial inspiration: the red gum or sweet gum tree, which is found in the eastern United States. The early settlers chewed the sticky sap, especially kids, who loved its sweet taste. The only problem: Getting the stuff out of the tree was virtually impossible to do without getting it all over yourself. So was getting it out of your hair and clothes—if you weren't careful, you could really *gum up the works*.

Americans travel 1,144,721,000 miles by air every day.

TAKE BY STORM

Meaning: "Make a big impression; become famous or popular virtually overnight."

Background: Today's politicians, movie stars, and war heroes take the world by storm...but the term itself dates back to the days when soldiers took fortified enemy positions *by storming them*.

TO BE BESIDE YOURSELF

Meaning: "Under great emotional stress."

Background: The ancient Greeks believed that when a person was under intense pressure, the soul literally left the body and was *beside itself*. (The word *ecstasy* has a similar meaning: Its Greek root means "to stand out of.")

GET YOUR SEA LEGS

Meaning: "To adjust to a new situation."

Background: The term dates back to the days when sailing ships ruled the high seas: a new sailor was said to have "gotten his sea legs" when he could walk steadily across the deck of a ship in stormy weather.

TO RUN AMOK

Meaning: "To behave in a wild, uncontrolled manner."

Background: The Malay word for "a person who has gone crazy" is *moq*. The first English sailors to visit Malaysia associated the word with the occasional insane people they saw there...and brought the word home with them.

DOUBLEHEADER

Meaning: "Two baseball games in a single afternoon."

Background: The name was borrowed from railroading—a train with two engines on it is also known as a doubleheader.

FLAG SOMETHING DOWN

Meaning: "To stop a moving vehicle, usually a taxi cab."

Background: Another train term: Railroad employees used to literally flag trains down—they stopped them by waving flags at the engineers.

On strike: The average American goes bowling 233 times in their lifetime.

TO TELL THE TRUTH

Are polygraphs accurate crime-fighting tools...or little more than modern-day witchcraft? You be the judge.

Police in Radnor, Pennsylvania, interrogated a suspect by placing a metal colander on his head and connecting it with a metal wire to a photocopy machine. The message, "He's lying," was placed in the copier and police pressed the copy button each time they believed the suspect wasn't telling the truth. Believing the 'lie detector' was working, the suspect confessed.

—*News of the Weird*

Can we ever *really* know for sure if someone is telling a lie? Most experts agree that the answer is no—but that hasn't stopped society from cooking up ways to sort out the liars from the honest people.

ANCIENT METHODS

• The Bedouins of the Arabian peninsula forced suspected liars to lick red-hot pokers with their tongues, on the assumption that liars would burn their tongues and truth tellers wouldn't. The method was primitive and barbaric—but it may have also been *accurate*, since the procedure measures the moisture content of the suspect's mouth—and dry mouths are often associated with nervousness caused by lying.

• The ancient Chinese forced suspected liars to chew a mouthful of rice powder and spit it out; if the rice was still dry, the suspect was deemed guilty.

• The ancient British used a similar trick: they fed suspects a large 'trial slice' of bread and cheese, and watched to see if he could swallow it. If a suspect's mouth was too dry to swallow, he was declared a liar and punished.

• The preferred method in India was to send the suspects into a dark room and have them pull on the tail of a sacred donkey, which was supposed to bray if the person was dishonest...at least that's what the suspects thought. The way the system *really* worked was that the investigators dusted the donkey's tail with black powder (which was impossible to see in the unlit room). Innocent people, the investigators reasoned, would pull the tail without hesitation...but the guilty person, figuring that no one could see them in the darkness, would only pretend to pull the tail but would not touch it at all.

MODERN METHOD

The first modern lie detector was invented by Cesare Lombroso, an Italian criminologist, in 1895. His device measured changes in pulse and blood pressure. Then, in 1914, another researcher named Vittorio Benussi invented a machine that measured changes in breathing rate. But it wasn't until 1921 that John A. Larson, a medical student at the University of California, invented a machine that measured pulse, blood pressure, and breathing rate simultaneously. His machine became known as a polygraph, because it measured three types of physiological changes. Today's polygraphs use these methods, as well as more sophisticated measurements.

THE QUESTIONS

The most common questioning method is called the Control Question Test (CQT), in which the polygraph operator asks three types of questions: neutral questions, key questions, and control questions.

• **Neutral questions** like "What kind of car do you drive?" are designed to measure the suspect's general level of nervousness, because nearly anyone who takes a polygraph test is going to be nervous.

• **Key, or "guilty," questions** quiz the suspect on information that only the guilty person would know. (For example: If the person taking the test were suspected of murdering someone, and the murder weapon was a knife, questions about knives would be considered key questions.)

• **Control, or "innocent," questions** would be indistinguishable from key questions by someone who did not have knowledge of the crime—but the guilty person would know. Questions about weapons not used in a murder would be considered control questions.

Pirates thought that wearing an earring in a pierced ear improved their eyesight.

An innocent person with no knowledge of the murder weapon would show the same level of nervousness during all the weapon questions—but the guilty person would be more nervous during questions about knives—and would be easy to identify using a polygraph...at least in theory.

BEATING THE SYSTEM

Modern-day lie detectors are pretty sophisticated, but they have the same flaw that the ancients methods did—they all assume that the liar, out of guilt or fear of discovery, will have some kind of involuntary physical response every time they lie...but that isn't necessarily the case, according to most experts. "I don't think there's any medical or scientific evidence which tends to establish that your blood pressure elevates, that you perspire more freely or that your pulse quickens when you tell a lie," says William G. Hundley, a defense lawyer.

Still, many people believe that the polygraph is a useful tool when used in concert with other investigative methods, especially when they're used on ordinary people who don't know how to cheat. "It's a great psychological tool," says Plato Cacheris, another defense lawyer. "You take the average guy and tell him you're going to give him a poly, and he's concerned enough to believe it will disclose any deception on his part." (Note: Cacheris is famous for having represented non-average guy Aldrich Ames, a CIA spy who passed a lie detector test in 1991 and then went on to sell more than $2.5 million worth of secrets to the Russians before he was finally caught in 1994.)

FAKIN' IT

Two tricks to help you beat a lie detector:

- Curl your toes or press your feet down against the floor while answering the "innocent" questions. It can raise the polygraph readings to the same range as the "guilty" questions, which can either make you appear innocent or invalidate the results.
- Stick a tack in your shoe and press your big toe against the sharp point during the "innocent" questions.

Both toe-curling and stepping on a tack during the innocent questions have the same effect: they raise the stress level of your body.

Sports stat: On average, for every 100,000 people who play football, 2,171 are seriously injured.

VIVE LA DIFFERENCE!

Researchers say that males and females are naturally different from one another in a number of unexpected ways. Here are a few of the things they've found out.

Women are more likely to smile than men when delivering bad news.

Toddler girls as young as two years old maintain eye contact with adults nearly twice as long as toddler boys do.

At the age of four months, infant girls can distinguish between photographs of people they know and don't know; most boys can't.

Did you have a nightmare last night? Women are twice as likely as men to say they did.

In households that have them, males control the TV remote control 55% of the time; women have control 34% of the time.

Doctors consider men obese when 25% of their body is composed of fat, and women obese when 30% is fat.

Boys fight more than girls do. The difference begins at about age two.

Fifty-nine percent of females—but only 4% of males—say they didn't enjoy the first time they had sex.

The average male brain is 14 percent larger than the average female brain.

Seventy-one percent of car-accident victims are male; only 29% are female.

On average, a man's skin ages 10 years more slowly than a woman's does.

In the year following a divorce, the average woman's standard of living falls 73%; the man's standard of living actually *rises* by 43%.

Male snow skiers are more likely to fall on their faces; female skiers are more likely to fall on their backs.

In one recent study, 36% of husbands surveyed said their wife "is like a god." Only 19% of women said the same thing about their husbands.

Women cry about five times as much as men; a male hormone may actually suppress tears.

Americans spend $1.5 billion on toothpaste (and $680 million on mouthwash) every year.

ACCIDENTALLY X-RATED

A lot of money is made on X-rated films, books, etc. But what happens when somebody's work unintentionally *winds up X-rated? That's actually a problem that some producers have to cope with. Here are a few examples.*

ACCIDENTALLY X-RATED MOVIE

In 1969, the movie rating system was still new. The X rating hadn't become a symbol of sexually explicit material yet—it just meant "adult subject matter." So when the Motion Picture Association of America gave *Midnight Cowboy*—the story of a male prostitute's (platonic) relationship with a down-and-out New York vagabond—an X rating, director John Schlesinger wasn't upset. In fact, he *approved of* the rating: He considered the film's subject matter too controversial for young audiences and didn't want to have to warn them away from the theatres himself; plus, he was afraid that without an "adult" rating, people might show up at theaters thinking the film was a genuine Western.

What Happened: *Midnight Cowboy* became the first X-rated film to play in top-flight movie houses and the only one ever to win an Oscar (for Best Picture, Best Director, and Best Screenplay). A few months after the film went into general release, the MPAA's Rating Commission decided to reserve the X-rating for "non-quality" films and officially changed *Midnight Cowboy*'s rating to R.

ACCIDENTALLY X-RATED CARTOONS

According to Hollywood legend, cartoonists in nearly every major movie studio have amused themselves by inserting one or two bawdy frames into "family" cartoon classics. In the theater, the frames went by much too fast for anyone to notice. But the laserdisc player enables people to view films frame by frame, and since their arrival, a number of things the public was never meant to see have been found in cartoons, new and old.

For example, in an old cartoon called *The Wabbit Who Came to Dinner*, Bugs steps out of the shower and wraps a towel around himself. According to Bill Givens in his book *Film Flubs II*, "There's a frame or two where an added bit of anatomy that you don't see in other Bugs cartoons seems to appear between his legs."

When *Who Framed Roger Rabbit?* was released on video/laserdisc, *Variety* magazine spilled the beans with a detailed examination of the film. They came up with two specific scenes to look for:

Scene #1: At the beginning of the film, Roger Rabbit is filming a cartoon with diaper-clad Baby Herman. Roger ruins the scene and Baby Herman stomps off the set, passing under a woman wearing a dress as he leaves. She screams and jumps away as he passes beneath her. According to *Variety*, "On screen, [the scene] looks playful. Advanced frame by frame on laserdisc, it's far from it."

Scene #2: Jessica Rabbit, Roger Rabbit's voluptuous wife, is riding through Toon Town in a taxi when the cab smashes into a lightpost. According to *Variety*, as Jessica is thrown from the cab she "spins in Kerrigan-like triple lutz fashion, with her trademark red dress hiking up. On the first scene, she appears to be wearing underwear. On the second spin, however, there are three frames which clearly show she's wearing nothing at all."

ACCIDENTAL X: REVENGE AND PRACTICAL JOKES

• In December 1994, a disgruntled video production worker of the UAV Corp., which distributes cartoon videos, added a two-minute scene from a movie called *Whore* to about 500 copies of the video, *Woody Woodpecker and Friends No. 3015*. The sabotage wasn't caught until the tapes were already in stores; the company had to recall all 20,000 copies that had been distributed.

• When Mark Twain sent his manuscript for *The Adventures of Huckleberry Finn* to the printers in the fall of 1884, they discovered that an engraved illustration of Uncle Silas "had been made to appear obscene." The engraving was so offensive (to Victorian eyes, anyway) that it had to be removed and a new one created and substituted in its place, causing the American edition to miss the 1884 Christmas season entirely. Had the mistake not been caught, the printer said at the time, "Mr. Clemens' credit for decency and morality would have been destroyed." The end result: *Huckleberry Finn* was released in the U.S. two months too late for Christmas ...and two months after the British version hit the shelves in England.

DUMB TV: THE "FLYING NUN" QUIZ

It was one of the most ridiculous sitcom plots in TV history: An American teenager gives up her life as a beach bunny and becomes Sister Bertrille at the Convent San Tanco, in Puerto Rico. Then she discovers that because she weighs only 90 pounds, wearing her order's bulky coronet (nun's hat) on windy days enables her to fly—a skill she uses to get into and out of trouble, fight crime, and occasionally assist the owner of a nearby casino. Believe it or not, "The Flying Nun" made a star out of 19-year-old actress Sally Field. Now in best BR tradition, we've decided to torture you with trivia questions about the show. But don't blame us—this quiz was devised by John Dollison, for his book, Pope Pourri.

1. What was the inspiration for the show?
(A) A real-life incident involving a small nun and a big hat.
(B) A novel about a flying nun.
(C) The TV shows "Bewitched" and "I Dream of Jeannie."
(D) Sally Field came up with the idea herself.

2. The part of Sister Bertrille was created for Sally Field...but she turned it down at first. Why?
(A) Fearful of scandal, the show's producers insisted that Field take a vow of chastity while she was on the show.
(B) Field had bad memories from her years in parochial school
(C) Field thought the role would restrict her too much...and besides, she wanted to be a movie star, not a TV star.

3. What made her change her mind and take the role?
(A) An intense religious experience
(B) Her movie career bit the dust.
(C) Pope Paul VI phoned Field personally and urged her to take the role before studio executives offered it to Annette Funicello.

4. How did the other nuns on the show try to keep Sister Bertrille from flying?

(A) Reverend Mother Plaseato (played by Madeline Sherwood) tied lead weights around her feet.
(B) They gave her a set of extra-heavy rosary beads.
(C) They tried to bulk her up with huge, heavy meals whenever possible.

5. How did officials in the Catholic Church respond to the show when it first went on the air?
(A) They condemned it.
(B) They refused to take a public stand.
(C) They liked it—and actually saw it as a recruiting film for nuns.

ANSWERS

No, we won't make you turn to the back of the book to find out the truth about Sister Bertrille. If you made it this far, you deserve a break.

1. (B) TV executive Max Wylie was flipping through a Doubleday catalog of recently published books one day in the mid-1960s looking for ideas for TV sitcoms. He came across a book called *The Fifteenth Pelican*, a story about a ninety-pound nun who could fly. Author Tere Rios got the idea for the book while travelling in 1955. "I saw a little Sister of Charity in her big white bonnet nearly blown off her feet in Paris," she later told reporters.

Wylie pitched the idea to Harry Ackerman, creator of the "Bewitched" TV series. Another show of his, "Gidget," had just gone off the air and he was looking for a new vehicle for Sally Field, the star of the show. "Bewitched," a show about a friendly witch with magic powers, had been a huge success; so had "I Dream of Jeanie," a show about a female genie with magical powers who marries an astronaut. Ackerman thought a similar show about a nun would be a hit...although he worried that giving a nun magical powers would be too controversial. So he stuck with *The Fifteenth Pelican*'s original premise and gave the nun special powers (brought on by high winds, her coronet, and the laws of aerodynamics) instead of magic ones.

The average Japanese drinks 4.8 gal. of liquor a year; the average American drinks 1.3 gal.

2. (C) "I didn't want to play a nun," Field told *TV Guide* in 1968. "You're not allowed to kiss or show your belly button." But that wasn't her only objection: her previous TV show, "Gidget," had fallen flat on its face, and Field mistakenly thought it was her fault. As *TV Guide* put it, "Sally came away with the feeling that she was somehow responsible for 'Gidget's' flop and no one would tell her why....She left the studio 'feeling defeated'...and embarked on a movie career, determined that TV should never darken her door again."

3. (B) Field tried out for the part of daughter Elaine Robinson in *The Graduate*...but Katherine Ross got the part. Then she tried out for the role of Neely in *Valley of the Dolls*...and lost it to Patty Duke. All of a sudden, another TV series didn't look so bad. "It was presumptuous to think I could step into movies," Field later recalled. "'Idiot,' I told myself, 'you're not Liz Taylor!' 'The Flying Nun' would give me time to learn and still keep me in the public eye. So—I changed my mind." (Money had a little to do with it, too. Studio executives cemented the deal by raising her pay from her $450-a-week "Gidget" salary to $4,000 a week.)

4. (B) Not your normal sitcom prop, but what do you expect?

5. (C) Studio executives were extremely worried about potential Catholic objections to "The Flying Nun" and went to great lengths to see that the church was not offended. They even gave special sneak previews of the pilot episode to high church officials all over the country, hoping to enlist their support for the show. "We just wanted to be sure the Catholic community dug it," one of the show's promoters told TV Guide in 1968....But their concerns were unfounded: Catholic Church officials loved the show and actually saw it as a much-needed recruiting film for nuns, whose numbers had been in decline since Vatican II. "The show is positioning nuns as human beings," one official with the National Catholic Office for Radio and Television said. "Only the studio, the agencies and the sponsors were worried. I guess they thought Catholics might stop buying toothpaste."

Or watching TV.

34% of U.S. men say meat makes up the largest portion of their diet; only 15% of women do.

Q & A: ASK THE EXPERTS

More random questions...and answers...from America's trivia experts.

SEEING THE LIGHT

Q: *What is a hologram? How is it different than a regular picture?*

A: "A hologram is a three-dimensional image produced with the use of laser light. Contrary to what you might think, when you look at something, you are not really viewing the object itself, but are instead looking at the light coming from the object. Because photographs are only able to record part of this light, the images they produce are limited to two dimensions. Using a laser, an object's illumination can be completely recorded, enabling it to be reproduced later in three dimensions." (From *Ask Me Something I Don't Know*, by Bill Adler, Jr. and Beth Pratt-Dewey)

DELICIOUS QUESTION

Q: *Why is New York called the Big Apple?*

A: "It appears more than likely that jazz musicians deserve the credit. Musicians of the 1930s, playing one night stands, coined their own terms not only for their music...but also for their travels, the people they met, the towns they stayed in. A town or city was an "apple." At that time a man named Charles Gillett was president of the New York City Convention and Visitors Bureau. Learning of the jazz term, he bragged, 'There are lots of "apples" in the U.S.A., but we're the best and the biggest. We're The Big Apple.'" (From *All Those Wonderful Names*, by J. N. Hook)

ABOUT YOUR BODY

Q: *How heavy are our bones?*

A: Our bones are a remarkable combination of strength and lightness. "In a 160-lb. man, only about 29 pounds—less than 20 percent—represent bone weight. Steel bars of comparable size would weigh at least four or five times as much." (From *Can Elephants Swim?* compiled by Robert M. Jones)

The end of the Cold War? Forty-eight U.S. spy rings were uncovered during the 1980s

BURNING QUESTION

Q: *What are first-, second-, and third-degree burns?*

A: "Burns are always serious because of the danger of infection while the damaged tissues are healing. In a first-degree burn, no skin is broken, but it is red and painful. In a second-degree burn, the burned area develops blisters and is very painful. One must try to avoid opening the blisters. In a third-degree burn, both the outer layer of the skin and the lower layer of flesh have been burned. This is the most serious of the three types, as the possibility of infection is greatest." (From *How Does a Fly Walk Upside Down*, by Martin M. Goldwyn)

BUSY THOUGHTS

Q: *Why doesn't a busy signal stop as soon as the person you're calling gets off the phone?*

A: "There's both a technical and a business reason that you can't just stay on the line and wait for the busy signal to stop. The technical reason is that the sound isn't coming from your friend over there on the other side of town, it's coming from the central switching office of the phone company. (The tone is generated by a gadget sensibly called the tone generator.) That said, the main reason you can't stick on the line is that the phone company doesn't want you to. You're tying up a line. So get off the phone." (From *Why Things Are, Volume II*, by Joel Aschenbach)

COLD FLASHES

Q: *Why do people get headaches when they eat ice cream too fast?*

A: "No one is quite sure what causes an ice cream headache (the official name for it). One likely guess is that it happens when ice cream (or other cold stuff) causes the blood vessels on the roof of your mouth to contract (i.e., shrink) a bit. Since the blood can't flow through these vessels as quickly as before, it backs up into the head, causing the other blood vessels to stretch. The result: pain." (From *Know It All*, by Ed Zotti)

BUT DON'T DRINK IT

Q: *Which contains more lemon, Lemon Pledge or Country Time Lemonade?*

A: According to *The Hidden Life of Groceries*, Lemon Pledge does.

Q: Where are the world's largest sculptures? A: Mt. Rushmore.

PRIMETIME PROVERBS

More TV wisdom from Primetime Proverbs: The Book of TV Quotes *by Jack Mingo and John Javna.*

ON DOCTORS

Sophia: "How come so many doctors are Jewish?"
Jewish Doctor: "Because their mothers are."

—*The Golden Girls*

ON EATING

"When a person eats fluffy eats, little cakes, pastry, and fancy little things, then that person is also fluffy. But when you eat meats and strong, heavy food, then you are also a strong person."

—Dr. Kurt von Stuffer (Sid Caesar), *Your Show of Shows*

"The way prices are going up, pretty soon indigestion is going to be a luxury."

—Larry, *Newhart*

ON EXPERIENCE

"I'm an experienced woman; I've been around....Well, all right, I might not've been around, but I've been... nearby."

—Mary Richards, *The Mary Tyler Moore Show*

ON FAMILY

"Her origins are so low, you'd have to limbo under her family tree."

—Minister (Eugene Levy), *SCTV*

ON FASHION

"There's something neat about a sweater with a hole. It makes you look like a tough guy."

—Beaver Cleaver, *Leave It to Beaver*

"If women dressed for men, the stores wouldn't sell much—just an occasional sun visor."

—Groucho Marx, *You Bet Your Life*

ON BEING FAT

"I love my blubber. It keeps me warm, it keeps me company, it keeps my pants up."

—Oscar Madison, *The Odd Couple*

Peter Marshall (the emcee): "Jackie Gleason recently revealed that he firmly believes in them and has actually seen them on at least two occasions. What are they?"
Charlie Weaver: "His feet."

—*Hollywood Squares*

Tired fact: During the work week, only 41% of Americans get 7 or more nightly hours of sleep.

LITTLE NAYIRAH'S TALE

Do you believe everything you read or see in the news? Here's a story that might shake you up. From It's a Conspiracy!, *by The National Insecurity Council.*

Who could forget the pretty young Kuwaiti refugee with tears running down her cheeks? While America was deciding whether to go to war against Iraq, on October 10, 1990, little "Nayirah" testified before a televised congressional hearing. Quietly sobbing at times, the teenager told how she had watched Iraqi troops storm a Kuwait City hospital, snatch 15 infants from their incubators, and leave "the babies to die on the cold floor." Americans were appalled. People across the country joined President Bush in citing the story as a good reason why America should go to war.

THE TRUTH OF THE MATTER

- As it turns out, Nayirah's story was a lie. Doctors at the Al-Adan Hospital in Kuwait City, where the incident allegedly took place, said it never happened.
- Congressional representatives conducting the hearing took pains to explain that Nayirah's last name was withheld "to protect her family from reprisals in occupied Kuwait." Also untrue. In fact, the young woman was not a refugee at all: she was the daughter of the Kuwaiti ambassador to the United States, and she likely wasn't in Kuwait at all when the atrocities supposedly happened.
- Actually, Nayirah had been coached by Hill and Knowlton, an American public relations firm headed by President Bush's former chief of staff, Craig Fuller. Hill and Knowlton selected her wardrobe, wrote her a script to memorize, and rehearsed with her for hours in front of video cameras.

DISINFORMING THE WORLD

- "Nayirah" was just one of many media stunts that sold the war to the American people, according to "Nightline" reporter Morgan

Strong in an article he wrote for *TV Guide* in 1992.

• A second Kuwaiti woman testified before a widely televised session of the UN while the world body was deciding whether to sanction force against Iraq. She was identified as simply another refugee. But it turns out that she was the wife of Kuwait's minister of planning and was herself a well-known TV personality in Kuwait.

• Strong asked a Kuwaiti exile leader why such a high-profile person was passed off as just another refugee. "Because of her professional experience," the Kuwaiti replied, "she is more believable." In her testimony, she indicated that her experience was firsthand. "Such stories...I personally have experienced," she said. But when interviewed later, in Saudi Arabia, she admitted that she had no direct knowledge of the events.

HILL AND KNOWLTON AT WORK

• Hill and Knowlton personnel were allowed to travel unescorted through Saudi Arabia at a time when news reporters were severely restricted by the U.S. Army. The PR firm's employees interviewed Kuwaiti refugees, looking for lurid stories and amateur videos that fit their political agenda. Kuwaitis with the most compelling tales were coached and made available to a press hamstrung by military restrictions. Happy for any stories to file, reporters rarely questioned the stories of Iraqi brutality that the refugees told them.

• Hill and Knowlton also supplied networks with videotapes that distorted the truth. One Hill and Knowlton tape purported to show Iraqis firing on peaceful Kuwaiti demonstrators...and that's the way the news media dutifully reported it. But the incident on tape was actually Iraqi soldiers *firing back* at Kuwaiti resistance fighters.

THE TRUTH

• Strong says: "These examples are but a few of the incidents of outright misinformation that found their way onto network news. It is an inescapable fact that much of what Americans saw on their news broadcasts, especially leading up to the Allied offensive against Iraqi-occupied Kuwait, was in large measure the contrivance of a public relations firm."

The double coconut palm produces the largest seeds (up to 60 lbs.) in the plant kingdom.

THE BERMUDA TRIANGLE

It's as famous as UFOs, as fascinating as the Abominable Snowman, as mysterious as the lost city of Atlantis. But is it real?

BACKGROUND

The next time you're looking at a map of the world, trace your finger from Key West, Florida, to Puerto Rico; from Puerto Rico to the island of Bermuda; and from there back to Florida. The 140,000-square-mile patch of ocean you've just outlined is the Bermuda Triangle. In the past 50 years, more than 100 ships and planes have disappeared there. That may sound like a lot, but it's actually about standard for a busy stretch of ocean.

"Besides," says Larry Kuche, author of *The Bermuda Triangle Mystery Solved*, "hundreds of planes and ships pass safely through the so-called triangle every day....It is no more logical to try to find a common cause for all the disappearances in the triangle than to try to find one cause for all the automobile accidents in Arizona."

Experts agree that the only real mystery about the Bermuda Triangle is why everyone thinks it's so mysterious.

THE DISAPPEARANCE THAT STARTED IT ALL

The "Lost Squadron." On December 15, 1945, Flight 19, a group of five U.S. Navy Avenger planes carrying 14 men, took off from the Fort Lauderdale Naval Air Station at 2 p.m. for a three-hour training mission off the Florida coast. Everything went well until about 3:40 p.m., when Lt. Charles C. Taylor, the leader of Flight 19, radioed back to Fort Lauderdale that both of his compasses had malfunctioned and that he was lost. "I am over land, but it's broken," he reported to base. "I am sure I'm in the Keys, but I don't know how far down and I don't know how to get to Fort Lauderdale." Shortly afterward he broke in with an eerier transmission: "We cannot see land....We can't be sure of any direction—even the ocean doesn't look as it should."

Over the next few hours, the tower heard numerous static-filled transmissions between the five planes. The last transmission came at 6:00 p.m., when a Coast Guard plane heard Taylor radio his colleagues: "All planes close up tight...will have to ditch unless landfall. When the first plane drops to 10 gallons we all go down together." That was his last transmission—that evening all five planes disappeared without a trace.

A few hours later, a search plane with a crew of 13 took off for the last reported position of the flight...and was never seen again. No wreckage or oil slick from any of the planes was ever found, prompting the Naval Board of Inquiry to observe that the planes "had disappeared as if they had flown to Mars."

A MYTH IS BORN

The Lost Squadron would probably be forgotten today if it hadn't been for a single news story published on September 16, 1950. An Associated Press reporter named E.V.W. Jones decided to occupy his time on a slow day by writing a story about the Lost Squadron and other ships and planes that had disappeared into the Atlantic Ocean off the Florida coast.

Dozens of newspapers around the country picked it up...and for some reason, it captured people's imaginations. Over the next few years the story was reprinted in tabloids, pulp magazines, pseudoscience journals, and "unexplained mysteries" books.

IT GETS A NAME

In 1964, Vincent Gaddis, another journalist, gave the story its *name*. He wrote an article in *Argosy* magazine called "The Deadly Bermuda Triangle" and listed dozens of ships that had disappeared there over the centuries, starting with the *Rosalie* (which disappeared in 1840) and ending with the yacht *Conne-mara IV* (which vanished in 1956). He also offered an explanation for the disappearances, speculating that they were caused by "space-time continua [that] may exist around us on the earth, inter-penetrating our known world," a pseudo-scientific way of suggesting that the planes and ships had disappeared into a third dimension.

Interest in the Bermuda Triangle hit a high point in 1974, when Charles Berlitz (grandson of the founder of Berlitz language schools) authored *The Bermuda Triangle: An Incredible Saga of Unexplained Disappearances*. Without presenting a shred of real evidence, he suggested the disappearances were caused by electromagnetic impulses generated by a 400-foot-tall pyramid at the bottom of the ocean. The book shot to the top of the bestseller list, inspir-

Q: What do Cleopatra and John Wilkes Booth have in common?

ing scores of copycat books, TV specials, and movies that kept the Bermuda Triangle myth alive for another generation.

DEBUNKING THE MYTH

Is there anything to the Bermuda Triangle theory? The U.S. government doesn't think so—the Coast Guard doesn't even bother to keep complete statistics on the incidents there and attributes the disappearances to the strong currents and violent weather patterns.

In 1985 an air-traffic controller named John Myhre came up with a plausible theory about the Lost Squadron's strange fate. A few years earlier he had been flipping through a book on the subject, when he came across a more complete record of the last radio communications between the five planes. Myhre was a pilot and had logged many hours flying off the coast of Florida. "When I ran across a more accurate version of Taylor's last transmissions," Myhre recounts, "I realized what had happened....The lead plane radioed that he was lost over the Florida Keys. Then he said he was over a single island and there was no land visible in any direction." Myhre believes the island Lt. Taylor reported "had to be Walker's Cay," an island that is not part of the Florida Keys:

> I've flown over it dozens of times and it's the only one of the hundreds of islands around Florida that's by itself out of sight of other land. And it's northwest of the Abacos, which, in fact, look very much like the Keys when you fly over them. Clearly if he thought he was in the Keys, he thought he could reach mainland by flying northeast. But if he was in the Abacos, a northeast course would just take him farther over the ocean.

*   *   *   *

MOVIE NOTE

The original Lost Squadron story became so embellished with new "facts" (Taylor's last words were reported to have been "I know where I am now...Don't come after me!...They look like they're from outer space!"), that filmmaker Stephen Spielberg included the Lost Squadron in a scene in *Close Encounters of the Third Kind*. The crew reappears on board the mother spaceship after being missing in action for decades.

NO RESPECT

Words to forget from comedian Rodney Dangerfield.

"We sleep in separate rooms, we have dinner apart, we take separate vacations—we're doing everything we can to keep our marriage together."

"I told my psychiatrist that everyone hates me. He said I was being ridiculous—everyone hasn't met me yet."

"If it weren't for pickpockets, I'd have no sex life at all."

"She was so old, when she went to school they didn't have history."

"I once asked my father if things were bad for him during the Depression. He said the first six months were bad, then he got used to me."

"My wife and I were happy for twenty years. Then we met."

"It's a good thing you're wearing a mustache. It breaks up the monotony of your face."

"I don't get no respect. No respect at all. Every time I get into an elevator the operator says the same thing: 'Basement?' No respect. When I was a kid we played hide-and-seek. They wouldn't even look for me. The other day I was standing in front of a big apartment house. The doorman asked me to get him a cab....I bought a used car—I found my wife's dress in the back seat."

"Last week I told my wife a man is like wine, he gets better with age. She locked me in the cellar."

"My wife's an Earth sign. I'm a water sign. Together we make mud."

"Always look out for Number One and be careful not to step in Number Two."

"I drink too much. Last time I gave a urine sample there was an olive in it."

"I broke up with my psychiatrist. I told him I had suicidal tendencies. He told me from now on I had to pay in advance."

INCOMPETENT CRIMINALS

A lot of Americans are worried about the growing threat of crime. Well, the good news is that there are plenty of crooks who are their own worst enemies. Here are a few true-life examples.

ARE WE HIGH YET?

When Nathan Radlich's house was burgled on June 4, 1993, thieves left his TV, his VCR, and even his watch. All they took was a "generic white cardboard box" of grayish white powder. A police spokesman said it looked similar to cocaine. "They probably thought they scored big," he mused.

The powder was actually the cremated remains of Radlich's sister, Gertrude, who had died three years earlier.

—From the *Fort Lauderdale Sun-Sentinel*

POOR PENMANSHIP

In 1992, 79-year-old Albert Goldsband walked into a San Bernardino, California, bank and handed the teller a note demanding money. When she couldn't read the note, he pulled out a toy gun. But the teller had already taken the note to her supervisor for help deciphering it.

Goldsband panicked and fled...to a nearby restaurant that was frequented by police officers. He was arrested immediately.

—From the *San Francisco Chronicle*

STUCK ON GLUE

RIO DE JANEIRO — Nov. 5, 1993. "A thief was found stuck to the floor of a factory Thursday after trying to steal glue in Belo Horizonte, 280 miles north of Rio, newspapers reported.

"Edilber Guimaeares, 19, stopped to sniff some of the glue he was stealing when two large cans fell to the floor, spilling over.

"When police were called Thursday morning, Guimaeares was glued to the floor, asleep."

—From the *San Francisco Examiner*

Seventy-three percent of women say they'd rather be "brilliant but plain" than "sexy but dumb."

MISTAKEN IDENTITY

"Warren Gillen, 26, was arrested for trying to rob a bank in Glasgow. Police put him in a lineup, but no one identified him. He was booked anyway after calling out from the lineup, 'Hey, don't you recognize me?' "

—From *More News of the Weird*

A CASE OF NERVES?

Lee W. Womble, 28, was spotted and picked up a few minutes after robbing the Lafayette Bank in Bridgeport, Connecticut.

Police said that even if they hadn't seen him, he would have been easy to identify; he had written his name on the note he handed the teller demanding money.

"He wrote his name on it twice—once on top of the other," said police. "He could have been trying to kill time. He could have been nervous or something. Who knows?"

—From the *Oakland Tribune*

WRONG TURN

"An alleged drunk driver who led police on a wild midnight chase landed in jail even before his arrest. His car crashed into the jail building.

"He didn't have too far to go from there,' said Police Capt. Mike Lanam. 'It was like a drive-up window.' "

—From the *Chicago Tribune*

EMPLOYMENT OPPORTUNITY

"A man accused of stealing a car was easy to track, police said, especially after they found his resume under one of the seats.

"Police discovered the handwritten resume when they looked through the stolen 1985 Chevrolet Celebrity they had recovered.

"Police then telephoned an employer listed on the resume for a different sort of reference."

—From the Associated Press

People with heart disease are 2.3 times more likely to have a heart attack when they're angry.

MONTHS OF THE YEAR

Here's where the names of the months come from.

JANUARY. Named for the Roman god *Janus*, a two-faced god who "opened the gates of heaven to let out the morning, and closed them at dusk." Janus was worshiped as the god of all doors, gates, and other entrances. Consequently, the opening month of the year was named after him.

FEBRUARY. The Roman "Month of Purification" got its name from *februarius*, the Latin word for purification. February 15 was set aside for the Festival of Februa, in which people repented and made sacrifices to the gods to atone for their wrongdoings.

MARCH. Named for Mars, the Roman god of war. The Roman empire placed great emphasis on wars and conquest, so until 46 B.C. this was the first month of the year.

APRIL. No one knows the origin of the name. One theory: it comes from *Aprilis* or *aphrilis*, which are corruptions of *Aphrodite*, the Greek name for Venus, the goddess of love. However, many experts think the month is named after the Latin verb *aperire*, which means "to open." (Most plants open their leaves and buds in April.)

MAY. Some people think the month is named after *Maia*, the mother of the god Mercury; other people think it was named in honor of the *Majores*, the older branch of the Roman Senate.

JUNE. It may have been named in honor of *Juno*, the wife of Jupiter; or it may have been named after the *Juniores*, the lower branch of the Roman Senate.

JULY. Named after Julius Caesar.

AUGUST. Named after Gaius Julius Caesar Octavianus, heir and nephew of Julius Caesar. The Roman Senate gave this Caesar the title of "Augustus," which means "revered," and honored him further by naming a month after him.

SEPTEMBER. Comes from the Latin word *septem*, which means "seven." September was the seventh month until about the year 700 B.C., when Numa Pompilius, the second Roman king, switched from a 304-day calendar to a 355-day lunar calendar.

OCTOBER. From *octo*, the Latin word for "eight." When Romans changed the calendar, they knew October was no longer the eighth month, and tried to rename it. Some candidates: *Germanicus* (after a general), *Antonius* (an emperor), *Faustina* (the emperor's wife), and *Herculeus* (after Emperor Commodus, who had nicknamed himself the "Roman Hercules.") None of the new names stuck.

NOVEMBER. From *novem*, the Latin word for "nine." November was also referred to as "blood-month." Reason: It was the peak season for pagan animal sacrifices.

DECEMBER. From *decem*, the Latin word for "ten." Attempts to rename it *Amazonius* in honor of the mistress of Emperor Commodius failed.

DAYS OF THE WEEK

When Anglo-Saxons invaded the British isles, they brought their language and pagan gods with them. The names of the days of the week are a legacy.

SUNDAY. Originally called *Sunnan daeg*, which, like today, meant "sun day."

MONDAY. Originally called *Monan daeg*, "moon day."

TUESDAY. *Tiwes daeg* was named in honor of Tiw, the Anglo-Saxon and Norse god of war.

WEDNESDAY. Named *Wodnes daeg* and dedicated to Woden, the king of the gods in Valhalla.

THURSDAY. *Thu(n)res daeg* commemorated Thor, the god of thunder, and the strongest and bravest god of them all.

FRIDAY. Originally named *Frige daeg* after Thor's mother Frigga, the most important goddess in Valhala. (That's one theory; the day may be also named after Freyja, the Norse goddess of love.)

SATURDAY. Named *Saeter daeg* in honor of Saturn, the Roman god of agriculture. It's the one day of the week whose name *isn't* derived from Anglo-Saxon/Norse myths.

THE JEEP STORY

Are you a 4-wheel-drive fanatic? Here's a story you'll like. It's about the vehicle that General George Marshall called "this country's most important contribution to World War II."

BACKGROUND

The U.S. Army of 1939 wasn't much like the one that won World War II six years later. Convinced that World War I had been "the war to end all wars," the U.S. government had cut military spending to the bone during the '30s. The army wasn't even *close* to bringing American troops into the automobile age yet. In fact, there weren't even enough vehicles to transport troops to the front lines. If the United States had gotten involved in a military action, most soldiers would have gone into battle either on foot or on *horseback*.

The problem drove officers nuts, particularly as another war in Europe began to look inevitable. "The humblest citizen rides proudly and swiftly to his work in his Model T or his shivering Chevrolet," one colonel complained to his superiors in 1940. "The infantryman alone, sole contemporary of the sodden coolie or the plodding Hindu, carries the supplies and implements of his trade upon his stooping back or loads them upon two-wheeled carts drawn by himself or by a harassed and hesitating mule."

THE CAR WARS

The army finally began to address the problem in 1940, when it drew up specifications for a zippy, 4-wheel-drive "low-silhouette scout car" large enough to carry four men and low enough to dodge enemy fire. It sent the specs to 135 different manufacturers, insisting that that the vehicle weigh no more than 1,300 lbs. and stand no taller than 3 feet high with its windshield folded down over the hood. Only two companies expressed interest: American Bantam of Butler, Pennsylvania, and Willys-Overland of Toledo, Ohio. Only American Bantam submitted a prototype to the military for testing.

The army liked the American Bantam model, but worried that the company, which had only 15 employees and no assembly plant, was too small to manufacture the hundreds of thousands of vehicles that would be needed. So it scheduled a special "field test" of the

American Bantam prototype, invited engineers from Willys-Overland and the Ford Motor Company to stop by as "observers"... and passed out the vehicle's blueprints to everyone who attended. The competition took the hint, and a few months later Ford and Willys delivered "remarkably similar" vehicles of their own. Willys-Overland won the contract. Later, when production demands outstripped even Willys's production capacity, Ford agreed to build the Willys model in its own factories. American Bantam spent the rest of the war building truck trailers and torpedo motors.

THE NAME GAME

When the first jeeps rolled off the assembly lines in 1941, they were known as "GPs," short for "general purpose." But they came to be known by other nicknames, including beetle bug, blitz buggy, Leaping Lena, beep, peep, and puddle jumper. Jeep was the one that stuck, not only because of the vehicle's initials but because of the 1930s *Popeye* cartoon character Jeep, who was "neither fowl nor beast, but knew all the answers and could do most anything."

The new vehicle was a hit, because *it* could do almost anything, too. As *Smithsonian* magazine put it, "Mounted with a machine gun, it became not just a means of transport, but a combat vehicle....They plowed snow and delivered mail to foxholes at the front. Their engines powered searchlights, their wheels agitated washtubs....With a special waterproofing kit, jeeps crawled through water up to their hoods....The army ordered an amphibious jeep (the seep) and a lightweight jeep for air drops (the fleep)."

COMING HOME

The jeep was so popular that when the war ended Willys-Overland trademarked the jeep as a Jeep (after a lengthy court battle with Ford) and began manufacturing models for the domestic market. But in the 1940s and 1950s, the public wanted big, luxurious cars. Jeep sales stayed sluggish until the 1970s. Then, for some reason, they began to pick up...and have kept getting stronger. In fact, in the 1980s, Chrysler bought American Motors just to get the Jeep line.

In the 1993-1994 model year, Americans bought over 1.4 million jeep-type vehicles—more than twice as many as were built during all of World War II.

Emergency call: In the U.S. you dial 911; in Stockholm, Sweden, you dial 90000.

INTERNATIONAL LAW

And you thought the U.S. legal system was strange...

Paris law forbids spinning tops on sidewalks...and staring at the mayor.

19th-century Scottish law required brides to be pregnant on their wedding day.

In England it's against the law to sue the queen—or to name your daughter "Princess" without her permission.

The law in Teruel, Spain, forbids taking hot baths on Sunday. (Cold baths are OK.)

In Rio de Janeiro, it's illegal to dance the samba in a tunnel.

Gun control: In Switzerland, the law *requires* you to keep guns and ammunition in your home.

Swedish law prohibits trained seals from balancing balls on their noses.

If you're arrested for drunken driving in Malaysia, you go to jail. (So does your wife.)

In Australia it's illegal to hire a woman under the age of 45 to work as a chorus girl.

In Reykjavik, Iceland, it's illegal to keep a dog as a pet.

If you curse within earshot of a woman in Egypt, the law says you forfeit two days' pay.

In pre-Islamic Turkey, if a wife let the family coffee pot run dry, her husband was free to divorce her.

The opposite was true in Saudi Arabia, where a woman was free to divorce her husband if he didn't keep her supplied with coffee.

Horses in Mukden, China, are required to wear diapers; their owners are required "to empty them at regular intervals into specially constructed receptacles."

Toronto, Canada, law requires pedestrians to give hand signals before turning.

English law forbids marrying your mother-in-law.

Red cars are outlawed in Shanghai, China...and other automobile colors are assigned according to the owner's profession.

WORD ORIGINS

You already know these words. But did you know where they come from?

Gossip: From *godsib*, which meant "godparent." (*Sibling* has the same root.) According to Morton S. Freeman in *The Story Behind the Word*, "The idea of gossip grew out of the regular meetings and intimate conversations of the *godsibbes*. What they talked about came to be called *godsibbes* or (as slurred) *gossip*."

Ignoramus: The Latin word which means "we do not know." By the 17th century the term referred almost exclusively to "ignorant, arrogant attorneys," thanks in large part to a 1615 play in which the main character was a stupid lawyer named Ignoramus.

Minimum: Comes from the Latin word *minium*, "red lead." "In medieval times," the book *Word Mysteries and Histories* reports, "chapter headings and other important divisions of a text were distinguished by being written in red, while the rest of the book was was written in black. . . . Sections of a manuscript were also marked off with large ornate initial capital letters, which were often decorated with small paintings. *Miniatura* was used to describe these paintings as well. Since the paintings were necessarily very tiny, *miniatura* came to mean 'a small painting or object of any kind.' "

Boor: Originally meant "farmer." (A "neighbor" was a near-farmer.) Originally the term had no pejorative meaning . . . but over time city dwellers, who fancied themselves as being more refined than their country cousins, interpreted the word to mean "ill-mannered," "unrefined," or "rude"—so much so that the original meaning was lost entirely.

Nickname: From the Middle English word *ekename*, which meant "additional name." Where did the "n" come from? From the definite article an, which frequently proceeded the word. Over time "an ekename" became "a nekename". . . and then finally "a nickname."

REVENGE!

While JFK was president, reporters quoted the Kennedy family motto a lot: "Don't get mad, get even." Well, we all want to get back at someone once in a while. These guys did—and did it well.

HERE, MY DEAR

Singer Marvin Gaye and Anna Gordy (sister of Motown founder Berry Gordy) had a bitter divorce battle. One of the terms of the settlement: Gaye had to give his ex-wife all the royalties from his next album. Gaye complied. He called the album *Here, My Dear,* and filled it with unrelenting, scathing attacks on her. Predictably, sales were a disappointing (to Anna and Motown) 400,000 copies. Added bonus: The episode got Gaye get out of his contract with Motown—something he desperately wanted. He signed with Columbia Records, where he produced some of the bestselling albums of his career.

NOTABLE EFFORT

"At a London party in the 1920s, Mrs. Ronald Greville slipped an inebriated butler a note saying, 'You are drunk. Leave the room at once.' He put the note on a silver tray and presented it to the guest of honor, British Foreign Secretary Austen Chamberlain."

—*Esquire* magazine

REWRITING HISTORY

In 1976, Robert Redford put together the film version of *All the President's Men,* the story of how two *Washington Post* reporters broke the Watergate scandal.

Post publisher Katherine Graham signed the contracts approving the project...then started worrying about her newspaper's image. She told her lawyers to try to stop the film—or at least keep the *Post*'s name out of it. This infuriated Redford.

"An early version of the script had referred to her as 'the unsung heroine' of the story,' " writes Stephen Bates, "and Patricia Neal had been considered for the role. Now Redford ordered that the Graham character be *eliminated.*" Redford left in only one reference to Graham: the scene in which "John Mitchell tells [reporter Carl]

Bernstein that, if a certain story is published, 'Katie Graham's gonna get her tit caught in a big fat wringer.'"

—*If No News, Send Rumors*

HAVE A CIGARETTE, DEAR?

BUCHAREST, Romania—"A man who was heckled by his wife to stop smoking left everything to her on condition she take up his habit as punishment for 40 years of 'hell.'

"Marin Cemenescu, who died at the age of 76, stipulated in his will that in order to inherit his house and $30,000 estate, his 63-year-old wife, Aneta, would have to smoke five cigarettes a day for the rest of her life.

" 'She could not stand to see me with a cigarette in my mouth, and I ended up smoking in the bathroom like a schoolboy,' Cemenescu wrote in his will. 'My life was hell.' "

—*San Francisco Chronicle*

DRUNKEN VEEP

When President Abe Lincoln ran for his second term of office, he dumped his first-term vice president, Hannibal Hamlin, in favor of Andrew Johnson. Hamlin wasn't too happy about it. But he did get a measure of revenge.

"The morning that Lincoln and Johnson were to be inaugurated," writes Steven Talley, "Hamlin stopped by Johnson's (formerly his) office. Johnson was ill with typhoid and quite nervous about [the event]. When he complained to Hamlin that he could stand a shot of whiskey, the teetotaler Hamlin immediately sent an aide for a bottle. Johnson poured himself a few extra-stiff drinks." Then Johnson gave one of the most embarrassing inaugural speeches in history—long, rambling, completely drunken. "No doubt," says Talley, "Hamlin acted as shocked as the rest of the crowd."

—*Bland Ambition*

WHAT ISLAND?

"In revenge for England's closing of the Libyan embassy in London, Col. Muammar el-Khadafy ordered that England be deleted from all Libyan maps in the mid-'80s. In its place, he put a new arm of the North Sea, bordered by Scotland and Wales."

—*More News of the Weird*

THE BARNEY STORY

Some dinosaurs are extinct...and others we only wish *were extinct—like Barney. You have to wonder why anyone thought the Barney blitz would succeed...and then you have to wonder why it did. Here's one version, written by Jack* Mingo*, the author of* How the Cadillac Got Its Fins.

How did Barney, a 6'4" inch purple-and-green dinosaur, capture the hearts and minds of two- and three-year-olds everywhere? It depends on who you ask.

THE LEGEND

The story told by the company—and reported in *Time* and other news sources, goes something like this:

Sheryl Leach, a simple mother and schoolteacher, was driving down the highway in Dallas in 1988 with her restless toddler Patrick, wondering how to get a little free time for herself.

At the time, the only thing that could hold Patrick's attention was a "Wee Sing" video featuring colorful characters and music. Suddenly, Leach had an inspiration: Why not try making a video herself? "How hard could it be?" she thought. "I could do that."

She got a schoolteacher friend named Kathy Parker to help, borrowed some money, and voila! Barney was born.

THE TRUTH

The real story makes Barney seem a little more like what he is—an extremely clever business venture.

Leach, the inspired mom, was actually working as a "software manager" for a successful religious and education publisher named DLM, Inc., which, umm, they forgot to mention was owned by her father-in-law, Richard Leach.

And Parker may have been a schoolteacher, but she was working as an "early childhood product manager" for the same company when Barney was born.

And hey, what a lucky break! DLM had just built video production facilities and was looking to branch into the lucrative kids' video market when Leach had her brainstorm. In fact, Leach's father-in-law invested $1 million to develop Barney and even provided the services of a video education specialist who was creating a real-estate training series for DLM at the time.

HOW BARNEY MADE IT TO TV

In *How the Cadillac Got Its Fins*, Jack Mingo writes: "DLM created eight videos starring Sandy Duncan; they sold more than four million copies. One of those copies came to the attention of the executive vice president for programming at Connecticut Public Broadcasting, Larry Rifkin.

"It was Super Bowl Sunday. Rifkin took his four-year-old daughter to the video store to rent some tapes so he could watch the game in peace. 'Leora walked out with "Barney and the Backyard Gang" and she watched the program and watched the program and watched the program. So I decided to take a look and see what it was she enjoying,' said Rifkin. He tracked down the manufacturer and made a deal to purchase 30 episodes for his station."

From there, the whole phenomenon just took off. Leach and Co. reportedly made $100 million from Barney in 1993 alone.

BARNEY VS. THE WORLD

Maybe it's the color purple...maybe it's that dippy voice. Whatever it is, Barney aroused some pretty potent passions.

For example:

• The Rev. Joseph Chambers, a North Carolina radio preacher, thinks Barney is proof that "America is under seige from the powers of darkness." He put out a pamphlet called *Barney the Purple Messiah*, charging that Barney is a New Age demon bent on introducing America's children to the occult.

• The University of Nebraska held a "Barney Bashing Day," which featured boxing with a Barney look-alike.

• In Worcester, Massachusetts, a college student jumped out of a car, shouted obscenities and assaulted a woman who had dressed as Barney to help celebrate the opening of a drug store. "I said, 'Why are you doing this to me?' " the woman told police, "And he said, 'Because we...hate Barney!' " One little boy who witnessed the attack said, "I'm going home to get my gun, Barney. And I'm going to shoot him."

Most popular junk food in New England: potato chips. In the Southeastern U.S.: cheese puffs.

MONUMENTAL MISTAKES

Many of our most treasured national landmarks and monuments were neglected—and sometimes almost destroyed—before anyone managed to rescue them. See if you can figure out what happened to them. Answers are on page 671.

1. Every year, thousands of people make the pilgimmage to Plymouth Rock. But for 150 years after the original Pilgrims landed, no one paid much attention to it. In the 1770s, pro-American rebels decided it was an historic American landmark and went to preserve it. Where did they find it?

A) 10 feet under water

B) buried in a roadway

C) in a pile of rocks on the outskirts of town

2. When this president died, his magnificent home and estate were sold to pay off his debts. A few years later, an observer described it as "nothing but ruin and change, rotting terraces, broken cabins, the lawn plowed up and cattle wandering among the Italian mouldering vases." What landmark was he talking about?

A) George Washington / Mount Vernon

B) Thomas Jefferson / Monticello

C) Andrew Jackson / The Hermitage

3. The Statue of Liberty was not immediately installed in New York Harbor, because there was no money available to build a base for it. What private source offered to pay for the base—but was refused?

A) The company that made Castoria laxative offered to pay for the base if they could put a huge advertisement on it.

B) Commodore Cornelius Vanderbilt offered to pay for it in exchange for the rights to run the ferry to and from Liberty Island.

C) The Daughters of the American Revolution offered to pay for it if the inscription welcoming immigrants was removed.

Twelve most-often-used letters in the alphabet: E, T, A, O, I, N, S, K, R, D, L, U.

4. As the country grew, the number of members in the House of Representatives grew. By 1857, the House had outgrown its chambers and moved to another wing of the Capitol. Today, the area contains statues of famous representatives. But in the late 1850s, it was occupied by:

A) a train station

B) a tourism information booth

C) a root beer stand

5. It was a dry-goods store from 1879 until the turn of the century. Then, in 1905, a hotel chain decided to buy the land, tear it down, and build a modern building on it. They offered $75,000 for it. The owner agreed to sell...unless the Texas legislature wanted to match the offer. But the legislature wouldn't authorize the funds to save it. Was it:

A) the Alamo

B) Sam Houston's birthplace

C) the Emma Lapham house, where the first baby was born to a Texas settler

6. Ford's Theater, where Lincoln was shot, is now a popular Lincoln museum and working theater. But it was almost demolished by:

A) John Ford himself, a Lincoln supporter who was heartbroken to have played any part in the assassination

B) The U.S. government, at Andrew Johnson's command. He thought it was in the nation's best interest to eliminate all memories of the tragedy.

C) An angry mob that gathered after the assassination. They wanted to burn it down, but were dispersed.

7. "Old Ironsides," the *U.S.S. Constitution*, is a tourist attraction afloat in the Boston Navy Yard today. But the famous ship was left to fall apart until 1927, when:

A) schoolchildren contributed their pennies to save it.

B) the Boston Red Sox played a series of exhibition games to save it.

C) Al Capone, striving for good publicity, donated the money to save it.

TRUE LIES: THE TONKIN INCIDENT

In 1964, Lyndon Johnson claimed that the U.S. was forced into the Vietnam War by an unprovoked North Vietnamese attack. Did it really happen that way—or was it a phony story to get the U.S. into the war? Here's a look at what happened, from It's a Conspiracy! *by The National Insecurity Council.*

Late in the evening on August 4, 1964, President Lyndon Johnson interrupted television programs on all three national networks with grim news. He announced that American destroyers off the coast of North Vietnam in the Gulf of Tonkin had been attacked twice by the North Vietnamese—without provocation.

He promised reprisals; in fact, he declared that U.S. planes were on their way to bomb North Vietnam as he spoke.

Three days later, President Johnson asked Congress to pass an emergency resolution that would authorize him to "take all necessary measures to repel any armed attack against the forces of the United States and to prevent further aggression."

Congress obliged: The Gulf of Tonkin Resolution passed 98-2 in the Senate, and Johnson used it to launch the longest war in American history—a war that cost more than $400 billion, killed 58,000 U.S. service people, and divided the country more than any other conflict since the Civil War.

Yet, as incredible as it seems, evidence now suggests that LBJ and his advisors wanted a war in Vietnam—and conspired to start it with a lie.

THE OFFICIAL STORY

First attack: August 2, 1964. According to government reports, three North Vietnamese PT boats, unprovoked and without warning, fired torpedoes and shells at the *Maddox*, a U.S. destroyer on patrol about 30 miles off the coast of North Vietnam. The destroyer and support aircraft fired back and drove them off.

Second attack: August 4, 1964. North Vietnamese PT boats made another "deliberate attack" on two United States destroyers

—the *Maddox* and the *Turner Joy*—which were patrolling international waters about 65 miles off the coast of North Vietnam. This attack was described as "much fiercer than the first one," lasting about three hours in rough seas, with bad weather and low visibility. The government said that American destroyers and aircraft fired on the vessels and sank at least two of them.

SUSPICIOUS FACTS

The First Attack

• The government lied about where the *Maddox* was and what it was doing on the night of the first attack:

✔ The *Maddox* wasn't in international waters. According to numerous reports, it was no farther than 10 miles—and possibly as close as four miles—from the North Vietnamese coast.

✔ It wasn't on a "routine patrol." The *Maddox* was providing cover for South Vietnamese gunboats attacking North Vietnamese radar stations in the Gulf of Tonkin. According to former CIA station chief John Stockwell, those gunboats were "manned with CIA crew" and had been raiding North Vietnam all summer.

• The government said the attack on the *Maddox* was "unprovoked." However, the *Maddox*'s log showed that it had fired first while North Vietnamese boats were still six miles away.

The Second Attack

• Many people doubt that the alleged August 4 attack ever occurred. They include:

✔ The *Maddox*'s captain, John Herrick. He radioed that reports of an enemy attack "appear very doubtful" and said there were "no actual sightings by *Maddox*."

✔ Commander Jim Stockdale, a navy pilot who responded to the *Maddox*'s distress calls. According to an October 1988 article in *The New American*, Stockdale "found the destroyers sitting in the water firing at—nothing....Not one American out there ever saw a PT boat. There was absolutely no gunfire except our own, no PT boat wakes, not a candle light, let alone a burning ship. No one could have been there and not have been seen on such a black night."

Twenty-three percent of Americans say it's OK for a wife to slap her husband.

✔ Pentagon planners who analyzed the information from Vietnam. "There was a great amount of uncertainty as to whether there was such an attack," recalls Daniel Ellsberg, who was working with the Pentagon at the time.

✔ President Lyndon Johnson. According to Stanley Karnow's *Vietnam: A History*, "Johnson privately expressed doubts only a few days after the second attack supposedly took place, confiding to an aide, 'Hell, those dumb sailors were just shooting flying fish.'"

• According to investigative reporter Jonathan Kwitny in his book *Endless Enemies*: "At one point things were so confused that the *Maddox* mistook the *Turner Joy* for a North Vietnamese ship and a gunner was ordered to fire at her point blank—which would have sunk her—but he refused the order pending an identity check. That was the closest that a U.S. ship came to being hit that night."

The Resolution

Although the Gulf of Tonkin Resolution was supposedly submitted "in response to this outrageous incident" (the second attack), the document had actually been drafted by William Bundy, Johnson's assistant secretary of state, three months earlier.

WHAT HAPPENED?

Did our government intentionally draw the U.S. into war? Kwitny writes: "What we know is entirely consistent with the possibility that the Tonkin Gulf Incident was a put-up job, designed to sucker the North Vietnamese into providing justification for a planned U.S. expansion of the war....The North Vietnamese had every reason to believe they were under attack before they approached a U.S. ship, and they certainly were under attack before they fired a shot. The press was lied to, and so misinformed the public. We were all lied to."

FOOTNOTE

The Tonkin Resolution was passed a few months before the 1964 presidential race between Johnson and Barry Goldwater. According to Kenneth Davis in his book *Don't Know Much About History*, "the Resolution not only gave Johnson the powers he needed to increase American commitment in Vietnam, but allowed him to blunt Goldwater's accusations that Johnson was 'timid before Communism.' "

Ten percent of Americans say it's OK for a husband to slap his wife.

THURBERISMS

The wit and wisdom of James Thurber, one of America's most respected humorists.

"It is better to have loafed and lost than never to have loafed at all."

"Love is blind, but desire just doesn't give a good goddamn."

"Well, if I called the wrong number, why did you answer the phone?"

"I hate women because they always know where things are."

"Seeing is deceiving. It's eating that's believing."

"You can fool too many of the people too much of the time."

"Early to rise and early to bed makes a male healthy, wealthy and dead."

"Humor is emotional chaos remembered in tranquility."

"It's a naive wine, without any breeding, but I think you'll be amused by its presumption."

"I have always thought of a dog lover as a dog who was in love with another dog."

"Some American writers who have known each other for years have never met in the day time or when both are sober."

"It's better to know some of the questions than all of the answers."

"You might as well fall flat on your face as lean too far backward."

"Love is what you've been through with somebody."

"All men kill the thing they hate, too, unless, of course, it kills them first."

"I'm 65 and I guess that puts me in with the geriatrics, but if there were fifteen months in every year, I'd only be 48."

"Sixty minutes of thinking of any kind is bound to lead to confusion and unhappiness."

"Boys are beyond the range of anybody's sure understanding, at least when they're between the ages of 18 months and 90 years."

In one recent study, 38% of American men said "they love their cars more than women."

THE NAKED TRUTH

People in this country get very strange when they take their clothes off. Check out these excerpts from newspaper articles contributed by BRI correspondent Peter Wing.

A BIG SURPRISE

"A male motorist told authorities yesterday that a naked, red-haired woman—'the largest woman you ever saw'—jumped out of the woods and attacked his car on a dark country road in northern Michigan.

After briefly terrorizing the motorist, the woman disappeared into the woods."

—**United Press International**

AND WHAT ABOUT KETCHUP?

LANSING, MICH — Oct. 16, 1981. "Two sisters who described their nude mustard-smeared joyride in a parcel delivery truck as a religious experience have been set free....A third sister was found mentally ill; sentencing in her case has been postponed.

"The three were arrested after driving off—nude except for their shoes and smeared with mustard—in a parked United Parcel Service truck. 'We were trying to find God,' one of the sisters explained."

—***San Francisco Chronicle***

THE CRISCO KID

"A Tifton, Georgia, man has been convicted of public indecency and placed on probation for slinging chunks of lard at women while driving a car in the nude."

—**Associated Press**

HOPPING AROUND THE NEIGHBORHOOD

SANTA CRUZ, CA— "A city police officer was investigating a complaint of a disturbance at a man's home when he spotted what looked like a tall, chocolate rabbit coming 'hippity hoppity' out of the yard. After a closer look, the officer discovered it was a 30-year-old female neighbor who had covered her nude body in chocolate glaze. She was disguised as the Easter bunny."

—**Associated Press**

More Oklahoma households own dogs than in any other state. Texas comes in second.

"FORTUNATE" SONS

We often assume that the children of rich or famous parents have it made. Maybe not. Here are a few stories to consider.

W.C. FIELDS, JR., *son of comedy great W.C. Fields*
As a child, Claude Fields hardly ever saw his father...or his father's money. W. C. Fields was as cheap as he was successful. He paid his estranged wife a paltry $60-a-week allowance and refused to contribute a cent to Claude's education. When he died, he left his wife and son only $10,000 each from his $800,000 estate, instructing that the rest be spent founding the W. C. Fields College for Orphan White Boys and Girls, Where No Religion of Any Sort Is to Be Preached. Claude, by then a successful lawyer, contested the will and won.

WILLIAM FRANKLIN, *son of Benjamin Franklin*
William picked up pro-British sentiments while living in London with his father in the 1750s and became an outspoken Royalist and opponent of American independence. Through his connections in the English aristocracy, he had himself appointed Royal Governor of New Jersey. In 1776, he was arrested for trying to rally opposition to the Declaration of Independence in the New Jersey colonial assembly. He languished in prison until 1778, they returned to London in 1782 when it became obvious that England was going to lose the war. Disinherited and shunned by his father (who died in 1790), William died in England in 1813.

HARILAL GANDHI, *son of Mahatma Gandhi*
"Men may be good," Mahatma Gandhi once observed, "but not necessarily their children." He was talking about Harilal Gandhi, his oldest son. But the Mahatma, who was as terrible a father as he was a great leader, had virtually abandoned his son by the time the lad was in his teens. Estranged from his father, widowed, and left to raise his four children alone, Harilal became a womanizer and an alcoholic. In 1936, he converted to Islam, which so deeply embarrassed the elder Gandhi that he issued a public letter condemning the conversion. "Harilal's apostasy is no loss to Hinduism," the letter read, "and his admission to Islam is a source of weakness to it, if

McDonald's restaurants reportedly make about 40% of their profits from "Happy Meals."

he remains the same wreck that he was before." Harilal remained a drunk in spite of his embracing a religion that forbade the consumption of alcohol, showing up drunk and disoriented at both his mother's funeral in 1944 and his father's in 1948. He died of tuberculosis six months after his father's death.

ALBERT FRANCIS CAPONE, JR., *son of Al Capone*
Believe it or not, Little Al was actually pretty honest. In the 1940s he even quit his job as a used-car salesman when he caught his boss turning back odometers. When the family assets were seized by the IRS after Big Al died in 1947, he had to drop out of college and make a living. So he opened a Miami restaurant with his mother.

In 1965, he was arrested for stealing two bottles of aspirin and some batteries from a supermarket. He pled no contest, telling the judge, "Everybody has a little larceny in him, I guess." A year later, still smarting from the publicity, Capone changed his name to Albert Francis.

ROMANO MUSSOLINI, *son of Italian dictator Benito Mussolini*
He was only 18 years old when his father fell from power at the end of World War II. So Romano spent much of his life in exile going to school, working as a poultry farmer, playing the piano, and developing a taste for jazz music. He eventually formed his own band, "The Romano Mussolini Jazz Band," and either because of talent or novelty was able to book performances around the world.

WILLIAM MURRAY, *son of Madalyn Murray O'Hair, the athiest whose 1963 Supreme Court case resulted in outlawing school prayer*
His mother's famous lawsuit was filed on William's behalf, so he wouldn't have to join in prayers with the rest of his ninth-grade class. But he converted to Christianity in the late 1970s after finding God in an Alcoholics Anonymous support group. William later became a Baptist preacher...and on at least one occasion was barred from preaching in a school auditorium by principals citing his own Supreme Court case.

RICHARD J. REYNOLDS II, *R.J.Reynolds tobacco fortune heir*
Died of emphysema in 1964. His son, Richard J. Reynolds III, died of emphysema in 1994. Patrick Reynolds (R. J. III's half-brother) sold his R.J. Reynolds stock and became an antismoking activist.

The average American today gets 20% less sleep than the average American did 100 years ago.

BUILDING THE PENTAGON

It isn't one of the Seven Wonders of the World, but it probably deserves to be. Here's the story of what was for decades the world's largest office building ...and what remains today "the most easily recognized building on Earth."

AMERICA GOES TO WAR

As the United States geared up for World War II in the late 1930s, military planners were concerned by the fact that the War Department was located in 17 buildings spread out all over Washington, D.C. Officers wasted hours each day traveling around town from one office to another. This made it almost impossible to plan America's defense quickly and efficiently. And the problem was expected to get much worse: In the second half of 1941 alone, the Department of the Army was expected to grow by 25%, enough to fill four more office buildings.

GETTING IN SHAPE

In July 1941, General Brehon Somervell, the army's chief of construction, gave a team of architects one weekend to come up with a plan for a building that would house the entire military, to be built on a compact site adjacent to Arlington National Cemetery. The architects probably would have preferred a traditional square design, but because a road cut through one corner of the property there wasn't enough room for a square building. So they designed a building with a pentagonal shape instead.

At first it looked like all of their work had been for nothing. When President Roosevelt learned of the intended site for the Pentagon, he insisted that it be moved farther away from Arlington National Cemetery so as not to desecrate the hallowed burial ground. The architects selected another site about 3/4 of a mile away, larger than the first site, but stuck with the original pentagonal shape. Why? According to historian R. Alton Lee:

> The original Pentagon pattern was retained for a number of reasons: it already was designed and there was the pressure of time; Army officers liked it because its shape was reminiscent of a 17th-century fortress; and any pattern close to a circular shape would permit the

greatest amount of office area within the shortest walking distance....Roosevelt agreed to the new site, but disliked the architectural design. Why not build a large, square, windowless building that could be converted during peace time into a storage area for archives or supplies? However, [Gen. Brehon Somervell, the officer in charge of construction] liked the pentagonal concept and, as time was vital, told the contractors to proceed....When the President discovered what was happening, construction had already begun.

THE HEIGHT

The architects also decided on a long, flat building instead of a tall, thin one like a skyscraper. Reason: It was faster and cheaper to build a building without elevators. Also, given that 20,000 to 30,000 people an hour would enter and leave the building during peak traffic times, connecting the floors with wide ramps enabled more people to get where they were going than stairs, elevators, or escalators ever could.

BUILDING THE BEHEMOTH

Because it seemed likely that the United States might enter the war at any moment, what took place next was one of the fastest and most massive construction projects ever attempted. Groundbreaking took place on August 11, 1941; soon afterward workers moved more than 5.5 million cubic yards of earth onto the site and then hammered 41,491 massive concrete piles (more than one for each person scheduled to move into the Pentagon) into the ground to form the foundation. Then they built the Pentagon building itself using more than 435,000 cubic yards of concrete made from sand and gravel dredged from the nearby Potomac River. Because speed was essential, 13,000 workers worked around the clock to get the building finished as quickly as possible. The pace was so rapid that rather than take the time to remove all of the heavy equipment after excavating the basement, contractors left some of it in place and entombed it in cement. And given the frantic pace of construction, the architects' drawings barely kept ahead of the construction crews.

The building wasn't built all at once: Each of the Pentagon's five sides was built independently of the others in clockwise order, with the occupants of each section moving in as soon as it was finished.

Q: What's the most popular amusement park on Earth? A: Tokyo Disneyland.

The last section was finally completed on January 15, 1943, just 16 months after the ground-breaking.

RANDOM PENTAGON FACTS

• Originally budgeted at $35 million, the building ultimately cost $70 million in 1942, about as much as a battleship. Despite the huge cost overruns and the last-minute changes in the plans, Congress barely let out a whimper when it authorized the additional funds needed to complete the building. World War II was in full swing, and even the most penny-pinching politicos kept silent out of fear of jeopardizing—or being *accused* of jeopardizing—the war effort.

• When the Pentagon was in its planning stages, Franklin Roosevelt insisted that the outside of the building not have any windows, believing it would look more dramatic. Furthermore, a windowless building would be easier to convert to civilian government use once the war was over. But munitions experts talked him out of it, explaining that walls with "blow-out" windows survive bombings better than solid masonry walls, which collapse entirely.

• The Pentagon is designed so that the offices are as close together as they possibly can be—even so, when the building first opened it quickly earned the nickname "Pantygon" because people walked their pants off getting from one place to another.

• To deal with the immense amount of vehicle traffic each working day, architects designed an elaborate system of over- and underpasses arranged into cloverleaf shapes, which enabled thousands of vehicles to drop off passengers and leave again without ever once stopping for a traffic light. The innovative cloverleaf over- and underpasses were so successful that they became a standard feature of the interstate highway system.

• The Pentagon has enough cafeterias and dining rooms to serve more than 17,500 meals a day…but has only 230 restrooms.

• It has 17.5 miles of corridors, 150 stairways, 4,200 clocks, 22,500 telephones connected by 100,000 miles of telephone cable, 25,000 employees, 2 hospitals, its own power and sewage plants, and the world's largest pneumatic tube system. But it only has one passenger elevator: the one that the Secretary of Defense uses to get from his parking space in the basement to his office.

DAVE'S WORLD

A few of our favorite quotes from comedian Dave Barry.

"The idea with natural childbirth is to avoid drugs so the mother can share the first intimate moments after birth with the baby and the father and the obstetrician and the standby anesthesiologist and the nurses and the person who cleans the room."

"I reached puberty at age thirty. At age twelve I looked like a fetus."

"Skiing combines outdoor fun with knocking down trees with your face."

"For most of history, baby-having was in the hands (so to speak) of women. Many fine people were born under this system. Things changed in the 1970s. The birth rate dropped sharply. Women started going to college and driving bulldozers and carrying briefcases and using words like 'debenture.' They didn't have time to have babies… Then young professional couples began to realize that their lives were missing something: a sense of stability, of companionship, of responsibility for another life. So they got Labrador retrievers. A little later they started having babies again, mainly because of the tax advantages."

"Dating means doing a lot of fun things you will never do again if you get married. The fun stops with marriage because you're trying to save money for when you split up your property."

"Isn't Muamar Khadafy the sound a cow makes when sneezing?"

"The First Amendment states that members of religious groups, no matter how small or unpopular, shall have the right to hassle you in airports."

"The Sixth Amendment states that if you are accused of a crime, you have the right to a trial before a jury of people too stupid to get out of jury duty."

40% of Americans take music lessons at some point in their lives; 7% take acting lessons.

POLITICALLY CORRECT NIGHTMARES

It's a good idea to be considerate to people with special needs. Unfortunately, "political correctness" can get ridiculous. Here are some more extreme examples.

GIRL TROUBLE. In October 1992, Shawn Brown, a sophomore at the University of Michigan, turned in a seven-page paper on opinion polls that he'd written for Professor Steven Rosenstone's "Introduction to American Politics." As reported by *Harper's* magazine, the following paragraph appeared in Brown's paper:

> Another problem with sampling polls is that some people desire their privacy and don't want to be bothered by a pollster. Let's say Dave Stud is entertaining three beautiful ladies in his penthouse when the phone rings. A pollster on the other end wants to know if we should eliminate the capital gains tax. Now, Dave is a knowledgeable businessperson who cares a lot about this issue. But since Dave is 'tied up' at the moment, he tells the pollster to 'bother' someone else. Now, this is perhaps a ludicrous example, but there is simply a segment of the population who wishes to be left alone.

The paper was graded by the professor's teaching assistant, a woman who was so outraged that she replied with these comments:

> You are right. This is ludicrous & inappropriate & OFFENSIVE. This is completely inappropriate for a serious political science paper. It completely violates the standard of non-sexist writing. Professor Rosenstone has encouraged me to interpret this comment as an example of sexual harassment and to take appropriate formal steps. I have chosen not to do so in this instance. However, any future comments, in a paper, in a class, or in any dealings with me, will be interpreted as sexual harassment and formal steps *will* be taken. Professor Rosenstone is aware of these comments—& is prepared to intervene. You are forewarned!

What would you do? Brown got out while he could. He dropped the course. Incredibly, the chair of the political science department later expressed her *support* for the teaching assistant's action.

In Boise, Idaho's 1985 mayoral election, Mr. Potatohead received four write-in votes.

SELLER BEWARE

According to a story in the *Washington Post*, here are a few standard terms that some real estate firms now feel they must avoid:

• *Executive*. It could be racist, since most corporate executives are white.

• *Sports enthusiasts*. It could discourage the disabled.

• *Quiet neighborhood*. It could be a code for "no children."

• *Master bedroom*. It suggests slavery.

• *Walk-in closets* and *spectacular view*. Some home buyers cannot walk or see.

POLITICALLY CORRECT COMMERCE

A few true-life PC adventures in advertising.

• Black Flag changed a commercial for insecticide "after a veterans' group protested the playing of taps over dead bugs."

• When Coca-Cola showed a group of women ogling a construction worker who strips off his shirt in a diet Coke commercial, the company was criticized for "reverse sexism."

• Burger King pulled a commercial showing "a mother teaching her grown son to memorize and recite the company's ad slogan to get a discount meal," after people complained the ad was unfair to people who had trouble memorizing things.

• When Aetna Life and Casualty depicted a wicked witch with green skin and a chin wart in a public-service advertisement for a measles vaccine, it was attacked by a "witches' rights group" for encouraging negative witch stereotypes.

SMALL NEWS ITEMS

• GRAND RAPIDS, MI—"A local striptease joint must build ramps on its stage to accommodate handicapped strippers, state officials have ruled."

• SAN FRANCISCO, CA—"A self-proclaimed witch who 'came out of the broom closet' two years ago is demanding that the [local] school district ban the fairy tale 'Hansel and Gretel' because it teaches children that it is acceptable to kill witches. 'They would not use a story that cast any other religion in a light like this,' she said."

A HANDY GUIDE TO THE END OF THE WORLD (Part III)

Here are the end-time prophesies of three familiar religions, from Uncle John's Indispensable Guide to the Year 2000.

CHRISTIANITY

Background: A 2000-year-old religion based on the teachings of Jesus Christ, considered the Son of God.

Signs Of The End: According to Dr. Douglas Ottati, an eminent Christian scholar, signs of the end are "very diverse...and can be very deceptive. One question that has to be answered," he says, "is: how dependable are they in the first place? Jesus Himself is often interpreted as having said that they're not very dependable." But not everyone agrees with that view; a number of events are regarded by many contemporary Christians as signs, based on *Revelation* and other parts of the *Bible*. A few examples:

• *The return of Jews to Israel.* Many consider the existence of the modern state of Israel to be a sign of the impending apocalypse.

• *The rise of China. Revelation* says an army of 200 million people will attack Israel at Armageddon. According to some sources, that's the current size of the Chinese army.

• *Development of computer technology. Revelation* says that in the end-times, only people with the mark of the Beast will be able to buy and sell goods. Some people think this could refer to computer technology such as bar codes.

• *The European Economic Community.* Many believe that the Antichrist must emerge from a united Europe.

When the World Ends: After much turmoil and strife, Christ will return and reign for a thousand-year period of peace. The battle of Armageddon will occur, evil will be defeated, and Judgment Day will arrive.

JUDAISM

Background: A 6,000-year-old monotheistic religion based on the Talmud (Jewish Oral Law) and the Torah (Written Law)—the first 5 books of the Old Testament.

Signs the End Is Near: The Messiah arrives. According to Rabbi Chaim Richman, this will be obvious, because "the world [will] be so drastically changed for the better that it [will] be absolutely incontestable!" For signs, he offers a list of "basic missions of the Messiah," including:

- "Cause the world to return to G-d and His teachings"
- "Oversee the rebuilding of Jerusalem, including the Temple, in the event that it has not yet been rebuilt."
- "Gather the Jewish people from all over the world and bring them home to the land of Israel."

When the World Ends: "Jews don't think in terms of the end of the world," says one scholar. "They think in terms of a new beginning. There's no cataclysm that marks this beginning. After the Messiah comes, people work in partnership with the Divine to bring about a better world."

ISLAM

Background: A religion founded in the 7th century by the prophet Muhammed. He experienced a series of divine visions which he wrote down in the *Koran*.

Signs The End Is Near: Mohammed Ali Ibn Zubair Ali says in *Signs of Qiyamah* that after the arrival of the Enlightened One, Imam Madhi, "the ground will cave in, fog or smoke will cover the skies for forty days. A night three nights long will follow the fog. After the night of three nights, the sun will rise in the west.The Beast from the Earth will emerge. The Beast will talk to people and mark the faces of people. A breeze from the south causes sores in the armpits of Muslims which they will die from. The Qur'an will be lifted from the hearts of the people."

When the World Ends: "The Imam...will create a world state....He will teach you simple living and high thinking. With such a start he will establish an empire of God in this world. He will be the final demonstration and proof of God's merciful wish to acquaint man with the right ways of life."

In 1658 the Virginia legislature passed a law outlawing lawyers.

TO SHAVE, OR NOT TO SHAVE?

Calling all men: It may come as a surprise, but shaving your beard is more than a social obligation. It's a grooming ritual that men have been messing around with since prehistoric times. Here are a few facts to ponder the next time you whip out that razor and start scrapin'.

PREHISTORIC SHAVING

• According to *Razor House*: "Cave paintings have shown that, contrary to popular opinion, early man went about his work clean-shaven, making good use of pieces of sharpened flint."

Shaving historian Eleanor Whitty adds:

• "The earliest razors discovered were flint blades made possibly as far back as 30,000 B.C. Flint could provide an extremely sharp edge for shaving. These were the first disposable shavers because flint becomes dull rather quickly."

• "Not only did early man cut and/or shave off body hair with flint, he also seemed to enjoy carving unusual artistic designs into his skin. If he added natural dyes and colors to these cuts, he ended up with a tattoo. Other stone shaving tools found were made during the Neolithic Period, or Late Stone Age."

• "With the Bronze Age and primitive metalworking, came razors made from iron, bronze and even gold."

ANCIENT SHAVING

• Egyptian pharaohs (around 4000 B.C.) were clean-shaven. All body hair, including beards, were considered a sign of "uncleanliness and negligence."

• The civilizations of Rome and Greece used iron blades with a long handle and developed the shape of the "open" or "cut-throat" razor which was the only practical razor until the 19th century.

• In Greece (around 500 B.C.) men cropped their hair very short and shaved their faces. Alexander the Great was largely responsible for this. Historians call him "obsessed with shaving." One reason: good military strategy. "He didn't want the enemy to be able to grab his soldiers' beards with one hand while stabbing them with the other." However, it was also a matter of aesthetics. Alexander even shaved during wartime, and "would not allow himself to be seen going into battle with a five o'clock shadow."

• Whitty reports that professional barbers were introduced to Rome about 300 B.C. by a businessman named Publicus Ticinius Maenas who he brought a few barbers with him from Sicily. It started a fad that lasted for hundreds of years.

• During this time, Whitty writes, "young Roman men about 21 years of age were actually *required* to have their first shave. To celebrate this official entry into manhood, they had an elaborate party-like ritual." Male friends were invited to watch, and brought gifts. The only Romans not required to go through this ritual were soldiers and young men training to become philosophers.

MODERN SHAVING

Razor House reports:

• "Advances in razor technology changed shaving habits in the 20th century. In 1900, most men were either shaved by the local barber (your trusted confidante, wielding a cut-throat razor), or periodically at home when required, rather than regularly. The barber's better-off customers would have personal sets of seven razors, labelled 'Sunday' to 'Saturday'."

• "The first 'safety' razor, a razor where the skin is protected from all but the very edge of the blade, was invented by a Frenchman, Jean-Jacques Perret, who was inspired by the joiner's plane. An expert on the subject, he also wrote a book called *Pogonotomy or the Art of Learning to Shave Oneself*. In the late 1820s, a similar razor was made in Sheffield and from the 1870s, a single-edge blade, mounted on a hoe-shaped handle was available in Britain and Germany."

• "The idea of a use-once, disposable blade (which didn't need re-sharpening) came from King Camp Gillette in 1895. It was suggested to him that the ideal way to make money was to sell a product that had to be replaced constantly—an early example of built-in obsolescence. However, producing a paper-thin piece of steel with a sharpened edge strong enough to remove a beard was a near technical impossibility at that time. Although patents were filed in 1901, it was not until 1903 that Gillette could go into business, with the assistance of his technical adviser, MIT's William Nickerson. He produced a grand total of 51 razors and 168 blades in that year.

SHAVING AND THE PRESIDENCY

• Our presidents were clean-shaven for the first half of the 19th century.

• Lincoln famously grew a beard just before taking office in 1860, and except for his successor, Andrew Johnson, who was clean-shaven, and Grover Cleveland, who had only a mustache, beards held sway for the rest of the century.

• For the record, Rutherford Hayes (1877-81) had the longest beard, and the last bearded president was Benjamin Harrison (1889-1892). (The public health experts at the turn of the century believed that beards carried germs into the home.)

FEAR OF SHAVING

New York Times in 1879 under the headline "Barbers Terrorize Public," which begins:

"The records of our insane asylums show the fearful effects wrought by the conversation of barbers. No less than 78 percent of the insane patients in public institutions in this state were in the habit of being shaved by barbers before they became insane. If this does not mean that to be shaved by a barber is to incur the risk of being talked into madness, statistics have no meaning."

HAIR FACTS

According to the Portland Oregonian*:*

• "Human beings have three times more body hair than chimpanzees."

• "Men's whiskers grow 5 to 6 inches a year."

• "The average guy devotes 2,965 hours over his lifetime to standing in front of a mirror and shaving—the equivalent of four months."

• In the matter of total facial-hair follicles, "people from Europe and the Middle East are hairiest, Asians the least hairy and Africans fall somewhere in between."

Taxi drivers and chauffeurs are more likely to be murdered on the job than anyone else.

NAME YOUR POISON

Here are the stories of how two popular alcoholic drinks got their names.

DRAMBUIE

Originally the personal liqueur of Prince Charles Edward (history's "Bonnie Prince Charlie"), who tried to overthrow King George II (1727-1760) in 1745. Charles's Scottish troops made it to within 80 miles of London, but they were ultimately beaten back and Charles was driven into hiding. In 1760 a member of the Mackinnon clan helped the prince escape to France. Charles was so grateful that he presented the man with the secret formula for his personal liqueur, which he called *an dram budheach*—which is Gaelic for "the drink that satisfies." The Mackinnons kept the drink to themselves for nearly a century and a half, but in 1906 Malcolm Mackinnon began selling it to the public under the shortened name Drambuie.

Historical Note: The recipe for Drambuie remains a family secret as closely held as the recipe for Coca-Cola—only a handful of Mackinnons know the recipe; to this day they mix the secret formula themselves.

CHAMPAGNE

Accidentally invented by Dom Perignon, a 17th-century monk in the Champagne region of France. Technically speaking, he didn't invent champagne—he invented *corks*, which he stuffed into the bottles of wine produced at his abbey in place of traditional cloth rag stoppers.

The cloth allowed carbon dioxide that formed during fermentation to escape, but the corks didn't—they were airtight and caused bubbles to form in the wine. Amazingly, Dom Perignon thought the bubbles were a sign of poor quality—and devoted his entire life to removing them, but he never succeeded.

Louis XIV took such a liking to champagne that he began drinking it exclusively. Thanks to his patronage, by the 1700s champagne was a staple of French cuisine.

Istanbul, which sits half in Europe and half in Asia, is the only city on two continents.

WHO HELPED HITLER?

Remember those movies about World War II, when everyone in America pitched in together to fight the Nazis? Well, here's some more amazing info from It's a Conspiracy!, *by The National Insecurity Council.*

While most Americans were appalled by the Nazis and the rearming of Germany in the 1930s, some of America's most powerful corporations were more concerned about making a buck from their German investments. Here are some examples of how U.S. industrialists supported Hitler and Nazi Germany.

GENERAL MOTORS

The Nazi connection: GM, which was controlled by the DuPont family during the 1940s, owned 80% of the stock of Opel AG, which made 30% of Germany's passenger cars.

Helping Hitler: When Hitler's panzer divisions rolled into France and Eastern Europe, they were riding in Opel trucks and other equipment. Opel earned GM a hefty $36 million in the ten years before war broke out, but because Hitler prohibited the export of capital, GM reinvested the profits in other German companies. At least $20 million was invested in companies owned or controlled by Nazi officials.

THE CURTISS-WRIGHT AVIATION COMPANY

The Nazi connection: Employees of Curtiss-Wright taught dive-bombing to Hitler's *Luftwaffe*.

Helping Hitler: When Hitler's bombers terrorized Europe, they were using American bombing techniques. The U.S. Navy invented dive-bombing several years before Hitler came to power, but managed to keep it a secret from the rest of the world by expressly prohibiting U.S. aircraft manufacturers from mentioning the technique to other countries. However, in 1934, Curtiss-Wright, hoping to increase airplane sales to Nazi Germany, found a way around the restriction: instead of *telling* the Nazis about dive-bombing, it *demonstrated* the technique in air shows. A U.S. Senate investigation concluded, "It is apparent that American aviation companies did their part to assist Germany's air armament."

Playboy's Playmate of the Month was originally called the "Sweetheart of the Month."

STANDARD OIL

The Nazi connection: The oil giant developed and financed Germany's synthetic fuel program in partnership with the German chemical giant I.G. Farben.

Helping Hitler: As late as 1934, Germany was forced to import as much as 85 percent of its petroleum from abroad. This meant that a worldwide fuel embargo could stop Hitler's army overnight. To get around this threat, Nazi Germany began converting domestic coal into synthetic fuel using processes developed jointly by Standard Oil and I.G. Farben.

• Standard taught I.G. Farben how to make tetraethyl-lead and add it to gasoline to make leaded gasoline. This information was priceless; leaded gas was essential for modern mechanized warfare. An I.G. Farben memo stated, "Since the beginning of the war we have been in a position to produce lead tetraethyl solely because, a short time before the outbreak of the war, the Americans established plants for us and supplied us with all available experience."

• A congressional investigation conducted after World War II found evidence that Standard Oil had conspired with I.G. Farben to block American research into synthetic rubber, in exchange for a promise that I.G. Farben would give Standard Oil a monopoly on its rubber-synthesizing process. The investigation concluded that "Standard fully accomplished I.G.'s purpose of preventing the United States production by dissuading American rubber companies from undertaking independent research in developing synthetic rubber processes."

HENRY FORD, founder of the Ford Motor Company

The Nazi connection: Ford was a big donor to the Nazi party.

Helping Hitler: Ford allegedly bankrolled Hitler in the early 1920s, at a time when the party had few other sources of income. In fact, the party might have perished without Ford's sponsorship. Hitler admired Ford enormously. In 1922, the *New York Times* reported, "The wall beside his desk in Hitler's private office is decorated with a large picture of Henry Ford." Ford never denied that he had bankrolled the Führer. In fact, Hitler presented him with Nazi Germany's highest decoration for foreigners, the Grand Cross of the German Eagle.

CHASE NATIONAL BANK (later Chase Manhattan Bank)

The Nazi connection: Chase operated branches in Nazi-occupied Paris and handled accounts for the German embassy as well as for German businesses operating in France.

Helping Hitler: As late as six months before the start of World War II in Europe, Chase National Bank worked with the Nazis to raise money for Hitler from Nazi sympathizers in the United States.

• Even after America entered the war, "the Chase Bank in Paris was the focus of substantial financing of the Nazi embassy's activities, with the full knowledge of [Chase headquarters in] New York. To assure the Germans of its loyalty to the Nazi cause...the Vichy branch of Chase at Chateauneuf-sur-Cher were strenuous in enforcing restrictions against Jewish property, even going so far as to refuse to release funds belonging to Jews because they anticipated a Nazi decree with retroactive provisions prohibiting such a release."

INTERNATIONAL TELEPHONE AND TELEGRAPH

The Nazi connection: IT&T owned substantial amounts of stock in several German armaments companies, including a 28% stake in Focke-Wolf, which built fighter aircraft for the German army.

Helping Hitler: Unlike General Motors, IT&T was permitted to repatriate the profits it made in Germany, but it chose not to. Instead, the profits were reinvested in the German armaments industry. According to *Wall Street and the Rise of Hitler*: "IT&T's purchase of a substantial interest in Focke-Wolf meant that IT&T was producing German planes used to kill Americans and their allies—and it made excellent profits out of the enterprise."

• The relationship with the Nazis continued even after the U.S. entered the war. According to *Trading with the Enemy*, the German army, navy, and air force hired IT&T to make "switchboards, telephones, alarm gongs, buoys, air raid warning devices, radar equipment, and 30,000 fuses per month for artillery shells used to kill British and American troops" *after* the bombing of Pearl Harbor. "In addition, IT&T supplied ingredients for the rocket bombs that fell on London...high frequency radio equipment, and fortification and field communication sets. Without this supply of crucial materials, it would have been impossible for the German air force to kill American and British troops."

Dwight D. Eisenhower wore two watches on his left arm and one on his right. (Even to bed.)

ELVIS: TOP GUN

Like many Americans, some of Elvis's favorite toys were his guns. And when he wasn't shooting, he liked to pretend he was a karate champ. Some details:

SHOT OFF THE CAN

You never knew when Elvis might get the urge to engage in a little shooting practice, so it paid to be on guard at *all* times.

On one memorable night, Elvis and some friends were relaxing in the Imperial Suite on the 30th floor of the Las Vegas Hilton after his show. "The very elegant Linda Thompson [Elvis's girlfriend] was sitting in the well-appointed and luxurious bathroom," writes Steve Dunleavy in *Elvis: What Happened?*, "when her reverie was rudely interrupted by a resounding blast. At the same time, a tiny rip appeared in the toilet paper on her right side [and] the mirror on the closet door splintered into shards of glass."

"I think Elvis was trying to hit a light holder on the opposite wall," explains Sonny West, Elvis's bodyguard. "Well, he's a lousy shot and he missed. The damn bullet went straight through the wall and missed Linda by inches. If she had been standing up next to the toilet paper holder, it would have gone right through her leg. If it had changed course or bounced off something, it could have killer her, man."

PLAYING IT SAFE

Elvis had hundreds of guns, and he liked to keep them loaded at all times. But he always left the first bullet chamber empty. "It is a habit he got from me," says Sonny West. "I had a friend who dropped his gun. It landed on the hammer...fired and hit him right through the heart, killing him instantly."

But Elvis had another reason. "Elvis knew what a real bad temper he had," says Sonny. "When he flashed, anything could happen. If he pulled the trigger in a rage, it would come up blank and give him just enough time to realize what on earth he was doing."

It paid off. One evening when the Elvis entourage was at the movies (Elvis rented the entire movie theater and brought his friends with him), Elvis went to the men's room and stayed there for a while. One of the group—a visitor who wasn't part of the regular "Memphis mafia"—started joking around, pounding on the bathroom door. West recalls:

"Elvis yells back 'Okay, man, okay.'

"But this guy just kept banging on the door....Apparently Elvis flashed. 'Goddammit!' he yelled as he charged out the door. Then he screamed, 'Who do you think you are, you m—f—r?,' whipped out his gun, pointed it right at the guy and pulled the trigger. Jesus, thank God, he didn't have a bullet in that chamber; otherwise, he would have blown the man's head clean off his shoulders."

CHOP! CHOP!

Elvis was fascinated with karate. He dreamed of making his own karate movie, starring himself as the evil karate master, and liked to drop in at various karate studios to shoot the breeze and work out.

Dave Hebler, a seventh-degree black-belt, remembers their first sparring session in *Elvis: What Happened?*:

"He came in with his usual entourage and shook hands all around. Then he wanted to show-off some moves. Within seconds ...it was obvious to me that one, Elvis didn't know half as much about karate as he thought he did; and two, he hardly knew where he was.

"He was moving very sluggishly and lurching around like a man who'd had far too much to drink....I mean he was actually tripping over and damn near falling on his butt.

"While I couldn't make him look like an expert, I tried to react to his moves in such a way that he wouldn't look half as bad as he could have." Hebler became a regular member of Elvis's entourage.

* * *

GOOD ADVICE

"Keep your temper. Do not quarrel with an angry person, but give him a soft answer. It is commanded by the Holy Writ, and, furthermore, it makes him madder than anything else you could say."

—***Anonymous***

HERE'S JAY

Thoughts from comedian Jay Leno, host of the "Tonight Show."

On the TV show "Thirtysomething": "First I see the wife and she's whining, 'What about my needs?' Then they cut to the husband and he's whining 'What about my needs?' And I'm sitting here saying, 'What about my needs?' I wanted to be entertained. Can't you blow up a car or something?"

"It is said that life begins when the fetus can exist apart from its mother. By this definition, many people in Hollywood are legally dead."

"National Condom Week is coming soon. Hey, there's a parade you won't want to miss."

"You're not famous until my mother has heard of you."

"On President's Day you stay home and you don't do anything. Sounds like *Vice* Presidents Day!"

"Wouldn't it be funny if there was nothing wrong with the [Hubble] telescope at all? It is just that the whole universe was fuzzy."

"A new report from the government says raw eggs may have salmonella and may be unsafe. In fact, the latest government theory says it wasn't the fall that killed Humpty Dumpty—he was dead before he hit the ground."

"The Supreme Court has ruled they cannot have a Nativity scene in Washington, D.C. This wasn't for any religious reasons. They couldn't find three wise men and a virgin."

"Here's an amazing story. A man in Orlando, Florida, was hit by eight cars in a row and only one stopped. The first seven drivers thought he was a lawyer. The eighth *was* a lawyer."

"New Year's Eve, where auld acquaintance be forgot. Unless, of course, those tests come back positive."

"I looked up the word 'politics' in the dictionary and it's actually a combination of two words; 'poli,' which means many, and 'tics,' which means bloodsuckers."

Good news for Heinz: 92% of U.S. household refrigerators contain at least one bottle of ketchup.

TIPS FOR TEENS

Teenage girls need all the advice they can get...so here's more priceless advice from a 1950s teen self-help book.

BLUE-RIBBON BABY-SITTING

Remember, mothers have a remarkable way of comparing notes on sitters. If you are serious about earning a few dollars, shape up!

A baby-sitting job is no time for watching TV programs not permitted at home. Act as if this is business. You are being paid. Arrange a definite time for sitting, and inform your family when they may expect you home.

Arrive on time, or a few minutes early to check facts before parents depart. Be sure you have a telephone number where parents, or a responsible adult, may be reached in an emergency.

Bring a book, your homework or knitting. Don't arm yourself with a long list of telephone numbers for a four-hour gab session. Don't treat your employer's refrigerator as a free raid on the local drive-in. Don't glue your nose to TV and overlook sleeping children. Check them every half hour.

Before bed, little ones often need a bottle. No cause for panic. The wiggles, small cries and faces are baby ways of saying, "Where's my nightcap?" Be prepared a few minutes before feeding time to avoid a long hungry roar.

Once the children are bedded down, stay fairly near the telephone. Light sleepers are frequently awakened by its ring.

Should the phone ring, answer as your employer directed. Be sure to write down messages. Never say, "This is Ann. The family is out, and I am baby-sitting with the children" to a stranger. Sad but true, this occasionally leads to harm to you or the children.

The Blue Ribbon Baby-Sitter is dependable and completely aware of her responsibility for others. Expect to be out of a job if you eat four hot dogs, two bottles of chilled cola, three packs of snacks, run up the phone bill with unnecessary calls to friends, or permit boy or girl friends to join you without permission!

DANGER: LEAVE YOUR GIRLFRIEND'S BOYFRIEND ALONE!

Are you the kind of girl who would dream up an elaborate and ridiculous plot to steal your girlfriend's boyfriend?

Perhaps the compulsion comes to you one day during a geometry test after you have borrowed a pencil from him because something is wrong with your ballpoint pen. You flunk the test. His darling smile keeps coming between you and the angles. At the end of the period, you return the pencil. He hands it back.

"Keep it," he says with a smile. "You'll probably need it in your next class, and I have another."

Another smile! The light in his eyes! You tremble with excitement. This is it! He loves you, and you love him. No one, not even your dearest girlfriend must stand between you.

After school you walk half a block behind him until both he and you are away from the crowds. Then you catch up and "just happen" to appear and join him. In a moment you "just happen" to stumble over nothing so that he must catch you in his arms.

He releases you quickly, a strange expression on his face, and then he strides ahead. You turn back toward your own home on the other side of town, overcome by the wonder of it all. You are sure the boy is too overcome by emotion to speak—that is why he went away so fast.

Unhappily, that evening you see him with your girlfriend. They are so engrossed in each other, neither sees you. Evidently the boy has spoken of your afternoon pursuit, however, for your girlfriend is cool toward you. In fact, you find yourself very lonely these days. You are a pitiful case because you are not only dishonest but ignorant.

SHOULD GIRLS TELEPHONE BOYS?

Careful, girls: In a poll of high-school boys more than two-thirds said they do not like to have girls call them on the telephone. They feel that this is a boy's privilege, and that a girl seems forward when she phones a boy. In fact, most say their families *tease* them about girls who call them at home.

THE DUMBEST WESTERN EVER MADE

There are plenty of worthless Westerns. But few can match this combination of two—count 'em—hilariously lousy films in one. Director Bill "One-Shot" Beaudine managed to capture the worst elements of both dumb Westerns and *cheesy monster movies and roll them into a single feature film.*

JESSE JAMES MEETS FRANKENSTEIN'S DAUGHTER, *Starring Narda Onyx, John Lupton, Cal Bolder, Estelita, Jim Davis and Steven Geray. Directed by William Beaudine.*

Background: William Beaudine was a film pioneer who began working for legendary director D.W. Griffith in 1909. During the the golden age of silent films, he became a director himself and churned out some of Hollywood's biggest hits. But he specialized in Westerns. In *Incredibly Strange Films*, Jim Morton writes:

> Beaudine hit his stride during the early days of Hollywood when studios were less devoted to big-budget productions and more interested in getting as many films as possible out to the American public. In those days, a western had an immediate audience. If it was a *Western*, it couldn't fail. These took anywhere from two days to two weeks to make. Beaudine dutifully churned them out, rarely lavishing much attention on any of them....One of the ways Beaudine kept his costs down (and his speed up) was by avoiding retakes whenever possible. He became so notorious for his refusal to reshoot a scene that he earned the nickname "One-Shot Beaudine." If a boom mike dipped into the frame, if a cowboy started to fall *before* he was shot—*oh well.*

Once, when told that he was behind schedule with a film, he responded: "You mean someone's actually waiting for this c--p?"

During the latter part of his career, Beaudine directed mostly TV shows—including more than 70 episodes of "Lassie." But in 1965, he directed two last films (both flicks in a drive-in double-feature). The first was called *Billy the Kid Meets Dracula*. This second, and worst, was *Jesse James Meets Frankenstein's Daughter*.

Beaudine, who wound up directing over 150 films, died in 1970.

Q: On average, how long is a giraffe's tongue? A: 14 inches.

At age 78, he was Hollywood's oldest working director...and he has the unusual distinction, for a B-film-meister, of having a star on the Hollywood Walk of Fame.

He certainly didn't get it for this movie.

The Plot: Dr. Maria Frankenstein and her brother Rudolf have settled in a small town in the Southwest. It's the perfect location—there's plenty of lightning to power her experiments, there are plenty of fresh young boys to experiment on, and the Austrian police will never find her there. (Seems she's been experimenting in Europe, too.)

As the film opens, all the Mexican peasants are leaving town—mostly to get away from Maria. Only one family remains, waiting for their son—who works at the Frankenstein hacienda—to get over "the sickness." Actually, Maria has operated on the boy, giving him the artificial brain her grandfather (she's really Frankenstein's *grand*daughter) created.

Rudolf is spooked by all this mad scientist stuff; he gives the boy poison rather than letting Maria succeed. Maria doesn't know what's going on—so she decides the boy was too weak; she needs a big, strong man to experiment on.

Well, it just so happens that Jesse James is riding around the countryside with a hulking doofus named Hank...and Hank has been shot during a robbery. He needs a doctor...so he and Jesse conveniently wind up at Frankenstein's hacienda.

To make a long story mercifully short: Maria gives Hank a new brain and calls him—what else?—Igor. Then she gets Igor to kill her brother. Then Igor kills Maria. Then Juanita, Jesse's girlfriend, kills Igor. Then the sheriff takes Jesse away. The End.

Don't Miss:

- ***The Frankenstein "hacienda"*** overlooking town. Viewed from Main Street, it's obviously a 20-foot-high painting. You've gotta see this one to appreciate it.
- ***The generic poison bottle.*** Rudolph poisons the boy with a beaker full of red water, labelled POISON. What kind of posion? Who knows? Who cares?
- ***The Indians riding by.*** Blissfully pointless footage cut in from some other B-film.

If you had to eat one food for the rest of your life, what would it be? In one study, 36% said pizza.

• ***The helmet.*** Maria uses it to activate the artificial brain. But it looks like a Rastafarian chemistry experiment, topped with a wire fence. Should win some sort of prize for low-budget props.

• ***Juanita.*** Played by actress Estelita Rodriguez, supposed to be a beautiful young girl…"even though she looks every one of her thirty-eight years."

IMMORTAL DIALOGUE

Maria: "What a fool I've been! I've allowed the duo-thermal impulsator to be attached only to the body! Let's see what Grandfather's notation says.... You see? The duo-thermal impulsator must also be attached to a living brain, to transmit living vibrations to the artificial brain!"

Rudolph: "But such a powerful electric impulse might prove fatal to the brain of a living person!"

Maria: "That chance I am willing to take!"

Maria: "It's because we've been forced to use the brains of children that we've failed. What we need is a man—a powerful man—a giant! Then we will succeed!"

Rudolph: "But what—what good will it do to succeed?"

Maria: "Imagine! We'll have someone to do our bidding who can't be put to death! Just as we have given it life, only we can take its life away!"

Rudolph: "Maria, we've already caused the deaths of three children, and violated the graves of others, just to make the experiments!"

Maria: "My, you're a humanitarian! You should have stayed in Europe and given pink pills to sweet old ladies!"

Maria: "This is the last artificial brain Grandfather Frankenstein made. The secret of how to make them died with him. If I fail in this last attempt, I too am willing to die!"

Rudolph: "Is it so terrible to fail?"

Maria: "You're a fool, Rudolph! We hold the secret of life in our hands!

Rudolph: "Maria, Maria! This has already cost Grandfather his life!"

Rocky Road ice cream was invented during the Depression as a "comment on the times."

IT'S A MIRACLE!

The tabloids are full of stories about people who see images of religious icons in everything from a lima bean to a smudge on a men's room floor. Could they be real? Who knows? But real or not, they can lead to some pretty weird—and occasionally destructive—situations. Here are the details of five widely reported "sightings" of the Virgin Mary, from John Dollison's book Pope-Pourri.

OUR LADY OF THE 1981 CAMARO

The Sighting: Brownsville, Texas. In September of 1993, a Texas man looked out the window of his house and saw a crowd of people pointing at the dusty hood of his 1981 Camaro. He went outside and asked what they were doing...and was told jubilantly that the Blessed Virgin had appeared in a dirt stain on the hood.

What Happened: To get rid of the throng, the man washed his car. But the image reappeared...and so did the crowds. "We've heard the people coming by to see the image won't let the owner move his car," a Brownsville police dispatcher told reporters. A church spokesperson told reporters: "If it leads people to prayer, that's good in itself."

OUR LADY OF THE AUTO PARTS STORE

The Sighting: Progreso, Texas. On December 3, 1990, the owner of the Progreso Auto Supply announced that the Virgin Mary had appeared in the concrete floor of the men's room shower.

What Happened: Within two weeks more than a thousand people a day were visiting the restroom to weep and pray. Few, if any, bought auto parts. Believers not only took the appearance seriously—some took Mary's unfortunate location, on the floor of an auto parts store shower, personally. "I feel guilty," one distraught woman declared. "I'm part to blame for where she is."

OUR LADY OF THE BACKYARD

The Sighting: In 1992 Marlboro, New Jersey citizen Joseph Januszkiewicz told the world that the Virgin Mary had appeared to him in his backyard on the first Sunday of each month and would keep doing so.

What Happened: The monthly visits attracted as many as ten thousand of the faithful to Marlboro (population 28,000)—costing the town as much as $21,000 in police patrols and "sanitation overtime" per visit. On September 25, 1992, the health department ordered Januszkiewicz to install ten portable toilets on his property to meet his pilgrims' nonspiritual needs. Health officials took the action after receiving "vivid accounts of people defecating in the woods and bushes."

OUR LADY OF COLD SPRING, KENTUCKY

The Sighting: In August 1992, Reverend LeRoy Smith of Saint Joseph Church in Cold Spring told his congregation that a visionary had predicted that the Virgin Mary would make an appearance at the church at midnight on September 1. He never identified the visionary. Six thousand people showed up to see if Mary would appear.

What Happened: Whether or not she did depends on who you ask. Some people saw her on the side of the church; others saw her in a nearby tree. One woman saw lights outside the church that she was sure represented the Blessed Virgin. But most people didn't see anything, including William Hughes, the local bishop. "I am convinced that nothing of a miraculous nature occurred," he reported the next day. Still, many of the spectators disagreed. A Ms. Dang voiced the opinion of many on hand when she commented to a reporter: "The bishop is a mortal man...and he could make a mistake."

OUR LADY OF MEDJUGORJE

The Sighting: In June 1981, two teenagers were sneaking cigarettes on the side of a hill overlooking Medjugorje in Bosnia-Herzegovina when the Virgin Mary appeared to them in the clouds. Four other teenagers made similar sightings not long afterwards (no word on what they were smoking), and the story spread around the world. Since then more than 15 million of the faithful have made pilgrimages to the site.

What Happened: Despite Medjugorje's immense popularity with pilgrims (before the Bosnian civil war it drew almost as many people as Fatima and Lourdes), the Vatican called the sightings bunk. They officially discouraged pilgrims from going there, and the local bishop denounced the sightings as "collective hallucinations." In a 1991 statement, nineteen of twenty Yugoslav bishops declared that "on the basis of research conducted so far, one cannot affirm that supernatural apparitions are involved." The pilgrims kept on coming, even as civil war raged...and a cottage industry of pizza parlors, hot dog stands, and foreign exchange booths sprang up to serve them. "The atmosphere is like Mary World," one Florida-based pilgrim told reporters. Even the outbreak of bloody civil war didn't stop visitors entirely. "I've had open-heart surgery, a ruptured appendix, a gall bladder removed, a back operation, a plugged carotid artery, an angioplasty, and I'm on my second pacemaker," another pilgrim told *The Wall Street Journal* while a fierce battle raged just outside of town. "You think I'm afraid of a little shooting?"

Unfortunately, people's excitement about the prospect of seeing the divine can have unexpectedly tragic consequences. Two more examples from Dollison's book:

OUR LADY OF BAZA, SPAIN

Background: In 1993 Sanchez Casas, an eighteen-year-old Spanish faith healer, announced that on June 11 the Virgin Mary would appear to any of his followers who "looked directly at the sun."

What Happened: On June 11, an estimated one thousand of his followers travelled to Baza, looked directly at the sun...and suffered severe eye damage. More than thirty people were hospitalized, and at least eight suffered permanent vision loss. (Casas pooh-poohed the stricken as "nonbelievers" who had "stared at the sun on the wrong day.")

OUR LADY OF DENVER, COLORADO

Background: In November 1991 a Denver woman announced to the world that the Blessed Virgin would appear at a shrine on Assumption Day—and that "great favors" would be rained upon those who witnessed the holy event. (How did the woman know? She said that Mary had told her so in a vision.)

What Happened: More than six thousand people—many of them elderly and infirm—traveled to the shrine in below-freezing temperatures to witness the "miracle" and spent the entire day staring into the sky waiting for something to happen. Nothing did...but as in Baza, some of the pilgrims looked directly at the sun. At least two dozen people suffered permanent loss of vision; others suffered permanent loss of faith. "Did you ever hear of people going to Jesus for a miracle," one partially blinded woman asked, "and coming away crippled?"

* * * *

...And Now For Some Health Info from the BRI

Skin cancer has become the most common form of cancer in the U.S. today...and nine times out of ten it's caused by too much exposure to the sun.

Know Your Risk

• If you sunburn easily and have a hard time getting tan, you're especially vulnerable to skin cancer. If you have fair skin, red or blonde hair, and light-colored eyes, you are at higher risk.

• If you got a severe, blistering sunburn during childhood, you're more likely to get the most deadly form of skin cancer later in life.

• If a member of your immediate family had skin cancer, you're at risk. About 10% of skin cancer cases run in families.

Protect Yourself

• Cut back on how much sun you get. Be most careful between 10 a.m. and 3 p.m., when the sun's UV rays are most intense.

• Wear a hat to protect your face and head (especially if you're bald). If possible, cover arms and legs. Be careful on overcast days; as much as 85% of the sun's ultraviolet rays can penetrate clouds.

• Use sunscreen, even if you're not on the beach. Apply it 30-45 minutes before exposure. Experts recommend a Sun Protection Factor (SPF) of at least 15. A higher rating isn't necessary, as long as you apply sunscreen liberally. An average adult should use about an ounce per application. Apply evenly to all exposed skin.

• Note: Sunscreens rated SPF 15 or higher contain ingredients that provide some protection against UVA.

In Bangkok, Thailand, ice skates are known as "hard water shoes."

UNCLE JOHN'S GOLDEN TURKEYS

Back in the 1980s, the Medved brothers introduced the term "golden turkeys" for unbelievably, hilariously bad films. Today there's a big subculture of people who love to watch them...and Uncle John is one. Here are two of his favorite grade Z films.

THE BEAST OF YUCCA FLATS (1961)

Written, Directed and Edited by Coleman Francis. Producted by Anthony Cardoza. Starring Tor Johnson, Conrad Brooks. Narration: Coleman Francis.

The Plot: Joseph Javorski, a Russian rocket scientist (played by hulking ex-wrestler Tor Johnson) escapes to America with secret documents. Javorski's destination: "Yucca Flats. And a meeting with top brass at the A-bomb testing grounds." When he gets there, he's chased into the desert by 2 KGB agents. Uh-oh there's an atomic test going on. An A-bomb goes off near the Russian trio; the spies are vaporized, but Tor is merely turned into a maniac. He spends the rest of the film wandering around the desert with a stick, looking for people to beat up and/or kill.

Commentary:

• *From "The Beast of Yucca Flats" website:* "As a fan of bad movies I have seen many of the greats in bad films, including the works of Ed Wood Jr., Larry (*Mars Needs Women*) Buchanan and Jerry (*Teenage Zombies*) Warren....But I have never seen a worse film than this....As soon as I saw it I knew my search (for the world's worst movie) was over. Since then I have seen it over and over...and each time it still amazes me.

Don't Miss:

• ***The Narrator.*** There's almost no dialogue, and no synchronized soundtrack. Instead, there's an "omniscient narrator," dubbed in after the film was completed. Ken Begg writes in *Jabootu's Bad Movie Universe*:

> Adding to the laughs is some of the most mind-boggling narration

"Honcho" is a Japanese word that means "squad leader." It was Americanized after WWII.

this side of the master, Ed Wood himself. Getting to watch Tor run around in ragged clothing, like TV's *Incredible Hulk*, is a treat for any Bad Movie connoisseur. The ponderous, repetitive narration about Mankind, Science, Justice and other Big Topics so solemnly intoned here is the cherry on the sundae.

Some examples:

—"Touch a button. Things happen. A scientist becomes a beast."

—"Jim Archer. Joe's partner. Another man caught in the frantic race for the betterment of mankind. Progress."

—"Jim Archer. Wounded parachuting on Korea. Jim and Joe try to keep the desert roads safe for travelers. Seven days a week."

—"Shockwaves of an A-bomb. A once powerful, humble man. Reduced to...nothing."

—"Joseph Javorski. Respected scientist. Now a fiend. Prowling the wastelands. A prehistoric beast in a nuclear age. Kill. Kill, just to be killing."

— "Vacation time. People travel east. West. North or south. The Radcliffs travel east, with two small boys, adventurous boys. Nothing bothers some people. Not even Flying Saucers."

—"Boys from the City. Not yet caught by the Whirlwind of Progress. Feed soda pop to the thirsty pigs."

• The "'exciting' car chase..." How many inconsistencies can *you* find? Here's Ken Begg's (Jabootu's) analysis:

> The scene immediately cuts from daytime to nighttime. Plus the scenery keeps changing (when the film isn't so dark that you can't see what's going on). First, they're driving through a forest. Then the desert. Then they're still in the desert, but on a road. Then on a road bordered by mountains. Then on a road where the other side's bordered by mountains. This goes on for some minutes. They drive past a plywood sign obviously made for the film (by somebody's kid, by the look of it) that reads "Yucca Flats." (Wow!)

THE CRAWLING EYE (1958)

Starring Forrest Tucker, Janet Munro, Laurence Payne, Jennifer Jayne, Warren Mitchell

The Plot: A mysterious radioactive cloud covers Mt. Trollenberg in the Swiss Alps. Meanwhile, mountain climbers are turning up decapitated. What's going on? United Nations investigator Alan Brooks is sent to find out. He and his psychic girlfriend Anne (who "slips in and out of unintentionally hilarious trances") discover "giant paper mache eyeballs with ultra-cheap tentacles," er, space aliens who want to take over our planet. Brooks finally figures out that the creatures like it cold, and gets rid of them with the help of a few "U.N. fire bombs" (molotov cocktails and napalm!).

Commentary:

From "Rotten Tomatoes" (Dennis Schwartz):

"May be a good film to see on late night cable TV while you're hoisting a few at the bar. In fact, every character in the film has either a brandy or a Scotch to drink at some time—when they're shook up or about to climb the mountain...or just to be sociable. So they might know something about this film [we] don't—such as, it might be best to have a few nips while viewing to enhance the "quality" of the film. Not that I'm an advocate of drinking, but what the hell...it can't hurt in this case."

From "The Bad Movie Report":

- "This film had a couple of things going for it, not least of which was that Anne is really attractive. Unfortunately they made this movie in 1958 so she dresses like June Cleaver....
- "Things I learned from this movie:
  - —Villagers have something to say about everything
  - —Clouds that are stationary and radioactive are bad news
  - —Foreboding music does not belong in a scene involving empty beds
  - —Do not open a [backpack] that is just lying around on a mountainside; odds are there's a head in it
  - —Zombies created by freezing aliens melt away when killed."

BONUS: Scene to Watch For. "As the villagers flee to the observatory, a child of about four somehow manages to cover what appears to be several miles in a matter of minutes to retrieve her ball. This scene is obviously contrived so that (a) we can get our first look at the enemy and (b) Forrest Tucker can do a manly rescue in the very nick." ***—Elizabeth Burton***

Military spending: Among other things, the U.S. military operates 234 golf courses.

TWAIN'S THOUGHTS

We included Mark Twain quotes in the original Bathroom Reader. *There are so many good ones, we couldn't resist including a few more.*

"Under certain circumstances, profanity provides a relief denied even to prayer."

"Why is it that we rejoice at a birth and grieve at a funeral? It is because we are not the person involved."

"The man who doesn't read good books has no advantage over the man who can't read them."

"It is easier to stay out than get out."

"In the first place, God made idiots. That was for practise. Then he made school boards."

"To eat is human. To digest divine."

"Most writers regard the truth as their most valuable possession, and therefore are most economical in its use."

"If you tell the truth you don't have to remember anything."

"I am different from Washington; I have a higher, grander standard of principle. Washington could not lie. I *can* lie, but I won't."

"Few things are harder to put up with than a good example."

"Heaven goes by favour. If it went by merit, you would stay out and your dog would go in."

"There are two times in a man's life when he should not speculate: when he can't afford it and when he can."

"Modesty died when clothes were born."

"We should be careful to get out of an experience only the wisdom that is in it—and stop there; lest we be like the cat that sits down on a hot stove-lid. She will never sit down on a hot stove-lid again—and that is well; but also she will never sit down on a cold one anymore."

"Never learn to do anything. If you don't learn,you'll always find someone else to do it for you."

Four health clinics around the world specialize in bad breath. (Two are in Philadelphia.)

WORD ORIGINS

Here are a few more words we all use—and where they come from…

Orangutan: From a Malay phrase that means "man of the forest."

Candidate: In ancient Rome a *candidatus* was "a person clothed in white." Roman politicians wore white togas to symbolize "humility and purity of motive."

Idiot: From the Greek word *idiotes*, which means "private people" or "people who do not hold public office."

Outlandish: Described the unfamiliar behavior of foreigners, also known as *outlanders*.

Eleven: The Germanic ancestor of the word, *ain-lif*, translates as "one left [over]." That's what happens when you count to ten on your fingers and still have one left over.

Twelve: Means "two left over."

Pirate: From the Greek word for "attacker."

Bus: Shortened from the French phrase *voiture omnibus*, "vehicle for all."

Taxi: Shortened from *taximeter-cabriolet*. *Cabriolet* was the name given to two-wheeled carriages…and *taximeter* was the device that "measured the charge."

Bylaw: A descendant of the Old Norse term *byr log*, which meant "village law."

Obvious: Comes from the Latin words *ob viam*, which mean "in the way." Something that's obvious is so clear to see that you can't help but stumble across it.

Hazard: From the Arabic words *al-zahr*, "a die," the name of a game played with dice. Then as now, gambling was *hazardous* to your financial health.

Scandal: From the Greek word for "snare, trap, or stumbling block."

The #1 song of 1959 was "Mack the Knife," by Bobby Darin.

THE STRANGE FATE OF THE DODO BIRD

The dodo bird has been labled the "mascot of extinction" and the "poster child for endangered species." Here's a look at the ill-fated fowl.

BACKGROUND

You may have heard of the dodo—or been called one—but you've never seen one. *Webster's New World Dictionary* offers three definitons for dodo:"foolish, stupid"; "an old-fashioned person, a fogy"; and "a large bird, now extinct, that had a hooked bill, a short neck and legs, and rudimentary wings useless for flying."

In fact, the dodo, now synonymous with stupidity, was the first animal species acknowledged to have been forced into extinction by man. It was probably one of the fastest extinctions in history.

MAIRITIUS IS "DISCOVERED"

Portuguese mariners first landed on Mauritius, a small island 400 miles east of Madagascar in the Indian Ocean, in about 1507. There they encountered a strange, flightless bird. Weighing more than 50 lbs., it was slightly larger than a turkey, as sluggish as a turtle, and remarkably stupid. The Portugese named it *duodo* or "simpleton."

Dutch settlers were the next Westerners to arrive on the island; they called the dodo *dodaers* ("fat asses") and even *Walghvögel* ("nauseus bird"), because the bird tasted terrible. "Greasie stomachs may seeke after them," one taster remarked in 1606, "but to the delicate they are offensive and of no nourishment."

THE DODO'S SECRET

Centuries of isolation from other animals and the absence of any natural enemies on Mauritius had deprived the dodo of its instinct for survival. For example:

• The dodo didn't bother to build nests for its eggs. It just laid them on the ground wherever it happened to be at the time...and just walked off afterward, abandoning the egg to whatever fate befell it. This wasn't a bad strategy when there were no predators around. But in time, humans brought monkeys, rats, pigs, and dogs to the island. They feasted on the eggs they found.

• It had no fear of humans. The early Mauritian settlers literally had to walk around the birds, or shove them aside with their feet when they walked around the island. If the settlers were hungry, they just killed the birds and ate them; others of the species would watch dumbly.

THE DISAPPEARING DODO

Dodos were plentiful in 1507, when man first arrrived, but by 1631 they were already quite scarce.

No one knows precisely when the dodo went extinct, but when the Frenchman François Leguat inventoried the wildlife of Mauritius in 1693, he made no mention of any bird resembling it—although he did note ominously that the wild boars (introduced by Western settlers) devoured "all the young animals they catch."

MISSED OPPORTUNITY

Was the dodo's extinction inevitable? Some experts say no. They point to animals such as domesticated cows, which flourish even though they're "slow, weak, stupid, and altogether uncompetitive." They think that if dodos had lasted for one more generation, they might have been successfully domesticated.

According to one account:

> On several occasions during the 17th century, living birds were brought from the Indian Ocean to Europe, and some of these were exhibited to the public. Even during the century in which it became extinct, the species aroused great interest in Europe. Had Dodos survived for a few more decades, colonies might perhaps have established themselves in European parks and gardens. Today, Dodos might be as common as peacocks in ornamental gardens the world over! Instead, all that remains are a few bones and pieces of skin, a collection of pictures of varying quality, and a series of written descriptions [that are] curiously inadequate in the information they convey.

THE LAST DODO

Not only are there no *live* dodos, there aren't even any *dead* ones left. The last stuffed specimen, collected by John Tradescant, a 17th-century horticulturist and collector of oddities, was donated to Ashmolean Museum at Oxford University after his death. It remained there until 1755. "In that year," *Horizon* magazine reported in 1971,

> the university...considered what to do with the dodo, which was probably stuffed with salt and sand, by then altogether tatty, and, who knows, maybe lice-infested. [Museum instructions] said: "That as any particular [specimen] grows old and perishing the Keeper may remove it into one of the closets or other repository, and some other to be substituted." The dodo was removed, and burned. Some thoughtful soul preserved the head and one foot, but there was, of course, no other bird to be substituted. The dodo was extinct.

OUT OF SIGHT, OUT OF MIND

So little was known about the dodo that by the middle of the 19th century, nearly 100 years after the Oxford University specimen was thrown out, people believed it had never existed, and had been merely "a legend like the unicorn."

It took a little digging to prove otherwise. "In 1863," recounts Errol Fuller in his book *Extinct Birds*, "a persistent native of Mauritius, George Clark, realizing the island's volcanic soil was too hard to hold fossils, decided that some dodo bones might have been washed up by rains on the muddy delta near the town of Mahebourg. He led an excavation that yielded a great quantity of dodo bones, which were assembled into complete skeletons and sent to the museums of the world. Joy! The dodo lived again."

LEWIS CARROLL'S DODO

Today, the most famous dodo bird is probably the one in *Alice in Wonderland*. Perhaps because the dodo is a symbol of stupidity, Lewis Carroll used it to parody politicians. His dodo is a windbag, runs aimlessly, and placates the masses with other people's assets...then ceremoniously gives some of them back to the original owner.

ALICE & THE DODO

When Alice became a giant in Wonderland, she began to cry. Her tears turned into a flood that swept away everything—including a strange menagerie of birds, mice, and other creatures. Finally the flood subsided and the dripping-wet animals wanted to get dry. First, a mouse tried reciting English history ("The driest thing I know') When that didn't work, the Dodo made a suggestion. Here's the passage in which the dodo appears:

THE DODO SPEAKS

"How are you getting on now, my dear?" the mouse said, turning to Alice as it spoke.

"As wet as ever," said Alice in a melancholy tone. "it doesn't seem to dry me at all."

"In that case,' said the Dodo solemnly, rising to its feet, "I move that the meeting adjourn, for the immediate adoption of more energetic remedies—"

"Speak English!" said the Eaglet. "I don't know the meaning of half those long words, and, what's more, I don't believe you do either!' And the Eaglet bent down its head to hide a smile: some of the other birds tittered audibly.

"What I was going to say," said the Dodo in an offended tone, "was, that the best thing to get us dry would be a Caucus-race."

"What is a Caucus-race?" said Alice; Not that she much wanted to know, but the Dodo had paused as if it thought that somebody ought to speak, and no one else seemed inclined to say anything.

"Why," said the Dodo, "the best way to explain it is to do it." *(And, as you might like to try the thing yourself some winter day, I'll tell you how the Dodo managed it.)*

THE CAUCUS RACE

First it marked out a race-course, in a sort of circle ("the exact shape doesn't matter," it said) and then all the party were placed along the course, here and there. There was no "One, two, three, and away!" but they began running when they liked, and left off when they liked, so that it was not easy to know when the race was over. However, when they had been running half an hour or so, and were quite dry again, the Dodo suddenly called out "The race is

Men are three times more likely than women to commit suicide after an unhappy love affair.

over!" and they all crowded round it, panting, and asking, "But who has won?"

This question the Dodo could not answer without a great deal of thought, and it stood for a long time with one finger pressed upon its forehead (the position in which you usually see Shakespeare, in the pictures of him), while the rest waited in silence. At last the Dodo said "Everybody has won, and all must have prizes."

ALICE IS SELECTED

"But who is to give the prizes?" quite a chorus of voices asked.

"Why, she, of course," said the Dodo, pointing to Alice with one finger; and the whole party at once crowded round her, calling out, in a confused way, "Prizes! Prizes!"

Alice had no idea what to do, and in despair she put her hand in her pocket, and pulled out a box of comfits...and handed them round as prizes. There was exactly one a-piece, all round.

"But she must have a prize herself, you know," said the Mouse.

"Of course," the Dodo replied very gravely. "What else have you got in your pocket?" it went on, turning to Alice.

"Only a thimble," said Alice sadly.

"Hand it over here," said the Dodo.

Then they all crowded round her once more, while the Dodo solemnly presented the thimble, saying "We beg your acceptance of this elegant thimble"; and, when it had finished this short speech, they all cheered.

Alice thought the whole thing very absurd, but they all looked so grave that she did not dare to laugh; and, as she could not think of anything to say, she simply bowed, and took the thimble, looking as solemn as she could.

Alice begins talking about her cat, and the animals nervously slink away. The Dodo never appears again.

Frank House, a catcher for the Kansas City Athletics, was nicknamed "Pig."

ANSWERS

Here are the solutions to our brain teasers, games, and quizzes.

WHAT DOES IT SAY?, PAGE 244

1. *John Underwood, Andover, Mass.* (JOHN under WOOD, and over MASS)

2. I thought I heard a noise outside, but it was *nothing after all* (0 after ALL)

3. Let's have *an understanding* (AN under STANDING)

4. *Look around you.* (LOOK around U)

5. "Remember," she said to the group, "*united we stand, divided we fall.*" (United WESTAND, divided WE FALL)

6. "Why'd he do that?" Jesse asked. "Well, son," I said, "he's a *mixed-up kid.*" (DKI = kid)

7. Texas? I love *wide-open spaces.* (S P A C E S)

8. "Drat! My watch broke. Time to get it *repaired.*" (RE paired)

9. "I remember the 1960s," she said, *looking backward.* (GNIKOOL = "looking" spelled backward)

10. No, we're not living together anymore. It's a *legal separation.* (L E G A L)

11. Haven't seen him in a while. He's *far away from home.* (FAR away from HOME)

12. Careful, I warned my sister. He's a *wolf in sheep's clothing* (WOLF inside WOOL)

13. "How do I get out of here?" he asked. I said, "Just calm down and put the *car in reverse.*" (R A C = car spelled backward)

14. I tried to teach her, but no luck. I guess she's a *backward child.* (DLIHC = *child* spelled backward)

15. When it's raining, *she meets me under an umbrella.* (SHE meets ME under AN UMBRELLA)

THE GODZILLA QUIZ, PAGE 264

1. C) They added Raymond Burr, casting him as Steve Martin, a reporter who remembers the whole incident as a flashback. It starts off with Burr in a hospital bed, recalling the horror he's seen. Then, throughout the film, footage of Burr is cleverly inserted to make it seem as though he's interacting with the Japanese cast.

2. C) *Gigantis*; it was illegal to use the name Godzilla. Warner Bros. brought the film into America, but they forgot to secure the rights to the name Godzilla, so they couldn't legally use it. In this film, by the way, Godzilla crushes Osaka instead of Tokyo, and begins his long tradition of monster-fighting (he takes on a giant creature called Angorus).

3. B) A giant cockroach and a robot with a buzz saw in his stomach. The seatopioans, stationed under the sea, are using a metal bird monster with a buzz saw (Gaigan) and a giant cockroach (Megalon—described as a "metal monster insect with drill arms") to fight Godzilla on the surface. Godzilla can't take them on alone. He teams up with Jet Jaguar, a cyborg who can change size to fight monsters.

4. B) A giant moth. The thing is Mothra, who starred in its own film a few years earlier. Godzilla kills Mothra—but a giant egg on display at a carnival hatches, and two "junior Mothras" emerge. They spin a cocoon around Godzilla and dump him in the ocean.

5. A) He fought a Godzilla robot from outer space. The film was originally called *Godzilla vs. the Bionic Monster*, presumably to cash in on the popularity of the "Six Million Dollar Man" TV show. But the owners of that TV show sued, and the title was changed to *Godzilla vs. the Cosmic Monster*.

6. C) A three-headed dragon. To defeat them, Godzilla takes a partner again—this time Angorus, his foe from *Gigantis*.

7. A) The Smog Monster—a 400-foot blob of garbage. The smog monster flies around, leaving a trail of poisonous vapors that cause people to drop like flies, especially at discos where teens are danc-

There is a town in Newfoundland, Canada called Dildo.

ing to anti-pollution songs. Don't miss the smash tune, "Save the Earth."

8. B) To show a little kid how to fight bullies. The boy falls asleep and dreams he travels to Monster Island, where Godzilla and his son teach him how to defend himself.

9. C) A giant lobster. Actually, he might be a giant shrimp. It's hard to tell. His strength: He can regenerate a limb every time one is torn off.

10. C) It was Godzilla's son. Imagine that—Godzilla's a parent!

AUNT LENNA'S PUZZLES, PAGE 320

1. The accountant and lawyer were women. Steve is a man's name.

2. The answers are WHOLESOME and ONE WORD.

AUNT LENNA'S PUZZLES, PAGE 359

1. He couldn't have heard where she was going if he was deaf.

2. 99-99/99

3. His wife was on a life-support system. When he pushed the elevator button, he realized the power had gone off.

4. The first man, who saw the smoke, knew first; the second man, who heard it, knew second; the third man, who saw the bullet, knew last. The speed of light travels faster than the speed of sound, and the speed of sound travels faster than a bullet.

5. Her shoes. Check it out against the woman's laments—it makes sense.

The flu was first described by Hippocrates, in 412 B.C.

6. Let's start with the grandmothers and grandfathers. That's 4. They're all mothers and fathers, so if there are 3 mothers and 3 fathers, we have 2 new people—1 mother, 1 father—for a total of 6.

The 2 mothers-in-law and fathers-in-law are the grandparents, so we don't count them again. The son-in-law and daughter-in-law are the 2 additional parents, so we don't count them again, either The 2 sons and 2 daughters are their children—which makes 10 people.

AUNT LENNA'S PUZZLES, PAGE 397

1. She's talking about the amount of bills, not the year. 1,993 bills are worth exactly $1 more than more than 1,992 bills.

2. They were traveling at different times.

3. Noel (No "L").

4. She grabbed one of the stones and quickly let it "slip" from her hands. Then, because she "couldn't find" the stone she'd dropped, she just looked in the bag to see what was left. It was a black stone, of course...which meant she'd won the bet.

5. Cut them into quarters with two cuts...then stack the quarters on top of each other and cut once. Eight pieces, three cuts.

6. She wrote:

qoodqodqo

Elvis collected statuettes of Joan of Arc and Venus de Milo.

ACRONYMANIA, P. 457

1. Zone Improvement Plan Code
2. Deoxyribo Nucleic Acid
3. Dead On Arrival
4. Erhard Seminars Training (or Eastern Standard Time)
5. (Department of) Housing and Urban Development
6. INTERnational Criminal POLice Organization
7. Keep It Simple Stupid
8. Light Amplification by Stimulated Emission of Radiation
9. UNIVersal Automatic Computer
10. NAtional BIScuit COmpany
11. National Aeronautics and Space Administration
12. New England Confectionary COmpany
13. Not In My BackYard
14. National Organization of Women
15. Organization of Petroleum Exporting Countries
16. Office of Special Housing Assistance
17. QUASi-StellAR Radio Source
18. Research ANd Development Corp.
19. Run Batted In
20. Rapid Eye Movement
21. Self-Contained Underwater Breathing Apparatus
22. Sealed With A Kiss
23. TriNiTrotoluene
24. United Nations Educational Scientific and Cultural Organization
25. United Nations International Children's Emergency Fund
26. Computerized Axial Tomography scan
27. Airborne Warning And Control System
28. Absent WithOut Leave
29. Compact Disc—Read Only Memory
30. Mobile Army Surgical Hospital
31. Will COmply
32. SOund Navigation And Ranging
33. Situation Normal, All Fouled (or F———) Up
34. North Atlantic Treaty Organization
35. Strategic Arms Limitation Talks
36. RAdio Detection And Ranging

According to one survey, Danes spent $166 million on prostitutes in 1993.

37. Subsonic Cruise Unarmed Decoy
38. Strategic Air Command
39. What You See Is What You Get
40. Women's Army Corps
41. SEa-Air-Land unitS
42. MicroSoft Disk Operating System
43. NORth American Air Defense Command
44. Tele-Active Shock Electronic Repulsion
45. Random Access Memory
46. Waste Of Money, Brains, And Time
47. Also Known As
48. CANada Oil, Low Acid

TEST YOUR "BEVERLY HILLBILLIES" IQ, PAGE 489

1. B) Still smarting from the cancellation of a sitcom called "The Bob Cummings Show" in 1959, Paul Henning, a TV executive, took his wife and mother-in-law on a 14,000-mile automobile trip through the eastern half of the United States. Henning was trying to get his mind off business, but it didn't work—the places he visited kept giving him ideas for new shows. After touring a Civil War site, he thought of creating a sit-com around the concept of an 1860s family that somehow lands in the 1960s...but he couldn't think of a believable way to transport them through time. He later explained:

> I wondered how, without being too magic, such a thing could be accomplished. I subsequently read a little bit about someone trying to build a road through a remote section of the Ozark Mountains and how the residents would try to stop the building of the road. They didn't want to have access. Part of that, I'm sure, was that a lot of them made their living moonshining and they didn't want "fereners," as they called it, coming in the remote places.

Turning the concept around, Henning thought that hillbillies moving to California was a good idea for a sit-com. He jotted down some ideas and showed them to executives of Filmways Television over lunch; by the end of the meeting the series had been sold.

2. A) "I told [Filmways] the concept," Henning later recalled. "These hillbillies strike oil and move to a sophisticated urban center, which I first imagined to be New York. But then I got to thinking of the cost of filming in New York and how it wouldn't work. Where else could they land? I thought of Beverly Hills, which is about as sophisticated as you can get on the West Coast."

The U.S. Congress didn't make "The Star Spangled Banner" the national anthem until 1931.

3. C) Henning and "Beverly Hillbillies" producer Al Simon spent months hitting every hillbilly band and hoedown looking for an authentic hillbilly to play the part of Granny. "Finally," he recalls, "we found someone and thought, 'Gee, this woman's great. This is gonna work out. She sounded great when we talked to her. She said she'd have her nephew, with whom she stayed, help her with the reading. When she came in and faced those cameras, she froze. She couldn't read! She was illiterate, but she disguised it cleverly."

Actress Bea Benaderet got ahold of the script and pleaded with Henning for an audition to play the part of Granny. He told her she was too "well built" for the part. "And when we did the test, she had seen Irene [Ryan] ready to go and do her thing. She said, 'There's your Granny!' " Henning disagreed. "At first they said I was too young," Ryan later recalled, "but I said 'If you get anybody older than I am, she'll be too old to do the series.' " She got the part—and Bea Benaderet got the part of Cousin Pearl. (*Note:* Did her voice sound oddly familiar to you when you watched the show? She also played the voice of Betty Rubble on "The Flintstones" cartoon show from 1960 to 1964.)

4. B) Bailey "wasn't happy anywhere he was," Henning recalls. "He complained a lot, but he played the part perfectly." The other cast members remember him as arrogant, publicity hungry, willing to argue over just about anything, and frequently insulting, even in public. Paul Henning's wife Ruth remembers one particular incident:

> We were going to a bank opening in Independence, Missouri....Ray got loaded on the plane and when we arrived at Paul's sister's house, a big, historical, Victorian-style home, Ray made a loud remark that it looked like a whorehouse. When Paul's sister stepped out on the porch to greet us, Ray said, "Are you the madam?"

"He alienated himself from everybody," one press agent recalls. "Sometimes people hated to be around him, he complained so much." But according to one California bank official, he was popular in the banking industry nonetheless. "The bankers all love him," the official told *TV Guide* in 1970, "which is unusual considering the way bankers have always been portrayed....I have yet to hear a banker complain about the character of Drysdale." Even so, Bailey's attitude may have cost him his career: according to news reports published after his death, Buddy Ebsen had refused to offer

Fully 50% of the Netherlands—including its two largest cities—lie below sea level.

him work on his new series, "Barnaby Jones". Bailey spent his last years unemployed and bitter. He died of a heart attack in 1980.

5. B) During one break in shooting in 1966, Douglas starred opposite Elvis Presley in his film *Frankie and Johnnie*...and according to some reports, fell in love with the King. "She didn't realize every girl he worked with fell in love with him. She really flipped out," Paul Henning recalls.

6. B) Critics almost uniformly hated the show. "We're liable to be Beverly Hillbillied to death," one observer sniffed, "please write your Congressman." Another complained that "'Beverly Hillbillies' aims low...and hits its target." But the show was an unprecedented hit with viewers. It shot to the #1 ratings slot after only five weeks on the air and quickly became the most-watched show in TV history.

7. A) The part of Jed Clampett was made with Buddy Ebsen in mind, but he didn't want the part. "My agent had mentioned the hillbillies," he later recalled, "but I wanted to run the other way. I had played a lot of hillbillies, and I just didn't want to get trapped again in that kind of getup with long hair and whiskers."

8. B) The owners were happy for the first three seasons...but only because they had insisted that Filmways keep their address a secret. But in the beginning of the fourth season, *TV Guide* got ahold of the address and published it, and the house, known as the Kirkeby Mansion, instantly became one of the hottest tourist stops in L.A. The wife of the owner went nuts. "She had been just beleaguered by tourists," Henning later recalled. "She had to get security people, shut her gates...it was a terrible mess. People would actually walk into her house and ask for Granny. Can you imagine?...The tragedy was that we were just about to go to color. This broke before we had a chance to film the exteriors in color. That was a real blow. We had to promise to stay away."

9. B) Tate, who later became famous as one of the murder victims of Charles Manson, played typist Janet Trego in several episodes and even dated Max Baer (Jethro) for a time. She later won the part as one of Cousin Pearl's daughters on "Petticoat Junction," but was replaced by another actress when *Playboy* magazine published nude photos of her that had been taken before she got the part. "When we first got her," director Joe Depew remembers, "She was

Average U.S. family income in 1915: $687 a year.

very amateurish. It was hard for her to read a line. Then she went to [acting] school and she learned a lot. She was a very pleasant girl and extremely beautiful...a real tragedy."

10. B) Granny was Granny Moses...just like the painter.

PRESIDENTIAL QUIZ, PAGE 542

1. (c) Carnegie, the steel magnate (1835-1919).

2. (d) Because liquor, as well as tobacco and profanity, was banished from the White House, Mrs. Hayes was also known as "Lemonade Lucy." At one official dinner, it was said, "the water flowed like champagne."

3. (a) Our eighth president (and Andrew Jackson's second vice president) was born in New York in Kinderhook in 1782 and inaugurated in 1837. The first seven presidents were, of course, born in English colonies.

4. (c) By a special act of Congress, the former representative (North Carolina, 1811-1816) and senator (Alabama, 1819-1844, 1848-1852) took the oath in Havana as President Franklin Pierce's vice president. King (1786-1853) died a month later, before the first session of the 33rd Congress was held, and so never got to preside over the Senate, the vice president's principal role at the time.

5. (b) The only president to sit on the high bench was appointed in 1921 by President Warren G. Harding. Ill health forced his resignation nine years later, a month before he died.

6. (b) And only one president remained a bachelor: James Buchanan (1791-1868). Grover Cleveland (1837-1908), who had, as a young bachelor in Buffalo, fathered a child, was a bachelor still when he was first elected president in 1884, but married his ward midway through his first term.

7. (c) "The more I see of the czar, the kaiser, and the mikado," Roosevelt declared, "the better I am content with democracy."

8. (d) The polio-stricken governor of New York State flew in a flimsy trimotor airplane from Albany to Chicago in 1932 to accept his nomination.

9. (b) It was in 1906, after yellow fever had been licked in the Canal Zone. The 25th president was also the first president to ride in an automobile, fly in an airplane, and dive into the sea in a submarine. "You must remember," a British diplomat sighed, "that the president is about six." The Rough Rider (1858-1919) also wrote 40 books, and left politics for almost two years in bereavement when his mother and his first wife died on the same day in 1884.

10. (b) George Washington, Andrew Jackson, William Henry Harrison, Zachary Taylor, Ulysses S. Grant, and Dwight D. Eisenhower. Five other professional soldiers have been nominated for the presidency: Benjamin Lincoln, Winfield Scott, John Fremont, George McClellan, and Winfield Scott Hancock.

11. (a) Abraham Lincoln.

THE NUMBERS GAME, PAGE 566

1. 7 = Wonders of the Ancient World
2. 1001 = Arabian Nights
3. 12 = Signs of the Zodiac
4. 54 = Cards in a Deck (with the Jokers)
5. 9 = Planets in the Solar System
6. 88 = Piano Keys
7. 13 = Stripes on the American Flag
8. 32 = Degrees Fahrenheit, at Which Water Freezes
9. 90 = Degrees in a Right Angle
10. 99 = Bottles of Beer on the Wall
11. 18 = Holes on a Golf Course
12. 8 = Sides on a Stop Sign
13. 3 = Blind Mice (See How They Run)
14. 4 = Quarts in a Gallon
15. 1 = Wheel on a Unicycle
16. 5 = Digits in a Zip Code
17. 24 = Hours in a Day
18. 57 = Heinz Varieties

Nearly 40% of the people who get plastic surgery are between 35 and 55 years old.

19. 11 = Players on a Football Team
20. 1000 = Words That a Picture Is Worth
21. 29 = Days in February in a Leap Year
22. 64 = Squares on a Chessboard
23. 40 = Days and Nights of the Great Flood
24. 2 = To Tango
25. 76 = Trombones in a Big Parade
26. 8 = Great Tomatoes in a Little Bitty Can
27. 101 = Dalmatians
28. 23 = Skidoo
29. 4 = He's a Jolly Good Fellow (yes, it's a trick)
30. 16 = Men on a Dead Man's Chest
31. 12 = Days of Christmas
32. 5 = Great Lakes
33. 7 = Deadly Sins
34. 2.5 = Children in a Typical American Family
35. 1, 2, 3 = Strikes You're Out at the Old Ball Game
36. 3 = Men in a Tub
37. 13 = Baker's Dozen

MONUMENTAL MISTAKES, PAGE 615

1) B. Buried in a roadway. By the time anyone looked for it, say the Whitcombs in *Oh Say Can You See*, "the rock was partially buried in the middle of a roadway leading to a wharf and had to be dug out and hauled to the town square. In the course of several additional moves, the rock fell from a wagon and had to be cemented together."

Tourists were upset that the rock wasn't at the ocean, where the pilgims were supposed to have stepped onto it. So the citizens of Plymouth obliged them, and moved it near the water in 1920.

2) B. Thomas Jefferson/Monticello. A northerner did buy Monticello and restore a part of it, but then the Civil War broke out, and the Confederates confiscated the property and stored grain and cows in it. In 1878 it was described as "desolation and ruin...a standing monument to the ingratitude of the great Republic." Believe it or not, the real effort to save Monticello didn't begin until 1923.

3) A. The company that made Castoria laxative. They agreed to give $25,000 "provided that for the period of one year you permit us to place across the top of the pedestal the word *Castoria*." Imagine how the history of the United States might have been affected if immigrants entering New York harbor had seen, in that inspiring first glimpse of America, an ad for laxatives. What lasting impression would it have made? It boggles the mind. Fortunately, they were turned down.

4) C. A root beer stand. One representative wrote at the time: "I look to see where [John C.] Calhoun sat and where [Henry] Clay sat and I find a woman selling oranges and root beer." In 1864 they turned it into Statuary Hall.

5) A. The Alamo. This landmark, where Davy Crockett and company died fighting against the Mexican Army in 1836, was originally a Spanish mission. When the Mexicans took the Alamo they tried to burn it down. Then they left it, and people who lived nearby took stones from the buildings whenever they liked. In the mid-1800s, the U.S. Army used the Alamo as a barracks. But in 1879, it was turned into a grocery/mercantile store. When a real estate syndicate tried to buy it in 1905, the Daughters of the Republic of Texas lobbied the state government to match the offer. They were turned down. It took a private donor—a 22-year-old cattle heiress—to come up with the funds to save it.

6) C. An angry mob that gathered after the assassination. The federal government bought it from John Ford for $100,000 and used it as an office and a storage area. Unfortunately, Lincoln wasn't the only one to die there. In 1893, twenty office workers were killed, and sixty-eight injured, when the building collapsed. It was unoccupied until 1964, when money was appropriated to restore the building to its 1865 condition.

7) A. Schoolchildren contributed their pennies to save it. The boat got its nickname not because its sides were made of iron, but because its thick wood sides seemed to deflect cannonballs during battle in the War of 1812. After the war, it was abandoned to rot—but in 1830, it was refurbished and used for training. Then, in 1927, it needed work again, and a drive to restore it was led by American schoolchildren.

* * *

MORE HOLLYWOOD-ISMS

More funny and inciteful observations taken from Star Speak: Hollywood on Everything, *by Doug McClelland.*

'I don't do the Hollywood party scene anymore. You can't go home and say to the kid, "Hi, here's a little switch: Daddy's going to throw up on you!"

—Robin Williams

"The most important thing in acting is honesty. Once you've learned to fake that, you're in."

—Samuel Goldwyn

"Actors are cattle. Disney probably has the right idea. He draws them in and if he doesn't like them he tears them up."

—Alfred Hitchcock

"It was funny, before we started shooting Police Woman someone said, "Have you ever played sleuths before?" And I said, "Oh, many times." What I thought he meant was sluts!"

—Angie Dickinson

"Acting is not an important job in the scheme of things. Plumbing is."

—Spencer Tracy

"A wife lasts only for the length of a marriage, but an ex-wife is there for the rest of your life."

—Woody Allen

"I am a very good housekeeper. Each time I get a divorce I keep the house."

—Zsa Zsa Gabor

Life span: A butterfly lives for about six months.

No Bathroom Is Complete Without...

The Best of Uncle John's Bathroom Reader®!

- *All your favorites— the funniest, oddest, most intriguing articles, quotes, and trivia from volumes 1–7*
- *522 pages—it's the biggest and best!*
- *Available for $16.95*

A Truly Satisfying Experience for the Connoisseur of Bathroom Reading

AVAILABLE AT YOUR LOCAL BOOKSTORE!

or from the BRI at:

P.O. Box 1117,
Ashland, Oregon 97520

www.bathroomreader.com *or* bathread@mind.net

Your Search Is Over!

Uncle John's Giant 10th Anniversary Bathroom Reader®!

Celebrate 10 years of America's
Bestselling Bathroom Reader Series

- *504 pages of all new material! Over twice as long as the regular Readers!*
- *Introducing the "Extended Sitting" section for those times when you know you're going to be sitting for a while.*
- *All for only $16.95!*

A Truly Satisfying Experience for the Connoisseur of Bathroom Reading

Available at your local bookstore
or from the BRI at:
P.O. Box 1117,
Ashland, OR 97520
www.bathroomreader.com *or* bathread@mind.net

Uncle John's Bathroom Reader series

—— Order Info ——

Uncle John's ***Supremely Satisfying*** *Bathroom Reader*,
Copyright © 2001. $16.95 (Available Nov. 2001)

Uncle John's ***All-Purpose Extra Strength*** *Bathroom Reader*,
Copyright © 2000. $16.95

Uncle John's ***Absolutely Absorbing*** *Bathroom Reader*,
Copyright © 1999. $16.95

Uncle John's ***Great Big*** *Bathroom Reader*,
Copyright © 1998. $16.95

Uncle John's ***Giant*** *10th Anniversary Bathroom Reader*,
Copyright © 1997. $16.95

Uncle John's ***Ultimate*** *Bathroom Reader (#8)*,
Copyright © 1996. $12.95

The ***Best of*** *Uncle John's Bathroom Reader*,
Our favorites from *BRs #1 – #7.*
Copyright © 1995. $16.95

Uncle John's ***Legendary Lost*** *Bathroom Reader*,
BRs #5, #6, & #7
Copyright © 1999. $18.95

* NOTE: The first four *Bathroom Readers* are published by St. Martin's Press, New York.

For bulk orders, wholesale prices, and credit card orders, go to our website: *www.bathreader.com* or call (800) 284-3580. For orders under ten books, just send a check (including S & H) to the address below:

U.S. Shipping & Handling rates:
• 1 book (book rate): add $3.50 • 2 – 3 books: add $4.50
• 4 – 5 books: add $5.50 • 6 – 10 books: add $1.00 per book.

Bathroom Readers' Press
PO Box 1117, Ashland, Oregon 97520
Phone: 541-488-4642 Fax: 541-482-6159

If you like reading our books...
try

VISITING THE BRI'S WEBSITE!

www.unclejohn.com
or
www.bathroomreader.com

- Visit "The Throne Room"—a great place to read!
- Receive our *irregular* newsletters via email
- Submit your favorite articles and facts
- Suggest ideas for future editions
- Order additional BRI books
- Become a BRI member

Go With the Flow!

THE LAST PAGE

FELLOW BATHROOM READERS:

The fight for good bathroom reading should never be taken loosely—we must sit firmly for what we believe in, even while the rest of the world is taking pot shots at us.

We've proven we're not simply a flush-in-the-pan...writers and publishers will soon find their resistance unrolling.

So we invite you to take the plunge: Sit Down and Be Counted! by joining the Bathroom Readers' Institute. Send a self-addressed, stamped envelope to: BRI, PO Box 1117, Ashland, Oregon 97520. Or contact us through our website at: *www.bathroomreader.com*. You'll receive your attractive free membership card and a copy of the BRI newsletter (sent out irregularly via email), receive discounts when ordering directly through the BRI, and earn a permanent spot on the BRI honor roll!

⚘ ⚘ ⚘

UNCLE JOHN'S NEXT BATHROOM READER IS IN THE WORKS!

Well, we've survived (barely) another year of satisfying your bathroom reading needs, but don't fret—there's more on the way. In fact, there are a few ways *you* can contribute to the next volume:

• Is there a subject you'd like to see us research? Write to us or contact us through our website (*www.bathroomreader.com*) and let us know. We aim to please.

• Have you seen or read an article you'd recommend as quintessential bathroom reading? Or is there a passage in a book or website that you want to share with us and other BRI members? Tell us how to find it. If you're the first to suggest it and we publish it in the next volume, there's a free book in it for you.

Well, we're out of space, and when you've gotta go, you've gotta go. Hope to hear from you soon. Meanwhile, remember:

Go with the flow!